Organizational Behavior Seventh Edition

John R. Schermerhorn, Jr.
Ohio University

James G. Hunt
Texas Tech University

Richard N. Osborn
Wayne State University

ORGANIZATIONAL BEHAVIOR 7TH edition

ISBN   0-471-22819-2 (ebook)
        0-471-42063-8 (print version)

Brief Contents

SECTION ONE 1

Organizational Behavior Today 3
Learning About Organizational Behavior 5
Organizations as Work Settings 7
Organizational Behavior and Management 9
Ethics and Organizational Behavior 12
Workforce Diversity 15
Demographic Differences 17
Aptitude and Ability 18
Personality 19
Personality Traits and Classifications 21
Values and Attitudes 27
Managing Diversity and Individual Differences 31
The Perceptual Process 32
Common Perceptual Distortions 37
Managing the Perceptual Process 40
Attribution Theory 41
The Concept of Organizational Culture 43
Observable Aspects of Organizational Culture 48
Values and Organizational Culture 49
Managing Organizational Culture 52
Organizational Development Process and Applications 54
Change in Organizations 59
Planned Change Strategies 62
Resistance to Change 64

Footnotes 67
Source Notes 71

SECTION TWO 73

High Performance Context of Organizational Behavior 75
What is a High Performance Organization? 78

Management Challenges of High Performance Organizations 81
Illustrative Case: Creating a High Performance Organization 84
Groups in Organizations 87
Stages of Group Development 90
Input Foundations of Group Effectiveness 92
Group and Intergroup Dynamics 95
Decision Making in Groups 96
High Performance Teams 100
Team Building 103
Improving Team Processes 105
Teams and the High Performance Workplace 110
Decision Making Process 114
Decision Making Models 115
Intuition, Judgment, and Creativity 118
Managing the Decision-Making Process 120
Technology, Culture, and Ethics in Decision Making 124
Conflict 127
Managing Conflict 130
Negotiation 135
Negotiation Strategies 137

Footnotes 140
Source Notes 144

SECTION THREE 145

What Is Motivation? 147
Reinforcement 148
Content Theories of Motivation 155
Process Theories 159
Integrating the Motivation Theories 162
Dynamics of Stress 165

Footnotes 168
Source Notes 169

SECTION FOUR 171

Power 173
Empowerment 181
Organizational Politics 183
Political Action and the Manager 186
The Nature of Communication 190
Essentials of Interpersonal Communication 192
Communication Barriers 195
Organizational Communication 197
Communication and the High Performance Workplace 200

Footnotes 203
Source Notes 204

SECTION FIVE 205

Organizational Behavior and Globalization 207
Cultures and Cultural Diversity 209
Globalization and People at Work 214
A Global View of Organizational Learning 219
Technology and Job Design 220
Goal Setting and Job Design 222
Alternative Work Arrangements 225
Organizational Design and Size 228
Operations Technology and Organizational Design 229
Information Technology and Organizational Design 231
Environment and Organizational Design 234
Strategy and Organizational Design 237

Footnotes 238
Source Notes 241

THE OB SKILLS WORKBOOK   243

The FST©MPANY Collection   245

ARTICLE 1 The Company of the Future Robert B. Reich   245
ARTICLE 2 Life In The Fast Lane Chuck Salter   252
ARTICLE 3 Danger: Toxic Company Alan M. Webber   255
ARTICLE 4 Learning for a Change Alan M. Webber   258

Cases for Critical Thinking   265

CASE 1 Drexler's Bar-B-Que Forest F. Aven, Jr., V. Jean Ramsey   265
CASE 2 Sun Microsystems: "We're the dot in .com" David S. Chappell   267
CASE 3 Crossing Borders Bernardo M. Ferdman, Plácida I. Gallegos and the Kaleel Jamison Consulting Group, Inc.   270
CASE 4 Never on a Sunday Anne C. Cowden   272
CASE 5 MAGREC, Inc. Mary McGarry, Barry R. Armandi   273
CASE 6 It Isn't Fair Barry R. Armandi   275
CASE 7 Amoco's Global Human Resource Systems Ellen Ernst Kossek   277
CASE 8 I'm Not in Kansas Anymore Anne C. Cowden   279
CASE 9 The Forgotten Group Member Franklin Ramsoomair   280
CASE 10 NASCAR's Racing Teams David S. Chappell   281
CASE 11 First Community Financial Mark Osborn   284
CASE 12 Mission Management and Trust Mark Osborn   285

CASE 13 Motorola: Is a High Performance Culture Enough? David S. Chappell   287
CASE 14 Perot Systems: Can a High Performance Company Have a Human Side?   289
CASE 15 Power or Empowerment at GM? Aneil Mishra, Karen Mishra, and Kim Cameron   293
CASE 16 The Poorly Informed Walrus Barbara McCain   296
CASE 17 Johnson and Johnson: Futuristic Decision Making David S. Chappell   297
CASE 18 American Airlines David S. Chappell   299
CASE 19 The New Vice President   303

Experiential Exercises   306

My Best Manager   306
Graffiti Needs   307
My Best Job   307
What Do You Value in Work?   307
My Asset Base   308
Expatriate Assignments   309
Cultural Cues   311
Prejudice in Our Lives   312
How We View Differences   313
Alligator River Story   313
Teamwork & Motivation   314
The Downside of Punishment   315
Annual Pay Raises   316
Tinker Toys   317
Job Design Preferences   318
My Fantasy Job   319
Eggsperiential Exercises   319
Scavenger Hunt – Team Building   320
Work Team Dynamics   321
Identifying Group Norms   321
Workgroup Culture   322
The Hot Seat   323

Organizations Alive!   324
Fast Food Technology   325
Alien Invasion   326
Interview a Leader   327
Leadership Skills Inventories   328
Leadership and Participation in Decision Making   329
My Best Manager: Revisited   330
Active Listening   331
Upward Appraisal   331
"360" Feedback   332
Role Analysis Negotiation   332
Lost at Sea   333
Entering the Unknown   334
Vacation Puzzle   335
The Ugli Orange   336
Force-Field Analysis   336

Self-Assessment Inventories   338

Managerial Assumptions   338
A 21st-Century Manager   339
Turbulence Tolerance Test   340
Global Readiness Index   341
Personal Values   342
Intolerance for Ambiguity   343
Two-Factor Profile   345
Are You Cosmopolitan?   345
Group Effectiveness   346
Organizational Design Preference   347
Which Culture Fits You?   347
Least Preferred Coworker Scale   348
Leadership Style   349
"TT" Leadership Style   350
Empowering Others   351
Machiavellianism   352
Personal Power Profile   353
Your Intuitive Ability   354
Decision-Making Biases   355
Conflict Management Styles   356
Your Personality Type   357
Time Management Profile   358

Contents

SECTION ONE   1

Organizational Behavior Today   3
What Is Organizational Behavior?   3
Shifting Paradigms of Organizational Behavior   3
Organizational Behavior and Diversity   4

Learning About Organizational Behavior   5
Organizational Behavior and the Learning Imperative   5
Scientific Foundations of Organizational Behavior   5
Interdisciplinary Body of Knowledge   5
Use of Scientific Methods   6
Focus on Application   6
Contingency Thinking   6

Organizations as Work Settings   7
Purpose, Mission, and Strategies   7
People and Work Systems   8

Organizational Behavior and Management   9
The Nature of Managerial Work   9
The Management Process   9
Managerial Roles and Networks   10
Managerial Skills and Competencies   11
Technical Skills   11
Human Skills   12
Conceptual Skills   12

Ethics and Organizational Behavior   12
Ways of Thinking About Ethical Behavior   12
Ethical Dilemmas in the Workplace   13
Organizational Social Responsibility   14
Work and the Quality of Life   14

Workforce Diversity   15
Equal Employment Opportunity   16
Managing Diversity   16

Demographic Differences   17
Gender   17
Age   17
Able-Bodiedness   18
Racial and Ethnic Groups   18

Aptitude and Ability   18

Personality   19
Personality Determinants and Development   19

Personality Traits and Classifications   21
Social Traits   22
Personal Conception Traits   22
Locus of Control   22
Authoritarianism/Dogmatism   23
Machiavellianism   24
Self-Monitoring   25
Emotional Adjustment Traits   25
Type A and Type B Orientation   25
Personality and Self-Concept   26

Values and Attitudes   27
Values   27
Sources and Types of Values   27
Patterns and Trends in Values   29
Attitudes   29
Attitudes and Behavior   30
Attitudes and Cognitive Consistency   31

Managing Diversity and Individual Differences   31

The Perceptual Process   32
Factors Influencing the Perceptual Process   33
The Perceiver   33
The Setting   33
The Perceived   34
Stages of the Perceptual Process   34
Attention and Selection   35
Organization   35
Interpretation   36
Retrieval   36
Response to the Perceptual Process   36

Common Perceptual Distortions   37
Stereotypes or Prototypes   37
Halo Effects   38
Selective Perception   38
Projection   38
Contrast Effects   39
Self-Fulfilling Prophecy   39

Managing the Perceptual Process   40
Impression Management   40
Distortion Management   40

Attribution Theory   41
Attribution Errors   42

vi ■ Contents

Attributions Across Cultures   42

The Concept of Organizational Culture   43
Functions and Components of Organizational Culture   43
External Adaptation   43
Internal Integration   44
Dominant Culture, Subcultures, and Countercultures   45
Importing Subcultures   46
Valuing Cultural Diversity   46
Levels of Cultural Analysis   47

Observable Aspects of Organizational Culture   48
Stories, Rites, Rituals, and Symbols   48
Cultural Rules and Roles   49
The Evolution of Shared Meanings from Observable Culture   49

Values and Organizational Culture   49
Management Philosophy   50
Organizational Myths   50
National Culture Influences   51

Managing Organizational Culture   52
Building, Reinforcing, and Changing Culture   52
Continuous Cultural Development   53

Organizational Development Process and Applications   54
Underlying Assumptions of OD   54
Shared Values and Principles Underlying OD   55
Action Research Foundations of OD   55
Organizational Development Interventions   56
Organizationwide Interventions   56
Group and Intergroup Interventions   58
Individual Interventions   58
OD and the Continuous Cultural Evolution   59

Change in Organizations   59
Planned and Unplanned Change   60
Organizational Forces and Targets for Change   60
Phases of Planned Change   61
Unfreezing   61
Changing   62
Refreezing   62

Planned Change Strategies   62
Force—Coercion   62
Rational Persuasion   63
Shared Power   64

Resistance to Change   64
Why People Resist Change   64
Resistance to the Change Itself   65
Resistance to the Change Strategy   65
Resistance to the Change Agent   65
How to deal with Resistance   65

Footnotes   67
Source Notes   71

SECTION TWO   73

High Performance Context of Organizational Behavior   75
OB and Changing Customer Expectations   75
OB and the Changing Workforce   75
OB and Changing Organizations   77

What is a High Performance Organization?   78
Emphasis on Intellectual Capital   78
Key Components of High Performance Organizations   79
Employee Involvement   79
Self-Directing Work Teams   79
Integrated Production Technologies   80
Organizational Learning   80
Total Quality Management   80

Management Challenges of High Performance Organizations   81
Environmental Linkages   81
Internal Integration   81
Middle Manager Roles   82
High Level Leadership   83
Greenfield Sites Versus Redesigns   83

Illustrative Case: Creating a High Performance Organization   84
Change Leadership   84
Total Systems Commitment   85
Implementation Processes   85

Groups in Organizations   87
What Is an Effective Group   87
Unique Contributions of Groups   87
Formal Groups   89
Informal Groups   90

Stages of Group Development   90
Forming Stage   90
Storming Stage   90
Norming Stage   91
Performing Stage   91
Adjourning Stage   92

Input Foundations of Group Effectiveness   92
Tasks   93
Goals, Rewards, and Resources   93
Technology   93
Membership Characteristics   94
Group Size   95

Group and Intergroup Dynamics   95
What Goes on within Groups   95
What Goes on between Groups   96

Decision Making in Groups   96
How Groups Make Decisions   97
Assets and Liabilities of Group Decision Making   98
Groupthink   98

How to Improve Group Decision Making   99
    Brainstorming   99
    Nominal Group Technique   99
    Delphi Technique   100
    Computer-Mediated Decision Making   100

High Performance Teams   100
    Types of Teams   100
    The Nature of Teamwork   101
    Diversity and Team Performance   102

Team Building   103
    How Team Building Works   103
    Approaches to Team Building   104

Improving Team Processes   105
    New Member Problems   105
    Task and Maintenance Leadership   105
    Roles and Role Dynamics   106
    Positive Norms   107
    Team Cohesiveness   108
        Conformity to Norms   109
        Influencing Cohesiveness   109

Teams and the High Performance Workplace   110
    Problem-Solving Teams   110
    Cross-Functional Teams   111
    Virtual Teams   111
    Self-Managing Teams   112
        How Self-Managing Teams Work   112
        Operational Implications of Self-Managing Teams   113

Decision Making Process   114
    Decision Environments   114
    Types of Decisions   115

Decision Making Models   115
    Classical and Behavioral Decision Theory   116
    The Garbage Can Model   117
    Decision Making Realities   118

Intuition, Judgment, and Creativity   118
    Judgmental Heuristics   119
    Creativity Factors   120

Managing the Decision-Making Process   120
    Choosing Problems to Address   121
    Deciding Who Should Participate   121
    Knowing When to Quit – Eliminating Escalating Commitments   123

Technology, Culture, and Ethics in Decision Making   124
    Information Technology and Decision Making   124
    Cultural Factors and Decision Making   125
    Ethical Issues and Decision Making   126

Conflict   127
    Types of Conflict   127
    Levels of Conflict   127

Functional and Dysfunctional Conflicts   128
    Culture and Conflict   129

Managing Conflict   130
    Stages of Conflict   130
    Causes of Conflict   131
    Indirect Conflict Management Approaches   132
        Reduced Interdependence   132
        Appeals to Common Goals   132
        Hierarchical Referral   133
        Altering Scripts and Myths   133
    Direct Conflict Management Approaches   133
        Lose—Lose Conflict   134
        Win—Lose Conflict   134
        Win—Win Conflict   135

Negotiation   135
    What is Negotiation?   135
    Negotiation Goals and Outcomes   135
    Ethical Aspects of Negotiation   136
    Organizational Settings for Negotiation   136
    Culture and Negotiation   136

Negotiation Strategies   137
    Distributive Negotiation   137
    Integrative Negotiation   138
    How to Gain Integrative Agreements   138
        Attitudinal Foundations   139
        Behavioral Foundations   139
        Information Foundations   139
    Common Negotiation Pitfalls   139
    Third-Party Roles in Negotiation   140

Footnotes   140
Source Notes   144

SECTION THREE   145

What Is Motivation   147
    Reinforcement, Content, and Process Theories   147
    Motivation Across Cultures   147

Reinforcement   148
    Classical and Operant Conditioning   148
    Reinforcement Strategies   150
        Positive Reinforcement   150
        Negative Reinforcement (Avoidance)   152
        Punishment   153
        Extinction   153
        Summary of Reinforcement Strategies   153
    Reinforcement Perspectives: Usage and Ethical Issues   154

Content Theories of Motivation   155
    Hierarchy of Needs Theory   155

ERG Theory   156
Acquired Needs Theory   157
Two-Factor Theory   157

Process Theories   159
Equity Theory   159
Expectancy Theory   160

Integrating the Motivation Theories   162
Job Satisfaction   162
Job Satisfaction, Retention and Performance   163
Argument: Satisfaction Causes Performance   163
Argument: Performance Causes Satisfaction   163
Argument: Rewards Cause Both Satisfaction and
Performance   164
Integrated Model of Motivation   164

Dynamics of Stress   165
Sources of Stress   165
Work-Related Stressors   165
Nonwork and Personal Stressors   166
Stress and Performance   166
Stress and Health   167
Stress Management   167

Footnotes   168
Source Notes   169

SECTION FOUR   171

Power   173
Position Power   173
Personal Power   174
Acquiring and Using Power and Influence   175
Building Position Power   175
Building Personal Power   176
Combined Building of Position and Personal Power   176
Turning Power into Relational Influence   177
Power, Formal Authority, and Obedience   178
The Milgram Experiments   178
Obedience and the Acceptance of Authority   179
Obedience and the Zone of Indifference   180

Empowerment   181
The Power Keys to Empowerment   181
Changing Position Power   182
Expanding the Zone of Indifference   182
Power as an Expanding Pie   182

Organizational Politics   183
The Two Traditions of Organizational Politics   183
The Double-Edged Sword of Organizational Politics   184
Organizational Politics and Self-Protection   184
Avoidance   185

Redirecting Responsibility   185
Defending Turf   186

Political Action and the Manager   186
Political Action and Subunit Power   187
Political Action in the Chief Executive Suite   187
Resource Dependencies   188
Organizational Governance   188

The Nature of Communication   190
The Communication Process   190
Feedback and Communication   192

Essentials of Interpersonal Communication   192
Effective and Efficient Communication   192
Nonverbal Communication   193
Active Listening   194

Communication Barriers   195
Physical Distractions   195
Semantic Problems   195
Mixed Messages   196
Cultural Differences   196
Absence of Feedback   196
Status Effects   197

Organizational Communication   197
Formal and Informal Channels   197
Communication Flows and Directions   198
Communication Networks   199

Communication and the High Performance Workplace   200
Changing Technologies   201
Complex Social Context   202

Footnotes   203
Source Notes   204

SECTION FIVE   205

Organizational Behavior and Globalization   207
A Global Economy   207
Regional Economic Alliances   208
Global Quality Standards   209
Global Managers   209

Cultures and Cultural Diversity   209
Popular Dimensions of Culture   210
Language   210
Time Orientation   210
Use of Space   211
Religion   211
Values and National Cultures   212
Understanding Cultural Differences   213

Globalization and People at Work   214
Multinational Employers   215

Multicultural Workforces   215
Expatriate Work Assignments   216
Ethical Behavior Across Cultures   217

A Global View of Organizational Learning   219
Are Management Theories Universal?   219
Best Practices Around the World   220

Technology and Job Design   220
Automation and Robotics   220
Flexible Manufacturing Systems   221
Electronic Offices   221
Work-Flow and Process Reengineering   222

Goal Setting and Job Design   222
Goal Setting Theory   222
Goal Setting Guidelines   222
Goal Setting and MBO   224

Alternative Work Arrangements   225
Compressed Work Weeks   225
Flexible Working Hours   225
Job Sharing   226
Work at Home and the Virtual Office   227
Part-Time Work   227

Organizational Design and Size   228
The Simple Design for Smaller Units and Firms   228

Operations Technology and Organizational Design   229
Thompson's View of Technology   229
Woodward's View of Technology   230
Where Operations Technology Dominates: The Adhocracy   230

Information Technology and Organizational Design   231
Information Technology as a Substitute   231
Information Technology as a Capability for Learning   232
Information Technology as a Strategic Capability   233

Environment and Organizational Design   234
Environmental Complexity   235
Environmental Richness   235
Environmental Interdependence   236
Uncertainty and Volatility   236
Using Alliances Where Environmental Factors Dominate   236

Strategy and Organizational Design   237
Competency-Based Strategies   238

Footnotes   238
Source Notes   241

THE OB SKILLS WORKBOOK   243

The F𝖠ST C𝖮MPANY Collection   245

ARTICLE 1   The Company of the Future   Robert B. Reich
245

Money Makes It Mutual   246
Mission Makes a Difference   247
Learning Makes You Grow   248
Fun Makes It Fresh   249
Pride Makes It Special   250
Balance Makes It Sustainable   250
The 21st-Century Company   252

ARTICLE 2   Life In The Fast Lane   Chuck Salter   **252**
It Sounds a Lot Like Auto Racing   252
New Teams Should Do Things in New Ways   253
You Win as a Team   253
Push for Perfection – but Accept Imperfection   254
To Speed Up, Slow Down   254
Don't Strut Your Stuff   254
To Win the Race, Drive by Different Rules   254
Face Down Your Toughest Competitor: Success   255

ARTICLE 3   Danger: Toxic Company   Alan M. Webber   **255**
The One Guaranteed Way to Get a 30% to 40% Productivity Gain   255
"Welcome to the Toxic Workplace! We Fire at Will!"   256
A Place Where People Come to Work to Get Rich Enough to Quit   256
Toxic Flextime: "Work any 18 Hours You Want."   256
What's the Difference Between a Factor of Production and a Human Being?   256
If Your Company Is So Great, Why Doesn't Anyone Want to Work There?   256
Which is Better Business – Paying Signing Bonuses or Treating People Right?   257
When You Look at Your People, What Do You See – Expenses or Assets?   257
Why Nothing Changes #1: Wishing Doesn't Make It So   257
Why Nothing Changes #2: Memory Is No Substitute for Thinking   258
How to Make Something Change: Start with You   258

ARTICLE 4   Learning for a Change   Alan M. Webber   **258**
What's Your Assessment of the Performance of Large-Scale Change Efforts over the Past Decade?   259
Why Haven't There Been More Successful Change Efforts?   259
So What Is the Deeper Explanation for the Failure of Corporate Change Efforts?   259
What Implications Does a Machine Mind-Set Have for Companies that Seek to Undergo Change?   260
Where, Specifically, Does the Mechanical Approach Go Wrong in Effecting Change?   260
What Happens When You See a Company as a Part of Nature?   260
How Does Challenging the Idea of the Hero-Leader Promote Change?   261
If the Idea of the Hero-Leader Takes Us in the Wrong Direction, What's the Right Direction?   261
What's the Best Way to Begin Creating Change?   262
After a Pilot Group Forms, What Are the Next Steps?   262

In Your New Book, You Identify the 10 Challenges of Change. Why focus on Challenges? 263

Back to the First Question: A Decade after *The Fifth Discipline* Appeared, Do You Think that Big Companies Can Change? 263

Sidebar: The 10 Challenges of Change 263

Sidebar: Chronology of Learning Organization Concepts 264

Cases for Critical Thinking 265

CASE 1 **Drexler's Bar-B-Que** Forest F. Aven, Jr., V. Jean Ramsey **265**
Review Questions 267

CASE 2 **Sun Microsystems: "We're the dot in .com"** David S. Chappell **267**
Sun Microsystems 267
Hard to Find Where the Sun Don't Shine 268
Java-Powered Net "Appliances" 268
Sun-AOL-Netscape 269
Review Questions 270
References 270

CASE 3 **Crossing Borders** Bernardo M. Ferdman, Plácida I. Gallegos and the Kaleel Jamison Consulting Group, Inc. **270**
Review Questions 271

CASE 4 **Never on a Sunday** Anne C. Cowden **272**
Review Questions 272

CASE 5 **MAGREC, Inc.** Mary McGarry, Barry R. Armandi **273**
Background 273
Pat's Dilemma 273
Review Questions 275

CASE 6 **It Isn't Fair** Barry R. Armandi **275**
Review Questions 277

CASE 7 **Amoco's Global Human Resource Systems** Ellen Ernst Kossek **277**
Review Questions 279

CASE 8 **I'm Not in Kansas Anymore** Anne C. Cowden **279**
Review Questions 280

CASE 9 **The Forgotten Group Member** Franklin Ramsoomair **280**
Review Questions 281

CASE 10 **NASCAR's Racing Teams** David S. Chappell **281**
NASCAR 281
Jeff Gordon – Racing Sensation 282
The High Performance TEAM 282
Review Questions 283
References 283

CASE 11 **First Community Financial** Mark Osborn **284**
Review Questions 285

CASE 12 **Mission Management and Trust** Mark Osborn **285**
Review Questions 286

CASE 13 **Motorola: Is a High Performance Culture Enough?** David S. Chappell **287**
The Evolution of Motorola 287

The Importance of Organizational Culture to Motorola 287
So What Went Wrong? 288
Review Questions 289
References 289

CASE 14 **Perot Systems: Can a High Performance Company Have a Human Side?** **289**
A Rich History 290
The New Face of Leadership? 291
Can a High Performance Company Have a Human Side? 292
The IPO 293
Review Questions 293
References 293

CASE 15 **Power or Empowerment at GM?** Aneil Mishra, Karen Mishra, and Kim Cameron **293**
Introduction 293
Background 294
Current Situation 294
Conclusion 295
Review Questions 296
References 296

CASE 16 **The Poorly Informed Walrus** Barbara McCain **296**
Review Questions 297

CASE 17 **Johnson and Johnson: Futuristic Decision Making** David S. Chappell **297**
Johnson and Johnson 297
FrameworkS at J&J 298
Does it Work? 299
Review Questions 299
References 299

CASE 18 **American Airlines** David S. Chappell **299**
The Airline Industry 300
Carrier Classifications 300
American Airlines 300
The Pilot "Sickout" 301
Where Do They Go From Here 302
Review Questions 302
References 302

CASE 19 **The New Vice President** **303**
Part A 303
Review Questions 303
Part B 303
Review Questions 304
Part C 304
Review Questions 304
Part D 304
Questions 305
Conclusion 305

Experiential Exercises 306

EXERCISE 1 **My Best Manager** **306**
Procedure 306

EXERCISE 2 **Graffiti Needs Assessment: Involving Students in the First Class Session** Barba K. Goza **307**
Procedure 307

EXERCISE 3 **My Best Job**   **307**
Procedure   307
EXERCISE 4 **What Do You Value in Work**   **307**
Procedures   307
EXERCISE 5 **My Asset Base**   **308**
Procedure   308
EXERCISE 6 **Expatriate Assignments** Robert E. Ledman
309
Procedure   309
Descriptions of Family Members   310
EXERCISE 7 **Cultural Cues** Susan Rawson Zacur and
W. Alan Randolph   **311**
Introduction   311
Procedure   311
EXERCISE 8 **Prejudice in Our Lives** Susan Schor, Annie McKee
and Ariel Fishman   **312**
Procedure   312
EXERCISE 9 **How We View Differences** Barbara Walker
313
Introduction   313
Procedure   313
Question   313
EXERCISE 10 **Alligator River Story**   **313**
The Alligator River Story   313
Procedure   314
EXERCISE 11 **Teamwork and Motivation** Dr. Barbara McCain
314
Procedure   314
Worksheet   315
EXERCISE 12 **The Downside of Punishment** Dr. Barbara McCain
315
Procedure   315
EXERCISE 13 **Annual Pay Raises**   **316**
Procedure   316
EXERCISE 14 **Tinker Toys** Bonnie McNeely   **317**
Procedure   317
EXERCISE 15 **Job Design Preferences**   **318**
Procedure   318
EXERCISE 16 **My Fantasy Job** Lady Hanson   **319**
Instructions   319
EXERCISE 17 **Eggsperiential Exercise** Dr. Barbara McCain
319
Materials Needed   319
Procedure   320
EXERCISE 18 **Scavenger Hunt – Team Building**
Michael R. Manning and Paula J. Schmidt   **320**
Introduction   320
Procedure   320
Items for Scavenger Hunt   320
EXERCISE 19 **Work Team Dynamics**   **321**
Introduction   321
Procedure   321
EXERCISE 20 **Identifying Group Norms**   **321**
Procedure   321
Scoring   322

EXERCISE 21 **Workgroup Culture** Conrad N. Jackson   **322**
Procedure   322
EXERCISE 22 **The Hot Seat** Barry R. Armandi   **323**
Procedure   323
EXERCISE 23 **Organizations Alive!** Bonnie L. McNeely
324
Procedure   325
EXERCISE 24 **Fast Food Technology** D. T. Hall and F.S. Hall
325
Introduction   325
Procedure   325
EXERCISE 25 **Alien Invasion**   **326**
Procedure   326
EXERCISE 26 **Interview a Leader** Bonnie McNeely   **327**
Procedure   327
Interview Questionnaire   327
EXERCISE 27 **Leadership Skills Inventories**   **328**
Procedure   328
EXERCISE 28 **Leadership and Participation in Decision
Making**   **329**
Procedure   329
EXERCISE 29 **My Best Manager: Revisited** J. Marcus Maier
330
Procedure   330
EXERCISE 30 **Active Listening** Robert Ledman   **331**
Procedure   331
EXERCISE 31 **Upward Appraisal**   **331**
Procedure   331
EXERCISE 32 **"360" Feedback** Timothy J. Serey   **332**
Introduction   332
Procedure   332
EXERCISE 33 **Role Analysis Negotiation** Paul Lyons   **332**
Introduction   332
Procedure   333
EXERCISE 34 **Lost At Sea**   **333**
Introduction   333
Procedure   334
EXERCISE 35 **Entering the Unkown** Michael R. Manning,
Conrad N. Jackson, and Paula S. Weber   **334**
Procedure   334
EXERCISE 36 **Vacation Puzzle** Barbar G. McCain and
Mary Khalili   **335**
Procedure   335
EXERCISE 37 **The Ugli Orange**   **336**
Introduction   336
Procedure   336
EXERCISE 38 **Force-Field Analysis**   **336**
Procedure   336

Self-Assessment Inventories   338

ASSESSMENT 1 **Managerial Assumptions**   **338**
Instructions   338
Scoring   339
Interpretation   339

ASSESSMENT 2 A 21st-Century Manager **339**
   Instructions   339
   Scoring   339
   Interpretation   339

ASSESSMENT 3 Turbulence Tolerance Test **340**
   Instructions   340
   Scoring   341
   Interpretation   341

ASSESSMENT 4 Global Readiness Index **341**
   Instructions   341
   Interpretation   342
   Scoring   342

ASSESSMENT 5 Personal Values **342**
   Instructions   342
   Scoring   343
   Interpretation   343

ASSESSMENT 6 Intolerance for Ambiguity **343**
   Instructions   343
   Scoring   344
   Interpretation   344

ASSESSMENT 7 Two-Factor Profile **345**
   Instructions   345
   Scoring   345
   Interpretation   345

ASSESSMENT 8 Are You Cosmopolitan? **345**
   Instructions   345
   Scoring and Interpretation   346

ASSESSMENT 9 Group Effectiveness **346**
   Instructions   346
   Scoring   346
   Interpretation   346

ASSESSMENT 10 Organizational Design Preference **347**
   Instructions   347
   Scoring   347
   Interpretation   347

ASSESSMENT 11 Which Culture Fits You? **347**
   Instructions   347
   Scoring   348
   Interpretation   348

ASSESSMENT 12 Least Preferred Coworker Scale **348**
   Instructions   348
   Scoring   348
   Interpretation   348

ASSESSMENT 13 Leadership Style **349**
   Instructions   349
   Scoring   350

ASSESSMENT 14 "TT" Leadership Style **350**
   Instructions   350
   Scoring   350
   Interpretation   351

ASSESSMENT 15 Empowering Others **351**
   Instructions   351
   Scoring   351
   Interpretation   351

ASSESSMENT 16 Machiavellianism **352**
   Instructions   352
   Scoring and Interpretation   352

ASSESSMENT 17 Personal Power Profile Marcus Maier **353**
   Instructions   353
   Scoring   354
   Interpretation   354

ASSESSMENT 18 Your Intuitive Ability **354**
   Instructions   354
   Scoring   355
   Interpretation   355

ASSESSMENT 19 Decision-Making Biases **355**
   Instructions   355
   Scoring   356
   Interpretation   356

ASSESSMENT 20 Conflict Management Styles **356**
   Instructions   356
   Scoring   356
   Interpretation   357

ASSESSMENT 21 Your Personality Type **357**
   Instructions   357
   Scoring   357
   Interpretation   357

ASSESSMENT 22 Time Mangement Profile **358**
   Instructions   358
   Scoring   358
   Interpretation   358

Section One

Section One

Organizational Behavior Today

People at work in organizations today are part of a new era. The institutions of society and the people who make them work are challenged in many and very special ways. Society at large increasingly expects high performance and high quality of life to go hand-in-hand, considers ethics and social responsibility core values, respects the vast potential of demographic and cultural diversity among people, and accepts the imprint of a globalization on everyday living and organizational competitiveness. In this new era of work and organizations, the body of knowledge we call "organizational behavior" offers many insights of great value.

■ WHAT IS ORGANIZATIONAL BEHAVIOR?

Formally defined, **organizational behavior**— OB for short—is the study of individuals and groups in organizations. Learning about OB will help you develop a better work-related understanding about yourself and other people. It can also expand your potential for career success in the dynamic, shifting, complex, and challenging *new* workplaces of today...and tomorrow.

■ **Organizational behavior** is the study of individuals and groups in organizations.

■ SHIFTING PARADIGMS OF ORGANIZATIONAL BEHAVIOR

Progressive workplaces today look and act very differently from those of the past. They have new features, they approach work processes in new ways, and they serve different customer and client markets. The last decade of the twentieth century was especially dramatic in both the nature and pace of change. One observer called it a "revolution that feels something like this: scary, guilty, painful, liberating, disorienting, exhilarating, empowering, frustrating, fulfilling, confusing, challenging. In other words, it feels very much like chaos."[1] But what began as a revolution has become everyday reality as we start a new century. Intense global competition, highly interdependent national economies, constantly emerging computer and information technologies, new forms of organizations, and shifting population demographics are now part of the norm. Today we are surrounded by both change and its implications for organizations—just look at the new world of electronic commerce,[2] and for individuals—look also at the demand for competencies with new technologies and commitment to continuous personal improvement.[3] What remains is the struggle to deal best with these changes, individually and institutionally, and to keep up the pace as further changes emerge.[4]

In an article entitled "The Company of the Future," Harvard Professor and former Secretary of Labor Robert Reich says: "Everybody works for somebody or something—be it a board of directors, a pension fund, a venture capitalist, or a traditional boss. Sooner or later you're going to have to decide who you want to work for."[5] In making this decision, you will want to join a progressive workplace that reflects values consistent with your own. This book can help you prepare for such choices in full recognition that our transition to the new century includes these trends:[6]

Trends in the new workplace

- Demise of "command-and-control"—with increasing competitiveness in organizational environments, traditional hierarchical structures are proving too unwieldy, slow, and costly to do well.
- Emergence of new workforce expectations—a new generation of workers is bringing with it less tolerance for hierarchy, more informality, and concerns for performance merit rather than status.
- Increasing impact of information technologies—organizations are now burgeoning with computers, and the consequent implications for information utilization are far reaching and substantial.
- Belief in empowerment—a dynamic and complex environment places a premium on knowledge, experience, and commitment, all of which thrive in high-involvement and participatory work settings.
- Emphasis on teamwork—organizations today are less vertical and more horizontal in focus; driven by complex environments and customer demands, work is increasingly team based with a focus on peer contributions.
- Concern for work-life balance—as society increases in complexity, organizations are paying more attention to how members balance the sometimes-conflicting demands and priorities of work and personal affairs.

■ ORGANIZATIONAL BEHAVIOR AND DIVERSITY

■ **Workforce diversity** involves differences based on gender, race and ethnicity, age, and able-bodiedness.

An important watchword in the twenty-first century is **workforce diversity**— the presence of differences based on gender, race and ethnicity, age, and able-bodiedness.[7] Success in the new workplace requires a set of skills for working successfully with a broad mix of people from different racial and ethnic backgrounds, of different ages and genders, and of different domestic and national cultures. *Valuing diversity* is an OB theme. It refers to managing and working with others in full respect for their individual differences. Interpersonal sensitivity and cultural respect are indispensable to valuing diversity.

■ The **glass ceiling effect** is a hidden barrier limiting advancement of women and minorities in organizations.

Even though valuing diversity is emphasized in our books and classrooms, much remains to be accomplished. A **glass ceiling effect** acts as a hidden barrier limiting the career advancement of minorities and women in some situations. A *Harvard Business Review* forum on "Race in the U.S. Workplace," for example, included these opening statements: "Many people of color themselves still struggle with the closed doors of institutional racism...ignorance and prejudice have by no means disappeared from the U.S. workforce." The article went on to conclude: "Yet there are signs of headway."[8] A recent study of 860 U.S. companies indicates that the number of African-Americans serving as board directors increased 18 percent in a two-year period; the number of women directors increased 4 percent.[9] Yet, as one indicator of lingering disparities in diversity representation in the executive ranks, women are reported as holding only about 11 percent of corporate officerships in Fortune 500 companies (see The Effective Manager 1.1). They also earn as senior executives only 68 cents to the dollar earned by the highest-paid men.[10]

Learning About Organizational Behavior

We live and work in a knowledge-based economy that is continually laced with the winds of change. This places a great premium on "learning" by organizations as well as individuals. Only the learners, so to speak, will be able to maintain the pace and succeed in a constantly changing environment.[11]

■ ORGANIZATIONAL BEHAVIOR AND THE LEARNING IMPERATIVE

Consultants and scholars emphasize **organizational learning** as the process of acquiring knowledge and utilizing information to adapt successfully to changing circumstances.[12] Organizations must be able to change continuously and positively while searching continuously for new ideas and opportunities. The same is true for each of us. We must strive for continuous improvement to keep pace with a dynamic and complex environment.

Life-long learning is a popular concept these days, and the message is relevant. You can and must learn from day-to-day work experiences, conversations with colleagues and friends, counseling and advice from mentors, success models, training seminars and workshops, and the information available in the popular press and mass media. This book contains a special section, *The Organizational Behavior Workbook*, designed specifically to help you begin this process. Included in the workbook are many opportunities for you, individually and in student study groups, to analyze readings and cases, participate in experimental exercises, and complete skills-assessment inventories to advance your learning.

> ■ **Organizational learning** is the process of acquiring knowledge and using information to adapt successfully to changing circumstances.

■ SCIENTIFIC FOUNDATIONS OF ORGANIZATIONAL BEHAVIOR

As far back as a century ago, consultants and scholars were giving increased attention to the systematic study of management. Although most attention was initially on physical working conditions, principles of administration, and industrial engineering principles, by the 1940s the focus had broadened to include the essential human factor. This gave impetus to research dealing with individual attitudes, group dynamics, and the relationships between managers and workers. Eventually, the discipline of organizational behavior emerged as a broader and encompassing approach. Today, it continues to evolve as a discipline devoted to scientific understanding of individuals and groups in organizations, and of the performance implications of organizational structures, systems, and processes.[13]

Interdisciplinary Body of Knowledge   OB is an interdisciplinary body of knowledge with strong ties to the behavioral sciences—psychology, sociology,

Figure 1.1
Research methods in organizational behavior.

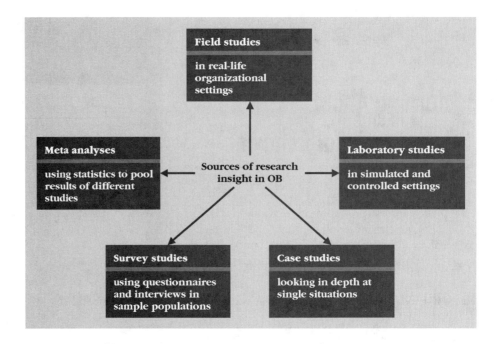

and anthropology, as well as to allied social sciences—such as economics and political science. Organizational behavior is unique, however, in its devotion to applying and integrating these diverse insights to achieve a better understanding of human behavior in organizations.

Use of Scientific Methods   OB uses scientific methods to develop and empirically test generalizations about behavior in organizations. Figure 1.1 describes research methodologies commonly used. Scientific thinking is important to OB researchers and scholars for these reasons: (1) the process of data collection is controlled and systematic; (2) proposed explanations are carefully tested; and (3) only explanations that can be scientifically verified are accepted. Research concepts and designs in OB are explained further in the module "Research Methods in Organizational Behavior."

Focus on Application   The field of organizational behavior focuses on applications that can make a real difference in how organizations and people in them perform. Outcome or dependent variables studied by researchers, for example, include task performance, job satisfaction, job involvement, absenteeism, and turnover. It is in this sense that OB is an applied social science that can ultimately help to improve the functioning of organizations and the work experiences of their members. Among the practical questions addressed by the discipline and in this book are: How should rewards such as merit pay raises be allocated? When should jobs be designed for individuals and for groups? What are the ingredients of successful teamwork? How can organizational cultures be changed? Should decisions be made by individual, consultative, or group methods? In a negotiation, what is the best way to achieve "win-win" outcomes?

Contingency Thinking   Rather than assume that there is one "best" or universal way to manage people and organizations, OB recognizes that management practices must be tailored to fit the exact nature of each situation. Using a **contingency approach**, researchers try to identify how different situations can best be understood and handled. We recognize that culture can affect how OB theories and concepts apply in different countries.[14] What works well in one culture may not work as well in another. Other important contingency variables addressed in this book include environment, technology, task, structure, and people.

■ The **contingency approach** seeks ways to meet the needs of different management situations.

Organizations as Work Settings

The study of organizational behavior must be framed in an understanding of organizations as work settings. An **organization** is formally defined as a collection of people working together in a division of labor to achieve a common purpose. This definition describes a wide variety of clubs, voluntary organizations, and religious bodies, as well as entities such as small and large businesses, labor unions, schools, hospitals, and government agencies. The insights and applications of OB can be applied to help all such organizations perform up to expectations as social institutions.

■ **Organizations** are collections of people working together to achieve a common purpose.

■ PURPOSE, MISSION, AND STRATEGIES

The *core purpose* of an organization may be stated as the creation of goods or services for customers. Nonprofit organizations produce services with public benefits, such as health care, education, judicial processing, and highway maintenance. Large and small for-profit businesses produce consumer goods and services such as automobiles, banking, travel, gourmet dining, and accommodations.

Missions and *mission statements* focus the attention of organizational members and external constituents on the core purpose.[15] For example, the pharmaceutical giant Merck states that its purpose is "to preserve human life." The retailer Wal-Mart states that it seeks "to give ordinary folk the chance to buy the same things as rich people."[16] Increasingly, mission statements are written to communicate a clear *vision* in respect to long-term goals and future aspirations. The corporate vision at America West Airlines expresses the desire "to be known for its focus on customer service and its high performance culture."[17] Bold and challenging visions can attract attention and help draw members together in the quest for high performance. As Robert Reich states in his description of the company of the future: "Talented people want to be part of something that they can believe in, something that confers meaning on their work, on their lives—something that involves a mission."[18]

Given a sense of purpose and a vision, organizations pursue action *strategies* to accomplish them. The variety of mergers and acquisitions common in business today, such as the Daimler-Chrysler combination, are examples of corporate strategies to achieve and sustain advantage in highly competitive environments. In this context, strategies must be both well formulated and well implemented for the organization to succeed.[19] The plan alone is insufficient to the broader strategic goal: To get and stay ahead of the competition. It is here, at the level of action, that the field of organizational behavior becomes especially important. A knowledge of OB is essential to effective strategy implementation. Things happen in organizations because of the efforts of people, and how people work together in organizations is what OB is all about.

■ PEOPLE AND WORK SYSTEMS

When CEO Richard Kovacevic of Norwest was asked to comment on the bank's performance, he said: "Our success has to do with execution…talented, professional, motivated people who care…that's our competitive advantage."[20] Leaders of today's organizations recognize the importance of putting people first. They understand the new significance of the old concept—people are an organization's most critical assets.

One of the important directions in OB today is the emphasis on **intellectual capital** as represented by the sum total of knowledge, expertise, and dedication of an organization's workforce.[21] It recognizes that even in the age of high technology, people are the indispensable **human resources** whose knowledge and performance advance the organization's purpose, mission, and strategies. Only through human efforts can the great advantages be realized from other *material resources* of organizations such as technology, information, raw materials, and money. A recent *Fortune* survey of America's most-admired firms goes so far as to report that "the single best predictor of overall success was a company's ability to attract, motivate, and retain talented people."[22]

Today's strategic emphasis on customer-driven and market-driven organizations places great significance on understanding the relationship between an organization and its environment. As shown in Figure 1.2, organizations can be viewed as **open systems** that obtain resource inputs from the environment and transform them into outputs that are returned to the environment in the form of finished goods or services. If everything works right, the environment values these outputs and creates a continuing demand for them. This sustains operations and allows the organization to survive and prosper over the long run. But things can and sometimes do go wrong in the organization/environment relationship. If the value chain breaks down and an organization's goods or services become unpopular, it will sooner or later have difficulty obtaining the resources it needs to operate. In the extreme case, it will be forced out of existence.

■ **Intellectual capital** is the sum total of knowledge, expertise, and energy available from organizational members.

■ **Human resources** are the people who do the work that helps organizations fulfill their missions.

■ **Open systems** transform human and material resource inputs into finished goods and services.

**Figure 1.2
Organization and environment relationships.**

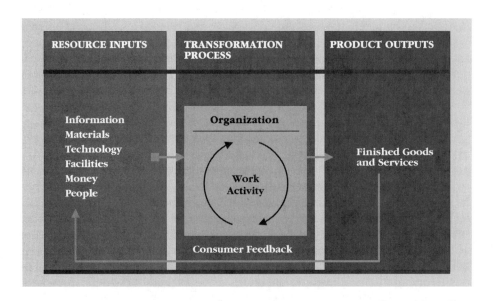

Organizational Behavior and Management

Regardless of your career direction and entry point, the field of organizational behavior will someday become especially important as you try to master the special challenges of working as a **manager**. In all organizations, managers perform jobs that involve directly supporting the work efforts of others. Being a manager is a unique challenge that carries distinct performance responsibilities. Managers help other people get important things done in timely, high-quality, and personally satisfying ways. In the new workplace, this is accomplished more through "helping" and "supporting" than through traditional notions of "directing" and "controlling." Indeed, the word "manager" is increasingly being linked in the new workplace to roles described by such titles as "coordinator," "coach," or "team leader."[23]

■ **Managers** are formally responsible for supporting the work efforts of other people.

■ THE NATURE OF MANAGERIAL WORK

Anyone who serves as a manager or team leader assumes a unique responsibility for work that is accomplished largely through the efforts of other people. The result is a very demanding and complicated job that has been described by researchers in the following terms.[24] *Managers work long hours.* A work week of more than the standard 40 hours is typical. The length of the work week tends to increase as one advances to higher managerial levels; heads of organizations often work the longest hours. *Managers are busy people.* Their work is intense and involves doing many different things on any given workday. The busy day of a manager includes a shifting mix of incidents that require attention, with the number of incidents being greatest for lower-level managers. *Managers are often interrupted.* Their work is fragmented and variable. Interruptions are frequent, and many tasks must be completed quickly. *Managers work mostly with other people.* In fact, they spend little time working alone. Time spent with others includes working with bosses, peers, subordinates, subordinates of their subordinates, as well as outsiders, such as customers, suppliers, and the like. *Managers are communicators.* In general, managers spend a lot of time getting, giving, and processing information. Their work is often face-to-face verbal communication that takes place during formal and informal meetings. Higher level managers typically spend more time in scheduled meetings than do lower level managers.

■ THE MANAGEMENT PROCESS

An *effective manager* is one whose organizational unit, group, or team consistently achieves its goals while members remain capable, committed, and enthusiastic. This definition focuses attention on two key results. The first is *task performance*—the quality and quantity of the work produced or the services provided by the work unit as a whole. The second is *job satisfaction*—how people feel about their work and the work setting. Just as a valuable machine should not be allowed to break down for lack of proper maintenance, the valuable contributions of the human resource should never be lost for lack of proper care. Accordingly, OB directs a manager's attention to such matters as job satisfaction, job involvement, and organizational commitment, as well as measures of actual task performance.

Figure 1.3
The management process of planning, organizing, leading, and controlling.

The job of any manager or team leader is largely one of adding value to the work setting by doing things that help others to accomplish their tasks. A traditional and still relevant way of describing this job is as a set of tasks or functions that must be performed constantly and often simultaneously. As shown in Figure 1.3, these four *functions of management* are planning, organizing, leading, and controlling. They form a framework for managerial action that can be described as follows:[25]

- **Planning**—Defining goals, setting specific performance objectives, and identify the actions needed to achieve them.
- **Organizing**—Creating work structures and systems, and arranging resources to accomplish goals and objectives.
- **Leading**—Instilling enthusiasm by communicating with others, motivating them to work hard, and maintaining good interpersonal relations.
- **Controlling**—Ensuring that things go well by monitoring performance and taking corrective action as necessary.

■ MANAGERIAL ROLES AND NETWORKS

In what has become a classic study of managerial behavior, Henry Mintzberg moved beyond this functional description and identified three sets of roles that managers must be prepared to perform on a daily basis.[26] These roles are shown in Figure 1.4. In the first category are *interpersonal roles* that involve working directly with other people. They include hosting and attending official ceremonies (figurehead), creating enthusiasm and serving people's needs (leader), and maintaining contacts with important people and groups (liaison). The *informational roles* involve exchanging information with other people. They include seeking out relevant information (monitor), sharing relevant information with insiders (disseminator), and sharing relevant information with outsiders (spokesperson).

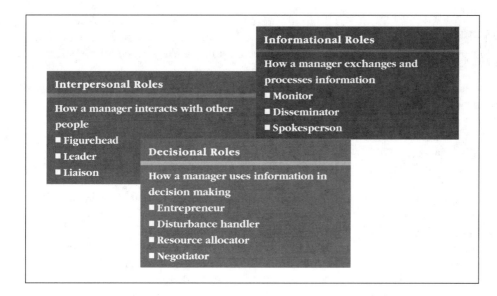

Figure 1.4
**Ten roles of effective
managers.**

The *decisional roles* involve making decisions that affect other people. They include seeking out problems to solve and opportunities to explore (entrepreneur), helping to resolve conflicts (disturbance handler), allocating resources to various uses (resource allocator), and negotiating with other parties (negotiator).

Essential to these roles and to all managerial work are good interpersonal relationships with a wide variety of people, both inside and outside the organization.[27] Managers and team leaders should be able to develop, maintain, and work well within *task networks*—of specific job-related contacts, *career networks*—of career guidance and opportunity resources and *social networks*—of trustworthy friends and peers.[28]

■ MANAGERIAL SKILLS AND COMPETENCIES

A *skill* is an ability to translate knowledge into action that results in a desired performance. Robert Katz divides the essential managerial skills into three categories: technical, human, and conceptual.[29] He further suggests that the relative importance of these skills varies across the different levels of management. Technical skills are considered more important at entry levels of management, where supervisors and team leaders must deal with job-specific problems. Senior executives are concerned more with issues of organizational purpose, mission, and strategy. Broader, more ambiguous, and longer term decisions dominate attention at these higher levels, and conceptual skills gain in relative importance. Human skills, which are strongly grounded in the foundations of organizational behavior, are consistent in their importance across all managerial levels.

Technical Skills   A **technical skill** is an ability to perform specialized tasks. Such ability derives from knowledge or expertise gained from education or experience. This skill involves proficiency at using select methods, processes, and procedures to accomplish tasks. Perhaps the best current example is skill in using the latest communication and information technologies. In the "high-tech" workplaces of today, technical proficiency in word processing, database management, spreadsheet analysis, E-mail, and communications networks are often

■ **Technical skill** is an ability to perform specialized tasks.

OB Across Functions

FINANCE

New CFO Key to Turnaround

With a strong background in finance and information systems, Deborah Hopkins also drew upon her people skills and experience with diversity and mentoring programs when taking on her new job as CFO of Boeing Aircraft. One of her first public events was a company retreat attended by 280 corporate executives. She presented basic financial formulas carefully, concerned that her audience not think she was talking beneath them. The praise flowed, and many attendees thanked her for clarifying basic business concepts. Hopkins has the experience and skills to make a difference at Boeing by teaching the managers about business, increasing the sophistication of managerial decision making, and helping to increase the integration of accounting and financial systems. Harry Stonecipher, Boeing's President and CEO, says that Hopkins is "a good communicator and she knows what she is talking about." This combination of technical and human skills is beneficial for both Boeing and Hopkins's career.

hiring prerequisites. Some technical skills require preparatory education, whereas others are acquired through specific training and on-the-job experience.

Human Skills Central to managerial work and team leadership are **human skills**, or the ability to work well with other people. They emerge as a spirit of trust, enthusiasm, and genuine involvement in interpersonal relationships. A person with good human skills will have a high degree of self-awareness and a capacity for understanding or empathizing with the feelings of others. People with this skill are able to interact well with others, engage in persuasive communications, deal successfully with disagreements and conflicts, and more. Human skills are indispensable in the new age of organizations where traditions of hierarchy and vertical structures are giving way to lateral relations and peer structures.[30]

Conceptual Skills All good managers are able to view the organization or situation as a whole and to solve problems to the benefit of everyone concerned. This capacity to analyze and solve complex and interrelated problems is a **conceptual skill**. It involves the ability to see and understand how the whole organizational system works, and how the parts are interrelated. Conceptual skill is used to identify problems and opportunities, gather and interpret relevant information, and make good problem-solving decisions that serve the organization's purpose.

■ **Human skill** is the ability to work well with other people.

■ **Conceptual skill** is the ability to analyze and solve complex problems.

■ **Ethical behavior** is morally accepted as "good" and "right."

Ethics and Organizational Behavior

The word "ethics" is important in OB. **Ethical behavior** is that accepted as morally "good" and "right," as opposed to "bad" or "wrong," in a particular setting.[31] Is it ethical to withhold information that might discourage a job candidate from joining your organization? Is it ethical to ask someone to take a job you know will not be good for his or her career progress? Is it ethical to ask so much of someone that they continually have to choose between "having a 'career' and having a 'life'?" The list of questions can go on and on, but an important point remains: The public is increasingly demanding that people in organizations and the organizations themselves all act in accordance with high ethical and moral standards.

■ WAYS OF THINKING ABOUT ETHICAL BEHAVIOR

Ethical behavior conforms not only to the dictates of law but also to a broader moral code that is common to society as a whole. Just exactly what moral code governs a person's choices, however, is a subject of debate. At least four ways of thinking about ethical behavior in and by organizations can be identified.

The *utilitarian view* considers ethical behavior to be that which delivers the greatest good to the greatest number of people. Those who subscribe to the results-oriented utilitarian logic assess the moral aspects of their decisions in terms of the consequences they create. Utilitarianism believes that the needs of the many outweigh the needs of the few. From such a perspective, it may be ethical to close a factory in one town in order to keep the parent corporation profitable and operating in several other towns.

The *individualism view* considers ethical behavior to be that which is best for an individual's long-term self-interests. In principle, at least, someone who acts unethically in the short run—such as by denying a qualified minority employee a promotion, should *not* succeed in the long run because the short-run action will not be tolerated. Thus, if everyone operated with long-term self-interest in mind, their short-run actions would be ethical.

The *moral-rights view* considers ethical behavior to be that which respects fundamental rights shared by all human beings. This view is tied very closely to the principle of basic human rights, such as those of life, liberty, and fair treatment by law. In an organization, this principle is reflected in such issues as rights to privacy, due process, and freedom of speech. Ethical behavior does not violate any of these fundamental human rights.

The *justice view* considers ethical behavior to be that which is fair and impartial in its treatment of people. It is based on the concept of equitable treatment for all concerned. In OB, two issues address this view of ethical behavior.[32] **Procedural Justice** is the degree to which the rules and procedures specified by policies are properly followed in all cases under which they are applied. In a sexual harassment case, for example, this may mean that required hearings are held for every case submitted for administrative review. **Distributive justice** is the degree to which all people are treated the same under a policy, regardless of race, ethnicity, gender, age, or any other demographic characteristic. In a sexual harassment case, this might mean that a complaint filed by a man against a woman would receive the same hearing as one filed by a woman against a man.

■ **Procedural justice** is the degree to which policies and procedures are properly followed.

■ **Distributive justice** is the degree to which all people are treated the same under a policy.

■ An **ethical dilemma** requires a person to choose among actions that offer possible benefits while also violating ethical standards.

■ ETHICAL DILEMMAS IN THE WORKPLACE

An **ethical dilemma** is a situation in which a person must decide whether or not to do something that, although benefiting them or the organization, or both, may be considered unethical. It is difficult to predict exactly what ethical dilemmas you will someday face. However, research suggests that people at work often encounter such dilemmas in their relationships with superiors, subordinates, customers, competitors, suppliers, and regulators. Common issues underlying the dilemmas involve honesty in communications and contracts, gifts and entertainment, kickbacks, pricing practices, and employee terminations.[33] More and more organizations are offering ethics training programs that offer advice (see The Effective Manager 1.2) for handling ethical dilemmas.[34] In addition, the training helps partici-

THE EFFECTIVE MANAGER 1.2

HOW TO DEAL WITH ETHICAL DILEMMAS

1. Recognize and clarify the dilemma.
2. Get all the possible facts.
3. List all of your options.
4. Test each option by asking:
   Is it legal? Is it right? Is it beneficial?
5. Make your decision.
6. Double check your decision by asking:
   How will I feel if my family finds out? How will I feel if this is printed in the newspaper?
7. Then, and only then, take action.

pants learn how to identify and deal with these common rationalizations that are sometimes used to help justify actual or potential misconduct.[35]

- Pretending the behavior is not really unethical or illegal.
- Excusing the behavior by saying it's really in the organization's or your best interest.
- Assuming the behavior is okay because no one else is expected to find out about it.
- Presuming your superiors will support and protect you if anything should go wrong.

■ ORGANIZATIONAL SOCIAL RESPONSIBILITY

■ **Social responsibility** is the obligation of organizations to behave in ethical and moral ways.

Closely related to the ethics of workplace behavior is **social responsibility**—the obligation of organizations to behave in ethical and moral ways as institutions of the broader society. This concept suggests that members must ensure that their ethical frameworks extend to the organization as a whole. Managers and leaders should commit organizations to actions that are consistent with both the quest for high productivity and the objective of corporate social responsibility. Unfortunately, it doesn't always turn out this way. Some years ago, for example, two Beech-nut senior executives were sentenced to jail for their roles in a notorious case of organizational wrongdoing. The scandal involved the sale of adulterated apple juice for infants. Although the bottles were labeled "100% fruit juice," the contents turned out to be a blend of chemical ingredients. This case, like many others that make the daily news, came to public awareness because of a *whistleblower*—someone within the organization who exposes the wrongdoings of others in order to preserve high ethical standards.[36]

■ WORK AND THE QUALITY OF LIFE

In many ways, the study of organizational behavior is a search for practical ideas on how to help organizations achieve high performance outcomes while always acting in an ethical and socially responsible manner. A central concern in this quest must be the well being of an organization's entire workforce—this means everyone, not just the managers. The term **quality of work life**, or QWL, is a prominent indicator in OB of the overall quality of human experience in the workplace. It is a reminder that high performance in any work setting can and should be accomplished by high levels of job satisfaction.

■ **Quality of work life** is the overall quality of human experiences in the workplace.

A commitment to QWL can be considered a core value of OB. The stage was set very early in the life of the discipline by theorists with a strong human orientation, such as Douglas McGregor.[37] He contrasted what he called *Theory X assumptions*—that people basically disliked work, needed direction, and avoided responsibility, with *Theory Y assumptions*—that people liked work, were creative, and accepted responsibility. For McGregor, Theory Y assumptions were the most appropriate and tended to create positive *self-fulfilling prophecies*. That is, when people were treated well at work, the likelihood was that they would respond positively and as expected.

Today the many concepts and theories discussed in OB reflect QWL and Theory Y themes. The hallmarks of excellence in management and organizations now include *empowerment*—involving people from all levels of responsibility in decision making; *trust*—redesigning jobs, systems, and structures to give people more personal discretion in their work; *rewards*—building reward systems that are fair, relevant, and consistent, while contingent on work performance; *responsiveness*—making the work setting more pleasant and supportive of individual needs and family responsibilities; and **work-life balance**—making sure that the demands of the job are a reasonable fit with one's personal life and non-work responsibilities.[38]

A commitment to QWL is consistent with respect for what was earlier called the intellectual capital of an organization. It involves putting people first in any list of organizational priorities. The next discussion will continue to explore how people help to build high performance organizations. For now, consider the leadership challenge posed in these comments made by Jeffrey Pfeffer in his book, *The Human Equation: Building Profits by Putting People First.*[39]

> The key to managing people in ways that lead to profits, productivity, innovation, and real organizational learning ultimately lie in how you think about your organization and its people…. When you look at your people, do you see costs to be reduced?… Or, when you look at your people do you see intelligent, motivated, trustworthy individuals—the most critical and valuable strategic assets your organization can have?

Workforce Diversity

A majority of Fortune 500 companies, including Colgate Palmolive, Corning, and Quaker Oats, are now providing incentives for executives to deal successfully with workforce diversity.[40] **Workforce diversity** refers to the presence of individual human characteristics that make people different from one another.[41] More specifically, this diversity comprises key demographic differences among members of a given workforce, including gender, race and ethnicity, age, and able-bodiedness. Sometimes they also encompass other factors, such as marital status, parental status, and religion.[42] The challenge is how to manage workforce diversity in a way that both respects the individual's unique perspectives and contributions and promotes a shared sense of organization vision and identity.

Workforce diversity is increasing in both the United States and Canada, as it is in much of the rest of the world. For example, in the United States, between 1990 and 2005, about 50 percent of the new entrants to the labor force will be women and racial and ethnic groups such as African Americans, Latinos, and Asians. At the same time, those 55 and older are projected to make up nearly 15 percent of the labor force. All of this is in sharp contrast to the traditional, younger, mostly white American male, labor force. Canadian and U.K. trends for women are similar.[43]

As the workforce becomes increasingly diverse, the possibility of stereotyping and discrimination increases and managing diversity becomes more important. **Stereotyping** occurs when one thinks of an individual as belonging to a group or category—for instance, elderly person—and the characteristics commonly associated with the group or category are assigned to the individual in question—for instance, older people aren't creative. Demographic characteristics may serve as the basis of stereotypes that obscure individual differences and prevent people

■ **Work-life balance** deals with the demands from one's work and personal affairs.

■ **Workforce diversity** is differences based on gender, race and ethnicity, age and able-bodiedness.

OB Across Functions

HUMAN RESOURCE MANAGEMENT

Special Recruiting for Project Management

The Vera Institute of Justice was approached by the U.S. Immigration and Naturalization Service (INS) to help with a problem. On any given day INS had 80,000 people in deportation proceedings, but only 8000 beds in its detention facilities. Vera made a counterproposal to create a community supervision program along with a new screening system for detention, allowing INS to better use its space *and* improve compliance for those immigrants released. Four staff, two at Vera and two recruited for their special functional knowledge of the project area, served as a cross-functional team and devoted five months to planning for the project. The heart of the plan was a screening process to determine those immigrants whom it was safe to release and who had an incentive to appear for INS hearings. The plan was reviewed at a project meeting where all the other project directors, plus planners and key administrators met to assess it. Ultimately, INS accepted a three-year demonstration project, paying Vera $2 million per year. A national advisory board of numerous experts is involved with evaluating the project. If it appears successful, Vera will move ahead and use a similar process to develop or demonstrate eight additional programs.

from getting to know others as individuals and accurately assessing their performance potential. If you believe that older people are not creative, for example, you may mistakenly decide not to assign a very inventive 60-year-old person to an important task force.

Discrimination against certain people in the organization is not only a violation of U.S., Canadian, and European Union (EU) laws, but it is also counterproductive because it prevents the contributions of people who are discriminated against from being fully utilized. Many firms are increasingly recognizing that a diverse workforce that reflects societal differences helps bring them closer to their customers.

■ EQUAL EMPLOYMENT OPPORTUNITY

Equal employment opportunity involves both workplace nondiscrimination and affirmative action. Employment decisions are nondiscriminatory when there is no intent to exclude or disadvantage legally protected groups. *Affirmative action* is a set of remedial actions designed to compensate for proven discrimination or correct for statistical imbalances in the labor force (e.g., local workers are 90 percent Hispanic, and your organization employs only 10 percent Hispanics).[44]

The most comprehensive statute prohibiting employment discrimination is Title VII of the Civil Rights Act of 1964. This act prohibits employers from discriminating against any individual with respect to compensation, terms, or conditions of employment because of race, color, religion, sex, or national origin. Affirmative action plans are required of federal government agencies and federal contractors, as well as organizations found to be in noncompliance with equal employment opportunity provisions. Many organizations also have implemented voluntary affirmative action plans.[45]

Affirmative action is legally driven by federal, state and provincial, and local laws, as well as numerous court cases. It requires written reports containing plans and statistical goals for specific groups of people in terms of such employment practices as hiring, promotions, and layoffs.[46]

■ MANAGING DIVERSITY

The concept of managing diversity in organizations emphasizes appreciation of differences in creating a setting where everyone feels valued and accepted. An organization's success or progress in managing diversity can be monitored by organizational surveys of attitudes and perceptions, among other means. Managing diversity assumes that groups will retain their own characteristics and will shape the firm as well as be shaped by it, creating a common set of values that will strengthen ties with customers, enhance recruitment, and the like. Sometimes, diversity management is resisted because of fear of change and discomfort with differences. To deal with this resistance, some countries, such as Canada, have laws designed to encourage the management of diversity at the provincial level through Employment Equity Legislation.[47]

Demographic Differences

Demographic characteristics are the background characteristics that help shape what a person becomes. Such attributes may be thought of in both current terms—for example, an employee's current medical status—and historical terms—for instance, where and how long a person has worked at various jobs. Demographic characteristics of special interest from equal employment opportunity and workplace diversity considerations include gender, age, race, ethnicity, and able-bodiedness.

■ **Demographic characteristics** are the background variables (e.g. age, gender) that help shape what a person becomes over time.

■ GENDER

The research on working women in general tells us that there are very few differences between men and women that affect job performance (see The Effective Manager 1.3). Thus, men and women show no consistent differences in their problem-solving abilities, analytical skills, competitive drive, motivation, learning ability, or sociability. However, women are reported to be more conforming and to have lower expectations of success than men do. And, women's absenteeism rates tend to be higher than those of men. This latter finding may change, however, as we see men starting to play a more active role in raising children; absenteeism is also likely to be less frequent as telecommuting, flexible working hours, and the like become more prevalent.[48] In respect to pay, women's earnings have risen slowly from 59 percent of men's in 1975 to 76 percent most recently.[49] Certainly, this rise is not consistent with the doubling of women in the labor force since 1970.[50]

■ AGE

The research findings concerning age are particularly important given the aging of the workforce. People 50 years old and older account for 85 percent of the projected labor force growth between 1990 and 2005.[51] Older workers are susceptible to being stereotyped as inflexible and undesirable in other ways. In some cases, workers as young as age forty are considered to be "old" and complain that their experience and skills are no longer valued. Age-discrimination lawsuits are increasingly common in the United States.[52] Such discrimination also operates in Britain, where 44 percent of older managers say they have experienced age discrimination.[53] On the other hand, small businesses in particular tend to value

---

THE EFFECTIVE MANAGER 1.3

TIPS IN DEALING WITH MALE AND FEMALE MANAGERS

- Do not assume that male and female managers differ in personal qualities.
- Make sure that policies, practices, and programs minimize gender differences in managers' job experiences.
- Do not assume that management success is more likely for either females or males.
- Recognize that there will be excellent, good, and poor managers within each gender.
- Understand that success requires the best use of human talent, regardless of gender.

older workers for their experience, stability and low turnover. Research is consistent with these preferences and also shows lower avoidable absences.[54] Finally, to the extent age is linked to experience or job tenure, there is a positive relationship between seniority and performance. More experienced workers tend to have low absence rates and relatively low turnover.[55]

■ ABLE-BODIEDNESS

Even though recent studies report that disabled workers do their jobs as well, or better than, nondisabled workers, nearly three quarters of severely disabled persons are reported to be unemployed. Almost 80 percent of those with disabilities say they want to work.[56] Once again, the expected shortage of traditional workers is predicted to lead to a reexamination of hiring policies. More firms are expected to give serious consideration to hiring disabled workers, particularly given that the cost of accommodating these workers has been shown to be low.[57]

■ RACIAL AND ETHNIC GROUPS

Consistent with some current literature, we use the term *racial and ethnic groups* to reflect the broad spectrum of employees of differing ethnicities or races who make up an ever-increasing portion of the new workforce.[58] Of particular significance in the American workplace is diversity reflected in an increasing proportion of African Americans, Asian Americans and Hispanic Americans. Projections by the Bureau of Labor Statistics estimate that they will constitute 27% of the workforce by the year 2005. The Hudson Institute extends this projection to 32% by the year 2020. The potential for stereotypes and discrimination to adversely affect career opportunities and progress for members of these and other minority groups must be recognized.

Even though employment decisions based on demographic differences are allowable under Title VII if they can be justified as bona fide occupational qualifications reasonable to normal business operations, race cannot be one of these. Case law has shown that these qualifications are always extremely difficult to justify.[59] In any event the flight attendant job is a case in point. When the airlines failed to show why men could not perform flight attendant duties as well as females, gender restrictions on hiring were lifted.

Aptitude and Ability

■ **Aptitude** represents a person's capability of learning something.

■ **Ability** reflects a person's existing capacity to perform the various tasks needed for a given job.

Demographic characteristics are sometimes used erroneously as stereotypes in place of assessing a person's true aptitude or ability. **Aptitude** represents a person's capability of learning something, whereas **ability** reflects a person's existing capacity to perform the various tasks needed for a given job and includes both relevant knowledge and skills.[60] In other words, aptitudes are potential abilities, whereas abilities are the knowledge and skills that an individual currently possesses.

Aptitudes and abilities are important considerations for a manager when initially hiring or selecting candidates for a job. We are all acquainted with various tests used to measure mental aptitudes and abilities. Some of these provide an overall intelligent quotient (IQ) score (e.g., the Stanford-Binet IQ Test). Others provide measures of more specific competencies that are required of people entering various educational programs or career fields. You have probably taken the ACT or SAT college entrance tests. Such tests are designed to facilitate the screening and selection of applicants for educational programs or jobs. In addition to mental aptitudes and abilities, some jobs, such as firefighters and police, require tests for physical abilities. Muscular strength and cardiovascular endurance are two of many physical ability dimensions.[61]

For legal purposes, demonstrated evidence must be presented that those scoring more favorably on the tests will tend to be more successful in their educational program, career field, or job performance than those with lower scores. In other words, there must be a fit between specific aptitudes and abilities and job requirements. If you want to be a surgeon, for instance, and cannot demonstrate good hand–eye coordination, there will not be a good ability–job fit. Such a fit is so important that it is a core concept on managing human resources.

Personality

In addition to demographics and aptitude and ability, a third important individual attribute is personality. The term **personality** represents the overall profile or combination of characteristics that capture the unique nature of a person as that person reacts and interacts with others. As an example, think of a person who was the billionaire founder of a fast-growing, high-tech computer company by the time he was 30; who in his senior year in high school had turned selling newspapers into enough of a business to buy a BMW; who told his management team that his daughter's first words were "Daddy kill-IBM, Gateway, Compaq;" who learned from production mistakes and brought in senior managers to help his firm; and who is so private he seldom talks about himself: In other words, think of Michael Dell, the founder of Dell Computer, and his personality.[62]

Personality combines a set of physical and mental characteristics that reflect how a person looks, thinks, acts, and feels. Sometimes attempts are made to measure personality with questionnaires or special tests. Frequently, personality can be implied from behavior alone, such as by the actions of Michael Dell. Either way, personality is an important individual characteristic for managers to understand. An understanding of personality contributes to an understanding of organizational behavior in that we expect a predictable interplay between an individual's personality and his or her tendency to behave in certain ways.

■ **Personality** represents the overall profile or combination of characteristics that capture the unique nature of a person as that person reacts and interacts with others.

■ PERSONALITY DETERMINANTS AND DEVELOPMENT

Just what determines personality? Is personality inherited or genetically determined, or is it formed by experience? You may have heard someone say something like, "She acts like her mother." Similarly, someone may argue that "Bobby is the way he is because of the way he was raised." These two arguments illustrate the nature/nurture controversy: Is personality determined by heredity, that is, by genetic endowment, or by one's environment? As Figure 1.5 shows, these two forces actually operate in combination. Heredity consists of those factors that are determined at conception, including physical characteristics, gender, and personality factors. Environment consists of cultural, social, and situational factors.

The impact of heredity on personality continues to be the source of considerable debate. Perhaps the most general conclusion we can draw is that heredity sets the limits on just how much personality characteristics can be developed; environment determines development within these limits. For instance, a person could be born with a tendency toward authoritarianism, and that tendency could be reinforced in an authoritarian work environment. These limits appear to vary from one characteristic to the next and across all characteristics there is about a 50–50 heredity–environment split.[63]

As we show throughout this book, *cultural values and norms* play a substantial role in the development of an individual's personality and behaviors. Contrast the individualism of U.S. culture with the collectivism of Mexican culture, for example.[64] Social factors reflect such things as family life, religion, and the many kinds of formal and informal groups in which people participate throughout their lives—friendship groups, athletic groups, as well as formal work groups. Finally, the demands of differing *situational factors* emphasize or constrain different aspects of an individual's personality. For example, in class you are likely to rein in your high spirits and other related behaviors encouraged by your personality. However, at a sporting event, you may be jumping up, cheering, and loudly criticizing the referees.

The **developmental approaches** of Chris Argyris, Daniel Levinson, and Gail Sheehy systematically examine the ways personality develops across time. Argyris notes that people develop along a continuum of dimensions from immaturity to maturity as shown in Figure 1.6. He believes that many organizations treat mature adults as if they were still immature and this creates many problems in terms of bringing out the best in employees. Levinson and Sheehy maintain that an individual's personality unfolds in a series of stages across time. Sheehy's model, for example, talks about three stages—ages 18–30, 30–45, and 45–85+. Each of these has a crucial impact on the worker's employment and career. The

■ **Developmental Approaches** are systematic models of ways in which personality develops across time.

**Figure 1.5
Heredity and environmental linkage with personality.**

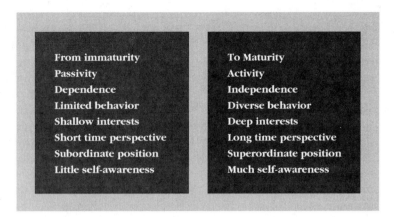

Figure 1.6
Argyris's Maturity–
Immaturity Continuum.

implications are that personalities develop over time and require different managerial responses. Thus, needs and other personality aspects of people initially entering an organization change sharply as they move through different stages or toward increased maturity.[65]

Personality Traits and Classifications

Numerous lists of personality traits—enduring characteristics describing an individual's behavior, have been developed, many of which have been used in OB research and can be looked at in different ways. First, recent research has examined people using extensive lists of personality dimensions and distilled them into the "Big Five:"[66]

- *Extraversion*—Outgoing, sociable, assertive
- *Agreeableness*—Good-natured, trusting, cooperative
- *Conscientiousness*—Responsible, dependable, persistent
- *Emotional stability*—Unworried, secure, relaxed
- *Openness to experience*—Imaginative, curious, broad-minded

The "Big Five" personality dimensions

Standardized personality tests determine how positively or negatively an individual scores on each of these dimensions. For instance, a person scoring high on openness to experience tends to ask lots of questions and to think in new and unusual ways. You can consider a person's individual personality profile across the five dimensions. In terms of job performance, research has shown that conscientiousness predicts job performance across five occupational groups of professions—engineers, police, managers, sales, and skilled and semiskilled employees. Predictability of the other dimensions depends on the occupational group. For instance, not surprisingly, extraversion predicts performance for sales and managerial positions.

A second approach to looking at OB personality traits is to divide them into social traits, personal conception traits, and emotional adjustment traits, and then to consider how those categories come together dynamically.[67]

■ SOCIAL TRAITS

Social traits are surface-level traits that reflect the way a person appears to others when interacting in various social settings. Problem-solving style, based on the work of Carl Jung, a noted psychologist, is one measure representing social traits.[68] It reflects the way a person goes about gathering and evaluating information in solving problems and making decisions.

Information gathering involves getting and organizing data for use. Styles of information gathering vary from sensation to intuitive. *Sensation-type individuals* prefer routine and order and emphasize well-defined details in gathering information; they would rather work with known facts than look for possibilities. By contrast, *intuitive-type individuals* prefer the "big picture." They like solving new problems, dislike routine, and would rather look for possibilities than work with facts.

The second component of problem solving, *evaluation*, involves making judgments about how to deal with information once it has been collected. Styles of information evaluation vary from an emphasis on feeling to an emphasis on thinking. *Feeling-type individuals* are oriented toward conformity and try to accommodate themselves to other people. They try to avoid problems that may result in disagreements. *Thinking-type individuals* use reason and intellect to deal with problems and downplay emotions.

When these two dimensions (information gathering and evaluation) are combined, four basic problem-solving styles result: sensation-feeling (SF), intuitive-feeling (IF), sensation-thinking (ST), and intuitive-thinking (IT), together with summary descriptions, as shown in Figure 1.7.

Research indicates that there is a fit between the styles of individuals and the kinds of decisions they prefer. For example, STs (sensation-thinkers) prefer analytical strategies—those that emphasize detail and method. IFs (intuitive-feelers) prefer intuitive strategies—those that emphasize an overall pattern and fit. Not surprisingly, mixed styles (sensation-feelers or intuitive-thinkers) select both analytic and intuitive strategies. Other findings also indicate that thinkers tend to have higher motivation than do feelers and that individuals who emphasize sensations tend to have higher job satisfaction than do intuitives. These and other findings suggest a number of basic differences among different problem-solving styles, emphasizing the importance of fitting such styles with a task's information processing and evaluation requirements.[69]

Problem-solving styles are most frequently measured by the (typically 100-item) *Myers–Briggs Type Indicator (MBTI)*, which asks individuals how they usually act or feel in specific situations. Firms such as Apple, AT&T, and Exxon, as well as hospitals, educational institutions, and military organizations, have used the Myers–Briggs for various aspects of management development.[70]

■ PERSONAL CONCEPTION TRAITS

The *personal conception traits* represent the way individuals tend to think about their social and physical setting as well as their major beliefs and personal orientation concerning a range of issues.

Locus of Control   The extent to which a person feels able to control his or her own life is concerned with a person's internal–external orientation and is measured by Rotter's locus of control instrument.[71] People have personal con-

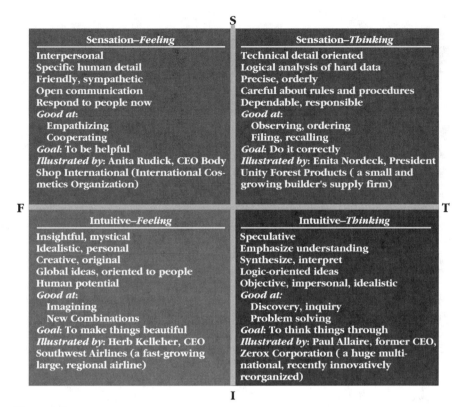

Figure 1.7
Four problem-solving style summaries.

ceptions about whether events are controlled primarily by themselves, which indicates an internal orientation, or by outside forces, such as their social and physical environment, which indicates an external orientation. Internals, or persons with an internal locus of control, believe that they control their own fate or destiny. In contrast, externals, or persons with an external locus of control, believe that much of what happens to them is beyond their control and is determined by environmental forces.

In general, externals are more extroverted in their interpersonal relationships and are more oriented toward the world around them. Internals tend to be more introverted and are more oriented toward their own feelings and ideas. Figure 1.8 suggests that internals tend to do better on tasks requiring complex information processing and learning, as well as initiative. Many managerial and professional jobs have these kinds of requirements.

Authoritarianism/Dogmatism Both "authoritarianism" and "dogmatism" deal with the rigidity of a person's beliefs. A person high in **authoritarianism** tends to adhere rigidly to conventional values and to obey recognized authority. This person is concerned with toughness and power and opposes the use of subjective feelings. An individual high in **dogmatism** sees the world as a threatening place. This person regards legitimate authority as absolute and accepts or rejects others according to how much they agree with accepted authority. Supe-

■ **Authoritarianism** is a tendency to adhere rigidly to conventional values and to obey recognized authority.

■ **Dogmatism** leads a person to see the world as a threatening place and regard authority as absolute.

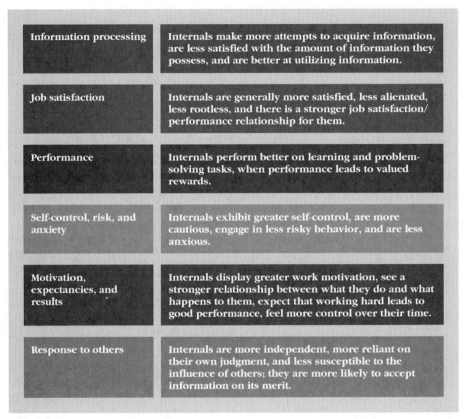

Information processing	Internals make more attempts to acquire information, are less satisfied with the amount of information they possess, and are better at utilizing information.
Job satisfaction	Internals are generally more satisfied, less alienated, less rootless, and there is a stronger job satisfaction/performance relationship for them.
Performance	Internals perform better on learning and problem-solving tasks, when performance leads to valued rewards.
Self-control, risk, and anxiety	Internals exhibit greater self-control, are more cautious, engage in less risky behavior, and are less anxious.
Motivation, expectancies, and results	Internals display greater work motivation, see a stronger relationship between what they do and what happens to them, expect that working hard leads to good performance, feel more control over their time.
Response to others	Internals are more independent, more reliant on their own judgment, and less susceptible to the influence of others; they are more likely to accept information on its merit.

Figure 1.8
Some ways in which internals differ from externals.

riors who possess these latter traits tend to be rigid and closed. At the same time, dogmatic subordinates tend to want certainty imposed upon them.[72]

From an ethical standpoint, we can expect highly authoritarian individuals to present a special problem because they are so susceptible to authority that in their eagerness to comply they may behave unethically.[73] For example, we might speculate that many of the Nazis who were involved in war crimes during World War II were high in authoritarianism or dogmatism; they believed so strongly in authority that they followed their unethical orders without question.

Machiavellianism The third personal conceptions dimension is Machiavellian-ism, which owes its origins to Niccolo Machiavelli. The very name of this sixteenth-century author evokes visions of a master of guile, deceit, and opportunism in interpersonal relations. Machiavelli earned his place in history by writing *The Prince*, a nobleman's guide to the acquisition and use of power.[74] The subject of Machiavelli's book is manipulation as the basic means of gaining and keeping control of others. From its pages emerges the personality profile of a Machiavellian—someone who views and manipulates others purely for personal gain.

Psychologists have developed a series of instruments called Mach scales to measure a person's Machiavellian orientation.[75] A high-Mach personality is someone who tends to behave in ways consistent with Machiavelli's basic principles. Such individuals approach situations logically and thoughtfully and are even capable of lying to achieve personal goals. They are rarely swayed by loyalty, friendships, past promises, or the opinions of others, and they are skilled at influencing others.

Research using the Mach scales provides insight into the way high and low Machs may be expected to behave in various situations. A person with a "cool" and "detached" high-Mach personality can be expected to take control and try to exploit loosely structured environmental situations but will perform in a perfunctory, even detached, manner in highly structured situations. Low Machs tend to accept direction imposed by others in loosely structured situations; they work hard to do well in highly structured ones. For example, we might expect that, where the situation permitted, a high Mach would do or say whatever it took to get his or her way. In contrast, a low Mach would tend to be much more strongly guided by ethical considerations and would be less likely to lie or cheat or to get away with lying or cheating.

Self-Monitoring   A final personal conceptions trait of special importance to managers is self-monitoring. **Self-monitoring** reflects a person's ability to adjust his or her behavior to external, situational (environmental) factors.[76]

High self-monitoring individuals are sensitive to external cues and tend to behave differently in different situations. Like high Machs, high self-monitors can present a very different appearance from their true self. In contrast, low self-monitors, like their low-Mach counterparts, aren't able to disguise their behaviors—"what you see is what you get." There is also evidence that high self-monitors are closely attuned to the behavior of others and conform more readily than do low self-monitors.[77] Thus, they appear flexible and may be especially good at responding to the kinds of situational contingencies emphasized throughout this book. For example, high self-monitors should be especially good at changing their leadership behavior to fit subordinates with high or low experience, tasks with high or low structure, and so on.

■ **Self-monitoring** reflects a person's ability to adjust his or her behavior to external, situational (environmental) factors.

■ EMOTIONAL ADJUSTMENT TRAITS

The **emotional adjustment traits** measure how much an individual experiences emotional distress or displays unacceptable acts. Often the person's health is affected. Although numerous such traits are cited in the literature, a frequently encountered one especially important for OB is the Type A/Type B orientation.

■ **Emotional adjustment traits** measure how much an individual experiences emotional distress or displays unacceptable acts.

Type A and Type B Orientation   To get a feel for this orientation, take the following quiz and then read on.[78] Circle the number that best characterizes you on each of the following pairs of characteristics.

Casual about appointments	1 2 3 4 5 6 7 8	Never late
Not competitive	1 2 3 4 5 6 7 8	Very competitive
Never feel rushed	1 2 3 4 5 6 7 8	Always feel rushed
Take one thing at a time	1 2 3 4 5 6 7 8	Try to do many things
Do things slowly	1 2 3 4 5 6 7 8	Do things fast
Express my feelings	1 2 3 4 5 6 7 8	Hold in my feelings
Many outside interests	1 2 3 4 5 6 7 8	Few outside interests

Total your points for the seven items in the quiz. Multiply this total by 3 to arrive at a final score. Use this total to locate your Type A/Type B orientation on the following list.

FINAL POINTS	A/B ORIENTATION
Below 90	B
90–99	B+
100–105	A-
106–119	A
120 or more	A+

■ **Type A orientations** are characterized by impatience, desire for achievement, and perfectionism.

■ **Type B orientations** are characterized by an easy going and less competitive nature than Type A.

Individuals with a **Type A orientation** are characterized by impatience, desire for achievement, and perfectionism. In contrast, those with **Type B orientations** are characterized as more easygoing and less competitive in relation to daily events.[79]

Type A people tend to work fast and to be abrupt, uncomfortable, irritable, and aggressive. Such tendencies indicate "obsessive" behavior, a fairly widespread—but not always helpful—trait among managers. Many managers are hard-driving, detail-oriented people who have high performance standards and thrive on routine. But when such work obsessions are carried to the extreme, they may lead to greater concerns for details than for results, resistance to change, overzealous control of subordinates, and various kinds of interpersonal difficulties, which may even include threats and physical violence. In contrast, Type B managers tend to be much more laid back and patient in their dealings with co-workers and subordinates.

■ PERSONALITY AND SELF-CONCEPT

■ **Personality dynamics** are the ways in which an individual integrates and organizes social traits, values and motives, personal conceptions, and emotional adjustment.

■ **Self-concept** is the view individuals have of themselves as physical, social, and spiritual or moral beings.

Collectively, the ways in which an individual integrates and organizes the previously discussed categories and the traits they contain are referred to as **personality dynamics**. It is this category that makes personality more than just the sum of the separate traits. A key personality dynamic in your study of OB is the self-concept.

We can describe the **self-concept** as the view individuals have of themselves as physical, social, and spiritual or moral beings.[80] It is a way of recognizing oneself as a distinct human being. A person's self-concept is greatly influenced by his or her culture. For example, Americans tend to disclose much more about themselves than do the English; that is, Americans' self-concept is more assertive and talkative.[81]

Two related—and crucial—aspects of the self-concept are self-esteem and self-efficacy. *Self-esteem* is a belief about one's own worth based on an overall self-evaluation.[82] People high in self-esteem see themselves as capable, worthwhile, and acceptable and tend to have few doubts about themselves. The opposite is true of a person low in self-esteem. Some OB research suggests that, whereas high self-esteem generally can boost performance and human resource maintenance, when under pressure, people with high self-esteem may become boastful and act egotistically. They also may be overconfident at times and fail to obtain important information.[83]

Self-efficacy, sometimes called the "effectance motive," is a more specific version of self-esteem; it is an individual's belief about the likelihood of successfully completing a specific task. You could be high in self-esteem, yet have a feeling of low self-efficacy about performing a certain task, such as public speaking.

Values and Attitudes

Joining demographic and personality characteristics as important individual difference characteristics are values and attitudes.

■ VALUES

Values can be defined as broad preferences concerning appropriate courses of action or outcomes. As such, values reflect a person's sense of right and wrong or what "ought" to be.[84] "Equal rights for all" and "People should be treated with respect and dignity" are representative of values. Values tend to influence attitudes and behavior. For example, if you value equal rights for all and you go to work for an organization that treats its managers much better than it does its workers, you may form the attitude that the company is an unfair place to work; consequently, you may not produce well or may perhaps leave the company. It's likely that if the company had had a more equalitarian policy, your attitude and behaviors would have been more positive.

Sources and Types of Values   Parents, friends, teachers, and external reference groups can all influence individual values. Indeed, peoples' values develop as a product of the learning and experience they encounter in the cultural setting in which they live. As learning and experiences differ from one person to another, value differences result. Such differences are likely to be deep seated and difficult (though not impossible) to change; many have their roots in early childhood and the way a person has been raised.[85]

The noted psychologist Milton Rokeach has developed a well-known set of values classified into two broad categories.[86] **Terminal values** reflect a person's preferences concerning the "ends" to be achieved; they are the goals individuals would like to achieve during their lifetime. Rokeach divides values into 18 terminal values and 18 instrumental values, as summarized in Figure 1.9. **Instrumental values** reflect the "means" for achieving desired ends. They represent how you might go about achieving your important end states, depending on the relative importance you attached to the instrumental values.

Illustrative research shows, not surprisingly, that both terminal and instrumental values differ by group (for example, executives, activist workers, and union members).[87] These preference differences can encourage conflict or agreement when different groups have to deal with each other.

Another frequently used classification of human values has been developed by psychologist Gordon Allport and his associates. These values fall into six major types:[88]

- *Theoretical*—Interest in the discovery of truth through reasoning and systematic thinking.
- *Economic*—Interest in usefulness and practicality, including the accumulation of wealth.
- *Aesthetic*—Interest in beauty, form, and artistic harmony.
- *Social*—Interest in people and love as a human relationship.

■ **Values** can be defined as broad preferences concerning appropriate courses of action or outcomes.

■ **Sources and types of values** Parents, friends, teachers, and external reference groups can all influence individual values.

■ **Terminal values** reflect a person's preferences concerning the "ends" to be achieved.

■ **Instrumental values** reflect a person's beliefs about the means for achieving desired ends.

Allport's six value categories

Figure 1.9
Rokeach value survey.

Terminal Values	Instrumental Values
A comfortable life (and prosperous)	Ambitious (hardworking)
An exciting life (stimulating)	Broad-minded (open-minded)
A sense of accomplishment (lasting contibution)	Capable (competent, effective)
A world at peace (free of war and conflict)	Cheerful (lighthearted, joyful)
A world of beauty (beauty of nature and the arts)	Clean (neat, tidy)
Equality (brotherhood, equal opportunity)	Courageous (standing up for beliefs)
Family security (taking care of loved ones)	Forgiving (willing to pardon)
Freedom (independence, free choice)	Helpful (working for others' welfare)
Happiness (contentedness)	Honest (sincere, truthful)
Inner harmony (freedom from inner conflict)	Imaginative (creative, daring)
Mature love (sexual and spiritual intimacy)	Independent (self-sufficient, self-reliant)
National security (attack protection)	Intellectual (intelligent, reflective)
Pleasure (leisurely, enjoyable life)	Logical (rational, consistent)
Salvation (saved, eternal life)	Loving (affectionate, tender)
Self-respect (self-esteem)	Obedient (dutiful, respectful)
Social recognition (admiration, respect)	Polite (courteous, well mannered)
True friendship (close companionship)	Responsible (reliable, dependable)
Wisdom (mature understanding of life)	Self-controlled (self-disciplined)

- *Political*—Interest in gaining power and influencing other people.
- *Religious*—Interest in unity and in understanding the cosmos as a whole.

Once again, groups differ in the way they rank order the importance of these values, as shown in the following.[89]

- *Ministers*—Religious, social, aesthetic, political, theoretical, economic.
- *Purchasing Executive*—Economic, theoretical, political, religious, aesthetic, social.
- *Industrial Scientists*—Theoretical, political, economic, aesthetic, religious, social.

The previous value classifications have had a major impact on the values literature, but they were not specifically designed for people in a work setting. A more recent values schema, developed by Maglino and associates, is aimed at people in the workplace:[90]

Maglino and associates value categories

- *Achievement*—Getting things done and working hard to accomplish difficult things in life.
- *Helping and Concern for Others*—Being concerned with other people and helping others.
- *Honesty*—Telling the truth and doing what you feel is right.
- *Fairness*—Being impartial and doing what is fair for all concerned.

■ **Value congruence** occurs when individuals express positive feelings upon encountering others who exhibit values similar to their own.

These four values have been shown to be especially important in the workplace; thus, the framework should be particularly relevant for studying values in OB.

In particular, values can be influential through **value congruence**, which occurs when individuals express positive feelings upon encountering others who exhibit values similar to their own. When values differ, or are *incongruent*, conflicts over such things as goals and the means to achieve them may result. The

Maglino et al. value schema was used to examine value congruence between leaders and followers. The researchers found greater follower satisfaction with the leader when there was such congruence in terms of achievement, helping, honesty, and fairness values.[91]

Patterns and Trends in Values   We should also be aware of applied research on values trends over time. Daniel Yankelovich, for example, is known for his informative public opinion polls.[92] Among North American workers, Yankelovich notes a movement away from valuing economic incentives, organizational loyalty, and work-related identity and toward valuing meaningful work, pursuit of leisure, and personal identity and self-fulfillment. Yankelovich believes that the modern manager must be able to recognize value differences and trends among people at work. For example, he reports finding higher productivity among younger workers who are employed in jobs that match their values and/or who are supervised by managers who share their values, reinforcing the concept of value congruence.

In a nationwide sample, managers and human-resource professionals were asked to identify the work-related values they believed to be most important to individuals in the workforce, both now and in the near future.[93] The nine most popular values named were: recognition for competence and accomplishments; respect and dignity; personal choice and freedom; involvement at work; pride in one's work; lifestyle quality; financial security; self-development; and health and wellness. These values are especially important for managers because they indicate some key concerns of the new workforce. Even though each individual worker places his or her own importance on these values, and even though the United States today has by far the most diverse workforce in its history, this overall characterization is a good place for managers to start when dealing with workers in the new workplace. It is important to note, however, that, although values are individual preferences, many tend to be shared within cultures and organizations.

■ ATTITUDES

Attitudes are influenced by values and are acquired from the same sources as values: friends, teachers, parents, and role models. Attitudes focus on specific people or objects, whereas values have a more general focus and are more stable than attitudes. "Employees should be allowed to participate" is a value; your positive or negative feeling about your job because of the participation it allows is an attitude. Formally defined, an **attitude** is a predisposition to respond in a positive or negative way to someone or something in one's environment. For example, when you say that you "like" or "dislike" someone or something, you are expressing an attitude. It's important to remember that an attitude, like a value, is a hypothetical construct; that is, one never sees, touches, or actually isolates an attitude. Rather, attitudes are *inferred* from the things people say, informally or in formal opinion polls or through their behavior.

Figure 1.10 shows attitudes as accompanied by antecedents and results.[94] The beliefs and values antecedents in the figure form the **cognitive component** of an attitude: the beliefs, opinions, knowledge, or information a person possesses. **Beliefs** represent ideas about someone or something and the conclusions people draw about them; they convey a sense of "what is" to an individual. "My job lacks responsibility" is a belief shown in the figure. Note that the beliefs may

■ **Attitude** is a predisposition to respond in a positive or negative way to someone or something in one's environment.

■ The **cognitive component** of an attitude reflects the beliefs, opinions, knowledge, or information a person possesses.

■ **Beliefs** represent ideas about someone or something and the conclusions people draw about them.

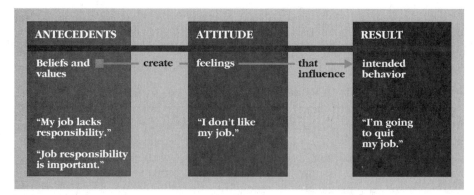

Figure 1.10
A work-related example of the three components of attitudes.

or may not be accurate. "Responsibility is important" is a corresponding aspect of the cognitive component, which reflects an underlying value.

The **affective component** of an attitude is a specific feeling regarding the personal impact of the antecedents. This is the actual attitude itself, such as "I don't like my job." The **behavioral component** is an intention to behave in a certain way based on your specific feelings or attitudes. This intended behavior is a result of an attitude and is a predisposition to act in a specific way, such as "I'm going to quit my job."

Attitudes and Behavior   You should recognize that the link between attitudes and behavior is tentative. An attitude results in *intended* behavior; this intention may or may not be carried out in a given circumstance.

In general, the more specific attitudes and behaviors are, the stronger the relationship. For example, say you are a French-Canadian webmaster and you are asked about your satisfaction with your supervisor's treatment of French-Canadian webmasters. You also indicate the strength of your intent to look for another webmaster job in a similar kind of organization within the next six months. Here, both the attitude and the behavior are specifically stated (they refer to French-Canadian webmasters, and they identify a given kind of organization over a specific time period). Thus, we would expect to find a relatively strong relationship between these attitudes and how aggressively you actually start looking for another webmaster job.

It is also important that a good deal of freedom be available to carry out the intent. In the example just given, the freedom to follow through would be sharply restricted if the demand for webmasters dropped substantially.

Finally, the attitude and behavior linkage tends to be stronger when the person in question has had experience with the stated attitude. For example, assuming you are a business administration or management major, the relationship between your course attitude and/or your intent to drop the course and your later behavior of actually doing so would probably be stronger in your present OB course than in the first week of your enrollment in an advanced course in nuclear fission.[95]

Even though attitudes do not always predict behavior, the link between attitudes and potential or intended behavior is important for managers to under-

■ The **affective component** of an attitude is a specific feeling regarding the personal impact of the antecedents.

■ The **behavioral component** is an intention to behave in a certain way based on your specific feelings or attitudes.

stand. Think about your work experiences or conversations with other people about their work. It is not uncommon to hear concerns expressed about someone's "bad attitude." These concerns typically reflect displeasure with the behavioral consequences with which the poor attitude is associated. Unfavorable attitudes in the form of low job satisfaction can result in costly labor turnover, absenteeism, tardiness, and even impaired physical or mental health. One of the manager's responsibilities, therefore, is to recognize attitudes and to understand both their antecedents and their potential implications.

Attitudes and Cognitive Consistency   Leon Festinger, a noted social psychologist, uses the term **cognitive dissonance** to describe a state of inconsistency between an individual's attitudes and his or her behavior.[96] Let's assume that you have the attitude that recycling is good for the economy but you don't recycle. Festinger predicts that such an inconsistency results in discomfort and a desire to reduce or eliminate it by (1) changing the underlying attitude, (2) changing future behavior, or (3) developing new ways of explaining or rationalizing the inconsistency.

■ **Cognitive dissonance** describes a state of inconsistency between an individual's attitude and behavior.

Two factors that influence which of the above choices tend to be made are the degree of control a person thinks he or she has over the situation and the magnitude of the rewards involved. In terms of control, if your boss won't let you recycle office trash, you would be less likely to change your attitude than if you voluntarily chose not to recycle. You might instead choose the rationalization option. In terms of rewards, if they are high enough, rewards tend to reduce your feeling of inconsistency: If I'm rewarded even though I don't recycle, the lack of recycling must not be so bad after all.

Managing Diversity and Individual Differences

Dealing with diversity and individual differences has to be included among the most important issues challenging all managers in the quest for high performance and organizational competitiveness. This is true not only in the United States but also in Canada, European Union countries, and several countries in Asia.[97] Only the details differ.

So how do managers deal with all this? To convey the flavor of what some of the more progressive employers have done in managing diversity, let's now consider Boston-based Harvard Pilgrim Health Care (HPHC). Barbara Stern is the vice president of diversity.[98] She argues that what has traditionally been a "soft" issue is now becoming a business necessity in terms of better serving customers, understanding markets, and obtaining full benefit from staff talents. Each year, HPHC attempts to increase its diversity in terms of the proportion of women and racial minorities by 0.5 percent, which allows for continuous improvement. Such improvement raised the proportion of minority new hires from 14 to 28 percent over four years, and the total minority employees went from 16 to 21 percent over the same period.

The Perceptual Process

A spectacular completed pass during the 1982 National Football Conference championship game helped propel Joe Montana, former San Francisco 49er quarterback, into the legendary status he enjoys today. The reverse effect apparently occurred for Danny White, Dallas Cowboys' quarterback. He fumbled in the final minute of the same game and never obtained the status of his predecessor, Roger Stauback, even though White took the Cowboys to the championship game three years in a row.[99]

■ **Perception** is the process through which people receive, organize, and interpret information from their environment.

This example illustrates the notion of **perception**, the process by which people select, organize, interpret, retrieve, and respond to information from the world around them.[100] This information is gathered from the five senses of sight, hearing, touch, taste, and smell. As Montana, White, and Stauback can attest, perception and reality are not necessarily the same thing. The perceptions or responses of any two people are also not necessarily identical, even when they are describing the same event.

Through perception, people process information inputs into responses involving feelings and action. Perception is a way of forming impressions about oneself, other people, and daily life experiences. It also serves as a screen or filter through which information passes before it has an effect on people. The quality or accuracy of a person's perceptions, therefore, has a major impact on his or her responses to a given situation.

Perceptual responses are also likely to vary between managers and subordinates. Consider Figure 1.11, which depicts contrasting perceptions of a perfor-

Figure 1.11
Contrasting perceptions between managers and their subordinates: The case of the performance appraisal interview.

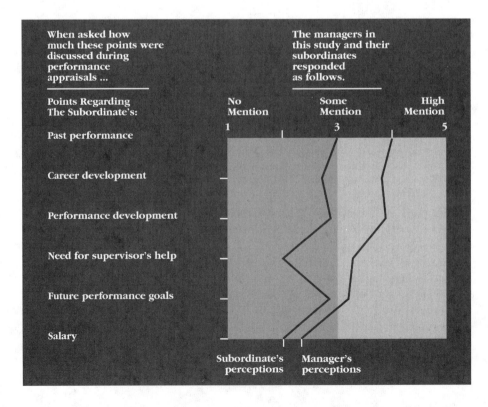

mance appraisal between managers and subordinates. Rather substantial differences exist in the two sets of perceptions; the responses can be significant. In this case, managers who perceive that they already give adequate attention to past performance, career development, and supervisory help are unlikely to give greater emphasis to these points in future performance appraisal interviews. In contrast, their subordinates are likely to experience continued frustration because they perceive that these subjects are not being given sufficient attention.

■ FACTORS INFLUENCING THE PERCEPTUAL PROCESS

The factors that contribute to perceptual differences and the perceptual process among people at work are summarized in Figure 1.12 and include characteristics of the *perceiver*, the *setting*, and the *perceived*.

The Perceiver   A person's past experiences, needs or motives, personality, and values and attitudes may all influence the perceptual process. A person with a strong achievement need tends to perceive a situation in terms of that need. If you see doing well in class as a way to help meet your achievement need, for example, you will tend to emphasize that aspect when considering various classes. By the same token, a person with a negative attitude toward unions may look for antagonisms even when local union officials make routine visits to the organization. These and other perceiver factors influence the various aspects of the perceptual process.

The Setting   The physical, social, and organizational context of the perceptual setting also can influence the perceptual process. Kim Jeffrey, the recently appointed CEO of Nestle's Perrier, was perceived by his subordinates as a frightening figure when he gave vent to his temper and had occasional confrontations with them. In the previous setting, before he was promoted, Jeffrey's flare-ups

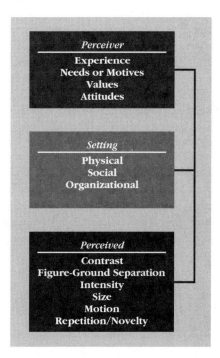

**Figure 1.12
Factors influencing the perceptual process.**

had been tolerable; now they caused intimidation, so his subordinates feared to express their opinions and recommendations. Fortunately, after he received feedback about this problem, he was able to change his subordinates' perceptions in the new setting.[101]

**Figure 1.13
Figure–ground
illustration.**

The Perceived   Characteristics of the perceived person, object, or event, such as contrast, intensity, figure–ground separation, size, motion, and repetition or novelty, are also important in the perceptual process. For example, one mainframe computer among six PCs or one man among six women will be perceived differently than one of six mainframe computers or one of six men—where there is less contrast. Intensity can vary in terms of brightness, color, depth, sound, and the like. A bright red sports car stands out from a group of gray sedans; whispering or shouting stands out from ordinary conversation. The concept is known as figure–ground separation, and it depends on which image is perceived as the background and which as the figure. For an illustration, look at Figure 1.13. What do you see? Faces or a vase?

In the matter of size, very small or very large people tend to be perceived differently and more readily than average-sized people. Similarly, in terms of motion, moving objects are perceived differently from stationary objects. And, of course, advertisers hope that ad repetition or frequency will positively influence peoples' perception of a product. Television advertising blitzes for new models of personal computers are a case in point. Finally, the novelty of a situation affects its perception. A purple-haired teenager is perceived differently from a blond or a brunette, for example.

■ STAGES OF THE PERCEPTUAL PROCESS

So far we have discussed key factors influencing the perceptual process. Now we'll look at the stages involved in processing the information that ultimately determines a person's perception and reaction, as shown in Figure 1.14. The infor-

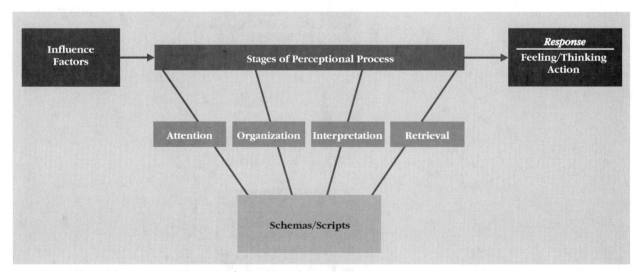

**Figure 1.14
The perceptual process.**

mation-processing stages are divided into information attention and selection; organization of information; information interpretation; and information retrieval.

Attention and Selection   Our senses are constantly bombarded with so much information that if we don't screen it, we quickly become incapacitated with information overload. *Selective screening* lets in only a tiny proportion of all of the information available. Some of the selectivity comes from controlled processing—consciously deciding what information to pay attention to and what to ignore. In this case, the perceivers are aware that they are processing information. Think about the last time you were at a noisy restaurant and screened out all the sounds but those of the person with whom you were talking.

In contrast to controlled processing, screening can also take place without the perceiver's conscious awareness. For example, you may drive a car without consciously thinking about the process of driving; you may be thinking about a problem you are having with your course work instead. In driving the car, you are affected by information from the world around you, such as traffic lights and other cars, but you don't pay conscious attention to that information. Such selectivity of attention and automatic information processing works well most of the time when you drive, but if a nonroutine event occurs, such as an animal darting into the road, you may have an accident unless you quickly shift to controlled processing.

Organization   Even though selective screening takes place in the attention stage, it is still necessary to find ways to organize the information efficiently. **Schemas** help us do this. Schemas are cognitive frameworks that represent organized knowledge about a given concept or stimulus developed through experience.[102] A self schema contains information about a person's own appearance, behavior, and personality. For instance, a person with a decisiveness schema tends to perceive himself or herself in terms of that aspect, especially in circumstances calling for leadership.

Person schemas refer to the way individuals sort others into categories, such as types or groups, in terms of similar perceived features. The term *prototype*, or *stereotype*, is often used to represent these categories; it is an abstract set of features commonly associated with members of that category. Once the prototype is formed, it is stored in long-term memory; it is retrieved when it is needed for a comparison of how well a person matches the prototype's features. For instance, you may have a "good worker" prototype in mind, which includes hard work, intelligence, punctuality, articulateness, and decisiveness; that prototype is used as a measure against which to compare a given worker. Stereotypes may be regarded as prototypes based on such demographic characteristics as gender, age, able-bodiedness, and racial and ethnic groups.

A *script schema* is defined as a knowledge framework that describes the appropriate sequence of events in a given situation.[103] For example, an experienced manager would use a script schema to think about the appropriate steps involved in running a meeting. Finally, *person-in-situation schemas* combine schemas built around persons (self and person schemas) and events (script schemas).[104] Thus, a manager might organize his or her perceived information in a meeting around a decisiveness schema for both himself or herself and a key participant in the meeting. Here, a script schema would provide the steps and their sequence in the meeting; the manager would push through the steps deci-

■ **Schemas** are cognitive frameworks that represent organized knowledge about a given concept or stimulus developed through experience.

sively and would call on the selected participants periodically throughout the meeting to respond decisively. Note that, although this approach might facilitate organization of important information, the perceptions of those attending might not be completely accurate because decisiveness of the person-in-situation schema did not allow the attendees enough time for open discussion.

As you can see in Figure 1.14, schemas are not important just in the organizing stage; they also affect other stages in the perception process. Furthermore, schemas rely heavily on automatic processing to free people up to use controlled processing as necessary. Finally, as we will show, the perceptual factors described earlier, as well as the distortions, to be discussed shortly, influence schemas in various ways.

Interpretation   Once your attention has been drawn to certain stimuli and you have grouped or organized this information, the next step is to uncover the reasons behind the actions. That is, even if your attention is called to the same information and you organize it in the same way your friend does, you may interpret it differently or make different attributions about the reasons behind what you have perceived. For example, as a manager, you might attribute compliments from a friendly subordinate to his being an eager worker, whereas your friend might interpret the behavior as insincere flattery.

Retrieval   So far, we have discussed the stages of the perceptual process as if they all occurred at the same time. However, to do so ignores the important component of memory. Each of the previous stages forms part of that memory and contributes to the stimuli or information stored there. The information stored in our memory must be retrieved if it is to be used. This leads us to the retrieval stage of the perceptual process summarized in Figure 1.14.

All of us at times can't retrieve information stored in our memory. More commonly, our memory decays, so that only some of the information is retrieved. Schemas play an important role in this area. They make it difficult for people to remember things not included in them. For example, based on your prototype about the traits comprising a "high performing employee" (hard work, punctuality, intelligence, articulateness, and decisiveness), you may overestimate these traits and underestimate others when you are evaluating the performance of a subordinate whom you generally consider good. Thus, you may overestimate the person's decisiveness since it is a key part of your high performance prototype.

Indeed, people are as likely to recall nonexistent traits as they are to recall those that are really there. Furthermore, once formed, prototypes may be difficult to change and tend to last a long time.[105] Obviously, this distortion can cause major problems in terms of performance appraisals and promotions, not to mention numerous other interactions on and off the job. By the same token, such prototypes allow you to "chunk" information and reduce overload. Thus, prototypes are a double-edged sword.

■ RESPONSE TO THE PERCEPTUAL PROCESS

Throughout this section, we have shown how the perceptual process influences numerous OB responses. Figure 1.14 classifies such responses into thoughts and feelings and actions. For example, in countries such as Mexico, bosses routinely greet their secretaries with a kiss, and that is expected behavior. In contrast, in this country your thoughts and feelings might be quite different about such behavior. You might very well perceive this as a form of sexual harassment. As you cover the other OB topics in the book, you also should be alert to the importance of perceptual responses covering thoughts, feelings, and actions.

Common Perceptual Distortions

Figure 1.15 shows some common kinds of distortions that can make the perceptual process inaccurate and affect the response. These are stereotypes and prototypes, halo effects, selective perception, projection, contrast effects, and self-fulfilling prophecy.

■ STEREOTYPES OR PROTOTYPES

Earlier, when discussing person schemas, we described stereotypes, or prototypes, as useful ways of combining information in order to deal with information overload. At the same time, we pointed out how stereotypes can cause inaccuracies in retrieving information, along with some further problems. In particular, stereotypes obscure individual differences; that is, they can prevent managers from getting to know people as individuals and from accurately assessing their needs, preferences, and abilities. We compared these stereotypes with research results and showed the errors that can occur when stereotypes are relied on for decision making. Nevertheless, stereotypes continue to exist at the board of directors level in organizations. A recent survey from 133 Fortune 500 firms showed that female directors were favored for membership on only the relatively peripheral public affairs committee in these organizations. Males were favored for membership on the more important compensation, executive, and finance committee, even when the females were equally or more experienced than their male counterparts.[106]

Here, we reiterate our previous message: Both managers and employees need to be sensitive to stereotypes; they also must attempt to overcome them and recognize that an increasingly diverse workforce can be a truly competitive advantage.

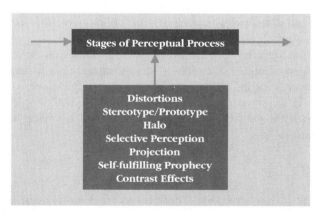

Figure 1.15
Distortions occurring in perceptual process stages.

■ HALO EFFECTS

A **halo effect** occurs when one attribute of a person or situation is used to develop an overall impression of the individual or situation. Like stereotypes, these distortions are more likely to occur in the organization stage of perception. Halo effects are common in our everyday lives. When meeting a new person, for example, a pleasant smile can lead to a positive first impression of an overall "warm" and "honest" person. The result of a halo effect is the same as that associated with a stereotype, however: Individual differences are obscured.

Halo effects are particularly important in the performance appraisal process because they can influence a manager's evaluations of subordinates' work performance. For example, people with good attendance records tend to be viewed as intelligent and responsible; those with poor attendance records are considered poor performers. Such conclusions may or may not be valid. It is the manager's job to try to get true impressions rather than allowing halo effects to result in biased and erroneous evaluations.

■ SELECTIVE PERCEPTION

Selective perception is the tendency to single out those aspects of a situation, person, or object that are consistent with one's needs, values, or attitudes. Its strongest impact occurs in the attention stage of the perceptual process. This perceptual distortion is identified in a classic research study involving executives in a manufacturing company.[107] When asked to identify the key problem in a comprehensive business policy case, each executive selected problems consistent with his or her functional area work assignments. For example, most marketing executives viewed the key problem area as sales, whereas production people tended to see the problem as one of production and organization. These differing viewpoints would affect how the executive would approach the problem; they might also create difficulties once these people tried to work together to improve things.

More recently, 121 middle- and upper-level managers attending an executive development program expressed broader views in conjunction with an emphasis on their own function. For example, a chief financial officer indicated an awareness of the importance of manufacturing, and an assistant marketing manager recognized the importance of accounting and finance along with their own functions.[108] Thus, this more current research demonstrated very little perceptual selectivity. The researchers were not, however, able to state definitively what accounted for the differing results.

These results suggest that selective perception is more important at some times than at others. Managers should be aware of this characteristic and test whether or not situations, events, or individuals are being selectively perceived. The easiest way to do this is to gather additional opinions from other people. When these opinions contradict a manager's own, an effort should be made to check the original impression.

■ PROJECTION

Projection is the assignment of one's personal attributes to other individuals; it is especially likely to occur in the interpretation stage of perception. A classic projection error is illustrated by managers who assume that the needs of their subordinates and their own coincide. Suppose, for example, that you enjoy responsibility and achievement in your work. Suppose, too, that you are the newly appointed manager of a group whose jobs seem dull and routine. You may move quickly to expand these jobs to help the workers achieve increased satisfaction from more challenging tasks because you want them to experience things that you, personally, value in work. But this may not be a good decision. If you project your needs onto the subordinates, individual differences are lost. Instead of designing the subordinates' jobs to fit their needs best, you have designed their jobs to fit your needs. The problem is that the subordinates may be quite satisfied and productive doing jobs that seem dull and routine to you. Projection can be controlled through a high degree of self-awareness and empathy—the ability to view a situation as others see it. In contrast with the usual negative effects of projection just described, there sometimes can be a positive ethical impact.

■ CONTRAST EFFECTS

Earlier, when discussing the perceived, we mentioned how a red sports car would stand out from others because of its contrast. Here, we show the perceptual distortion that can occur when, say, a person gives a talk following a strong speaker or is interviewed for a job following a series of mediocre applicants. We can expect a **contrast effect** to occur when an individual's characteristics are contrasted with those of others recently encountered who rank higher or lower on the same characteristics. Clearly, both managers and employees need to be aware of the possible perceptual distortion the contrast effect may create in many work settings.

■ **Contrast effects** occur when an individual's characteristics are contrasted with those of others recently encountered who rank higher or lower on the same characteristics.

■ SELF-FULFILLING PROPHECY

A final perceptual distortion that we consider is the **self-fulfilling prophecy**—the tendency to create or find in another situation or individual that which you expected to find in the first place. Self-fulfilling prophecy is sometimes referred to as the "Pygmalion effect," named for a mythical Greek sculptor who created a statue of his ideal mate and then made her come to life.[109] His prophecy came true! Through self-fulfilling prophecy, you also may create in the work situation that which you expect to find.

■ **Self-fulfilling prophecy** is the tendency to create or find in another situation or individual that which one has expected to find.

Self-fulfilling prophecy can have both positive and negative results for you as a manager. Suppose you assume that your subordinates prefer to satisfy most of their needs outside the work setting and want only minimal involvement with their jobs. Consequently, you are likely to provide simple, highly structured jobs designed to require little involvement. Can you predict what response the subordinates would have to this situation? Their most likely response would be to show the lack of commitment you assumed they would have in the first place. Thus, your initial expectations are confirmed as a self-fulfilling prophecy.

Self-fulfilling prophecy can have a positive side, however (see The Effective Manager 1.4). Students introduced to their teachers as "intellectual bloomers"

THE EFFECTIVE MANAGER 1.4

CREATING POSITIVE SELF-FULFILLING PROPHECIES FOR EMPLOYEES

- Create a warmer interpersonal climate between your subordinates and you.
- Give more performance feedback to subordinates—make it as positive as possible, given their actual performance.
- Spend more time helping subordinates learn job skills.
- Provide more opportunities for subordinates to ask questions.

do better on achievement tests than do their counterparts who lack such a positive introduction. A particularly interesting example of the self-fulfilling prophecy is that of Israeli tank crews. One set of tank commanders was told that according to test data some members of their assigned crews had exceptional abilities but others were only average. In reality, the crew members were assigned randomly, so that the two test groups were equal in ability. Later, the commanders reported that the so-called exceptional crew members performed better than the "average" members. As the study revealed, however, the commanders had paid more attention to and praised the crew members for whom they had the higher expectancies.[110] The self-fulfilling effects in these cases argue strongly for managers to adopt positive and optimistic approaches to people at work.

Managing the Perceptual Process

To be successful, managers must understand the perceptual process, the stages involved, and the impact the perceptual process can have on their own and others' responses. They must also be aware of what roles the perceiver, the setting, and the perceived have in the perceptual process. Particularly important with regard to the perceived is the concept of impression management—for both managers and others.

■ IMPRESSION MANAGEMENT

Impression management is a person's systematic attempt to behave in ways that will create and maintain desired impressions in the eyes of others. First impressions are especially important and influence how people respond to one another. Impression management is influenced by such activities as associating with the "right people," doing favors to gain approval, flattering others to make oneself look better, taking credit for a favorable event, apologizing for a negative event while seeking a pardon, agreeing with the opinions of others, downplaying the severity of a negative event, and doing favors for others.[111] Successful managers learn how to use these activities to enhance their own images, and they are sensitive to their use by their subordinates and others in their organizations. In this context job titles are particularly important.

■ DISTORTION MANAGEMENT

During the attention and selection stage, managers should be alert to balancing automatic and controlled information processing. Most of their responsibilities, such as performance assessment and clear communication, will involve controlled processing, which will take away from other job responsibilities. Along with more controlled processing, managers need to be concerned about increasing the frequency of observations and about getting representative information rather than simply responding to the most recent information about a subordinate or a production order, for instance. Some organizations, including large farms, have responded to the need for representative and more accurate information by utilizing current technology. In addition, managers should not fail to seek out disconfirming information that will help provide a balance to their typical perception of information.

The various kinds of schemas and prototypes and stereotypes are particularly important at the information organizing stage. Managers should strive to broaden their schemas or should even replace them with more accurate or complete ones.

At the interpretation stage, managers need to be especially attuned to the impact of attribution on information; we discuss this concept further in the section on managing the attributional process. At the retrieval stage, managers should be sensitive to the fallibility of memory. They should recognize the tendency to overrely on schemas, especially prototypes or stereotypes that may bias information stored and retrieved.

Throughout the entire perception process managers should be sensitive to the information distortions caused by halo effects, selective perception, projection, contrast effects, and self-fulfilling prophecy, in addition to the distortions of stereotypes and prototypes.

Attribution Theory

■ **Attribution theory** is the attempt to understand the cause of an event, assess responsibility for outcomes of the event, and assess the personal qualities of the people involved.

Earlier in the section we mentioned attribution theory in the context of perceptual interpretation. **Attribution theory** aids in this interpretation by focusing on how people attempt to (1) understand the causes of a certain event, (2) assess responsibility for the outcomes of the event, and (3) evaluate the personal qualities of the people involved in the event.[112] In applying attribution theory, we are especially concerned with whether one's behavior has been internally or externally caused. Internal causes are believed to be under an individual's control—you believe Jake's performance is poor because he is lazy. External causes are seen as outside a person—you believe Kellie's performance is poor because her machine is old.

According to attribution theory, three factors influence this internal or external determination: distinctiveness, consensus, and consistency. *Distinctiveness* considers how consistent a person's behavior is across different situations. If Jake's performance is low, regardless of the machine on which he is working, we tend to give the poor performance an internal attribution; if the poor performance is unusual, we tend to assign an external cause to explain it.

Consensus takes into account how likely all those facing a similar situation are to respond in the same way. If all the people using machinery like Kellie's have poor performance, we tend to give her performance an external attribution. If other employees do not perform poorly, we attribute internal causation to her performance.

Consistency concerns whether an individual responds the same way across time. If Jake has a batch of low-performance figures, we tend to give the

OB Across Functions

PUBLIC RELATIONS

Enhancing Public Image Perception Through Benchmarking

Although nationally acclaimed for its artistic quality and considered on a par with other major ballet companies, the Boston Ballet felt it lagged behind in fund-raising ability. It also worried that the perception of its image among Boston cultural institutions was too weak to support a major fund-raising expansion. The Ballet's board chair, John Humphrey, led a benchmarking effort focusing on how other organizations manage or change their public image. He established a cross-functional committee of trustees and professional staff. The committee ultimately chose three best-practice benchmark organizations in different fields: a ballet company, a museum, and a fast-growing Boston-based bakery chain—all noted for their excellent public images. Committee members developed a questionnaire and conducted followup interviews in these organizations to find out characteristics and activities that led to their superb public image perceptions. From this information, the committee made action recommendations for the Boston Ballet. Many of the recommendations were accepted, including the creation of a comprehensive image campaign for the Ballet, developed by a major Boston public relations firm, *pro bono*.

poor performance an internal attribution. In contrast, if Jake's low performance is an isolated incident, we attribute it to an external cause.

■ ATTRIBUTION ERRORS

In addition to these three influences, two errors have an impact on internal versus external determination—the *fundamental attribution error* and the *self-serving bias*.[113] Figure 1.16 provides data from a group of health-care managers.[114] When supervisors were asked to identify, or attribute, causes of poor performance among their subordinates, the supervisors more often chose the individual's internal deficiencies—lack of ability and effort—rather than external deficiencies in the situation—lack of support. This demonstrates a **fundamental attribution error**—the tendency to underestimate the influence of situational factors and to overestimate the influence of personal factors in evaluating someone else's behavior. When asked to identify causes of their own poor performance, however, the supervisors overwhelmingly cited lack of support—an external, or situational, deficiency. This indicates a **self-serving bias**—the tendency to deny personal responsibility for performance problems but to accept personal responsibility for performance success.

To summarize, we tend to overemphasize other people's internal personal factors in their behavior and to underemphasize external factors in other people's behavior. In contrast, we tend to attribute our own success to our own internal factors and to attribute our failure to external factors.

The managerial implications of attribution theory can be traced back to the fact that perceptions influence responses. For example, a manager who feels that subordinates are not performing well and perceives the reason to be an internal lack of effort is likely to respond with attempts to "motivate" the subordinates to work harder; the possibility of changing external, situational factors that may remove job constraints and provide better organizational support may be largely ignored. This oversight could sacrifice major performance gains. Interestingly, because of the self-serving bias, when they evaluated their own behavior, the supervisors in the earlier study indicated that their performance would benefit from having better support. Thus, the supervisors' own abilities or willingness to work hard were not felt to be at issue.

■ ATTRIBUTIONS ACROSS CULTURES

Research on the self-serving bias and fundamental attribution error has been done in cultures outside the United States with unexpected results.[115] In Korea, for example, the self-serving bias was found to be negative; that is, Korean managers

■ **Fundamental attribution error** is the tendency to underestimate the influence of situational factors and to overestimate the influence of personal factors in evaluating someone else's behavior.

■ **Self-serving bias** is the tendency to deny personal responsibility for performance problems but to accept personal responsibility for performance success.

Figure 1.16
Health-care managers' attributions of causes for poor performance.

Cause of Poor Performance by Their Subordinates	Most Frequent Attribution	Cause of Poor Performance by Themselves
7	Lack of *ability*	1
12	Lack of *effort*	1
5	Lack of *support*	23

attribute work group failure to themselves—"I was not a capable leader"—rather than to external causes. In India, the fundamental attribution error overemphasizes external rather than internal causes for failure. Africans attribute negative consequences—driving away fish and angering mermaids into creating squalls—to women but apparently not to men. Why these various differences occurred is not clear, but differing cultural values appear to play a role. Finally, there is some evidence that U.S. females may be less likely to emphasize the self-serving bias than males.[116]

Certain cultures, such as the United States, tend to overemphasize internal causes and underemphasize external causes. Such overemphasis may result in negative attributions toward employees. These negative attributions, in turn, can lead to disciplinary actions, negative performance evaluations, transfers to other departments, and overreliance on training, rather than focusing on such external causes as lack of workplace support.[117] Employees, too, take their cues from managerial misattributions and, through negative self-fulfilling prophecies, may reinforce managers' original misattributions. Employees and managers alike (see The Effective Manager 1.5) can be taught attributional realignment to help deal with such misattributions.[118]

THE EFFECTIVE MANAGER 1.5

KEYS IN MANAGING PERCEPTIONS AND ATTRIBUTIONS

- Be self-aware.
- Seek a wide range of differing information.
- Try to see a situation as others would.
- Be aware of different kinds of schemas.
- Be aware of perceptual distortions.
- Be aware of self and other impression management.
- Be aware of attribution theory implications.

The Concept of Organizational Culture

Organizational or corporate culture is the system of shared actions, values, and beliefs that develops within an organization and guides the behavior of its members.[119] In the business setting, this system is often referred to as the *corporate culture*. Just as no two individual personalities are the same, no two organizational cultures are identical. Most significantly, management scholars and consultants increasingly believe that cultural differences can have a major impact on the performance of organizations and the quality of work life experienced by their members.

■ FUNCTIONS AND COMPONENTS OF ORGANIZATIONAL CULTURE

Through their collective experience, members of an organization solve two extremely important survival issues.[120] The first is the question of external adaptation: What precisely needs to be accomplished, and how can it be done? The second is the question of internal integration: How do members resolve the daily problems associated with living and working together?

External Adaptation **External adaptation** involves reaching goals and dealing with outsiders. The issues concerned are tasks to be accomplished, methods used to achieve the goals, and methods of coping with success and failure.

■ **Organizational or corporate culture** is the system of shared actions, values, and beliefs that develops within an organization and guides the behavior of its members.

■ **External adaptation** involves reaching goals and dealing with outsiders. Issues concerned are tasks to be accomplished, methods used to achieve the goals, and methods of coping with success and failure.

Through their shared experiences, members may develop common views that help guide their day-to-day activities. Organizational members need to know the real mission of the organization, not just the pronouncements to key constituencies, such as stockholders. Members will naturally develop an understanding of how they contribute to the mission via interaction. This view may emphasize the importance of human resources, the role of employees as cogs in a machine, or a cost to be reduced.

Closely related to the organization's mission and view of its contribution are the questions of responsibility, goals, and methods. For instance, at 3M, employees believe that it is their responsibility to innovate and contribute creatively. They see these responsibilities reflected in achieving the goal of developing new and improved products and processes.

Each collection of individuals in an organization also tends to (1) separate more important from less important external forces; (2) develop ways to measure their accomplishments; and (3) create explanations for why goals are not always met. Daimler-Chrysler's managers, for example, have moved away from judging their progress against specific targets to estimating the degree to which they are moving a development process forward. Instead of blaming a poor economy or upper level managers for the firm's failure to reach a goal, Daimler-Chrysler managers have set hard goals that are difficult to reach and have redoubled their efforts to improve participation and commitment.[121]

The final issues in external adaptation deal with two important, but often neglected, aspects of coping with external reality. First, individuals need to develop acceptable ways of telling outsiders just how good they really are. At 3M, for example, employees talk about the quality of their products and the many new, useful products they have brought to the market. Second, individuals must collectively know when to admit defeat. At 3M, the answer is easy for new projects: At the beginning of the development process, members establish "drop" points at which to quit the development effort and redirect it.[122]

In sum, external adaptation involves answering important instrumental or goal-related questions concerning coping with reality: What is the real mission? How do we contribute? What are our goals? How do we reach our goals? What external forces are important? How do we measure results? What do we do if specific targets are not met? How do we tell others how good we are? When do we quit?

Internal Integration   The corporate culture also provides answers to the problems of internal integration. *Internal integration* deals with the creation of a collective identity and with finding ways of matching methods of working and living together.

The process of internal integration often begins with the establishment of a unique identity; that is, each collection of individuals and each subculture within the organization develops some type of unique definition of itself. Through dialogue and interaction, members begin to characterize their world. They may see it as malleable or fixed, filled with opportunity or threatening. Real progress toward innovation can begin when group members collectively believe that they can change important parts of the world around them and that what appears to be a threat is actually an opportunity for change.[123]

Three important aspects of working together are (1) deciding who is a member and who is not; (2) developing an informal understanding of acceptable and unacceptable behavior; and (3) separating friends from enemies. Effective total quality management holds that subgroups in the organization need to view their immediate supervisors as members of the group who are expected to represent them to friendly higher managers.

To work together effectively, individuals need to decide collectively how to allocate power, status, and authority. They need to establish a shared understanding of who will get rewards and sanctions for specific types of actions. Too often, managers fail to recognize these important aspects of internal integration. For example, a manager may fail to explain the basis for a promotion and to show why this reward, the status associated with it, and the power given to the newly promoted individual are consistent with commonly shared beliefs.

Collections of individuals need to work out acceptable ways to communicate and to develop guidelines for friendships. Although these aspects of internal integration may appear esoteric, they are vital. To function effectively as a team, individuals must recognize that some members will be closer than others; friendships are inevitable. However, the basis for friendships can be inappropriately restricted. At the U.S. Department of Interior, for example, recent budget cuts may have had a beneficial effect. At one time, the political appointees could be found eating together in their own executive dining room. Now, all employees eat at the Interior Department lunchroom, and even the political appointees are making new friends with the career civil servants.

In sum, internal integration involves answers to important questions associated with living together. What is our unique identity? How do we view the world? Who is a member? How do we allocate power, status, and authority? How do we communicate? What is the basis for friendship? Answering these questions is important to organizational members because the organization is more than a place to work; it is a place where individuals spend much of their adult life.[124]

■ DOMINANT CULTURE, SUBCULTURES, AND COUNTERCULTURES

Smaller firms often have a single dominant culture with a unitary set of shared actions, values, and beliefs. Most larger organizations contain several subcultures as well as one or more countercultures.[125] **Subcultures** are groups of individuals with a unique pattern of values and philosophy that is not inconsistent with the organization's dominant values and philosophy.[126] Interestingly, strong subcultures are often found in high performance task forces, teams, and special project groups in organizations. The culture emerges to bind individuals working intensely together to accomplish a specific task. For example, there are strong subcultures of stress engineers and liaison engineers in the Boeing Renton plant. These highly specialized groups must solve knotty technical issues to ensure that Boeing planes are safe. Though distinct, these groups of engineers share in the dominant values of Boeing.

In contrast, **countercultures** have a pattern of values and a philosophy that reject the surrounding culture.[127] When Stephen Jobs reentered Apple computer as its interim CEO, he quickly formed a counterculture within Apple. Over the next 18 months, numerous clashes occurred as the followers of the old CEO (Gil Amelio) fought to maintain their place. Jobs won and Apple won. His counterculture became dominant.

Within an organization, mergers and acquisitions may produce countercultures. Employers and managers of an acquired firm may hold values and assump-

■ **Subcultures** are unique patterns of values and philosophies within a group that are consistent with the dominant culture of the larger organization or social system.

■ **Countercultures** are the patterns of values and philosophies that outwardly reject those of the larger organization or social system.

tions that are quite inconsistent with those of the acquiring firm. This is known as the "clash of corporate cultures."[128] When Coca-Cola bought Columbia Pictures, the soft-drink company found out too late that the picture business was quite different from selling beverages. It sold Columbia, with its unique corporate culture, to Sony rather than fight a protracted clash of cultures.[129]

Importing Subcultures   Every large organization imports potentially important subcultural groupings when it hires employees from the larger society. In North America, for instance, subcultures and countercultures may naturally form based on ethnic, racial, gender, generational, or locational similarities. In Japanese organizations, subcultures often form based on the date of graduation from a university, gender, or geographic location. In European firms, ethnicity and language play an important part in developing subcultures, as does gender. In many less developed nations, language, education, religion, or family social status are often grounds for forming societally popular subcultures and countercultures.

The difficulty with importing groupings from the larger societies lies in the relevance these subgroups have to the organization as a whole. At the one extreme, senior managers can merely accept these divisions and work within the confines of the larger culture. There are three primary difficulties with this approach. First, subordinated groups, such as members of a specific religion or ethnic group, are likely to form into a counterculture and to work more diligently to change their status than to better the firm. Second, the firm may find it extremely difficult to cope with broader cultural changes. For instance, in the United States the expected treatment of women, ethnic minorities, and the disabled has changed dramatically over the last 20 years. Firms that merely accept old customs and prejudices have experienced a greater loss of key personnel and increased communication difficulties, as well as greater interpersonal conflict, than have their more progressive counterparts. Third, firms that accept and build on natural divisions from the larger culture may find it extremely difficult to develop sound international operations. For example, many Japanese firms have had substantial difficulty adjusting to the equal treatment of women in their U.S. operations.[130]

Valuing Cultural Diversity   Managers can work to eradicate all naturally occurring subcultures and countercultures. Firms are groping to develop what Taylor Cox calls the multicultural organization. The multicultural organization is a firm that values diversity but systematically works to block the transfer of societally based subcultures into the fabric of the organization.[131] Because Cox focuses on some problems unique to the United States, his prescription for change may not apply to organizations located in other countries with much more homogeneous populations.

Cox suggests a five-step program for developing the multicultural organization. First, the organization should develop pluralism with the objective of multibased socialization. To accomplish this objective, members of different naturally occurring groups need to school one another to increase knowledge and information and to eliminate stereotyping. Second, the firm should fully integrate its structure so that there is no direct relationship between a naturally occurring group and any particular job—for instance, there are no distinct male or female jobs. Third, the firm must integrate the informal networks by eliminating barriers and increasing participation. That is, it must break down existing societally based informal groups. Fourth, the organization should break the linkage between naturally occurring group identity and the identity of the firm. In other words, the firm should not be just for the young, old, men, women, and so on. Fifth, the organization must actively work to eliminate interpersonal conflict based on either the group identity or the natural backlash of the largest societally based grouping.

The key problems associated with fully implementing Cox's program are separating the firm from the larger culture in which it must operate and eliminating some societally based groupings that are relevant for achieving the firm's goals. For instance, the U.S. military is barred from fully implementing Cox's recommendations simply because it is not currently legal to put women into all combat roles. The issue of generational groupings provides another example. Implementing Cox's recommendations would call for 20 year olds to be represented proportionally in the senior management ranks; most corporations want and need the judgment honed by experience. However, astute senior managers are recognizing that they may be out of touch with younger employees. For example, Robert Hausman, chairman of Coventry Industries of Boca Raton, Florida routinely meets young employees once a month over pizza.[132]

■ LEVELS OF CULTURAL ANALYSIS

Three important levels of cultural analysis in organizations are: observable culture, shared values, and common assumptions.[133] These levels may be envisioned as layers. The deeper one gets, the more difficult it is to discover the culture.

The first level concerns *observable culture,* or "the way we do things around here." These are the methods the group has developed and teaches to new members. The observable culture includes the unique stories, ceremonies, and corporate rituals that make up the history of a successful work group.

The second level of analysis recognizes that *shared values* can play a critical part in linking people together and can provide a powerful motivational mechanism for members of the culture. Many consultants suggest that organizations should develop a "dominant and coherent set of shared values."[134] The term *shared* in cultural analysis implies that the group is a whole. Every member may not agree with the shared values, but they have all been exposed to them and have often been told they are important. At Hewlett-Packard, for example, "quality" is part of everyone's vocabulary. The firm was founded on the belief that everyone could make a creative contribution to developing quality products.

At the deepest level of cultural analysis are common assumptions, or the taken-for-granted truths that collections of corporate members share as a result of their joint experience. It is often extremely difficult to isolate these patterns, but doing so helps explain why culture invades every aspect of organizational life.

OB Across Functions

MARKETING

Marketing at a High Performance Organization: Hewlett-Packard

A corporation with nearly 125,000 employees and with sales approaching $50 billion, Hewlett-Packard (HP) is a leader in many information technology fields. Throughout its international product line advertising there is a constant repetition of an HP core value—quality. For instance, in 1999 HP launched its first advertising campaign on behalf of its European channel partners to support the Connect Programme—a program designed to bring better account management, increased business opportunities, and higher profitability to some of HP's international marketing partners. To qualify, retailers and resellers must meet a number of quality criteria for both their technical and sales staff. Then they become members of the Connect Programme group. The theme of the marketing campaign—"Connect with our family of skilled resellers"—urges European, Middle Eastern, and African IT executives to trust in HP dealers.

Observable Aspects of Organizational Culture

Important parts of an organization's culture emerge from the collective experience of its members. These emergent aspects of the culture help make it unique and may well provide a competitive advantage for the organization. Some of these aspects may be directly observed in day-to-day practices. Others may have to be discovered—for example, by asking members to tell stories of important incidents in the history of the organization. We often learn about the unique aspects of the organizational culture through descriptions of specific events.[135] By observing employee actions, listening to stories, and asking members to interpret what is going on, one can begin to understand the organization's culture.

■ STORIES, RITES, RITUALS, AND SYMBOLS

Organizations are rich with stories of winners and losers, successes and failures. Perhaps one of the most important stories concerns the founding of the organization. The founding story often contains the lessons learned from the heroic efforts of an embattled entrepreneur, whose vision may still guide the firm. The story of the founding may be so embellished that it becomes a **saga**—a heroic account of accomplishments.[136] Sagas are important because they are used to tell new members the real mission of the organization, how the organization operates, and how individuals can fit into the company. Rarely is the founding story totally accurate, and it often glosses over some of the more negative aspects of the founders. Such is the case with Nike.

If you have job experience, you may well have heard stories concerning the following questions: How will the boss react to a mistake? Can someone move from the bottom to the top of the company? What will get me fired? These are common story topics in many organizations.[137] Often, the stories provide valuable hidden information about who is more equal than others, whether jobs are secure, and how things are really controlled. In essence, the stories begin to suggest how organizational members view the world and live together. Some of the most obvious aspects of organizational culture are rites and rituals. **Rites** are standardized and recurring activities that are used at special times to influence the behaviors and understanding of organizational members; **rituals** are systems of rites. It is common, for example, for Japanese workers and managers to start their workdays together with group exercises and singing of the "company song." Separately, the exercises and song are rites. Together, they form part of a ritual. In other settings, such as the Mary Kay Cosmetics company, scheduled ceremonies reminiscent of the Miss America pageant (a ritual) are used regularly to spotlight positive work achievements and reinforce high performance expectations with awards, including gold and diamond pins and fur stoles.

Rituals and rites may be unique to particular groups within the organization. Subcultures often arise from the type of technology deployed by the unit, the specific function being performed, and the specific collection of specialists in the unit. The boundaries of the subculture may well be maintained by a unique language. Often, the language of a subculture, and its rituals and rites, emerge from the group as a form of jargon. In some cases, the special language starts to move outside the firm and begins to enter the larger society. For instance, an ad for a Hewlett-

■ **Sagas** are embellished heroic accounts of the story of the founding of an organization.

■ **Rites** are standardized and recurring activities used at special times to influence the behaviors and understanding of organizational members.

■ **Rituals** are systems of rites.

Packard hand-held computer read: "All the features you need are built right in. MS-DOS, Lotus 1-2-3...and a 512 K RAM version of the HP 95LX." Not everyone found this a user-friendly ad, but it did appeal to knowledgeable individuals.[138]

Another observable aspect of corporate culture centers on the symbols found in organizations. A **cultural symbol** is any object, act, or event that serves to transmit cultural meaning. Good examples are the corporate uniforms worn by UPS and Federal Express delivery personnel. Although many such symbols are quite visible, their importance and meaning may not be.

■ **A cultural symbol** is any object, act, or event that serves to transmit cultural meaning.

■ CULTURAL RULES AND ROLES

Organizational culture often specifies when various types of actions are appropriate and where individual members stand in the social system. These cultural rules and roles are part of the normative controls of the organization and emerge from its daily routines.[139] For instance, the timing, presentation, and methods of communicating authoritative directives are often quite specific to each organization. In one firm, meetings may be forums for dialogue and discussion, where managers set agendas and then let others offer new ideas, critically examine alternatives, and fully participate. In another firm, the "rules" may be quite different: The manager goes into the meeting with fixed expectations. Any new ideas, critical examinations, and the like are expected to be worked out in private before the meeting takes place. The meeting is a forum for letting others know what is being done and for passing out orders on what to do in the future.

■ THE EVOLUTION OF SHARED MEANINGS FROM OBSERVABLE CULTURE

What you see as an outside observer may or may not be what organizational members see. You may see NASA personnel on television filling the tanks of a booster rocket for the space shuttle. If you could ask the workers directly what they are doing, you might be surprised by the answer. They are not just filling booster tanks; they are assisting with an important part of exploring space. Through interaction with one another, and as reinforced by the rest of the organization, the workers have infused a larger shared meaning—or sense of broader purpose—into their tasks. In this sense, organizational culture is a "shared" set of meanings and perceptions that are created and learned by organizational members in the course of interactions.[140] This set of shared meanings may be accompanied by shared values.

Values and Organizational Culture

To describe more fully the culture of an organization, it is necessary to go deeper than the observable aspects. To many researchers and managers, shared common values lie at the very heart of organization culture. Shared values help turn routine activities into valuable, important actions, tie the corporation to the important values of society, and may provide a very distinctive source of competitive advantage. In organizations, what works for one person is often taught to new members as the correct way to think and feel. Important values are then attributed to these solutions to everyday problems. By linking values and actions, the organization taps into some of the strongest and deepest realms of the individual. The tasks a person performs are given not only meaning but value; what one does is not only workable but correct, right, and important.

Some successful organizations share some common cultural characteristics.[141] Organizations with "strong cultures" possess a broadly and deeply shared value system. Unique, shared values can provide a strong corporate identity, enhance collective commitment, provide a stable social system, and reduce the need for formal and bureaucratic controls. A strong culture can be a double-edged sword, however. A strong culture and value system can reinforce a singular view of the organization and its environment. If dramatic changes are needed, it may be very difficult to change the organization. General Motors may have a "strong" culture, for example, but the firm faces enormous difficulty in its attempts to adapt its ways to a dynamic and highly competitive environment.

In many corporate cultures, one finds a series of common assumptions known to most everyone in the corporation: "We are different." "We are better at…." "We have unrecognized talents." Cisco Systems at the opening of this chapter provides an excellent example. Senior managers often share common assumptions, such as, "We are good stewards." "We are competent managers." "We are practical innovators." Like values, such assumptions become reflected in the organizational culture.

■ MANAGEMENT PHILOSOPHY

■ **Management philosophy** is a philosophy that links key goal-related issues with key collaboration issues to come up with general ways by which the firm will manage its affairs.

A **management philosophy** links key goal-related issues with key collaboration issues and comes up with a series of general ways by which the firm will manage its affairs.[142] A well-developed management philosophy is important because (1) it establishes generally understood boundaries on all members of the firm; (2) it provides a consistent way of approaching new and novel situations; and (3) it helps hold individuals together by assuring them of a known path toward success. Wal-Mart has a clearly identified management philosophy linking growth and profitability with customer service and individual employee commitment. Each manager runs "a store within a store," supported by more senior management and corporate buyers. This concept both liberates individuals to try new initiatives and binds their efforts within managerial constraints and purchasing realities. Once, the homespun comments of legendary CEO Sam Walton helped to help bind individuals together; now managers evoke his memory. The philosophy is expressed in some old-fashioned values, such as customer service, frugality, hard work, and service toward employees.

Elements of the management philosophy may be formally documented in a corporate plan, a statement of business philosophy, or a series of goals (see The Effective Manager 1.6). Yet, it is the unstated but well-understood fundamentals these written documents signify that form the heart of a well-developed management philosophy.

■ ORGANIZATIONAL MYTHS

■ An **organizational myth** is an unproven and often unstated belief that is accepted uncritically.

In many firms, the management philosophy is supported by a series of organizational myths. **Organizational myths** are unproven and often unstated beliefs that are accepted uncritically. In a study of safety in nuclear power plants, senior managers were asked whether they felt there was a tradeoff between safeness and efficiency. The response was clear: A safe plant is an efficient plant. Yet, most of these executives had seen data showing that measures of safeness and efficiency were quite independent. To admit there was a tradeoff raised the issue of making choices between efficiency and safety. All wanted to believe that to do one was to promote the other.[143]

Whereas some may scoff at these organizational myths and want to see rational, hard-nosed analysis replace mythology, each firm needs a series of managerial myths.[144] Myths allow executives to redefine impossible problems into more manageable components. Myths can facilitate experimentation and creativity, and they allow managers to govern. For instance, senior executives are not just decision makers or rational allocators of resources. All organization members hope these individuals will also be fair, just, and compassionate.

■ NATIONAL CULTURE INFLUENCES

Widely held common assumptions may often be traced to the larger culture of the corporation's host society.[145] The difference between Sony's corporate emphasis on group achievements and Zenith's emphasis on individual engineering excellence, for example, can be traced to the Japanese emphasis on collective action versus the U.S. emphasis on individualism.

National cultural values may also become embedded in the expectations of important organizational constituencies and in generally accepted solutions to problems. When moving across national cultures, managers need to be sensitive to national cultural differences so that their actions do not violate common assumptions in the underlying national culture. In Japan and Western Europe, for example, executives are expected to work cooperatively with government officials on an informal basis. Informal business-government relations that are perfectly acceptable in these countries are considered influence peddling in the United States. Whereas some South American executives expect to pay directly for some government services, in the United States such payments are considered bribes.

Inappropriate actions that violate common assumptions drawn from national culture can have an important impact on performance and may alienate organizational members, even if managers have the best intentions. To improve morale at General Electric's new French subsidiary, Chi. Generale de Radiologie, American managers invited all the European managers to a "get acquainted" meeting near Paris. The Americans gave out colorful T-shirts with the GE slogan, "Go for One," a typical maneuver in many American training programs. The French resented the T-shirts. One outspoken individual said, "It was like Hitler was back, forcing us to wear uniforms. It was humiliating."

THE EFFECTIVE MANAGER 1.6

ELEMENTS OF STRONG CORPORATE CULTURES

- A widely shared real understanding of what the firm stands for, often embodied in slogans.
- A concern for individuals over rules, policies, procedures, and adherence to job duties.
- A recognition of heroes whose actions illustrate the company's shared philosophy and concerns.
- A belief in ritual and ceremony as important to members and to building a common identity.
- A well-understood sense of the informal rules and expectations so that employees and managers understand what is expected of them.
- A belief that what employees and managers do is important and that it is important to share information and ideas.

Managing Organizational Culture

The culture should be considered as critical as structure and strategy in establishing the organizational foundations of high performance. Good managers are able to reinforce and support an existing strong culture; good managers are also able to help build resilient cultures in situations where they are absent. For instance, CEO Mike Walsh of Union Pacific has brought a new and fresh approach to the firm with what *Fortune* Magazine called an "introverted corporate culture." Cultural changes under Walsh's leadership included the empowerment of managers at all levels. A typical response: "We were so elated the company was willing to give new authority that we wanted it to work."

Two broad strategies for managing the corporate culture have received considerable attention in the OB literature. One strategy calls for managers to help modify observable culture, shared values, and common assumptions directly. A second strategy involves the use of organizational development techniques to modify specific elements of the culture.

■ BUILDING, REINFORCING, AND CHANGING CULTURE

Managers can modify the visible aspects of culture, such as the language, stories, rites, rituals, and sagas. They can change the lessons to be drawn from common stories and even encourage individuals to see the reality they see. Because of their positions, senior managers can interpret situations in new ways and can adjust the meanings attached to important corporate events. They can create new rites and rituals. This takes time and enormous energy, but the long-run benefits can also be great.

Top managers, in particular, can set the tone for a culture and for cultural change. Managers at Aetna Life and Casualty Insurance built on its humanistic traditions to provide basic skills to highly motivated but underqualified individuals. Even in the highly cost-competitive steel industry, Chairperson F. Kenneth Iverson of Nucor built on basic entrepreneurial values in U.S. society to reduce the number of management levels by half. And at Procter and Gamble, Richard Nicolosi evoked the shared values for greater participation in decision making dramatically to improve creativity and innovation.

Each of these examples illustrates how managers can help foster a culture that provides answers to important questions concerning external adaptation and internal integration. Recent work on the linkages among corporate culture and financial performance reaffirms the importance of an emphasis on helping employees adjust to the environment. It also suggests that this emphasis alone is not sufficient. Neither is an emphasis solely on stockholders or customers associated with long-term economic performance. Instead, managers must work to emphasize all three issues simultaneously. This emphasis on customers, stockholders, and employees comes at a cost of emphasizing management. Large offices, multimillion-dollar salaries, golden parachutes (protections for executives if the firm is bought by others), as well as the executive plane, dining room, and country club are out.

Early research on culture and culture change often emphasized direct attempts to alter the values and assumptions of individuals by resocializing them—that is, trying to change their hearts so that their minds and actions would follow.[146] The goal was to establish a clear, consistent organizationwide consensus. More recent work suggests that this unified approach of working through values may not be either possible or desirable.

Trying to change people's values from the top down without also changing how the organization operates and recognizing the importance of individuals does not work very well. Take a look at Cisco Systems. Here managers realize that keeping a dynamic, change-oriented and fun culture is a mix of managerial actions, decisions about technology, and initiatives from all employees. The values are not set and imposed from someone on high. The shared values emerge, and they are not identical across all of Cisco's operating sites. Subtle but important differences emerge across their operations in Silicon Valley, the North Carolina operation, and the Australian setting.

It is also a mistake for managers to attempt to revitalize an organization by dictating major changes and ignoring shared values. Although things may change a bit on the surface, a deeper look often shows whole departments resisting change and many key people unwilling to learn new ways. Such responses may indicate that the managers responsible are insensitive to the effects of their proposed changes on shared values. They fail to ask whether the changes are contrary to the important values of participants within the firm, a challenge to historically important corporatewide assumptions, and inconsistent with important common assumptions derived from the national culture, outside the firm. Note the example of Stephen Jobs at Apple earlier in this section. He did not make all the changes. Rather, he worked with others to make changes in strategy, structure, products, and marketing and to build on deep-seated common assumptions that long-term employees shared.

Few executives are able to reshape common assumptions or "the taken-for-granted truths" in a firm without taking drastic, radical action. Roger Smith of General Motors realized this challenge and established a new division to produce the Saturn.

At Harley Davidson, a new senior management team had to replace virtually all of the company's middle managers in order to establish a new, unique, and competitive culture. All too often, however, executives are unable to realize that they, too, can be captured by the broadly held common assumptions within their firms. Just as executives in Eastern European firms must reexamine the philosophical foundation of their firms as their countries adopt market economies, so must managers in the United States and other Western nations, as they anticipate the exciting challenges of a new century.

■ CONTINUOUS CULTURAL DEVELOPMENT

To keep the culture fresh and competitive, the challenge today is to engage in a process of continuous self-assessment and planned change in order to stay

---

THE EFFECTIVE MANAGER 1.7

PICKING A FIRM BY ITS CULTURE

One study suggests that there are four dominant types of corporate cultures:

1. Academies—individuals are carefully moved through training programs for career development.
2. Fortresses—individuals are asked to engage in a turnaround and a fight for corporate survival.
3. Clubs—seniority, loyalty, status, commitment, and "fitting in" are most important.
4. Baseball teams—talent and performance are considered critical.

■ **Organization develop-ment (OD)** is the applica-tion of behavioral science knowledge in a long-range effort to improve an organi-zation's ability to cope with change in its external envi-ronment and increase its problem-solving capabilities.

abreast of problems and opportunities in a complex and demanding environ-ment. **Organization development (OD)** is a comprehensive approach to planned change that is designed to improve the overall effectiveness of organi-zations. Formally defined, OD is the application of behavioral science knowl-edge in a long-range effort to improve an organization's ability to cope with change in its external environment and to increase its internal problem-solving capabilities.[147]

Organization development is used to improve performance in organizations of many types, sizes, and settings. It includes a set of tools with which any man-ager who is concerned about achieving and maintaining high levels of produc-tivity will want to be familiar. Because of its comprehensive nature and scientific foundations, OD was frequently implemented with the aid of an external consul-tant. As OD techniques have been combined with a better understanding of or-ganizational culture, its basic concepts can and should be used routinely by all managers.

Organizational Development Processes and Applications

Organizational development provides a set of well-proven methods for develop-ing and changing what cultural analyses call *external adaptation* and *internal integration*. Importantly, OD seeks to achieve change in such a way that the or-ganization's members become more active and confident in taking similar steps to maintain the culture and longer run organization effectiveness. A large part of any OD program's success in this regard rests with its assumptions, values and action research foundations.

■ UNDERLYING ASSUMPTIONS OF OD

The organizational development foundations for achieving change are rooted in underlying assumptions about individuals, groups, and organizations. At the in-dividual level, OD is guided by principles that reflect an underlying respect for people and their capabilities. It assumes that individual needs for growth and de-velopment are most likely to be satisfied in a supportive and challenging work environment. It also assumes that most people are capable of taking responsibil-ity for their own actions and of making positive contributions to organizational performance.

At the *group level*, OD is guided by principles that reflect a belief that groups can be good for both people and organizations. It assumes that groups help their members satisfy important individual needs and can also be helpful in support-ing organizational objectives. And it assumes that effective groups can be created by people working in collaboration to meet individual and organizational needs.

At the *organizational level*, OD is guided by principles that show a respect for the complexity of an organization as a system of interdependent parts. It as-sumes that changes in one part of the organization will affect other parts as well. And it assumes that organizational structures and jobs can be designed to meet the needs of individuals and groups as well as those of the organization.

SHARED VALUES AND PRINCIPLES UNDERLYING OD

Organizational development offers a systematic approach to planned change in organizations which addresses two main goals: outcome goals (mainly issues of external adaptation) and process goals (mainly issues of internal integration). Outcome goals include achieving improvements in task performance by improving external adaptation capabilities. In OD, these goals focus on what is actually accomplished through individual and group efforts. Process goals include achieving improvements in such things as communication, interaction, and decision making among an organization's members. These goals focus on how well people work together, and they stress improving internal integration.

In pursuit of these goals, OD is intended to help organizations and their members by (1) creating an open problem-solving climate throughout an organization, (2) supplementing formal authority with that of knowledge and competence, (3) moving decision making to points where relevant information is available, (4) building trust and maximizing collaboration among individuals and groups, (5) increasing the sense of organizational "ownership" among members, and (6) allowing people to exercise self-direction and self-control at work.[148] Thus, using OD implicitly involves these values. That is, organization development is designed to improve the contributions of individual members in achieving the organizational goals, and it seeks to do so in ways that respect the organization's members as mature adults who need and deserve high-quality experiences in their working lives.

ACTION RESEARCH FOUNDATIONS OF OD

Organizational development practitioners refer to **action research** as the process of systematically collecting data on an organization, feeding it back to the members for action planning, and evaluating results by collecting and reflecting on more data after the planned actions have been taken. This is a data-based and collaborative approach to problem solving and organizational assessment. When used in the OD process, action research helps identify action directions that may enhance an organization's effectiveness. In a typical action-research sequence depicted in Figure 1.17, the sequence is initiated when someone senses a performance gap and decides to analyze the situation systematically for the problems and opportunities it represents. The process continues through the following steps: data gathering, data feedback, data analysis, and action planning. It continues to the point at which action is taken and results are evaluated. The evaluation or reassessment stage may or may not generate another performance gap. If it does, the action-research cycle begins anew.

Figure 1.18 identifies one set of frameworks that can assist OD practitioners in accomplishing the required diagnoses. These foundations apply the open systems framework and OB concepts with which you are already familiar from earlier parts of this book. At the organizational level, the figure indicates that effectiveness must be understood with respect to forces in the external environment and major organizational aspects, such as strategy, technology, structure, culture, and management systems. At the group level, effectiveness is viewed in a context of forces in the internal environment of the organization and major group aspects, such as tasks, membership, norms, cohesiveness, and group processes. At the individual level, effectiveness is considered in relationship to the internal

■ **Action research** is the process of systematically collecting data on an organization, feeding it back for action planning, and evaluating results by collecting and reflecting on more data.

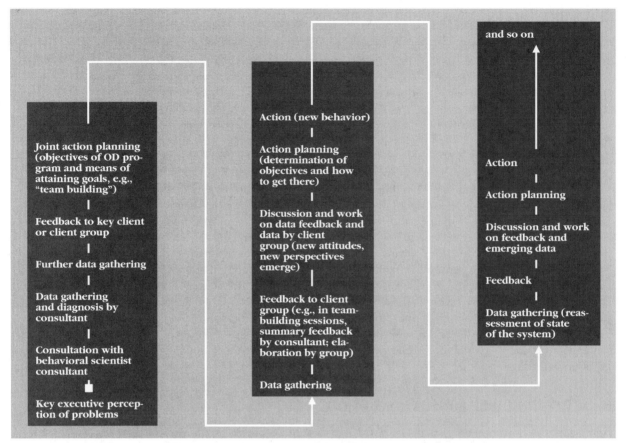

Figure 1.17
An action-research model for organization development.

environment of the work group and individual aspects, such as tasks, goals, needs, and interpersonal relationships.

■ ORGANIZATIONAL DEVELOPMENT INTERVENTIONS

The action research process should engage members of an organization in activities designed to accomplish the required diagnoses and to develop and implement plans for constructive change. Action research, data collection, and the diagnostic foundations should come together through the choice and use of OD "interventions." **Organizational development interventions** are activities initiated by the consultant to facilitate planned change and to assist the client system in developing its own problem-solving capabilities. With less formality, many of these techniques are also now being used by managers to help understand and improve their own operations. Major OD interventions can be categorized with respect to their major impact at the organizational, group, and individual levels of action.[149]

Organizationwide Interventions An effective organization is one that achieves its major performance objectives while maintaining a high quality of work life for its members. OD interventions designed for systemwide application include the following.

■ **Organization development interventions** are activities initiated to support planned change and improve work effectiveness.

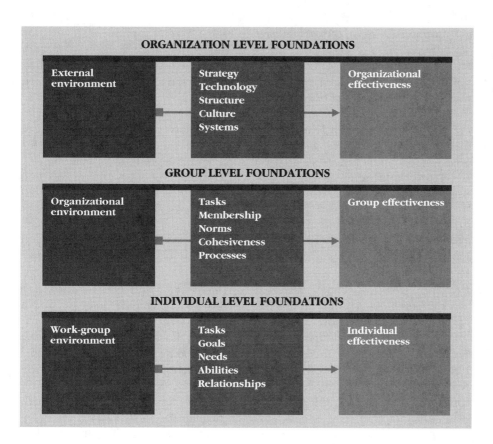

Figure 1.18
Diagnostic foundations of organization development and OD techniques: concerns for individual, group, and organizational effectiveness.

Survey feedback begins with the collection of data via questionnaire responses from organization members, or a representative sample of such responses. The data are then presented, or fed back, to the members. They subsequently engage in a collaborative process to interpret the data and to develop action plans in response.

Confrontation meetings are designed to help determine quickly how an organization may be improved and to take initial actions to better the situation.[150] The intervention involves a one-day meeting conducted by an OD facilitator for a representative sample of organizational members, including top management. In a structured format, the consultant asks participants to make individual lists of what they feel can be done to improve things. Then, through a series of small-group work sessions and sharing of results, these ideas are refined into a tentative set of actions that top management then endorses for immediate implementation. The major trick here is to get senior managers to propose changing their part of the firm. Confrontation meetings fail if all the proposed changes call for adjustments by subordinates without any alterations by the top managers.

Structural redesign involves realigning the structure of the organization or major subsystems to improve performance. It includes examining the best fit between structure, technology, and environment. In today's highly dynamic environments, in light of the increasing involvement of organizations in international operations and with rapid changes in information technology, a structure can easily grow out of date. Thus, structural redesign is an important OD intervention that can be used to help maintain the best fit between organizational structures and situational demands.

■ **Survey feedback** begins with the collection of data via questionnaires from organization members or a representative sample of them.

■ A **confrontation meeting** helps determine how an organization may be improved and start action toward improvement.

■ **Structural redesign** involves realigning the structure of the organization or major subsystem in order to improve performance.

■ **Collateral organization** involves a representative set of members in periodic small-group, problem-solving sessions.

■ **Team building** is designed to gather and analyze data on the functioning of a group and implement changes to increase its operating effectiveness.

■ **Process consultation** helps a group improve on such things as norms, cohesiveness, decision-making methods, communication, conflict, and task and maintenance activities.

■ **Intergroup team building** helps groups improve their working relationships with one another and experience improved group effectiveness.

■ **Role negotiation** is a process through which individuals clarify expectations about what each should be giving and receiving as group members.

■ **Job redesign** creates long-term congruence between individual goals and organizational career opportunities.

Collateral organization is designed to make creative problem solving possible by pulling a representative set of members out of the formal organization structure to engage in periodic small-group problem-solving sessions.[151] These collateral, or "parallel," structures are temporary and exist only to supplement the activities of the formal structure.

Group and Intergroup Interventions   OD interventions at the group level are designed to improve group effectiveness. The major interventions at this level are team building, process consultation, and intergroup team building.

Team building involves a manager or consultant engaging the members of a group in a series of activities designed to help them examine how the group functions and how it may function better. Like survey feedback at the organizational level, team building involves some form of data collection and feedback. The key elements, however, are a collaborative assessment of the data by all members of the group and the achievement of consensus regarding what may be done to improve group effectiveness. Team building is often done at "retreats" or off-site meetings, where group members spend two to three days working intensely together on this reflection–analysis–planning process.

Process consultation involves structured activities that are facilitated by an OD practitioner and is designed to improve group functioning. Process consultation has a more specific focus than does team building, however; its attention is directed toward the key "processes" through which members of a group work with one another. The process consultant is concerned with helping a group function better on such things as norms, cohesiveness, decision-making methods, communication, conflict, and task and maintenance activities.

Intergroup team building is a special form of team building. It is designed to help two or more groups improve their working relationships with one another and, it is hoped, to experience improved group effectiveness as a result. Here, the OD practitioner engages the groups or their representatives in activities that increase awareness of how each group perceives the other. Given this understanding, collaborative problem solving can improve coordination between the groups and encourage more mutual support of one another as important components in the total organization.

Individual Interventions   Task performance and job satisfaction are important concerns with respect to improving individual effectiveness in the workplace. OD interventions at this level of attention range from those that address personal issues to those that deal more with specific job and career considerations. Individual-level OD interventions include the following.

Role negotiation is a means of clarifying what individuals expect to give and receive of one another in their working relationship. Because roles and personnel change over time, role negotiation can be an important way to maintain task understandings among individuals in an organization. This kind of understanding is quite easily accomplished by helping people who work together clarify what they need from one another to do their jobs well.

Job redesign is the process of creating long-term congruence between individual goals and organizational career opportunities. A good example is the Hackman and Oldham diagnostic approach to job enrichment.[152] Recall that this approach involves (1) analyzing the core characteristics of a job or group of jobs, (2) analyzing the needs and capabilities of workers in those jobs, and (3) taking action to adjust the core job characteristics either to enrich or to simplify the jobs to best match individual preferences.

Career planning takes the form of structured opportunities for individuals to work with their managers or staff experts from the personnel or human resources department on career issues. They may map career goals, assess personal development needs, and actively plan short-term and long-term career moves. Increasingly, career planning is becoming a major part of the support that highly progressive organizations provide for their members.

■ **Career planning** creates long-term congruence between individual goals and organizational career opportunities.

OD and the Continuous Cultural Evolution   Today, a new wave of successful high-tech firms exemplifies the use of organization development assumptions, values, and techniques without using the term OD. It is not that such firms as Cisco Systems or Starbucks are trying to force change on their employees. Rather, the managers in these systems take a very practical approach to managing culture. They realize that both external adaptation and internal integration are important for a variety of subcultures within their firms. They use OD intervention techniques to improve both. They do not dictate values or set common assumptions in isolation but with their fellow employees. They are working with others to help nurture and guide the continual evolution of organizational culture from day to day.

Change in Organizations

"Change" is the watchword of the day for many, if not most, organizations. Some of this change may be described as *radical change*, or frame-breaking change.[153] This is change that results in a major overhaul of the organization or its component systems. In today's business environments, such radical changes are often initiated by a critical event, such as a new CEO, a new ownership brought about by merger or takeover, or a dramatic failure in operating results. When it occurs in the life cycle of an organization, radical change is intense and all-encompassing.

Another common form of organizational change is *incremental change*, or frame-bending change. This type of change, being part of an organization's natural evolution, is frequent and less traumatic. Typical changes of this type include the introduction of new products, new technologies, and new systems and processes. Although the nature of the organization remains relatively the same, incremental change builds on the existing ways of operating to enhance or extend them in new directions. The capability of improving continuously through incremental change is an important asset in today's demanding environments.

The success of both radical and incremental change in organizations depends in part on **change agents** who lead and support the change processes. These are individuals and groups who take responsibility for changing the existing behavior patterns of another person or social system. Although change agents sometimes are hired as consultants from outside the organization, any manager or leader in today's dynamic times is expected to act in a change agent capacity. Indeed, this responsibility is increasingly defined even more specifically as essential to the leadership role. Simply put, being an effective change agent means being a great "change leader."[154]

■ **Change agents** are people who take action to change the behavior of people and systems.

■ PLANNED AND UNPLANNED CHANGE

■ **Unplanned change** occurs spontaneously and without a change agent's direction.

Not all change in organizations is the result of a change agent's direction. **Unplanned changes** occur spontaneously or randomly. They may be disruptive, such as a wildcat strike that ends in a plant closure, or beneficial, such as an interpersonal conflict that results in a new procedure designed to smooth the flow of work between two departments. When the forces of unplanned change begin to appear, the appropriate goal is to act quickly to minimize any negative consequences and maximize any possible benefits. In many cases, unplanned changes can be turned into good advantage.

■ **Planned change** is intentional and occurs with a change agent's direction.

In contrast, **planned change** is the result of specific efforts by a change agent. It is a direct response to someone's perception of a *performance gap*—a discrepancy between the desired and actual state of affairs. Performance gaps may represent problems to be resolved or opportunities to be explored. Most planned changes may be regarded as efforts intended to deal with performance gaps in ways that benefit an organization and its members. The processes of continuous improvement require constant vigilance to spot performance gaps— both problems and opportunities—and to take action to resolve them.

OB Across Functions

OPERATIONS

Building Support for Organizational Transformations

Change doesn't come easy in most circumstances, and the larger the organization the more difficult the process often becomes. At Royal Dutch/Shell you'll find some 100,000+ employees and operations spread worldwide. When Steve Miller took over as group managing director, he found that a two-year-old effort to transform the company was bogged down. It was designed to start at the top and progress throughout the firm level by level. Miller decided to tackle the resistant bureaucracy by actively involving employees from the front line. Through "grassroots" leadership, he set out to work as directly as possible with a cross section of Shell employees from over 25 countries. The response was quick and positive. Miller and his management team found that the employees were willing to participate. Their energies spread to the levels above, and the change processes were reinvigorated. Through communication, empowerment, and respect for ideas and experience, Miller tapped what may be an organization's most important change asset—its people. But you don't get the advantages if you aren't willing to step out of the executive office, meet the people doing all types of jobs on the front line, and then ask the right questions. Sincerity and trust, of course, add the final ingredients to grassroots change leadership.

■ ORGANIZATIONAL FORCES AND TARGETS FOR CHANGE

The forces for change driving organizations of all types and sizes are ever present in and around today's dynamic work settings.[155] They are found in the *organization–environment relationship*, with mergers, strategic alliances, and divestitures among the examples of organizational attempts to redefine their relationships with challenging social and political environments. They are found in the *organizational life cycle*, with changes in culture and structure among the examples of how organizations must adapt as they evolve from birth through growth and toward maturity. They are found in the *political nature of organizations*, with changes in internal control structures, including benefits and reward systems, that attempt to deal with shifting political currents.

Planned change based on any of these forces can be internally directed toward a wide variety of organizational components. As shown in Figure 1.19, these targets include organizational purpose, strategy, structure, and people, as well as objectives, culture, tasks, and technology. When considering these targets, however, it must be recognized that they are highly intertwined in the workplace. Changes in any one are likely to require or involve changes in others. For example, a change in the basic *tasks*—what it is that people do, is almost inevitably accompanied by a change in *technology*—the way in which tasks are accomplished. Changes in tasks and technology usu-

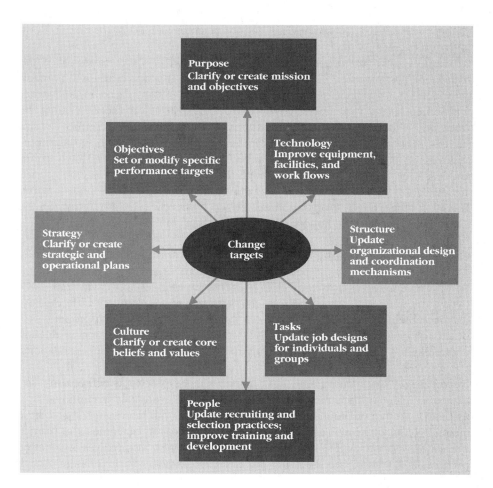

Figure 1.19
Organizational targets
for planned change.

ally require alterations in structures, including changes in the patterns of authority and communication as well as in the roles of workers. These technological and structural changes can, in turn, necessitate changes in the knowledge, skills, and behaviors of *people*—the members of the organization.[156] In all cases, of course, tendencies to accept easy-to-implement, but questionable, "quick fixes" to problems should be avoided.[157]

■ PHASES OF PLANNED CHANGE

Psychologist Kurt Lewin recommends that any change effort be viewed as a process with three distinct phases—unfreezing, changing, and refreezing, all of which must be well handled for a change to be successful.[158] He also suggests that we may become easily preoccupied with the changing phase and neglect the importance of the unfreezing and refreezing stages.

Unfreezing   In Lewin's model, **unfreezing** is the managerial responsibility of preparing a situation for change. It involves disconfirming existing attitudes and behaviors to create a felt need for something new. Unfreezing is facilitated by environmental pressures, declining performance, recognition of a problem, or awareness that someone else has found a better way, among other things. Many

■ **Unfreezing** is the stage at which a situation is prepared for change.

changes are never tried or they fail simply because situations are not properly unfrozen to begin with.

Large systems seem particularly susceptible to what is sometimes called the *boiled frog phenomenon*.[159] This refers to the notion that a live frog will immediately jump out when placed in a pan of hot water. When placed in cold water that is then heated very slowly, however, the frog will stay in the water until the water boils the frog to death. Organizations, too, can fall victim to similar circumstances. When managers fail to monitor their environments, recognize the important trends, or sense the need to change, their organizations may slowly suffer and lose their competitive edge. Although the signals that change may be needed are available, they aren't noticed or given any special attention—until it is too late. In contrast, the best organizations are led by people who are always on the alert and understand the importance of "unfreezing" in the change process.

■ **Changing** is the stage in which specific actions are taken to create change.

Changing The **changing** stage involves taking action to modify a situation by changing things, such as the people, tasks, structure, or technology of the organization. Lewin believes that many change agents are prone to an activity trap. They bypass the unfreezing stage and start changing things prematurely or too quickly. Although their intentions may be correct, the situation has not been properly prepared for change. This often leads to failure. Changing something is difficult enough in any situation, let alone having to do so without the proper foundations.

■ **Refreezing** is the stage in which changes are reinforced and stabilized.

Refreezing The final stage in the planned change process is **refreezing**. Designed to maintain the momentum of a change and eventually institutionalize it as part of the normal routine, refreezing secures the full benefits of long-lasting change. Refreezing involves positively reinforcing desired outcomes and providing extra support when difficulties are encountered. It involves evaluating progress and results, and assessing the costs and benefits of the change. And it allows for modifications to be made in the change to increase its success over time. When all of this is not done and refreezing is neglected, changes are often abandoned after a short time or incompletely implemented.

Planned Change Strategies

Managers and other change agents use various means for mobilizing power, exerting influence over others, and getting people to support planned change efforts. As described in Figure 1.20, each of these strategies builds from the various bases of social power. Note in particular that each power source has somewhat different implications for the planned change process.[160]

■ FORCE–COERCION

■ A **force–coercion strategy** uses authority, rewards, and punishments to create change.

A **force–coercion strategy** uses legitimacy, rewards, or punishments as primary inducements to change. That is, the change agent acts unilaterally to "command" change through the formal authority of his or her position, to induce change via an offer of special rewards, or to bring about change via threats of punishment. People respond to this strategy mainly out of the fear of being punished if they do not comply with a change directive or out of the desire to gain a reward if they do. Compliance is usually temporary and continues only as long

Figure 1.20
Power bases, change strategies, and predicted change outcomes.

as the change agent and his or her legitimate authority are visible, or as long as the opportunities for rewards and punishments remain obvious.

Your actions as a change agent using the force–coercion strategy might match the following profile.

> You believe that people who run things are basically motivated by self-interest and by what the situation offers in terms of potential personal gains or losses. Since you feel that people change only in response to such motives, you try to find out where their vested interests lie and then put the pressure on. If you have formal authority, you use it. If not, you resort to whatever possible rewards and punishments you have access to and do not hesitate to threaten others with these weapons. Once you find a weakness, you exploit it and are always wise to work "politically" by building supporting alliances wherever possible.[161]

■ RATIONAL PERSUASION

Change agents using a **rational persuasion strategy** attempt to bring about change through the use of special knowledge, empirical support, or rational arguments. This strategy assumes that rational people will be guided by reason and self-interest in deciding whether or not to support a change. Expert power is mobilized to convince others that the change will leave them better off than before. It is sometimes referred to as an *empirical-rational strategy* of planned change. When successful, this strategy results in a longer lasting, more internalized change than does force–coercion.

As a change agent taking the rational persuasion approach to a change situation, you might behave as follows.

> You believe that people are inherently rational and are guided by reason in their actions and decision making. Once a specific course of action is demonstrated to be in a person's self-interest, you assume that reason and rationality will cause the person to adopt it. Thus, you approach change with the objective of communicating—through information and facts—the essential "desirability" of change from the perspective of the person whose behavior you seek to influence. If this logic is effectively communicated, you are sure of the person's adopting the proposed change.[162]

■ A **rational persuasion strategy** uses facts, special knowledge, and rational argument to create change.

■ SHARED POWER

■ A **shared-power strategy** uses participatory methods and emphasizes common values to create change.

A **shared-power strategy** actively and sincerely involves the people who will be affected by a change in planning and making key decisions relating to this change. Sometimes called a *normative-reeducative approach*, this strategy tries to develop directions and support for change through involvement and empowerment. It builds essential foundations, such as personal values, group norms, and shared goals, so that support for a proposed change emerges naturally. Managers using normative-reeducative approaches draw upon the power of personal reference and also share power by allowing others to participate in planning and implementing the change. Given this high level of involvement, the strategy is likely to result in a longer lasting and internalized change.

As a change agent who shares power and adopts a normative-reeducative approach to change, you are likely to fit this profile:

> You believe that people have complex motivations. You feel that people behave as they do as a result of sociocultural norms and commitments to these norms. You also recognize that changes in these orientations involve changes in attitudes, values, skills, and significant relationships, not just changes in knowledge, information, or intellectual rationales for action and practice. Thus, when seeking to change others, you are sensitive to the supporting or inhibiting effects of group pressures and norms. In working with people, you try to find out their side of things and to identify their feelings and expectations.[163]

Resistance to Change

■ **Resistance to change** is an attitude or behavior that shows unwillingness to make or support a change.

In organizations, **resistance to change** is any attitude or behavior that indicates unwillingness to make or support a desired change. Change agents often view any such resistance as something that must be "overcome" in order for change to be successful. This is not always the case, however. It is helpful to view resistance to change as feedback that the change agent can use to facilitate gaining change objectives.[164] The essence of this constructive approach to resistance is to recognize that when people resist change, they are defending something important and that appears threatened by the change attempt.

■ WHY PEOPLE RESIST CHANGE

People have many reasons to resist change. The Effective Manager 1.8 identifies fear of the unknown, insecurity, lack of a felt need to change, threat to vested interests, contrasting interpretations, and lack of resources, among other possibilities. A work team's members, for example, may resist the introduction of advanced workstation computers because they have never used the operating system and are apprehensive. They may wonder whether the new computers will eventually be used as justification for "getting rid" of some of them; or they may believe that they have

THE EFFECTIVE MANAGER 1.8

EIGHT REASONS
FOR RESISTING CHANGE

1. Fear of the unknown
2. Lack of good information
3. Fear for loss of security
4. No reasons to change
5. Fear for loss of power
6. Lack of resources
7. Bad timing
8. Habit

been doing their jobs just fine and do not need the new computers to improve things. These and other viewpoints often create resistance to even the best and most well-intended planned changes.

Resistance to the Change Itself   Sometimes a change agent experiences resistance to the change itself. People may reject a change because they believe it is not worth their time, effort, or attention. To minimize resistance in such cases, the change agent should make sure that everyone who may be affected by a change knows specifically how it satisfies the following criteria.[165]

- *Benefit*—The change should have a clear relative advantage for the people being asked to change; it should be perceived as "a better way."
- *Compatibility*—The change should be as compatible as possible with the existing values and experiences of the people being asked to change.
- *Complexity*—The change should be no more complex than necessary; it must be as easy as possible for people to understand and use.
- *Triability*—The change should be something that people can try on a step-by-step basis and make adjustments as things progress.

Criteria for successful changes

Resistance to the Change Strategy   Change agents must also be prepared to deal with resistance to the change strategy. Someone who attempts to bring about change via force–coercion, for example, may create resistance among individuals who resent management by "command" or the use of threatened punishment. People may resist a rational persuasion strategy in which the data are suspect or the expertise of advocates is not clear. They may resist a shared-power strategy that appears manipulative and insincere.

Resistance to the Change Agent   Resistance to the change agent is directed at the person implementing the change and often involves personality and other differences. Change agents who are isolated and aloof from other persons in the change situation, who appear self-serving, or who have a high emotional involvement in the changes are especially prone to such problems. Research also indicates that change agents who differ from other persons in the change situation on such dimensions as age, education, and socioeconomic factors may encounter greater resistance to change.[166]

■ HOW TO DEAL WITH RESISTANCE

An informed change agent has many options available for dealing positively with resistance to change, in any of its forms.[167] The first approach is through *education and communication*. The objective is to educate people about a change before it is implemented and to help them understand the logic of the change. Education and communication seem to work best when resistance is based on inaccurate or incomplete information. A second way is the use of *participation and involvement*. With the goal of allowing others to help design and implement the changes, this approach asks people to contribute ideas and advice or to work on task forces or committees that may be leading the change. This is especially useful when the change agent does not have all the information needed to successfully handle a problem situation.

Facilitation and support involves providing assistance—both emotional and material, for people experiencing the hardships of change. A manager using this approach actively listens to problems and complaints, provides training in the new ways, and helps others to overcome performance pressures. Facilitation and support is highly recommended when people are frustrated by work constraints and difficulties encountered in the change process. A *negotiation and agreement* approach offers incentives to actual or potential change resistors. Tradeoffs are arranged to provide special benefits in exchange for assurances that the change will not be blocked. It is most useful when dealing with a person or group that will lose something of value as a result of the planned change.

Manipulation and cooptation makes use of covert attempts to influence others, selectively providing information and consciously structuring events so that the desired change occurs. In some cases, leaders of the resistance may be "bought off" with special side deals to gain their support. Manipulation and cooptation are common when other tactics do not work or are too expensive. Finally, *explicit or implicit coercion* employs the force of authority to get people to accept change. Often, resistors are threatened with a variety of undesirable consequences if they do not go along as planned. This may be done, for example, in crisis situations when speed is of the essence.

Figure 1.21 summarizes additional insights into how and when each of these methods may be used to deal with resistance to change. Regardless of the chosen strategy, it is always best to remember that the presence of resistance typically suggests that something can be done to achieve a better fit among the change, the situation, and the people affected. A good change agent deals with resistance to change by listening to feedback and acting accordingly.

Method	Use when	Advantages	Disadvantages
Education & communication	People lack information or have inaccurate information	Creates willingness to help with the change	Can be very time consuming
Participation & involvement	Other people have important information and/or power to resist	Adds information to change planning; builds commitment to the change	Can be very time consuming
Facilitation & support	Resistance traces to resource or adjustment problems	Satisfies directly specific resource or adjustment needs	Can be time consuming; can be expensive
Negotiation & agreement	A person or group will "lose" something because of the change	Helps avoid major resistance	Can be expensive; can cause others to seek similar "deals"
Manipulation & cooptation	Other methods don't work or are too expensive	Can be quick and inexpensive	Can create future problems if people sense manipulation
Explicit & implicit coercion	Speed important and change agent has power	Quick; overpowers resistance	Risky if people get "mad"

Figure 1.21
Methods for dealing with resistance to change.

Footnotes

1 John Huey, "Managing in the Midst of Chaos," *Fortune* (April 5, 1993), pp. 38–48. See also Tom Peters, *Thriving on Chaos* (New York: Knopf, 1991); Jay R. Galbraith, Edward E. Lawler III, and Associates, *Organizing for the Future: The New Logic for Managing Organizations* (San Francisco: Jossey-Bass, 1993); William H. Davidow and Michael S. Malone, *The Virtual Corporation: Structuring and Revitalizing the Corporation of the 21st Century* (New York: Harper Business, 1993); Charles Handy, *The Age of Unreason* (Boston: Harvard Business School Press, 1990) and *The Age of Paradox* (Boston: Harvard Business School Press, 1994). Peter Drucker, *Managing in a Time of Great Change* (New York: Truman Talley, 1995); and Tom Peters, "The Brand Called You," *Fast Company* (August/September 1997).

2 See Gary Hamel and Jeff Sampler, "The e-Corporation," *Fortune* (December 7, 1998), pp. 79–90; and David Kirkpatrick, "The E-Ware War," *Fortune* (December 7, 1998), pp. 115–117.

3 See Daniel H. Pink, "Free Agent Nation," *Fast Company* (December 1997), pp. 131ff; and Tom Peters, "The Brand Called You," *Fast Company* (August/September 1997).

4 Thomas Petzinger, Jr., "A New Model for the Nature of Business: It's Alive!" *Wall Street Journal* (February 26, 1999), pp. B1, B4.

5 Robert B. Reich, "The Company of the Future," *Fast Company* (November 1998), p. 124ff.

6 Based on Jay A. Conger, *Winning 'em Over: A New Model for Managing in the Age of Persuasion* (New York: Simon & Schuster, 1998), pp. 180–181; Stewart D. Friedman, Perry Christensen, and Jessica DeGroot, "Work and Life: The End of the Zero-Sum Game, *Harvard Business Review* (November–December 1998): 119–129; and C. Argyris, "Empowerment: The Emperor's New Clothes," *Harvard Business Review*, (May–June 1998): 98–105.

7 The foundation report on diversity in the American workplace is *Workforce 2000: Work and Workers in the 21st Century* (Indianapolis: Hudson Institute, 1987). For comprehensive discussions, see Martin M. Chemers, Stuart Oskamp, and Mark A. Costanzo, *Diversity in Organizations: New Perspectives for a Changing Workplace* (Beverly Hills, CA,: Sage, 1995); and Robert T. Golembiewski, *Managing Diversity in Organizations* (Tuscaloosa, AL: University of Alabama Press, 1995).

8 David A. Thomas and Suzy Wetlaufer, "A Question of Color: A Debate on Race in the U.S. Workplace," *Harvard Business Review* (September–October 1997): 118–132.

9 "Change at the Top," *Wall Street Journal* (March 9, 1999), p. B12.

10 Catalyst Survey 1998 as reported in "Executive Pay Gap Widens," Associated Press, New York, and appearing in *The Columbus Dispatch* (November 10, 1998), p. 2C; and "You've Come a Short Way, Baby," *Business Week* (November 23, 1998), pp. 82–88. For a look at corporate best practices, see Catalyst, *Advancing Women in Business: The Catalyst Guide* (San Francisco: Jossey-Bass, 1998).

11 James G. March, *The Pursuit of Organizational Intelligence* (Malden, MA: Blackwell, 1999).

12 See Peter Senge, *The Fifth Discipline* (New York: Harper, 1990); D. A. Garvin, "Building a Learning Organization," *Harvard Business Review* (November/December 1991): 78–91; Chris Argyris, *On Organizational Learning*, 2nd ed. (Malden, MA: Blackwell, 1999).

13 See Jay W. Lorsch ed., *Handbook of Organizational Behavior* (Englewood Cliffs, NJ: Prentice Hall, 1987), for a general overview.

14 Geert Hofstede, "Cultural Constraints in Management Theories," *Academy of Management Executive*, 7 (1993): 81–94.

15 For more on mission statements see Patricia Jones and Larry Kahaner, *Say It and Live It: The 50 Corporate Mission Statements That Hit the Mark* (New York: Currency/Doubleday, 1995) and John Graham and Wendy Havlick, *Mission Statements: A Guide to the Corporate and Nonprofit Sectors* (New York: Garland Publishers, 1995).

16 James C. Collins and Jerry I. Porras, "Building Your Company's Vision," *Harvard Business Review* (September–October 1996): 65–77.

17 America West Airlines corporate Web site: www.americawest.com.

18 Reich, op. cit. (1998).

19 See Michael E. Porter, *Competitive Strategy: Techniques for Analyzing Industries and Competitors* (New York: Free Press, 1980) and *Competitive Advantage: Creating and Sustaining Superior Performance* (New York: Free Press, 1986); Gary Hamel and C. K. Prahalad, "Strategic Intent," *Harvard Business Review* (May–June 1989): 63–76; and Richard A. D'Aveni, *Hyper-Competition: Managing the Dynamics of Strategic Maneuvering* (New York: Free Press, 1994).

20 Quote from Jeffrey Pfeffer, *The Human Equation: Building Profits by Putting People First* (Boston: Harvard Business School Press, 1998).

21 See Dave Ulrich, "Intellectual Capital = Competence x Commitment," *Harvard Business Review* (Winter 1998): 15–26.

22 "What Makes a Company Great?" *Fortune* (October 26, 1998), p. 218.

23 See Brian Dumaine, "The New Non-Manager Managers," *Fortune* (February 22, 1993), pp. 80–84; and Walter Kiechel III, "How We Will Work in the Year 2000," *Fortune* (May 17, 1993), p. 38.

24 This review is from Henry Mintzberg, *The Nature of Managerial Work* (New York: Harper & Row, 1973). For related and further developments, see Morgan W. McCall, Jr., Ann M. Morrison, and Robert L. Hannan, *Studies of Managerial Work: Results and Methods, Technical Report No. 9* (Greensboro, NC: Center for Creative Leadership, 1978); John P. Kotter, *The General Managers* (New York: Free Press, 1982); Fred Luthans, Stuart Rosenkrantz, and Harry Hennessey, "What Do Successful Managers Really Do?" *Journal of Applied Behavioral Science* 21, No. 2, (1985): 255–270; Robert E. Kaplan, *The Warp and Woof of the General Manager's Job Technical Report No. 27* (Greensboro, NC: Center for Creative Leadership, 1986); and Fred Luthans, Richard M. Hodgetts, and Stuart A. Rosenkrantz, *Real Managers* (New York: HarperCollins, 1988).

25 John R. Schermerhorn, Jr., *Management*, 6th ed. (New York: Wiley, 1999).

26 Mintzberg, op. cit., 1973. See also Henry Mintzberg, *Mintzberg on Management* (New York: Free Press, 1989) and "Rounding Out the Manager's Job," *Sloan Management Review* (Fall 1994): 11–26.

27 Kotter, op. cit. (1982); John P. Kotter, "What Effective General Managers Really Do," *Harvard Business Review*, 60 (November/December 1982): 161. See Kaplan, op. cit., 1984.

28 Herminia Ibarra, "Managerial Networks," Teaching Note #9-495-039, Harvard Business School Publishing, Boston, MA.

29 Robert L. Katz, "Skills of an Effective Administrator, *Harvard Business Review*, 52 (September/October 1974): 94. See also Richard E. Boyatzis, *The Competent Manager: A Model for Effective Performance* (New York: Wiley, 1982).

30 Conger, op. cit., (1998).

31 A good overview is available in Linda K. Trevino and Katherine J. Nelson, *Managing Business Ethics*, 2nd ed. (New York: Wiley, 1999).

32 See Blair Sheppard, Roy J. Lewicki, and John Minton, *Organizational Justice: The Search for Fairness in the Workplace* (New York: Lexington Books, 1992); and Jerald Greenberg, *The Quest for Justice on the Job: Essays and Experiments* (Thousand Oaks, CA: Sage Publications, 1995); Robert Folger and Russell Cropanzano, *Organizational Justice and Human Resource Management* (Thousand Oaks, CA: Sage, 1998).

33 See Steven N. Brenner and Earl A. Mollander, "Is the Ethics of Business Changing?" *Harvard Business Review* 55 (January/February 1977): 50–57; Saul W. Gellerman, "Why 'Good' Managers Make Bad Ethical Choices," *Harvard Business Review* 64 (July/August 1986): 85–90; Barbara Ley Toffler, *Tough Choices: Managers Talk Ethics* (New York: John Wiley, 1986); Justin G. Longnecker, Joseph A. McKinney, and Carlos W. Moore, "The Generation Gap in Business Ethics," *Business Horizons,* 32 (September/October 1989): 9–14; John B. Cullen, Vart Victor, and Carroll Stephens, "An Ethical Weather Report: Assessing the Organization's Ethical Climate," *Organizational Dynamics* (Winter 1990): 50–62; Dawn Blalock, "Study Shows Many Execs Are Quick to Write Off Ethics," *Wall Street Journal* (March 26, 1996), p. C1.

[34] Developed in part from Alan L. Otten, "Ethics on the Job: Companies Alert Employees to Potential Dilemmas," *Wall Street Journal* (July 14, 1986), p. 17.

[35] Based on Gellerman, op. cit. (1986).

[36] For research on whistleblowers, see Paula M. Miceli and Janet P. Near, *Blowing the Whistle* (New York: Lexington, 1992).

[37] Douglas McGregor, *The Human Side of Enterprise* (New York: McGraw-Hill, 1960).

[38] David A. Nadler and Edward E. Lawler III, "Quality of Work Life: Perspectives and Directions," *Organizational Dynamics* 11 (1983): 22–36; the discussion of QWL, in Thomas G. Cummings and Edgar F. Huse, *Organizational Development and Change* (St. Paul, MN: West, 1990); and Stewart D. Friedman, Perry Christensen, and Jessica DeGroot, "Work and Life: The End of the Zero-Sum Game," *Harvard Business Review* (November–December 1998): 119–129.

[39] Pfeffer, *The Human Equation: Building Profits by Putting People First*, op. cit., p. 292.

[40] J. Laabs, "Interest in Diversity Training Continues to Grow," *Personnel Journal* (October 1993), p. 18.

[41] L. R. Gomez-Mejia, D. B. Balkin, and R. L. Cardy, *Managing Human Resources* (Englewood Cliffs, NJ: Prentice-Hall, 1995), p. 154.

[42] John P. Fernandez, *Managing a Diverse Workforce* (Lexington, MA: D. C. Heath, 1991); D. Jamieson and Julia O'Mara, *Managing Workplace 2000* (San Francisco: Jossey-Bass, 1991).

[43] T. G. Exner, "In and Out of Work," *American Demographics* (June 1992), p. 63, and A. N. Fullerton, "Another Look at the Labor Force," *Monthly Labor Review* (November 1993), p. 34; M. K. Foster and B. J. Orser, "A Marketing Perspective on Women in Management," *Canadian Journal of Administrative Sciences*, Vol. 11, No. 4 (1994), pp. 339–345; L. Gardenswartz and A. Rowe, "Diversity Q & A," *Mosaics* (March/April, 1998), p. 3.

[44] Linda A. Krefting and Frank J. Kryzstofiak, "Looking Like America: Potential Conflicts Between Workplace Diversity Initiatives and Equal Opportunity Compliance in the U.S.," Working paper (Lubbock, TX: Texas Tech University, 1998), p. 10.

[45] Krefting and Kryzstofiak, p. 10.

[46] The following discussion is based on L. Gardenswartz and A. Rowe, *Managing Diversity: A Complete Desk Reference and Planning Guide* (Homewood, IL: Business One Irwin, 1993), p. 405.

[47] Gardenswartz and Rowe, *Managing Diversity*, p. 405; Michelle N. Martinez, "Equality Effort Sharpens Bank's Edge," *HR Magazine* (January 1995), pp. 38–43.

[48] See E. Maccoby and C. N. Jacklin, *The Psychology of Sex Differences* (Stanford, CA: Stanford University press, 1974); G. N. Powell, *Women and Men in Management* (Beverly Hills, CA: Sage Publications, 1988); T. W. Mangione, "Turnover—Some Psychological and Demographic Correlates," in R. P. Quinn and T. W. Mangione (eds.), *The 1969–70 Survey of Working Conditions* (Ann Arbor: University of Michigan Survey Research Center, 1973); R. Marsh and H. Mannari, "Organizational Commitment and Turnover: A Predictive Study," *Administrative Science Quarterly* (March 1977), pp. 57–75; R. J. Flanagan, G. Strauss, and L. Ulman, "Worker Discontent and Work Discontent and Work Place Behavior," *Industrial Relations* (May 1974), pp. 101–23; K. R. Garrison and P. M. Muchinsky, "Attitudinal and Biographical Predictions of Incidental Absenteeism," *Journal of Vocational Behavior* (April 1977), pp. 221–230; G. Johns, "Attitudinal and Nonattitudinal Predictions of Two Forms of Absence from Work," *Organizational Behavior and Human Performance* (December 1978), pp. 431–44; R. T. Keller, "Predicting Absenteeism from Prior Absenteeism, Attitudinal Factors, and Nonattitudinal Factors," *Journal of Applied Psychology* (August 1983), pp. 536–540.

[49] Gomez-Mejia, Balkin, and Cardy, p. 171.

[50] "The Growing Influence of Women," *Workplace Visions* (Sept./Oct. 1998), p. 2.

[51] American Association of Retired Persons, *The Aging Work Force* (Washington, DC: AARP, 1995), p. 3.

[52] Nina Monk, "Finished at Forty," *Fortune* (February 1, 1999), pp. 50–58.

[53] *Mosaics*, Vol. 3, No. 2 (March/April 1997), p. 3.

[54] Paul Mayrand, "Older Workers: A Problem or the Solution?" *AARP Textbook Authors' Conference Presentation* (October 1992), p. 29; G. M. McEvoy and W. F. Cascio, "Cumulative Evidence of the Relationship Between Employee Age and Job Performance," *Journal of Applied Psychology* (February 1989), pp. 11–17.

[55] Robbins, Ch. 2.

[56] See Fernandez, p. 236; *Mosaics*, Vol. 4, No. 2 (March–April, 1998), p. 4.

[57] Fernandez; *Mosaics* (March–April, 1998).

[58] See Taylor H. Co and Stacy Blake, "Managing Cultural Diversity: Implications for Organizational Competitiveness," *Academy of Management Executive*, Vol. 5, No. 3 (1991), p. 45.

[59] Krefting and Krzystofiak, p. 14.

[60] Larry L. Cummings and Donald P. Schwab, *Performance in Organizations: Determinants and Appraisal* (Glenview, IL: Scott, Foresman, 1973), p. 8.

[61] See J. Hogan, "Structure of Physical Performance in Occupational Tasks," *Journal of Applied Psychology*, Vol. 76 (1991), pp. 495–507.

[62] R. Jacob, "The Resurrection of Michael Dell," *Fortune* (August 1995), pp. 117–128.

[63] See N. Brody, *Personality: In Search of Individuality* (San Diego, CA: Academic Press, 1988), pp. 68–101; C. Holden, "The Genetics of Personality," *Science* (August 7, 1987), pp. 598–601.

[64] See Geert Hofstede, *Culture's Consequences: International Differences in Work-Related Values*, abridged ed. (Beverly Hills: Sage Publications, 1984).

[65] Chris Argyris, *Personality and Organization* (New York: Harper & Row, 1957); Daniel J. Levinson, *The Seasons of a Man's Life* (New York: Alfred A. Knopf, 1978); Gail Sheehy, *New Passages* (New York: Ballantine Books, 1995).

[66] M. R. Barrick and M. K. Mount, "The Big Five Personality Dimensions and Job Performance: A Meta Analysis," *Personnel Psychology*, Vol. 44 (1991), pp. 1–26, and "Autonomy as a Moderator of the Relationships Between the Big Five Personality Dimensions and Job Performance," *Journal of Applied Psychology* (February 1993), pp. 111–118.

[67] See Jim C. Nunnally, *Psychometric Theory*, 2nd ed. (New York: McGraw Hill, 1978), Ch. 14.

[68] See David A. Whetten and Kim S. Cameron, *Developing Management Skills*, 3rd ed. (New York: Harper Collins, 1995), p. 72.

[69] Raymond G. Hunt, Frank J. Krzystofiak, James R. Meindl, and Abdalla M. Yousry, "Cognitive Style and Decision Making," *Organizational Behavior and Human Decision Processes*, Vol. 44, No. 3 (1989), pp. 436–453. For additional work on problem-solving styles, see Ferdinand A. Gul, "The Joint and Moderating Role of Personality and Cognitive Style on Decison Making," *Accounting Review* (April 1984), pp. 264–277; Brian H. Kleiner, "The Interrelationship of Jungian Modes of Mental Functioning with Organizational Factors: Implications for Management Development," *Human Relations* (November 1983), pp. 997–1012; James L. McKenney and Peter G. W. Keen, "How Managers' Minds Work," *Harvard Business Review* (May/June 1974), pp. 79–90.

[70] Some examples of firms using the Myers-Briggs Indicators are J. M. Kunimerow and L. W. McAllister, "Team Building with the Myers-Briggs Type Indicator: Case Studies," *Journal of Psychological Type*, Vol. 15 (1988), pp. 26–32; G. H. Rice, Jr. and D. P. Lindecamp, "Personality Types and Business Success of Small Retailers," *Journal of Occupational Psychology*, Vol. 62 (1989), pp. 177–182; and B. Roach, *Strategy Styles and Management Types: A Resource Book for Organizational Management Consultants* (Stanford, CA: Balestrand Press, 1989).

[71] J. B. Rotter, "Generalized Expectancies for Internal versus External Control of Reinforcement," *Psychological Monographs*, Vol. 80 (1966), pp. 1–28.

[72] Don Hellriegel, John W. Slocum, Jr., and Richard W. Woodman, *Organizational Behavior*, 5th ed. (St. Paul, MN: West, 1989), p. 46.

[73] See John A. Wagner III and John R. Hollenbeck, *Management of Organizational Behavior* (Englewood Cliffs, NJ: Prentice-Hall, 1992), Ch. 4.

[74] Niccolo Machiavelli, *The Prince*, trans. George Bull (Middlesex, UK: Penguin, 1961).

[75] Richard Christie and Florence L. Geis, *Studies in Machiavellianism* (New York: Academic Press, 1970).

[76] See M. Synder, *Public Appearances/Private Realities: The Psychology of Self-Monitoring* (New York: W. H. Freeman, 1987).

[77] Snyder.

[78] Adapted from R. W. Bortner, "A Short Scale: A Potential Measure of Pattern A Behavior," *Journal of Chronic Diseases* Vol. 22 (1969). Used by permission.

[79] See Meyer Friedman and Ray Roseman, *Type A Behavior and Your Heart* (New York: Alfred A. Knopf, 1974). For another view, see Walter Kiechel III, "Attack of the Obsessive Managers," *Fortune* (February 16, 1987), pp. 127–128.

[80] Viktor Gecas, "The Self-Concept," in Ralph H. Turner and James F. Short, Jr. (eds.), Vol. 8, *Annual Review of Sociology* (Palo Alto, CA: Annual Review, 1982), p. 3. Also see Arthur P. Brief and Ramon J. Aldag, "The 'Self' in Work Organizations: A Conceptual Review," *Academy of Management Review* (January 1981), pp. 75–88; and Jerry J. Sullivan, "Self Theories and Employee Motivation," *Journal of Management* (June 1989), pp. 345–363.

[81] Compare Philip Cushman, "Why the Self Is Empty," *American Psychologist* (May 1990), pp. 599–611.

[82] Based in part on a definition in Gecas, p. 3.

[83] Suggested by J. Brockner, *Self-Esteem at Work* (Lexington, MA: Lexington Books, 1988) p. 144; and Wagner and Hollenbeck, pp. 100–101.

[84] See P. E. Jacob, J. J. Flink, and H. L. Schuchman, "Values and Their Function in Decisionmaking," *American Behavioral Scientist,* Vol. 5, Suppl. 9 (1962), pp. 6–38.

[85] See M. Rokeach and S. J. Ball Rokeach, "Stability and Change in American Value Priorities, 1968–1981," *American Psychologist* (May 1989), pp. 775–784.

[86] Milton Rokeach, *The Nature of Human Values* (New York: Free Press, 1973).

[87] See W. C. Frederick and J. Weber, "The Values of Corporate Managers and Their Critics: An Empirical Description and Normative Implications," in W. C. Frederick and L. E. Preston (eds.), *Business Ethics: Research Issues and Empirical Studies* (Greenwich, CT: JAI Press, 1990), pp. 123–144.

[88] Gordon Allport, Philip E. Vernon, and Gardner Lindzey, *Study of Values* (Boston: Houghton Mifflin, 1931).

[89] Adapted from R. Tagiuri, "Purchasing Executive: General Manager or Specialist?" *Journal of Purchasing* (August 1967), pp. 16–21.

[90] Bruce M. Maglino, Elizabeth C. Ravlin, and Cheryl L. Adkins, "Value Congruence and Satisfaction with a Leader: An Examination of the Role of Interaction," unpublished manuscript (Columbia, SC: University of South Carolina, 1990), pp. 8–9.

[91] Maglino, Ravlin, and Adkins.

[92] Daniel Yankelovich, *New Rules! Searching for Self-Fulfillment in a World Turned Upside Down* (New York: Random House, 1981); Daniel Yankelovich, Hans Zetterberg, Burkhard Strumpel, and Michael Shanks, *Work and Human Values: An International Report on Jobs in the 1980s and 1990s* (Aspen, CO: Aspen Institute for Humanistic Studies, 1983).

[93] See Jamieson and O'Mara, pp. 28–29.

[94] Compare Martin Fishbein and Icek Ajzen, *Belief, Attitude, Intention and Behavior: An Introduction to Theory and Research* (Reading, MA: Addison-Wesley, 1975).

[95] See A W. Wicker, "Attitude versus Action: The Relationship of Verbal and Overt Behavioral Responses to Attitude Objects," *Journal of Social Issues* (Autumn 1969), pp. 41–78.

[96] Leon Festinger, *A Theory of Cognitive Dissonance* (Palo Alto, CA: Stanford University Press, 1957).

[97] H. W. Lane and J. J. DiStefano (eds.), *International Management Behavior* (Scarborough, Ontario: Nelson Canada, 1988), pp. 4–5; Z. Abdoolcarim, "How Women Are Winning at Work," *Asian Business* (November 1993), pp. 24–29.

[98] Michelle Neely Martinez, "Health Care Firm Seeks to Measure Diversity," *HR News* (October 1997), p. 6.

[99] "Clark's Catch Engraved in NFL Lore," *Lubbock Avalanche-Journal* (January 11, 1992), p. D5.

[100] H. R. Schiffmann, *Sensation and Perception: An Integrated Approach*, 3rd ed. (New York: Wiley, 1990).

[101] Example from John A. Wagner III and John R. Hollenbeck, *Organizational Behavior* 3rd ed. (Upper Saddle River, NJ: Prentice-Hall, 1998), p. 59.

[102] See M. W. Levine and J. M. Shefner, *Fundamentals of Sensation and Perception*; Georgia T. Chao and Steve W. J. Kozlowski, "Employee Perceptions on the Implemention of Robotic Manufacturing Technology," *Journal of Applied Psychology,* Vol. 71 (1986), pp. 70–76; Steven F. Cronshaw and Robert G. Lord, "Effects of Categorization, Attribution, and Encoding Processes in Leadership Perceptions," *Journal of Applied Psychology,* Vol. 72 (1987), pp. 97–106.

[103] See Robert Lord, "An Information Processing Approach to Social Perception's, Leadership, and Behavioral Measurement in Organizations," in B. M. Staw and L. L. Cummings (eds.), *Research in Organizational Behavior*, Vol. 7 (Greenwich, CT: JAI Press, 1985), pp. 87–128; T. K. Srull and R. S. Wyer, *Advances in Social Cognition* (Hillsdale, NJ: Erlbaum, 1988); U. Neisser, *Cognition and Reality* (San Francisco: W. H. Freeman, 1976), p. 112.

[104] See J. G. Hunt, *Leadership: A New Synthesis* (Newbury Park, CA: Sage Publications, 1991), Ch. 7; R. G. Lord and R. J. Foti, "Schema Theories, Information Processing, and Organizational Behavior," in H. P. Sims, Jr., and D. A. Gioia (eds.), *The Thinking Organization* (San Francisco: Jossey-Bass, 1986), pp. 20–48; S. T. Fiske and S. E. Taylor, *Social Cognition* (Reading, MA: Addison-Wesley, 1984).

[105] See J. S. Phillips, "The Accuracy of Leadership Ratings: A Categorization Perspective," *Organizational Behavior and Human Performance,* Vol. 33 (1984), pp. 125–138; J. G. Hunt, B. R. Baliga, and M. F. Peterson, "Strategic Apex Leader Scripts and an Organizational Life Cycle Approach to Leadership and Excellence," *Journal of Management Development,* Vol. 7 (1988), pp. 61–83.

[106] D. Bilimoria and S. K. Piderit, "Board Committee Membership Effects of Sex-Biased Bias," *Academy of Management Journal,* Vol. 37 (1994), pp. 1453–1477.

[107] Dewitt C. Dearborn and Herbert A. Simon, "Selective Perception: A Note on the Departmental Indentification of Executives," *Sociometry,* Vol. 21 (1958), pp. 140–144.

[108] J. P. Walsh, "Selectivity and Selective Perception: An Investigation of Managers' Belief Structures and Information Processing," *Academy of Management Journal,* Vol. 24 (1988), pp. 453–470.

[109] J. Sterling Livingston, "Pygmalion in Management," *Harvard Business Review* (July/August 1969).

[110] D. Eden and A. B. Shani, "Pygmalian Goes to Boot Camp," *Journal of Applied Psychology,* Vol. 67 (1982), pp. 194–199.

[111] See B. R. Schlenker, *Impression Management: The Self-Concept, Social Identity, and Interpersonal Relations* (Monterey, CA: Brooks/Cole, 1980); W. L. Gardner and M. J. Martinko, "Impression Management in Organizations," *Journal of Management* (June 1988), p. 332; R. B. Cioldini, "Indirect Tactics of Image Management: Beyond Banking," in R. A. Giacolini and P. Rosenfeld (eds.), *Impression Management in the Organization* (Hillsdale, NJ: Erlbaum, 1989), pp. 45–71.

[112] See H. H. Kelley, "Attribution in Social Interaction," in E. Jones, et al. (eds.), *Attribution: Perceiving the Causes of Behavior* (Morristown, NJ: General Learning Press, 1972).

[113] See Terence R. Mitchell, S. G. Green, and R. E. Wood, "An Attribution Model of Leadership and the Poor Performing Subordinate," in Barry Staw and Larry L. Cummings (eds.), *Research in Organizational Behavior* (New York: JAI Press, 1981), pp. 197–234; John H. Harvey and Gifford Weary, "Current Issues in Attribution Theory and Research," *Annual Review of Psychology,* Vol. 35 (1984), pp. 427–459.

[114] Data reported in John R. Schermerhorn, Jr., "Team Development for High Performance Management," *Training & Development Journal,* Vol. 40 (Nov. 1986), pp. 38–41.

[115] R. M. Steers, S. J. Bischoff, and L. H. Higgins, "Cross Cultural Management Research," *Journal of Management Inquiry* (Dec. 1992), pp. 325–326; J. G. Miller, "Culture and the Development of Everyday Causal Explanation," *Journal of Personality and Social Psychology,* Vol. 46 (1984), pp. 961–978.

[116] A. Maass and C. Volpato, "Gender Differences in Self-Serving Attributions About Sexual Experiences," *Journal of Applied Psychology,* Vol. 19 (1989), pp. 517–542.

[117] See J. M. Crant and T. S. Bateman, "Assignment of Credit and Blame for Performance Outcomes," *Academy of Management Journal* (February 1993), pp. 7–27; E. C. Pence, W. E. Pendelton, G. H. Dobbins, and J. A. Sgro, "Effects of Causal Explanations and Sex Variables on Recommendations for Corrective Actions Following Employee Failure," *Organizational Behavior and Human Performance* (April 1982), pp. 227–240.

[118] See F. Forsterling, "Attributional Retraining: A Review," *Psychological Bulletin* (Nov. 1985), pp. 496–512.

[119] Edgar Schein, "Organizational Culture," *American Psychologist*, Vol. 45 (1990), pp. 109–119; and E. Schein, *Organizational Culture and Leadership* (San Francisco: Jossey-Bass, 1985).

[120] Schein (1990).

[121] From an interview with Daimler-Chrysler employees after the consummation of the merger between Chrysler and Daimler by Richard Osborn.

[122] This example was reported in an interview with Edgar Schein, "Corporate Culture Is the Real Key to Creativity," *Business Month* (May 1989), pp. 73–74.

[123] For early work, see T. Deal and A. Kennedy, *Corporate Culture* (Reading, MA: Addison-Wesley, 1982); and Peters and R. Waterman, *In Search of Excellence* (New York: Harper & Row, 1982), while more recent studies are summarized in Joanne Martin and Peter Frost, "The Organizational Culture War Games: The Struggle for Intellectual Dominance," in Stewart R. Clegg, Cynthia Hardy, and Walter R. Nord (eds.), *Handbook of Organizational Studies* (London: Sage Publications, 1996), pp. 599–621.

[124] Schein (1985).

[125] For an extended discussion, see J. M. Beyer and H. M. Trice, "How an Organization's Rites Reveal Its Culture," *Organizational Dynamics* (Spring 1987), pp. 27–41.

[126] A. Cooke and D. M. Rousseau, "Behavioral Norms and Expectations: A Quantitative Approach to the Assessment of Organizational Culture," *Group and Organizational Studies* 13 (1988), pp. 245–273.

[127] Martin and C. Siehl, "Organization Culture and Counterculture," *Organizational Dynamics* 12 (1983), pp. 52–64.

[128] Ibid.

[129] "Is Sony Finally Getting the Hang of Hollywood?" *Business Week* (September 7, 1992), p. 76.

[130] See Pfeffer (1998).

[131] Taylor Cox, Jr., "The Multicultural Organization," *Academy of Management Executive,* Vol. 2, No. 2 (May 1991), pp. 34–47.

[132] Carl Quintanilla, "DU-UDE: CEOs, Feeling Out of Touch with Junior Employees, Try to Get 'Withit'" *Wall Street Journal* (November 10, 1998), p. 1.

[133] Schein (1985), pp. 52–57.

[134] Peters and Waterman (1982).

[135] Schein (1990).

[136] H. Gertz, *The Interpretation of Culture* (New York: Basic Books, 1973).

[137] Beyer and Trice (1987).

[138] *Business Week* (November 23, 1992), p. 117.

[139] H. M. Trice and J. M. Beyer, "Studying Organizational Cultures Through Rites and Ceremonials," *Academy of Management Review,* Vol. 3 (1984), pp. 633–669.

[140] J. Martin, M. S. Feldman, M. J. Hatch, and S. B. Sitkin, "The Uniqueness Paradox in Organizational Stories," *Administrative Science Quarterly,* Vol. 28 (1983), pp. 438–453.

[141] Deal and Kennedy (1982).

[142] This section is based on R. N. Osborn and C. C. Baughn, *An Assessment of the State of the Field of Organizational Design* (Alexandria, VA: U.S. Army Research Institute, 1994).

[143] Osborn and Baughn (1994).

[144] R. N. Osborn and D. Jackson, "Leaders, River Boat Gamblers or Purposeful Unintended Consequences," *Academy of Management Journal,* Vol. 31 (1988), pp. 924–947.

[145] G. Hofstede and M. H. Bond, "The Confucius Connection: From Cultural Roots to Economic Growth," *Organizational Dynamics,* Vol. 16 (1991): 4–21.

[146] Martin and Frost (1996).

[147] Warner Burke, *Organization Development* (Reading, MA: Addison-Wesley, 1987); Wendell L. French and Cecil H. Bell, Jr., *Organization Development*, 4th ed. (Englewood Cliffs, NJ: Prentice-Hall, 1990); Edgar F. Huse and Thomas G. Cummings, *Organization Development and Change*, 4th ed. (St. Paul, MN: West, 1989).

[148] Warren Bennis, "Using Our Knowledge of Organizational Behavior," in Lorsch, pp. 29–49.

[149] Excellent overviews are found in Cummings and Huse (1989), pp. 32–36, 45; and French and Bell (1990).

[150] Richard Beckhard, "The Confrontation Meeting," *Harvard Business Review,* Vol. 45 (March/April 1967), pp. 149–155.

[151] See Dale Zand, "Collateral Organization: A New Change Strategy," *Journal of Applied Behavioral Science* 10 (1974): 63–89; Barry A. Stein and Rosabeth Moss Kanter, "Building the Parallel Organization," *Journal of Applied Behavioral Science*, Vol. 16 (1980), pp. 371–386.

[152] J. Richard Hackman and Greg R. Oldham, *Work Redesign* (Reading, MA: Addison-Wesley, 1980).

[153] See David Nadler and Michael Tushman, *Strategic Organizational Design* (Glenview, IL: Scott, Foresman, 1988); and Noel M. Tichy, "Revolutionize Your Company," *Fortune* (December 13, 1993), pp. 114–118.

[154] Jay A. Conger, Edward E. Lawler III, and Gretchen M. Spreitzer (eds.), *The Leaders Change Handbook* (San Francisco: Jossey-Bass, 1999).

[155] Rosabeth Moss Kanter, Barry A. Stein, and Todd D. Jick, "Meeting the Challenges of Change," *World Executive's Digest* (May 1993), pp. 22–27.

[156] The classic description of organizations on these terms is by Harold J. Leavitt, "Applied Organizational Change in Industry: Structural, Technological and Humanistic Approaches," in James G. March (ed.), *Handbook of Organizations* (Chicago: Rand McNally, 1965). This application is developed from Robert A. Cooke, "Managing Change in Organizations," in Gerald Zaltman (ed.), *Management Principles for Nonprofit Organizations* (New York: American Management Association, 1979). See also David A. Nadler, "The Effective Management of Organizational Change," in Jay W. Lorsch (ed.), *Handbook of Organizational Behavior* (Englewood Cliffs, NJ: Prentice-Hall, 1987), pp. 358–369.

[157] See, for example, Ralph H. Kilmann, *Beyond the Quick Fix* (San Francisco: Jossey-Bass, 1984); Noel M. Tichy and Mary Anne Devanna, *The Transformational Leader* (New York: Wiley, 1986); and Peter M. Senge, *The Fifth Discipline: The Art & Practice of the Learning Organization* (New York: Doubleday, 1990).

[158] Kurt Lewin, "Group Decision and Social Change," in G. E. Swanson, T. M. Newcomb, and E. L. Hartley (eds.), *Readings in Social Psychology* (New York: Holt, Rinehart & Winston, 1952), pp. 459–473.

[159] Tichy and Devanna (1986), p. 44.

[160] The change strategies are described in Robert Chin and Kenneth D. Benne, "General Strategies for Effecting Changes in Human Systems," in Warren G. Bennis, Kenneth D. Benne, Robert Chin, and Kenneth E. Corey (eds.), *The Planning of Change*, 3rd ed. (New York: Holt, Rinehart & Winston, 1969), pp. 22–45.

[161] Example developed from an exercise reported in J. William Pfeiffer and John E. Jones, *A Handbook of Structured Experiences for Human Relations Training*, Vol. II (La Jolla, CA: University Associates, 1973).

[162] Ibid.

[163] Ibid.

[164] Donald Klein, "Some Notes on the Dynamics of Resistance to Change: The Defender Role," in Bennis et al. (eds.), *The Planning of Change* (1969), pp. 117–124.

[165] See Everett M. Rogers, *Communication of Innovations*, 3rd ed. (New York: Free Press, 1993).

[166] Ibid.

[167] John P. Kotter and Leonard A. Schlesinger, "Choosing Strategies for Change," *Harvard Business Review*, Vol. 57 (March/April 1979), pp. 109–112.

Source Notes

Information from Jeff Cole, "New Boeing CFO's Assignment: Signal a Turnaround," *Wall Street Journal* (January 26, 1999), pp. B1, B4.

Trilogy information from Robert B. Reich, "The Company of the Future," *Fast Company* (November 1998), p. 124ff; corporate Web site.

Florida A & M University. Diana Kunde, "Black University, Corporations Find Close Ties Benefit Everyone," *The Columbus Dispatch* (October 5, 1998), p. 4).

Great Plains Software information from Robert B. Reich, "The Company of the Future," *Fast Company* (November 1998), p. 124ff.

Information from Timothy D. Schellhardt, "In a Factory Schedule, Where Does Religion Fit In?" *Wall Street Journal* (March 4, 1999), pp. B1, B12.

Information from Christine W. Letts, William P. Ryan, and Allen Grossman, *High Performance Nonprofit Organizations* (New York: Wiley, 1999), pp. 69–70.

Information from "Allstate Creating a World-Class Diversity Program," *BNAC Communicator*, Vol. 15 (Fall 1997), pp. 1 and 6.

Information from Sharon Johnson, "Hospitals Prepare for the International Marketplace," *New York Times Advertising Supplement* (November 12, 1995), p. WF7.

Information from Gary N. Powell, "One More Time: Do Female and Male Managers Differ?" *Academy of Management Executive*, Vol. 4, No. 3 (1990), p. 74.

Information from John P. Fernandez, *Managing a Diverse Workforce* (Lexington, MA: D. C. Heath, 1991); D. Jamieson and Julia O'Mara, *Managing Workplace 2000* (San Francisco: Jossey-Bass, 1991).

Information from Janie Shockley and Coy Gayle, "Diversity on the Border," *MOSAICS; SHRM Focuses on Workplace Diversity* (July/August, 1997), p. 5.

Information from Sharon Johnson, "Hospitals Prepare for the International Marketplace," *New York Times Advertising Supplement* (November, 12, 1995), p. WF16-WF17.]

Information from Bernice Kanner, "Successful Entrepreneurs Share Important Personality Attributes," *Lubbock-Avalanche-Journal* (November 22, 1998), p. 13A.

Information from J. M. Kunimerow and L. W. McAllister, "Team Building with the Myers-Briggs Type Indicator: Case Studies," *Journal of Psychological Type*, Vol. 15 (1988), pp. 26–32.

Information from Sang M. Lee, Snagjim Yoo, and Tosca M. Lee, "Korean Chaebol: Corporate Values and Strategies," *Organizational Dynamics* (Spring 1991), p. 40.

Information from John Cloud, "Why Coors Went Soft," *Time* (November 2, 1998), p. 70.

See Michelle Neely Martinez, "Health Care Firm Seeks to Measure Diversity," *HR News* (October 1997), p. 6.

Chris Argyris, *Personality and Organization* (New York: Harper & Row, 1957).

Information from R. P. McIntyre and M. M. Capen, "A Cognitive Style Perspective on Ethical Questions," *Journal of Business Ethics* 12 (1993): 631; and D. Hellriegel, J. Slocum, and Richard Woodman, *Organizational Behavior*, 7th ed. (Minneapolis: West Publishing, 1995), Ch. 4.

Information from M. Rokeach, *The Nature of Human Values* (New York: The Free Press, 1973).

Information from "Vormawha Holds Unique Position as Africa's First Female Sea Captain", *Lubbock Avalanche-Journal* (January 3, 1996), p. 4B.

Data reported in Edward E. Lawler III, Allan M. Mohrman, Jr., and Susan M. Resnick, "Performance Appraisal Revisited," *Organizational Dynamics*, Vol. 13 (Summer 1984), pp. 20–35.

Information from Elizabeth Langton, "Simulated Mayhem Training," *Lubbock Avalanche-Journal* (December 8, 1998), p. 8A.

Information from Kevin Rubens, "Changes in Russia Challenge HR," *HR Magazine* (November 1995), p. 72.

Information from "Marketing Excellence Ontario Award Recipient, 1995 Entrepreneur of the Year," *Canadian Business* (November 1995), pp. 11–12, and information concerning the M.A.C. AIDS Fund (May 1999).

J. Sterling Livingston, "Pygmalion in Management," *Harvard Business Review* (July/August 1969); D. Eden and A. B. Shani, "Pygmalion Goes to Boot Camp," *Journal of Applied Psychology*, Vol. 67 (1982), pp. 194–199.

Information from Christine W. Letts, William P. Ryan, and Allen Grossman, *High Performance Non-profit Organizations* (New York: Wiley, 1999), pp. 93–96.

Information from *Lubbock Avalanche-Journal* (November 19, 1988), p. 1E.

Information from *Lubbock Avalanche-Journal* (March 2, 1997), pp. 1–2H.

Information from "Corporate Identity", *Lubbock Avalanche-Journal* (July 12, 1998), pp. 1–2E.

Data reported in John R. Schermerhorn, Jr, "Team Development for High Performance Management," *Training and Development Journal*, Vol. 40 (Nov. 1986), pp. 38–41.

Information from B. R. Schlinker, *Impression Management: The Self-Concept, Social Identity, and Interpersonal Relations* (Monterey, CA: Brooks/Cole, 1980).

http.www.cisco.com/; Shawn Tully, "How Cisco Mastered the Net," *Fortune* (August 17, 1998); Albert Pang, "E-commerce Bonanza: Is It Real or Imagined?" *Internet Computing* (February 9, 1998); Thomas l. Friedman, "The Internet Wars," *New York Times* (April 11, 1998), pp .

From interviews with Fred Fernandez.

www.hp.com.

Time David Kirpatrick, "The Second Coming of Apple," *Fortune* (November 9, 1998); Brent Schlender, "The Three Faces of Steve," *Fortune* (November 9, 1998), pp. 8, 27.

Based on work by Jeffrey Sonnenfeld, as reported by Carol Hymowitz, "Which Corporate Culture Fits You?" *Wall Street Journal* (July 17, 1989), p. B1.]

Copyright 1969 by the Regents of the University of California. Reprinted from *California Management Review* 12, No. 2 (1996), p. 26, Figure 1, by permission of the Regents.

John R. Schermerhorn, Jr., *management*, 4th ed. (New York: Wiley, 1999), p. 381. Used by permission.

Richard Pascale, "Change How You Define Leadership and You Change How You Run a Company," *Fast Company, The Professor Series* (Boston: Fast Company, 1998).

General Motors: Information from Craig S. Smith, "GM Seeks Ways to Boost Viability of New China Plant," *The Asian Wall Street Journal* (December 16, 1998), p. 1.

Unilever: Information from Darren McDermott and Fara Warner, "Unilever Finds Brisk Business," *The Asian Wall Street Journal* (November 20, 1998), p. 1.

Red Roof Inns: Information from Mike Pramik, "Wellness Programs Give Businesses Healthy Bottom Line," *The Columbus Dispatch* (January 18, 1999), pp. 10–11.

Lonnie Johnson: Information from Patricia J. Mays, "Gun Showers Wealth on Inventor," *The Columbus Dispatch* (January 24, 1999), p. 6B.

John R. Schermerhorn, Jr., *Management for Productivity*, 4th ed. (New York: Wiley, 1996), p. 661. Used by permission.

Section Two

Section Two

High Performance Context of Organizational Behavior

Some critical forces in the emerging high performance context involve changing customer expectations, the changing workforce, and changing organizations.

■ OB AND CHANGING CUSTOMER EXPECTATIONS

Only those organizations that deliver what customers want in terms of quality, service, and cost will prosper in today's highly competitive environments. This continues to be an age of **total quality management** (TQM)—management dedicated to ensuring that an organization and all of its members are committed to high quality, continuous improvement, and customer satisfaction. *Quality* in this sense means that customers' needs are met and that all tasks are done right the first time. An important hallmark of the total quality concept is **continuous improvement**—the belief that anything and everything done in the workplace should be continually evaluated by asking two questions: (1) Is this necessary? (2) If so, can it be done better?[1]

Consistent with this approach is the creation of customer-driven organizations that are dedicated to quality and service. Figure 2.1 expresses this notion in the form of an *upside-down pyramid* view of organizations. The figure focuses attention on total quality service to customers and clients by placing them at the top of the organization. Managing from this point of view requires that workers operate in ways that directly affect customers and clients; it requires that team leaders and middle managers do things that directly support the workers; and it requires that top managers clarify the organizational mission and objectives, set strategies, and make adequate resources available.[2]

> ■ **Total quality management** is total commitment to high quality results, continuous improvement, and meeting customer needs.

> ■ **Continuous improvement** is the belief that anything and everything done in the workplace should be continually improved.

■ OB AND THE CHANGING WORKFORCE

The American workforce is becoming more and more diverse with an increasing proportion of women, persons of color, and older employees. Trends in Canada and the European Union are similar.[3] Besides more diversity, two especially important and contradictory workforce characteristics are (1) the impact of **Generation X** or *"Gold-Collar" workers* (those born between 1965 and 1977), and (2) the impact of poor educational preparation of some high school graduates. In fact, U.S. test scores were the lowest in one comparison of 16 industrialized countries.[4] Both characteristics present a current OB challenge but in very different ways.

> ■ **Generation X workers** are those born between 1965 and 1977 who are knowledge workers in short supply.

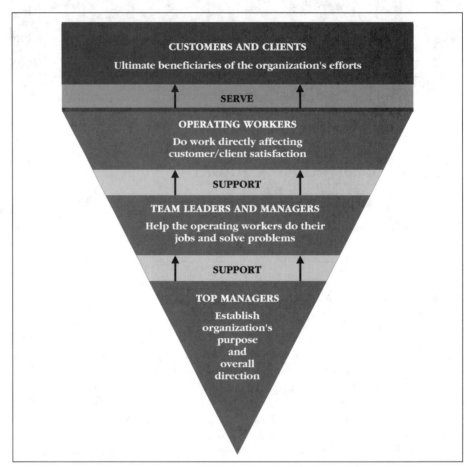

Figure 2.1
The "upside-down pyramid" view of organizations and management.

■ **Empowerment** allows individuals or groups to make decisions that affect them or their work.

■ **Knowledge workers** employees whose major task is to produce new knowledge, typically through computer-oriented means.

Figure 2.2 shows that Gold-Collar Generation X workers demand a lot of the company. They want challenge on the job and flexibility in work schedules; some even want to work at home. But they also want to work in teams, and they are interested in **empowerment**—being allowed as an individual or group to make decisions that affect their work. These needs, wants, and desires are likely to be strongest for **knowledge workers**—employees whose major task is to produce new knowledge, typically through computer-oriented means—and other jobs with workers in high demand and low supply. At the millennium, this condition is widespread throughout the U.S. economy, with unemployment rates the lowest in many years.[5] The level of skills and abilities among many of these workers allows them to function well in highly challenging jobs and work settings.[6]

At the opposite end of the spectrum are those high school graduates who score poorly on standardized tests and enter the workforce with skills deficiencies. In the United States, an alarming number of them require considerable basic skills training in math, writing, and reasoning to get them up to speed in many of today's organizations.[7] In a knowledge-driven economy, high costs are

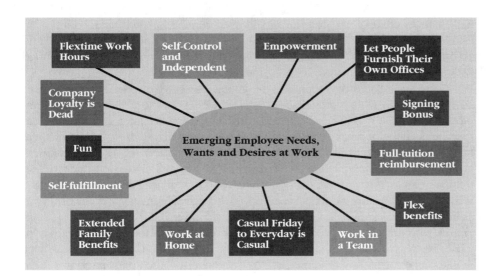

associated with such remedial training and the individuals can suffer long-term career disadvantages.

■ OB AND CHANGING ORGANIZATIONS

The last decade may well be remembered as the one that fundamentally changed the way people work.[8] We experienced the stresses of downsizing and restructuring; we gained sensitivity to the peaks and valleys of changing economic times; and we witnessed the advent of the Internet with its impact on both people and organizations. Truly progressive organizations, however, are doing much more than simply cutting employees and adding technology to reduce the scale of operations in the quest for productivity. They are changing the very essence of the way things are done, and they are adding new meaning to the traditional notions of employer–employee relationships.

One characteristic of this new and fast-paced world of organizations is constant change which carries with it an emphasis on reinventing ways of doing things and continuously improving in all aspects of operations. Many organizations have pursued **process reengineering** which rethinks and radically redesigns business processes to stimulate innovation and change and improve critical performance measures such as cost, quality, service, and speed.[9] Organizations facing these new demands are being asked to "start over"—to forget how things were done in the past and to ask only how they should be done to best meet critical performance measures. Answers to these questions are used to redesign activities and workflows in order to give better value to both internal and external customers.

New information technology has seen an explosion of activity in what may become a benchmark of twenty-first-century organizations—**electronic commerce** in which business is transacted through the Internet. The popular Web-based bookseller Amazon.com is but one spectacular example of emerging **E-corporations** that utilize the Internet and information technologies to support enterprise-wide computer integration of all aspects of operations.[10] In an increasingly "Net-centric" world, technology-driven *network organizations* operate as vir-

■ **Process reengineering** is the total rethinking and redesigning of organizational process to improve performance and innovation and involves analyzing, streamlining, and reconfiguring actions and tasks to achieve work goals.

■ **Electronic commerce** is where business is transacted through the Internet.

■ **E-corporations** utilize the Internet and information technologies to support enterprise-wide computer integration of operations.

tual alliances of suppliers, customers, and even competitors, who link with the latest electronic information technologies and share such things as skills, costs, and access to global markets.[11] These alliances are formed, utilized, and disbanded with ease, all in quick response to business opportunities.

These and related developments are giving rise to what some call a *free-agent economy*, one in which individuals contract their services to a shifting mix of employers over time.[12] British scholar and consultant Charles Handy describes the career implications of what he calls the **shamrock organization**.[13] A shamrock, the Irish national emblem, has three leaves per stem. Each leaf represents a different group of people. The first leaf is a core group of workers made up of permanent, full-time employees with critical skills, who follow standard career paths. This is a relatively small group, perhaps made up of those who remain after major downsizing of a more traditional organization. The second leaf is a group of outside operators who are engaged contractually by the core group to perform a variety of jobs essential to the daily functioning of the organization. Many of these jobs would be performed by full-time staff, (e.g., human resource personnel) in a more traditional organization. The third leaf is a group of part-timers who can be hired temporarily by the core group as the needs of the business grow and who can just as easily be let go when business falls. Today's college graduates must be prepared to succeed in the second and third leaves, not just the first.

■ **Shamrock organizations** are firms that operate with a core group of permanent workers supplemented by outside contractors and part-time workers.

What Is a High Performance Organization?

The free-agent economy and shamrock organization are one aspect of the rapidly changing context of OB. Another is the **high performance organization**, introduced earlier as one intentionally designed to bring out the best in people and thereby produce organizational capability that delivers sustainable organizational results. Instead of treating people as disposable parts of constantly shifting temporary alliances, HPOs place people first.[14] They are regarded as the crucial resource in providing the capability to deliver sustainable high performance results.

■ The **high performance organization** is intentionally designed to bring out the best in people and produce sustainable organizational results.

■ EMPHASIS ON INTELLECTUAL CAPITAL

The essential foundation for the high performance organization is **intellectual capital**, defined in Section 1, as represented by the sum total of knowledge, expertise, and dedication of an organization's workforce.[15] In this sense, even in the days of high technology, people are the indispensable *human resources* whose contributions advance the organization's purpose, mission, and strategies. To utilize this intellectual capital, HPOs often organize their flow of work around the key business processes and often create work teams within these processes.[16] They follow human-resource policies directed toward enhancing employee flexibility, skills, knowledge, and motivation.[17] At the same time, high performance organizations involve fewer levels of management and change the way managers operate. They become much less directive order-givers and instead emphasize coaching, integrating the work of work teams with each other, and facilitating the work of the teams so that they can best complete their jobs and meet customer expectations.[18]

■ **Intellectual capital** is represented by the sum total of knowledge, expertise, and energy available from organization members.

■ KEY COMPONENTS OF HIGH PERFORMANCE ORGANIZATIONS

A high performance organization's specific form depends on its setting—for example, an HPO bank would have a form different than an auto manufacturer's.[19] But, most high performance organizations include the five components shown in Figure 2.3. The key HPO components are: employee involvement, self-directing work teams, integrated production technologies, organizational learning, and total quality management.

Employee Involvement   The amount of decision making delegated to workers at all levels reflects **employee involvement**. This can be visualized as a continuum.[20] At one end is no involvement (workers just do their jobs) or parallel involvement (there are such things as suggestion boxes, roundtable discussions concerning the jobs, and quality circles—members of a quality circle meet regularly to find ways to achieve continuous improvement of quality operations). In the middle is moderate involvement or participative management (there are increased responsibilities for making day-to-day job decisions). At the opposite end from low involvement is high involvement, or what we earlier termed empowerment—where, you will recall, there is worker responsibility for making decisions regarding themselves and their work. Typically, these decisions are of great latitude regarding virtually all aspects of the job. Increased use of employee involvement came from the realization that positive benefits could come from allowing employees' input into how their jobs were done. Research shows that employee productivity and various aspects of satisfaction tend to be higher with more involvement.[21]

■ **Employee involvement** is the amount of decision making delegated to employees.

Self-Directing Work Teams   Teams or workgroups that are empowered to make decisions about planning, doing, and evaluating their work are **self-directing work teams**. They sometimes have other names, such as self-managing or self-leading work teams, or autonomous work groups. We discuss them thoroughly later. There are at least two reasons for their role in high performance or-

■ **Self-directing work teams** are teams that are empowered to make decisions about planning, doing, and evaluating their work.

Figure 2.3
Five components of a high performance organization.

ganizations. First, the importance of tapping employee expertise and knowledge is now well-recognized. Second, there has been an increased need for employees to manage themselves as organizations have downsized and restructured for greater competitiveness.[22] Self-directing work teams strongly affect employee satisfaction and commitment and moderately affect performance.[23]

Integrated Production Technologies All organizations use technology to combine the use of resources, knowledge, and techniques and create a product or service output. The concept of **integrated production technologies** focuses on providing flexibility in manufacturing and services and involves job-design and information systems. Key aspects of integrated production technologies typically involve the use of just-in-time production or service systems, and a heavy emphasis on computers to assist in designing products or services, controlling equipment in production processes, and integrating the business functions.

> ■ **Integrated production technologies** focus on providing flexibility in manufacturing and services and involve job design and information systems as a part of the technology.

Just-in-time systems involve working closely with suppliers to make sure just the right amount of material is available to do the job. At Honeywell, for example, this is done by having the materials suppliers work in the Honeywell plants to see that the inventory level is appropriate. McDonald's does it by keeping only a very small (just-in-time) supply of hamburgers on hand to service its customers.[24]

Computer usage includes integrating such business functions as order entry and accounting with computer-aided design of the product or service and computer-aided production to help control workflow and other product or service aspects. For example, the Technology/Clothing Technology Corporation has developed a computer design process that will allow clothing manufacturers to create "custom" clothing and then to use computers to translate the final design specifications into instructions for manufacturing the item.[25] K2 Corporation, a large U.S. manufacturer of skis, uses these approaches in producing its custom-ordered skis.[26] These design and production functions are often integrated via computer into the just-in-time systems and the integration of business functions so that placing the order, designing it, producing it, and making sure an appropriate level of parts is available are all assisted by computer.

Organizational Learning Section 1 introduced *organizational learning* as a way for organizations to adapt to their settings and to gather information to anticipate future changes.[27] High performance organizations with the characteristics in this section, are designed for organizational learning. They integrate information into the organization's memory for availability and use in new situations.[28] The need for such learning resulted from the realization that traditional, hierarchically structured organizations were not very good at anticipating environmental changes or at sharing information across functions such as production, marketing, and engineering.

Total Quality Management As introduced earlier, total quality management involves a total commitment to high-quality results, continuous improvement, and meeting customer needs. The initial push for TQM as far back as the mid-1980s tended to apply it in separate, narrowly focused groups emphasizing various aspects of quality. These groups met separately from the workers' regular jobs. Now total quality management has become a tightly integrated part of HPOs where an emphasis on employee involvement and self management encourages all workers to do their own quality planning and checking.

Management Challenges of High Performance Organizations

The journey toward becoming an HPO presents many challenges. Responding to these challenges calls for a very strong leadership commitment. For those organizations that have made the HPO commitment, it has been well worth the effort. Studies of some 1100 companies across a 30-year period show some interesting results. First, bottom-line financial performance tends to increase 30 to 50 percent over a three- to five-year time period. Second, this bottom-line financial performance has increased by a minimum of 3 to 7 percent per year faster than in traditional organizations.[29] These results, however, are dependent upon the mastery of the following challenges.

■ ENVIRONMENTAL LINKAGES

Like other organizations, high performance organizations are open systems influenced by the rapidly moving *external environment* with its global emphasis and rapidly changing customer expectations. Among the most important *inputs* are the organizational worksite's problems and opportunities and the organization's purpose, mission, and strategy, along with its vision. HPOs typically develop a mission and vision package that ties these elements together and integrates them with the organization's core values.[30] In a true HPO, this vision/direction package must involve employees and managers at all organization levels. This blending is crucial to ensuring a high level of acceptance by everybody in the organization. This high level of mutual acceptance is a key difference between HPOs and other more traditional organizations. The previously mentioned *HPO components*—employee involvement, self-directed work teams, integrated manufacturing technologies, organizational learning, and total quality management—make unique contributions to the transformation of inputs into outputs.

The *outputs* basically consist of individual, group, and organizational effectiveness and contributions to society. Organizational effectiveness looks at how well the HPO has done financially and what the quality of work life is for members of the organization. The latter includes satisfaction, commitment to the organization, and many other measures of this kind. Contributions to society are those the organization is making to society through charitable contributions, volunteer activities by managers and workers, and many other similar activities.[31]

This open systems perspective therefore means that the inputs, transformation processes, and outputs are all influenced by the external environment and all influence each other. Thus, there is feedback from the outputs to the transformation components and inputs, and there is continual adjustment to meet the environmental demands.

■ INTERNAL INTEGRATION

A difficult challenge is the integration of all five HPO components. For example, the self-directing teams must include the integrated production system in their plans and operations. Often the teams are heavily involved in the system's design. Similarly, the teams also must include total quality management considerations as part of their functioning. At the same time, they must build organizational learning and employee involvement functions and activities. In successful HPOs there is a fit among all these activities and functions, as there is with the open system inputs and outputs.

Unlike traditional organizations, in which design emanates from the top down, the design of an HPO involves a combination of top-down and bottom-up decision making. Successful design calls for a strong and sustained emphasis from the top supported by various design teams comprised of people from all levels of the organization. It also calls for staying on course in dealing with the inevitable problems introduced by change. Organizations able to do this can reap the kinds of benefits we discuss in the concluding section.

■ **HPO "islands"** are HPO units engulfed by organizations or units that do not function as HPOs and may even be opposed to them.

Sometimes **HPO "islands"** exist within a larger, more traditional organization. HPO islands are engulfed by organizations or units that do not function as HPOs and may even be opposed to them. Saturn Corporation within General Motors is one such example. Originally set up to help serve as an example for the rest of the corporation, Saturn has been in a constant struggle to maintain itself as a true HPO.[32] Some influential executives from GM and the United Auto Workers Union have not supported Saturn because they have been concerned about losing the control they maintain elsewhere in GM's more traditional organization.[33]

In spite of these internal pressures, Saturn has been quite successful as a high performance organization. At the same time, external market forces have made it very difficult for Saturn to continue its success. Well-run HPOs have generally been better able to withstand these negative pressures than have traditional ones, however.[34]

■ MIDDLE MANAGER ROLES

Middle managers must also address a number of challenges to build a true high performance organization. Many will be asked to help implement one or more of the components described earlier to help move their organization on the journey toward becoming an HPO. As an example, creating self-directing work teams can provide resistance at both manager and employee levels.[35] A key concern is that middle managers in traditional organizations may be asked to implement a change that eliminates some or all of their job.[36] Many of these functions have been shifted to the teams themselves, and the middle managers must carve out new roles and adjust their traditional role as a source of direction.

THE EFFECTIVE MANAGER 2.1

MANAGERIAL CHALLENGES OF HIGH PERFORMANCE ORGANIZATIONS

- Employee concern with effectiveness
- Employee self-direction
- Employee concern with organization design
- Challenging jobs and/or work teams
- Intense peer and customer feedback
- Financial rewards and recognition

Although many Generation X employees may welcome new self-managing team environments, other workers, particularly those lacking the appropriate educational skills, may offer resistance. Some employees do not believe that working in teams is a fair way to work, and some do not like the additional challenge of teams. There is also a strong preference among many employees, especially in the United States, to do individual work. A key challenge for middle managers in implementing any of these components (see The Effective Manager 2.1) is to help deal with possible employee resistance.[37]

Another challenge for middle managers is to resolve the tensions that may exist between or among the various components. For example, in an organization on a journey toward an HPO, the total quality management component may reflect the separate, narrowly focused groups emphasizing various aspects of quality. These groups typically have lots of management control. In contrast, an employee involvement component in this same organization involves considerable worker empowerment across a great many issues, and not just quality. To reconcile the demands of these two different HPO components is very difficult for both managers and employees. The middle managers and the employees will need to be extensively trained to handle their new role in an HPO. Middle managers also will require lots of training and they must help with the design and implementation of training for other employees.[38] This much or more training is needed for employees to be able to perform their new duties and to keep up with increasing competition.

■ HIGH LEVEL LEADERSHIP

The first challenge for upper level management is to decide how far to go in becoming an HPO. Many organizations implement only one or two of the components above and are not true HPOs. They are traditional organizations with some HPO components. How far they attempt to go depends on the environment and input factors, as well as on how strongly the top level values and is committed to a true HPO. For example, HPOs are particularly useful in constantly changing environments that demand innovation. Some firms, such as Procter and Gamble, place a strong value on HPOs, and top management has a strong commitment to them.[39] Many managers simply do not want to make this kind of commitment and instead are satisfied with trying to implement one or two components or sometimes just a small portion of a single component.

Another challenge for senior managers is the internationalization of U.S. business practices. In a number of countries where status, power, and prestige are inherent in work-related values (e.g., Malaysia, Italy, Mexico) it can be very difficult to implement HPO components like self-directing teams and employee involvement. In addition, workers with the appropriate abilities and education may not be available.[40] Finally, training and development of middle managers is a challenge. As we have stated, they no longer perform many of the managerial duties in traditional organizations.

■ GREENFIELD SITES VERSUS REDESIGNS

A final challenge is the question of starting a high performance organization from scratch or redesigning a traditional organization to become one. Those started

---

OB Across Functions
PRODUCT DEVELOPMENT

Customer Input Through Quality Function Deployment

Firms are increasingly using cross-functional teams to deploy the voice of the customer through all stages of the product development process. These teams have the skills to design the product, write engineering specifications, purchase materials, and prepare plans for production preparation and completion. For example, Wiremold, an electrical goods manufacturer in West Hartford, Connecticut, uses three-member design teams. These teams have a marketer, a design/product engineer, and a production engineer. The teams interview their customers—electrical contractors and architects—about their needs. These interviews lead to a broad, preliminary definition of the product. Then the teams interview other customers over and over as the product begins to develop on team members' computer screens and in their minds. When this process started, the designers did not want a production engineer involved in discussions. Ultimately, however, the process worked so well that the team could see the product through the customer's eye, and the importance of having each of the product design functions represented became obvious.

The quality function deployment process cut the design process from three years to less than six months at Wiremold. Sales increased by 150 percent by creating new market niches and grabbing customers from competitors that were not using cross-functional teams and the quality function deployment process. *www.wiremold.com*

■ **Greenfield sites** are those HPO sites started from scratch at a new site.

from scratch at a new site are called **greenfield sites**. Saturn Corporation is an example. It took ten years to develop Saturn from its original conception until its plant opened. During that period, everything was designed from the ground up—typical for greenfield sites.[41] In contrast, redesigns start out as more traditional organizations and try to change these designs to work toward becoming an HPO.

Organizations that have implemented new designs have experienced an average financial increase of about 10 percent a year. In contrast, organizations that have redesigned themselves have realized average increases of 6.8 percent a year. Traditional organizations that have not been redesigned have seen improvements of 3.8 percent a year.[42] So, although all three design types have experienced financial increases in response to external and internal pressures, the HPO designs have done the best.

Illustrative Case: Creating a High Performance Organization

One organization that is moving toward becoming a high performance organization is VF Corporation.[43] Called a "stealth giant" because it touches peoples' lives in dozens of ways without their being aware of it, VF Corporation makes Lee, Wrangler, Britannia, and Rustler jeans and sells about $2 billion of jeans a year—more than any other organization. The firm, 100 years old and headquartered in Greensboro, North Carolina is undergoing a far-reaching redesign.

■ CHANGE LEADERSHIP

In total, VF Corp. makes 17 brands of different kinds of apparel and had total sales of $5.5 billion in a recent reporting period. Until recently, each brand operated as an independent division, with its own purchasing, production, marketing and computer systems. The brands are sold in mass-market retail outlets, such as Wal-Mart and Target, as well as department stores such as Macy's.

When Mackey McDonald took over as chief executive officer, he was determined to shake up the firm. VF had long been a steady, but not spectacular performer. Its sales were almost flat and costs were increasing, its information systems costs alone rising more than 10 percent per year. Each of the brands had its own system and the systems were not able to communicate with each other. The divisions did not coordinate raw material ordering or manufacturing to maximize output. They also often competed for the same buyers. The corporation had many small-company disadvantages and few of the large-company advantages.

McDonald set a goal of $7 billion in sales within four years. He articulated a vision of "consumerization" which would tailor the firm's production and distribution systems to serve customers with maximum efficiency. VF no longer would have to depend on fuzzy national and regional forecasts, which often created shortages or gluts in inventories. McDonald said, "We had a tremendous opportunity to compete on knowledge." He envisioned using what is called a "micromarketing system" that would be able to predict that, say, a particular Wal-Mart store would sell a given number of Wranglers with a 34 inch waist size, in a given color, at the beginning of summer. VF would then make sure the jeans were in stock, so that sales would not be lost to competitors. To do this and the other things needed to carry out the vision, VF would move far toward becoming an enterprise or E-corporation. It also would be taking giant steps toward becoming a high performance organization. Let us now look at the steps taken to become a true HPO.

■ TOTAL SYSTEMS COMMITMENT

The environment facing VF Corporation was becoming increasingly complex, global, and fast moving. Low-priced foreign goods were increasing across many of VF's brands. Competitors, such as Levi Strauss, were attempting to move toward consumerization.[44] VF's sales had pretty much plateaued, and costs were increasing. These and other pressures were pushing the firm to take steps to deal with the external environmental changes.

As a response to these pressures, as well as the internal-coordination ones mentioned earlier, McDonald put forth his consumerization vision and $7 billion sales goal. McDonald's first step to establish a vision/direction setting package was to bring together 50 VF managers. They fanned out across the country looking for best practices to emulate. Firms such as Proctor & Gamble, 3M, and Caterpillar were visited.

The management group then almost literally locked itself into a conference room for about six months and developed new business processes for VF. The firm reorganized the 17 brands into five "coalitions": intimates, jeanswear (including workwear), playwear, knitwear, and international operations and marketing. It also moved the headquarters to North Carolina and set up a new unit to coordinate the coalitions. This unit was called VF Services and, in addition to coordinating the technology across the coalitions, VF Services oversaw some accounting, procurement, and human resources operations, all as part of the E-corporation, high-tech system. To indicate the division's importance, its head was appointed as a division president and also was a long-term VF employee.

■ IMPLEMENTATION PROCESSES

The next step was to develop implementation processes for product development, production planning, and distribution. This also required development of crucial processes for routing information from unit to unit, at the employee level, departmental level, coalition level and wherever else such information was needed. At this point, VF turned to a number of outside enterprise resource planning software vendors to help tie together the above systems and vision/direction setting package, while also modifying the systems to suit its own needs. Figure 2.4 shows a simplified version of the VF enterprise-wide integrated information systems.

The figure emphasizes integrated production technology. Its core is the enterprise resource planning (ERP) function which handles order management, production planning, materials management, and finance modules, all with sophisticated software programs. All the other functions—product-development, micromarketing, warehouse control—manufacturing control, capacity and raw materials planning, and forecasting tie into ERP and to each other. Each uses its own software. The system is designed to tie together everything from raw material ordering to supplying retailers with appropriately designed and manufactured apparel products in a timely manner.

This integrated production technology component was central to the vision/ direction setting package put together by CEO McDonald and his 50 key executives, in response to the changing environment. In terms of employee involvement, we also know that 50 key executives were involved. There also is evidence that the company's computer personnel were strongly involved. We do not know how involved the production employees were and we have no information here on the extent to which self-directing work teams were used.

In terms of organizational learning, it probably will be enhanced by the enterprise-wide planning system. The system records and feeds back information across the enterprise in a very systematic way. At the same time, considerable training time is devoted to the managers and employees. For example, the VF employees responsible for getting only a single one of the software modules running have each undergone at least 14 weeks of training. They spend time at vendor organizations as well as in VF. Vendor employees also spend considerable long-term time in VF Corporation.

Figure 2.4 shows the extensive feedback among the modules in the production component. At the same time, the production component will provide financial feedback as well as whatever output information management deems to be important. Likewise, as indicated above, we are told there is feedback

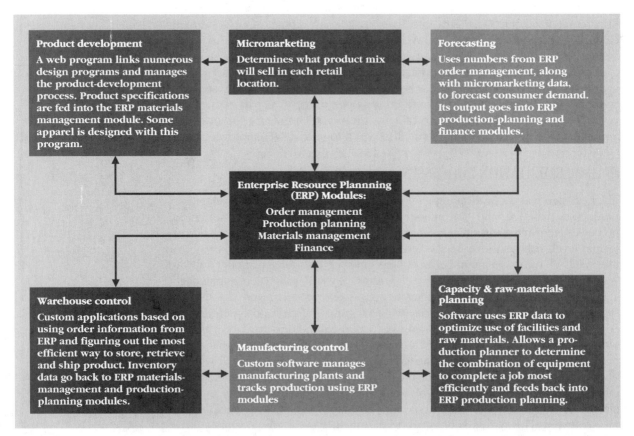

Figure 2.4
Simplified VF Corporation enterprise-wide integrated information systems.

between the production technology component and the total quality and organizational learning components, and it is reasonable to assume with the other components as well. We also can assume that, for total quality management, computerized systems should provide a great deal of assistance.

In summary, this once-traditional organization that has used an E-corporation approach as a starting point on a journey that could lead to becoming a high performance organization. VF Corporation has demonstrated some of the characteristics of such an organization, but only time will tell whether or not it achieves its goals.

Groups in Organizations

A **group** may be defined as a collection of two or more people who work with one another regularly to achieve common goals. In a true group, members are mutually dependent on one another to achieve common goals, and they interact with one another regularly to pursue those goals over a sustained period of time.[45] Groups are good for both organizations and their members, helping to accomplish important tasks and to maintain a high-quality workforce. Consultant and management scholar Harold J. Leavitt is a well-known advocate for the power and usefulness of groups.[46] Recently, he has described "hot groups" that thrive in conditions of crisis and competition and whose creativity and innovativeness generate extraordinary returns.[47]

■ **Groups** involve two or more people working together regularly to achieve common goals.

■ WHAT IS AN EFFECTIVE GROUP?

An **effective group** is one that achieves high levels of task performance, member satisfaction and team viability.[48] With regard to *task performance*, this group achieves its performance goals—in the standard sense of quantity, quality, and timeliness of work results. For a permanent work group, such as a manufacturing team, this may mean meeting daily production targets. For a temporary group, such as a new policy task force, this may involve meeting a deadline for submitting a new organizational policy to the company president. With regard to *member satisfaction*, an effective group is one whose members believe that their participation and experiences are positive and meet important personal needs. They are satisfied with their tasks, accomplishments, and interpersonal relationships. With regard to *team viability*, the members are sufficiently satisfied to continue working well together on an ongoing basis and/or to look forward to working together again at some future point in time. The group in this way has all-important long-term performance potential.

■ **Effective groups** achieve high levels of task, performance, member satisfaction and team viability.

■ UNIQUE CONTRIBUTIONS OF GROUPS

Effective groups help organizations accomplish important tasks. In particular, they offer the potential for **synergy**—the creation of a whole that is greater than the sum of its parts. When synergy occurs, groups accomplish more than the total of their members' individual capabilities. Group synergy is necessary for orga-

■ **Synergy** is the creation of a whole greater than the sum of its parts.

nizations to become competitive and achieve long-term high performance in today's dynamic times.[49]

The Effective Manager 2.2 lists in general the benefits groups can bring to organizations. More specifically, groups often have three performance advantages over individuals acting alone.[50] First, when there is no clear "expert" in a particular task or problem, groups seem to make better judgments than does the average individual alone. Second, when problem solving can be handled by a division of labor and the sharing of information, groups are typically more successful than individuals. And third, because of their tendencies to make riskier decisions, groups can be more creative and innovative than individuals.

In addition, groups are important settings where people learn from one another and share job skills and knowledge.[51] The learning environment and the pool of experience within a group can be used to solve difficult and unique problems. This is especially helpful to newcomers who often need help in their jobs. When group members support and help each other in acquiring and improving job competencies, they may even make up for deficiencies in organizational training systems.

Groups are also able to satisfy the needs of members. They offer opportunities for social interaction and can provide individuals with a sense of security in available work assistance and technical advice. They can provide emotional support in times of special crisis or pressure, and allow for ego involvement in group goals and activities.

At the same time that they have enormous performance potential, groups can also have problems. One concern is **social loafing**, also known as the *Ringelmann effect*. It is the tendency of people to work less hard in a group than they would individually.[52] Max Ringlemann, a German psychologist, pinpointed the phenomenon by asking people to pull on a rope as hard as they could, first alone and then in a group.[53] He found that average productivity dropped as more people joined the rope-pulling task. He acknowledged two reasons why people may not work as hard in groups as they would individually: (1) their individual contribution is less noticeable in the context of the group, and (2) they prefer to see others carry the workload. Some considerations in dealing with social loafing or trying to prevent it from occurring include:

- Define member roles and tasks to maximize individual interests
- Link individual rewards to performance contributions to the group
- Raise accountability by identifying individuals' performance contributions to the group

■ **Social loafing** occurs when people work less hard in groups than they would individually.

How to handle social loafing

■ **Social facilitation** is the tendency for one's behavior to be influenced by the presence of others in a group.

Another issue in group work is **social facilitation**—the tendency for one's behavior to be influenced by the presence of others in a group or social setting.[54] In general, *social facilitation theory* indicates that working in the presence of others creates an emotional arousal or excitement that stimulates behavior and therefore affects performance. Arousal tends to work positively when one is proficient with the task. Here, the excitement leads to extra effort at doing something that already comes quite naturally. An example is the play of a world-class athlete in front of an enthusiastic "hometown" crowd. But the effect of social facilitation can be negative when the task is not well learned. You may know this best in the context of public speaking. When asked to speak in front of a class or larger audience, you may well stumble as you try hard in public to talk about an unfamiliar topic.

■ FORMAL GROUPS

There are many ways in the new workplace for groups to be used to great advantage. A **formal group** is officially designated to serve a specific organizational purpose. An example is the work unit headed by a manager and consisting of one or more direct reports. The organization creates such a group to perform a specific task, which typically involves the use of resources to create a product such as a report, decision, service, or commodity.[55] The head of a formal group is responsible for the group's performance accomplishments, but all members contribute the required work. Also, the head of the group plays a key "linking-pin" role that ties it horizontally and vertically with the rest of the organization.[56]

Formal groups may be permanent or temporary. *Permanent work groups*, or *command groups* in the vertical structure, often appear on organization charts as departments (e.g., market research department), divisions (e.g., consumer products division), or teams (e.g., product-assembly team). Such groups can vary in size from very small departments or teams of just a few people to large divisions employing a hundred or more people. In all cases, permanent work groups are officially created to perform a specific function on an ongoing basis. They continue to exist until a decision is made to change or reconfigure the organization for some reason.

In contrast, *temporary work groups* are *task groups* specifically created to solve a problem or perform a defined task. They often disband once the assigned purpose or task has been accomplished.[57] Examples are the many temporary committees and task forces that are important components of any organization. Indeed, today's organizations tend to make more use of *cross-functional teams* or *task forces* for special problem-solving efforts. The president of a company, for example, might convene a task force to examine the possibility of implementing flexible work hours for nonmanagerial employees. Usually, such temporary groups appoint chairpersons or heads who are held accountable for results, much as is the manager of a work unit. Another common form is the *project team* that is formed, often cross-functionally, to complete a specific task with a well-defined end point. Examples include installing a new E-mail system and introducing a new product modification.[58]

Information technology is bringing a new type of group into the workplace. This is the *virtual group*, a group whose members convene and work together electronically via networked computers. In this new age of the Internet and intranets, and more, virtual groups will become increasingly common in organizations. Facilitated by ever-advancing team-oriented software, or groupware, members of virtual groups can do the same things as members of face-to-face groups. They can share information, make decisions, and complete tasks. The

■ **Formal groups** are officially designated for a specific organizational purpose.

important role of virtual groups or teams in the high performance workplace is discussed later.

■ INFORMAL GROUPS

Informal groups emerge without being officially designated by the organization. They form spontaneously and are based on personal relationships or special interests, and not on any specific organizational endorsement. They are commonly found within most formal groups. *Friendship groups,* for example, consist of persons with natural affinities for one another. They tend to work together, sit together, take breaks together, and even do things together outside of the workplace. *Interest groups* consist of persons who share common interests. These may be job-related interests, such as an intense desire to learn more about computers, or nonwork interests, such as community service, sports, or religion.

Informal groups often help people get their jobs done. Through their network of interpersonal relationships, they have the potential to speed up the work flow as people assist each other in ways that formal lines of authority fail to provide. They also help individuals satisfy needs that are thwarted or otherwise left unmet in a formal group. In these and related ways, informal groups can provide their members with social satisfactions, security, and a sense of belonging.

Stages of Group Development

Whether one is part of a formal work unit, a temporary task force, or a virtual team, the group itself passes through different stages in its life cycle.[59] Furthermore, depending on the stage the group has reached, the leader and members can face very different challenges. Figure 2.5 describes five stages of group development: (1) forming, (2) storming, (3) norming, (4) performing, and (5) adjourning.[60]

■ FORMING STAGE

In the *forming stage* of group development, a primary concern is the initial entry of members to a group. During this stage, individuals ask a number of questions as they begin to identify with other group members and with the group itself. Their concerns may include: "What can the group offer me?" "What will I be asked to contribute?" "Can my needs be met at the same time I contribute to the group?" Members are interested in getting to know each other and discovering what is considered acceptable behavior, in determining the real task of the group, and in defining group rules.

■ STORMING STAGE

The *storming stage* of group development is a period of high emotionality and tension among the group members. During this stage, hostility and infighting may occur, and the group typically experiences many changes. Coalitions or cliques may form as individuals compete to impose their preferences on the group and to achieve a desired status position. Outside demands, including premature expectations for performance results, may create uncomfortable pres-

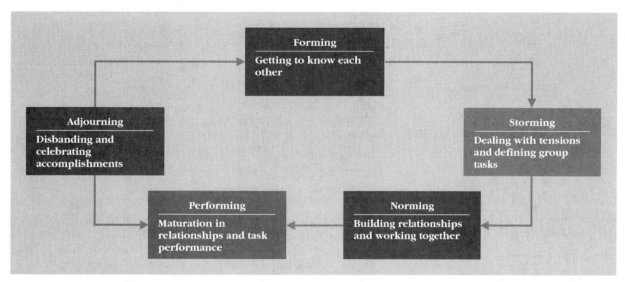

Figure 2.5
Five stages of group development.

sures. In the process, membership expectations tend to be clarified, and attention shifts toward obstacles standing in the way of group goals. Individuals begin to understand one another's interpersonal styles, and efforts are made to find ways to accomplish group goals while also satisfying individual needs.

■ NORMING STAGE

The *norming stage* of group development, sometimes called initial integration, is the point at which the group really begins to come together as a coordinated unit. The turmoil of the storming stage gives way to a precarious balancing of forces. With the pleasures of a new sense of harmony, group members will strive to maintain positive balance. Holding the group together may become more important to some than successfully working on the group's tasks. Minority viewpoints, deviations from group directions, and criticisms may be discouraged as group members experience a preliminary sense of closeness. Some members may mistakenly perceive this stage as one of ultimate maturity. In fact, a premature sense of accomplishment at this point needs to be carefully managed as a "stepping stone" to the next higher level of group development.

■ PERFORMING STAGE

The *performing stage* of group development, sometimes called total integration, marks the emergence of a mature, organized, and well-functioning group. The group is now able to deal with complex tasks and handle internal disagreements in creative ways. The structure is stable, and members are motivated by group goals and are generally satisfied. The primary challenges are continued efforts to improve relationships and performance. Group members should be able to adapt successfully as opportunities and demands change over time. A group that

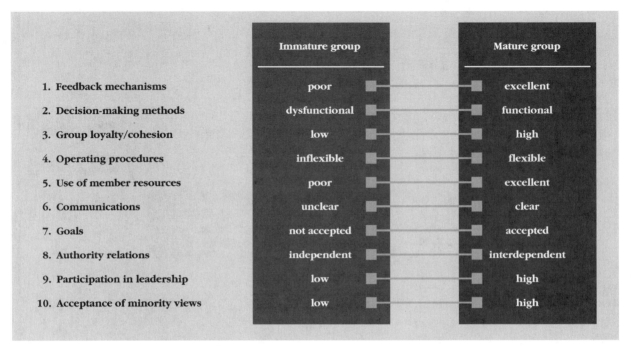

Figure 2.6
Ten criteria for measuring the maturity of a group.

has achieved the level of total integration typically scores high on the criteria of group maturity shown in Figure 2.6.

■ ADJOURNING STAGE

A well-integrated group is able to disband, if required, when its work is accomplished. The *adjourning stage* of group development is especially important for the many temporary groups that are increasingly common in the new workplace, including task forces, committees, project teams and the like. Members of these groups must be able to convene quickly, do their jobs on a tight schedule, and then adjourn—often to reconvene later if needed. The members' willingness to disband when the job is done and to work well together in future responsibilities, group or otherwise, is an important long-run test of group success.

Input Foundations of Group Effectiveness

An organization's success depends largely on the performance of its internal networks of formal and informal groups. Groups in this sense are an important component of the *human resources* and *intellectual capital* of organizations.[61] Like individuals, group contributions are essential if the organization is to prosper through high performance over the long run.

The systems model in Figure 2.7 shows how groups, like organizations, pursue effectiveness by interacting with their environments to transform resource inputs into product outputs.[62] The inputs are the initial "givens" in any group

Figure 2.7
The work group as an open system transforming resource inputs into product outputs.

situation. They are the foundations for all consequent action. As a general rule-of-thumb, the stronger the input foundations the better the chances for long-term group effectiveness. Key group inputs include the nature of the task, goals, rewards, resources, technology, membership diversity, and group size.

■ TASKS

Tasks place different demands on groups, with varying implications for group effectiveness. The *technical demands* of a group's task include its routineness, difficulty, and information requirements. The *social demands* of a task involve relationships, ego involvement, controversies over ends and means, and the like. Tasks that are complex in technical demands require unique solutions and more information processing; those that are complex in social demands involve difficulties reaching agreement on goals or methods for accomplishing them. Naturally, group effectiveness is harder to achieve when the task is highly complex.[63] To master complexity, group members must apply and distribute their efforts broadly and actively cooperate to achieve desired results. When their efforts are successful at mastering complex tasks, however, group members tend to experience high levels of satisfaction with the group and its accomplishments.

■ GOALS, REWARDS, AND RESOURCES

Appropriate goals, well-designed reward systems, and adequate resources are all essential to support long-term performance accomplishments. A group's performance, much as an individual's performance, can suffer when goals are unclear, insufficiently challenging, or arbitrarily imposed. It can also suffer if goals and rewards are focused too much on individual instead of group outcomes. And it can suffer if adequate budgets, the right facilities, good work methods and procedures, and the best technologies are not available. By contrast, having the right goals, rewards, and resources can be a strong launching pad for group success.

■ TECHNOLOGY

Technology provides the means to get work accomplished. It is always necessary to have the right technology available for the task at hand. The nature of the work-flow technology can also influence the way group members interact with one another while performing their tasks. It is one thing to be part of a group that crafts products to specific customer requests; it is quite another to be part of a group whose members staff one section of a machine-paced assembly line. The former technology permits greater interaction among group members. It will probably create a closer knit group with a stronger sense of identity than the one formed around one small segment of an assembly line.

■ MEMBERSHIP CHARACTERISTICS

To achieve success a group must have the right skills and competencies available for group problem solving. Although talents alone cannot guarantee desired results, they establish an important baseline of performance potential. When the input competencies are insufficient, a group's performance limits will be difficult to overcome.

In *homogeneous groups* where members are very similar to one another, members may find it very easy to work together. But they may also suffer performance limitations if their collective skills, experiences and perspectives are not a good match for complex tasks. In *heterogeneous groups* whose members vary in age, gender, race, ethnicity, experience, culture, and the like, a wide pool of talent and viewpoints is available for problem-solving. But this diversity may also create difficulties as members try to define problems, share information, and handle interpersonal conflicts. These difficulties may be quite pronounced in the short run, but once members learn how to work together, the diversity can be turned into enhanced performance potential.[64]

Researchers identify what is called the **diversity–consensus dilemma**—the tendency for increasing diversity among group members to make it harder for group members to work together, even though the diversity itself expands the skills and perspectives available for problem solving.[65] The challenge to group effectiveness in a multinational team, for example, is to take advantage of the diversity without suffering process disadvantages.[66]

The mix of personalities is also important in a group or team. The **FIRO-B theory** (with "FIRO" standing for fundamental interpersonal orientation) helps to identify differences in how people relate to one another based on their needs to express and receive feelings of inclusion, control, and affection.[67] Developed by William Schutz, the theory points out that groups whose members are compatible on these needs are likely to be more effective than groups whose members are more incompatible on them. Symptoms of incompatibilities in a group include withdrawn members, open hostilities, struggles over control, and domination of the group by a few members. Schutz states the management implications of the FIRO-B theory this way: "If at the outset we can choose a group of people who can work together harmoniously, we shall go far toward avoiding situations where a group's efforts are wasted in interpersonal conflicts."[68]

Another source of diversity in group membership is *status*—a person's relative rank, prestige, or standing in a group. Status within a group can be based on any number of factors, including age, work seniority, occupation, education, performance, or standing in other groups. **Status congruence** occurs when a person's position within the group is equivalent to ones held outside of the group. Problems are to be expected when status incongruence is present and someone's position in the group does not reflect the outside status. In high-power distance cultures such as Malaysia, for example, the chair of a committee is expected to be

■ The **diversity–consensus dilemma** is the tendency for diversity in groups to create process difficulties even as it offers improved potential for problem solving.

■ **FIRO-B theory** examines differences in how people relate to one another based on their needs to express and receive feelings of inclusion, control, and affection.

■ **Status congruence** involves consistency between a person's status within and outside of a group.

the highest-ranking member of the group. When such status congruity is present, members can feel comfortable for the group to proceed with its work. If the senior member is not appointed to head the committee, discomfort will ensue and difficulties in group performance are likely. Similar problems might occur, for example, when a young college graduate is appointed to chair a project group composed of senior and more experienced workers.

■ GROUP SIZE

The size of a group, as measured by the number of its members, can make a difference in a group's effectiveness. As a group becomes larger, more people are available to divide up the work and accomplish needed tasks. This can boost performance and member satisfaction, but only up to a point. As a group continues to grow in size, communication and coordination problems often set in. Satisfaction may dip, and turnover, absenteeism, and social loafing may increase. Even logistical matters, such as finding time and locations for meetings, become more difficult for larger groups and can affect performance negatively.[69]

A good size for problem-solving groups is between five and seven members. A group with fewer than five may be too small to adequately share responsibilities. With more than seven, individuals may find it harder to participate and offer ideas. Larger groups are also more prone to possible domination by aggressive members and have tendencies to split into coalitions or subgroups.[70] Groups with an odd number of members find it easier to use majority voting rules to resolve disagreements. When speed is required, this form of conflict management is useful, and odd-numbered groups may be preferred. But when careful deliberations are required and the emphasis is more on consensus, such as in jury duty or very complex problem solving, even-numbered groups may be more effective unless an irreconcilable deadlock occurs.[71]

Group and Intergroup Dynamics

The effectiveness of any group, as previously depicted in Figure 2.7, requires more than the correct inputs. It always depends in part on how well members work together to utilize these inputs to produce the desired outputs. When we speak about people "working together" in groups, we are dealing with issues of **group dynamics**—the forces operating in groups that affect the way members relate to and work with one another. From the perspective of an open system, group dynamics are the *processes* through which inputs are transformed into outputs.

■ **Group dynamics** are the forces operating in groups that affect the ways members work together.

■ WHAT GOES ON WITHIN GROUPS

George Homans described a classic model of group dynamics involving two sets of behaviors—required and emergent. In a work group, *required behaviors* are those formally defined and expected by the organization.[72] For example, they may include such behaviors as punctuality, customer respect, and assistance to co-workers. *Emergent behaviors* are those that group members display in addition to what the organization asks of them. They derive not from outside expectations but from personal initiative. Emergent behaviors often include things that people do beyond formal job requirements and that help get the job done in the best ways possible. Rarely can required behaviors be specified so perfectly that they meet all the demands that arise in a work situation. This makes emergent behaviors so essential. An example might be someone taking the time to send an E-mail to an absent member to keep her informed about what happened during a group meeting. The concept of empowerment, often discussed in this book as essential to the high performance workplace, relies strongly on unlocking this positive aspect of emergent behaviors.

Homans' model of group dynamics also describes member relationships in terms of activities, interactions, and sentiments, all of which have their required and emergent forms. *Activities* are the things people do or the actions they take in groups while working on tasks. *Interactions* are interpersonal communications and contacts. *Sentiments* are the feelings, attitudes, beliefs, or values held by group members.

■ WHAT GOES ON BETWEEN GROUPS

■ **Intergroup dynamics** are relationships between groups cooperating and competing with one another.

The term **intergroup dynamics** refers to the dynamics that take place between two or more groups. Organizations ideally operate as cooperative systems in which the various components support one another. In the real world, however, competition and intergroup problems often develop within an organization and have mixed consequences. On the negative side—such as when manufacturing and sales units don't get along, intergroup dynamics may divert energies as members focus more on their animosities toward the other group than on the performance of important tasks.[73] On the positive side, competition among groups can stimulate them to work harder, become more focused on key tasks, develop more internal loyalty and satisfaction, or achieve a higher level of creativity in problem solving. Japanese companies, for example, often use competitive themes to motivate their organization-wide workforces. At Sony, it has been said that the slogan "BMW" stands for "Beat Matsushita Whatsoever."[74]

Organizations and their managers go to great lengths to avoid the negative and achieve the positive aspects of intergroup dynamics. Groups engaged in destructive competition, for example, can be refocused on a common enemy or a common goal. Direct negotiations can be held among the groups, and members can be trained to work more cooperatively. It is important to avoid win–lose reward systems in which one group must lose something in order for the other to gain. Rewards can be refocused on contributions to the total organization and on how much groups help one another. Also, cooperation tends to increase as interaction between groups increases.

Decision Making in Groups

One of the most important activities engaged in by any group is *decision making*—the process of choosing among alternative courses of action. Obviously, the quality and timeliness of decisions made and the processes through which they are arrived at can have an important impact on group effectiveness.

■ HOW GROUPS MAKE DECISIONS

Edgar Schein, a noted scholar and consultant, has worked extensively with groups to analyze and improve their decision-making processes.[75] He observes that groups may make decisions through any of the following six methods: lack of response, authority rule, minority rule, majority rule, consensus, or unanimity.

In *decision by lack of response*, one idea after another is suggested without any discussion taking place. When the group finally accepts an idea, all others have been bypassed and discarded by simple lack of response rather than by critical evaluation. In *decision by authority rule*, the chairperson, manager, or leader makes a decision for the group. This can be done with or without discussion and is very time efficient. Whether the decision is a good one or a bad one, however, depends on whether or not the authority figure has the necessary information and on how well other group members accept this approach. In *decision by minority rule*, two or three people are able to dominate or "railroad" the group into making a decision to which they agree. This is often done by providing a suggestion and then forcing quick agreement by challenging the group with such statements as: "Does anyone object?... No? Well, let's go ahead then."

One of the most common ways groups make decisions, especially when early signs of disagreement set in, is *decision by majority rule*. Here, formal voting may take place, or members may be polled to find the majority viewpoint. This method parallels the democratic political system and is often used without awareness of its potential problems. The very process of voting can create coalitions. That is, some people will be "winners," and others will be "losers" when the final vote is tallied. Those in the minority—the "losers," may feel left out or discarded without having had a fair say. As a result, they may be less enthusiastic about implementing the decision of the "winners." Lingering resentments may impair group effectiveness in the future.

Another alternative is *decision by consensus*. Formally defined, **consensus** is a state of affairs whereby discussion leads to one alternative being favored by most members and the other members agreeing to support it. When a consensus is reached, even those who may have opposed the chosen course of action know that they have been listened to and have had a fair chance to influence the outcome. Consensus, as suggested by the guidelines in The Effective Manager 2.3, does not require unanimity. What it does require is the opportunity for any dissenting members to feel they have been able to speak, and that their voices have been heard.[76]

A *decision by unanimity* may be the ideal state of affairs. Here, all group members agree totally on the course of action to be taken. This is a "logically perfect" group decision method that is extremely difficult to attain in actual practice. One reason that groups sometimes turn to authority decisions, majority vot-

■ **Consensus** is a group decision that has the expressed support of most members.

THE EFFECTIVE MANAGER 2.3

GUIDELINES FOR GROUP CONSENSUS

1. Don't argue blindly; consider others' reactions to your points.
2. Don't change your mind just to reach quick agreement.
3. Avoid conflict reduction by voting, coin tossing, and bargaining.
4. Try to involve everyone in the decision process.
5. Allow disagreements to surface so that information and opinions can be deliberated.
6. Don't focus on winning versus losing; seek alternatives acceptable to all.
7. Discuss assumptions, listen carefully, and encourage participation by everyone.

ing, or even minority decisions is the difficulty of managing the group process to achieve consensus or unanimity.[77]

■ ASSETS AND LIABILITIES OF GROUP DECISION MAKING

The best groups don't limit themselves to just one decision-making method, using it over and over again regardless of circumstances. Instead, they change decision methods to best fit the problem and situation at hand. Indeed, an important group leadership skill is helping a group choose the "right" decision method—that is, the one providing for a timely and quality decision and to which the members are highly committed. This choice should be made with a full awareness of the assets and liabilities of group decision making. For example, the *potential advantages of group decision making* include:[78]

Advantages of group decision making

1. *Information*—more knowledge and expertise is applied to solve the problem.
2. *Alternatives*—a greater number of alternatives are examined, avoiding tunnel vision.
3. *Understanding and acceptance*—the final decision is better understood and accepted by all group members.
4. *Commitment*—there is more commitment among all group members to make the final decision work.

We also know that groups can experience problems when they are making decisions. The *potential disadvantages of group decision making* include:[79]

Disadvantages of group decision making

1 *Social pressure to conform*—individuals may feel compelled to go along with the apparent wishes of the group.
2. *Minority domination*—the group's decision may be forced or "railroaded" by one individual or a small coalition.
3. *Time demands*—with more people involved in the dialogue and discussion, group decisions usually take longer to make than individual decisions.

■ GROUPTHINK

■ **Groupthink** is the tendency of cohesive group members to lose their critical evaluative capabilities.

An important potential problem in group decision making, identified by social psychologist Irving Janis, is **groupthink**—the tendency of members in highly cohesive groups to lose their critical evaluative capabilities.[80] Janis believes that, because highly cohesive groups demand conformity, their members tend to become unwilling to criticize one another's ideas and suggestions. Desires to hold the group together and to avoid unpleasant disagreements lead to an overemphasis on agreement and an underemphasis on critical discussion. The possible result is a poor decision. Janis suggests that groupthink played a role in the lack of preparedness of U.S. forces at Pearl Harbor in World War II. It has also been linked to U.S. decision making during the Vietnam War and to the space shuttle *Challenger* disaster.

Group leaders and members must be on guard to spot the symptoms of groupthink and take any necessary action to prevent its occurrence.[81] The Effective Manager 2.4 identifies steps that can be taken to avoid groupthink. Among them, for example, President Kennedy chose to absent himself from certain strategy discussions by his cabinet during the Cuban Missile crisis. Reportedly, this facilitated discussion and helped to improve decision making as the crisis was successfully resolved.

■ HOW TO IMPROVE GROUP DECISION MAKING

In order to take full advantage of the group as a decision-making resource, care must be taken to manage group dynamics to balance individual contributions and group operations.[82] A particular concern is with the process losses that often occur in free-flowing meetings, such as a committee deliberation or a staff meeting on a specific problem. In these settings the risk of social pressures to conformity, domination, time pressures, and even highly emotional debates may detract from the purpose at hand. They are also settings in which special group decision techniques may be used to advantage.[83]

Brainstorming In **brainstorming**, group members actively generate as many ideas and alternatives as possible, and they do so relatively quickly and without inhibitions. Four rules typically govern the brainstorming process. First, *all criticism is ruled out.* No one is allowed to judge or evaluate any ideas until the idea-generation process has been completed. Second, *"freewheeling" is welcomed.* The emphasis is on creativity and imagination; the wilder or more radical the ideas, the better. Third, *quantity is wanted.* The emphasis is also on the number of ideas; the greater the number, the more likely a superior idea will appear. Fourth, *"piggy-backing" is good.* Everyone is encouraged to suggest how others' ideas can be turned into new ideas or how two or more ideas can be joined into still another new idea. Typical results include enthusiasm, involvement, and a free flow of ideas useful in creative problem solving.

Nominal Group Technique In any group, there will be times when the opinions of members differ so much that antagonistic arguments will develop during free-wheeling discussions. At other times the group will be so large that open discussion and brainstorming are awkward to manage. In such cases, a form of structured group decision making called the **nominal group technique** may be helpful.[84] It puts people in small groups of six to seven members and asks everyone to respond individually and in writing to a "nominal question" such as: "What should be done to improve the effectiveness of this work team?" Everyone is encouraged to list as many alternatives or ideas as they can. Next, participants read aloud their responses to the nominal question in round-robin fashion. The recorder writes each response on large newsprint as it is offered. No criticism is allowed. The recorder asks for any questions that may clarify items on the newsprint. This is again done in round-robin fashion, and no evaluation is allowed. The goal is simply to make sure that everyone present fully understands each response. A structured voting procedure is then used to prioritize responses

THE EFFECTIVE MANAGER 2.4

HOW TO AVOID GROUPTHINK

- Assign the role of critical evaluator to each group member.
- Have the leader avoid seeming partial to one course of action.
- Create subgroups to work on the same problem.
- Have group members discuss issues with outsiders and report back.
- Invite outside experts to observe and react to group processes.
- Assign someone to be a "devil's advocate" at each meeting.
- Write alternative scenarios for the intentions of competing groups.
- Hold "second-chance" meetings after consensus is apparently achieved.

■ **Brainstorming** involves generating ideas through "freewheeling" and without criticism.

■ The **nominal group technique** involves structured rules for generating and prioritizing ideas.

to the nominal question. The nominal group procedure allows ideas to be evaluated without risking the inhibitions, hostilities, and distortions that may occur in an open meeting.

Delphi Technique A third group decision approach, the **Delphi technique**, was developed by the Rand Corporation for use in situations where group members are unable to meet face to face. In this procedure, a series of questionnaires are distributed to a panel of decision makers, who submit initial responses to a decision coordinator. The coordinator summarizes the solutions and sends the summary back to the panel members, along with a follow-up questionnaire. Panel members again send in their responses, and the process is repeated until a consensus is reached and a clear decision emerges.

Computer-Mediated Decision Making Today's information and computer technologies enable group decision making to take place across great distances with the support of group decision support systems. The growing use of *electronic brainstorming* is one example of the trend toward virtual meetings. Assisted by special software, participants use personal computers to enter ideas at will, either through simultaneous interaction or over a period of time. The software compiles and disseminates the results. Both the nominal group and Delphi techniques also lend themselves to computer mediation. Electronic approaches to group decision making can offer several advantages, including the benefits of anonymity, greater number of ideas generated, efficiency of recording and storing for later use, and ability to handle large groups with geographically dispersed members.[85]

■ The **Delphi technique** involves generating decision-making alternatives through a series of survey questionnaires.

High Performance Teams

When we think of the word "teams," a variety of popular sporting teams usually comes to mind. Work groups can also be considered as teams to the extent that they meet the demands of this definition. A **team** is a small group of people with complementary skills, who work actively together to achieve a common purpose for which they hold themselves collectively accountable.[86]

Teams are one of the major forces behind today's revolutionary changes in organizations. Management scholar Jay Conger calls the team-based organization the management system of the future, the business world's response to the need for speed in an ever more competitive environment.[87] He cites the example of an American jet engine manufacturer that switched to cross-functional teams instead of traditional functional work units. The firm cut the time required to design and produce new engines by 50 percent. Conger says: "Cross-functional teams are speed machines."[88] Clearly, we need to know more about such teams and teamwork in organizations.

■ **Teams** are groups of people who work actively together to achieve a purpose for which they are all accountable.

■ TYPES OF TEAMS

A major challenge in any organization is to turn formal groups into true high performance teams in any of the following settings.[89] First, there are *teams that recommend things*. Established to study specific problems and recommend solutions to them, these teams typically work with a target completion date and disband once their purpose has been fulfilled. They are temporary groups including task forces, ad hoc committees, project teams, and the like. Members of these teams must be able to learn quickly how to work well together, accomplish the assigned task, and make good action recommendations for followup work by other people.

Second, there are *teams that run things*. These management teams consist of people with the formal responsibility for leading other groups. These teams may exist at all levels of responsibility, from the individual work unit composed of a team leader and team members to the top management team composed of a CEO and other senior executives. Teams can add value to work processes at any level and offer special opportunities for dealing with complex problems and uncertain situations. Key issues addressed by top management teams, for example, include identifying overall organizational purposes, goals, and values, crafting strategies, and persuading others to support them.[90]

Third, there are *teams that make or do things*. These are functional groups and work units that perform ongoing tasks, such as marketing or manufacturing. Members of these teams must have good long-term working relationships with one another, solid operating systems, and the external support needed to achieve effectiveness over a sustained period of time. And they need energy to keep up the pace and meet the day-to-day challenges of sustained high performance.

■ THE NATURE OF TEAMWORK

All teams need members who believe in team goals and are motivated to work with others actively to accomplish important tasks—whether those tasks involve recommending things, making or doing things, or running things. Indeed, an essential criterion of a true team is that the members feel "collectively accountable" for what they accomplish.[91]

This sense of collective accountability sets the stage for real **teamwork**, where team members actively working together in such a way that all their respective skills are well utilized to achieve a common purpose.[92] A commitment to teamwork is found in the willingness of every member to "listen and respond constructively to views expressed by others, give others the benefit of the doubt, provide support, and recognize the interests and achievements of others."[93] Teamwork of this type is the central foundation of any high performance team. But developing it is a challenging leadership task, regardless of the setting. It takes a lot more work to build a well-functioning team, than to simply assign members to the same group and then expect them to do a great job.[94] See for example, The Effective Manager 2.5.

High performance teams have specific characteristics that allow them to excel at teamwork and achieve special performance advantages. First, *high performance teams have strong core values* that help guide their attitudes and behaviors in directions consistent with the team's purpose. Such values act as

■ **Teamwork** occurs when group members work together in ways that utilize their skills well to accomplish a purpose.

THE EFFECTIVE MANAGER 2.5

HOW TO CREATE A HIGH-PERFORMING TEAM

- Communicate high-performance standards.
- Set the tone in the first team meeting.
- Create a sense of urgency.
- Make sure members have the right skills.
- Establish clear rules for team behavior.
- As a leader, model expected behaviors.
- Find ways to create early "successes."
- Continually introduce new facts and information.
- Make sure members spend a lot of time together.
- Give positive feedback and reward high performance.

OB Across Functions

RESEARCH & DEVELOPMENT

Working Together Across Cultures

"Something magical happens," says John Thomas, project engineer in the Science and Technology's Process Modeling and Measurement Directorate, when Corning scientists from the Fontainebleau Research Center in France and those at Sullivan Park solve a problem together. This is not because they've entered some big melting pot where everyone thinks the same. No, that "something magical" comes from an environment that honors, and even demands, the different perspectives inherent in the two cultures. "Europeans are very creative thinkers, they take time to really reflect on a problem to come up with the very best theoretical solution," states Thomas. "Americans are more tactical and practical—we want to get down to developing a working solution as soon as possible." His partner at the Fontainebleau Research Center in France, Patrick Herveé, summarizes the difference this way: "The French are more focused on ideas and concepts. If we get blocked in the execution of those ideas, we give up. Not the Americans. They pay more attention to details, processes and time schedules. They make sure they are prepared and have involved everyone in the planning process so that they won't get blocked. But it's best if you mix the two approaches. In the end, you will achieve the best results."

an internal control system for a group or team and can substitute for much of the outside direction that a supervisor might otherwise provide. Second, *high performance teams turn a general sense of purpose into specific performance objectives.* Whereas a shared sense of purpose gives general direction to a team, commitment to specific performance results— such as reducing the time of getting the product to market by half, makes this purpose truly meaningful. Specific objectives provide a focus for solving problems and resolving conflicts, and they set standards for measuring results and obtaining performance feedback. They also help group members understand the need for "collective" versus purely individual efforts. Third, members of *high performance teams have the right mix of skills*, including technical skills, problem-solving and decision-making skills, and interpersonal skills. Finally, *high performance teams possess creativity.* In the new workplace, teams must use their creativity to assist organizations in continuous improvement of operations—including productivity and customer service—and in continuous development of new products, services, and markets.

■ DIVERSITY AND TEAM PERFORMANCE

In order to create and maintain high performance teams, all of the various elements of group effectiveness must be addressed and successfully managed. Among them, membership diversity as an important input to group and team dynamics carries special significance in today's workplace.[95] When team members are homogeneous, that is, when members are alike in respect to such things as age, gender, race, ethnicity, experience, ethnicity and culture, there are certain potential benefits. It will probably be easy for them to quickly build social relationships and begin the interactions needed to work harmoniously together. On the other hand, the homogeneity may be limiting in terms of ideas, viewpoints, and creativity. With team diversity in terms of demography, experiences, and cultures, by contrast, comes a rich pool of information, talent, and varied perspectives that can help improve problem solving and increase creativity. These assets are especially valuable when the team is working on complex and very demanding tasks.

Research indicates that diversity among team members may create performance difficulties early in the team's life or stage of development. This occurs when interpersonal stresses and conflicts relating to diversity slow down group processes such as relationship building, problem definition, and information sharing.[96] But even though diverse teams may struggle in the short run to resolve these issues, they are also likely to develop enhanced performance potential once things are worked out.[97] Although it may take a bit more time and effort to create teamwork from foundations of diversity, longer-term gains in creativity and performance can make it all worthwhile. Teamwork rich in diversity is one of the great advantages of high performance organizations.

Team Building

Teamwork doesn't always happen naturally in a group. It is something that team members and leaders must work hard to achieve. In the sports world, for example, coaches and managers focus on teamwork when building new teams at the start of each season. And as you are aware, even experienced teams often run into problems as a season progresses. Members slack off or become disgruntled; some have performance "slumps;" some are traded to other teams. Even world-champion teams have losing streaks, and the most talented players can lose motivation at times, quibble among themselves, and end up contributing little to team success. When these things happen, the owners, managers, and players are apt to examine their problems, take corrective action to rebuild the team, and restore the teamwork needed to achieve high performance results.

Work groups and teams have similar difficulties. When newly formed, they must master challenges in the early stages of group development. Even when they are mature, most work teams encounter problems of insufficient teamwork at different points in time. When difficulties occur, or as a means of preventing them from occurring, a systematic process of **team building** can help. This is a sequence of planned activities designed to gather and analyze data on the functioning of a group and to initiate changes designed to improve teamwork and increase group effectiveness.[98]

■ **Team building** is a collaborative way to gather and analyze data to improve teamwork.

■ HOW TEAM BUILDING WORKS

The action steps and continuous improvement theme highlighted in Figure 2.8 are typical of most team-building approaches. The process begins when someone no-

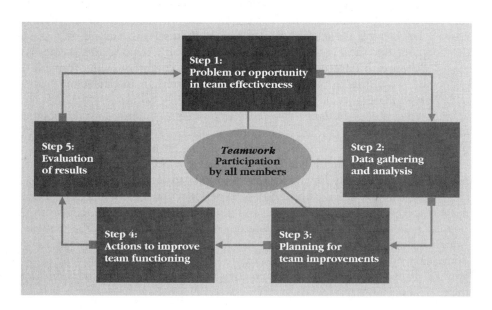

**Figure 2.8
The team-building
process.**

tices that a problem exists or may develop with team effectiveness. Members then work together to gather data relating to the problem, analyze these data, plan for improvements, and implement the action plans. The entire team-building process is highly collaborative. Everyone is expected to participate actively as group operations are evaluated and decisions are made on what needs to be done to improve the team's functioning in the future. This process can and should become an ongoing part of any team's work agenda. It is an approach to continuous improvement that can be very beneficial to long-term team effectiveness.

Team-building is participatory, and it is data based. Whether the data are gathered by questionnaire, interview, nominal group meeting, or other creative methods, the goal is to get good answers to such questions as: "How well are we doing in terms of task accomplishment?"... "How satisfied are we as individual members with the group and the way it operates?" There are a variety of ways for such questions to be asked and answered in a collaborative and motivating manner.

■ APPROACHES TO TEAM BUILDING

In the *formal retreat approach*, team building takes place during an off-site "retreat." During this retreat, which may last from one to several days, group members work intensively on a variety of assessment and planning tasks. They are initiated by a review of team functioning using data gathered through survey, interviews, or other means. Formal retreats are often held with the assistance of a consultant, who is either hired from the outside or made available from in-house staff. Team-building retreats are quite common and offer opportunities for intense and concentrated efforts to examine group accomplishments and operations.

Not all team building is done in a formal retreat format or with the assistance of consultants. In a *continuous improvement approach*, the manager, team leader, or group members themselves take responsibility for regularly engaging in the team-building process. This method can be as simple as periodic meetings that implement the team-building steps; it can also include self-managed formal retreats. In all cases, the team members commit themselves to monitoring group development and accomplishments continuously and making the day-to-day changes needed to ensure team effectiveness. Such continuous improvement of teamwork is essential to the total quality and total service management themes so important to organizations today.

In addition, the *outdoor experience approach* is an increasingly popular team-building activity that may be done on its own or in combination with other approaches. The outdoor experience places group members in a variety of physically challenging situations that must be mastered through teamwork, not individual work. By having to work together in the face of difficult obstacles, team members are supposed to experience increased self-confidence, more respect for others' capabilities, and a greater commitment to teamwork. A popular sponsor of team building through outdoor experience is the Outward Bound Leadership School, but many others exist. For a group that has never done team building before, outdoor experience can be an exciting way to begin; for groups familiar with team building, it can be a way of further enriching the experience.

Improving Team Processes

Like many changes in the new workplace, the increased emphasis on teams and teamwork is a major challenge for people used to more traditional ways of working. As more and more jobs are turned over to teams and as more and more traditional supervisors are asked to function as team leaders, special problems relating to team processes may arise. As teams become more integral to organizations, multiple and shifting memberships can cause complications. Team leaders and members alike must be prepared to deal positively with such issues as introducing new members, handling disagreements on goals and responsibilities, resolving delays and disputes when making decisions, and reducing friction and interpersonal conflicts. Given the complex nature of group dynamics, team building in a sense is never done. Something is always happening that creates the need for further leadership efforts to help improve team processes.

■ NEW MEMBER PROBLEMS

Special difficulties are likely to occur when members first get together in a new group or work team, or when new members join an existing one. Problems often arise as new members try to understand what is expected of them while dealing with anxiety and discomfort in a new social setting. New members, for example, may worry about: *Participation*—"Will I be allowed to participate?" *Goals*—"Do I share the same goals as others?" *Control*—"Will I be able to influence what takes place?" *Relationships*—"How close do people get?" *Processes*—"Are conflicts likely to be upsetting?"

Edgar Schein points out that people may try to cope with individual entry problems in self-serving ways that may hinder group operations.[99] He identifies three behavior profiles that are common in such situations. The *tough battler* is frustrated by a lack of identity in the new group and may act aggressively or reject authority. This person wants answers to the question: "Who am I in this group?" The *friendly helper* is insecure, suffering uncertainties of intimacy and control. This person may show extraordinary support for others, behave in a dependent way, and seek alliances in subgroups or cliques. The friendly helper needs to know whether she or he will be liked. The *objective thinker* is anxious about how personal needs will be met in the group. This person may act in a passive, reflective, and even single-minded manner while struggling with the fit between individual goals and group directions.

■ TASK AND MAINTENANCE LEADERSHIP

Research in social psychology suggests that the achievement of sustained high performance by groups requires that both "task needs" and "maintenance needs" be met.[100] Although anyone formally appointed as group leader should help fulfill these needs, all members should also contribute. This responsibility for **distributed leadership** in group dynamics is an important requirement of any high performance team.[101]

Figure 2.9 describes group **task activities** as the various things members do that directly contribute to the performance of important group tasks. They include

■ **Distributed leadership** is the sharing of responsibility for meeting group task and maintenance needs.

■ **Task activities** directly contribute to the performance of important tasks.

Figure 2.9
Task and maintenance leadership in group team dynamics.

activities such as initiating discussion, sharing information, asking information of others, clarifying something that has been said, and summarizing the status of a deliberation.[102] If these task activities are not adequate, the group will have difficulty accomplishing its objectives. By contrast, in an effective group, members contribute important task activities as needed and as building blocks for performance success.

■ **Maintenance activities** support the emotional life of the team as an ongoing social system.

Maintenance activities support the group's social and interpersonal relationships. They help the group stay intact and healthy as an ongoing social system. A member contributes maintenance leadership, for example, by encouraging the participation of others, trying to harmonize differences of opinion, praising the contributions of others, and agreeing to go along with a popular course of action. When maintenance leadership is poor, members become dissatisfied with one another and their group membership. This sets the stage for conflicts that can drain energies otherwise needed for task performance. In an effective group, by contrast, maintenance activities help sustain the relationships needed for group members to work well together over time.

In addition to helping meet a group's task and maintenance needs, group members share the additional responsibility of avoiding *disruptive behaviors*—behaviors that harm the group process. Full participation in distributed leadership means taking individual responsibility for avoiding the following types of behaviors, and helping others do the same:

Disruptive behaviors that harm teams

1. Being overly aggressive toward other members.
2. Withdrawing and refusing to cooperate with others.
3. Horsing around when there is work to be done.
4. Using the group as a forum for self-confession.
5. Talking too much about irrelevant matters.
6. Trying to compete for attention and recognition.

■ ROLES AND ROLE DYNAMICS

■ A **role** is a set of expectations for a team member or person in a job.

In groups and teams, new and old members alike need to know what others expect of them and what they can expect from others. A **role** is a set of expectations associated with a job or position on a team. When roles are unclear or conflictive, performance problems can occur. Groups and work teams sometimes experience problems that are caused by difficulties in defining and managing the roles of members.

Role ambiguity occurs when a person is uncertain about his or her role. To do any job well, people need to know what is expected of them. In new group or team situations, role ambiguities may create problems as members find that their work efforts are wasted or unappreciated by others. Even on mature groups and teams, the failure of members to share expectations and listen to one another may at times create a similar lack of understanding. Being asked to do too much or too little can also create problems. **Role overload** occurs when too much is expected and the individual feels overwhelmed with work. **Role underload** occurs when too little is expected and the individual feels underutilized. Any group benefits from clear and realistic expectations regarding the contributions of each member.

Role conflict occurs when a person is unable to meet the expectations of others. The individual understands what needs to be done but for some reason cannot comply. The resulting tension can reduce job satisfaction and affect both work performance and relationships with other group members. Four common forms of role conflict are: (1) *Intrasender role conflict* occurs when the same person sends conflicting expectations. (2) *Intersender role conflict* occurs when different people send conflicting and mutually exclusive expectations. (3) *Person–role conflict* occurs when one's personal values and needs come into conflict with role expectations. (4) *Interrole conflict* occurs when the expectations of two or more roles held by the same individual become incompatible, such as the conflict between work and family demands.

One way of managing role dynamics in any group or work setting is by *role negotiation*. This is a process through which individuals negotiate to clarify the role expectations each holds for the other. Sample results from an actual role negotiation are shown in Figure 2.10. Note the "give and take" between negotiators.

■ POSITIVE NORMS

The **norms** of a group or team represent ideas or beliefs about how members are expected to behave. They can be considered as "rules" or "standards" of con-

■ **Role ambiguity** occurs when someone is uncertain about what is expected of him or her.

■ **Role overload** occurs when too much work is expected of the individual.

■ **Role underload** occurs when too little work is expected of the individual.

■ **Role conflict** occurs when someone is unable to respond to role expectations that conflict with one another.

Forms of role conflict

■ **Norms** are rules or standards for the behavior of group members.

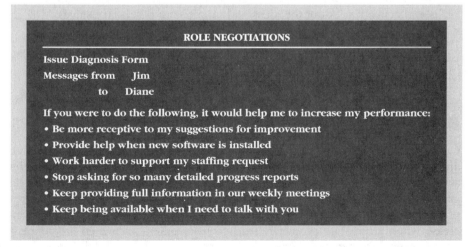

Figure 2.10
A sample role negotiations agreement.

THE EFFECTIVE MANAGER 2.6

SEVEN STEPS TO POSITIVE NORMS

1. Act as a positive role model.
2. Hold meetings to agree on goals.
3. Select members who can and will perform.
4. Provide support and training for members.
5. Reinforce and reward desired behaviors.
6. Hold meetings for feedback and performance review.
7. Hold meetings to plan for improvements.

duct.[103] Norms help clarify the expectations associated with a person's membership in a group. They allow members to structure their own behavior and to predict what others will do; they help members gain a common sense of direction; and they reinforce a desired group or team culture. When someone violates a group norm, other members typically respond in ways that are aimed at enforcing the norm. These responses may include direct criticisms, reprimands, expulsion, and social ostracism.

Managers, task force heads, committee chairs, and team leaders must all try to help their groups adopt positive norms that support organizational goals (see The Effective Manager 2.6). A key norm in any setting is the *performance norm*, which conveys expectations about how hard group members should work. Other norms are important too. In order for a task force or a committee to operate effectively, for example, norms regarding attendance at meetings, punctuality, preparedness, criticism, and social behaviors are needed. Groups also commonly have norms regarding how to deal with supervisors, colleagues, and customers, as well as norms establishing guidelines for honesty and ethical behaviors. The following list shows how everyday conversations can lend insight into the various types of norms that operate with positive and negative implications for groups and organizations.[104]

Types of group norms

- *Organizational and personal pride norms*—"It is a tradition around here for people to stand up for the company when others criticize it unfairly" (positive); "In our company, they are always trying to take advantage of us" (negative).

- *High-achievement norms*—"On our team, people always try to work hard" (positive); "There's no point in trying harder on our team, nobody else does" (negative).

- *Support and helpfulness norms*—"People on this committee are good listeners and actively seek out the ideas and opinions of others" (positive); "On this committee it's dog-eat-dog and save your own skin" (negative).

- *Improvement and change norms*—"In our department people are always looking for better ways of doing things" (positive); "Around here, people hang on to the old ways even after they have outlived their usefulness" (negative).

■ TEAM COHESIVENESS

■ **Cohesiveness** is the degree to which members are attracted to a group and motivated to remain a part of it.

Group or team **cohesiveness** is the degree to which members are attracted to and motivated to remain part of it.[105] Cohesiveness tends to be high when members are similar in age, attitudes, needs, and backgrounds. It is also high in groups of small size, where members respect one another's competencies, agree on common goals, and work on interdependent tasks. Cohesiveness tends to increase when groups are physically isolated from others and when they experience performance success or crisis.

Persons in a highly cohesive group value their membership and strive to maintain positive relationships with other group members. In this sense, cohe-

Figure 2.11
How cohesiveness and conformity to norms affect group performance.

sive groups and teams are good for their members. In contrast to less cohesive groups, members of highly cohesive ones tend to be more energetic when working on group activities, less likely to be absent, and more likely to be happy about performance success and sad about failures. Cohesive groups generally have low turnover and satisfy a broad range of individual needs, often providing a source of loyalty, security, and esteem for their members.

Conformity to Norms   Even though cohesive groups are good for their members, they may or may not be good for the organization. Figure 2.11 demonstrates the performance implications for a basic *rule of conformity in group dynamics*: the more cohesive the group, the greater the conformity of members to group norms.

When the performance norms are positive in a highly cohesive work group or team, the resulting conformity to the norm should have a positive effect on task performance as well as member satisfaction. This is a "best-case" situation for everyone. When the performance norms are negative in a highly cohesive group, however, the same power of conformity can have undesirable results. As shown in the figure, this creates a "worst-case" situation for the organization. Although team members are highly motivated to support group norms, the organization suffers from poor performance results. In between these two extremes are mixed-case situations in which a lack of cohesion fails to rally strong conformity to the norm. With its strength reduced, the outcome of the norm is somewhat unpredictable and performance will most likely fall on the moderate or low side.

Influencing Cohesiveness   Team leaders and managers must be aware of the steps they can take to build cohesiveness, such as in a group that has positive norms but suffers from low cohesiveness. They must also be ready to deal with situations when cohesiveness adds to the problems of negative and hard-to-

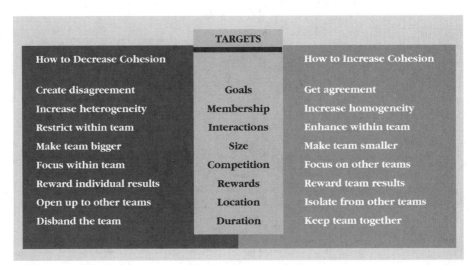

Figure 2.12
Ways to increase and decrease group cohesiveness.

change performance norms. Figure 2.12 shows how group cohesiveness can be increased or decreased by making changes in group goals, membership composition, interactions, size, rewards, competition, location, and duration.

Teams and the High Performance Workplace

When it was time to re-engineer its order-to-delivery process to eliminate an uncompetitive and costly 26-day cycle time, Hewlett-Packard turned to a team. In just nine months they slashed the time to eight days, improved service, and cut costs. How did they do it? Team leader Julie Anderson says: "We took things away: no supervisors, no hierarchy, no titles, no job descriptions…the idea was to create a sense of personal ownership." Says a team member: "…no individual is going to have the best idea, that's not the way it works—the best ideas come from the collective intelligence of the team."[106]

Just like this example from Hewlett-Packard, organizations everywhere in the new workplace are finding creative ways of using teams to solve problems and make changes to improve performance. The watchwords of these new approaches to teamwork are empowerment, participation, and involvement, and the setting is increasingly described as an organization that looks and acts much more "lateral" or "horizontal" than vertical.[107]

■ PROBLEM-SOLVING TEAMS

■ Members of **employee involvement teams** meet regularly to examine work-related problems and opportunities.

One way organizations can use teams is in creative problem solving. The term **employee involvement team** applies to a wide variety of teams whose members meet regularly to collectively examine important workplace issues. They discuss ways to enhance quality, better satisfy customers, raise productivity, and improve the quality of work life. In this way, employee involvement teams mobilize the full extent of workers' know-how and gain the commitment needed to fully implement solutions.

A special type of employee involvement group is the **quality circle**, or QC for short. It is a small group of persons who meet periodically (e.g., an hour or so, once a week) to discuss and develop solutions for problems relating to quality, productivity, or cost.[108] QCs are popular in organizations around the world, but cannot be seen as panaceas for all of an organization's ills. To be successful, members of QCs should receive special training in group dynamics, information gathering, and problem analysis techniques. Leaders of quality circles should also be trained in participation and team building. Any solutions to problems should be jointly pursued by QC members and organizational management. QCs work best in organizations that place a clear emphasis on quality in their mission and goals, promote a culture that supports participation and empowerment, encourage trust and willingness to share important information, and develop a "team spirit."

■ Members of a **quality circle** meet regularly to find ways for continuous improvement of quality operations.

■ CROSS-FUNCTIONAL TEAMS

In today's organizations, teams are essential components in the achievement of more horizontal integration and better lateral relations. The **cross-functional team**, consisting of members representing different functional departments or work units, plays an important role in this regard. Traditionally, many organizations have suffered from what is often called the **functional silos problem**. This problem occurs when members of functional units stay focused on matters internal to the function and minimize their interactions with members of other functions. In this sense, the functional departments or work units create artificial boundaries or "silos" that discourage rather than encourage more integrative thinking and active coordination with other parts of the organization.

■ **Cross-functional teams** bring together persons from different functions to work on a common task.

■ The **functional silos problem** is when persons working in different functions fail to communicate and interact with one another.

The new team-based organizations are designed to help break down this problem and improve lateral communication.[109] Members of cross-functional teams can solve problems with a positive combination of functional expertise and integrative or total systems thinking. They do so with the great advantages of better information and more speed. Boeing, for example, used this concept to great advantage in designing and bringing to market the 777 passenger jet.[110] A complex network of cross-functional teams brought together design engineers, mechanics, pilots, suppliers, and even customers to manage the "design/build" processes.

■ VIRTUAL TEAMS

Until recently, teamwork was confined in concept and practice to those circumstances in which members could meet face-to-face. Now, the advent of new technologies and sophisticated computer programs known as groupware have changed all that. **Virtual teams**, introduced in the last chapter as ones whose members meet at least part of the time electronically and with computer support, are a fact of life.[111] The real world of work in businesses and other organizations today involves a variety of electronic communications that allow people to work together through computer mediation, and often separated by vast geographical space. *Groupware*, in popular forms such as Lotus Domino, Microsoft Exchange and Netscape SuiteSpot, allows for virtual meetings and group decision making

■ A **virtual team** convenes and operates with members linked together electronically via networked computers.

in a variety of forms and situations.[112] This is further supported by advancements in conferencing and collaboration, including audio, data, and video conferencing alternatives.[113]

Virtual teams offer a number of potential advantages. They bring cost-effectiveness and speed to teamwork where members are unable to meet easily face-to-face. They also bring the power of the computer to bear on typical team needs for information processing and decision making.[114] With the computer as the "go-between" for virtual team members, however, group dynamics can emerge with a slightly different form than found in face-to-face settings.[115] Although technology can help to overcome great distance in making communication possible among a group of people, it may also create teams whose members do not share much, if any, direct "personal" contact. Whereas this may have an advantage of focusing interaction and decision making on facts and objective information rather than emotional considerations, it also may increase risks as decisions are made in a limited social context. Virtual teams may suffer from less social rapport and less direct interaction among members.

Just as with any form of teamwork, virtual teams rely on the efforts and contributions of their members as well as organizational support to achieve effectiveness. Teamwork in any form always takes work. The same stages of development, the same input considerations, and same process requirements are likely to apply in a virtual team as with any team. Where possible, the advantages of face-to-face and virtual teamwork should be combined for maximum benefit. The computer technology should also be appropriate and team members should be well trained in using it.[116]

■ SELF-MANAGING TEAMS

■ **Self-managing teams** are empowered to make decisions about planning, doing, and evaluating their daily work.

A high-involvement work group design that is increasingly well-established today is known as the **self-managing team**. These are small groups empowered to make the decisions needed to manage themselves on a day-to-day basis.[117] Although there are different variations of this theme, members of a true self-managing work team make decisions on scheduling work, allocating tasks, training for job skills, evaluating performance, selecting new team members, and controlling quality of work. Members are collectively held accountable for the team's overall performance results.

How Self-Managing Teams Work Self-managing teams, also called *self-directed teams* or *empowered teams*, are permanent and formal elements in the organizational structure. They replace the traditional work group headed by a supervisor. What differentiates self-managing teams from the more traditional work group is that the team members assume duties otherwise performed by a manager or first-line supervisor. The team members, not a supervisor, perform and are collectively accountable for such activities as planning and work scheduling, performance evaluation, and quality control.

A self-managing team should probably include between 5 and 15 members. The teams must be large enough to provide a good mix of skills and resources, but small enough to function efficiently.

■ **Multiskilling** occurs when team members are trained in skills to perform different jobs.

Members must have substantial discretion in determining work pace and in distributing tasks. This is made possible, in part, by **multiskilling**, whereby team members are trained in performing more than one job on the team. In self-managing teams, each person is expected to perform many different jobs—even all of the team's jobs, as needed. The more skills someone masters, the higher the base pay. Team members themselves conduct the job training and certify one another as having mastered the required skills.

Operational Implications of Self-Managing Teams   The expected benefits of self-managing teams include productivity and quality improvements, production flexibility and faster response to technological change, reduced absenteeism and turnover, and improved work attitudes and quality of work life. But these results are not guaranteed. Like all organizational changes, the shift to self-managing teams can encounter difficulties. Structural changes in job classifications and management levels will have consequent implications for supervisors and others used to more traditional ways. Simply put, with a self-managing team you don't need the formal first-line supervisor anymore. The possible extent of this change is shown in Figure 2.13, where the first level of supervisory management has been eliminated and replaced by self-managing teams. Note also that many of the supervisor's traditional tasks are reallocated to the team.

For persons used to more traditional work, the new arrangement can be challenging; for managers learning to deal with self-managing teams rather than individual workers, the changeover can be difficult; for any supervisors displaced by self-managing teams, the implications are even more personal and threatening.

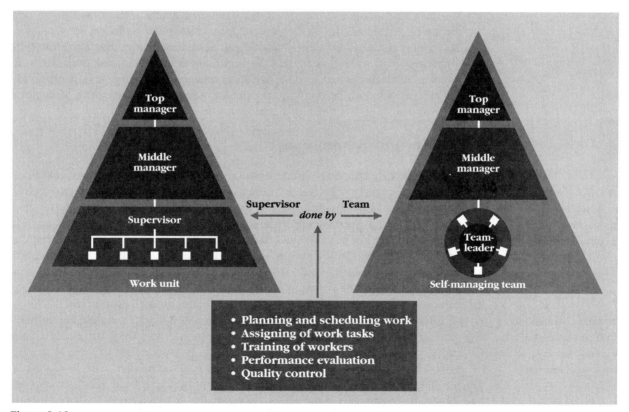

Figure 2.13
Organizational and management implications of self-managing teams.

Given this situation, a question must be asked: *Should all work groups operate as self-managing teams?* The best answer is "No." Self-managing teams are probably not right for all organizations, work situations, and people. They have great potential, but they also require a proper setting and support. At a minimum, the essence of any self-managing team—high involvement, participation, and empowerment, must be consistent with the values and culture of the organization.

Decision Making Process

■ **Decision making** is choosing a course of action to deal with a problem.

Formally defined, **decision making** is the process of choosing a course of action for dealing with a problem or opportunity.[118] The five basic steps involved in systematic decision making are:

Five steps in decision making

1. Recognize and define the problem or opportunity.
2. Identify and analyze alternative courses of action, and estimate their effects on the problem or opportunity.
3. Choose a preferred course of action.
4. Implement the preferred course of action.
5. Evaluate the results and follow up as necessary.

We must also recognize that in settings where substantial change and many new technologies prevail, this step-by-step approach may not be followed. Occasionally, a nontraditional sequence works and yields superior performance over the traditional view. We also think it is important to consider the ethical consequences of decision making. To understand when and where to use the traditional or novel decision techniques calls for a further understanding of decision environments and the types of decisions to be made.

■ DECISION ENVIRONMENTS

■ **Certain environments** provide full information on the expected results for decision-making alternatives.

Problem-solving decisions in organizations are typically made under three different conditions or environments: certainty, risk, and uncertainty.[119] **Certain environments** exist when information is sufficient to predict the results of each alternative in advance of implementation. When a person invests money in a savings account, for example, absolute certainty exists about the interest that will be earned on that money in a given period of time. Certainty is an ideal condition for managerial problem solving and decision making. The challenge is simply to locate the alternative offering the best or ideal solution. Unfortunately, certainty is the exception instead of the rule in decision environments.

■ **Risk environments** provide probabilities regarding expected results for decision-making alternatives.

Risk environments exist when decision makers lack complete certainty regarding the outcomes of various courses of action, but they are aware of the probabilities associated with their occurrence. A *probability*, in turn, is the degree of likelihood of an event's occurrence. Probabilities can be assigned through objective statistical procedures or through personal intuition. For instance, managers can make statistical estimates of quality rejects in production runs, or a senior production manager can make similar estimates based on past experience. Risk is a common decision environment in today's organizations.

Uncertain environments exist when managers have so little information on hand that they cannot even assign probabilities to various alternatives and their possible outcomes. This is the most difficult of the three decision environments. Uncertainty forces decision makers to rely heavily on individual and group creativity to succeed in problem solving. It requires unique, novel, and often totally innovative alternatives to existing patterns of behavior. Responses to uncertainty are often heavily influenced by intuition, educated guesses, and hunches. Furthermore, an uncertain decision environment may also be characterized as a rapidly changing organizational setting in terms of (a) external conditions, (b) the information technology requirements called for to analyze and make decisions, and (c) the personnel influencing problem and choice definitions. This has been called an **organized anarchy**, a firm or division in a firm in a transition characterized by very rapid change and lack of a legitimate hierarchy and collegiality. Although this was once a very unique setting, many high-tech firms and those with expanding global operations share many of the characteristics of an organized anarchy.

■ TYPES OF DECISIONS

The many routine and nonroutine problems in the modern workplace call for different types of decisions. Routine problems arise on a regular basis and can be addressed through standard responses, called **programmed decisions**. These decisions simply implement solutions that have already been determined by past experience as appropriate for the problem at hand. Examples of programmed decisions are reordering inventory automatically when stock falls below a predetermined level and issuing a written reprimand to someone who violates a certain personnel procedure.

Nonroutine problems are unique and new, having never been encountered before. Because standard responses are not available, these circumstances call for creative problem solving. These **nonprogrammed decisions** are specifically crafted or tailored to the situation at hand. Higher level managers generally spend a greater proportion of their decision-making time on nonroutine problems. An example is a senior marketing manager who has to respond to the introduction of a new product by a foreign competitor. Although past experience may help deal with this competitive threat, the immediate decision requires a creative solution based on the unique characteristics of the present market situation.

For firms in or characterized by "organized anarchy," we also suggest there is a third class of decisions called associative choices. **Associative choices** are decisions that can be loosely linked to nagging continual problems but that were not specifically developed to solve the problem. Given the chaotic nature of the setting, the necessity to take action as opposed to waiting, and the ability of employees to make nearly any "decision" work, a stream of associative choices may be used to improve the setting, even though the problems are not solved.

■ Uncertain environments provide no information to predict expected results for decision-making alternatives.

■ Organized anarchy is a firm or division in a firm in a transition characterized by very rapid change and lack of a legitimate hierarchy.

■ Programmed decisions are determined by past experience as appropriate for a problem at hand.

■ Nonprogrammed decisions are created to deal uniquely with a problem at hand.

■ Associative choices are decisions that can be loosely linked to nagging continual problems but that were not specifically developed to solve the problem.

Decision Making Models

The field of organizational behavior historically emphasizes two alternative approaches to decision making—classical and behavioral (see Figure 2.14).[120]

Figure 2.14
Decision making viewed from the classical and behavioral perspectives.

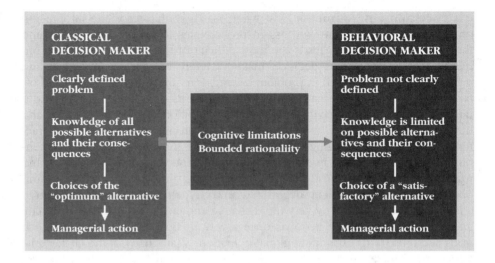

CLASSICAL DECISION MAKER

Clearly defined problem

Knowledge of all possible alternatives and their consequences

Choices of the "optimum" alternative

Managerial action

Cognitive limitations
Bounded rationaliity

BEHAVIORAL DECISION MAKER

Problem not clearly defined

Knowledge is limited on possible alternatives and their consequences

Choice of a "satisfactory" alternative

Managerial action

■ **Classical decision theory** views decision makers as acting in a world of complete certainty.

■ **Behavioral decision theory** views decision makers as acting only in terms of what they perceive about a given situation.

Classical decision theory models view the manager as acting in a world of complete certainty. **Behavioral decision theory** models accept the notion of bounded rationality and suggests that people act only in terms of what they perceive about a given situation.

■ CLASSICAL AND BEHAVIORAL DECISION THEORY

Ideally, the manager faces a clearly defined problem, knows all possible action alternatives and their consequences, and then chooses the alternative that offers the best, or "optimum," solution to the problem. This optimizing style is an ideal way to make decisions. This classical approach is normative and prescriptive, and is often used as a model for how managers should make decisions.

Behavioral scientists are cautious about applying classical decision theory to many decision situations. They recognize that the human mind is a wonderful creation, capable of infinite achievements. But they also recognize that human beings have *cognitive limitations* that restrict their information-processing capabilities. Information deficiencies and overload compromise the ability of decision makers to achieve complete certainty and otherwise operate according to the classical model. Human decision makers also operate with *bounded rationality*.[121] Bounded rationality is a short-hand term suggesting that, while individuals are reasoned and logical, humans have their limits. Individuals interpret and make sense of things within the context of their personal situation. They engage in decision making "within the box" of a simplified view of a more complex reality. This makes it difficult to realize the ideal of classical decision making. As a result, the classical model does not give a full and accurate description of how most decisions are made in organizations.[122]

Classical decision theory does not appear to fit today's chaotic world of globalizing high-tech organizations, yet it would be a mistake to dismiss it and the types of progress that can be made with classical models. Classical models can be used toward the bottom of many firms. For instance, even the most high-tech firm faces many clearly defined problems with known alternatives where firms have already selected an optimal solution. That a firm's managers don't know the answer may make it appear nonclassical when, in fact, it should not be.

As noted above, **behavioral decision theory** models accept the notion of bounded rationality and suggest that people act only in terms of what they perceive about a given situation. Because these perceptions are frequently imperfect, most organizational decision making does not take place in a world of complete certainty. Rather, the behavioral decision maker is viewed as acting most often under uncertain conditions and with limited information. Organizational decision makers face problems that are often ambiguous, and they have only partial knowledge of the available action alternatives and their consequences. This leads to a phenomenon which Herbert Simon has described as **satisficing**—decision makers choose the first alternative that appears to give an acceptable or a satisfactory resolution of the problem. As Simon states: "Most human decision making, whether individual or organizational, is concerned with the discovery and selection of satisfactory alternatives; only in exceptional cases is it concerned with the discovery and selection of optimal decisions."[123]

■ **Satisficing** is choosing the first alternative that appears to give an acceptable or satisfactory resolution of the problem.

■ THE GARBAGE CAN MODEL

A third view of decision making stems from the so-called **garbage can model**.[124] In this view, the main components of the choice process—problems, solutions, participants, and choice situations—are all mixed up together in the "garbage can" of the organization. In many organizations where the setting is stable and the technology is well known and fixed, tradition, strategy, and the administrative structure help order the contents of the garbage can. Specific problems can be matched to specific solutions, an orderly process can be maintained, and the behavior view of decision making may be appropriate.

■ **Garbage can model** views the main components of the choice process—problems, solutions, participants, and choice situations—as all mixed up together in the garbage can of the organization.

But when the setting is dynamic, the technology is changing, demands are conflicting or the goals are unclear, things can get mixed up. More action than thinking can take place. Solutions emerge as "potential capabilities"—capabilities independent of problems or opportunities. Solutions often emerge not to solve specific problems but as lessons learned from the experience of other organizations. These new solution/capabilities may be in the form of new employees, new technical experts, consultants, or reports on best practices. Many solutions might well be implemented even if they cannot be tied to a specific problem. Solutions may also be implemented when no other solution has solved a persistent, chronic problem. Although implemented solutions change the organization, they are unlikely to solve specific problems.

The garbage can model highlights an important feature of decision making in many large organizations. Choice making and implementation may be done by quite different individuals. Often, the job of subordinates is to make the decisions of senior managers work. They must interpret the intentions of their bosses as well as solve local problems. Implementation becomes an opportunity to instill many changes related to the choice of more senior executives. So what is chosen gets implemented along with many other changes. The link between choice and implementation may become even weaker when senior managers are vague or do not vigorously follow up on implementation. The net result from those actually implementing the decision is the appearance that what was chosen does not exactly match what is implemented.

There is a final aspect of the garbage can view. Many problems go unsolved. That is, all organizations have chronic, persistent deficiencies that never seem to get much better. In a garbage can view, this is because decision makers cannot agree to match these problems with solutions, make a choice, and implement it on a timely and consistent basis; nor do they know how to resolve chronic problems. It is only when a problem and a solution "bump into one another" under a decision maker willing to implement a choice that problems, solutions, and choice come together as expected under other views. Thus, one key job challenge for the astute manager is to make the appropriate linkages among problems and solutions.

■ DECISION MAKING REALITIES

All three of these models highlight specific features of the complex choice processes managers must engage in as professionals. A key difference between a manager's ability to make an optimum decision in the classical style and the manager's tendency to make a satisfying decision in the behavioral style is the availability of information. The organizational realities of bounded rationality and cognitive limitations affect the way people define problems, identify action alternatives, and choose preferred courses of action. By necessity, most decision making in organizations involves more than the linear and step-by-step rational choice that models often suggest. The process may not be as chaotic as the garbage can models; yet it is often not as rational as even a behavioral view suggests. In real organizations, decisions must be made under risk and uncertainty. Decisions must be made to solve nonroutine problems. And decisions must be made under the pressures of time and information limitations.

Intuition, Judgment, and Creativity

Choices always bear the unique imprint of the individuals who make them, the politics within the organization, and the challenges facing its decision makers. In reality, intuition, judgment, and creativity are as critical as understanding how decisions can be made.

A key element in decision making under risk and uncertainty is intuition. **Intuition** is the ability to know or recognize quickly and readily the possibilities of a given situation.[125] Intuition adds elements of personality and spontaneity to decision making. As a result, it offers potential for creativity and innovation.

In an earlier time, scholars carried on a vigorous debate regarding how managers should plan and make decisions.[126] On one side of the issue were those who believed that planning could be accomplished in a systematic step-by-step fashion. On the other side were those who believed that the very nature of managerial work made this hard to achieve in actual practice. We now know that managers favor verbal communication. Thus, they are more likely to gather data and to make decisions in a relational or interactive way than in a systematic step-by-step fashion.[127] Managers often deal with impressions. Thus, they are more likely to synthesize than to analyze data as they search for the "big picture" in order to redefine

■ **Intuition** is the ability to know or recognize quickly the possibilities of a situation.

problems and link problems with a variety of solutions. Managers work fast, do a variety of things, and are frequently interrupted. Thus, they do not have a lot of quiet time alone to think, plan, or make decisions systematically (see The Effective Manager 2.7).

Are managers correct when they favor the more intuitive and less systematic approach? The more chaotic environments and technologies of many of today's organizations press for this emphasis on intuition. Unfortunately, many business firms are better at implementing the common solutions of others than uniquely solving their problems. Since managers do work in chaotic settings, this reality should be accepted and decision makers should be confident in using their intuitive skills. However, they should combine analytical and intuitive approaches to create new and novel solutions to complex problems.

THE EFFECTIVE MANAGER 2.7

WAYS TO IMPROVE INTUITION

Relaxation Techniques
• Drop the problem for a while.
• Spend some quiet time by yourself.
• Try to clear your mind.

Mental Exercises
• Use images to guide your thinking.
• Let ideas run freely without a specific goal.

■ JUDGMENTAL HEURISTICS

Judgment, or the use of one's intellect, is important in all aspects of decision making. When we question the ethics of a decision, for example, we are questioning the "judgment" of the person making it. Research shows that people are prone to mistakes using biases that often interfere with the quality of decision making.[128] These can be traced to the use of **heuristics**—simplifying strategies or "rules of thumb" used to make decisions. Heuristics serve a useful purpose in making it easier to deal with uncertainty and limited information in problem situations. But they can also lead to systematic errors that affect the quality, and perhaps the ethical implications, of any decisions made. It is helpful to understand the common judgmental heuristics of availability, representativeness, and anchoring and adjustment.[129]

■ **Heuristics** are simplifying strategies or "rules of thumb" used to make decisions.

The **availability heuristic** involves assessing a current event based on past occurrences that are easily available in one's memory. An example is the product development specialist who bases a decision not to launch a new product on her recent failure with another product offering. In this case, the existence of a past product failure has negatively, and perhaps inappropriately, biased the decision maker's judgment of how to best handle the new product.

■ The **availability heuristic** bases a decision on recent events relating to the situation at hand.

The **representativeness heuristic** involves assessing the likelihood that an event will occur based on its similarity to one's stereotypes of similar occurrences. An example is the team leader who selects a new member not because of any special qualities of the person, but only because the individual comes from a department known to have produced high performers in the past. In this case, it is the individual's current place of employment—and not his or her job qualifications—that is the basis for the selection decision.

■ The **representativeness heuristic** bases a decision on similarities between the situation at hand and stereotypes of similar occurrences.

The **anchoring and adjustment heuristic** involves assessing an event by taking an initial value from historical precedent or an outside source, and then incrementally adjusting this value to make a current assessment. An example is the executive who makes salary increase recommendations for key personnel by simply adjusting their current base salaries by a percentage amount. In this case, the existing base salary becomes an "anchor" that drives subsequent salary increases. In some situations this anchor may be inappropriate, such as the case of

■ The **anchoring and adjustment heuristic** bases a decision on incremental adjustments to an initial value determined by historical precedent or some reference point.

■ The **confirmation trap** is the tendency to seek confirmation for what is already thought to be true and to not search for disconfirming information.

■ The **hindsight trap** is a tendency to overestimate the degree to which an event that has already taken place could have been predicted.

■ **Creativity** generates unique and novel responses to problems. Individual decisions are made by one individual on behalf of a group.

an individual whose market value has become substantially higher than is reflected by the base salary plus increment.

In addition to using the common judgmental heuristics, decision makers are also prone to more general biases in decision making. One bias is the **confirmation trap**, whereby the decision maker seeks confirmation for what is already thought to be true and neglects opportunities to acknowledge or find disconfirming information. A form of selective perception, this bias involves seeking only those cues in a situation that support a preexisting opinion. A second bias is the **hindsight trap**, whereby the decision maker overestimates the degree to which he or she could have predicted an event that has already taken place. One risk of hindsight is that it may foster feelings of inadequacy or insecurity in dealing with future decision situations.

■ CREATIVITY FACTORS

Creativity in decision making involves the development of unique and novel responses to problems and opportunities. In a dynamic environment full of nonroutine problems, creativity in crafting decisions often determines how well people and organizations do in response to complex challenges.[130]

We examined the group as an important resource for improving creativity in decision making. Indeed, making good use of such traditional techniques as brainstorming, nominal groups, and the Delphi method can greatly expand the creative potential of people and organizations. The addition of new computer-based group meeting and decision-making techniques extends this great potential even further.

Creative thinking may unfold in a series of five stages. First is *preparation*.[131] Here people engage in the active learning and day-to-day sensing required to deal successfully with complex environments. The second stage is *concentration*, whereby actual problems are defined and framed so that alternatives can be considered for dealing with them. In the third stage, *incubation*, people look at the problems in diverse ways that permit the consideration of unusual alternatives, avoiding tendencies toward purely linear and systematic problem solving. The fourth stage is *illumination* in which people respond to flashes of insight and recognize when all pieces to the puzzle suddenly fit into place. The fifth and final stage is *verification*, which proceeds with logical analysis to confirm that good problem-solving decisions have really been made.[132]

All of these stages of creativity need support and encouragement in the organizational environment. However, creative thinking in decision making can be limited by a number of factors. Judgmental heuristics like those just reviewed can limit the search for alternatives. When attractive options are left unconsidered, creativity can be limited. Cultural and environmental blocks can also limit creativity. This occurs when people are discouraged from considering alternatives viewed as inappropriate by cultural standards or inconsistent with prevailing norms.

Managing the Decision-Making Process

As suggested by our discussion of creativity, people working at all levels, in all areas, and in all types and sizes of organizations are not supposed to simply make decisions. They must make *good* decisions—the right decisions in the right way at the right time.[133] Managing the decision-making process involves choices itself. Critical choices include which "problems" to work on, who to involve and how to involve them as well as when to quit.

■ CHOOSING PROBLEMS TO ADDRESS

Most people are too busy and have too many valuable things to do with their time to personally make the decisions on every problem or opportunity that comes their way. The effective manager and team leader knows when to delegate decisions to others, how to set priorities, and when to abstain from acting altogether. When faced with the dilemma of whether or not to deal with a specific problem, asking and answering the following questions can sometimes help.[134]

Is the problem easy to deal with? Small and less significant problems should not get the same time and attention as bigger ones. Even if a mistake is made, the cost of decision error on small problems is also small. *Might the problem resolve itself?* Putting problems in rank order leaves the less significant for last. Surprisingly, many of these less important problems resolve themselves or are solved by others before you get to them. One less problem to solve leaves decision-making time and energy for other uses. *Is this my decision to make?* Many problems can be handled by other persons. They should be delegated to people who are best prepared to deal with them; ideally, they should be delegated to people whose work they most affect. Finally, *is this a solvable problem within the context of the organization?* The astute decision maker recognizes the difference between problems that realistically can be solved and those that are simply not solvable for all practical purposes.

■ DECIDING WHO SHOULD PARTICIPATE

A mistake commonly made by many new managers and team leaders is presuming that they must solve every problem by making every decision themselves. In practice, good organizational decisions are made by individuals acting alone, by individuals consulting with others, and by groups of people working together.

When individual decisions, also called **authority decisions**, are made, the manager or team leader uses information that he or she possesses and decides what to do without involving others. This decision method often reflects the prerogatives of a person's position of formal authority in the organization. For instance, in deciding a rotation for lunch hours in a retail store, the manager may post a schedule. In **consultative decisions**, by contrast, inputs on the problem are solicited from other persons. Based on this information and its interpretation, the decision maker arrives at a final choice. To continue the example, the manager may tell subordinates that a lunch schedule is needed and ask them when they would like to schedule their lunch and why before making the decision. In other cases, true **group decisions** can be made by both consulting with others and allowing them to help make the final choice. To complete the example, the manager may hold a meeting to get everyone's agreement on a lunch schedule or a system for deciding how to make the schedule.

Victor Vroom, Phillip Yetton, and Arthur Jago have developed a framework for helping managers choose which of these decision-making methods is

■ **Authority decisions** are made by the manager or team leader without involving others using information that he or she possesses.

■ **Consultative decisions** are made by one individual after seeking input from or consulting with members of a group.

■ **Group decisions** are made by all members of the group.

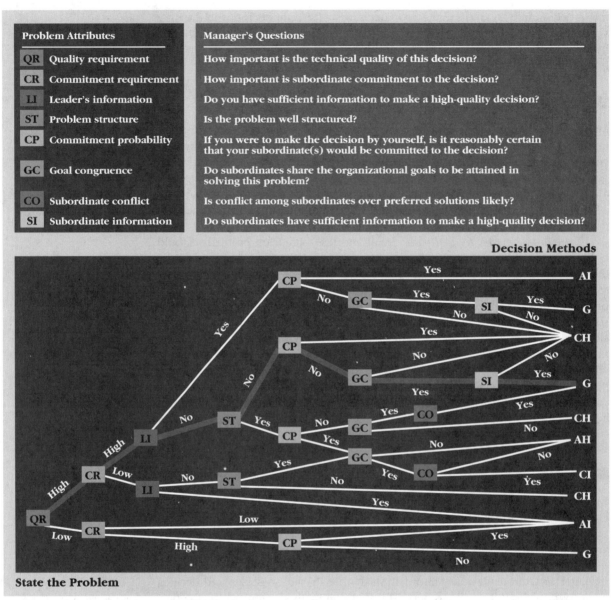

Problem Attributes		Manager's Questions
QR	Quality requirement	How important is the technical quality of this decision?
CR	Commitment requirement	How important is subordinate commitment to the decision?
LI	Leader's information	Do you have sufficient information to make a high-quality decision?
ST	Problem structure	Is the problem well structured?
CP	Commitment probability	If you were to make the decision by yourself, is it reasonably certain that your subordinate(s) would be committed to the decision?
GC	Goal congruence	Do subordinates share the organizational goals to be attained in solving this problem?
CO	Subordinate conflict	Is conflict among subordinates over preferred solutions likely?
SI	Subordinate information	Do subordinates have sufficient information to make a high-quality decision?

Figure 2.15
Selecting alternative decision-making methods: The Vroom and Jago decision process flowchart.

most appropriate for various problem situations.[135] (See Figure 2.15.) The central proposition in their model is that the decision-making method used should always be appropriate to the problem being solved. The challenge is to know when and how to implement each of the possible methods as the situation demands. They further clarify individual, consultative, and group decision options as follows.

Decision-making methods

- **AI** (*first variant on the authority decision*): The manager solves the problem or makes the decision alone, using information available at that time.

- **AII** (*second variant on the authority decision*): The manager obtains the necessary information from subordinate(s) or other group members and then decides on the problem solution. The manager may or may not tell subordinates what the problem is before obtaining the information from them. The subordinates provide the necessary information but do not generate or evaluate alternatives.

- **CI** (*first variant on the consultative decision*): The manager shares the problem with relevant subordinates or other group members individually, getting their ideas and suggestions without bringing them together as a group. The manager then makes a decision that may or may not reflect the subordinates' input.

- **CII** (*second variant on the consultative decision*): The manager shares the problem with subordinates or other group members, collectively obtaining their ideas and suggestions. The manager then makes a decision that may or may not reflect the subordinates' input.

- **G** (*the group or consensus decision*): The manager shares the problem with the subordinates as a total group and engages the group in consensus seeking to arrive at a final decision.

In the most recent version of this decision-making framework, Vroom and Jago use the flowchart shown in Figure 2.15 to help managers analyze problem situations and choose the most appropriate decision-making methods. Key issues involve the quality requirements of a decision, the availability and location of the relevant information, the commitments needed to fully implement the decision, and the amount of time available. Although this model appears complex and cumbersome, its underlying logic offers a useful decision-making discipline. Try it by working through Figure 2.15 for an organizational problem with which you are familiar. The analysis forces you to recognize how time, quality requirements, information availability, and subordinate acceptance issues can affect decision outcomes. It also reminds you that all of the decision methods are important and useful. The key to effectively managing participation in decision making is first knowing when to use each decision method and then knowing how to implement each of them well.

■ KNOWING WHEN TO QUIT— ELIMINATING ESCALATING COMMITMENTS

The organization's natural desire to continue on a selected course of action reinforces some natural tendencies among decision makers.[136] Once the agonizing process of making a choice is apparently completed, executives make public commitments to implementation, and implementation begins, managers are often reluctant to change their minds and admit a mistake. Instead of backing off, the tendency is to press on to victory. This is called **escalating commitment**— continuation and renewed efforts on a previously chosen course of action, even though it is not working. Escalating commitment is reflected in the popular adage, "If at first you don't succeed, try, try, again."

In beginning Finance courses, students learn about the fallacy of sunk costs. Money committed and spent is gone. The decision to continue is just that—a decision. It needs to be based on what investment is needed and the returns on that investment. This is one of the most difficult aspects of decision making to

■ **Escalating commitment** is the tendency to continue a previously chosen course of action even when feedback suggests that it is failing.

convey to executives simply because so many of these executives rose to their positions by turning apparently losing courses of action into winners.[137] The tendency to escalate commitments often outweighs the willingness to disengage from them. Decision makers may rationalize negative feedback as a temporary condition, protect their egos by not admitting that the original decision was a mistake, or characterize any negative results as a "learning experience" that can be overcome with added future effort.[138]

The self-discipline required to admit mistakes and change direction, however, is sometimes difficult to achieve. Escalating commitments are a form of decision entrapment that leads people to do things that the facts of a situation do not justify. We should be proactive in spotting "failures" and more open to reversing decisions or dropping plans that do not appear to be working.[139] But again, this is easier said than done. Good decision makers know when to call it quits. They are willing to reverse previous decisions and stop investing time and other resources in unsuccessful courses of action. As the late W. C. Fields is said to have muttered, "If at first you don't succeed, try, try, again. Then quit."

Technology, Culture, and Ethics in Decision Making

In today's environments, the problems facing organizational decision makers seem to get ever more complex. For example, consider the following workplace trends:[140]

Key workplace trends

- Businesses are becoming smaller in size; they are doing more outsourcing and employing fewer full-time workers.

- New, more flexible, and adaptable organizational forms are replacing the traditional pyramid structures.

- Multifunctional understanding is increasingly important as organizations emphasize lateral coordination.

- Workers with both technical knowledge and team skills are becoming increasingly sought after.

- The nature of "work" is in flux as jobs change fast, require continuous learning, and are less bound by the "9 to 5" tradition.

Each of these trends is changing who, when, where, and how decision making is accomplished. We face difficult stresses and strains as the quest for higher and higher productivity challenges the needs, talents, and opportunities of people at work. Complexities in the decision making process include issues of information technology, culture and ethics.

■ INFORMATION TECHNOLOGY AND DECISION MAKING

■ **Artificial intelligence** is the study of how computers can be programmed to think like the human brain.

As we have discussed throughout this book, today's organizations are becoming ever more sophisticated in applying information technologies. Eventually, developments in the field of **artificial intelligence** (AI), the study of how computers can be programmed to think like the human brain, will allow computers to displace many decision makers.[141] Nobel Laureate and decision scientist Herbert Simon is convinced that computers will someday be more intelligent than humans.

Already, the applications of AI to organizational decision making are significant. We have access to decision-making support from expert systems that reason like human experts and follow "either-or" rules to make deductions. For example, if you call an advertised 800 number to apply for a home equity loan, you will not get a human but a computer program to take all the necessary information and provide confirmation of a loan. On the factory floor, decision support systems schedule machines and people for maximum production efficiencies.

In the very near future, fuzzy logic that reasons beyond either-or choices and neural networks that reason inductively by simulating the brain's parallel processing capabilities will become operational realities to move beyond simple programmed decisions. Uses for such systems may be found everywhere from hospitals where they will check on medical diagnoses to investment houses where they will analyze potential investment portfolios to a wide and growing variety of other settings.[142]

Computer support for group decision making, including developments with the Internet and with intranets, has broken the decision-making meeting out of the confines of face-to-face interactions. With the software now available, problems can be defined and decisions can be made through virtual teamwork by people in geographically dispersed locations. We know that group decision software can be especially useful for generating ideas, such as in electronic brainstorming, and for improving the time efficiency of decisions. People working under electronically mediated conditions tend to stay focused on tasks and avoid the interpersonal conflicts and other problems common in face-to-face deliberations. On the negative side, decisions made by "electronic groups" carry some risks of being impersonal and perhaps less compelling in terms of commitments to implementation and follow-through. There is evidence, moreover, that use of computer technology for decision making is better accepted by today's college students than by persons who are already advanced in their organizational careers.[143]

What new information technology will not do is deal with the issues raised by the garbage can model. The information technologies promise a more orderly world where the process of choosing conforms more to the traditional models with an extension of the normal boundaries of rationality. For us, what is still on the information technology horizon are the most important decisions that come before the classical and standard approaches. These are pre-decision choices that are heavily influenced by cultural factors and ethics.

■ CULTURAL FACTORS AND DECISION MAKING

Fons Trompenaars notes that culture is "the way in which a group of people solves problems."[144] It is only reasonable to expect that as cultures vary so too will choices concerning what is to be solved and how. For example, there are historical cultural preferences for solving problems. The approach favored in this chapter emphasizes the North American view stressing decisiveness, speed, and individual selection of alternatives. This view speaks more to choice and less to implementation. Yet, the garbage can view suggests that implementation can proceed almost separately from other aspects of decision making.

Other cultures place less emphasis on individual choice than on developing implementations that work. They start with what is workable and better rather than with the classical and behavioral comparison of current conditions with some ideal.[145] If a change can improve the current situation, even if it is not apparently directed toward a problem identified by senior management, subordinate managers may work together to implement it. And then senior management may be informed of the success of the change. To emphasize the importance of smooth implementation over grand decision making, corporations may adopt systems similar to the Japanese ringi system where lower-levels indicate their written approval of proposals prior to formal implementation. Written approval is an issue not of whether the change should be done but whether it is feasible for the group to implement.[146]

The more important role of culture in decision making concerns not how problems are solved but which concerns are elevated to the status of problems solvable within the firm. For instance, the very fact that a procedure is old may make it more suspect in the United States than in France.[147] Far too many of our views maybe dictated by Western bureaucratic thinking.[148] Not all cultures are as pluralistic, bluntly competitive, or impersonal as that of the United States. In other parts of the world, personal loyalties may drive decisions, and preserving harmony may be considered more important than achieving a bit more efficiency. In short, problems may be more person centered and socially defined than bureaucratically proscribed.

■ ETHICAL ISSUES AND DECISION MAKING

The subject of ethical behavior in the workplace cannot be overemphasized, and it is worth reviewing once again the framework for ethical decision making first introduced in Section 1. An *ethical dilemma* was defined as a situation in which a person must decide whether or not to do something that, although personally or organizationally beneficial, may be considered unethical and perhaps illegal. Often, ethical dilemmas are associated with risk and uncertainty, and with nonroutine problem situations. Just how decisions are handled under these circumstances, ones that will inevitably appear during your career, may well be the ultimate test of your personal ethical framework.

Effective Manager 1.2 in Section 1 introduced a useful decision-making checklist for resolving ethical dilemmas. Before any decision is made the checklist tests the preliminary decision with stiff questions.[149] First, it would have you ask: "Is my action legal? Is it right? Is it beneficial?" Second, it would have you ask: "How would I feel if my family found out about this? How would I feel if my decision were printed in the local newspaper?" Only after these questions are asked and satisfactorily answered, does the model suggest you should take action.

When it comes to the ethics of decision making, the criteria individuals use to define problems and the values that underlie these criteria must be considered.[150] Moral conduct is involved in choosing problems, deciding who should be involved, estimating the impacts of alternatives, and selecting an alternative for implementation.

Moral conduct does not arise from after-the-fact embarrassment. As Fineman suggests, "If people are unable to anticipate shame or guilt before they act in particular ways, then moral codes are invalid.... Decisions may involve lying, deceit, fraud, evasion of negligence—disapproved of in many cultures. But ethical monitoring and control go beyond just the pragmatics of harm."[151] In other words, when you are the decision maker, decision making is not just a choice process followed by implementation for the good of the organization. It involves your values and your morality whether or not you think it should. Thus, effective implemented choices need to not only solve a problem or capitalize on choices but also match your values and help others. It is little wonder, then, that decision making will likely be the biggest challenge of your organizational career.[152]

Conflict

Conflict occurs whenever disagreements exist in a social situation over issues of substance or whenever emotional antagonisms create frictions between individuals or groups.[153] Managers and team leaders can spend considerable time dealing with conflict, including conflicts in which the manager or leader is directly involved as one of the principal actors.[154] In other situations, the manager or leader may act as a mediator, or third party, whose job it is to resolve conflicts between other people. In all cases, a manager and team leader must be comfortable with the interpersonal conflict. This includes being able to recognize situations that have the potential for conflict and to deal with these situations in ways that will best serve the needs of both the organization and the people involved.[155]

■ **Conflict** occurs when parties disagree over substantive issues or when emotional antagonisms create friction between them.

■ TYPES OF CONFLICT

Conflict as it is experienced in the daily workplace involves at least two basic forms. **Substantive conflict** is a fundamental disagreement over ends or goals to be pursued and the means for their accomplishment.[156] A dispute with one's boss over a plan of action to be followed, such as the marketing strategy for a new product, is an example of substantive conflict. When people work together day in and day out, it is only normal that different viewpoints on a variety of substantive workplace issues will arise. At times people will disagree over such things as group and organizational goals, the allocation of resources, the distribution of rewards, policies and procedures, and task assignments. Dealing with such conflicts successfully is an everyday challenge for most managers.

■ **Substantive conflict** involves fundamental disagreement over ends or goals to be pursued and the means for their accomplishment.

By contrast, **emotional conflict** involves interpersonal difficulties that arise over feelings of anger, mistrust, dislike, fear, resentment, and the like.[157] This conflict is commonly known as a "clash of personalities." Emotional conflicts can drain the energies of people and distract them from important work priorities. They can emerge from a wide variety of settings and are common among co-workers as well as in superior–subordinate relationships. The latter form of emotional conflict is perhaps the most upsetting organizational conflict for any person to experience. Unfortunately, competitive pressures in today's business environment and the resulting emphasis on downsizing and restructuring have created more situations in which the decisions of a "tough" boss can create emotional conflict.

■ **Emotional conflict** involves interpersonal difficulties that arise over feelings of anger, mistrust, dislike, fear, resentment, and the like.

■ LEVELS OF CONFLICT

When dealing personally with conflicts in the workplace, the relevant question becomes: "How well prepared are you to encounter and deal successfully with conflicts of various types?" People at work may encounter conflict at the intrapersonal level (conflict within the individual), the interpersonal level (individual-to-individual conflict), the intergroup level, or the interorganizational level.

Some conflicts that affect behavior in organizations involve the individual alone. These **intrapersonal conflicts** often involve actual or perceived pressures from incompatible goals or expectations of the following types: *Approach–approach conflict* occurs when a person must choose between two positive and equally attractive alternatives. An example is having to choose between a valued promotion in the organization or a desirable new job with another firm. *Avoidance–avoidance conflict* occurs when a person must choose between two negative and equally unattractive alternatives. An example is being asked either to accept a job transfer to another town in an undesirable location or to have one's employment with an organization terminated. *Approach–avoidance conflict* occurs when a person must decide to do something that has both positive and negative consequences. An example is being offered a higher paying job whose responsibilities entail unwanted demands on one's personal time.

Interpersonal conflict occurs between two or more individuals who are in opposition to one another. It may be substantive or emotional or both. Two persons debating each other aggressively on the merits of hiring a job applicant is an example of a substantive interpersonal conflict. Two persons continually in disagreement over each other's choice of work attire is an example of an emotional interpersonal conflict.

Intergroup conflict that occurs among members of different teams or groups can also have substantive and/or emotional underpinnings. Intergroup conflict is quite common in organizations, and it can make the coordination and integration of task activities very difficult.[158] The classic example is conflict among functional groups or departments, such as marketing and manufacturing, in organizations. The growing use of cross-functional teams and task forces is one way of trying to minimize such conflicts and promote more creative and efficient operations.

Interorganizational conflict is most commonly thought of in terms of the competition and rivalry that characterizes firms operating in the same markets. A good example is the continuing battle between U.S. businesses and their global rivals. But interorganizational conflict is a much broader issue than that represented by market competition alone. Consider, for example, disagreements between unions and the organizations employing their members; between government regulatory agencies and the organizations subject to their surveillance; between organizations and those who supply them with raw materials.

■ FUNCTIONAL AND DYSFUNCTIONAL CONFLICTS

Conflict in organizations can be upsetting both to the individuals directly involved and to others affected by its occurrence. It can be quite uncomfortable, for example, to work in an environment in which two co-workers are continually hostile toward each other. In OB, however, the two sides to conflict shown in Figure 2.16 are recognized—the functional or constructive side, and the dysfunctional or destructive side.

Functional conflict, alternatively called *constructive conflict*, results in positive benefits to individuals, the group, or the organization. On the positive side, conflict can bring important problems to the surface so that they can be addressed. It can cause decisions to be considered carefully and perhaps reconsidered to ensure that the right path of action is being followed. It can increase the amount of

■ Intrapersonal conflict occurs within the individual because of actual or perceived pressures from incompatible goals or expectations.

■ Interpersonal conflict occurs between two or more individuals in opposition to each other.

■ Intergroup conflict occurs among groups in an organization.

■ Interorganizational conflict occurs between organizations.

■ Functional conflict results in positive benefits to the group.

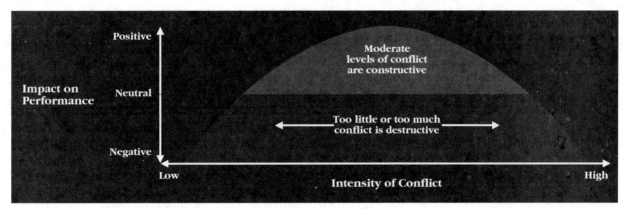

Figure 2.16
The two faces of conflict: functional conflict and dysfunctional conflict.

information used for decision making. And it can offer opportunities for creativity that can improve individual, team, or organizational performance. Indeed, an effective manager is able to stimulate constructive conflict in situations in which satisfaction with the status quo inhibits needed change and development.

Dysfunctional conflict, or *destructive conflict*, works to the individual's, group's, or organization's disadvantage. It diverts energies, hurts group cohesion, promotes interpersonal hostilities, and overall creates a negative environment for workers. This occurs, for example, when two employees are unable to work together because of interpersonal differences (a destructive emotional conflict) or when the members of a committee fail to act because they cannot agree on group goals (a destructive substantive conflict). Destructive conflicts of these types can decrease work productivity and job satisfaction and contribute to absenteeism and job turnover. Managers must be alert to destructive conflicts and be quick to take action to prevent or eliminate them or at least minimize their disadvantages.

■ **Dysfunctional conflict** works to the group's or organization's disadvantage.

■ CULTURE AND CONFLICT

Society today shows many signs of wear and tear in social relationships. We experience difficulties born of racial tensions, homophobia, gender gaps, and more. All trace in some way to tensions among people who are different in some ways from one another. They are also a reminder that culture and cultural differences must be considered for their conflict potential.

Among the popular dimensions of culture discussed in Section 5, for example, substantial differences may be noted in time orientation. When persons from short-term cultures such as the United States try to work with persons from long-term cultures such as Japan, the likelihood of conflict developing is high. The same holds true when individualists work with collectivists and when persons from high-power distance work with those from low-power distance cultures.[159] In each case, individuals who are not able to recognize and respect the impact of culture on behavior may contribute to the emergence of dysfunctional situations. On the other hand, by approaching a cross-cultural work situation with sensitivity and respect, one can find ways to work together without great difficulty and even with the advantages that constructive conflict may offer.

Managing Conflict

■ **Conflict resolution** occurs when the reasons for a conflict are eliminated.

Conflict can be addressed in many ways, but the important goal is to achieve or set the stage for true **conflict resolution**—a situation in which the underlying reasons for a given destructive conflict are eliminated. The process begins with a good understanding of causes and recognition of the stage to which conflict has developed.

■ STAGES OF CONFLICT

Most conflicts develop in stages, as shown in Figure 2.17. Managers should recognize that unresolved prior conflicts help set the stage for future conflicts of the same or related sort. Rather than try to deny the existence of conflict or settle on a temporary resolution, it is always best to deal with important conflicts so that they are completely resolved.[160] *Conflict antecedents* establish the conditions from which conflicts are likely to develop. When the antecedent conditions become the basis for substantive or emotional differences between people or groups, the stage of *perceived conflict* exists. Of course, this perception may be held by only one of the conflicting parties. It is important to distinguish between perceived and *felt conflict*. When conflict is felt, it is experienced as tension that motivates the person to take action to reduce feelings of discomfort. For conflict to be resolved, all parties should both perceive it and feel the need to do something about it.

When conflict is expressed openly in behavior, it is said to be manifest. A state of *manifest conflict* may be resolved by removing or correcting its antecedents. It can also be suppressed. With suppression, no change in antecedent

Figure 2.17
The stages of conflict.

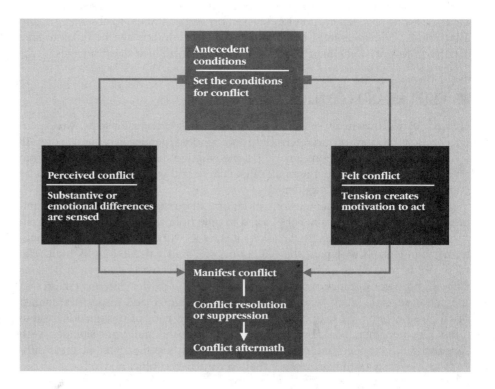

conditions occurs; the manifest conflict behaviors are controlled. For example, one or both parties may choose to ignore the conflict in their dealings with one another. *Suppression* is a superficial and often temporary form of conflict resolution. Indeed, we have already noted that unresolved and suppressed conflict fall into this category. Both may continue to fester and cause future conflicts over similar issues. For the short run, however, they may represent the best a manager can achieve until antecedent conditions can be changed.

Unresolved substantive conflicts can result in sustained emotional discomfort and escalate into dysfunctional emotional conflict between individuals. In contrast, truly resolved conflicts may establish conditions that reduce the potential for future conflicts or make it easier to deal with them. Thus, any manager should be sensitive to the influence of *conflict aftermath* on future conflict episodes.

■ CAUSES OF CONFLICT

The process of dealing successfully with conflict begins with a recognition of several types of conflict situations. *Vertical conflict* occurs between hierarchical levels. It commonly involves supervisor–subordinate disagreements over resources, goals, deadlines, or performance results. *Horizontal conflict* occurs between persons or groups at the same hierarchical level. These disputes commonly involve goal incompatibilities, resource scarcities, or purely interpersonal factors. A common variation of horizontal conflict is *line–staff conflict*. It often involves disagreements over who has authority and control over certain matters such as personnel selection and termination practices.

Also common to work situations are *role conflicts* that occur when the communication of task expectations proves inadequate or upsetting. This often involves unclear communication of work expectations, excessive expectations in the form of job overloads, insufficient expectations in the form of job underloads, and incompatibilities among expectations from different sources.

Work-flow interdependencies are breeding grounds for conflicts. Disputes and open disagreements may erupt among people and units who are required to cooperate to meet challenging goals.[161] When interdependence is high—that is, when a person or group must rely on task contributions from one or more others to achieve its goals—conflicts often occur. You will notice this, for example, in a fast-food restaurant, when the people serving the food have to wait too long for it to be delivered from the cooks. Conflict also escalates when individuals or groups lack adequate task direction or goals. *Domain ambiguities* involve misunderstandings over such things as customer jurisdiction or scope of authority. Conflict is likely when individuals or groups are

OB Across Functions

PURCHASING

Conflict Management in Supplier Relationships

Suppliers and manufacturers in the United States have often experienced conflict over price, quality, and service. By contrast, the Japanese are known for working together creatively to turn this potentially destructive relationship into constructive conflict. Recently, U.S. firms are attempting much the same to maintain global competitiveness. In fact, you certainly know that Chrysler was bought by Germany's Daimler Benz and the combined firm is highly regarded in a very competitive industry. What you may not know is that part of the foundation for Chrysler's success was set in the supplier relationships developed by the firm's vice president for purchasing, Thomas T. Stallkamp. He says: "When you start to see your suppliers as experts, then they become valuable partners instead of a switchable commodity." Under Stallkamp's leadership, Chrysler eliminated competitive bidding to gain supplier contracts. Instead, Chrysler gave suppliers detailed specifications and asked them to meet the specifications and cut costs. In return, the firm agreed to share the savings with the suppliers and to give long-term purchase contracts. Part of Chrysler's overall TQM approach, this cooperative approach to supplier relationships called SCORE—Supplier Cost Reduction Effort, has been credited with over 4600 cost-saving ideas and actual savings of some $235 million.

placed in ambiguous situations where it is difficult for them to understand just who is responsible for what.

Actual or perceived *resource scarcity* can foster destructive competition. When resources are scarce, working relationships are likely to suffer. This is especially true in organizations that are experiencing downsizing or financial difficulties. As cutbacks occur, various individuals or groups try to position themselves to gain or retain maximum shares of the shrinking resource pool. They are also likely to try to resist resource redistribution, or to employ countermeasures to defend their resources from redistribution to others.

Finally, *power or value asymmetries* in work relationships can create conflict. They exist when interdependent people or groups differ substantially from one another in status and influence or in values. Conflict resulting from asymmetry is prone to occur, for example, when a low-power person needs the help of a high-power person, who does not respond; when people who hold dramatically different values are forced to work together on a task; or when a high-status person is required to interact with and perhaps be dependent on someone of lower status.

■ INDIRECT CONFLICT MANAGEMENT APPROACHES

Indirect conflict management approaches share the common ground of avoiding direct dealings with personalities. They include reduced interdependence, appeals to common goals, hierarchical referral, and alterations in the use of mythology and scripts.

Reduced Interdependence   When work-flow conflicts exist, managers can adjust the level of interdependency among units or individuals.[162] One simple option is *decoupling*, or taking action to eliminate or reduce the required contact between conflict parties. In some cases, the units' tasks can be adjusted to reduce the number of required points of coordination. The conflicting units can then be separated from one another, and each can be provided separate access to valued resources. Although decoupling may reduce conflict, it may also result in duplication and a poor allocation of valued resources.

Buffering is another approach that can be used when the inputs of one group are the outputs of another group. The classic buffering technique is to build an inventory, or buffer, between the two groups so that any output slowdown or excess is absorbed by the inventory and does not directly pressure the target group. Although it reduces conflict, this technique is increasingly out of favor because it increases inventory costs. This consequence is contrary to the elements of "just-in-time" delivery that is now valued in operations management.

Conflict management can be facilitated by assigning people to serve as formal *linking pins* between groups that are prone to conflict.[163] Persons in linking-pin roles, such as project liaison, are expected to understand the operations, members, needs, and norms of their host group. They are supposed to use this knowledge to help their group work better with other groups in order to accomplish mutual tasks. Though expensive, this technique is often used when different specialized groups, such as engineering and sales, must closely coordinate their efforts on complex and long-term projects.

Appeals to Common Goals   An *appeal to common goals* can focus the attention of potentially conflicting parties on one mutually desirable conclusion. By elevating the potential dispute to a common framework wherein the parties recognize their mutual interdependence in achieving common goals, petty disputes can be put in perspective. However, this can be difficult to achieve when prior performance is poor and individuals or groups disagree over how to improve performance. In this negative situation, the manager needs to remember the attributional tendency of individuals to blame poor performance on others or on external conditions. In this case, conflict resolution begins by making sure that the parties take personal responsibility for improving the situation.

Hierarchical Referral   *Hierarchical referral* makes use of the chain of command for conflict resolution. Here, problems are simply referred up the hierarchy for more senior managers to reconcile. Whereas hierarchical referral can be definitive in a given case, it also has limitations. If conflict is severe and recurring, the continual use of hierarchical referral may not result in true conflict resolution. Managers removed from day-to-day affairs may fail to diagnose the real causes of a conflict, and conflict resolution may be superficial. Busy managers may tend to consider most conflicts as results of poor interpersonal relations and may act quickly to replace a person with a perceived "personality" problem.[164]

Altering Scripts and Myths   In some situations, conflict is superficially managed by *scripts*, or behavioral routines that become part of the organization's culture.[165] The scripts become rituals that allow the conflicting parties to vent their frustrations and to recognize that they are mutually dependent on one another via the larger corporation. An example is a monthly meeting of "department heads," held presumably for purposes of coordination and problem solving but that actually becomes just a polite forum for superficial agreement.[166] Managers in such cases know their scripts and accept the difficulty of truly resolving any major conflicts. By sticking with the script, expressing only low-key disagreement and then quickly acting as if everything has been resolved, for instance, the managers publicly act as if problems are being addressed. Such scripts can be altered to allow and encourage active confrontation of issues and disagreements.

■ DIRECT CONFLICT MANAGEMENT APPROACHES

Figure 2.18 describes the five approaches to conflict management from the perspective of their relative emphasis on cooperativeness and assertiveness in the relationship. Consultants and academics generally agree that true conflict resolution can occur only when the underlying substantive and emotional reasons for the conflict are identified and dealt with through a solution that allows all conflicting parties to "win."[167] (See The Effective Manager 2.8.) This important issue of "Who wins?" can be addressed from the perspective of each conflicting party.

THE EFFECTIVE MANAGER 2.8

WHEN TO USE CONFLICT MANAGEMENT STYLES

- Collaboration and problem solving is preferred to gain true conflict resolution when time and cost permit.
- Avoidance may be used when an issue is trivial or more important issues are pressing, or when people need to cool down temporarily and regain perspective.
- Authoritative command may be used when quick and decisive action is vital or when unpopular actions must be taken.
- Accommodation may be used when issues are more important to others than to yourself or when you want to build "credits" for use in later issues.
- Compromise may be used for temporary settlements to complex issues or to arrive at expedient solutions when time is limited.

Figure 2.18
Five ways to manage conflict.

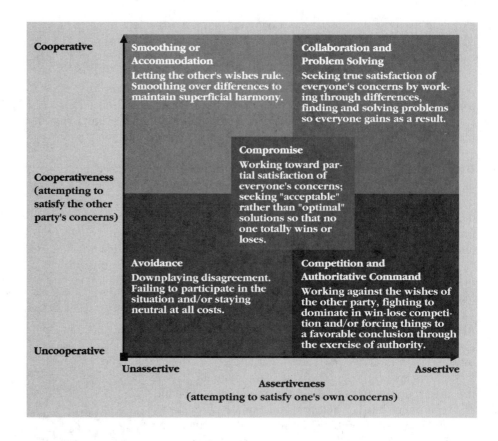

■ **Avoidance** involves pretending a conflict does not really exist.

■ **Accommodation** or **smoothing** involves playing down differences and finding areas of agreement.

■ **Compromise** occurs when each party gives up something of value to the other.

■ **Competition** seeks victory by force, superior skill, or domination.

■ **Authoritative command** uses formal authority to end conflict.

Lose–Lose Conflict   *Lose–lose conflict* occurs when nobody really gets what he or she wants. The underlying reasons for the conflict remain unaffected and a similar conflict is likely to occur in the future. Lose–lose conflicts often result when there is little or no assertiveness and conflict management takes these forms. **Avoidance** is an extreme form of inattention; everyone simply pretends that the conflict does not really exist and hopes that it will go away. **Accommodation**, or **smoothing** as it is sometimes called, involves playing down differences among the conflicting parties and highlighting similarities and areas of agreement. This peaceful coexistence ignores the real essence of a given conflict and often creates frustration and resentment. **Compromise** occurs when each party gives up something of value to the other. As a result of no one getting its full desires, the antecedent conditions for future conflicts are established.

Win–Lose Conflict   In *win–lose conflict*, one party achieves its desires at the expense and to the exclusion of the other party's desires. This is a high-assertiveness and low-cooperativeness situation. It may result from outright **competition** in which a victory is achieved through force, superior skill, or domination by one party. It may also occur as a result of **authoritative command**, whereby a formal authority simply dictates a solution and specifies what is gained and what is lost by whom. Win–lose strategies fail to address the root causes of the conflict and tend to suppress the desires of at least one of the conflicting parties. As a result, future conflicts over the same issues are likely to occur.

Win–Win Conflict *Win–win conflict* is achieved by a blend of both high cooperativeness and high assertiveness.[168] **Collaboration** or **problem solving** involves a recognition by all conflicting parties that something is wrong and needs attention. It stresses gathering and evaluating information in solving disputes and making choices. Win–win conditions eliminate the reasons for continuing or resurrecting the conflict since nothing has been avoided or suppressed. All relevant issues are raised and openly discussed. The ultimate test for a win–win solution is whether or not the conflicting parties see that the solution (1) achieves each other's goals, (2) is acceptable to both parties, and (3) establishes a process whereby all parties involved see a responsibility to be open and honest about facts and feelings. When success is achieved, true conflict resolution has occurred.

Although collaboration and problem solving are generally favored, one limitation is the time and energy it requires. It is also important to realize that both parties to the conflict need to be assertive and cooperative in order to develop a win–win joint solution. Finally, collaboration and problem solving may not be feasible if the firm's dominant culture does not place a value on cooperation.[169]

■ **Collaboration** involves recognition that something is wrong and needs attention through problem solving.

■ **Problem solving** uses information to resolve disputes.

Negotiation

Talk about conflict! Picture yourself trying to make a decision in the following situation: You have ordered a new state-of-the-art notebook computer for a staff member in your department. At about the same time another department ordered a different brand. Your boss indicates that only one brand will be ordered. Of course, you believe the one chosen by your department is the best.

■ WHAT IS NEGOTIATION?

This is just a sample of the many situations that involve managers and others in **negotiation**—the process of making joint decisions when the parties involved have different preferences.[170] Negotiation has special significance in work settings, where disagreements are likely to arise over such diverse matters as wage rates, task objectives, performance evaluations, job assignments, work schedules, work locations, and more.

■ **Negotiation** is the process of making joint decisions when the parties involved have different preferences.

■ NEGOTIATION GOALS AND OUTCOMES

In negotiation two important goals must be considered: substance and relationship goals. *Substance goals* deal with outcomes that relate to the "content" issues under negotiation. The dollar amount of a wage agreement in a collective bargaining situation is one example. *Relationship goals* deal with outcomes that relate to how well people involved in the negotiation and any constituencies they may represent are able to work with one another once the process is concluded. An example is the ability of union members and management representatives to work together effectively after a contract dispute has been settled.

Unfortunately, many negotiations result in damaged relationships because the negotiating parties become preoccupied with substance goals and self-interests. In contrast, *effective negotiation* occurs when substance issues are resolved

THE EFFECTIVE MANAGER 2.9

CRITERIA OF AN EFFECTIVE NEGOTIATION

1. *Quality*—The negotiation results offer a "quality" agreement that is wise and satisfactory to all sides.
2. *Harmony*—The negotiation is "harmonious" and fosters rather than inhibits good interpersonal relations.
3. *Efficiency*—The negotiation is "efficient" and no more time consuming or costly than absolutely necessary.

and working relationships are maintained or even improved. It results in overlapping interests and joint decisions that are "for the better" of all parties. Three criteria for effective negotiation are described in The Effective Manager 2.9.

∎ ETHICAL ASPECTS OF NEGOTIATION

To maintain good working relationships in negotiations, managers and other involved parties should strive for high ethical standards. This goal may be side tracked by an over emphasis on self-interests. The motivation to behave ethically in negotiations is put to the test by each party's desire to "get more" than the other from the negotiation, and/or with a belief that there are insufficient resources to satisfy all parties.[171] After the heat of negotiations dies down, the parties involved often try to rationalize or explain away questionable ethics as unavoidable, harmless, or justified. Such after-the-fact rationalizations may be offset by long-run negative consequences, such as not being able to achieve one's wishes again the next time. At the very least, the unethical party may be the target of revenge tactics by those who were disadvantaged. Furthermore, once some people have behaved unethically in one situation, they may become entrapped by such behavior and prone to display it again in the future.[172]

∎ ORGANIZATIONAL SETTINGS FOR NEGOTIATION

Managers and team leaders should be prepared to participate in at least four major action settings for negotiations. In *two-party negotiation* the manager negotiates directly with one other person. In *group negotiation* the manager is part of a team or group whose members are negotiating to arrive at a common decision. In *intergroup negotiation* the manager is part of a group that is negotiating with another group to arrive at a decision regarding a problem or situation affecting both. And in *constituency negotiation* the manager is involved in negotiation with other persons, with each party representing a broader constituency. A common example of constituency negotiation involves representatives of management and labor negotiating a collective bargaining agreement.

∎ CULTURE AND NEGOTIATION

The existence of cultural differences in time orientation, individualism-collectivism, and power distance can have a substantial impact on negotiation. For example, when American businesses try to negotiate quickly with Chinese counterparts, they often do so with the goal of getting definitive agreements that will govern a working relationship. Culture isn't always on their side. A typical Chinese approach to negotiation might move much more slowly, require the development of good interpersonal relationships prior to reaching any agreement, display reluctance to commit everything to writing, and anticipate that any agreement reached will be subject to modification as future circumstances may require.[173] All this is quite the opposite of the typical expectations of negotiators used to the individualist and short-term American culture.

Negotiation Strategies

Managers and other workers frequently negotiate with one another over access to scarce organizational resources. These resources may be money, time, people, facilities, equipment, and so on. In all such cases, the general approach to or strategy for the negotiation can have a major influence on its outcomes. In **distributive negotiation**, the focus is on "positions" staked out or declared by conflicting parties. Each party is trying to claim certain portions of the available "pie." In **integrative negotiation**, sometimes called *principled negotiation*, the focus is on the "merits" of the issues. Everyone involved tries to enlarge the available pie rather than stake claims to certain portions of it.[174]

■ DISTRIBUTIVE NEGOTIATION

In distributive bargaining approaches, the participants would each ask the question: "Who is going to get this resource?" This question, and the way in which it frames subsequent behavior, will have a major impact on the negotiation process and outcomes. A case of distributive negotiation usually unfolds in one of two directions, neither of which yields optimal results. *"Hard" distributive negotiation* takes place when each party holds out to get its own way. This leads to competition, whereby each party seeks dominance over the other and tries to maximize self-interests. The hard approach may lead to a win–lose outcome in which one party dominates and gains. Or it can lead to an impasse.

"Soft" distributive negotiation, by contrast, takes place when one party is willing to make concessions to the other to get things over with. In this case, one party tries to find ways to meet the other's desires. A soft approach leads to accommodation in which one party gives in to the other, or to compromise in which each party gives up something of value in order to reach agreement. In either case at least some latent dissatisfaction is likely to develop. Even when the soft approach results in compromise (e.g., splitting the difference between the initial positions equally), dissatisfaction may exist since each party is still deprived of what it originally wanted.

Figure 2.19 introduces the case of the graduating senior negotiating a job offer with a corporate recruiter.[175] The example illustrates the basic elements of classic two-party negotiation in distributive contexts. To begin, look at the situation from the graduate's perspective. She has told the recruiter that she would like a salary of $45,000; this is her initial offer. But she also has in mind a minimum reservation point of $35,000—the lowest salary that she will accept for this job. Thus, she communicates a salary request of $45,000 but is willing to accept one as low as $35,000. The situation is somewhat reversed from the recruiter's perspective. His initial offer to the graduate is $30,000, and his maximum reservation point is $40,000; this is the most he is prepared to pay.

The **bargaining zone** is defined as the range between one party's minimum reservation point and the other party's maximum reservation point. In Figure 2.19, the bargaining zone is $40,000–$45,000. This is a positive bargaining zone since the

■ **Distributive negotiation** focuses on positions staked out or declared by the parties involved who are each trying to claim certain portions of the available pie.

■ **Integrative negotiation** focuses on the merits of the issues, and the parties involved try to enlarge the available pie rather than stake claims to certain portions of it.

■ The **bargaining zone** is the zone between one party's minimum reservation point and the other party's maximum reservation point in a negotiating situation.

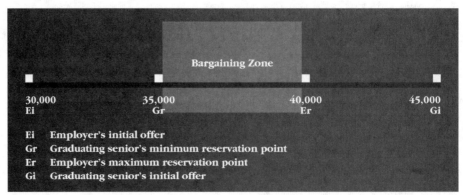

Figure 2.19
An example of the bargaining zone in classic two-party negotiation.

reservation points of the two parties overlap. Whenever a positive bargaining zone exists, bargaining has room to unfold. Had the graduate's minimum reservation point been greater than the recruiter's maximum reservation point (for example, $42,000), no room would have existed for bargaining. Classic two-party bargaining always involves the delicate tasks of first discovering the respective reservation points (one's own and the other's) and then working toward an agreement that lies somewhere within the resulting bargaining zone and is acceptable to each party.

■ INTEGRATIVE NEGOTIATION

In the integrative approach to negotiation, participants would ask: "How can the resource best be utilized?" Notice that this question is very different from the one described for distributive negotiation. It is much less confrontational, and it permits a broader range of alternatives to be considered in the process. From the outset there is much more of a "win–win" orientation.

At one extreme, integrative negotiation may involve selective avoidance, in which both parties realize that there are more important things on which to focus their time and attention. The time, energy, and effort needed to negotiate may not be worth the rewards. Compromise can also play a role in the integrative approach, but it must have an enduring basis. This is most likely to occur when the compromise involves each party giving up something of perceived lesser personal value to gain something of greater value. For instance, in the classic two-party bargaining case over salary, both the graduate and the recruiter could expand the negotiation to include the starting date of the job. Since it will be a year before the candidate's first vacation, she may be willing to take a little less money if she can start a few weeks later. Finally, integrative negotiation may involve true collaboration. In this case, the negotiating parties engage in problem solving to arrive at a mutual agreement that maximizes benefits to each.

■ HOW TO GAIN INTEGRATIVE AGREEMENTS

Underlying the integrative or principled approach is negotiation based on the merits of the situation. The foundations for gaining truly integrative agreements rest in supportive attitudes, constructive behaviors, and good information.[176]

Attitudinal Foundations   There are three attitudinal foundations of integrative agreements. First, each party must approach the negotiation with a *willingness to trust* the other party. This is a reason why ethics and maintaining relationships are so important in negotiations. Second, each party must convey a *willingness to share information* with the other party. Without shared information, effective problem solving is unlikely to occur. Third, each party must show a *willingness to ask concrete questions* of the other party. This further facilitates information sharing.

Behavioral Foundations   During a negotiation, all behavior is important for both its actual impact and the impressions it leaves behind. Accordingly, the following behavioral foundations of integrative agreements must be carefully considered and included in any negotiator's repertoire of skills and capabilities:

- The ability to separate the people from the problem to avoid allowing emotional considerations to affect the negotiation.
- The ability to focus on interests rather than positions.
- The ability to avoid making premature judgments.
- The ability to keep the acts of alternative creation separate from their evaluation.
- The ability to judge possible agreements on an objective set of criteria or standards.

Behavioral foundations of integrative agreements

Information Foundations   The information foundations of integrative agreements are substantial. They involve each party becoming familiar with the BATNA, or "best alternative to a negotiated agreement." That is, each party must know what he or she will do if an agreement can't be reached. This requires that both negotiating parties identify and understand their personal interests in the situation. They must know what is really important to them in the case at hand, and they must come to understand the relative importance of the other party's interests. As difficult as it may seem, each party must achieve an understanding of what the other party values, even to the point of determining its BATNA.

■ COMMON NEGOTIATION PITFALLS

The negotiation process is admittedly complex on cultural and many other grounds. It is further characterized by all the possible confusions of sometimes volatile interpersonal and group dynamics. Accordingly, negotiators need to guard against some common negotiation pitfalls.[177]

First, is the tendency in negotiation to stake out your position based on the assumption that in order to gain your way, something must be subtracted from the other party's way. This *myth of the fixed pie* is a purely distributive approach to negotiation. The whole concept of integrative negotiation is based on the premise that the pie can sometimes be expanded or utilized to the maximum advantage of all parties, not just one.

Second, because parties to negotiations often begin by stating extreme demands, the possibility of *escalating commitment* is high. That is, once demands have been stated, people become committed to them and are reluctant to back down. Concerns for protecting one's ego and saving face may lead to nonrational escalation of conflict. Self-discipline is needed to spot this tendency in one's own behavior as well as in others.

Third, negotiators often develop *overconfidence* that their positions are the only correct ones. This can lead them to ignore the other party's needs. In some cases, negotiators completely fail to see merits in the other party's position—merits that an outside observer would be sure to spot. Such overconfidence makes it harder to reach a positive common agreement.

Fourth, communication problems can cause difficulties during a negotiation. It has been said that "negotiation is the process of communicating back and forth for the purpose of reaching a joint decision."[178] This process can break down because of a *telling problem*—the parties don't really talk to one another, at least not in the sense of making themselves truly understood. It can also be damaged by a *hearing problem*—the parties are unable or unwilling to listen well enough to understand what each other is saying. Indeed, positive negotiation is most likely when each party engages in active listening and frequently asks questions to clarify what the other is saying. Each party occasionally needs to "stand in the other party's shoes" and to view the situation from their perspective.[179]

■ THIRD-PARTY ROLES IN NEGOTIATION

■ In **arbitration** a neutral third party acts as judge with the power to issue a decision binding on all parties.

Negotiation may sometimes be accomplished through the intervention of third parties, such as when stalemates occur and matters appear unresolvable under current circumstances. In **arbitration**, such as the salary arbitration now common in professional sports, this third party acts as the "judge" and has the power to issue a decision that is binding on all parties. This ruling takes place after the arbitrator listens to the positions advanced by the parties involved in a dispute. In **mediation** a neutral third party tries to engage the parties in a negotiated solution through persuasion and rational argument. This is a common approach in labor–management negotiations, where trained mediators acceptable to each side are called in to help resolve bargaining impasses. Unlike arbitrator, the mediator is not able to dictate a solution.

■ In **mediation** a neutral third party tries to engage the parties in a negotiated solution through persuasion and rational argument.

Footnotes

[1] "What Makes a Company Great?" *Fortune* (October 26, 1998), p. 218.

[2] See Thomas A. Stewart, "Planning a Career Without Managers," *Fortune* (March 20, 1995), pp. 72–80.

[3] Workplace Visions (September/October 1998), p. 2.

[4] Lester Thurow, *Head to Head: The Coming Economic Battle among Japan, Europe, and America* (New York: Morrow, 1992) and Barry A. Macy, *Successful Strategic Change* (San Francisco: Barrett-Koehler, in press).

[5] "Unemployment Falls 4.2 Percent to 29-Year Low," *Lubbock Avalanche-Journal* (April 3, 1999), p. E-1.

[6] Nina Munk, "The New Organization Man," *Fortune* (March 16, 1998), pp. 63–64.

[7] Thurow.

[8] See, for example, Jay R. Galbraith, Edward E. Lawler III, and Associates, *Organizing for the Future: The New Logic for Managing Organizations* (San Francisco: Jossey-Bass, 1993); and Peter Drucker, *Managing in a Time of Great Change* (New York: Truman Talley, 1995).

[9] Michael Hammer and James Champy, *Reengineering the Corporation* (New York: Harper Collins, 1993).

[10] See Gary Hammel and Jeff Sampler, "The e-Corporation," *Fortune* (December 7, 1998), pp. 79–90; and David Kirkpatrick, "The E-Ware War," *Fortune* (December 7, 1998), pp. 115–117.

[11] William H. Davidow and Michael S. Malone, *The Virtual Corporation: Structuring and Revitalizing the Corporation of the 21st Century* (New York: Harper Business, 1993). Also, Andrew Kupfer, "Alone Together: Will Being Wired Set Us Free?" *Fortune* (March 20, 1995), pp. 94–104.

[12] See Daniel H. Pink, "Free Agent Nation," *Fast Company* (December, 1997), pp. 131ff; and Tom Peters, "The Brand Called You," *Fast Company* (August/September 1997).

[13] Charles Handy, *The Age of Unreason* (Boston: Harvard Business School Press, 1990). See also his later book, *The Age of Paradox* (Boston: Harvard Business School Press, 1994).

[14] Jeffrey Pfeffer, *The Human Equation: Building Profits by Putting People First* (Boston: Harvard Business School Press, 1998).

[15] See Dave Ulrich, "Intellectual Capital = Competence x Commitment," *Harvard Business Review* (Winter 1998), pp. 15–26.

[16] Bradley L. Kirksman, Kevin B. Lowe, and Dianne P. Young, "The Challenge in High Performance Work Organizations," *Journal of Leadership Studies*, Vol. 5, No. 2 (Spring 1998): 3–15.

[17] Kirksman, Lowe, and Young, p. 5.

[18] Ibid.

[19] Ibid.; see also Course Notes for Management 5371 (1999).

[20] Kirksman, Lowe, and Young, pp. 5, 6.

[21] Ibid., p. 5.

[22] C. B. Gibson and B. L. Kirksman, "Our Past, Present and Future in Teams: The Role of the Human Resources Professional in Managing Team Performance," in A. L. Kraut and A. K. Korman (eds.), *Changing Concepts and Practices for Human Resources Management: Contributions from Industrial Organizational Psychology* (San Francisco: Jossey-Bass, in press).

[23] P. S. Goodman, R. Devadas, and T. L. Hughson, "Groups and Productivity: Analyzing the Effectiveness of Self Managing Work Teams," in J. P. Campbell and R. J. Campbell (eds.), *Productivity in Organizations: New Perspectives from Industrial and Organizational Psychology* (San Francisco: Jossey-Bass, 1988), pp. 295–237.

[24] Robert E. Markland, Shawnee K. Vickery, and Robert A. Davis, *Operations Management,* 2nd ed. (Cincinnati, OH: Southwestern Publishing, 1998), p. 646.

[25] Lee J. Kraijewski and Larry R. Ritzman, *Operations Management*, 5th ed. (Reading, MA: Addison-Wesley, 1989), pp. 158–159.

[26] Ibid.

[27] See D. A. Garvin, "Building a Learning Organization," *Harvard Business Review* (July–August 1993): 78–91; and Danny Miller, "A Preliminary Typology of Organizational Learning: Synthesizing the Literature," *Journal of Management*, Vol. 22, No. 3 (1996), pp. 485–505.

[28] Kirksman, Lowe, and Young pp. 6–7.

[29] Macy, *Successful Strategic Change.*

[30] Macis, Course Notes, (Spring 1999).

[31] See Jack O'Toole, *Forming the Future: Lessons from the Saturn Corporation* (Cambridge, MA: Basil Blackwell, 1996), p. 15.

[32] Kirksman, Lowe, and Young, pp. 7–12.

[33] Ibid.

[34] Ibid., p. 9.

[35] Macy, Course Notes (Spring 1999).

[36] Ibid.

[37] Kirksman, Lowe, and Young, pp. 10–12.

[38] O'Toole, p. 15.

[39] See B. A. Macy and J. Izumi, "Organizational Change, Design, and Work Innovation: A Meta-Analysis of 131 North American Field Studies—1961–1991," in W. A. Pasmore and R. W. Woodman (eds.), *Research in Organizational Change and Development*, Vol. 7 (Greenwich, CT: Jai Press, 1993), pp. 235–311.

[40] Macy, Course Notes (Spring 1999).

[41] O'Toole.

[42] Macy, *Successful Strategic Change.*

[43] The discussion in this section is based heavily on Eryn Brown, "VF Corp. Changes Its Underware," *Fortune* (December 7, 1998), pp. 115–118.

[44] Nina Monk, "How Levi's Trashed a Great American Brand," *Fortune* (April 12, 1999), pp. 82–91.

[45] For a good discussion of groups and teams in the workplace, see Jon R. Katzenbach and Douglas K. Smith, "The Discipline of Teams," *Harvard Business Review* (March–April, 1993), pp. 111–120.

[46] Harold J. Leavitt and Jean Lipman-Blumen, "Hot Groups," *Harvard Business Review* (July–August 1995), pp. 109–116.

[47] See, for example, Edward E. Lawler, III, *High-Involvement Management* (San Francisco: Jossey-Bass, 1986).

[48] Information from "Empowerment That Pays Off," *Fortune* (March 20, 1995), pp. 145–146; and Alex Taylor III, "The Germans Take Charge; Creating DaimlerChrysler Was a Coup for Jurgen Schrempp, But Can He Make the New Company Work?" *Fortune* (January 11, 1999), p. 92.

[49] Marvin E. Shaw, *Group Dynamics: The Psychology of Small Group Behavior*, 2nd ed. (New York: McGraw-Hill, 1976).

[50] D. A. Kravitz and B. Martin, "Ringelmann Rediscovered," *Journal of Personality and Social Psychology*, Vol. 50 (1986), pp. 936–941.

[51] David M. Herold, "The Effectiveness of Work Groups," in Steven Kerr, ed., *Organizational Behavior* (New York: Wiley, 1979), p. 95.

[52] A classic article is by Richard B. Zajonc, "Social Facilitation," *Science*, Vol. 149 (1965), pp. 269–274.

[53] Gerald Salancik and Jeffrey Pfeffer, "A Social Information Processing Approach to Job Attitude and Task Design," *Administrative Science Quarterly*, Vol. 23 (1978), pp. 224–253.

[54] David M. Herold, "The Effectiveness of Work Groups," in Steven Kerr, ed., *Organizational Behavior* (New York: Wiley, 1979), p. 95.

[55] Rensis Likert, *New Patterns of Management* (New York: McGraw-Hill, 1961).

[56] For a good discussion of task forces, see James Ware, "Managing a Task Force," Note 478-002, Harvard Business School, 1977.

[57] See "The Corporate Jungle Spawns a New Species: The Project Manager," *Fortune* (July 10, 1995), pp. 179–180.

[58] Information from Myron Maget, "Who's Winning the Information Revolution?" *Fortune* (November 30, 1992), pp. 110–117; and Paul Taylor, "Big Names Drawn by High Skills and Low Cost Levels," *The Financial Times* (December 2, 1998), p. 2.

[59] See, for example, Leland P. Bradford, *Group Development*, 2nd ed. (San Francisco: Jossey-Bass, 1997).

[60] J. Steven Heinen and Eugene Jacobson, "A Model of Task Group Development in Complex Organization and a Strategy of Implementation," *Academy of Management Review*, Vol. 1 (October 1976), pp. 98–111; Bruce W. Tuckman, "Developmental Sequence in Small Groups," *Psychological Bulletin*, Vol. 63 (1965), pp. 384–399; and Bruce W. Tuckman and Mary Ann C. Jensen, "Stages of Small Group Development Revisited," *Group & Organization Studies*, Vol. 2 (1977), pp. 419–427.

[61] Dave Ulrich, "Intellectual Capital = Competence × Commitment," *Sloan Management Review* (Winter 1998), pp. 15–26.

[62] See J. Richard Hackman, "The Design of Work Teams," in Jay W. Lorsch (ed.), *Handbook of Organizational Behavior* (Englewood Cliffs, NJ: Prentice Hall, 1987), pp. 343–357.

[63] Herold, op. cit. (1979). See also the discussion of group tasks in Stewart, Manz, and Sims, op. cit. (1999), pp. 142–143.

[64] Ilgen, et al., op. cit. (1997); and Warren Watson, "Cultural Diversity's Impact on Interaction Process and Performance," *Academy of Management Journal*, Vol. 16 (1993).

[65] L. Argote and J. E. McGrath, "Group Processes in Organizations: Continuity and Change" in C. L. Cooper and I. T. Robertson (eds.), *International Review of Industrial and Organizational Psychology* (New York: Wiley, 1993), pp. 333–389.

[66] See Daniel R. Ilgen, Jeffrey A. LePine, and John R. Hollenbeck, "Effective Decision Making in Multinational Teams," in P. Christopher Earley and Miriam Erez (eds.), *New Perspectives on International Industrial/Organizational Psychology* (San Francisco: New Lexington Press, 1997), pp. 377–409.

[67] William C. Schutz, *FIRO: A Three-Dimensional Theory of Interpersonal Behavior* (New York: Rinehart, 1958).

[68] William C. Schutz, "The Interpersonal Underworld," *Harvard Business Review*, Vol. 36 (July–August, 1958), p. 130.

[69] Katzenbach and Smith, op. cit. (1993).

[70] E. J. Thomas and C. F. Fink, "Effects of Group Size," in Larry L. Cummings and William E. Scott (eds.), *Readings in Organizational and Human Performance* (Homewood, IL: Irwin, 1969), pp. 394–408.

[71] Shaw, op. cit. (1976).

[72] George C. Homans, *The Human Group* (New York: Harcourt Brace, 1950).

[73] For a discussion of intergroup dynamics, see Schein, op. cit. (1988), pp. 106–115.

[74] "Producer Power," *The Economist* (March 4, 1995), p. 70.

[75] This discussion is developed from Schein, op. cit. (1988), pp. 69–75.

[76] Ibid., p. 73.

[77] Developed from guidelines presented in the classic article by Jay Hall, "Decisions, Decisions, Decisions," *Psychology Today* (November 1971), pp. 55–56.

[78] Norman R.F. Maier, "Assets and Liabilities in Group Problem Solving," *Psychological Review*, Vol. 74 (1967), pp. 239–249.

[79] Ibid.

[80] Irving L. Janis, "Groupthink," *Psychology Today* (November 1971), pp. 43–46; Irving L. Janis, *Groupthink*, 2nd ed. (Boston: Houghton Mifflin, 1982). See also J. Longley and D. G. Pruitt, "Groupthink: A Critique of Janis' Theory," in L. Wheeler (ed.), *Review of Personality and Social Psychology* (Beverly Hills, CA: Sage Publications, 1980); Carrie R. Leana, "A Partial Test of Janis's Groupthink Model: The Effects of Group Cohesiveness and Leader Behavior on Decision Processes," *Journal of Management*, Vol. 11, No. 1 (1985), pp. 5–18. See also Jerry Harvey, "Managing Agreement in Organizations: The Abilene Paradox," *Organizational Dynamics* (Summer 1974), pp. 63–80.

[81] Janis, op. cit. (1982).

[82] Gayle W. Hill, "Group versus Individual Performance: Are N1 1 Heads Better Than One?" *Psychological Bulletin*, Vol. 91 (1982), pp. 517–539.

[83] These techniques are well described in George P. Huber, *Managerial Decision Making* (Glenview, IL: Scott, Foresman, 1980); and Andre L. Delbecq, Andrew L. Van de Ven, and David H. Gustafson, *Group Techniques for Program Planning: A Guide to Nominal Groups and Delphi Techniques* (Glenview, IL: Scott, Foresman, 1975); and William M. Fox, "Anonymity and Other Keys to Successful Problem-Solving Meetings," *National Productivity Review*, Vol. 8 (Spring 1989), pp. 145–156.

[84] Delbecq et al., op. cit. (1975); Fox, op. cit. (1989).

[85] R. Brent Gallupe and William H. Cooper, "Brainstorming Electronically," *Sloan Management Review* (Fall 1993), pp. 27–36.

[86] Jon R. Katzenbach and Douglas K. Smith, "The Discipline of Teams," *Harvard Business Review* (March–April 1993a), pp. 111–120; and Jon R. Katzenbach and Douglas K. Smith, *The Wisdom of Teams: Creating the High-Performance Organization* (Boston: Harvard Business School Press, 1993b).

[87] Jay A. Conger, *Winning 'em Over: A New Model for Managing in the Age of Persuasion* (New York: Simon & Schuster, 1998).

[88] Ibid., p. 191.

[89] Katzenbach and Smith, op. cit. (1993a and 1993b).

[90] See also Jon R. Katzenbach, "The Myth of the Top Management Team," *Harvard Business Review*, Vol. 75 (November–December 1997), pp. 83–91.

[91] Katzenbach and Smith, op. cit. (1993a and 1993b).

[92] For a good overview, see Greg L. Stewart, Charles C. Manz, and Henry P. Sims, *Team Work and Group Dynamics* (New York: Wiley, 1999).

[93] Katzenbach and Smith, op. cit. (1993a), p. 112.

[94] Developed from ibid. (1993a), pp. 118–119.

[95] See Stewart et al., op. cit. (1999), pp. 43–44.

[96] See Daniel R. Ilgen, Jeffrey A. LePine, and John R. Hollenbeck, "Effective Decision Making in Multinational Teams," in P. Christopher Earley and Miriam Erez (eds.), *New Perspectives on International Industrial/Organizational Psychology* (San Francisco: New Lexington Press, 1997), pp. 377–409.

[97] Ilgen, et al., op. cit. (1997); and Warren Watson, "Cultural Diversity's Impact on Interaction Process and Performance," *Academy of Management Journal*, Vol. 16 (1993).

[98] For a good discussion of team building, see William D. Dyer, *Team Building*, 3rd ed. (Reading, MA: Addison-Wesley, 1995).

[99] Developed from a discussion by Edgar H. Schein, *Process Consultation* (Reading, MA: Addison-Wesley, 1969), pp. 32–37; Edgar H. Schein, *Process Consultation: Volume I* (1988), pp. 40–49.

[100] The classic work is Robert F. Bales, "Task Roles and Social Roles in Problem-Solving Groups," in Eleanor E. Maccoby, Theodore M. Newcomb, and E. L. Hartley (eds.), *Readings in Social Psychology* (New York: Holt, Rinehart & Winston, 1958).

[101] Schein, op. cit. (1988).

[102] For a good description of task and maintenance functions, see John J. Gabarro and Anne Harlan, "Note on Process Observation," Note 9-477-029 (Harvard Business School, 1976).

[103] See Daniel C. Feldman, "The Development and Enforcement of Group Norms," *Academy of Management Review*, Vol. 9 (1984), pp. 47–53.

[104] See Robert F. Allen and Saul Pilnick, "Confronting the Shadow Organization: How to Select and Defeat Negative Norms," *Organizational Dynamics* (Spring 1973), pp. 13–17; Alvin Zander, *Making Groups Effective* (San Francisco: Jossey-Bass, 1982), Ch. 4; Daniel C. Feldman, op. cit. (1984).

[105] For a summary of research on group cohesiveness, see Marvin E. Shaw, *Group Dynamics* (New York: McGraw-Hill, 1971), pp. 110–112, 192.

[106] Information from Stratford Sherman, "Secrets of HP's 'Muddled' Team," *Fortune* (March 18, 1996), pp. 116–120.

[107] See Jay R. Galbraith and Edward E. Lawler III, "The Challenges of Change: Organizing for Competitive Advantage," in Susan Albers Mohrman, Jay R. Galbraith, Edward E. Lawler III, and Associates, *Tomorrow's Organization: Crafting Winning Capabilities in a Dynamic World* (San Francisco: Jossey-Bass, 1998).

[108] See Kenichi Ohmae, "Quality Control Circles: They Work and Don't Work," *Wall Street Journal* (March 29, 1982), p. 16; Robert P. Steel, Anthony J. Mento, Benjamin L. Dilla, Nestor K. Ovalle, and Russell F. Lloyd, "Factors Influencing the Success and Failure of Two Quality Circles Programs," *Journal of Management*, Vol. 11, No. 1 (1985), pp. 99–119; Edward E. Lawler III, and Susan A. Mohrman, "Quality Circles: After the Honeymoon," *Organizational Dynamics*, Vol. 15, No. 4 (1987), pp. 42–54.

[109] See Jay R. Galbraith, *Designing Organizations* (San Francisco: Jossey-Bass, 1998).

[110] Jerry Yoram Wind and Jeremy Main, *Driving Change: How the Best Companies Are Preparing for the 21st Century* (New York: The Free Press, 1998), p. 135.

[111] Jessica Lipnack and Jeffrey Stamps, *Virtual Teams: Reaching Across Space, Time, and Organizations with Technology* (New York: Wiley, 1997).

[112] For a review of some alternatives, see Jeff Angus and Sean Gallagher, "Virtual Team Builders—Internet-Based Teamware Makes It Possible to Build Effective Teams from Widely Dispersed Participants," *Information Week* (May 4, 1998).

[113] Christine Perey, "Conferencing and Collaboration: Real-World Solutions for Business Communications," *Business Week*, special advertising section (1999).

[114] R. Brent Gallupe and William H. Cooper, "Brainstorming Electronically," *Sloan Management Review* (Fall 1993), pp. 27–36.

[115] William M. Bulkeley, "Computerizing Dull Meetings Is Touted as an Antidote to the Mouth That Bored," *Wall Street Journal* (January 28, 1992), pp. B1, B2.

[116] See Gallupe and Cooper, op. cit. (1993).

[117] For early research on related team concepts, see Richard E. Walton, "How to Counter Alienation in the Plant," *Harvard Business Review* (November–December 1972), pp. 70–81; Richard E. Walton, "Work Innovations at Topeka: After Six Years," *Journal of Applied Behavior Science*, Vol. 13 (1977), pp. 422–431; Richard E. Walton, "The Topeka Work System: Optimistic Visions, Pessimistic Hypotheses, and Reality," in Zager and Rosow (eds.), *The Innovative Organization*, Ch. 11.

[118] For concise overviews, see Susan J. Miller, David J. Hickson, and David C. Wilson, "Decision-Making in Organizations," in Stewart R. Clegg, Cynthia Hardy, and Walter R. Nord (eds.), *Handbook of Organizational Studies* (London: Sage Publications, 1996), pp. 293–312; George P. Huber, *Managerial Decision Making* (Glenview, IL: Scott, Foresman, 1980).

[119] This section is based on Michael D. Choen, James G. March, and Johan P. Olsen, "The Garbage Can Model of Organizational Choice," *Administrative Science Quarterly* 17 (1972): 1–25 and James G. March and Herbert A. Simon, *Organizations* (New York: Wiley, 1958), pp. 137–142.

[120] This traditional distinction is often attributed to Herbert Simon, *Administrative Behavior* (New York: Free Press, 1945), but an available

source is Herbert Simon, *The New Science of Management Decision* (New York: Harper & Row, 1960).

[121] Ibid.

[122] Also see Mary Zey (ed.), *Decision Making: Alternatives to Rational Choice Models* (Thousand Oaks, CA: Sage Publications, 1992).

[123] Simon, *Administrative Behavior.*

[124] For discussions, see Cohen, March, and Olsen (1972); Miller, Hickson, and Wilson (1996); and Michael Masuch and Perry LaPontin, "Beyond Garbage Cans: An AI Model of Organizational Choice," *Administrative Science Quarterly* 34 (1989): 38–67.

[125] Weston H. Agor, *Intuition in Organizations* (Newbury Park, CA: Sage Publications, 1989).

[126] Henry Mintzberg, "Planning on the Left Side and Managing on the Right," *Harvard Business Review* 54 (July/August 1976): 51–63.

[127] See Weston H. Agor, "How Top Executives Use Their Intuition to Make Important Decisions," *Business Horizons* 29 (January/February 1986): 49–53; and Agor (1989).

[128] The classic work in this area is found in a series of articles by D. Kahneman and A. Tversky, "Subjective Probability: A Judgement of Representativeness," *Cognitive Psychology* 3 (1972): 430–454; "On the Psychology of Prediction," *Psychological Review* 80 (1973): 237–251; "Prospect Theory: An Analysis of Decision under Risk," *Econometrica* 47 (1979): 263–291; "Psychology of Preferences," *Scientific American* (1982): 161–173; "Choices, Values, Frames" *American Psychologist* 39 (1984): 341–350.

[129] Definitions and subsequent discussion based on Max H. Bazerman, *Judgement in Managerial Decision Making*, 3rd ed. (New York: Wiley, 1994).

[130] Cameron M. Ford and Dennis A. Gioia, *Creative Action in Organizations* (Thousand Oaks, CA: Sage Publications, 1995).

[131] G. Wallas, *The Art of Thought* (New York: Harcourt, 1926). Cited in Bazerman (1994).

[132] E. Glassman, "Creative Problem Solving," *Supervisory Management* (January 1989): 21–26; and B. Kabanoff and J. R. Rossiter, "Recent Developments in Applied Creativity," *International Review of Industrial and Organizational Psychology* 9 (1994): 283–324.

[133] Information from Kenneth Labich, "Nike vs. Reebok," *Fortune* (September 18, 1995), pp. 90–106.

[134] James A. F. Stoner, *Management*, 2nd ed. (Englewood Cliffs, NJ: Prentice-Hall, 1982), pp. 167–168.

[135] Victor H. Vroom and Philip W. Yetton, *Leadership and Decision Making* (Pittsburgh: University of Pittsburgh Press, 1973); Victor H. Vroom and Arthur G. Jago, *The New Leadership* (Englewood Cliffs, NJ: Prentice-Hall, 1988).

[136] Barry M. Staw, "The Escalation of Commitment to a Course of Action," *Academy of Management Review* 6 (1981): 577–587; Barry M. Staw and Jerry Ross, "Knowing When to Pull the Plug," *Harvard Business Review* 65 (March/April 1987): 68–74. See also Glen Whyte, "Escalating Commitment to a Course of Action: A Reinterpretation," *Academy of Management Review* 11 (1986): 311–321.

[137] Joel Brockner, "The Escalation of Commitment to a Failing Course of Action: Toward Theoretical Progress," *Academy of Management Review* 17 (1992): 39–61; J. Ross and B. M. Staw, "Organizational Escalation and Exit: Lessons from the Shoreham Nuclear Power Plant," *Academy of Management Journal* 36 (1993): 701–732.

[138] Bazerman (1994), pp. 79–83.

[139] See Brockner (1992); Ross and Staw (1993); and J. Z. Rubin, "Negotiation: An Introduction to Some Issues and Themes," *American Behavioral Scientist* 27 (1983): 135–147.

[140] See "Computers That Think Are Almost Here," *Business Week* (July 17, 1995): 68–73.

[141] A. R. Dinnis and J. S. Valacich, "Computer Brainstorms: Two Heads Are Better Than One," *Journal of Applied Psychology* (February 1994): 77–86.

[142] For an expanded discussion of such ethical frameworks for decision making, see Linda A. Travino and Katherine A. Nelson, *Managing Business Ethics* (New York: Wiley, 1995).

[143] B. Kabanoff and J. R. Rossiter, "Recent Developments in Applied Cre-

[144] Fons Trompenaars, *Riding the Waves of Culture: Understanding Cultural Diversity in Business* (London: Nicholas Brealey Publishing, 1993), p. 6.

[145] See ibid., pp. 58–59.

[146] For a good discussion of decision making in Japanese organizations, see Min Chen, *Asian Management Systems* (New York: Routledge, 1995).

[147] Nancy J. Adler, *International Dimensions of Organizational Behavior*, 2nd ed. (Boston: PWS-Kent, 1991).

[148] See Miller, Hickson, and Wilson (1996).

[149] We would like to thank Kristi M. Lewis for emphasizing the importance of identifying criteria and weighing criteria and urging us to include this section on ethics.

[150] Stephen Fineman, "Emotion and Organizing," in Clegg, Hardy, and Nord *Handbook of Organizational Studies*, pp. 542–580.

[151] For an expanded discussion of ethical frameworks for decision making, see Linda A. Travino and Katherine A. Nelson, *Managing Business Ethics* (New York: Wiley, 1995); Saul W. Gellerman, "Why 'Good' Managers Make Bad Ethical Choices," *Harvard Business Review* 64 (July/August 1986): 85–90 and Barbara Ley Toffler, *Tough Choices: Managers Talk Ethics* (New York: Wiley, 1986).

[152] Ibid.

[153] One of the classic discussions is by Richard E. Walton, *Interpersonal Peacemaking: Confrontations and Third-Party Consultation* (Reading, MA: Addison-Wesley, 1969).

[154] Kenneth W. Thomas and Warren H. Schmidt, "A Survey of Managerial Interests with Respect to Conflict," *Academy of Management Journal* 19 (1976): 315–318.

[155] For a good overview see Richard E. Walton, *Managing Conflict: Interpersonal Dialogue and Third Party Roles*, 2nd ed. (Reading, MA: Addison-Wesley, 1987) and Dean Tjosvold, *The Conflict-Positive Organization: Stimulate Diversity and Create Unity* (Reading, MA: Addison-Wesley, 1991).

[156] Walton (1969).

[157] Ibid.

[158] Richard E. Walton and John M. Dutton, "The Management of Interdepartmental Conflict: A Model and Review," *Administrative Science Quarterly* 14 (1969): 73–84.

[159] Geert Hofstede, *Culture's Consequences: International Differences in Work-Related Values* (Beverly Hills, CA: Sage Publications, 1980) and Geert Hofstede, "Cultural Constraints in Management Theories," *Academy of Management Executive* 7 (1993): 81–94.

[160] These stages are consistent with the conflict models described by Alan C. Filley, *Interpersonal Conflict Resolution* (Glenview, IL: Scott, Foresman, 1975); and Louis R. Pondy, "Organizational Conflict: Concepts and Models," *Administrative Science Quarterly* 12 (September 1967): 269–320.

[161] Information from "Capitalizing on Diversity: Navigating the Seas of the Multicultural Workforce and Workplace," *Business Week*, Special Advertising Section (December 4, 1998).

[162] Walton and Dutton (1969).

[163] Rensis Likert and Jane B. Likert, *New Ways of Managing Conflict* (New York: McGraw-Hill, 1976).

[164] See Jay Galbraith, *Designing Complex Organizations* (Reading, MA: Addison-Wesley, 1973); David Nadler and Michael Tushman, *Strategic Organizational Design* (Glenview, IL: Scott, Foresman, 1988).

[165] E. M. Eisenberg and M. G. Witten, "Reconsidering Openness in Organizational Communication," *Academy of Management Review* 12 (1987): 418–426.

[166] R. G. Lord and M. C. Kernan, "Scripts as Determinants of Purposeful Behavior in Organizations," *Academy of Management Review* 12 (1987): 265–277.

[167] See Filley (1975); and L. David Brown, *Managing Conflict at Organizational Interfaces* (Reading, MA: Addison-Wesley, 1983).

[168] Ibid., pp. 27, 29.

[169] For discussions, see Robert R. Blake and Jane Strygley Mouton, "The Fifth Achievement," *Journal of Applied Behavioral Science* 6 (1970): 413–427; Kenneth Thomas, "Conflict and Conflict Management," in M. D. Dunnett (ed.), *Handbook of Industrial and Organizational Behavior* (Chicago: Rand McNally, 1976), pp. 889–935; and Kenneth W. Thomas, "Toward Multi-Dimensional Values in Teaching: The Examples of Conflict Behaviors," *Academy of Management Review* 2 (1977): 484–490.

[170] For an excellent overview, see Roger Fisher and William Ury, *Getting to Yes: Negotiating Agreement Without Giving In* (New York: Penguin, 1983). See also James A. Wall, Jr., Negotiation: Theory and Practice (Glenview, IL: Scott, Foresman, 1985).

[171] Roy J. Lewicki and Joseph A. Litterer, *Negotiation* (Homewood, IL: Irwin, 1985), pp. 315–319.

[172] Ibid., pp. 328–329.

[173] For a good discussion, see Michael H. Bond, *Behind the Chinese Face* (London: Oxford University Press, 1991); and Richard D. Lewis, *When Cultures Collide*, Chapter 23 (London: Nicholas Brealey Publishing, 1996).

[1774] Following discussion based on Fisher and Ury (1983); and Lewicki and Litterer, (1985).

[175] This example is developed from Max H. Bazerman, *Judgment in Managerial Decision Making*, 2nd ed. (New York: Wiley, 1991), pp. 106–108.

[176] For a detailed discussion, see Fisher and Ury (1983), and Lewicki and Litterer (1985).

[177] Developed from Bazerman (1991), pp. 127–141.

[178] Fisher and Ury (1983), p. 33.

[179] Lewicki and Litterer (1985), pp. 177–181.

Source Notes

Information from William B. Brenneman, J. Bernard Keys, and Robert M. Fulmer, "Learning Across a Living Company: The Shell Companies' Experiences," *Organizational Dynamics* (Summer 1998), pp. 67–68.

Information from Katharine Mieszkowski, "Web Commerce As If Customers Mattered," *Fast Company* (November 1998), pp. 98ff.

Information from Eric Sundstrom and Associates, *Supporting Work Team Effectiveness* (San Francisco: Jossey-Bass, 1999), pp. 218–223.

Information from Rhonda Thompson, "An Employee's View of Empowerment," *HR Focus* (July 1993), p. 14.

Information from Eric Sundstrom and Associates, *Supporting Work Team Effectiveness* (San Francisco: Jossey-Bass, 1999), p. 233.

Information from a personal visit to the Benevia plant (October 15–17, 1997), by J. G. Hunt.

Information from Leonard D. Goodstein and Howard E. Butz, "Customer Value: The Linchpin of Organizational Change," *Organizational Dynamics* (Summer 1998), pp. 26–27.

Information from Jack O'Toole, *Forming the Future: Lessons from the Saturn Corporation* (Cambridge, MA: Blackledge, 1996), Ch. 5, 1–5.

Information from Barry A. Macy, *Successful Strategic Change* (San Francisco: Barrett-Koehler, in press).

Developed from E. E. Lawler III, "Total Quality Management and Employee Involvement: Are They Compatible?" *Academy of Management Executive*, Vol. 8, No. 1 (1994), pp. 68–76.

Information from B. A. Macy, *Successful Strategic Change* (San Francisco: Barrett-Koehler, in press).

Adapted from Bradley L. Kirkman, Kevin B. Lowe, and Dianne P. Young, "The Challenge of Leadership in High Performance Work Organizations," *Journal of Leadership Studies*, Vol. 5, No. 2, (1998), p. 8.

Based on Eryn Brown, "VF Corp. Changes Its Underware," *Fortune* (December 7, 1998), p. 117.

Sony: Information from "Videoconferencing by Sony, Naturally," Business Week (November 16, 1998), special advertising section.

EDS: Information from Eric Matson, "The Seven Sins of Deadly Meetings," *Fast Company Handbook of the Business Revolution* (New York: Fast Company, 1997), p. 31.

W. L. Gore & Associates: Information from Shelley Branch, "The 100 Best Companies to Work for in America," *Fortune* (January 11, 1999), p. 126.

Information from Jennifer Scott, "More Workers Have Option of Taking Stock in Company," *The Columbus Dispatch* (January 25, 1999), pp. 10–11.

Developed from Edgar H. Schein, *Process Consultation*, Vol. 1. Copyright © 1988 (Addison-Wesley Publishing Company), Chapter 6.

Excerpted from "Employee Case Study," Corning Glass Works, located on the corporate Web site at http://www.corning.com/company_info/index.html. Used by permission.

Charles Schwab & Co.: Information from Eric Matson, "The Seven Sins of Deadly Meetings," *Fast Company Handbook of the Business Revolution* (New York: Fast Company, 1997), p. 31.

John R. Schermerhorn, Jr., *Management*, 5th ed. (New York: Wiley, 1996), p. 274. Used by permission.

PNCBank.com.

PNCBank.com/whoarewe/corpinfo/officers.html.

Nokia Annual Report, 1997, p. 22.

"The Brain Behind the Brain," *Business Week* (July 17, 1995), p. 71.

Analog.com/publications/DSP; Otis Port and Paul C. Judge, "Chips That Mimic the Human Senses," *Business Week* (November 30, 1998), pp. 158–159.

Information from Mary Scott, "Odwalla, Inc.," *Business Ethics* (November/December 1995), p. 35.

Reprinted from Victor H. Vroom and Arthur G. Jago, *The New Leadership* (Englewood Cliffs, NJ: Prentice-Hall, 1988), p. 184. Used by permission of the authors.

John R. Schermerhorn, Jr., *Management*, 6th ed. (New York: Wiley, 199), p. 341. Used by permission.

Honda Motors: Information from "Capitalizing on Diversity: Navigating the Seas of the Multicultural Workforce and Workplace," *Business Week*, Special Advertising Section (December 4, 1998).

Sun Microsystems: Information from Sue Shellenbarger, "More Managers Find a Happy Staff Leads to Happy Customers," *The Wall Street Journal* (December 23, 1998), p. B1.

HRM News: Information from Carol Kleiman, "Performance Review Comes 'Full Circle'," *The Columbus Dispatch* (January 31, 1999), p. 29I.

Deloitte Touche: Information from Sue Shellenbarger, "Three Myths that Make Managers Push Staff to the Edge of Burnout," *The Wall Street Journal* (March 17, 1999), pl. B1.

EEOC: Information from "Suspect Age Bias? Try Proving It," *Fortune* (February 1, 1999), p. 58.

Section Three

Section Three

What Is Motivation?

If asked to identify a major concern or problem at work, a manager is very likely to cite "motivational" need to do something that will encourage people to work harder to do "what I want." Formally defined, **motivation** refers to the individual forces that account for the direction, level, and persistence of a person's effort expended at work. *Direction* refers to an individual's choice when presented with a number of possible alternatives (e.g., whether to exert effort toward product quality or toward product quantity). *Level* refers to the amount of effort a person puts forth (e.g., a lot or a little). *Persistence* refers to the length of time a person sticks with a given action (e.g., to try to achieve product quantity and give up when it is found difficult to attain).

■ **Motivation** refers to forces within an individual that account for the level, direction, and persistence of effort expended at work.

■ REINFORCEMENT, CONTENT, AND PROCESS THEORIES

The theories of motivation can be divided into three broad categories.[1] **Reinforcement theories** emphasize the linkage between individual behavior and some specific outcomes to show how managers can alter the direction, level, or persistence of individual actions. They focus on the observable rather than what is inside an employee's head. Thus, reinforcement views place a premium on observing individuals to see which work-related outcomes are highly valued. By altering when, where, how, and why some types of rewards are given, the manager can change the apparent motivation of employees by providing a systematic set of consequences to shape behavior. **Content theories** focus primarily on individual needs—the physiological or psychological deficiencies that we feel a compulsion to reduce or eliminate. These theories suggest that the manager's job is to create a work environment that responds positively to individual needs. They help to explain how poor performance, undesirable behaviors, low satisfaction, and the like can be caused by "blocked" needs or needs that are not satisfied on the job. **Process theories** focus on the thought or cognitive processes that take place within the minds of people and that influence their behavior. Whereas a content approach may identify job security as an important need for an individual, a process approach probes further to identify why the person behaves in particular ways relative to available rewards and work opportunities. Ultimately, we use the insights of three sets of theories to offer an integrated view of motivational dynamics that should be useful in any work setting.[2]

■ **Reinforcement theories** emphasize the means through which operant conditioning takes place.

■ **Content theories** profile different needs that may motivate individual behavior.

■ **Process theories** seek to understand the thought processes that determine behavior.

■ MOTIVATION ACROSS CULTURES

Before we examine the motivation theories in detail, an important caveat is in order. Motivation is a key concern in firms across the globe. However, North

American theories (and these are the only ones discussed in this section) are subject to cultural limitations.[3] The determinants of motivation and the best ways to deal with it are likely to vary considerably across Asia, South America, Eastern Europe, and Africa. Individual values and attitudes—both important aspects of motivation—have strong cultural foundations. What proves "motivational" as a reward in one culture, for example, might not work in another. We should be sensitive to these issues and avoid being parochial or ethnocentric by assuming that people in all cultures are motivated by the same things in the same ways.[4]

Reinforcement

■ **Reinforcement** is the administration of a consequence as a result of behavior.

In OB, reinforcement has a very specific meaning that has its origin in some classic studies in psychology.[5] **Reinforcement** is the administration of a consequence as a result of a behavior. Managing reinforcement properly can change the direction, level, and persistence of an individual's behavior. To understand this idea, we need to review some of the concepts on conditioning and reinforcement you learned in your basic psychology course. We will then move on to applications.

■ CLASSICAL AND OPERANT CONDITIONING

■ **Classical conditioning** is a form of learning through association that involves the manipulation of stimuli to influence behavior.

Recall that Ivan Pavlov studied classical conditioning. **Classical conditioning** is a form of learning through association that involves the manipulation of stimuli to influence behavior. The Russian psychologist "taught" dogs to salivate at the sound of a bell by ringing the bell when feeding the dogs. The sight of the food naturally caused the dogs to salivate. Eventually, the dogs "learned" to associate the bell ringing with the presentation of meat and to salivate at the ringing of the bell alone. Such "learning" through association is so common in organizations that it is often ignored until it causes considerable confusion. Take a look at Figure 3.1. The key is to understand a stimulus and a conditioned stimulus. A

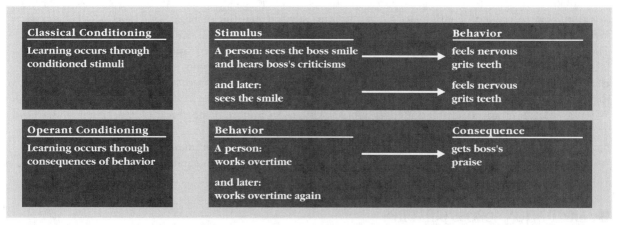

Figure 3.1
Differences between classical and operant conditioning approaches.

stimulus is something that incites action and draws forth a response (the meat for the dogs). The trick is to associate one neutral potential stimulus (the bell ringing) with another initial stimulus that already affects behavior (the meat). The once-neutral stimulus is called a *conditioned stimulus* when it affects behavior in the same way as the initial stimulus. In Figure 3.1, the boss's smiling becomes a conditioned stimulus because of its linkage to his criticisms.

Operant conditioning, popularized by B. F. Skinner, is an extension of the classical case to much more practical affairs.[6] It includes more than just a stimulus and a response behavior. **Operant conditioning** is the process of controlling behavior by manipulating its consequences. Classical and operant conditioning differ in two important ways. First, control in operant conditioning is via manipulation of consequences. Second, operant conditioning calls for examining antecedents, behavior, and consequences. The *antecedent* is the condition leading up to or "cueing" behavior. For example, in Figure 3.1, an agreement between the boss and the employee to work overtime as needed is an antecedent. If the employee works overtime, this would be the *behavior* while the *consequence* would be the boss's praise.

If a boss wants a behavior to be repeated, such as working overtime, she must manipulate the consequences. The basis for manipulating consequences is E. L. Thorndike's law of effect.[7] The **law of effect** is simple but powerful: behavior that results in a pleasant outcome is likely to be repeated while behavior that results in an unpleasant outcome is not likely to be repeated. The implications of this law are rather straightforward. If, as a supervisor, you want more of a behavior, you must make the consequences for the individual positive.

Note that the emphasis is on consequences that can be manipulated rather than on consequences inherent in the behavior itself. OB research often emphasizes specific types of rewards that are considered by the reinforcement perspective to influence individual behavior. *Extrinsic rewards* are positively valued work outcomes that are given to the individual by some other person. They are important external reinforcers or environmental consequences that can substantially influence a person's work behaviors through the law of effect. Figure 3.2 presents a sample of extrinsic rewards that managers can allocate to their subordinates.[8] Some of these rewards are contrived, or planned, rewards that have direct costs and budgetary implications. Examples are pay increases and cash bonuses. A second category includes natural rewards that have no cost other

■ A **stimulus** is something that incites action.

■ **Operant conditioning** is the process of controlling behavior by manipulating, or "operating" on, its consequences.

■ The **law of effect** is the observation that behavior that results in a pleasing outcome is likely to be repeated; behavior that results in an unpleasant outcome is not likely to be repeated.

Figure 3.2
A sample of extrinsic rewards allocated by managers.

than the manager's personal time and efforts. Examples are verbal praise and recognition in the workplace.

■ REINFORCEMENT STRATEGIES

We now bring the notions of classical conditioning, operant conditioning, reinforcement, and extrinsic rewards together to show how the direction, level, and persistence of individual behavior can be changed. This combination is called "OB Mod" after its longer title of **organization behavior modification**. **OB Mod** is the systematic reinforcement of desirable work behavior and the nonreinforcement or punishment of unwanted work behavior. OB Mod includes four basic reinforcement strategies: positive reinforcement, negative reinforcement (or avoidance), punishment, and extinction.[9]

Positive Reinforcement   B. F. Skinner and his followers advocate **positive reinforcement**—the administration of positive consequences that tend to increase the likelihood of repeating the desirable behavior in similar settings. For example, a Texas Instruments manager nods to a subordinate to express approval after she makes a useful comment during a sales meeting. Obviously, the boss wants more useful comments. Later, the subordinate makes another useful comment, just as the boss hoped she would.

To begin using a strategy of positive reinforcement, we need to be aware that positive reinforcers and rewards are not necessarily the same. Recognition, for example, is both a reward and a potential positive reinforcer. Recognition becomes a positive reinforcer only if a person's performance later improves. Sometimes, rewards turn out not to be positive reinforcers. For example, a supervisor at Boeing might praise a subordinate in front of other group members for finding errors in a report. If the group members then give the worker the silent treatment, however, the worker may stop looking for errors in the future. In this case, the supervisor's "reward" does not serve as a positive reinforcer.

To have maximum reinforcement value, a reward must be delivered only if the desired behavior is exhibited. That is, the reward must be contingent on the desired behavior. This principle is known as the **law of contingent reinforcement**. In the previous Texas Instruments example, the supervisor's praise was contingent on the subordinate's making constructive comments. Finally, the reward must be given as soon as possible after the desired behavior. This is known as the **law of immediate reinforcement**.[10] If the TI boss waited for the annual performance review to praise the subordinate for providing constructive comments, the law of immediate reinforcement would be violated.

Now that we have presented the general concepts, it is time to address two important issues of implementation.[11] First, what do you do if the behavior approximates what you want but is not exactly on target? Second, is it necessary to provide reinforcement each and every time? These are issues of shaping and scheduling, respectively.

Shaping   If the desired behavior is specific in nature and is difficult to achieve, a pattern of positive reinforcement, called shaping, can be used. **Shaping** is the creation of a new behavior by the positive reinforcement of successive approxi-

■ **Organization behavior modification (OB Mod)** is the systematic reinforcement of desirable work behavior and the nonreinforcement or punishment of unwanted work behavior.

■ **Positive reinforcement** is the administration of positive consequences that tend to increase the likelihood of repeating the behavior in similar settings.

■ The **law of contingent reinforcement** is the view that, for a reward to have maximum reinforcing value, it must be delivered only if the desired behavior is exhibited.

■ The **law of immediate reinforcement** states that the more immediate the delivery of a reward after the occurrence of a desirable behavior, the greater the reinforcing effect on behavior.

■ **Shaping** is the creation of a new behavior by the positive reinforcement of successive approximations to the desired behavior.

mations leading to the desired behavior. For example, new machine operators in the Ford Motor casting operation in Ohio must learn a complex series of tasks in pouring molten metal into the casting in order to avoid gaps, overfills, or cracks.[12] The molds are filled in a three-step process, with each step progressively more difficult than its predecessor. Astute master craftspersons first show neophytes how to pour the first step and give praise based on what they did right. As the apprentices gain experience, they are given praise only when all of the elements of the first step are completed successfully. Once the apprentices have mastered the first step, they progress to the second. Reinforcement is given only when the entire first step and an aspect of the second step are completed successfully. Over time, apprentices learn all three steps and are given contingent positive rewards immediately for a complete casting that has no cracks or gaps. In this way, behavior is shaped gradually rather than changed all at once.

Scheduling Positive Reinforcement   Positive reinforcement can be given according to either continuous or intermittent schedules. **Continuous reinforcement** administers a reward each time a desired behavior occurs. **Intermittent reinforcement** rewards behavior only periodically. These alternatives are important because the two schedules may have very different impacts on behavior. In general, continuous reinforcement elicits a desired behavior more quickly than does intermittent reinforcement. Thus, in the initial training of the apprentice casters, continuous reinforcement would be important. At the same time, continuous reinforcement is more costly in the consumption of rewards and is more easily extinguished when reinforcement is no longer present. In contrast, behavior acquired under intermittent reinforcement lasts longer upon the discontinuance of reinforcement than does behavior acquired under continuous reinforcement. In other words, it is more resistant to extinction. Thus, as the apprentices master an aspect of the pouring, the schedule is switched from continuous to intermittent reinforcement.

As shown in Figure 3.3, intermittent reinforcement can be given according to fixed or variable schedules. *Variable schedules* typically result in more consistent patterns of desired behavior than do fixed reinforcement schedules. *Fixed interval schedules* provide rewards at the first appearance of a behavior after a given time has elapsed. *Fixed ratio schedules* result in a reward each time a certain number of the behaviors have occurred. A *variable interval schedule* rewards behavior at random times, while a *variable ratio schedule* rewards behavior after a random number of occurrences. For example, as the apprentices perfect their technique for a stage of pouring castings, the astute masters switch to a variable ratio reinforcement.

Let's look at an example from Drankenfeld Colors, Washington, Pennsylvania, with 250 employees. The absentee rate of these employees was very low, and in a recent year 44 percent of the employees had perfect attendance records. The firm wanted to use positive reinforcement to showcase perfect attendance, even though attendance was already so positive. Consequently, it gave monetary awards of $50 for perfect attendance at 6 and 12 months, with a $25 bonus for a full year of perfect attendance. In addition, the firm entered employees with perfect attendance into a sweepstakes drawing at special award banquets. The winners received an all-expense-paid trip for two to a resort. Perfect attendance increased from 44 percent to 62 percent in the program's first year.[13]

■ **Continuous reinforcement** is a reinforcement schedule that administers a reward each time a desired behavior occurs.

■ **Intermittent reinforcement** is a reinforcement schedule that rewards behavior only periodically.

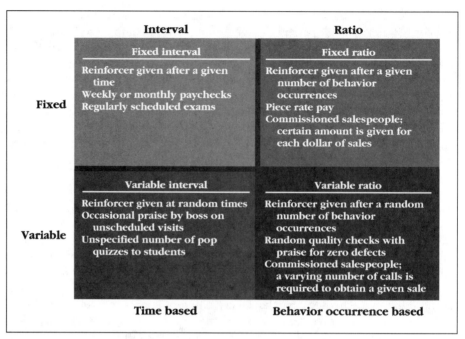

Figure 3.3
Four types of intermittent reinforcement schedules.

Let's consider what kind of reinforcement scheduling was used in this program. A strong argument can be made that a fixed ratio schedule was used, in conjunction with a variable ratio schedule. The first schedule rewarded attendance behaviors occurring within 6 months and 12 months, or the specific number of workday attendance occurring within these periods. Thus, for each period during which a perfect number of attendance days occurred, a person received an award—a fixed ratio schedule one.

The second schedule focuses on eligibility for the drawing. It is a variable ratio because a random number of perfect attendance days must pass before a specific employee receives a trip. Maintaining perfect attendance to qualify for the drawing is similar to playing a slot machine. In this variable ratio system, players keep putting coins in the machines because they don't have any idea when they will hit the jackpot.[14] Lotteries similar to Drankenfeld's have been used by firms as different as new car dealerships and New York Life Insurance.[15]

Negative Reinforcement (Avoidance)   A second reinforcement strategy used in OB Mod is **negative reinforcement** or avoidance—the withdrawal of negative consequences, which tends to increase the likelihood of repeating the desirable behavior in similar settings. For example, a manager at McDonald's regularly nags a worker about his poor performance and then stops nagging when the worker does not fall behind one day. We need to focus on two aspects here: the negative consequences followed by the withdrawal of these consequences when desirable behavior occurs. The term negative reinforcement comes from this withdrawal of the negative consequences. This strategy is also sometimes called avoidance because its intent is for the person to avoid the negative conse-

■ **Negative reinforcement** is the withdrawal of negative consequences, which tends to increase the likelihood of repeating the behavior in a similar setting; it is also known as avoidance.

quence by performing the desired behavior. For instance, we stop at a red light to avoid a traffic ticket or a worker who prefers the day shift is allowed to return to that shift if she performs well on the night shift.

Punishment A third OB Mod strategy is punishment. Unlike positive reinforcement and negative reinforcement, punishment is not intended to encourage positive behavior but to discourage negative behavior. Formally defined, **punishment** is the administration of negative consequences or the withdrawal of positive consequences that tend to reduce the likelihood of repeating the behavior in similar settings. The first type of punishment is illustrated by a Burger King manager who assigns a tardy worker to an unpleasant job, such as cleaning the restrooms. An example of withdrawing positive consequences is a Burger King manager who docks the employee's pay when she is tardy.

Some scholarly work illustrates the importance of punishment by showing that punishment administered for poor performance leads to enhanced performance without a significant effect on satisfaction. However, punishment seen by the workers as arbitrary and capricious leads to very low satisfaction, as well as low performance.[16] Thus, punishment can be handled poorly, or it can be handled well. Of course, the manager's challenge is to know when to use this strategy and how to use it correctly.

Finally, punishment may be offset by positive reinforcement received from another source. It is possible for a worker to be reinforced by peers at the same time that the worker is receiving punishment from the manager. Sometimes the positive value of such peer support is so great that the individual chooses to put up with the punishment. Thus, the undesirable behavior continues. As many times as a experienced worker may be verbally reprimanded by a supervisor for playing jokes on new employees, for example, the "grins" offered by other workers may well justify continuation of the jokes in the future.

Does all of this mean that punishment should never be administered? Of course not. The important things to remember are to administer punishment selectively and then to do it right.

Extinction The final OB Mod reinforcement strategy is **extinction**—the withdrawal of the reinforcing consequences for a given behavior. For example, Jack is often late for work, and his co-workers cover for him (positive reinforcement). The manager instructs Jack's co-workers to stop covering for him, withdrawing the reinforcing consequences. The manager has deliberately used extinction to get rid of an undesirable behavior. This strategy decreases the frequency of or weakens the behavior. The behavior is not "unlearned"; it simply is not exhibited. Since the behavior is no longer reinforced, it will reappear if reinforced again. Whereas positive reinforcement seeks to establish and maintain desirable work behavior, extinction is intended to weaken and eliminate undesirable behavior.

Summary of Reinforcement Strategies Figure 3.4 summarizes and illustrates the use of each OB Mod strategy. They are all designed to direct work behavior toward practices desired by management. Both positive and negative reinforcement are used to strengthen the desirable behavior of improving work quality when it occurs. Punishment is used to weaken the undesirable behavior of high error rate and involves either administering negative consequences or withdraw-

■ **Punishment** is the administration of negative consequences that tend to reduce the likelihood of repeating the behavior in similar settings.

■ **Extinction** is the withdrawal of the reinforcing consequences for a given behavior.

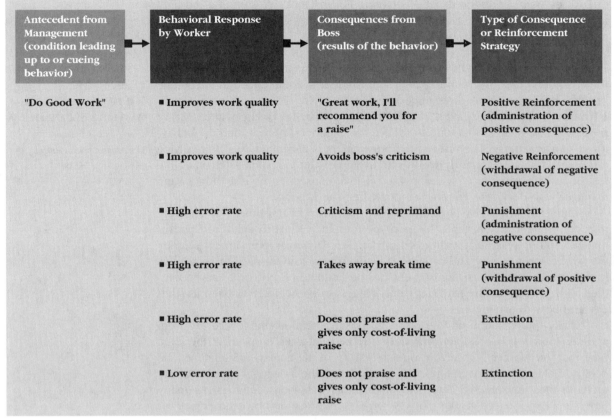

Antecedent from Management (condition leading up to or cueing behavior)	Behavioral Response by Worker	Consequences from Boss (results of the behavior)	Type of Consequence or Reinforcement Strategy
"Do Good Work"	■ Improves work quality	"Great work, I'll recommend you for a raise"	Positive Reinforcement (administration of positive consequence)
	■ Improves work quality	Avoids boss's criticism	Negative Reinforcement (withdrawal of negative consequence)
	■ High error rate	Criticism and reprimand	Punishment (administration of negative consequence)
	■ High error rate	Takes away break time	Punishment (withdrawal of positive consequence)
	■ High error rate	Does not praise and gives only cost-of-living raise	Extinction
	■ Low error rate	Does not praise and gives only cost-of-living raise	Extinction

Figure 3.4
Applying Reinforcement strategies.

ing positive consequences. Similarly, extinction is used deliberately to weaken the undesirable high error rate behavior when it occurs. Note also, however, that extinction is used inadvertently to weaken the desirable low error rate behavior. Finally, these strategies may be used in combination as well as independently.

■ REINFORCEMENT PERSPECTIVES: USAGE AND ETHICAL ISSUES

The effective use of reinforcement strategies can help manage human behavior at work. Testimony to this effect is found in the application of these strategies in many large firms, such as General Electric and B. F. Goodrich, and even in small firms, such as Mid-America Building Maintenance. Mid-America, a janitorial services firm in Wichita, Kansas, provides an incentive program to employees who work 90 consecutive workdays without an absence.[17] Reinforcement strategies are also supported by the growing number of consulting firms that specialize in reinforcement techniques.

Managerial use of these approaches is not without criticism, however. For example, some reports on the "success" of specific programs involve isolated cases that have been analyzed without the benefit of scientific research designs.

It is hard to conclude definitively whether the observed results were caused by reinforcement dynamics. In fact, one critic argues that the improved performance may well have occurred only because of the goal setting involved—that is, because specific performance goals were clarified, and workers were individually held accountable for their accomplishment.[18]

Another major criticism rests with the potential value dilemmas associated with using reinforcement to influence human behavior at work. For example, some critics maintain that the systematic use of reinforcement strategies leads to a demeaning and dehumanizing view of people that stunts human growth and development.[19] A related criticism is that managers abuse the power of their position and knowledge by exerting external control over individual behavior. Advocates of the reinforcement approach attack the problem head on: They agree that behavior modification involves the control of behavior, but they also argue that behavior control is an irrevocable part of every manager's job. The real question is how to ensure that any manipulation is done in a positive and constructive fashion.[20]

Content Theories of Motivation

Content theories, as noted earlier, suggest that motivation results from the individual's attempts to satisfy needs. Four of the better known content theories have been proposed by Abraham Maslow, Clayton Alderfer, David McClelland, and Frederick Herzberg. Each of these scholars offers a slightly different view of the needs individuals may bring with them to work.

■ HIERARCHY OF NEEDS THEORY

Abraham Maslow's **hierarchy of needs theory**, as shown in Figure 3.5, identifies five distinct levels of individual needs: from self-actualization and esteem, at the top, to social, safety, and physiological at the bottom.[21] Maslow assumes that some needs are more important than others and must be satisfied before the other needs can serve as motivators. For example, physiological needs must be satisfied before safety needs are activated, safety needs must be satisfied before social needs are activated, and so on.

Maslow's view is quite popular in U.S. firms because it appears easily implemented. Unfortunately, however, research evidence fails to support the existence of a precise five-step hierarchy of needs. The needs more likely operate in a flexible hierarchy. Some research suggests that **higher order needs** (esteem and self-actualization) tend to become more important than **lower order needs** (psychological, safety, and social) as individuals move up the corporate ladder.[22] Other studies report that needs vary according to a person's career stage, the size of the organization, and even geographical location.[23] There is also no consistent evidence that the satisfaction of a need at one level decreases its importance and increases the importance of the next higher need.[24] Finally, when the hierarchy of needs is examined across cultures, values such as those discussed in Section 2 become important.[25] For instance, social needs tend to dominate in more collectivist societies, such as Mexico and Pakistan.[26]

■ Maslow's **hierarchy of needs theory** offers a pyramid of physiological, safety, social, esteem, and self-actualization needs.

■ **Higher order needs** in Maslow's hierarchy are esteem and self-actualization.

■ **Lower order needs** in Maslow's hierarchy are physiological, safety, and social.

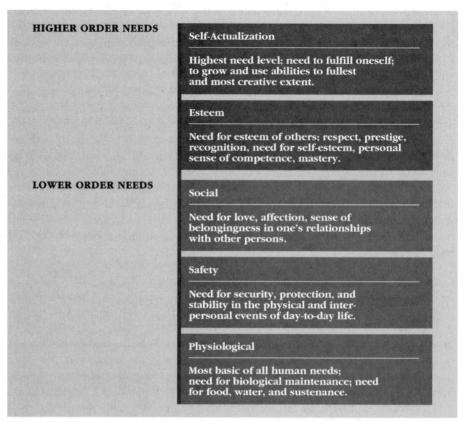

Figure 3.5
Higher order and lower order needs in Maslow's hierarchy of needs.

■ ERG THEORY

■ Alderfer's **ERG theory** identifies existence, relatedness, and growth needs.

■ **Existence needs** are desires for physiological and material well-being.

■ **Relatedness needs** are desires for satisfying interpersonal relationships.

■ **Growth needs** are desires for continued personal growth and development.

Clayton Alderfer's **ERG theory** is also based on needs but differs from Maslow's theory in three basic respects.[27] First, the theory collapses Maslow's five need categories into three: **existence needs**—desire for physiological and material well-being; **relatedness needs**—desire for satisfying interpersonal relationships; and **growth needs**—desire for continued personal growth and development. Second, whereas Maslow's theory argues that individuals progress up the "needs" hierarchy, ERG theory emphasizes a unique *frustration-regression* component. An already satisfied lower level need can become activated when a higher level need cannot be satisfied. Thus, if a person is continually frustrated in his or her attempts to satisfy growth needs, relatedness needs can again surface as key motivators. Third, unlike Maslow's theory, ERG theory contends that more than one need may be activated at the same time.

Even though more research is needed to shed more light on its validity, the supporting evidence on ERG theory is encouraging.[28] In particular, the theory's allowance for regression back to lower level needs is a valuable contribution to our thinking. It may help to explain why in some settings, for example, workers' complaints focus on wages, benefits, and working conditions—things relating to existence needs. Although these needs are important, their importance may be exaggerated because the workers' jobs cannot otherwise satisfy relatedness and growth needs. ERG theory thus offers a more flexible approach to understanding human needs than does Maslow's strict hierarchy.

■ ACQUIRED NEEDS THEORY

In the late 1940s, psychologist David I. McClelland and his co-workers began experimenting with the Thematic Apperception Test (TAT) as a way of measuring human needs.[29] The TAT is a projective technique that asks people to view pictures and write stories about what they see. In one case, McClelland showed three executives a photograph of a man sitting down and looking at family photos arranged on his work desk. One executive wrote of an engineer who was daydreaming about a family outing scheduled for the next day. Another described a designer who had picked up an idea for a new gadget from remarks made by his family. The third described an engineer who was intently working on a bridge-stress problem that he seemed sure to solve because of his confident look.[30] McClelland identified three themes in these TAT stories, with each corresponding to an underlying need that he believes is important for understanding individual behavior. These needs are (1) **need for achievement (nAch)**—the desire to do something better or more efficiently, to solve problems, or to master complex tasks; (2) **need for affiliation (nAff)**—the desire to establish and maintain friendly and warm relations with others; and (3) **need for power (nPower)**—the desire to control others, to influence their behavior, or to be responsible for others.

McClelland posits that these three needs are acquired over time, as a result of life experiences. He encourages managers to learn how to identify the presence of nAch, nAff, and nPower in themselves and in others and to be able to create work environments that are responsive to the respective need profiles.

The theory is particularly useful because each need can be linked with a set of work preferences. A high-need achiever will prefer individual responsibilities, challenging goals, and performance feedback. A high-need affiliator is drawn to interpersonal relationships and opportunities for communication. The high need-for-power type seeks influence over others and likes attention and recognition. If these needs are truly acquired, it may be possible to acquaint people with the need profiles required to succeed in various types of jobs. For instance, McClelland found that the combination of a moderate to high need for power and a lower need for affiliation is linked with senior executive success. High nPower creates the willingness to have influence or impact on others; lower nAff allows the manager to make difficult decisions without undue worry over being disliked.[31]

Research lends considerable insight into nAch in particular and includes some especially interesting applications in developing nations. For example, McClelland trained businesspeople in Kakinda, India, to think, talk, and act like high achievers by having them write stories about achievement and participate in a business game that encouraged achievement. The businesspeople also met with successful entrepreneurs and learned how to set challenging goals for their own businesses. Over a two-year period following these activities, the participants from the Kakinda study engaged in activities that created twice as many new jobs as those who hadn't received the training.[32]

■ TWO-FACTOR THEORY

Frederick Herzberg took a different approach to examining motivation. He simply asked workers to report the times they felt exceptionally good about their

■ **Need for achievement (nAch)** is the desire to do better, solve problems, or master complex tasks.

■ **Need for affiliation (nAff)** is the desire for friendly and warm relations with others.

■ **Need for power (nPower)** is the desire to control others and influence their behavior.

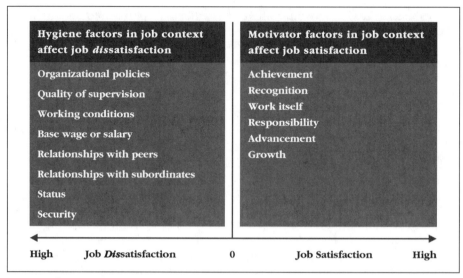

Figure 3.6
Sources of dissatisfaction and satisfaction in Herzberg's two-factor theory.

jobs and the times they felt exceptionally bad about them.[33] As shown in Figure 3.6, Herzberg and his associates noted that the respondents identified somewhat different things when they felt good or bad about their jobs. From this study they developed the **two-factor theory**, also known as the motivator-hygiene theory, which portrays different factors as primary causes of job satisfaction and job dissatisfaction.

According to this theory, **hygiene factors** are sources of job dissatisfaction. These factors are associated with the job context or work setting; that is, they relate more to the environment in which people work than to the nature of the work itself. Among the hygiene factors shown on the left in Figure 3.6 perhaps the most surprising is salary. Herzberg found that low salary makes people dissatisfied, but that paying them more does not necessarily satisfy or motivate them. In the two-factor theory, job satisfaction and job dissatisfaction are totally separate dimensions. Therefore, improving a hygiene factor, such as working conditions, will not make people satisfied with their work; it will only prevent them from being dissatisfied.

To improve job satisfaction, the theory directs attention to an entirely different set of factors—the **motivator factors** shown on the right in Figure 3.6. These factors are related to job content—what people actually do in their work. Adding these satisfiers or motivators to people's jobs is Herzberg's link to performance. These factors include sense of achievement, recognition, and responsibility.

According to Herzberg, when these opportunities are not available, low job satisfaction causes a lack of motivation and performance suffers. He suggests the technique of job enrichment as a way of building satisfiers into job content. For now, the notion is well summarized in this statement by Herzberg: "If you want people to do a good job, give them a good job to do."[34]

OB scholars continue to debate the merits of the two-factor theory and its applications.[35] Many are unable to confirm the theory. Many criticize it as being method bound. This is a serious criticism, for the scientific approach requires

■ Herzberg's **two-factor theory** identifies job context as the source of job dissatisfaction and job content as the source of job satisfaction.

■ **Hygiene factors** in job context, the work setting, are sources of job dissatisfaction.

■ **Motivator factors** in job content, the tasks people actually do, are sources of job satisfaction.

that theories be verifiable under different research methods. Furthermore, this theory, just like the other content theories, fails to account for individual differences, to link motivation and needs to both satisfaction and performance, or to consider cultural and professional differences.[36]

The content theories remain popular in management circles because of their simplicity and the direct apparent linkage from needs to behavior. At the same time, none of the theories links needs directly to motivated behavior desired by the manager. Rather, managers just misinterpret the theories and often inappropriately assume that they know the needs of their subordinates. Thus, we advise extreme care in simplistic application of content theories. We will return to these theories when we incorporate satisfaction into the discussion of motivation.

Process Theories

The various content theories emphasize the "what" aspects of motivation. That is, they tend to look for ways to improve motivation by dealing with activated or deprived needs. They do not delve formally into the thought processes through which people choose one action over another in the workplace. *Process theories* focus on thought processes. Although there are many process theories, we will concentrate on equity and expectancy theory.

■ Adams' **equity theory** posits that people will act to eliminate any felt inequity in the rewards received for their work in comparison with others.

■ EQUITY THEORY

Equity theory is based on the phenomenon of social comparison and is best applied to the workplace through the writing of J. Stacy Adams.[37] Adams argues that when people gauge the fairness of their work outcomes relative to others, any perceived inequity is a motivating state of mind. Perceived inequity occurs when someone believes that the rewards received for their work contributions compare unfavorably to the rewards other people appear to have received for their work. When such perceived inequity exists, the theory states that people will be motivated to act in ways that remove the discomfort and restore a sense of felt equity.

Felt negative inequity exists when an individual feels that he or she has received relatively less than others have in proportion to work inputs. *Felt positive inequity* exists when an individual feels that he or she has received relatively more than others have. When either feeling exists, the individual will likely engage in one or more of the following behaviors to restore a sense of equity.

THE EFFECTIVE MANAGER 3.1

STEPS FOR MANAGING THE EQUITY PROCESS

- Recognize that equity comparisons are inevitable in the workplace.
- Anticipate felt negative inequities when rewards are given.
- Communicate clear evaluations of any rewards given.
- Communicate an appraisal of performance on which the reward is based.
- Communicate comparison points appropriate in the situation.

How to restore perceived equity

- Change work inputs (e.g., reduce performance efforts).
- Change the outcomes (rewards) received (e.g., ask for a raise).

- Leave the situation (e.g., quit).
- Change the comparison points (e.g., compare self to a different co-worker).
- Psychologically distort the comparisons (e.g., rationalize that the inequity is only temporary and will be resolved in the future).
- Take actions to change the inputs or outputs of the comparison person (e.g., get a co-worker to accept more work).

The equity comparison intervenes between the allocation of rewards and the ultimate impact on the recipients. What may seem fair and equitable to a group leader, for example, might be perceived as unfair and inequitable by a team member after comparisons are made with other teammates. Furthermore, such feelings of inequity are determined solely by the individual's interpretation of the situation. It is not the reward-giver's intentions that count, but it is how the recipient perceives the reward that will determine actual motivational outcomes.

Research indicates that people who feel they are overpaid (perceived positive inequity) increase the quantity or quality of their work, whereas those who feel they are underpaid (perceived negative inequity) decrease the quantity or quality of their work.[38] The research is most conclusive with respect to felt negative inequity. It appears that people are less comfortable when they are underrewarded than when they are overrewarded. Such results, however, are particularly tied to individualistic cultures in which self-interests tend to govern social comparisons. In more collectivist cultures, such as those of many Asian countries, the concern often runs more for equality than equity. This allows for solidarity with the group and helps to maintain harmony in social relationships.[39]

■ EXPECTANCY THEORY

■ Vroom's **expectancy theory** argues that work motivation is determined by individual beliefs regarding effort/performance relationships and work outcomes.

Victor Vroom's **expectancy theory** posits that motivation is a result of a rational calculation.[40] A person is motivated to the degree that he or she believes that (1) effort will yield acceptable performance, (2) performance will be rewarded, and (3) the value of the rewards is highly positive. The interactive combination of all three influences motivation. (See Figure 3.7.) Thus, some key concepts are defined in terms of probabilities.

■ **Expectancy** is the probability that work effort will be followed by performance accomplishment.

- The probability assigned by an individual that work effort will be followed by a given level of achieved task performance is called **expectancy**. Expectancy would equal 0 if the person felt it were impossible to achieve the given performance level; it would equal 1 if a person were 100 percent certain that the performance could be achieved.

■ **Instrumentality** is the probability that performance will lead to various work outcomes.

- **Instrumentality** is the probability assigned by the individual that a given level of achieved task performance will lead to various work outcomes. Instrumentality also varies from 0 to 1. (Strictly speaking, Vroom's treatment of instrumentality would allow it to vary from −1 to +1. We use the probability definition here and the 0 to +1 range for pedagogical purposes; it is consistent with the instrumentality notion.)

■ **Valence** is the value to the individual of various work outcomes.

- **Valence** is the value attached by the individual to various work outcomes. Valences form a scale from −1 (very undesirable outcome) to +1 (very desirable outcome). Vroom posits that motivation (*M*), expectancy (*E*), instrumen-

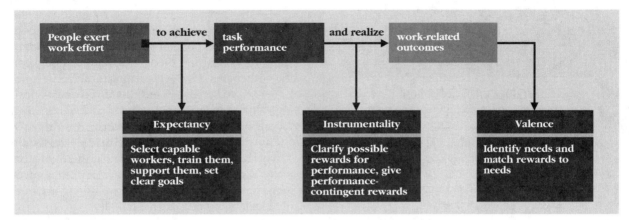

Figure 3.7
Key terms and managerial implications of Vroom's expectancy theory.

tality (I), and valence (V) are related to one another by the equation: $M = (E) \times (I) \times (V)$. This multiplier effect means that the motivational appeal of a given work path is sharply reduced whenever any one or more of these factors approaches the value of zero. Conversely, for a given reward to have a high and positive motivational impact as a work outcome, the expectancy, instrumentality, and valence associated with the reward all must be high and positive.

Suppose that a manager is wondering whether or not the prospect of earning a merit raise will be motivational to an employee. Expectancy theory predicts that motivation to work hard to earn the merit pay will be low if *expectancy* is low—a person feels that he or she cannot achieve the necessary performance level. Motivation will also be low if *instrumentality* is low—the person is not confident a high level of task performance will result in a high merit pay raise. Motivation will also be low if *valence* is low—the person places little value on a merit pay increase. And motivation will be low if any combination of these exists. Thus, the multiplier effect requires managers to act to maximize expectancy, instrumentality, and valence when seeking to create high levels of work motivation. A zero at any location on the right side of the expectancy equation will result in zero motivation.

Expectancy logic argues that a manager must try to intervene actively in work situations to maximize work expectancies, instrumentalities, and valences that support organizational objectives.[41] To influence expectancies, managers should select people with proper abilities, train them well, support them with needed resources, and identify clear performance goals. To influence instrumentality, managers should clarify performance–reward relationships and confirm these relationships when rewards are actually given for performance accomplishments. To influence valences, managers should identify the needs that are important to each individual and then try to adjust available rewards to match these needs.

A great deal of research on expectancy theory has been conducted, and review articles are available.[42] Although the theory has received substantial sup-

■ **Extrinsic rewards** are given to the individual by some other person in the work setting.

■ **Intrinsic rewards** are received by the individual directly through task performance.

port, specific details, such as the operation of the multiplier effect, remain subject to some question. One of the more popular modifications of Vroom's original version of the theory distinguishes between work outcomes for calculating valence.[43] Researchers have separated **extrinsic rewards**—positively valued work outcomes given to the individual by some other person—from intrinsic rewards (see The Effective Manager 3.2). **Intrinsic rewards** are positively valued work outcomes that the individual receives directly as a result of task performance. A feeling of achievement after accomplishing a particularly challenging task is an example.

Expectancy theory does not specify exactly which rewards will motivate particular groups of workers. In this sense, the theory allows for the fact that the rewards and their link with performance are likely to be seen as quite different in different cultures. It helps to explain some apparently counterintuitive findings. For example, a pay raise motivated one group of Mexican workers to work fewer hours. They wanted a certain amount of money in order to enjoy things other than work rather than just more money. A Japanese sales representative's promotion to manager of a U.S. company adversely affected his performance. His superiors did not realize that the promotion embarrassed him and distanced him from his colleagues.[44]

Integrating The Motivation Theories

As you can see rewards, needs, cognitions, satisfaction, and performance are all integral to the discussion of motivation. Understanding the linkage between satisfaction and performance will help integrate all the views we have discussed.

■ JOB SATISFACTION

■ **Job satisfaction** is the degree to which individuals feel positively or negatively about their jobs.

Formally defined, **job satisfaction** is the degree to which individuals feel positively or negatively about their jobs. It is an attitude or emotional response to one's tasks as well as to the physical and social conditions of the workplace. At first glance, and from the perspective of Herzberg's two-factor theory, some aspects of job satisfaction should be motivational and lead to positive employment relationships and high levels of individual job performance. But as we will discuss, the issues are more complicated than this conclusion suggests.

On a daily basis, managers must be able to infer the job satisfaction of others by careful observation and interpretation of what they say and do while going about their jobs. Sometimes, it is also useful to examine more formally the levels of job satisfaction among groups of workers, especially through formal interviews or questionnaires. Increasingly, other methods are being used as well such as focus groups and computer-based attitude surveys.[45]

Among the many available job satisfaction questionnaires that have been used over the years, two popular ones are the Minnesota Satisfaction Questionnaire (MSQ) and the Job Descriptive Index (JDI).[46] Both address aspects of satisfaction with which good managers should be concerned for the people reporting to them. For example, the MSQ measures satisfaction with working conditions, chances for advancement, freedom to use one's own judgment, praise for doing a good job, and feelings of accomplishment, among others. The five facets of job satisfaction measured by the JDI are:

- *The work itself*—responsibility, interest, and growth.
- *Quality of supervision*—technical help and social support.
- *Relationships with co-workers*—social harmony and respect.
- *Promotion opportunities*—chances for further advancement.
- *Pay*—adequacy of pay and perceived equity vis-à-vis others.

Five facets of job satisfaction

■ JOB SATISFACTION, RETENTION AND PERFORMANCE

The importance of job satisfaction can be viewed in the context of two decisions people make about their work. The first is the decision to belong—that is, to join and remain a member of an organization. The second is the decision to perform—that is, to work hard in pursuit of high levels of task performance. Not everyone who belongs to an organization performs up to expectations.

The decision to belong concerns an individual's attendance and longevity at work. In this sense, job satisfaction influences *absenteeism*, or the failure of people to attend work. In general, workers who are satisfied with the job itself have more regular attendance and are less likely to be absent for unexplained reasons than are dissatisfied workers. Job satisfaction can also affect turnover, or decisions by people to terminate their employment. Simply put, dissatisfied workers are more likely than satisfied workers to quit their jobs.[47]

What is the relationship between job satisfaction and performance? There is considerable debate on this issue, with three alternative points of view evident: (1) satisfaction causes performance, (2) performance causes satisfaction, and (3) rewards cause both performance and satisfaction.[48]

Argument: Satisfaction Causes Performance   If job satisfaction causes high levels of performance, the message to managers is quite simple: To increase employees' work performance, make them happy. Research, however, indicates that no simple and direct link exists between individual job satisfaction at one point in time and work performance at a later point. This conclusion is widely recognized among OB scholars, even though some evidence suggests that the relationship holds better for professional or higher level employees than for non-professionals or those at lower job levels. Job satisfaction alone is not a consistent predictor of individual work performance.

Argument: Performance Causes Satisfaction   If high levels of performance cause job satisfaction, the message to managers is quite different. Rather than focusing first on peoples' job satisfaction, attention should be given to helping people achieve high performance; job satisfaction would be expected to follow. Research indicates an empirical relationship between individual performance measured at a certain time period and later job satisfaction. A basic model of this relationship, based on the work of Edward E. Lawler and Lyman Porter, maintains that performance accomplishment leads to rewards that, in turn, lead to satisfaction.[49] In this model rewards are intervening variables; that is, they "link" performance with later satisfaction. In addition, a moderator variable—perceived equity of rewards—further affects the relationship. The moderator indicates that performance will lead to satisfaction only if rewards are perceived as equitable. If an individual feels that his or her performance is unfairly rewarded, the performance–causes–satisfaction relationship will not hold.

Argument: Rewards Cause Both Satisfaction and Performance   This final argument in the job satisfaction–performance controversy is the most compelling. It suggests that a proper allocation of rewards can positively influence both performance and satisfaction. The key word in the previous sentence is *proper*. Research indicates that people who receive high rewards report higher job satisfaction. But research also indicates that performance-contingent rewards influence a person's work performance. In this case, the size and value of the reward vary in proportion to the level of one's performance accomplishment. Large rewards are given for high performance; small or no rewards are given for low performance. And whereas giving a low performer only small rewards initially may lead to dissatisfaction, the expectation is that the individual will make efforts to improve performance in order to obtain greater rewards in the future.

The point is that managers should consider satisfaction and performance as two separate but interrelated work results that are affected by the allocation of rewards. Whereas job satisfaction alone is not a good predictor of work performance, well-managed rewards can have a positive influence on both satisfaction and performance.

■ INTEGRATED MODEL OF MOTIVATION

Figure 3.8 outlines the integrated view. Note that the figure has much in common with Vroom's expectancy theory and the Porter–Lawler framework just dis-

Figure 3.8
An integrated model of individual motivation to work.

cussed.[50] In the figure, job performance and satisfaction are separate, but potentially interdependent, work results. Performance is influenced most directly by individual attributes such as ability and experience, organizational support such as resources and technology, and work effort—the point at which an individual's level of motivation comes directly to bear. Individual motivation directly determines work effort, and the key to motivation is the ability to create a work setting that positively responds to individual needs and goals. Whether or not a work setting proves motivational for a given individual depends on the availability of rewards and their perceived value. Note also the importance of contingent rewards, reflecting the law of contingent reinforcement. Recall also the importance of immediacy in rewarding.

The content theories enter the model as the guide to understanding individual attributes and identifying the needs that give motivational value to the possible rewards. When the individual experiences intrinsic rewards for work performance, motivation will be directly and positively affected. Motivation can also occur when job satisfactions result from either extrinsic or intrinsic rewards that are felt to be equitably allocated. When felt negative inequity results, satisfaction will be low and motivation will be reduced.

With this discussion of reinforcement, content, and process theories, you should have a better understanding of motivation. Although it will always be difficult to motivate employees, the knowledge in this section should help you reach toward higher performance and satisfaction. Finally, the integrating model rests on cultural assumptions, so that the meaning of the concepts may be culturally specific. The importance of various intrinsic and extrinsic rewards may well differ across cultures, as may the aspects of performance that are highly valued.

Dynamics of Stress

The processes of change and innovation often create new and increased pressures on the people involved. **Stress** must be understood as a state of tension experienced by individuals facing extraordinary demands, constraints, or opportunities.[51]

■ **Stress** is tension from extraordinary demands, constraints, or opportunities.

■ SOURCES OF STRESS

Any look toward your career future in today's dynamic times must include an awareness that stress is something you, as well as others, are sure to encounter.[52] **Stressors** are the wide variety of things that cause stress for individuals. Some stressors can be traced directly to what people experience in the workplace, whereas others derive from nonwork and personal factors.

■ **Stressors** are things that cause stress.

Work-Related Stressors   Without doubt work can be stressful, and job demands can disrupt one's work-life balance. A study of two-career couples, for example, found some 43 percent of men and 34 percent of women reporting that they worked more hours than they wanted to.[53] We know that work-related stress can come from many sources—from excessively high or low task demands, role conflicts or ambiguities, poor interpersonal relations, or career progress that is either too slow or too fast. A list of common stressors includes the following:

- *Task demands*—being asked to do too much or being asked to do too little.

- *Role ambiguities*—not knowing what one is expected to do or how work performance is evaluated.

- *Role conflicts*—feeling unable to satisfy multiple, possibly conflicting, performance expectations.

- *Ethical dilemmas*—being asked to do things that violate the law or personal values.

- *Interpersonal problems*—experiencing bad relationships or working with others who do not get along.

- *Career developments*—moving too fast and feeling stretched; moving too slowly and feeling plateaued.

- *Physical setting*—being bothered by noise, lack of privacy, pollution, or other unpleasant working conditions.

Nonwork and Personal Stressors   A less obvious, though important, source of stress for people at work is the "spillover" effect from forces in their nonwork lives. Family events (e.g., the birth of a new child), economic difficulties (e.g., the sudden loss of a big investment), and personal affairs (e.g., a separation or divorce) can all be extremely stressful. Since it is often difficult to completely separate work and nonwork lives, stress of this nonwork sort can affect the way people feel and behave on the job as well as away from it.

Another set of stressors includes personal factors, such as individual needs, capabilities, and personality. Stress can reach a destructive state more quickly for example, when experienced by highly emotional people or by those with low self-esteem. People who perceive a good fit between job requirements and personal skills seem to have a higher tolerance for stress than do those who feel less competent as a result of a person–job mismatch.[54] Basic aspects of personality are also important. The achievement orientation, impatience, and perfectionism of individuals with Type A personalities, for example, often create stress for them in work settings that others find relatively stress-free.[55]

■ STRESS AND PERFORMANCE

■ **Constructive stress** has a positive impact on both attitudes and performance.

■ **Destructive stress** has a negative impact on both attitudes and performance.

Stress isn't always negative as an influence on our lives. It has two faces—one positive and one negative.[56] **Constructive stress**, or *eustress*, acts in a positive way. Moderate levels of stress by prompting increased work effort, stimulating creativity, and encouraging greater diligence. You may know such stress as the tension that causes you to study hard before exams, pay attention, and complete assignments on time in a difficult class. **Destructive stress**, or *distress*, is dysfunctional for both the individual and the organization. Too much stress can overload and break down a person's physical and mental systems resulting in absenteeism, turnover, errors, accidents, dissatisfaction, reduced performance, unethical behavior and even illness. Stanford scholar and consultant Jeffrey Pfeffer, for example, criticizes organizations that suffer from such excessive practices for creating *toxic workplaces*.[57] A toxic company implicitly says to its employees: "We're going to put you in an environment where you have to work in a style and at a pace that is not sustainable. We want you to come in here and burn yourself out. Then you can leave."[58]

■ STRESS AND HEALTH

As is well known, stress can impact a person's health. It is a potential source of both anxiety and frustration, which can harm the body's physiological and psychological well-being over time.[59] Health problems associated with stress include heart attack, stroke, hypertension, migraine headache, ulcers, substance abuse, overeating, depression, and muscle aches. As noted in The Effective Manager 3.3, managers and team leaders should be alert to signs of excessive stress in themselves and their co-workers. Key symptoms to look for are changes from normal patterns—changes from regular attendance to absenteeism, from punctuality to tardiness, from diligent work to careless work, from a positive attitude to a negative attitude, from openness to change to resistance to change, or from cooperation to hostility.

THE EFFECTIVE MANAGER 3.3

SIGNS OF EXCESSIVE STRESS

- Change in eating habits
- Change in alcohol consumption or smoking
- Unhealthy feelings—aches and pains, upset stomach
- Restlessness, inability to concentrate, sleeping problems
- Tense, uptight, fidgety, nervous feelings
- Disoriented, overwhelmed, depressed, irritable feelings

■ STRESS MANAGEMENT

Stress prevention is the best first-line strategy in the battle against stress. It involves taking action to keep stress from reaching destructive levels in the first place. Personal and nonwork stressors must be recognized so that action can be taken to prevent them from adverse impact. Persons with Type A personalities, for example, may exercise self-discipline; supervisors of Type A employees may try to model a lower key, more relaxed approach to work. Family problems may be partially relieved by a change of work schedule; the anxiety caused by pressing family concerns may be reduced by simply knowing that your supervisor understands.

Once stress has reached a destructive point, special techniques of **stress management** can be implemented. This process begins with the recognition of stress symptoms and continues with actions to maintain a positive performance edge. The term **wellness** is increasingly used these days. Personal wellness involves the pursuit of one's physical and mental potential through a personal health promotion program.[60] The concept recognizes individual responsibility to enhance and maintain wellness through a disciplined approach to physical and mental health. It requires attention to such factors as smoking, weight, diet, alcohol use, and physical fitness. Organizations can benefit from commitments to support personal wellness. A University of Michigan study indicates that firms have saved up to $600 per year per employee by helping them to cut the risk of significant health problems.[61] Arnold Coleman, CEO of Healthy Outlook Worldwide, a health fitness consulting firm, states: "If I can save companies 5 to 20 percent a year in medical costs, they'll listen. In the end you have a well company and that's where the word 'wellness' comes from."[62]

■ **Stress prevention** involves minimizing the potential for stress to occur.

■ **Stress management** takes an active approach to deal with stress that is influencing behavior.

■ **Wellness** involves maintaining physical and mental health to better deal with stress when it occurs.

Organizations that build positive work environments and make significant investments in their employees are best positioned to realize the benefits of their full talents and work potential. As Pfeffer says: "All that separates you from your competitors are the skills, knowledge, commitment, and abilities of the people who work for you." Organizations that treat people right will get high returns...."[63] That, in essence, is what the study of organizational behavior is all about.

Footnotes

[1] Information from Greg Southam, "Unusual Approach Builds a Winner; Company Owner Rejects Traditional Management Teachings," *The Edmonton Journal* (November 30, 1994), p. D6.

[2] See John P. Campbell, Marvin D. Dunnette, Edward E. Lawler III, and Karl E. Weick, Jr., *Managerial Behavior Performance and Effectiveness* (New York: McGraw-Hill, 1970), Ch. 15.

[3] For a review article that identifies a still-relevant need for more integration among motivation theories, see Terrence R. Mitchell, "Motivation—New Directions for Theory, Research and Practice," *Academy of Management Review* 7 (January 1982): 80–88.

[4] Geert Hofstede, "Cultural Constraints in Management Theories," *Academy of Management Executive* 7 (February 1993): 81–94.

[5] Geert Hofstede, *Culture's Consequences: International Differences in Work-Related Values*, abridged ed. (Beverly Hills, CA: Sage Publications, 1984).

[6] For good overviews of reinforcement-based views, see W. E. Scott, Jr., and P. M. Podsakoff, *Behavioral Principles in the Practice of Management* (New York: Wiley, 1985); Fred Luthans and Robert Kreitner, *Organizational Behavior Modification and Beyond* (Glenview, IL: Scott, Foresman, 1985).

[7] Some of B. F. Skinner's work; see his *Walden Two* (New York: Macmillan, 1948), *Science and Human Behavior* (New York: Macmillan, 1953), and *Contingencies of Reinforcement* (New York: Appleton-Century-Crofts, 1969).

[8] E. L. Thorndike, *Animal Intelligence* (New York: Macmillan, 1911), p. 244.

[9] Adapted from Luthans and Kreitner, op. cit. (1985).

[10] This discussion is based on ibid.

[11] Both laws are stated in Keith L. Miller, *Principles of Everyday Behavior Analysis* (Monterey, CA: Brooks/Cole, 1975), p. 122.

[12] While some have used reinforcement as a springboard to discuss individual learning, we prefer to emphasize the cognitive or thinking aspects of learning.

[13] This example is based on a study by Barbara Price and Richard Osborn, "Shaping the Training of Skilled Workers," working paper (Detroit: Department of Management, Wayne State University, 1999).

[14] See John Putzier and Frank T. Novak, "Attendance Management and Control," *Personnel Administrator* (August 1989): 59–60.

[15] Robert Kreitner and Angelo Kiniki, *Organization Behavior*, 2nd ed. (Homewood, IL: Irwin, 1992).

[16] These have been used for years; see K. M. Evans, "On-the Job Lotteries: A Low-Cost Incentive That Sparks Higher Productivity," *Compensation and Benefits Review* 20, No. 4 (1988): 63–74; A. Halcrow, "Incentive! How Three Companies Cut Costs," *Personnel Journal* (February 1986), p. 12.

[17] A. R. Korukonda and James G. Hunt, "Pat on the Back Versus Kick in the Pants: An Application of Cognitive Inference to the Study of Leader Reward and Punishment Behavior," *Group and Organization Studies* 14 (1989): 299–234.

[18] See "Janitorial Firm Success Story Started with Cleaning Couple," *Lubbock Avalanche-Journal* (August 25, 1991), p. E7.

[19] Edwin A. Locke, "The Myths of Behavior Mod in Organizations," *Academy of Management Review* 2 (October 1977): 543–553. For a counterpoint, see Jerry L. Gray, "The Myths of the Myths about Behavior Mod in Organizations: A Reply to Locke's Criticisms of Behavior Modification," *Academy of Management Review* 4 (January 1979): 121–129.

[20] Robert Kreitner, "Controversy in OBM: History, Misconceptions, and Ethics," in Lee Frederiksen, ed., *Handbook of Organizational Behavior Management* (New York: Wiley, 1982), pp. 71–91.

[21] W. E. Scott, Jr., and P. M. Podsakoff, *Behavioral Principles in the Practice of Management* (New York: Wiley, 1985); also see W. Clay Hamner, "Reinforcement Theory and Contingency Management in Organizational Settings," in Richard M. Steers and Lyman W Porters (eds.), *Motivation and Work Behavior*, 4th ed. (New York: McGraw-Hill, 1987), pp. 139–165; Luthans and Kreitner, op. cit. (1985); Charles C. Manz and Henry P. Sims, Jr., *Superleadership* (New York: Berkley, 1990).

[22] Abraham Maslow, *Eupsychian Management* (Homewood, IL: Irwin, 1965), and *Motivation and Personality*, 2nd ed. (New York: Harper & Row, 1970).

[23] Lyman W. Porter, "Job Attitudes in Management: II. Perceived Importance of Needs as a Function of Job Level," *Journal of Applied Psychology* 47 (April 1963): 141–148.

[24] Douglas T. Hall and Khalil E. Nougaim, "An Examination of Maslow's Need Hierarchy in an Organizational Setting," *Organizational Behavior and Human Performance* 3 (1968): 12–35; Porter, op. cit. (1963); John M. Ivancevich, "Perceived Need Satisfactions of Domestic Versus Overseas Managers," 54 (August 1969): 274–278.

[25] Mahmoud A. Wahba and Lawrence G. Bridwell, "Maslow Reconsidered: A Review of Research on the Need Hierarchy Theory," *Academy of Management Proceedings* (1974): 514–520; Edward E. Lawler III and J. Lloyd Shuttle, "A Causal Correlation Test of the Need Hierarchy Concept," *Organizational Behavior and Human Performance* 7 (1973): 265–287.

[26] Nancy J. Adler, *International Dimensions of Organizational Behavior*, 2nd ed. (Boston: PWS-Kent, 1991), p. 153.

[27] Ibid.; Richard M. Hodgetts and Fred Luthans, *International Management* (New York: McGraw-Hill, 1991), Ch. 11.

[28] Clayton P. Alderfer, "An Empirical Test of a New Theory of Human Needs," *Organizational Behavior and Human Performance* 4 (1969): 142–175; Clayton P. Alderfer, *Existence, Relatedness, and Growth* (New York: Free Press, 1972); Benjamin Schneider and Clayton P. Alderfer, "Three Studies of Need Satisfaction in Organization," *Administrative Science Quarterly* 18 (1973): 489–505.

[29] Lane Tracy, "A Dynamic Living Systems Model of Work Motivation," *Systems Research* 1 (1984): 191–203; John Rauschenberger, Neal Schmidt, and John E. Hunter, "A Test of the Need Hierarchy Concept by a Markov Model of Change in Need Strength," *Administrative Science Quarterly* 25 (1980): 654–670.

[30] Sources pertinent to this discussion are David C. McClelland, *The Achieving Society* (New York: Van Nostrand, 1961); David C. McClelland, "Business, Drive and National Achievement," *Harvard Business Review* 40 (July/August 1962): 99–112; David C. McClelland, "That Urge to Achieve," *Think* (November/December 1966): 19–32; G. H. Litwin

and R. A. Stringer, *Motivation and Organizational Climate* (Boston: Division of Research, Harvard Business School, 1966), pp. 18–25.

[31] George Harris, "To Know Why Men Do What They Do: A Conversation with David C. McClelland," *Psychology Today* 4 (January 1971): 35–39.

[32] David C. McClelland and David H. Burnham, "Power Is the Great Motivator," *Harvard Business Review* 54 (March/April 1976): 100–110; David C. McClelland and Richard E. Boyatzis, "Leadership Motive Pattern and Long-Term Success in Management," *Journal of Applied Psychology* 67 (1982): 737–743.

[33] P. Miron and D. C. McClelland, "The Impact of Achievement Motivation Training in Small Businesses," *California Management Review* (Summer 1979): 13–28.

[34] The complete two-factor theory is well explained by Herzberg and his associates in Frederick Herzberg, Bernard Mausner, and Barbara Bloch Synderman, *The Motivation to Work*, 2nd ed. (New York: Wiley, 1967); and Frederick Herzberg, "One More Time: How Do You Motivate Employees?" *Harvard Business Review* 46 (January/February 1968): 53–62.

[35] From Herzberg, op. cit. (1968), pp. 53–62.

[36] See Robert J. House and Lawrence A. Wigdor, "Herzberg's Dual-Factor Theory of Job Satisfaction and Motivation: A Review of the Evidence and a Criticism," *Personnel Psychology* 20 (Winter 1967): 369–389; and Steven Kerr, Anne Harlan, and Ralph Stogdill, "Preference for Motivator and Hygiene Factors in a Hypothetical Interview Situation," *Personnel Psychology* 27 (Winter 1974): 109–124; Nathan King, "A Clarification and Evaluation of the Two-Factor Theory of Job Satisfaction," *Psychological Bulletin* (July 1970): 18–31; Marvin Dunnette, John Campbell, and Milton Hakel, "Factors Contributing to Job Satisfaction and Job Dissatisfaction in Six Occupational Groups," *Organizational Behavior and Human Performance* (May 1967): 143–174; R. J. House and L. Wigdor, "Herzberg's Dual Factor Theory of Job Satisfaction and Motivation: A Review of the Evidence and a Criticism," *Personnel Psychology* (Summer 1967): 369–389.

[37] Adler, op. cit. (1991), Ch 6; Nancy J. Adler and J. T. Graham, "Cross Cultural Interaction: The International Comparison Fallacy," *Journal of International Business Studies* (Fall 1989): 515–537; Frederick Herzberg, "Workers Needs: The Same around the World," *Industry Week* (September 27, 1987), pp. 29–32.

[38] See, for example, J. Stacy Adams, "Toward an Understanding of Inequality," *Journal of Abnormal and Social Psychology* 67 (1963): 422–436; and J. Stacy Adams, "Inequity in Social Exchange," in L. Berkowitz (ed.), *Advances in Experimental Social Psychology*, Vol. 2 (New York: Academic Press, 1965), pp. 267–300.

[39] Adams, op. cit. (1965).

[40] These issues are discussed in C. Kagitcibasi and J. W. Berry, "Cross-Cultural Psychology: Current Research and Trends," *Annual Review of Psychology* 40 (1989): 493–531.

[41] Victor H. Vroom, *Work and Motivation* (New York: Wiley, 1964).

[42] See Richard T. Mowday, "Equity Theory Predictions of Behavior in Organizations," in Richard M. Steers and Lyman W. Porter (eds.), *Motivation and Work Behavior*, 4th ed. (New York: McGraw-Hill, 1987), pp. 89–110.

[43] See Steers and Porter, op. cit. (1987); Gerald R. Salancik and Jeffrey Pfeffer, "A Social Information Processing Approach to Job Attitudes and Task Design," *Administrative Science Quarterly* 23 (June 1978): 224–253.

[44] See Terence R. Mitchell, "Expectancy Models of Job Satisfaction, Occupational Preference and Effort: A Theoretical, Methodological, and Empirical Appraisal," *Psychological Bulletin* 81 (1974): 1053–1077; Mahmoud A. Wahba and Robert J. House, "Expectancy Theory in Work and Motivation: Some Logical and Methodological Issues," *Human Relations* 27 (January 1974): 121–147; Terry Connolly, "Some Conceptual and Methodological Issues in Expectancy Models of Work Performance Motivation," *Academy of Management Review* 1 (October 1976): 37–47; Terrence Mitchell, "Expectancy-Value Models in Organizational Psychology," in N. Feather (ed.), *Expectancy, Incentive and Action* (New York: Erlbaum & Associates, 1980).

[45] See William E. Wymer and Jeanne M. Carsten, "Alternative Ways to Gather Opinions," *HR Magazine* 37, 4 (April 1992): 71–78.

[46] The Job Descriptive Index (JDI) is available from Dr. Patricia C. Smith, Department of Psychology, Bowling Green State University; the Minnesota Satisfaction Questionnaire (MSQ) is available from the Industrial Relations Center and Vocational Psychology Research Center, University of Minnesota.

[47] Barry M. Staw, "The Consequences of Turnover," *Journal of Occupational Behavior* 1 (1980): 253–273; John P. Wanous, *Organizational Entry* (Reading, MA: Addison-Wesley, 1980).

[48] Charles N. Greene, "The Satisfaction-Performance Controversy," *Business Horizons* 15 (1972): 31; Michelle T. Iaffaldano and Paul M. Muchinsky, "Job Satisfaction and Job Performance: A Meta-Analysis," *Psychological Bulletin* 97 (1985): 251–273; Greene, op. cit. (1972), pp. 31–41; Dennis Organ, "A Reappraisal and Reinterpretation of the Satisfaction-Causes-Performance Hypothesis," *Academy of Management Review* 2 (1977): 46–53; Peter Lorenzi, "A Comment on Organ's Reappraisal of the Satisfaction-Causes-Performance Hypothesis," *Academy of Management Review* 3 (1978): 380–382.

[49] Lyman W. Porter and Edward E. Lawler III, *Managerial Attitudes and Performance* (Homewood, IL: Irwin, 1968).

[50] This integrated model is consistent with the comprehensive approach suggested by Martin G. Evans, "Organizational Behavior: The Central Role of Motivation," in J. G. Hunt and J. D. Blair (eds.), *1986 Yearly Review of Management of the Journal of Management* 12 (1986): 203–222.

[51] Arthur P. Brief, Randall S. Schuler, and Mary Van Sell, *Managing Job Stress* (Boston: Little, Brown, 1981).

[52] A review of research is available in Steve M. Jex, *Stress and Job Performance* (Thousand Oaks, CA: Sage, 1998).

[53] "Couples Dismayed at Long Workdays, New Study Finds," *Columbus Dispatch* (January 23, 1999), p. 5A.

[54] See Orlando Behling and Arthur L. Darrow, *Managing Work-Related Stress* (Chicago: Science Research Associates, 1984).

[55] Meyer Friedman and Ray Roseman, *Type A Behavior and Your Heart* (New York: Alfred A. Knopf, 1974).

[56] See H. Selye, *The Stress of Life*, rev. ed. (New York: McGraw-Hill, 1976).

[57] Jeffrey Pfeffer, *The Human Equation: Building Profits by Putting People First* (Boston: Harvard Business School Press, 1998).

[58] Quotes are from Alan M. Webber, "Danger: Toxic Company," *Fast Company* (November 1998), p. 152.

[59] See John D. Adams, "Health, Stress, and the Manager's Life Style," *Group and Organization Studies*, Vol. 6 (September 1981), pp. 291–301.

[60] Robert Kreitner, "Personal Wellness: It's Just Good Business," *Business Horizons*, Vol. 25 (May/June 1982), pp. 28–35.

[61] Information from Mike Pramik, "Wellness Programs Give Businesses Healthy Bottom Line," *Columbus Dispatch* (January 18, 1999), pp. 10–11.

[62] Ibid.

[63] Pfeffer (1998).

Source Notes

www.omniroyal.com/.

www.Oglebaynorton.com; Jeremy Kahn, "A CEO Cuts His Own Pay," *Fortune* (October 26, 1998), pp. 56, 60, 64.

Starbucks.com/ and Starbucks.com/company mission.

www.patagonia.com; Patagonia Annual Report, 1998.

Section Four

Section Four

Power

In OB, **power** is defined as the ability to get someone to do something you want done or the ability to make things happen in the way you want them to. We examined leadership as a key power mechanism to make things happen. Now it is time to discusses other ways. The essence of power is control over the behavior of others.[1] Power is the force you use to make things happen in an intended way, whereas **influence** is what you have when you exercise power, and it is expressed by others' behavioral response to your exercise of power. Managers derive power from both organizational and individual sources. These sources are called *position power* and *personal power*, respectively.[2]

■ POSITION POWER

Three bases of power are available to a manager solely as a result of his or her position in the organization: reward, coercive, and legitimate power.

Reward power is the extent to which a manager can use extrinsic and intrinsic rewards to control other people. Examples of such rewards include money, promotions, compliments, or enriched jobs. Although all managers have some access to rewards, success in accessing and utilizing rewards to achieve influence varies according to the skills of the manager.

Power can also be founded on punishment instead of reward. For example, a manager may threaten to withhold a pay raise, or to transfer, demote, or even recommend the firing of a subordinate who does not act as desired. Such **coercive power** is the extent to which a manager can deny desired rewards or administer punishments to control other people. The availability of coercive power also varies from one organization and manager to another. The presence of unions and organizational policies on employee treatment can weaken this power base considerably.

The third base of "position" power is **legitimate power**, or formal authority. It stems from the extent to which a manager can use subordinates' internalized values or beliefs that the "boss" has a "right of command" to control their behavior. For example, the boss may have the formal authority to approve or deny such employee requests as job transfers, equipment purchases, personal time off, or overtime work. Legitimate power represents a special kind of power a manager has because subordinates believe it is legitimate for a person occupying the managerial position to have the right to command. If this legitimacy is lost, authority will not be accepted by subordinates. Since legitimate power is multifaceted and much of it may be "latent," some additional discussion is required.

■ **Power** is the ability to get someone else to do something you want done or the ability to make things happen or get things done the way you want.

■ **Influence** is a behavioral response to the exercise of power.

■ **Reward power** is the extent to which a manager can use extrinsic and intrinsic rewards to control other people.

■ **Coercive power** is the extent to which a manager can deny desired rewards or administer punishment to control other people.

■ **Legitimate power** or formal authority is the extent to which a manager can use the "right of command" to control other people.

One of the most important aspects of legitimacy is the access to and control of information. Indeed, some observers believe that information power should be listed as a separate source of power. In most organizations, the "right" to know and use information is restricted and confined by a series of rules and regulations. For instance, in most firms an individual's pay is not broadly known, nor are engineering drawings typically allowed outside engineering. Marketing plans may be "top secret," as is the latest evaluation of the boss. The nominal reason for controlling information is to protect the firm. The real reason is often to allow information holders to increase their power.

Underpinning legitimacy in most organizations is an implicit moral and technical order. As we will note later in this section, from the crib to the school to the corporation to retirement, individuals in our society are taught to obey "higher authority." In U.S. firms, "higher authority" means those close to the top of the corporate pyramid. In other societies, "higher authority" does not have a bureaucratic or organizational reference but consists of those with moral authority such as tribal chiefs, religious leaders, and the like. In firms, the legitimacy of those at the top increasingly derives from their positions as representatives for various constituencies. This is a technical or instrumental role, but many senior executives evoke social causes in their role as authority figures.

■ PERSONAL POWER

Personal power resides in the individual and is independent of that individual's position. Personal power is important in many well-managed firms. Three bases of personal power are expertise, rational persuasion, and reference.

Expert power is the ability to control another person's behavior through the possession of knowledge, experience, or judgment that the other person does not have but needs. A subordinate obeys a supervisor possessing expert power because the boss ordinarily knows more about what is to be done or how it is to be done than does the subordinate. Expert power is relative, not absolute.

Rational persuasion is the ability to control another's behavior because through the individual's efforts, the person accepts the desirability of an offered goal and a reasonable way of achieving it. Much of what a supervisor does day to day involves rational persuasion up, down, and across the organization. Rational persuasion involves both explaining the desirability of expected outcomes and showing how specific actions will achieve these outcomes.

Referent power is the ability to control another's behavior because the person wants to identify with the power source. In this case, a subordinate obeys the boss because he or she wants to behave, perceive, or believe as the boss does. This obedience may occur, for example, because the subordinate likes the boss personally and therefore tries to do things the way the boss wants them done. In a sense, the subordinate attempts to avoid doing anything that would interfere with the pleasing boss–subordinate relationship. A person's referent power can be enhanced when the individual taps into the moral order or shows a clearer long-term path to a morally desirable end. In common language, individuals with the ability to tap into these more esoteric aspects of corporate life have "charisma" and "the vision thing." Followership is not based on what the subordinate will get for specific actions or specific levels of performance, but on what the individual represents—a path toward a loftier future.

■ **Expert power** is the ability to control another's behavior because of the possession of knowledge, experience, or judgment that the other person does not have but needs.

■ **Rational persuasion** is the ability to control another's behavior because through the individual's efforts, the person accepts the desirability of an offered goal and a reasonable way of achieving it.

■ **Referent power** is the ability to control another's behavior because of the individual's desire to identify with the power source.

■ ACQUIRING AND USING POWER AND INFLUENCE

A considerable portion of any manager's time is directed toward what is called *power-oriented behavior*. Power-oriented behavior is action directed primarily at developing or using relationships in which other people are to some degree willing to defer to one's wishes.[3] Figure 4.1 shows three basic dimensions of power and influence with which a manager will become involved in this regard: downward, upward, and lateral. Also shown in the figure are some preliminary ideas for achieving success along each of these dimensions.

The effective manager is one who succeeds in building and maintaining high levels of both position and personal power over time. Only then is sufficient power of the right types available when the manager needs to exercise influence on downward, lateral, and upward dimensions.

Building Position Power   Position power can be enhanced when managers are able to demonstrate to others that their work units are highly relevant to organizational goals and are able to respond to urgent organizational needs. To increase centrality and criticality in the organization, managers may seek to acquire a more central role in the work flow by having information filtered through them, making at least part of their job responsibilities unique, expanding their network of communication contacts, and occupying an office convenient to main traffic flows.

Managers may also attempt to increase the relevance of their tasks and those of their unit to the organization. There are many ways to do this. Executives may attempt to become an internal coordinator within the firm or external representative. They may suggest their subordinates take on these roles, particularly when the firm is downsizing. When the firm is in a dynamic setting of changing technology, the executive may also move to provide unique services and information to other units. This is particularly effective if the executive moves his unit

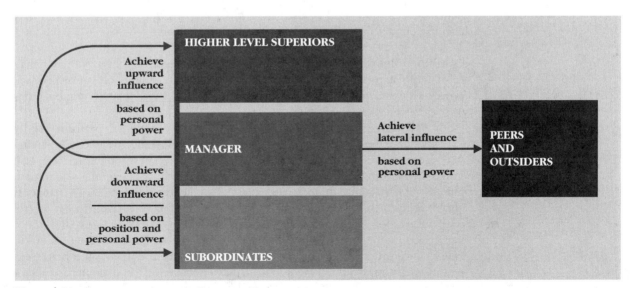

Figure 4.1
Three dimensions of managerial power and influence.

into becoming involved with decisions central to the organization's top-priority goals. To expand their position, managers may also delegate routine activities, expand the task variety and novelty for subordinates, initiate new ideas, and get involved in new projects. We will have more to say about this matter when discussing empowerment.

There are also ways managers attempt to build influence that may or may not have a positive effect on the organization. Managers may attempt to define tasks so that they are difficult to evaluate, such as by creating an ambiguous job description or developing a unique language for their work.

Building Personal Power   Personal power arises from the personal characteristics of the manager rather than from the location and other characteristics of his or her position in the organization's hierarchy of authority.

Three personal characteristics, expertise, political savvy, and likability, have special potential for enhancing personal power in an organization. The most obvious is *building expertise*. Additional expertise may be gained by advanced training and education, participation in professional associations, and involvement in the early stages of projects.

A somewhat less obvious way to increase personal power is to learn *political savvy*—better ways to negotiate, persuade individuals, and understand the goals and means they are most willing to accept. The novice believes that most individuals are very much the same, see the same goals, and will accept much the same paths toward these goals. The more astute individual recognizes important individual differences.

A manager's reference power is increased by characteristics that enhance his or her "*likability*" and create personal attraction in relationships with other people. These include pleasant personality characteristics, agreeable behavior patterns, and attractive personal appearance. The demonstration of sincere hard work on behalf of task performance can also increase personal power by enhancing both expertise and reference. A person who is perceived to try hard may be expected to know more about the job and thus be sought out for advice. A person who tries hard is also likely to be respected for the attempt and may even be depended on by others to maintain that effort.

Combined Building of Position and Personal Power   From a purely analytical standpoint, most sources of power can be traced to position power or personal power. However, many of the influential actions and behaviors are combinations of position and personal power.

Most managers attempt to increase the visibility of their job performance by (1) expanding the number of contacts they have with senior people, (2) making oral presentations of written work, (3) participating in problem-solving task forces, (4) sending out notices of accomplishment, and (5) generally seeking additional opportunities to increase personal name recognition. Most managers also recognize that, between superiors and subordinates, access to or control over information is an important element. A boss may appear to expand his or her expert power over a subordinate by not allowing the individual access to critical information. Although the denial may appear to enhance the boss's expert power, it may reduce the subordinate's effectiveness. In a similar manner a supervisor may also control access to key organizational decision makers. An individual's ability to contact key persons informally can offset some of this disadvantage. Furthermore, astute senior executives routinely develop "back channels" to lower-level individuals deep within the firm to offset the tendency of bosses to control information and access.

Expert power is often relational and embedded within the organizational context. Many important decisions are made outside formal channels and are substantially influenced by key individuals with the requisite knowledge. By developing and using coalitions and networks, an individual may build on their expert power. Though coalitions and networks, an individual may alter the flow of information and the context for analysis. By developing coalitions and networks, executives also expand their access to information and their opportunities for participation.

Executives also attempt to control, or at least influence, decision premises. A decision premise is a basis for defining the problem and for selecting among alternatives. By defining a problem in a manner that fits the executive's expertise, it is natural for that executive to be in charge of solving it. Thus, the executive subtly shifts his or her position power.

Executives who want to increase their power often make their goals and needs clear and bargain effectively to show that their preferred goals and needs are best. They do not show their power base directly but instead provide clear "rational persuasion" for their preferences. So the astute executive does not threaten or attempt to evoke sanctions to build power. Instead, he or she combines personal power with the position of the unit to enhance total power. As the organizational context changes, different personal sources of power may become more important alone and in combination with the individual's position power. So there is an art to building power.

■ TURNING POWER INTO RELATIONAL INFLUENCE

Using position and personal power well to achieve the desired influence over other people is a challenge for most managers. Practically speaking, there are many useful ways of exercising relational influence. The most common strategies involve the following:[4]

Reason	Using facts and data to support a logical argument.	**Strategies for exercising influence**
Friendliness	Using flattery, goodwill, and favorable impressions.	
Coalition	Using relationships with other people for support.	
Bargaining	Using the exchange of benefits as a basis for negotiation.	
Assertiveness	Using a direct and forceful personal approach.	
Higher authority	Gaining higher level support for one's requests.	
Sanctions	Using organizationally derived rewards and punishments.	

Research on these strategies suggests that reason is the most popular strategy overall.[5] In addition, friendliness, assertiveness, bargaining, and higher authority are used more frequently to influence subordinates than to influence supervisors. This pattern of influence attempts is consistent with our earlier contention that downward influence generally includes mobilization of both position and personal power sources, whereas upward influence is more likely to draw on personal power.

Little research is available on the subject of upward influence in organizations. This is unfortunate, since truly effective managers are able to influence their bosses as well as their subordinates. One study reports that both supervisors and subordinates view reason, or the logical presentation of ideas, as the most frequently used strategy of upward influence.[6] When queried on reasons for success and failure, however, the viewpoints of the two groups show both similarities and differences. The perceived causes of success in upward influence are similar for both supervisors and subordinates and involve the favorable content of the influence attempt, a favorable manner of its presentation, and the competence of the subordinate.[7] The two groups disagree on the causes of failure, however. Subordinates attribute failure in upward influence to the close-mindedness of the supervisor, unfavorable content of the influence attempt, and unfavorable interpersonal relationships with the supervisor. In contrast, supervisors attribute failure to the unfavorable content of the attempt, the unfavorable manner in which it was presented, and the subordinate's lack of competence.

■ POWER, FORMAL AUTHORITY, AND OBEDIENCE

As we have shown, power is the potential to control the behavior of others, and formal authority is the potential to exert such control through the legitimacy of a managerial position. Yet, we also know that people who seem to have power don't always get their way. Why do some people obey directives and others do not? More specifically, why should subordinates respond to a manager's authority, or "right to command," in the first place? Furthermore, given that subordinates are willing to obey, what determines the limits of obedience?

The Milgram Experiments The mythology of American independence and unbridled individualism is so strong we need to spend some time explaining how most of us are really quite obedient. So we turn to the seminal studies of Stanley Milgram on obedience.[8] Milgram designed experiments to determine the extent to which people obey the commands of an authority figure, even if they believe they are endangering the life of another person. Subjects, ranging in age from 20 to 50 and representing a diverse set of occupations (engineers, salespeople, schoolteachers, laborers, and others), were paid a nominal fee for participation in the project.

The subjects were falsely told that the purpose of the study was to determine the effects of punishment on learning. The subjects were to be the "teachers." The "learner" was a confederate of Milgram's, who was strapped to a chair in an adjoining room with an electrode attached to his wrist. The "experimenter," another confederate of Milgram's, was dressed in a gray laboratory coat. Appearing impassive and somewhat stern, the experimenter instructed the "teacher" to read a series of word pairs to the "learner" and then to reread the first word along with four other terms. The learner was supposed to indicate which of the four terms was in the original pair by pressing a switch that caused a light to flash on a response panel in front of the teacher.

The teacher was instructed to administer a shock to the learner each time a wrong answer was given. This shock was to be increased one level of intensity each time the learner made a mistake. The teacher controlled switches that ostensibly administered shocks ranging from 15 to 450 volts. In reality, there was no electric current in the apparatus, but the learners purposely "erred" often and responded to each level of "shock" in progressively distressing ways. If a "teacher" (subject) proved unwilling to administer a shock, the experimenter used the following sequential prods to get him or her to perform as requested: (1) "Please continue" or "Please go on"; (2) "The experiment requires that you continue"; (3) "It is absolutely essential that you continue"; and (4) "You have no choice, you must go on." Only when the "teacher" refused to go on after the fourth prod would the experiment be stopped. When would you expect the "teachers" to refuse to go on?

Milgram asked some of his students and colleagues the same question. Most felt that few, if any, of the subjects would go beyond the "very strong shock" level. Actually, 26 subjects (65 percent) continued to the end of the experiment and shocked the "learners" to the maximum. None stopped before 300 volts, the point at which the learner pounded on the wall. The remaining 14 subjects refused to obey the experimenter at various intermediate points.

Most people are surprised by these results, as was Milgram. The question is why other people would have a tendency to accept or comply with authoritative commands under such extreme conditions. Milgram conducted further experiments to try to answer this question. The subjects' tendencies toward compliance were somewhat reduced (1) when experimentation took place in a rundown office (rather than a university lab), (2) when the victim was closer, (3) when the experimenter was farther away, and (4) when the subject could observe other subjects. However, the level of compliance was still much higher than most of us would expect.

What does this mean for empowerment? Note the tendency for individuals to comply and be obedient—to switch off and merely do exactly what they are told to do. In many firms, employees are hired to be obedient; they are rewarded for being so, and they feel alienated when others seek to "empower them."

Obedience and the Acceptance of Authority   Direct defiance within organizational settings is quite rare, as is the individual who institutes new and different ways to get the job done. If the tendency to follow instructions is great and defiance is rare, then why do so many organizations appear to drift into apparent chaos?

The answer to this question can be found in work by the famous management writer Chester Barnard.[9] Barnard's argument focused on the "consent of the governed" rather than on the rights derived from ownership. He argued that subordinates accepted or followed a directive from the boss only under special circumstances.

All four of these circumstances must be met: (1) the subordinate can and must understand the directive; (2) the subordinate must feel mentally and physically capable of carrying out the directive; (3) the subordinate must believe that the directive is not inconsistent with the purpose of the organization; and (4) the subordinate must believe that the directive is not inconsistent with his or her personal interests.

These four conditions are very carefully stated. For instance, to accept and follow an order, the subordinate does not need to understand how the proposed action will help the organization. He or she only needs to believe that the requested action is not inconsistent with the purpose of the firm. The astute manager will not take these guidelines for granted. In giving directives, the astute manager recognizes that the acceptance of the request is not assured. When seeking empowerment, two of the biggest problems are embodied in Barnard's work. First, few employees understand what they are to do when a boss says they are empowered. They just do not understand what is to be done or what is to be accomplished. Second, many employees are deeply suspicious of management and need to know why empowerment is better for them or at least not inconsistent with their own interests. Continual lauding of the importance of empowerment for the firm does not satisfy this important factor.

Obedience and the Zone of Indifference Most people seek a balance between what they put into an organization (contributions) and what they get from an organization in return (inducements). Within the boundaries of the psychological contract, therefore, employees will agree to do many things in and for the organization because they think they should. In exchange for certain inducements, subordinates recognize the authority of the organization and its managers to direct their behavior in certain ways. Based on his acceptance view of authority, Chester Barnard calls this area in which directions are obeyed the "zone of indifference."[10]

A **zone of indifference** is the range of authoritative requests to which a subordinate is willing to respond without subjecting the directives to critical evaluation or judgment. Directives falling within the zone are obeyed. Requests or orders falling outside the zone of indifference are not considered legitimate under terms of the psychological contract. Such "extraordinary" directives may or may not be obeyed. This link between the zone of indifference and the psychological contract is shown in Figure 4.2.

The zone of indifference is not fixed. There may be times when a boss would like a subordinate to do things falling outside the zone. In this case, the manager must enlarge the zone to accommodate additional behaviors. In these

■ A **zone of indifference** is the range of authoritative requests to which a subordinate is willing to respond without subjecting the directives to critical evaluation or judgment.

Requested Action	Obey?
Work Sundays	No
Shop during lunch hour for boss	No
Make coffee for the office	?
Work 40 hours in the week	Yes
Do word processing	Yes
Schedule meetings	Yes
Maintain computer databases	Yes
Work occasional paid overtime	Yes
Compose letters and reports	?
Computerize member list for boss's country club	No
"Fudge" boss's expense accounts	No

Inside zone of indifference: Normal inducements sufficient

Outside zone of indifference: Extraordinary inducements required

Figure 4.2
Hypothetical psychological contract for a secretary.

attempts, a manager most likely will have to use more incentives than pure position power. In some instances, no power base may be capable of accomplishing the desired result. Consider your own zone of indifference and tendency to obey. When will you say "No" to your boss? When should you be willing to say "No"? At times, the situation may involve ethical dilemmas, where you may be asked to do things that are illegal, unethical, or both.

Research on ethical managerial behavior shows that supervisors can become sources of pressure for subordinates to do such things as support incorrect viewpoints, sign false documents, overlook the supervisor's wrongdoing, and do business with the supervisor's friends.[11] Most of us will occasionally face such ethical dilemmas during our careers. For now, we must simply remember that saying "No" or "refusing to keep quiet" can be difficult and potentially costly.

Empowerment

Empowerment is the process by which managers help others to acquire and use the power needed to make decisions affecting themselves and their work. More than ever before, managers in progressive organizations are expected to be good at (and highly comfortable with) empowering the people with whom they work. Rather than considering power to be something to be held only at higher levels in the traditional "pyramid" of organizations, this view considers power to be something that can be shared by everyone working in flatter and more collegial structures.

The concept of empowerment is part of the sweeping change being witnessed in today's corporations. Corporate staff is being cut back; layers of management are being eliminated; the number of employees is being reduced as the volume of work increases. What is left is a leaner and trimmer organization staffed by fewer managers who must share more power as they go about their daily tasks. Indeed, empowerment is a key foundation of the increasingly popular self-managing work teams and other creative worker involvement groups.

■ **Empowerment** is the process by which managers help others to acquire and use the power needed to make decisions affecting themselves and their work.

■ THE POWER KEYS TO EMPOWERMENT

One of the bases for empowerment is a radically different view of power itself. So far, our discussion has focused on power that is exerted over other individuals. In this traditional view, power is relational in terms of individuals. In contrast, the concept of empowerment emphasizes the ability to make things happen. Power is still relational, but in terms of problems and opportunities, not individuals. Cutting through all the corporate rhetoric on empowerment is quite difficult, since the term has become quite fashionable in management circles. Each individual empowerment attempt needs to be examined in light of how power in the organization will be changed (see The Effective Manager 4.1).

THE EFFECTIVE MANAGER 4.1

GUIDELINES FOR IMPLEMENTING EMPOWERMENT

1. Delegation of authority to lower levels should be clear and unambiguous.
2. Planning must be integrated and participative at all levels.
3. Managers at all levels, but especially the top, should exercise strong communication skills.

Changing Position Power　When an organization attempts to move power down the hierarchy, it must also alter the existing pattern of position power. Changing this pattern raises some important questions. Can "empowered" individuals give rewards and sanctions based on task accomplishment? Has their new right to act been legitimized with formal authority? All too often, attempts at empowerment disrupt well-established patterns of position power and threaten middle and lower level managers. As one supervisor said, "All this empowerment stuff sounds great for top management. They don't have to run around trying to get the necessary clearances to implement the suggestions from my group. They never gave me the authority to make the changes, only the new job of asking for permission."

Expanding the Zone of Indifference　When embarking on an empowerment program, management needs to recognize the current zone of indifference and systematically move to expand it. All too often, management assumes that its directive for empowerment will be followed; management may fail to show precisely how empowerment will benefit the individuals involved, however. Management at Montgomery Ward, for example, told salesclerks that they were "empowered" to accept merchandise returns. At the same time, management cut full-time staff, hired more part-time salespeople at minimum wage, and refused to consider offering full benefits to part-time workers. Although management wanted salesclerks to do more work, they cut their staff's zone of indifference by reducing the level of inducements. Now, in many Montgomery Ward stores, all merchandise returns are processed in one central location under the direct supervision of the store manager.

■ POWER AS AN EXPANDING PIE

Along with empowerment, employees need to be trained to expand their power and their new influence potential. This is the most difficult task for managers and a difficult challenge for employees, for it often changes the dynamic between supervisors and subordinates. The key is to change the concept of power within the organization from a view that stresses power over others to one that emphasizes the use of power to get things done. Under the new definition of power, all employees can be more powerful.

A clearer definition of roles and responsibilities may help managers empower others. For instance, senior managers may choose to concentrate on long-term, large-scale adjustments to a variety of challenging and strategic forces in the external environment. If top management tends to concentrate on the long term and downplay quarterly mileposts, others throughout the organization must be ready and willing to make critical operating decisions to maintain current profitability. By providing opportunities for creative problem solving coupled with the discretion to act, real empowerment increases the total power available in an organization. In other words, the top levels don't have to give up power in order for the lower levels to gain it. Note that senior managers must give up the illusion of control—the false belief that they can direct the actions of employees five or six levels of management below them.

The same basic arguments hold true in any manager–subordinate relationship. Empowerment means that all managers need to emphasize different ways of exercising influence. Appeals to higher authority and sanctions need to be replaced by appeals to reason. Friendliness must replace coercion, and bargaining must replace orders for compliance.

Given the all too familiar history of an emphasis on coercion and compliance within firms, special support may be needed for individuals so that they become comfortable in developing their own power over events and activities. What executives fear, and all too often find, is that employees passively resist empowerment by seeking directives they can obey or reject. The fault lies with the executives and the middle managers who need to rethink what they mean by power and rethink their use of traditional position and personal power sources. The key is to lead, not push; reward, not sanction; build, not destroy; and expand, not shrink. To expand the zone of indifference also calls for expanding the inducements for thinking and acting, not just for obeying.

Organizational Politics

Any study of power and influence inevitably leads to the subject of "politics." For many, this word may conjure up thoughts of illicit deals, favors, and special personal relationships. Perhaps this image of shrewd, often dishonest, practices of obtaining one's way is reinforced by Machiavelli's classic fifteenth-century work *The Prince*, which outlines how to obtain and hold power via political action. It is important, however, to adopt a perspective that allows politics in organizations to function in a much broader capacity.[12]

■ THE TWO TRADITIONS OF ORGANIZATIONAL POLITICS

There are two quite different traditions in the analysis of organizational politics. One tradition builds on Machiavelli's philosophy and *defines politics in terms of self-interest and the use of nonsanctioned means*. In this tradition, **organizational politics** may be formally defined as the management of influence to obtain ends not sanctioned by the organization or to obtain sanctioned ends through nonsanctioned influence means.[13] Managers are often considered political when they seek their own goals or use means that are not currently authorized by the organization or that push legal limits. Where there is uncertainty or ambiguity, it is often extremely difficult to tell whether a manager is being political in this self-serving sense.[14] For instance, was John Meriwether a great innovator when he established Long Term Capital Management (LTCM) as a hedge fund to bet on interest rate spreads?[15] At one time, the firm included 2 Nobel laureates and some 25 Ph.D.s. Or was he the consummate insider when he got the U.S. Federal Reserve to orchestrate a bailout when it looked like he would either go broke or lose control to a rich investor? Or as often happens in the world of corporate politics, could both of these statements be partially true?

The second tradition *treats politics as a necessary function resulting from differences in the self-interests of individuals*. Here, organizational politics is viewed as the art of creative compromise among competing interests. In the case of John Meriwether and LTCM, when it went bankrupt the country's financial leaders were concerned that it could cause a panic in the markets and so hurt everyone. So the Federal Reserve stepped in. That Meriwether did not lose everything was

■ **Organizational politics** is the management of influence to obtain ends not sanctioned by the organization or to obtain sanctioned ends through nonsanctioned means and the art of creative compromise among competing interests.

merely a byproduct of saving the whole financial system. In a heterogeneous society, individuals will disagree as to whose self-interests are most valuable and whose concerns should therefore be bounded by collective interests. Politics arise because individuals need to develop compromises, avoid confrontation, and live together. The same holds true in organizations, where individuals join, work, and stay together because their self-interests are served. Furthermore, it is important to remember that the goals of the organization and the acceptable means are established by organizationally powerful individuals in negotiation with others. Thus, organizational politics is also the use of power to develop socially acceptable ends and means that balance individual and collective interests.

■ THE DOUBLE-EDGED SWORD OF ORGANIZATIONAL POLITICS

The two different traditions of organizational politics are reflected in the ways executives describe their effects on managers and their organizations. In one survey, some 53 percent of those interviewed indicated that organizational politics enhanced the achievement of organizational goals and survival.[16] Yet, some 44 percent suggested that it distracted individuals from organizational goals. In this same survey, 60 percent of respondents suggested that organizational politics was good for career advancement; 39 percent reported that it led to a loss of power, position, and credibility.

Organizational politics is not automatically good or bad. It can serve a number of important functions, including overcoming personnel inadequacies, coping with change, and substituting for formal authority.

Even in the best managed firms, mismatches arise among managers who are learning, burned out, lacking in needed training and skills, overqualified, or lacking the resources needed to accomplish their assigned duties. Organizational politics provides a mechanism for circumventing these inadequacies and getting the job done. Organizational politics can facilitate adaptation to changes in the environment and technology of an organization.

Organizational politics can help identify such problems and move ambitious, problem-solving managers into the breach. It is quicker than restructuring. It allows the firm to meet unanticipated problems with people and resources quickly, before small headaches become major problems. Finally, when a person's formal authority breaks down or fails to apply to a particular situation, political actions can be used to prevent a loss of influence. Managers may use political behavior to maintain operations and to achieve task continuity in circumstances where the failure of formal authority may otherwise cause problems.

■ ORGANIZATIONAL POLITICS AND SELF-PROTECTION

Whereas organizational politics may be helpful to the organization as a whole, it is probably more commonly known and better understood in terms of self-protection.[17] Whether or not management likes it, all employees recognize that in any organization they must watch out for themselves first. In too many organizations, if the employee doesn't protect himself or herself, no one else will.

Individuals can employ three common strategies to protect themselves. They can (1) avoid action and risk taking, (2) redirect accountability and responsibility, or (3) defend their turf.

Avoidance   *Avoidance* is quite common in controversial areas where the employee must risk being wrong or where actions may yield a sanction. Perhaps the most common reaction is to "work to the rules." That is, employees are protected when they adhere strictly to all the rules, policies, and procedures or do not allow deviations or exceptions. Perhaps one of the most frustrating but effective techniques is to "play dumb." We all do this at some time or another. When was the last time you said, "Officer, I didn't know the speed limit was 35. I couldn't have been going 52."

Although working to the rules and playing dumb are common techniques, experienced employees often practice somewhat more subtle techniques of self-protection. These include depersonalization and stalling. Depersonalization involves treating individuals, such as customers, clients, or subordinates, as numbers, things, or objects. Senior managers don't fire long-term employees; the organization is merely "downsized" or "delayered." Routine stalling involves slowing down the pace of work to expand the task so that the individuals look as if they are working hard. With creative stalling, the employees may spend the time supporting the organization's ideology, position, or program and delaying implementation.

Redirecting Responsibility   Politically sensitive individuals will always protect themselves from accepting blame for the negative consequences of their actions. Again, a variety of well-worn techniques may be used for *redirecting responsibility.* "Passing the buck" is a common method employees and managers use. The trick here is to define the task in such a way that it becomes someone else's formal responsibility. The ingenious ways individuals can redefine an issue to avoid action and transfer responsibility are often amazing.

Both employees and managers may avoid responsibility by *buffing,* or *rigorous documentation.* Here, individuals take action only when all the paperwork is in place and it is clear that they are merely following procedure. Closely related to rigorous documentation is the "blind memo," which explains an objection to an action implemented by the individual. Here, the required action is taken, but the blind memo is prepared should the action come into question. Politicians are particularly good at this technique. They will meet with a lobbyist and then send a memo to the files confirming the meeting. Any relationship between what was discussed in the meeting and the memo is accidental.

As the last example suggests, a convenient method some managers use to avoid responsibility is merely to *rewrite history.* If a program is successful, the manager claims to have been an early supporter. If a program fails, the manager was the one who expressed serious reservations in the first place. Whereas a memo in the files is often nice to have to show one's early support or objections, some executives don't bother with such niceties. They merely start a meeting by recapping what has happened in such a way that makes them look good.

For the really devious, there are three other techniques for redirecting responsibility. One technique is to blame the problem on someone or some group that has difficulty defending themselves. Fired employees, outsiders, and opponents are often targets of such scapegoating. Closely related to scapegoating is blaming the problem on uncontrollable events. The really astute manager goes far beyond the old "the-dog-ate-my-homework" routine. A perennial favorite is, "Given the unexpected severe decline in the overall economy, firm profitability was only somewhat below reasonable expectations." Meaning, the firm lost a bundle.

Should these techniques fail, there is always another possibility: Facing apparent defeat, the manager can escalate commitment to a losing cause of action. That is, when all appears lost, assert your confidence in the original action, blame the problems on not spending enough money to implement the plan fully, and embark on actions that call for increased effort. The hope is that you will be promoted or retired by the time the negative consequences are recognized.

Defending Turf   Defending turf is a time-honored tradition in most large organizations. As noted earlier, managers seeking to improve their power attempt to expand the jobs their groups perform. Defending turf also results from the coalitional nature of organizations. That is, the organization may be seen as a collection of competing interests held by various departments and groups. As each group attempts to expand its influence, it starts to encroach on the activities of other groups. Turf protection can be seen more easily in the following analysis of political action and the manager.

Political Action and the Manager

Managers may gain a better understanding of political behavior by placing themselves in the positions of other persons involved in critical decisions or events. Each action and decision can be seen as having benefits for and costs to all parties concerned. Where the costs exceed the benefits, the manager may act to protect his or her position.

Figure 4.3 shows a sample payoff table for two managers, Lee and Leslie, in a problem situation involving a decision as to whether or not to allocate resources

Figure 4.3
Political payoff matrix for the allocation of resources on a sample project.

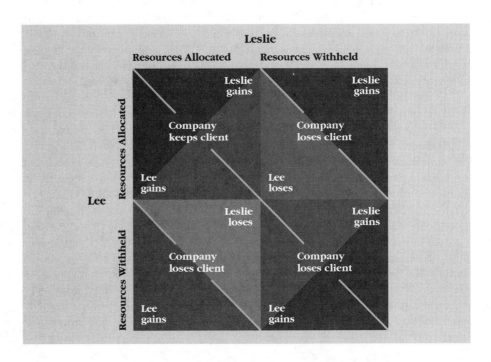

to a special project. If both managers authorize the resources, the project gets completed on time, and their company keeps a valuable client. Unfortunately, if they do this, both Lee and Leslie overspend their budgets. Taken on its own, a budget overrun would be bad for the managers' performance records. Assume that the overruns are acceptable only if the client is kept. Thus, if both managers act, both they and the company win, as depicted in the upper left block of the figure. Obviously, this is the most desirable outcome for all parties concerned.

Assume that Leslie acts, but Lee does not. In this case, the company loses the client, Leslie overspends the budget in a futile effort, but Lee ends up within budget. While the company and Leslie lose, Lee wins. This scenario is illustrated in the lower left block of the figure. The upper right block shows the reverse situation, where Lee acts but Leslie does not. In this case, Leslie wins, while the company and Lee lose. Finally, if both Lee and Leslie fail to act, each stays within the budget and therefore gains, but the company loses the client.

The company clearly wants both Lee and Leslie to act. But will they? Would you take the risk of overspending the budget, knowing that your colleague may refuse? The question of trust is critical here, but building trust among co-managers and other workers takes time and can be difficult. The involvement of higher level managers may be needed to set the stage better. Yet, in many organizations both Lee and Leslie would fail to act because the "climate" or "culture" too often encourages people to maximize their self-interest at minimal risks.

■ POLITICAL ACTION AND SUBUNIT POWER

Political action links managers more formally to one another as representatives of their work units. Five of the more typical lateral, intergroup relations in which you may engage as a manager are work flow, service, advisory, auditing, and approval.[18] Work-flow linkages involve contacts with units that precede or follow in a sequential production chain. Service ties involve contacts with units established to help with problems. For instance, an assembly-line manager may develop a service link by asking the maintenance manager to fix an important piece of equipment on a priority basis. In contrast, advisory connections involve formal staff units having special expertise, such as a manager seeking the advice of the personnel department on evaluating subordinates. Auditing linkages involve units that have the right to evaluate the actions of others after action has been taken, whereas approval linkages involve units whose approval must be obtained before action may be taken.

To be effective in political action, managers should understand the politics of subunit relations. Line units are typically more powerful than are staff groups, and units toward the top of the hierarchy are often more powerful than are those toward the bottom. In general, units gain power as more of their relations with others are of the approval and auditing types. Work-flow relations are more powerful than are advisory associations, and both are more powerful than are service relations.

■ POLITICAL ACTION IN THE CHIEF EXECUTIVE SUITE

From descriptions of the 1890s' robber barons such as Jay Gould to the actions of Microsoft's Bill Gates, Americans have been fascinated with the politics of the chief executive suite. An analytical view of executive suite dynamics may lift some of the mystery behind the political veil at the top levels in organizations.

Resource Dependencies Executive behavior can sometimes be explained in terms of resource dependencies—the firm's need for resources that are controlled by others.[19] Essentially, the resource dependence of an organization increases as (1) needed resources become more scarce, (2) outsiders have more control over needed resources, and (3) there are fewer substitutes for a particular type of resource controlled by a limited number of outsiders. Thus, one political role of the chief executive is to develop workable compromises among the competing resource dependencies facing the organization—compromises that enhance the executive's power. To create such compromises, executives need to diagnose the relative power of outsiders and to craft strategies that respond differently to various external resource suppliers.

For larger organizations, many strategies may center on altering the firm's degree of resource dependence. Through mergers and acquisitions, a firm may bring key resources within its control. By changing the "rules of the game," a firm may also find protection from particularly powerful outsiders. In the opening case, for instance, Netscape was seeking relief from the onslaught of Microsoft by appealing to the U.S. government. Markets may also be protected by trade barriers, or labor unions may be put in check by "right to work" laws. Yet, there are limits on the ability of even our largest and most powerful organizations to control all important external contingencies.

International competition has narrowed the range of options for chief executives; they can no longer ignore the rest of the world. Some may need to redefine fundamentally how they expect to conduct business. For instance, once U.S. firms could go it alone without the assistance of foreign corporations. Now, chief executives are increasingly leading them in the direction of more joint ventures and strategic alliances with foreign partners from around the globe. Such "combinations" provide access to scarce resources and technologies among partners, as well as new markets and shared production costs.

On the seamier side, there is a new wrinkle in the discussion of resource dependencies—executive pay. Traditionally, U.S. CEOs made about 30 times the pay of the average worker. This was similar to CEO pay scales in Europe and Japan.[20] Today many U.S. CEOs are making 3000 times the average pay of workers. How did they get so rich? CEOs may tie themselves to the short-term interests of powerful stockholders. Their pay may be directly linked to short-term stock price increases, even though CEOs are most often expected to focus on the long-term health of the firm. When a CEO downsizes, embarks on a merger campaign, or cuts such benefits as worker health care, short-term profits may jump dramatically and lift the stock price. Although the long-term health of the firm may be put in jeopardy, few U.S. CEOs seem able to resist the temptation. It is little wonder that there is renewed interest in how U.S. firms are governed.

■ **Organizational governance** is the pattern of authority, influence, and acceptable managerial behavior established at the top of the organization.

Organizational Governance **Organizational governance** refers to the pattern of authority, influence, and acceptable managerial behavior established at the top of the organization. This system establishes what is important, how issues will be defined, who should and should not be involved in key choices, and the boundaries for acceptable implementation.

Students of organizational governance suggest that a "dominant coalition" comprised of powerful organizational actors is a key to understanding a firm's governance.[21] Although one expects many top officers within the organization to be members of this coalition, the dominant coalition occasionally includes outsiders with access to key resources. Thus, analysis of organizational governance builds on the resource dependence perspective by highlighting the effective control of key resources by members of a dominant coalition.

This view of the executive suite recognizes that the daily practice of organizational governance is the development and resolution of issues. Through the governance system, the dominant coalition attempts to define reality. By accepting or rejecting proposals from subordinates, by directing questions toward the interests of powerful outsiders, and by selecting individuals who appear to espouse particular values and qualities, the pattern of governance is slowly established within the organization. Furthermore, this pattern rests, at least in part, on very political foundations.

Whereas organizational governance was an internal and a rather private matter in the past, it is now becoming more public and openly controversial. This was evidenced to some extent in the many well-publicized hostile takeovers of the 1980s and 1990s. Whereas some argue that senior managers don't represent shareholder interests well enough, others are concerned that they give too little attention to broader constituencies.

It has been estimated that the *Fortune* 500 corporations have cut some 8 million positions over the last 15 years of downsizing.[22] Managers and employees of these firms once felt confident that the management philosophy of their firm included their interests. In the new millennium, only a few employees seem to share this confidence. For instance, Boeing announced record production, near-record profits, and a merger with McDonnell-Douglas at the same time that it eliminated some 20,000 engineers from its home Seattle operations. Boeing eliminated almost all of the engineers hired in the last two years. As one critic caustically noted, "They ate their young to get executive bonuses." Obviously, Boeing is not a high performance organization.

Public concerns about U.S. corporations, especially those organizations with high-risk technologies such as chemical processing, medical technology, and integrated oil refineries, appear on the rise. For instance, Dow-Corning's survival is questionable because it has been accused of selling breast implants that cause immune system problems. Dow-Corning cites the lack of scientific evidence linking their product with such problems, but jury after jury is awarding damages to women who have had Dow-Corning implants and immune system problems. Without doubt juries are holding Dow-Corning management accountable.

Imbalanced organizational governance by some U.S. corporations may limit their ability to manage global operations effectively. Although U.S. senior managers may blame such externalities as unfavorable trade laws for their inability to compete in Japan or other Asian competitors, their critics suggest that it's just a lack of global operating savvy that limits the corporations these managers are supposed to be leading. Organizational governance is too closely tied to the short-term interests of stockholders and the pay of the CEO.

On a more positive note, there are bright spots suggesting that the governance of U.S. firms is extending well beyond the limited interests of the owners to include employees and into communities.

OB Across Functions
FINANCE
CFOs Don't Do Bad Either
The typical chief financial officer (CFO) receives about 34 percent of a CEO's (chief executive officer) compensation. A 1998 survey of the top-paid CFOs suggests some are not doing too badly, however. Scott Sullivan, CFO of World Com (now MCI World Com), received about $20 million in total direct compensation, while Early L. Mason of Compaq Computer was paid close to $16 million. The third highest paid CFO was Robert G. Scott of Morgan Stanley Dean Witter at over $12 million, followed by Donald Peterson of Lucent Technologies at over $10 million. Rounding out the top five was James Stewart of Cigna at a mere $9,457,400. The average cash compensation for all CFOs in the survey was over $360,000.

Cavanagh, Moberg, and Velasquez argue that organizational governance should have an ethical base.[23] They suggest that from the CEO to the lowest employee, a person's behavior must satisfy the following criteria to be considered ethical. First, the behavior must result in optimizing the satisfaction of people both inside and outside the organization to produce the greatest good for the greatest number of people. Second, the behavior must respect the rights of all affected parties, including the human rights of free consent, free speech, freedom of conscience, privacy, and due process. Third, the behavior must respect the rules of justice by treating people equitably and fairly, as opposed to arbitrarily.

There may be times when a behavior is unable to fulfill these criteria but can still be considered ethical in the given situation. This special case must satisfy the criterion of overwhelming factors, in which the special nature of the situation results in (1) conflicts among criteria (e.g., a behavior results in some good and some bad being done), (2) conflicts within criteria (e.g., a behavior uses questionable means to achieve a positive end), or (3) incapacity to employ the criteria (e.g., a person's behavior is based on inaccurate or incomplete information).

Choosing to be ethical often involves considerable personal sacrifice, and, at all corporate levels, it involves avoiding common rationalizations. CEOs and employees alike may justify unethical actions by suggesting that (1) the behavior is not really illegal and so could be moral; (2) the action appears to be in the firm's best interests; (3) the action is unlikely ever to be detected; and (4) it appears that the action demonstrates loyalty to the boss, the firm, or short-term stockholder interests. Whereas these rationalizations may appear compelling at the moment of action, each deserves close scrutiny if the firm's organizational governance system is to avoid falling into being dominated by the more unsavory side of organizational politics.

The Nature of Communication

Lucent Technologies, one of the major technology companies of our day, opened a recent annual report with these words: "There is a revolution going on in the communications industry." The report went on to note that over 900 million voice-mail messages are now exchanged every day, 2.7 trillion E-mails are sent in a year—some 5 million per minute—100 million Internet users come online in a year, and Internet traffic doubles every 100 days.[24] The figures are amazing, and the implications are clear. Appetites for information are growing by leaps and bounds, and the future of organizations is increasingly depending on their abilities to harness information and information technology for competitive advantage. At the center of all this stands the great demands and opportunities of the process we know as "communication."

■ THE COMMUNICATION PROCESS

■ **Communication** is the process of sending and receiving symbols with attached meanings.

It is useful to think of **communication** as a process of sending and receiving messages with attached meanings. The key elements in the communication process are illustrated in Figure 4.4. They include a *source*, who encodes an intended meaning into a message, and a *receiver*, who decodes the message into a perceived meaning.[25] The receiver may or may not give feedback to the source. Al-

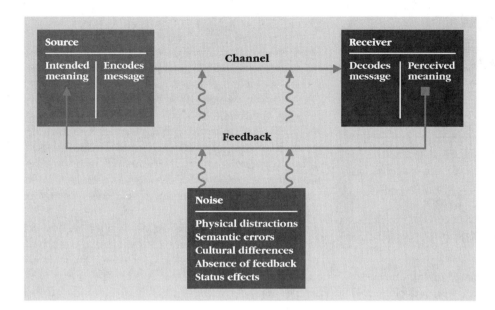

Figure 4.4
The communication process and possible sources of "noise."

though this process may appear to be very elementary, it is not quite as simple as it looks. **Noise** is the term used to describe any disturbance that disrupts it and interferes with the transference of messages within the communication process.

The information source is a person or group trying to communicate with someone else. The source seeks to communicate, in part, to change the attitudes, knowledge, or behavior of the receiver. A team leader, for example, may want to communicate with a division manager in order to explain why the team needs more time or resources to finish an assigned project. This involves *encoding*—the process of translating an idea or thought into a message consisting of verbal, written, or nonverbal symbols (such as gestures), or some combination of them. Such messages are transmitted through various **communication channels**, such as face-to-face meetings, electronic mail and other forms, written letters or memorandums, and telephone communications or voice-mail, among others. The choice of channel can have an important impact on the communication process. Some people are better at using certain channels over others, and some messages are better handled by specific channels. In the earlier case of the team leader communicating with the division manager, for example, it can make quite a difference whether the message is sent face to face, in a written memo, by voice-mail, or by E-mail.

The communication process is not completed just because a message is sent. The receiver is the individual or group of individuals to whom a message is directed. In order for meaning to be assigned to any received message, its contents must be interpreted through *decoding*. This process of translation is complicated by many factors, including the knowledge and experience of the receiver and his or her relationship with the sender. A message may also be interpreted with the added influence of other points of view, such as those offered by friends, co-workers, or organizational superiors. Ultimately, the decoding may result in the receiver interpreting a message in a way that is different from that originally intended by the source.

■ **Noise** is anything that interferes with the effectiveness of communication.

■ **Communication channels** are the pathways through which messages are communicated.

HOW TO GIVE CONSTRUCTIVE FEEDBACK

• Give directly and in a spirit of mutual trust.
• Be specific not general; use clear examples.
• Give when receiver is most ready to accept.
• Be accurate; check validity with others.
• Focus on things the receiver can control.
• Limit how much receiver gets at one time.

■ **Feedback** communicates how one feels about something another person has done or said.

■ FEEDBACK AND COMMUNICATION

Most receivers are well aware of the potential gap between the intended message of the source and the perceived meaning assigned to it by the recipient. One way in which these gaps are identified is through **feedback**, the process through which the receiver communicates with the sender by returning another message. The exchange of information through feedback can be very helpful in improving the communication process, and the popular advice to always "keep the feedback channels open" is good to remember.

In practice, giving "feedback" is often associated with one person communicating an evaluation of what another person has said or done. There is an art to giving this special type of feedback so that the receiver accepts it and uses it constructively (see The Effective Manager 4.2). Words that are intended to be polite and helpful can easily end up being perceived as unpleasant and even hostile. This risk is particularly evident in the performance appraisal process. A manager or team leader must be able to do more than just complete a written appraisal to document another person's performance for the record. To serve the person's developmental needs, feedback regarding the results of the appraisal—both the praise and the criticism, must be well communicated.[26]

Essentials of Interpersonal Communication

Organizations today are information rich. They are also increasingly "high-tech." But, we always need to remember that people still drive the system. And if people are to work together well and commit their mutual talents and energies to create high performance organizations, they must excel at interpersonal communication.

■ EFFECTIVE AND EFFICIENT COMMUNICATION

When people communicate with one another, at least two important things are at issue. One is the accuracy of the communication—an issue of effectiveness; the other is its cost—an issue of efficiency.

■ **Effective communication** is when the intended meaning equals the perceived meaning.

Effective communication occurs when the intended meaning of the source and the perceived meaning of the receiver are virtually the same.[27] Although this should be the goal in any communication, it is not always achieved. Even now, we worry about whether or not you are interpreting these written words exactly as we intend. Our confidence would be higher if we were face to face in class together and you could ask clarifying questions. Opportunities to offer feedback and ask questions are important ways of increasing the effectiveness of communication.

■ **Efficient communication** is low cost in its use of resources.

Efficient communication occurs at minimum cost in terms of resources expended. Time, for example, is an important resource. Picture your instructor taking the time to communicate individually with each student in your class about the course subject matter. It would be virtually impossible to do so. Even if it were possible, it would be very costly in terms of time. People at work often choose not to visit one another personally to communicate messages. Instead, they rely on the efficiency of written memos, posted bulletins, group meetings, E-mail, or voice-mail.

As efficient as these forms of communication may be, they are not always effective. A change in policy posted by efficient E-mail may save time for the sender, but it may not achieve the desired interpretations and responses. Similarly, an effective communication may not be efficient. For a business manager to visit each employee and explain a new change in procedures may guarantee that everyone understands the change, but it may also be prohibitively expensive in terms of the required time expenditure.

■ NONVERBAL COMMUNICATION

We all know that people communicate in ways other than the spoken or written word. Indeed, **nonverbal communication** that takes place through facial expressions, body position, eye contact, and other physical gestures is important both to understand and master. It is basically the act of speaking without using words. *Kinesics*, the study of gestures and body postures, has achieved a rightful place in communication theory and research.[28] The nonverbal side to communication can often hold the key to what someone is really thinking or meaning. It can also affect the impressions we make on others. Interviewers, for example, tend to respond more favorably to job candidates whose nonverbal cues, such as eye contact and erect posture, are positive than to those displaying negative nonverbal cues, such as looking down or slouching. The art of impression management during interviews and in other situations requires careful attention to both verbal and nonverbal aspects of communication, including one's dress, timeliness, and demeanor.

Nonverbal communication can also take place through the physical arrangement of space, such as that found in various office layouts. *Proxemics*, the study of the way space is utilized, is important to communication.[29] Figure 4.5 shows three different office arrangements and the messages they may communicate to visitors. Check the diagrams against the furniture arrangement in your office or

■ **Nonverbal communication** occurs by facial expressions, body motions, eye contact, and other physical gestures.

| "I am the boss!" | "I am the boss, but let's talk." | "Forget I'm the boss, let's talk." |

Figure 4.5
Furniture placement and nonverbal communication in the office.

THE EFFECTIVE MANAGER 4.3

GUIDELINES FOR ACTIVE LISTENING

1. Listen for content—try to hear exactly what is being said.
2. Listen for feelings—try to identify how the source feels about things.
3. Respond to feelings—let the source know that his or her feelings are recognized.
4. Note all cues—be sensitive to both verbal and nonverbal expressions.
5. Reflect back—repeat in your own words what you think you are hearing.

■ **Active listening**

encourages people to say what they really mean.

that of your instructor or a person with whom you are familiar. What are you/they saying to visitors by the choice of furniture placement?[30]

■ ACTIVE LISTENING

The ability to listen well is a distinct asset to anyone whose job involves a large proportion of time spent "communicating" with other people. After all, there are always two sides to the communication process: (1) sending a message, or "telling," and (2) receiving a message, or "listening." There is legitimate concern that too many people emphasize the telling and neglect the listening.[31] Everyone in the new workplace should develop good skills in **active listening**—the ability to help the source of a message say what he or she really means. The concept comes from the work of counselors and therapists, who are trained to help people express themselves and talk about things that are important to them.[32] Take a moment to more thoroughly consider the guidelines for active listening shown in The Effective Manager 4.3. Then read the conversations below. One involves active listening on the part of the branch manager; the other does not. How would you feel as the group leader in each case?[33]

Example 1

Group leader: Hey, Sal, I don't get this work order. We can't handle this today. What do they think we are?

Branch manager: But that's the order. So get it out as soon as you can. We're under terrific pressure this week.

Group Leader: Don't they know we're behind schedule already because of that software problem?

Branch manager: Look, I don't decide what goes on upstairs. I just have to see that the work gets out, and that's what I'm going to do.

Group leader: The team won't like this.

Branch manager: That's something you'll have to work out with them, not me.

Example 2

Group leader: Hey, Kelley, I don't get this work order. We can't handle this today. What do they think we are?

Branch manager: Sounds like you're pretty sore about it.

Group leader: I sure am. We're just about getting back to schedule while fighting that software breakdown. Now this comes along.

Branch manager: As if you didn't have enough work to do?

Group leader: Right, I don't know how to tell the team about this. They're under a real strain today. Seems like everything we do around here is rush, rush, rush.

Branch manager: I guess you feel like it's unfair to load anything more on them.

Group leader: Well, yes. But I know there must be plenty of pressure on everybody up the line. If that's the way it is, I'll get the word to them.

Branch manager: Thanks. If you'll give it a try, I'll do my best to hold with the schedule in the future.

The branch manager in Example 2 possesses active listening skills. She responded to the group leader's communication in a way that increased the flow of information. The manager learned more about the situation. The group leader felt better after having been able to really say what she thought, and after being heard!

Communication Barriers

It is important to understand six sources of noise that are common to most interpersonal exchanges: physical distractions, semantic problems, mixed messages, cultural differences, absence of feedback, and status effects. They were shown earlier in Figure 4.4 as potential threats to the communication process.

■ PHYSICAL DISTRACTIONS

Any number of physical distractions can interfere with the effectiveness of a communication attempt. Some of these distractions are evident in the following conversation between an employee, George, and his manager.[34]

> Okay, George, let's hear your problem (phone rings, boss picks it up, promises to deliver the report, "just as soon as I can get it done"). Uh, now, where were we—oh, you're having a problem with marketing. They (the manager's secretary brings in some papers that need immediate signatures; he scribbles his name and the secretary leaves)...you say they're not cooperative? I tell you what, George, why don't you (phone rings again, lunch partner drops by)...uh, take a stab at handling it yourself. I've got to go now.

Besides what may have been poor intentions in the first place, George's manager allowed physical distractions to create information overload. As a result, the communication with George suffered. This mistake can be eliminated by setting priorities and planning. If George has something to say, his manager should set aside adequate time for the meeting. In addition, interruptions such as telephone calls, drop-in visitors, and the like, should be prevented. At a minimum, George's manager could start by closing the door to the office and instructing his secretary not to disturb them.

■ SEMANTIC PROBLEMS

Semantic barriers to communication involve a poor choice or use of words and mixed messages. The following illustrations of the "bafflegab" that once tried to pass as actual "executive communication" are a case in point.[35]

A. "We solicit any recommendations that you wish to make, and you may be assured that any such recommendations will be given our careful consideration."

B. "Consumer elements are continuing to stress the fundamental necessity of a stabilization of the price structure at a lower level than exists at the present time."

■ The **KISS principle** stands for "keep it short and simple."

■ **Mixed messages** occur when words say one thing while nonverbal cues say something else.

One has to wonder why these messages weren't stated more simply as: (A) "Send us your recommendations. They will be carefully considered," and (B) "Consumers want lower prices." In this regard, the popular **KISS principle** of communication is always worth remembering: "Keep it short and simple."

■ MIXED MESSAGES

Mixed messages occur when a person's words communicate one thing while actions or "body language" communicate another. They are important to spot since nonverbals can add important insight into what is really being said in face-to-face communication.[36] For instance, someone may voice a cautious "Yes" during a business meeting at the same time that her facial expression shows stress and she begins to lean back in her chair. The body language in this case may suggest the existence of important reservations, even though the words indicate agreement.

■ CULTURAL DIFFERENCES

People must always exercise caution when they are involved in cross-cultural communication—whether between persons of different geographical or ethnic groupings within one country, or between persons of different national cultures. A common problem is *ethnocentrism*—the tendency to believe one's culture and its values are superior to those of others. It is often accompanied by an unwillingness to try to understand alternative points of view and to take the values they represent seriously. This mindset can easily create communication problems among people of diverse backgrounds.

The difficulties with cross-cultural communication are perhaps most obvious in respect to language differences. Advertising messages, for example, may work well in one country but encounter difficulty when translated into the language of another. Problems may accompany with the introduction of Ford's European model, the "Ka," in Japan. In Japanese, *Ka* means mosquito and analysts wonder if a car that is named for a disease-carrying pest can ever sell well.[37] Gestures may also be used quite differently in the various cultures of the world. For example, crossed legs in the United Kingdom are quite acceptable, but are rude in Saudia Arabia if the sole of the foot is directed toward someone. Pointing at someone to get their attention may be acceptable in Canada, but in Asia it is considered inappropriate.[38]

■ ABSENCE OF FEEDBACK

One-way communication flows from sender to receiver only, as in the case of a written memo or a voice-mail message. There is no direct and immediate feedback from the recipient. Two-way communication, by contrast, goes from sender to receiver and back again. It is characterized by the normal interactive conversations in our daily experiences. Research indicates that two-way communication is more accurate and effective than is one-way communication, even though it is also more costly and time consuming. Because of their efficiency, however, one-way forms of communication—memos, letters, E-mail, voice-mail, and the like are frequently used in work settings. One-way messages are easy for the sender but often frustrating for the receiver, who may be left unsure of just what the sender means or wants done.

■ STATUS EFFECTS

Status differences in organizations create potential communication barriers between persons of higher and lower ranks. On the one hand, given the authority of their positions, managers may be inclined to do a lot of "telling" but not much "listening." On the other hand, we know that communication is frequently biased when flowing upward in organizational hierarchies.[39] Subordinates may *filter* information and tell their superiors only what they think the boss wants to hear. Whether the reason is a fear of retribution for bringing bad news, an unwillingness to identify personal mistakes, or just a general desire to please, the result is the same: The higher level decision maker may end up taking the wrong actions because of biased and inaccurate information supplied from below. This is sometimes called the **MUM effect** in reference to tendencies to sometimes keep "mum" from a desire to be polite and a reluctance to transmit bad news.[40]

> ■ The **MUM effect** occurs when people are reluctant to communicate bad news.

To avoid such problems, managers and group leaders must develop trust in their working relationships with subordinates and team members, and take advantage of all opportunities for face-to-face communications. *Management by wandering around*, or **MBWA** for short, is now popularly acclaimed as one way to achieve this trust.[41] It simply means getting out of the office and talking to people regularly as they do their jobs. Managers who spend time walking around can greatly reduce the perceived "distance" between themselves and their subordinates. It helps to create an atmosphere of open and free-flowing communication between the ranks. As a result, more and better information is available for decision making, and the relevance of decisions to the needs of operating workers increases.

> ■ **MBWA** involves getting out of the office to directly communicate with others.

Organizational Communication

Communication among members of an organization, as well as between them and external customers, suppliers, distributors, alliance partners, and a host of outsiders, provides vital information for the enterprise. **Organizational communication** is the specific process through which information moves and is exchanged throughout an organization.[42] Information flows through both formal and informal structures, and it flows downward, upward, and laterally.

> ■ **Organizational communication** is the process by which information is exchanged in the organizational setting.

Today, more than ever before, computer technology plays a major role in how information is shared and utilized in organizations. Research in the area of *channel richness*, the capacity of a channel to convey information effectively, lends insight into how various channel alternatives may be used depending on the type of message to be conveyed. In general, the richest channels are face to face. Next are telephone, E-mail, written memos and letters. The leanest channels are posted notices and bulletins. When messages get more complex and open ended, richer channels are necessary to achieve effective communication; leaner channels work well for more routine and straightforward messages, such as announcing the location of a previously scheduled meeting.

■ FORMAL AND INFORMAL CHANNELS

Information flows in organizations through both formal and informal channels of communication. **Formal channels** follow the chain of command established by an

> ■ **Formal channels** follow the official chain of command.

■ **Informal channels** do not follow the chain of command.

■ A **grapevine** transfers information through networks of friendships and acquaintances.

organization's hierarchy of authority. For example, an organization chart indicates the proper routing for official messages passing from one level or part of the hierarchy to another. Because formal channels are recognized as authoritative, it is typical for communication of policies, procedures, and other official announcements to adhere to them. On the other hand, much "networking" takes place through the use of **informal channels** that do not adhere to the organization's hierarchy of authority.[43] They coexist with the formal channels but frequently diverge from them by skipping levels in the hierarchy or cutting across vertical chains of command. Informal channels help to create open communications in organizations and ensure that the right people are in contact with one another."[44]

One familiar informal channel is the **grapevine** or network of friendships and acquaintances through which rumors and other unofficial information are passed from person to person. Grapevines have the advantage of being able to transmit information quickly and efficiently. Grapevines also help fulfill the needs of people involved in them. Being part of a grapevine can provide a sense of security from "being in the know" when important things are going on. It also provides social satisfaction as information is exchanged interpersonally. The primary disadvantage of grapevines occurs when they transmit incorrect or untimely information. Rumors can be very dysfunctional, to both people and organizations. One of the best ways to avoid them is to make sure that key persons in a grapevine get the right information to begin with.

■ COMMUNICATION FLOWS AND DIRECTIONS

As shown in Figure 4.6, *downward communication* follows the chain of command top to bottom. One of its major functions is to inform. Lower level personnel need to know what higher levels are doing and to be regularly reminded of key policies, strategies, objectives, and technical developments. Of special importance is feedback and information on performance results. Sharing such information helps minimize the spread of rumors and inaccuracies regarding higher level intentions. It also helps create a sense of security and involvement among receivers, who feel they know the whole story. Unfortunately, a lack of adequate downward communication is often cited as a management failure. On the issue of corporate downsizing, for example, one sample showed that 64 percent of employees did not believe what management said, 61 percent felt uninformed about company plans, and 54 percent complained that decisions were not well explained.[45]

The flow of messages from lower to higher levels is *upward communication*. As shown in Figure 4.6, it serves several purposes. Upward communication keeps higher levels informed about what lower level workers are doing, what their problems are, what suggestions they have for improvements, and how they feel about the organization and their jobs. The employee surveys used by Sun Microsystems and mentioned in the chapter opener are examples. But, as you should recall, status effects can potentially interfere with the effectiveness of upward communication.

The importance of *lateral communication* in the new workplace has been a recurrent theme in this book. Today's customer-sensitive organizations need timely and accurate feedback and product information. To serve customer needs they must get the right information—and get it fast enough—into the hands of workers. Furthermore, inside the organization, people must be willing and able to communicate across departmental or functional boundaries and to listen to one

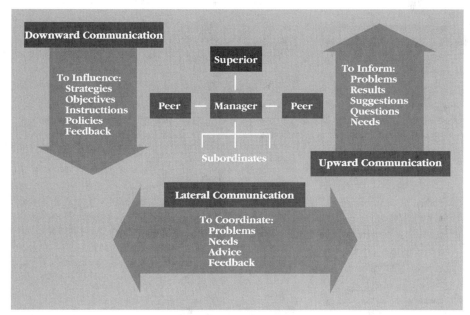

Figure 4.6
Directions for information flows in organizations.

another's needs as "internal customers." New organization designs are emphasizing lateral communication in the form of cross-departmental committees, teams, or task forces and the matrix organization. Among the developments is growing attention to *organizational ecology*—the study of how building design may influence communication and productivity by improving lateral communications.

∎ COMMUNICATION NETWORKS

Figure 4.7 depicts three interaction patterns and communication networks that are common within organizations.[46] Having the right interaction pattern and communication network can make a big difference in the way groups function and in the performance results they achieve.

Some work arrangements involve *interacting groups* whose members work closely together on tasks and in which close coordination of activities takes place. Information flows to everyone. This interaction pattern results in a **decentralized communication network** in which all group members communicate directly and share information with one another. Sometimes these are also referred to as all-channel or star communication networks.[47] They work best for complex and non-routine tasks. They also tend to create high levels of member satisfaction.

Other work arrangements involve *coacting groups* whose members work on tasks independently, while linked through some form of central coordination. The required work is divided up and then largely completed by individuals working alone. Each individual's activities are coordinated and results pooled by a central control point. Information flows to a central person and is redistributed. This creates a **centralized communication network**, with the central person serving as the "hub." Sometimes these are called wheel or chain communication networks. They work best when tasks are easily routinized or subdivided. In

∎ **Decentralized communication networks** link all group members directly with one another.

∎ **Centralized communication networks** link group members through a central control point.

Figure 4.7
Interaction patterns and communication networks in groups.

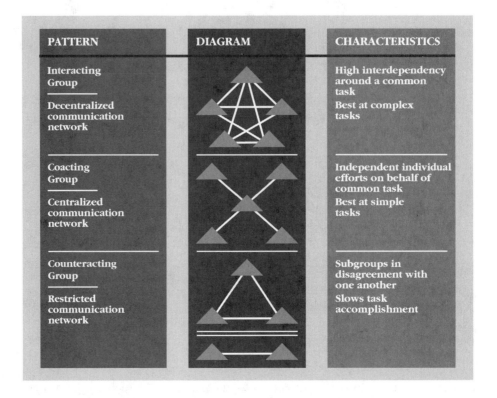

PATTERN	DIAGRAM	CHARACTERISTICS
Interacting Group Decentralized communication network		High interdependency around a common task Best at complex tasks
Coacting Group Centralized communication network		Independent individual efforts on behalf of common task Best at simple tasks
Counteracting Group Restricted communication network		Subgroups in disagreement with one another Slows task accomplishment

these groups, it is usually the central or "hub" person who experiences this satisfaction. After all, he or she alone is most involved in all aspects of group information processing.

Counteracting groups exist when subgroups disagree on some aspect of workplace operations. The subgroups may experience issue-specific disagreements—such as a temporary debate over the best means to achieve a goal, or the disagreements may be of longer-term duration—such as labor–management disputes. In either case, the resulting interaction pattern involves a **restricted communication network** in which polarized subgroups contest one another's positions and maintain sometimes antagonistic relations. As would be expected, communication between the groups is often limited and biased. Problems of destructive competition in intergroup dynamics are likely under such circumstances.

■ **Restricted communication networks** link subgroups that disagree with one another's positions.

Communication and the High Performance Workplace

One of the greatest changes in organizations and in everyday life in recent years has been the great explosion in new communication technologies. We have moved from the world of the telephone, mail, photocopying, and face-to-face meetings into one of voice-mail, E-mail, facsimile transmission, computer-mediated conferencing, and use of the Internet and Intranets. The ability to participate effectively in all forms of the electronic office and communications environment is well established as an essential career skill. The increasing importance of E-commerce is also transforming the very nature of business in modern society.[48]Given the pace and extensiveness of these dynamics, everyone must keep themselves up to date with the full range of information technologies and emerging issues in organizational communication.

■ CHANGING TECHNOLOGIES

The impact of the new technologies is discussed throughout this book with respect to job design and the growth of telecommuting, organizational design and the growth of network organizations, and teamwork and the availability of software for electronic meetings and decision making, among many other applications. Advances in information technology are allowing organizations to. (1) distribute information much faster than before; (2) make more information available than ever before; (3) allow broader and more immediate access to this information; (4) encourage participation in the sharing and use of information; and, (5) integrate systems and functions, and use information to link with environments in unprecedented ways.

The potential disadvantages of electronic communications must also be recognized. To begin, the technologies are largely impersonal; people interact with machines, not with one another. Electronics also removes nonverbal communications from the situation—aspects that may otherwise add important context to an interaction. In addition, the electronic medium can influence the emotional aspects of communication. Some argue, for example, that it is far easier to be blunt, overly critical, and insensitive when conveying messages electronically rather than face-to-face. The term "flaming" is sometimes used to describe rudeness in electronic communication. In this sense, the use of computer mediation may make people less inhibited and more impatient in what they say.[49]

Another risk of the new communication technologies is information overload. In some cases, too much information may find its way into the communication networks and E-mail systems and basically overload the systems—both organizational and individual. Individual users may have difficulty sorting the useful from the trivial and may become impatient while doing so.

In all this, one point remains undeniable: New communication technologies will continue to keep changing the nature of work and of office work in particular. The once-conventional office is fast giving way to new forms such as telecommuting and the use of electronic networks. Workers in the future will benefit as new technologies allow them to spend

OB Across Functions
MANAGEMENT INFORMATION SYSTEMS

Enterprise Resource Planning Builds the E-Corporation

Total enterprise integration is one of the big pushes these days. The emergence of the new "E-corporation" is a major competitive challenge in many industries. Consider the example of VF Corporation, which manufactures some $2 billion of jeans each year for major brands including Lee, Wrangler, Britannia, and Rustler. When Mackey McDonald took over as the firm's CEO his vision was to create a computer-savvy company that would use the latest in technologies to continually identify customer demographics, point-of-sale, and other relevant information to drive its production and distribution systems. In short, information and technology were to be used for competitive advantage. VF's integrated information systems begin with SAP software, which addresses resource planning at the corporate level and for the entire organization. SAP serves as the information systems hub and communicates with special software programs that individually deal with such needs as product development, micromarketing, forecasting, capacity and raw materials planning, manufacturing control, and warehouse control. It's all sophisticated and integrated, and with a purpose. The investment costs over $100 million, and VF is still working to get all the software systems in place. However, the goals of speed to market and cost efficiency are within reach. McDonald is confident that the returns will be high. After all, he began the process by involving employees from all levels of the firm in planning and identifying systems needs. He says: "Our people designed the products and the processes. That's why I think we can have success."

more time out of the traditional office and more time working with customers on terms that best fit individual needs.

■ COMPLEX SOCIAL CONTEXT

There are any number of issues affecting communication in the complex social context of organizations today. Of continuing interest, for example, is the study of male and female communication styles. In her book *Talking 9 to 5*, Deborah Tannen argues that men and women learn or are socialized into different styles and as a result often end up having difficulties communicating with one another.[50] She sees women more oriented toward relationship building in communication, for example, while men are more prone to seek status through communications.[51] Because people tend to surround themselves with those whose communication styles fit with their own, a further implication is that either women or men may dominate communications in situations where they are in the majority.[52]

More and more people are asking a question related to the prior discussion: "Are women better communicators than men?" A study by the consulting firm Lawrence A. Pfaff and Associates suggests they may well be.[53] The survey shows that supervisors rank women managers higher than men managers on communication, approachability, evaluations, and empowering others; their subordinates also rank women higher on these same items. A possible explanation is that early socialization and training better prepare women for the skills involved in communication and may make them more sensitive in interpersonal relationships. In contrast, men may be more socialized in ways that cause communication problems—such as aggression, competitiveness, and individualism.[54] In considering such possibilities, however, it is important to avoid gender stereotyping and to focus instead on the point of ultimate importance—how communication in organizations can be made most effective.[55]

Among the controversies in organizational communication today is the issue of *privacy*. An example is concern for eavesdropping by employers on employee use of electronic messaging in corporate facilities. Progressive organizations are developing internal policies regarding the privacy of employee communications, and the issue is gaining attention from legislators. A state law in Illinois now makes it legal for bosses to listen in on employees' telephone calls. But the law leaves the boundaries of appropriateness unclear. Such eavesdropping is common in some service areas such as airlines reservations, where union concerns are sometimes expressed in the context of "Big brother is watching you!"[56] The privacy issue is likely to remain controversial as communication technologies continue to make it easier for employers to electronically monitor the performance and communications of their workers.

Our society also struggles with the *political correctness* of communications in the workplace. The vocabulary of work is changing, and people are ever more on guard not to let their choice of words offend another individual or group. We now hear references to "people of color," the "physically challenged," and "seniors;" not too long ago these references may have been different, and they may be different again in the future. Organizations are taking notice of this issue and are offering more training to their members to help eliminate in any communications possible overtones of intolerance and insensitivity.

Footnotes

[1] John R. P. French and Bertram Raven, "The Bases of Social Power," in Dorwin Cartwright (ed.), *Group Dynamics: Research and Theory* (Evanston, IL: Row, Peterson, 1962), pp. 607–623.

[2] See French and Raven (1962).

[3] John P. Kotter, "Power, Success, and Organizational Effectiveness," *Organizational Dynamics* 6 (Winter 1978): 27; David A. Whetten and Kim S. Cameron, *Developing Managerial Skills* (Glenview, IL: Scott, Foresman, 1984), pp. 250–259.

[4] David Kipinis, Stuart M. Schmidt, Chris Swaffin-Smith, and Ian Wilkinson, "Patterns of Managerial Influence: Shotgun Managers, Tacticians, and Bystanders," *Organizational Dynamics* 12 (Winter 1984): 60, 61.

[5] Ibid., pp. 58–67; David Kipinis, Stuart M. Schmidt, and Ian Wilkinson, "Intraorganizational Influence Tactics: Explorations in Getting One's Way," *Journal of Applied Psychology* 65 (1980): 440–452.

[6] Warren K. Schilit and Edwin A. Locke, "A Study of Upward Influence in Organizations," *Administrative Science Quarterly*, 27 (1982): 304–316.

[7] Ibid.

[8] Stanley Milgram, "Behavioral Study of Obedience," in Dennis W. Organ (ed.), *The Applied Psychology of Work Behavior* (Dallas: Business Publications, 1978), pp. 384–398. Also see Stanley Milgram, "Behavioral Study of Obedience," *Journal of Abnormal and Social Psychology* 67 (1963): 371–378; Stanley Milgram, "Group Pressure and Action Against a Person," *Journal of Abnormal and Social Psychology* 69 (1964): 137–143; "Some Conditions of Obedience and Disobedience to Authority," *Human Relations* 1 (1965): 57–76; Stanley Milgram, *Obedience to Authority* (New York: Harper & Row, 1974).

[9] Chester Barnard, *The Functions of the Executive* (Cambridge, MA: Harvard University Press, 1938).

[10] Ibid.

[11] See Steven N. Brenner and Earl A. Mollander, "Is the Ethics of Business Changing?" *Harvard Business Review* 55 (February 1977): 57–71; Barry Z. Posner and Warren H. Schmidt, "Values and the American Manager: An Update," *California Management Review* 26 (Spring 1984): 202–216.

[12] Although the work on organizational politics is not extensive, useful reviews include a chapter in Robert H. Miles, *Macro Organizational Behavior* (Santa Monica, CA: Goodyear, 1980); Bronston T. Mayes and Robert W. Allen, "Toward a Definition of Organizational Politics," *Academy of Management Review* 2 (1977): 672–677; Gerald F. Cavanagh, Dennis J. Moberg, and Manuel Velasquez, "The Ethics of Organizational Politics," *Academy of Management Review* 6 (July 1981): 363–374; Dan Farrell and James C. Petersen, "Patterns of Political Behavior in Organizations," *Academy of Management Review* 7 (July 1982): 403–412; D. L. Madison, R. W. Allen, L. W. Porter, and B. T. Mayes, "Organizational Politics: An Exploration of Managers' Perceptions," *Human Relations* 33 (1980): 92–107.

[13] Mayes and Allen, "Toward a Definition of Organizational Politics," p. 675.

[14] Jeffrey Pfeffer, *Power in Organizations* (Marshfield, MA: Pitman, 1981), p. 7.

[15] Michael Sconcolfi, Anita Raghavan, and Mitchell Pacelle, "All Bets Are Off: How the Salesmanship and Brainpower Failed at Long Term Capital," *Wall Street Journal* (November 16, 1998), p. 1, 18–19.

[16] B. E. Ashforth and R. T. Lee, "Defensive Behavior in Organizations: A Preliminary Model," *Human Relations* (July 1990): 621–648; personal communication with Blake Ashforth, December 1998.

[17] See Pfeffer (1981); M. M. Harmon and R. T. Mayer, *Organization Theory for Public Administration* (Boston: Little, Brown, 1986); W. Richard Scott, *Organizations: Rational, Natural and Open Systems* (Englewood Cliffs, NJ: Prentice-Hall, 1987).

[18] Developed from James L. Hall and Joel L. Leldecker, "A Review of Vertical and Lateral Relations: A New Perspective for Managers," in Patrick Connor (ed.), *Dimensions in Modern Management*, 3rd ed. (Boston: Houghton Mifflin, 1982), pp. 138–146, which was based in part on Leonard Sayles, *Managerial Behavior* (New York: McGraw-Hill, 1964).

[19] See Jeffrey Pfeffer, *Organizations and Organization Theory* (Boston: Pitman, 1983); Jeffrey Pfeffer and Gerald R. Salancik, *The External Control of Organizations* (Englewood Cliffs, NJ: Prentice-Hall, 1978).

[20] R. N. Osborn, "A Comparison of CEO Pay in Western Europe, Japan and the U.S.," working paper (Detroit: Department of Management, Wayne State University, 1998).

[21] See the early work of James D. Thompson, *Organizations in Action* (New York: McGraw-Hill, 1967) and more recent studies by R. N. Osborn and D. H. Jackson, "Leaders, Riverboat Gamblers, or Purposeful Unintended Consequences in Management of Complex Technologies," *Academy of Management Journal* 31 (1988): 924–947; M. Hector, "When Actors Comply: Monitoring Costs and the Production of Social Order," *Acta Sociologica* 27 (1984): 161–183; T. Mitchell and W. G. Scott, "Leadership Failures, the Distrusting Public and Prospects for the Administrative State," *Public Administration Review* 47 (1987): 445–452.

[22] J. J. Jones, *The Downsizing of American Potential* (New York: Raymond Press, 1996).

[23] This discussion is based on Cavanagh, Moberg, and Velasquez (1981); and Manuel Velasquez, Dennis J. Moberg, and Gerald Cavanagh, "Organizational Statesmanship and Dirty Politics: Ethical Guidelines for the Organizational Politician," *Organizational Dynamics* 11 (1983): 65–79, both of which offer a fine treatment of the ethics of power and politics.

[24] Lucent Technologies, *1998 Annual Report*.

[25] Steve Axley, author of *Communication at Work: Management and the Communication-Intensive Organization* (Westport, CT: Quorum Books, 1996), points out that the ultimate meaning in any communication is created by the receiver or perceiver of the message.

[26] Developed from J. Stephen Morris, "How to Make Criticism Sessions Productive," *Wall Street Journal* (October 12, 1981), p. 24.

[27] See Axelrod (1996).

[28] See Richard L. Birdwhistell, *Kinesics and Context* (Philadelphia: University of Pennsylvania Press, 1970).

[29] Edward T. Hall, *The Hidden Dimension* (Garden City, NY: Doubleday, 1966).

[30] See D. E. Campbell, "Interior Office Design and Visitor Response," *Journal of Applied Psychology* 64 (1979): 648–653; P. C. Morrow and J. C. McElroy, "Interior Office Design and Visitor Response: A Constructive Replication," *Journal of Applied Psychology* 66 (1981): 646–650.

[31] M. P. Rowe and M. Baker, "Are You Hearing Enough Employee Concerns?" *Harvard Business Review* 62 (May/June 1984): 127–135.

[32] This discussion is based on Carl R. Rogers and Richard E. Farson, "Active Listening" (Chicago: Relations Center of the University of Chicago).

[33] Modified from an example in ibid.

[34] Richard V. Farace, Peter R. Monge, and Hamish M. Russell, *Communicating and Organizing* (Reading, MA: Addison-Wesley, 1977), pp. 97–98.

[35] The statements are from *Business Week* (July 6, 1981), p. 107.

[36] See A. Mehrabian, *Silent Messages* (Belmont, CA: Wadsworth, 1981).

[37] Information from "How Not to Do International Business," *Business Week* (April 12, 1999).

[38] See C. Barnum and N. Woliansky, "Taking Cues from Body Language," *Management Review* 78 (1989): 59; S. Bochner (ed.), *Cultures in Contact: Studies in Cross-Cultural Interaction* (London: Pergamon, 1982); A. Furnham and S. Bocher, *Culture Shock: Psychological Reactions to Unfamiliar Environments* (London: Methuen, 1986).

[39] This research is reviewed by John C. Athanassiades, "The Distortion of Upward Communication in Hierarchical Organizations," *Academy of Management Journal* 16 (June 1973): 207–226.

[40] F. Lee, "Being Polite and Keeping MUM: How Bad News is Communicated in Organizational Hierarchies," *Journal of Applied Social Psychology* 23 (1993): 1124–1149.

[41] Thomas J. Peters and Robert H. Waterman, Jr., *In Search of Excellence* (New York: Harper & Row, 1983).

[42] Portions of this section are adapted from John R. Schermerhorn, Jr., *Management*, 5th ed. (New York: Wiley, 1996), pp. 375–378. Used by permission.

[43] Networking is considered an essential managerial activity by Kotter (1982).

[44] Peters and Waterman (1983).

[45] *Business Week* (May 16, 1994), p. 8.

[46] The concept of interacting, coacting, and counteracting groups is presented in Fred E. Fiedler, *A Theory of Leadership Productivity* (New York: McGraw-Hill, 1967).

[47] Research on communication networks is found in Alex Bavelas, "Communication Patterns in Task-Oriented Groups," *Journal of the Acoustical Society of America* 22 (1950): 725–730. See also "Research on Communication Networks," as summarized in Marvin E. Shaw, *Group Dynamics: The Psychology of Small Group Behavior* (New York: McGraw-Hill, 1976), pp. 137–153.

[48] See "e.Biz: What Every CEO Should Know about Electronic Business," *Business Week*, Special Report (March 22, 1999).

[49] See C. Brod, *Technostress: The Human Cost of the Computer Revolution* (Reading, MA: Addison-Wesley, 1984); and G. Brockhouse, "I Have Seen the Future...," *Canadian Business* (August 1993): 43–45.

[50] Deborah Tannen, *Talking 9 to 5* (New York: Avon, 1995).

[51] Deborah Tannen, *You Just Don't Understand: Women and Men in Conversation* (New York: Ballantine Books, 1991).

[52] Deborah Tannen, "The Power of Talk: Who Gets Heard and Why," *Harvard Business Review* (September–October, 1995): 138–148.

[53] Reported by *Working Woman* (November 1995), p. 14.

[54] Ibid.

[55] For an editorial opinion, see Jayne Tear, "They Just Don't Understand Gender Dynamics," *Wall Street Journal* (November 20, 1995), p. A14.

[56] See "My Boss, Big Brother," *Business Week* (January 22, 1996), p. 56.

Source Notes

Linda Corman, "As Good as It Gets: The 1998 Compensation Survey," *CFO* (November 1998), pp. 41–54.

www.catalinamktg.com.

Based on information in John Lornic, "Managing When There Is No Middle," *Canadian Business* (June 1996), pp. 86–89, 94.

Littlecaesars.com; "New Ex Takes Reins at Hospice," *Detroit News* (October 25, 1998), p. C-l.

Eryn Brown, "VF Corp. Changes its Underware," *Fortune* (December 7, 1998), pp. 115–118; and "Stitching Together an E-Corporation," *Fortune* (December 7, 1998), p. 117.

Monsanto: Information from Timothy D. Schellhardt, "Monsanto Best on Box Buddies," *Wall Street Journal* (February 23, 1999), p. B1.

UAL: Information from "UAL: Labor Is My Co-Pilot," *Business Week* (March 1, 1999), p. 38.

American Express: New information from "The Rise of a Star," *Business Week* (December 21, 1998), pp. 60–68.

John R. Schermerhorn, Jr., *Management*, 5th ed. (New York: Wiley, 1996), p. 377. Used by permission.

Section Five

Section Five

Organizational Behavior and Globalization

Most organizations today must achieve high performance in the context of a competitive and complex global environment.[1] As we begin the twenty-first century, we find ourselves fully in the age of **globalization** with its complex economic networks of competition, resource supplies, and product markets transcending national boundaries and circling the globe.[2] None of us can have failed to notice its impact on organizations, the people who work in them, and our everyday lives. Consider the potential effects of globalization in terms of your own life and career: (1) You already purchase many products made by foreign firms; (2) you may someday work overseas in the foreign operation of a domestic firm; (3) you may someday work overseas as an expatriate employee of a foreign firm; and (4) you may someday work as a domestic employee of a foreign firm operating in your home country. The field of organizational behavior recognizes these realities and seeks to help you understand the performance implications of work in the global economy.

■ **Globalization** involves growing worldwide interdependence of resource suppliers, product markets, and business competition.

■ A GLOBAL ECONOMY

The rapid growth of information technology and electronic communications has heightened the average person's awareness of the global economy. The international news brings the entire world into our homes and our thoughts daily. An explosion of opportunities on the Internet allows us to share and gather information from global sources at low cost and from the convenience of our desktops— at home, while traveling, or at work. And, always, the transnational movement of products, trends, values, and innovations continues to change lifestyles at a rapid pace. At the same time that valuable skills and investments move from country to country, cultural diversity among the populations is increasing. Immigration is having profound implications for many nations. Tomorrow's employers will have even greater need to deal with *multicultural workforces*—those that draw workers from nontraditional labor sources and from ethnic backgrounds representing all corners of the globe.[3]

Domestic self-sufficiency is no longer a viable option for nations or businesses.[4] Commercial investments travel the trade routes of the world. Canadian businesses, for example, have their sights set on America, with some $65 billion already invested there. Germany is a large investor in the United States, with recent mergers creating the global giants Daimler Chrysler and Deutsche Bank-Bankers Trust. The Japanese are also large investors with ownership stakes in over 1500 U.S. factories, employing over 350,000 people.[5] Crossing the Atlantic to Scotland, with its low taxes, excellent infrastructure, and skilled workers, many high-technology firms like IBM have invested over $4.5 billion in what is now being called "Silicon Glen."[6] Global supplier networks play significant roles in the operations of many industries. The U.S. automobile industry, for example, imports Japanese, Mexican, and Brazilian engines; utilizes German instruments and British electronics; and employs Italian designers. Advances in technology make it possible for software developers in places like Bangalore, India, to work for global employers without ever having to leave home.

■ REGIONAL ECONOMIC ALLIANCES

The importance of regional economic alliances as forces in the global economy is undeniable.[7] First and foremost, the European Union (EU) is moving forward with its agendas of political, economic, and monetary union among member countries.[8] Remarkably, it has seen the advent of a new world currency, the Euro, which will replace the traditional currencies of many member nations. Within the EU, businesses from member countries have access to a market of some 400 million customers. Agreements to eliminate border controls and trade barriers, create uniform technical product standards, open government procurement contracts, and unify financial regulations are all designed to bring economic benefit and union to Europe, a region whose economy of some $6.5 trillion closely approaches the U.S.'s $8.0 trillion economy.[9]

The EU's counterpart in North America, the North American Free Trade Agreement (NAFTA), links the economies and customer markets of Canada, the United States, and Mexico in freer trade. NAFTA has been praised for uniting in trade a region with more potential customers than the European Union. It now looks forward to a future of expanded membership to other countries of the Americas. Some business and government leaders even speak of an all-encompassing Free Trade Agreement for the Americas (FTAA) by 2005. At present, the Caribbean Community (CARICOM) is seeking to negotiate free trade agreements with Latin American countries. In addition, the Andean Pact (linking Venezuela, Colombia, Ecuador, Peru, and Bolivia) and Mercosur (linking Brazil, Paraguay, Uruguay, and Argentina) are already active in South America.[10]

Similar regional economic partnerships are being forged in other parts of the globe as well. In Asia, the Asia-Pacific Economic Co-operation Forum (APEC) is a framework designed to produce joint economic development among countries of the Asia-Pacific basin. A region that has recently experienced economic turmoil with worldwide financial implications, Asia remains a world economic power and is the home of many world-class business competitors.[11] Japan's economic influence is ever-evident, as is China's whose might may well dominate the twenty-first century. Recent events have further confirmed the importance of other Asian countries, especially Taiwan, Singapore, South Korea, Malaysia, Thailand, and Indonesia. India, with its huge population, is an economy on the move and is recognized as a world-class supplier of software expertise.

Africa, led by developments in post-Apartheid South Africa, has also become an important member of the global economy. Countries like Uganda, Ivory Coast, Botswana, South Africa, and Ghana are now recognized as positive business prospects.[12] A report on sub-Saharan Africa recently concluded that the region's contextual problems are manageable and that the continent presents investment opportunities.[13] Coca-Cola, one of the American firms responding to this call, projects 15 percent growth rates as part of its business plan for Africa. Coca Cola's CEO M. Douglas Ivester says: "We see an Africa more directly accountable for its own destiny than it has for centuries."[14]

■ GLOBAL QUALITY STANDARDS

One indicator of the importance of business globalization is the quality designation "ISO," representing quality standards set by the International Standards Organization in Geneva, Switzerland. This mark of quality excellence has become a framework for quality assurance worldwide. The European Union and more than 50 countries, including the United States, Canada, and Mexico, have endorsed the ISO's quality standard. The certification is fast becoming a goal for companies around the world who want to do business in Europe and want to win reputations as total quality "world-class" manufacturers.

■ A **global manager** has the international awareness and cultural sensitivity needed to work well across national borders.

■ GLOBAL MANAGERS

Along with prior developments in globalization, the search is now also on for a new breed of manager—the **global manager**, someone who knows how to conduct business across borders.[15] Often multilingual, the global manager thinks with a world view; appreciates diverse beliefs, values, behaviors, and practices; and is able to map strategy accordingly. If you fit this description (see The Effective Manager 5.1), or soon will, get ready. Corporate recruiters are scrambling to find people with these skills and interests.

The global dimension in business and management, though pervasive, poses many complications to be overcome. Even high performers with proven technical skills at home may find that their styles and attitudes just don't work well overseas. Experienced international managers indicate that a "global mindset" of cultural adaptability, patience, flexibility, and tolerance are indispensable.[16] The failure rate for Americans in overseas assignments has been measured as high as 25 percent,[17] and a study criticizes British and German companies for giving inadequate preparation to staff sent abroad.[18]

THE EFFECTIVE MANAGER 5.1

ATTRIBUTES OF THE "GLOBAL MANAGER"

- Adapts well to different business environments.
- Respects different beliefs, values, and practices.
- Solves problems quickly in new circumstances.
- Communicates well with people from different cultures.
- Speaks more than one language.
- Understands different government and political systems.
- Conveys respect and enthusiasm when dealing with others.
- Possesses high technical expertise for a job.

Cultures and Cultural Diversity

The word "culture" is frequently used in organizational behavior in connection with the concept of corporate culture, the growing interest in workforce diversity, and the broad differences among people around the world. Specialists tend to agree that **culture** is the learned, shared way of doing things in a particular society. It is the way, for example, in which its members eat, dress, greet and treat one another, teach their children, solve everyday problems, and so on.[19] Geert Hofst-

■ **Culture** is the learned and shared way of thinking and acting among a group of people or society.

ede, a Dutch scholar and consultant, refers to culture as the "software of the mind," making the analogy that the mind's "hardware" is universal among human beings but the software of culture takes many different forms.[20] Indeed, we are not born with a culture; we are born into a society that teaches us its culture. And because a culture is shared by people, it helps to define the boundaries between different groups and affect how their members relate to one another.

■ POPULAR DIMENSIONS OF CULTURE

The popular dimensions of culture are those that are most apparent to the individual traveling abroad—for example, language, time orientation, use of space, and religion.[21]

Language   Perhaps the most conspicuous aspect of culture, and certainly the one the traveler notices first, is language. The languages of the world number into the thousands. Some, such as Maltese, are spoken by only a handful of people, whereas others, such as English, Spanish, and Chinese, are spoken by millions. Some countries, such as France and Malaysia, have one official language; others, such as Canada, Switzerland, and India, have more than one; and still others, like the United States, have none.

The centrality of language to culture is represented by the *Whorfian hypothesis*, which considers language as a major determinant of our thinking.[22] The vocabulary and structure of a language reflect the history of a society and can also reveal how members relate to the environment. Arabic, for example, has many different words for the camel, its parts, and related equipment. As you might expect, English is very poor in its ability to describe camels. The fact that many people apparently speak the same language, such as English, doesn't mean that they share the same culture. Some words spoken in one language fail to carry the same meaning from culture to culture or region to region. A "truck" in Chicago is a "lorry" in London; "hydro" in Calgary is "electric power" in Boston; grocery shoppers in the American Midwest put "pop" in their "sacks," East Coast shoppers put "soda" in their "bags."

The anthropologist Edward T. Hall notes important differences in the ways different cultures use language.[23] Members of **low-context cultures** are very explicit in using the spoken and written word. In these cultures, such as those of Australia, Canada, and United States, the message is largely conveyed by the words someone uses, and not particularly by the "context" in which they are spoken. In contrast, members of **high-context cultures** use words to convey only a limited part of the message. The rest must be inferred or interpreted from the context, which includes body language, the physical setting, and past relationships—all of which add meaning to what is being said. Many Asian and Middle Eastern cultures are considered high context, according to Hall, whereas most Western cultures are low context.

Time Orientation   Hall also uses time orientation to classify cultures.[24] In **polychronic cultures** people hold a traditional view of time that may be described as a "circle." This suggests repetition in the sense that time is "cyclical" and goes around and around. In this view time does not create pressures for immediate action or performance. After all, one will have another chance to pass the same way again. If an opportunity is lost today—no problem, it may return again

■ In **low-context cultures** messages are expressed mainly by the spoken and written word.

■ In **high-context cultures** words convey only part of a message, while the rest of the message must be inferred from body language and additional contextual cues.

■ In a **polychronic culture** people tend to do more than one thing at a time.

tomorrow. Members of polychronic cultures tend to emphasize the present and often do more than one thing at a time.[25] An important business or government official in a Mediterranean country, for example, may have a large reception area outside his or her office. Visitors wait in this area and may transact business with the official and others who move in and out and around the room, conferring as they go.

Members of **monochronic cultures** view time more as a "straight line." In this "linear" view of time, the past is gone; the present is here briefly; and the future is almost upon us. In monochronic cultures time is measured precisely and creates pressures for action and performance. People appreciate schedules and appointments and talk about "saving" and "wasting" time. Long-range goals become important, and planning is a way of managing the future. In contrast to the Mediterranean official in the last example, a British manager will typically allot a certain amount of time in her daily calendar to deal with a business visitor. During this time the visitor receives her complete attention. Only after one visitor leaves will another one be received, again based upon the daily schedule.

Use of Space   *Proxemics*, the study of how people use space to communicate, reveals important cultural differences.[26] Personal space can be thought of as the "bubble" that surrounds us, and its preferred size tends to vary from one culture to another. When others invade or close in on our personal space, we tend to feel uncomfortable. Then again, if people are too far away, communication becomes difficult.

<table>
<tr><td>

OB Across Functions

INFORMATION SYSTEMS

Going Global by Staying High Tech

There is no shortage of assistance for those small and medium-sized businesses that want to "go global." Indeed, the information needed to get started as an exporter and participant in the marketplaces of the world is available at the touch of a keyboard—on the Internet. Those looking for a starting point can go to *www.web.idirect.com/~tiger/supersit.htm*. To look up travel guides and location information in a minute, *www.go-global.com* is a useful site. International business is well catalogued at *www.fita.org*, and in-depth information on free trade zones where exports are free of customs duties is available at *www.imex.com/naftz.html*. The world of international business is a world of diverse peoples and cultures. The best of the best know how to work across cultures with respect and delight. Visit *www.bena.com/ewinters/xculture.html* for essays on a variety of cross-cultural business issues. And if you want to take a miniature course in exporting, check Deloitte Touche Tohmatsu's offering at *www.dtonline.com/expand/excover.htm*. This is a small sample of rich resources available to facilitate international business ventures. But you've got to be linked and willing to explore the Web to take full advantage of them. Information technology today provides the potential for competitive advantage through expanded global commerce. It's yours for the asking.

</td></tr>
</table>

Arabs and South Americans seem more comfortable talking at closer distances than do North Americans; Asians seem to prefer even greater distances. When a Saudi moves close to speak with a visiting Canadian executive, the visitor may back away to keep more distance between them. But the same Canadian may approach a Malaysian too closely when doing business in Kuala Lumpur, causing her or his host to back away. Cross-cultural misunderstandings due to different approaches to personal space are quite common.

In some cultures, often polychronic ones, space is organized in such a way that many activities can be carried out simultaneously. Spanish and Italian towns are organized around central squares (plazas or piazzas), whereas American towns typically have a traditional "Main Street" laid out in linear fashion. Similar cultural influences are seen in the layout of work space. Americans, who seem to prefer individual offices, may have difficulty adjusting to Japanese employers who prefer open floor plans.

Religion   Religion is also a major element of culture and can be one of its more visible manifestations. The influence of religion often prescribes rituals,

■ In a **monochronic culture** people tend to do one thing at a time.

holy days, and foods that can be eaten. Codes of ethics and moral behavior often have their roots in religious beliefs. The influence of religion on economic matters can also be significant.[27] In the Middle East, one finds interest-free "Islamic" banks that operate based on principles set forth in the Koran. In Malaysia, business dinners are scheduled after 8:00 P.M. so that Muslim guests can first attend to their evening prayer.

■ VALUES AND NATIONAL CULTURES

Cultures vary in their underlying patterns of values and attitudes. The way people think about such matters as achievement, wealth and material gain, risk and change, may influence how they approach work and their relationships with organizations. A framework developed by Geert Hofstede offers one approach for understanding how value differences across national cultures can influence human behavior at work. The five dimensions of national culture in his framework can be described as follows.[28]

Hofstede's dimensions of national cultures

■ **Power distance** is the willingness of a culture to accept status and power differences among its members.

■ **Uncertainty avoidance** is the cultural tendency to be uncomfortable with uncertainty and risk in everyday life.

■ **Individualism–collectivism** is the tendency of a culture's members to emphasize individual self-interests or group relationships.

■ **Masculinity–femininity** is the degree to which a society values assertiveness or relationships.

■ **Long-term/short-term orientation** is the degree to which a culture emphasizes long-term or short-term thinking.

1. **Power distance** is the willingness of a culture to accept status and power differences among its members. It reflects the degree to which people are likely to respect hierarchy and rank in organizations. Indonesia is considered a high–power distance culture, whereas Sweden is considered a relatively low–power distance culture.

2. **Uncertainty avoidance** is a cultural tendency toward discomfort with risk and ambiguity. It reflects the degree to which people are likely to prefer structured or unstructured organizational situations. France is considered a high–uncertainty avoidance culture, whereas Hong Kong is considered a low–uncertainty avoidance culture.

3. **Individualism–collectivism** is the tendency of a culture to emphasize individual versus group interests. It reflects the degree to which people are likely to prefer working as individuals or working together in groups. The United States is a highly individualistic culture, whereas Mexico is a more highly collectivist one.

4. **Masculinity–femininity** is the tendency of a culture to value stereotypical masculine or feminine traits. It reflects the degree to which organizations emphasize competition and assertiveness versus interpersonal sensitivity and concerns for relationships. Japan is considered a very masculine culture, whereas Thailand is considered a more feminine culture.

5. **Long-term/short-term orientation** is the tendency of a culture to emphasize values associated with the future, such as thrift and persistence, versus values that focus largely on the present. It reflects the degree to which people and organizations adopt long-term or short-term performance horizons. South Korea is high on long-term orientation, whereas the United States is a more short-term-oriented country.

The first four dimensions in Hofstede's framework were identified in an extensive study of thousands of employees of a multinational corporation operating in more than 40 countries.[29] The fifth dimension of long-term/short-term orientation was added from research conducted by cross-cultural psychologist Michael Bond and his colleagues using the Chinese Values Survey they developed.[30]

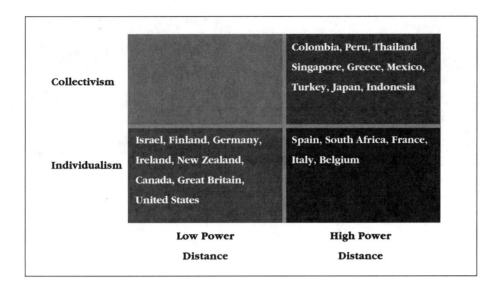

Figure 5.1
Sample country clusters on Hofstede's dimensions of individualism–collectivism and power distance.

Their research suggested the cultural importance of Confucian dynamism, with its emphasis on persistence, the ordering of relationships, thrift, sense of shame, personal steadiness, reciprocity, protection of "face," and respect for tradition.[31]

When using the Hofstede framework, it is important to remember that the five dimensions are interrelated and not independent.[32] National cultures may best be understood in terms of cluster maps or collages that combine multiple dimensions. For example, Figure 5.1 shows a sample grouping of countries based on individualism–collectivism and power distance. Note that high power distance and collectivism are often found together, as are low power distance and individualism. Whereas high collectivism may lead us to expect a work team in Indonesia to operate by consensus, the high power distance may cause the consensus to be heavily influenced by the desires of a formal leader. A similar team operating in more individualist and low power distance Great Britain or America might make decisions with more open debate, including expressions of disagreement with a leader's stated preferences.

■ UNDERSTANDING CULTURAL DIFFERENCES

To work well with people from different cultures, you must first understand your own culture. We are usually unaware of our own culture until we come into contact with a very different one. Knowing your own culture will help guard you against two problems that frequently arise in international dealings. One is the danger of *parochialism*—assuming that the ways of your culture are the only ways of doing things. The other is the danger of *ethnocentrism*—assuming that the ways of your culture are the best ways of doing things.[33] It is parochial for a traveling American businesswoman to insist that all of her business contacts speak English, whereas it is ethnocentric for her to think that anyone who dines with a spoon rather than a knife and fork lacks proper table manners.

A framework developed by Fons Trompenaars offers a useful vantage point for better understanding and, hopefully, dealing with cultural differences.[34] Working from a databank of respondents from 47 national cultures, he suggests that cultures vary in the way their members solve problems of three major types:

Canada, USA, Ireland	Universalism vs. Particularism	Indonesia, China, Venezuela
USA, Hungary, Russia	Individualism vs. Collectivism	Thailand, Japan, Mexico
Indonesia, Germany, Japan	Neutral vs. Affective	Italy, France, USA
Spain, Poland, USA	Specific vs. Diffuse	India, Great Britain, Egypt
Australia, Canada, Norway	Achievement vs. Ascription	Philippines, Pakistan, Brazil
Great Britain, Belgium, USA	Sequential vs. Synchronic	Malaysia, Venezuela, France

Figure 5.2
Sample country clusters on Trompenaars' framework for understanding cultural differences.

(1) relationships with people, (2) attitudes toward time, and (3) attitudes toward the environment.

Trompenaars identifies five major cultural differences in how people handle relationships with other people. The orientations, as illustrated in Figure 5.2, are:

How cultures deal with relationships among people

1. *Universalism versus particularism*—relative emphasis on rules and consistency, or relationships and flexibility.
2. *Individualism versus collectivism*—relative emphasis on individual freedom and responsibility, or group interests and consensus.
3. *Neutral versus affective*—relative emphasis on objectivity and detachment, or emotion and expressed feelings.
4. *Specific versus diffuse*—relative emphasis on focused and narrow involvement, or involvement with the whole person.
5. *Achievement versus prescription*—relative emphasis on performance-based and earned status, or ascribed status.

With regard to problems based on attitudes toward time, Trompenaars distinguishes between cultures with sequential versus synchronic orientations. Time in a sequential view is a passing series of events; in a synchronic view, it consists of an interrelated past, present, and future. With regard to problems based on attitudes toward the environment, he contrasts how different cultures may relate to nature in inner-directed versus outer-directed ways. Members of an inner-directed culture tend to view themselves separate from nature and believe they can control it. Those in an outer-directed culture view themselves as part of nature and believe they must go along with it.

Globalization and People at Work

OB scholars are increasingly sensitive to the need to better understand how management and organizational practices vary among the world's cultures. In this sense, we must be familiar with the importance of multinational employers, the diversity of multicultural workforces, and the special demands of international work assignments.

■ MULTINATIONAL EMPLOYERS

A true **multinational corporation**, or MNC, is a business firm that has extensive international operations in more than one foreign country. MNCs are more than just companies that "do business abroad;" they are global concerns—exemplified by Ford, Royal-Dutch Shell, Sony, and many others. The missions and strategies of MNCs are worldwide in scope. In the public sector, multinational organizations (MNOs) are those with nonprofit missions whose operations also span the globe. Examples are Amnesty International, the International Red Cross, the United Nations, and the World Wildlife Fund.

The truly global organization operates with a total world view and does not have allegiance to any one national "home." Futurist Alvin Toffler labels them *transnational organizations* that "may do research in one country, manufacture components in another, assemble them in a third, sell the manufactured goods in a fourth, deposit surplus funds in a fifth, and so on."[35] Although the pure transnational corporation may not yet exist, large firms like Nestle, Gillette, and Ford are striving hard to move in that direction. Greatly facilitating those moves are new information technologies, which allow organizations to operate through virtual linkages with components and suppliers located around the world.

The MNCs have enormous economic power and impact. Toffler, in particular, warns that "the size, importance, and political power of this new player in the global game has skyrocketed."[36] Their activities can bring both benefits and controversies to host countries. One example is in Mexico, where many *maquiladoras*, or foreign-owned plants, assemble imported parts and ship finished products to the United States. Labor is relatively inexpensive for the foreign operators, while Mexico benefits from industrial development, reduced unemployment, and increased foreign exchange earnings. But some complain about the downsides of *maquiladoras*—stress on housing and public services in Mexican border towns, inequities in the way Mexican workers are treated (wages, working conditions, production quotas) relative to their foreign counterparts, and the environmental impact of pollution from the industrial sites.[37]

■ MULTICULTURAL WORKFORCES

What is the best way to deal with a multicultural workforce? There are no easy answers. Styles of leadership, motivation, decision making, planning, organizing, leading, and controlling vary from country to country.[38] Managing a construction project in Saudi Arabia with employees from Asia, the Middle East, Europe, and North America working side by side will clearly present challenges different from those involved in a domestic project. Similarly, establishing and successfully operating a joint venture in Kazakhstan, Nigeria, or Vietnam will require a great deal of learning and patience. In these and other international settings, political risks and bureaucratic difficulties further complicate the already difficult process of working across cultural boundaries.

The challenges of managing across cultures, however, are not limited to international operations. In this connection, a new term has been coined—*domestic multiculturalism*, which describes cultural diversity within a given national population: This diversity will be reflected in the workforces of local organizations.[39] Los Angeles, for example, is a popular home to many immigrant groups. Some 20 percent of the city's school children speak other languages more flu-

■ A **multinational corporation** is a business with extensive international operations in more than one country.

ently than they speak English; in Vancouver, British Columbia, Chinese is also the mother tongue of some 20 percent of the population.

■ EXPATRIATE WORK ASSIGNMENTS

■ An **expatriate** works and lives in a foreign country for an extended time.

The human resources firm ComPsych reports there are over 350,000 Americans working abroad for U.S. employers.[40] People who work and live abroad for extended periods of time are referred to as **expatriates**. The cost of an expatriate worker can be very expensive for the employer. An executive earning $100,000 per year in the United States, for example, might cost her company more than $300,000 in the first year of an assignment in England—with the added cost tied to compensation, benefits, transfer, and other relocation expenses. Estimates are that a three-year expatriate assignment will cost the employer an average of $1 million.[41] To get the most out of the investment, progressive employers will maximize the potential of expatriate performance success by taking a variety of supportive actions.[42] They carefully recruit employees who have the right sensitivities and skills, provide them with good training and orientation to the foreign culture, actively support them while working abroad, give extra attention to the needs of the expatriate's family members, and pay careful attention to relocation when the expatriate and family return home.

Expatriates usually face their greatest problems when entering and working in a foreign culture, and when experiencing repatriation on the return home. Figure 5.3 illustrates phases in the typical expatriate work assignment, beginning with the initial assignment shock the person experiences upon being informed of a foreign posting. How recruitment, selection, and orientation are handled

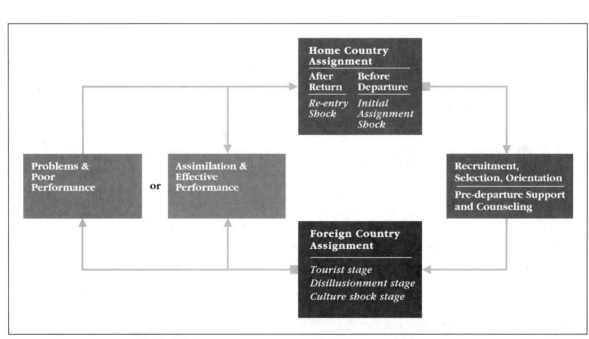

Figure 5.3
Stages in the expatriate international career cycle: potential adjustment problems in the home and foreign countries.

during this stage can have an important influence on the assignment's eventual success. Ideally, the employee, along with his or her spouse and family, is allowed to choose whether or not to accept the opportunity. Also ideally, proper pre-departure support and counseling are given to provide "realistic expectations" of what is to come.

The expatriate undergoes three phases of adjustment to the new country.[43] First is the *tourist stage*, in which the expatriate enjoys discovering the new culture. Second is the *disillusionment stage*, in which his or her mood is dampened as difficulties become more evident. Typical problems include conversing well in the local language and obtaining personal products and food supplies of preference. Third, the expatriate's mood often hits bottom in the stage of *culture shock*. Here confusion, disorientation, and frustration in the ways of the local culture and living in the foreign environment set in. If culture shock is well handled, the expatriate begins to feel better, function more effectively, and lead a reasonably normal life. If it isn't, work performance may suffer, even deteriorating to the point where a reassignment home may be necessary.

At the end of the expatriate assignment, perhaps after three or four years, the reentry process can also be stressful.[44] After an extended period away, the expatriate and his or her family have changed and the home country has changed as well. One does not simply "fall back in"; rather, it takes time to get used to living at home again. Furthermore, in too many instances little thought may be given to assigning the returned expatriate a job that matches his or her current skills and abilities. While abroad, the expatriate has often functioned with a great degree of independence—something that may or may not be possible at home. Problems caused by reentry shock can be minimized through careful planning. This includes maintaining adequate contact with the home office during the expatriate assignment as well as having all possible support for the move back. Employers should also identify any new skills and abilities, and assign returned expatriates to jobs commensurate with their abilities. As organizations utilize more and more expatriate assignments, their career planning and development systems must also operate on a global scale.

■ ETHICAL BEHAVIOR ACROSS CULTURES

The importance of ethical issues in organizational behavior and management has been discussed. In the international arena, special ethical challenges arise as a result of cultural diversity and the variation in governments and legal systems that characterize our world. Prominent current issues include corruption and bribery in international business practices, poor working conditions and the employment of child and prison labor in some countries, and the role of international business in supporting repressive governments that fail to protect and respect the basic human rights of citizens.[45]

In the United States, the Foreign Corrupt Practices Act of 1977 makes it illegal for firms to engage in corrupt practices overseas, such as giving bribes to government officials in order to obtain business contracts. In 1999, member countries of the Organization for Economic Development agreed to ban payoffs to foreign officials by their countries' businesses. The United States government is pushing for more countries to join the movement against bribe giving and taking, and suggestions have been made that the World Bank consider corruption as a criterion when making loan decisions.[46]

The term *sweatshop* is increasingly in the news these days, and refers to organizations that force workers to labor under adverse conditions that may include long work days, unsafe conditions, and even the use of child labor. A variety of advocacy groups are now active in campaigning against sweatshops, and a number of well-recognized firms have been the targets of their attention—including such well-recognized multinationals as Nike, Mattel, and Disney. Watchdog groups in Asia, for example, have criticized Disney for allowing some of its contract manufacturers in China to force workers to labor seven days a week, up to 16 hours a day, and at no overtime. Mattel has been accused of engaging subcontractors who run "sweatshop Barbie" assembly lines that include extra-long work hours and heavy fines for workers' mistakes. In response to such criticisms more multinational employers are engaging outside consultants to conduct social audits of their international operations, adopting formal codes of ethical practices governing subcontractors, and backing external codes of conduct such as *Social Accountability 8000*—a certificate awarded by the Council on Economic Priorities. Nike, Disney, and Mattell have each taken steps along these lines to ensure that products made under their name are manufactured under conditions that meet acceptable standards.[47] Worth considering is the following comment by Jack Sheinkman, President Emeritus of the Amalgamated Clothing and Textile Workers Union, and member of the Council on Economic Priorities Advisory Board:

> As business becomes ever-more global in scope and its links in the chain of production extend further, the task of rating corporate social responsibility has become more complex. So, too, has the safeguarding of workers' rights...especially when responsibility is shared among manufacturers, contractors, subcontractors, buying agents,...and other parties to business agreements which transcend time-zones, language barriers, and developing and industrialized country borders alike.[48]

A continuing issue for debate in this area of international business and management practices is the influence of culture on ethical behavior. Figure 5.4 presents a continuum that contrasts "cultural relativism" with "ethical imperialism." Business ethicist Thomas Donaldson describes **cultural relativism** as the position that there is no universal right way to behave and that ethical behavior is determined by its cultural context.[49] In other words, international business behavior is justified on the argument: "When in Rome do as the Romans do." If one accepts

■ **Cultural relativism** suggests that ethical behavior is determined by its cultural context.

Cultural relativism	Ethical imperialism
No culture's ethics are superior. The values and practices of the local setting determine what is right or wrong.	Certain absolute truths apply everywhere. Universal values transcend cultures in determining what is right or wrong.
When in Rome, do as the Romans do.	*Don't do anything you wouldn't do at home.*

Figure 5.4
The Extremes of Cultural Relativism and Ethical Imperialism in International Business Ethics.

cultural relativism, a sweatshop operation would presumably be okay as long as it was consistent with the laws and practices of the local culture. The opposite extreme on the continuum in Figure 5.4 reflects an absolutist or universalistic assumption that there is a single moral standard that fits all situations, regardless of culture and national location. In other words, if a practice such as child labor is not acceptable in one's home environment it shouldn't be engaged in elsewhere. Critics of the absolutist approach claim that it is a form of *ethical imperialism* because it attempts to impose external ethical standards unfairly or inappropriately on local cultures and fails to respect their needs and unique situations.

Donaldson suggests that there is no simple answer to this debate and warns against the dangers of both cultural relativism and ethical imperialism. He makes the case that multinational businesses should adopt core or threshold values to guide behavior in ways that respect and protect fundamental human rights in any situation. However, he also suggests that there is room beyond the threshold to adapt and tailor one's actions in ways that respect the traditions, foundations, and needs of different cultures.[50]

A Global View of Organizational Learning

Organizational learning was first defined in Section 1 as the process of acquiring the knowledge necessary to adapt to a changing environment. In the context and themes of this section, the concept can be extended to **global organizational learning**—the ability to gather from the world at large the knowledge required for long-term organizational adaptation. Simply stated, people from different cultures and parts of the world have a lot to learn from one another about organizational behavior and management.

■ **Global organizational learning** is the ability to gather from the world at large the knowledge required for long-term organizational adaptation.

■ ARE MANAGEMENT THEORIES UNIVERSAL?

One of the most important questions to be asked and answered in this age of globalization is whether or not management theories are universal. That is, can and should a theory developed in one cultural context be transferred and used in another? The answer according to Geert Hofstede is "no," at least not without careful consideration of cultural influences. Culture can influence both the development of a theory or concept and its application. As an example, Hofstede cites the issue of motivation. He notes that Americans have historically addressed motivation from the perspective of individual performance and rewards—consistent with their highly individualistic culture. However, concepts such as merit pay and job enrichment may not fit well in other cultures where high collectivism places more emphasis on teamwork and groups. Hofstede's point, and one well worth remembering, is that although we can and should learn from what is taking place in other cultures, we should be informed consumers of that knowledge. We should always factor cultural considerations into account when transferring theories and practices from one setting to the next.[51]

A good case in point relates to the interest generated some years ago in Japanese management approaches, and based upon the success experienced at the time by Japanese industry.[52] Japanese firms have traditionally been described as favoring *lifetime employment* with strong employee-employer loyalty, seniority pay, and company unions. Their operations have emphasized a *quality commitment*, the *use of teams* and *consensus decision making*, and career development based upon *slow promotions* and *cross-functional job assignments*.[53]

Although the Japanese economy and many of its firms have had problems of their own recently, management scholars and consultants recognize that many lessons can still be learned from their practices. However, we also recognize that cultural differences must be considered in the process.[54] Specifically, what works in Japan may not work as well elsewhere, at least not without some modifications. Japan's highly collectivist society, for example, contrasts markedly with the highly individualistic cultures of the United States and other Western nations. It is only reasonable to expect differences in their management and organizational practices.

■ BEST PRACTICES AROUND THE WORLD

An appropriate goal in global organizational learning is to identify the "best practices" found around the world. What is being done well in other settings may be of great value at home, whether that "home" is in Africa, Asia, Europe, North America, or anywhere else. Whereas the world at large once looked mainly to the North Americans and Europeans for management insights, today we recognize that potential "benchmarks" of excellence for high performance organizations can be discovered anywhere. For example, the influence of the Japanese approaches as a stimulus to global organizational learning is evident in many of the workplace themes with which you will become familiar in this book. These include growing attention to the value of teams and work groups, consensus decision making, employee involvement, flatter structures, and strong corporate cultures. These and related concepts and themes are well represented in today's high performance organizations.

As the field of organizational behavior continues to mature in its global research and understanding, we will all benefit from an expanding knowledge base that is enriched by cultural diversity. Organizational behavior is a science of contingencies, and one of them is culture. No one culture possesses all of the "right" answers to today's complex management and organizational problems. But a sincere commitment to global organizational learning can give us fresh ideas while still permitting locally appropriate solutions to be implemented with cultural sensitivity. This search for global understanding will be reflected in the following chapters as we move further into the vast domain of OB.

Technology and Job Design

■ **Sociotechnical systems** integrate people and technology into high performance work settings.

The concept of **sociotechnical systems** is used in organizational behavior to indicate the importance of integrating people and technology to create high performance work systems.[55] As computers and information technologies continue to dominate the modern workplace, this concept remains an important point of reference in incorporating new developments into job designs.

■ AUTOMATION AND ROBOTICS

As mentioned earlier, highly simplified jobs often cause problems because they offer little intrinsic motivation for the worker. Such tasks have been defined so narrowly that they lack challenge and lead to boredom when someone has to repeat them over and over again. Given the high technology now available, one way to tackle this problem is through complete **automation** where a machine is used to do the work previously accomplished by a human. This approach increasingly involves the use of robots, which are becoming ever more versatile and reliable. Also, robot prices are falling as the cost of human labor rises. Japan presently leads the world in robot use, with a ratio of one robot for every 36 people employed in manufacturing. The United States lags far behind, but its robot use is growing rapidly.[56] If you were to travel to Wolfsburg, Germany, you would find that Volkswagen's car plant is one of the world's largest and most highly automated. Robots do 80 percent of welding work and can be programmed to perform different tasks. Computers control the assembly line, adjusting production to fit schedules for different models and options.[57]

■ **Automation** allows machines to do work previously accomplished by people.

■ FLEXIBLE MANUFACTURING SYSTEMS

In **flexible manufacturing systems**, adaptive computer-based technologies and integrated job designs are used to shift work easily and quickly among alternative products. This approach is increasingly common, for example, in companies supporting the automobile industry with machined metal products, such as cylinder heads and gear boxes.[58] Here, a cellular manufacturing system contains a number of automated production machines that cut, shape, drill, and fasten together various metal components. The machines can be quickly changed from manufacturing one product to another.[59] Workers in flexible manufacturing cells perform few routine assembly-line tasks. Rather, they ensure that the operations are handled correctly, and they deal with the changeover from one product configuration to another. They develop expertise across a wide range of functions and the jobs are rich in potential for enriched core job characteristics.

■ **Flexible manufacturing systems** use adaptive technology and integrated job designs to easily shift production among alternative products.

■ ELECTRONIC OFFICES

Electronic office technology was the key when U.S. Healthcare, a large, private practice–based health maintenance organization (HMO), became interested in improving the quality of its health-care services. The company installed large electronic bulletin boards that monitored progress toward a range of performance goals. It also installed an E-mail system, put in robots to deliver the paper mail, and installed a computerized answering machine. Essentially, the company tried to automate as many tasks as possible to free people for more challenging work. Similarly, Mutual Benefit Life completely reorganized the way it serviced insurance application forms—once handled by as many as 19 people across five departments. Mutual created a new case manager position responsible for processing applications from their inception until policies were issued. Accompanying this radical change in job design were powerful PC-based workstations designed to assist decision making and connected to a variety of automated subsystems on a mainframe.[60]

Continuing developments in electronic offices offer job enrichment possibilities for those workers equipped to handle the technology. But those jobs can be stressful and difficult for those who do not have the necessary education or skills. One survey showed that even in highly developed countries like those in Europe, 54 percent of workers possessed inadequate skills to operate a computer; the proportion was about one-third in the United States.[61] People who work continuously with computers are also beginning to experience physical ailments associated with repetitious keyboarding and mouse movements. Clearly, the high technologies of the new workplace must be carefully integrated with the human factor.

■ WORK-FLOW AND PROCESS REENGINEERING

■ **Process reengineering** analyzes, streamlines, and reconfigures actions and tasks to achieve work goals.

One of the latest approaches for improving job designs and performance is based on the concept of **process reengineering**—the analysis, streamlining, and reconfiguration of actions and tasks required to reach a work goal.[62] The process design approach systematically breaks processes down into their specific components and subtasks, analyzes each for relevance and simplicity, and then does everything possible to reconfigure the process to eliminate wasted time, effort, and resources. A classic example might be the various steps required to gain approval for a purchase order to buy a new computer. The process reengineering approach looks at every step in the process, from searching for items and vendors to obtaining bids, completing necessary forms, securing required signatures and approvals, actually placing the order, and so on to the point at which the new computer arrives, is checked in, is placed into an equipment inventory, and then is finally delivered to the workplace. In all this, one simple question drives the reengineering approach: What is necessary and what can be eliminated?

Goal Setting and Job Design

Goals are important aspects of any job design. Without proper goals, employees may suffer a direction problem. Some years ago, for example, a Minnesota Vikings' defensive end gathered up an opponent's fumble. Then, with obvious effort and delight, he ran the ball into the wrong end zone. Clearly, the athlete did not lack motivation. Unfortunately, however, he failed to channel his energies toward the right goal. Similar problems are found in many work settings. They can be eliminated, or at least reduced, by the proper setting and clarification of task goals.

■ GOAL SETTING THEORY

■ **Goal setting** is the process of developing and setting motivational performance objectives.

Goals play an important part in high performance work environments. **Goal setting** is the process of developing, negotiating, and formalizing the targets or objectives that a person is responsible for accomplishing.[63] Over a number of years, Edwin Locke and his associates have developed a comprehensive framework linking goals to performance as shown in Figure 5.5. The model uses elements of expectancy theory from Section 3 to help clarify the implications of goal setting for performance while taking into account certain moderating conditions, such as ability and task complexity.

■ GOAL SETTING GUIDELINES

Research using and extending these predictions is now quite extensive. Indeed, more research has been done on goal setting than any other theory related to

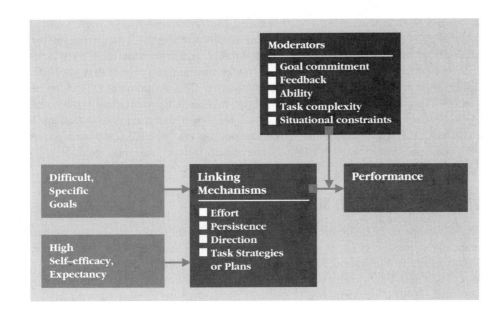

Figure 5.5
Essentials of the Locke
and Latham goal-setting
framework.

work motivation.[64] Nearly 400 studies have been conducted in several countries, including Australia, England, Germany, Japan, and the United States.[65] The basic precepts of goal-setting theory remain a most important source of advice for managing human behavior in the work setting.

Managerially speaking, the implications of the Locke and Latham model and related goal-setting research can be summarized as follows.[66] First, *difficult goals are more likely to lead to higher performance than are less difficult ones.* However, if the goals are seen as too difficult or impossible, the relationship with performance no longer holds. For example, you will likely perform better as a financial services agent if you have a goal of selling six annuities a week than if you have a goal of three. However, if your goal is 15 annuities a week, you may consider that as impossible to achieve, and your performance may well be lower than what it would be with a more realistic goal.

Second, *specific goals are more likely to lead to higher performance than are no goals or vague or very general ones.* All too often people work with very general goals such as the encouragement to "do your best." Research indicates that more specific goals, such as selling six computers a day, are much more motivational than a simple "do your best" goal.

Third, *task feedback, or knowledge of results, is likely to motivate people toward higher performance by encouraging the setting of higher performance goals.* Feedback lets people know where they stand and whether they are on course or off course in their efforts. For example, think about how eager you are to find out how well you did on an examination.

Fourth, *goals are most likely to lead to higher performance when people have the abilities and the feelings of self-efficacy required to accomplish them.* The individual must be able to accomplish the goals and feel confident in those abilities. To take the financial services example again, you may be able to do what's required to sell six annuities a week and feel confident that you can. If your goal is 15, however, you may believe that your abilities are insufficient to the task and thus lack the confidence to work hard enough to accomplish it.

Fifth, *goals are most likely to motivate people toward higher performance when they are accepted and there is commitment to them.* Participating in the goal-setting process helps build such acceptance and commitment. It helps create "ownership" of the goals. However, Locke and Latham report that goals assigned by someone else can be equally effective. The assigners are likely to be authority figures, and that can have an impact. The assignment also implies that the subordinate can actually reach the goal. Moreover, assigned goals often are a challenge and help define the standards people use to attain self-satisfaction with their performance. According to Locke and Latham, assigned goals lead to poor performance only when they are curtly or inadequately explained.

■ GOAL SETTING AND MBO

When we speak of goal setting and its potential to influence individual performance at work, the concept of *management by objectives*, or MBO, immediately comes to mind. The essence of MBO is a process of joint goal setting between a supervisor and a subordinate.[67] It involves managers working with their subordinates to establish performance goals and plans that are consistent with higher level work unit and organizational objectives. When this process is followed throughout an organization, MBO helps clarify the hierarchy of objectives as a series of well-defined means–end chains.

Figure 5.6 shows a comprehensive view of MBO. The concept is consistent with the notion of goal setting and its associated principles discussed above. Notice how joint supervisor–subordinate discussions are designed to extend participation from the point of establishing initial goals to the point of evaluating results in terms of goal attainment. In addition to these goal-setting steps, a successful MBO system calls for careful implementation. Not only must workers have the freedom to carry out the required tasks, managers should be prepared to actively support their efforts to achieve the agreed-upon goals.

Although a fair amount of research based on case studies of MBO success is available, few rigorously controlled studies have been done. What there is re-

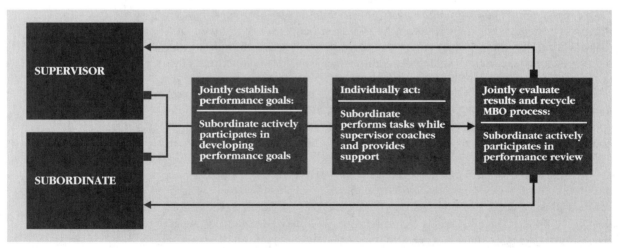

Figure 5.6
How the management by objectives process works.

ports mixed results.[68] In general, and as an application of goal-setting theory, MBO has much to offer. But it is by no means easy to start and keep going. Many firms have started and dropped the approach because of difficulties experienced early on. Among the specific problems it creates are too much paperwork documenting goals and accomplishments and too much emphasis on goal-oriented rewards and punishments, top-down goals, goals that are easily stated in objective terms, and individual instead of group goals. MBO also may need to be implemented organizationwide if it is to work well.

Alternative Work Arrangements

Alternative ways of scheduling time are becoming increasingly common in the workplace. These arrangements are essentially reshaping the traditional 40-hour week, 9 to 5 schedules where work is done on the premises. Virtually all such plans are designed to influence employee satisfaction and to help employees balance the demands of their work and nonwork lives.[69] They are becoming more and more important in fast-changing societies where demands for "work-life balance" and more "family-friendly" employers are growing ever more apparent.[70] For example, dual-career families with children, part-time students, older workers (retired or near retirement age), and single parents are all candidates for alternative work arrangements.

■ COMPRESSED WORK WEEKS

A **compressed work week** is any scheduling of work that allows a full-time job to be completed in fewer than the standard five days. The most common form of compressed work week is the "4/40" or 40 hours of work accomplished in four 10-hour days.

This approach has many possible benefits. For the worker added time off is a major feature of this schedule. The individual often appreciates increased leisure time, three-day weekends, free weekdays to pursue personal business, and lower commuting costs. The organization can benefit, too, in terms of lower employee absenteeism, and improved recruiting of new employees. But, there are also potential disadvantages. Individuals can experience increased fatigue from the extended workday and family adjustment problems. The organization can experience work scheduling problems and customer complaints because of breaks in work coverage. Some organizations may face occasional union opposition and laws requiring payment of overtime for work exceeding eight hours of individual labor in any one day. Overall reactions to compressed work weeks are likely to be most favorable for employees allowed to participate in the decision to adopt the new work week, who have their jobs enriched as a result of the new schedule, and who have strong higher-order needs in Maslow's hierarchy.[71]

■ FLEXIBLE WORKING HOURS

Another innovative work schedule, **flexible working hours** or flextime, gives individuals a daily choice in the timing of their work commitments. One such

■ A **compressed work week** allows a full-time job to be completed in less than five full workdays.

■ **Flexible working hours** give employees some daily choice in scheduling arrival and departure times from work.

THE EFFECTIVE MANAGER 5.2

FLEXTIME BENEFITS

For organizations:
Less absenteeism, tardiness, turnover
More commitment
Higher performance

For workers:
Shorter commuting time
More leisure time
More job satisfaction
Greater sense of responsibility

schedule requires employees to work four hours of "core" time but leaves them free to choose their remaining four hours of work from among flexible time blocks. One person, for example, may start early and leave early, whereas another may start later and leave later. This flexible work schedule is becoming increasingly popular and is a valuable alternative for structuring work to accommodate individual interests and needs.

Flextime increases individual autonomy in work scheduling and offers many opportunities and benefits (see The Effective Manager 5.2). It is a way for dual-career couples to handle children's schedules as well as their own; it is a way to meet the demands of caring for elderly parents or ill family members; it is even a way to better attend to such personal affairs as medical and dental appointments, home emergencies, banking needs, and so on. Proponents of this scheduling strategy argue that the discretion it allows workers in scheduling their own hours of work encourages them to develop positive attitudes and to increase commitment to the organization. A majority of American workplaces already have flextime programs, and the number is growing.[72] An Aetna manager, commenting on the firm's flexible working hours program, said: "We're not doing flexible work scheduling to be nice, but because it makes business sense."[73]

■ JOB SHARING

■ **Job sharing** allows one full-time job to be divided among two or more persons.

In **job sharing**, one full-time job is assigned to two or more persons who then divide the work according to agreed-upon hours. Often, each person works half a day, but job sharing can also be done on a weekly or monthly basis. Although it is practiced by only a relatively small percentage of employers, human-resource experts believe that job sharing is a valuable alternative work arrangement.[74]

Organizations benefit from job sharing when they can attract talented people who would otherwise be unable to work. An example is the qualified teacher who also is a parent. This person may be able to work only half a day. Through job sharing, two such persons can be employed to teach one class. Some job sharers report less burnout and claim that they feel recharged each time they report for work. The tricky part of this arrangement is finding two people who will work well with each other. When middle managers Sue Mannix and Charlotte Schutzman worked together at Bell Atlantic, for example, they faithfully coordinated each other's absences with Schutzman working Mondays, Tuesdays, and Wednesday mornings and Mannix working the rest of the work week.[75]

Job sharing should not be confused with a more controversial arrangement called *work sharing*. This occurs when workers agree to cut back on the number of hours they work in order to protect against layoffs. Workers may agree to voluntarily reduce 20 percent of hours worked and pay received, rather than have the employer cut 20 percent of the workforce during difficult economic times. Legal restrictions prohibit this practice in some settings.

■ WORK AT HOME AND THE VIRTUAL OFFICE

High technology is influencing yet another alternative work arrangement that is becoming increasingly visible in many employment sectors ranging from higher education to government and from manufacturing to services. **Telecommuting** describes work done at home or in a remote location via use of computers and advanced telecommunications linkages with a central office or other employment locations. This arrangement sometimes is called *flexiplace*. At IBM, Canada, flexiplace means working most of the time from a home office and coming into IBM corporate offices only for special meetings. In a practice known as *hoteling*, temporary offices are reserved for these workers during the times they visit the main office. Worldwide, some 20 percent of IBM's workforce of 270,000 employees spends two or more days a week working at home or visiting customers.[76]

The notion of telecommuting is more and more associated with the *virtual office*, where the individual works literally "from the road" and while traveling from place-to-place or customer-to-customer by car or airplane. In all cases, the worker remains linked electronically with the home office.[77] The number of workers who are telecommuting is growing daily; AT&T reports that some 55 percent of its managers telecommute, and Cisco Systems states that 66 percent of its workforce overall telecommutes.[78]

Telecommuting offers the individual the potential advantages of flexibility, the comforts of home, and choice of locations consistent with one's lifestyle. In terms of advantages to the organization, this alternative often produces cost savings and efficiency as well as employee satisfaction. On the negative side, telecommuters sometimes complain of isolation from co-workers, decreased identification with the work team, and technical difficulties with the computer linkages essential to their work arrangement. Yet overall, the practice continues to grow, with more organizations now offering special training in the *virtual management* of telecommuters. Increasingly too, managers are also telecommuting. At AT&T, for example, almost 30 percent of managers work at home at least one day per week.[79]

■ PART-TIME WORK

Part-time work has become an increasingly prominent and controversial work arrangement. In **temporary part-time work** an employee is classified as "temporary" and works less than the standard 40-hour work week. In **permanent part-time work** the person is considered a "permanent" member of the workforce but contributes fewer hours than the standard, typically 40-hour work week. For example, at Peet's Coffee and Tea, many of the loyal and satis-

■ **Telecommuting** is work at home or in remote locations and using computer and telecommunication linkages with the office.

■ **Temporary part-time work** is temporary work of fewer hours than the standard week.

■ **Permanent part-time work** is permanent work of fewer hours than the standard week.

OB Across Functions

BUSINESS LAW

New Hiring Practices Have Legal Implications

Flexibility is a watchword of the day in any consideration of work scheduling. The term applies not only to the needs of the workers who want more flexibility in their hours, but also to employers who want flexibility in expanding and contracting their workforces. It is here that the role of the part-time or temporary worker becomes important. When companies employ temporary workers on a regular basis, for at least a year or more, these workers are sometimes called "permatemps." New legal challenges in U.S. courts are raising important issues of labor law even as part-time and contingency workers become more integral to the human-resource strategies of many organizations. The question relates largely to the availability of benefits for permatemps, based on who is considered their true "employer." If the company is considered the employer, instead of the individual worker being considered an independent contractor, permatemps in effect become "common-law workers." As such, under federal pension laws they are eligible for the benefits available to other workers, unless they have been specifically excluded by policy. Benefits lawyers are watching current cases carefully, since the rulings could open the door for future lawsuits.

fied Peetniks fall into this category. By working at least 21 hours a week, they are considered permanent and gain access to important benefits otherwise denied to the temporary part-time workers.[80]

Usually, temporary part-timers are easily released and hired as needs dictate. Accordingly, many organizations use part-time work to hold down labor costs and to help smooth out peaks and valleys in the business cycle. Employers also may use part-time work to better manage what may be called "retention quality." These workers are highly skilled individuals committed to their careers who want to continue to develop professionally but who can only work part time. Part-time nurses, among others, fall in this category.[81]

The part-time work schedule can be a benefit to people who want to supplement other jobs or who want something less than a full work week for a variety of personal reasons. For someone who is holding two jobs, including at least one part time, the added burdens can be stressful and may affect performance in either one or both work settings. Furthermore, part-timers often fail to qualify for fringe benefits, such as health care, life insurance, and pensions, and they may be paid less than their full-time counterparts. Nevertheless, part-time work schedules are of growing practical importance because of the organizational advantages they offer.

Organizational Design and Size

■ **Organizational design** is the process of choosing and implementing a structural configuration for an organization.

Organizational design is the process of choosing and implementing a structural configuration.[82] The choice of an appropriate organizational design is contingent upon several factors, including the size of the firm, its operations and information technology, its environment, and the strategy it selects for growth and survival.

For many reasons, large organizations cannot be just bigger versions of their smaller counterparts. As the number of individuals in a firm increases arithmetically, the number of possible interconnections among them increases geometrically. In other words, the direct interpersonal contact among all members in a large organization must be managed. The design of small firms is directly influenced by its core operations technology, whereas larger firms have many core operations technologies in a wide variety of much more specialized units. In large organizations, a key to success is efficiency by economies of scale—production of products and services efficiently through repetition. Specialization of labor, equipment, and departments is one way of capturing the potential economies of scale. Increasing specialization calls for increased control and coordination to ensure that actions are directed toward common goals and linked together in a meaningful way. In short, larger organizations are often more complex than smaller firms. This additional complexity calls for a more sophisticated organizational design. Yet even very large organizations also rely on simple design elements.

■ THE SIMPLE DESIGN FOR SMALLER UNITS AND FIRMS

■ **Simple design** is a configuration involving one or two ways of specializing individuals and units.

The **simple design** is a configuration involving one or two ways of specializing individuals and units. That is, vertical specialization and control typically emphasize levels of supervision without elaborate formal mechanisms (e.g., rule books, policy manuals), and the majority of the control resides in the manager. Thus, the simple design tends to minimize the bureaucratic aspects and rest more heavily on the leadership of the manager.

The simple design is appropriate for many small firms, such as family businesses, retail stores, and small manufacturing firms.[83] The strengths of the simple design are simplicity, flexibility, and responsiveness to the desires of a central manager—in many cases, the owner. Because a simple design relies heavily on the manager's personal leadership, however, this configuration is only as effective as is the senior manager.[84]

Operations Technology and Organizational Design

Although the design of an organization should reflect its size, it must also be adjusted to fit technological opportunities and requirements.[85] That is, successful organizations are said to arrange their internal structures to meet the dictates of their dominant "technologies" or work flows and, more recently, information technology opportunities.[86] **Operations technology** is the combination of resources, knowledge, and techniques that creates a product or service output for an organization.[87] **Information technology** is the combination of machines, artifacts, procedures, and systems used to gather, store, analyze, and disseminate information for translating it into knowledge.[88]

For over 30 years, researchers in OB have chartered the links between operations technology and organizational design. For operations technology, two common classifications have received considerable attention: Thompson's and Woodward's classifications.

■ THOMPSON'S VIEW OF TECHNOLOGY

James D. Thompson classified technologies based on the degree to which the technology could be specified and the degree of interdependence among the work activities with categories called intensive, mediating, and long linked.[89] Under *intensive technology*, there is uncertainty as to how to produce desired outcomes. A group of specialists must be brought together interactively to use a variety of techniques to solve problems. Examples are found in a hospital emergency room or a research and development laboratory. Coordination and knowledge exchange are of critical importance with this kind of technology.

Mediating technology links parties that want to become interdependent. For example, banks link creditors and depositors and store money and information to facilitate such exchanges. Whereas all depositors and creditors are indirectly interdependent, the reliance is pooled through the bank. The degree of coordination among the individual tasks with pooled technology is substantially reduced, and information management becomes more important than coordinated knowledge application.

Under *long-linked technology*, also called mass production or industrial technology, the way to produce the desired outcomes is known. The task is broken down into a number of sequential steps. A classic example is the automobile

■ **Operations technology** is the combination of resources, knowledge, and techniques that creates a product or service output for an organization.

■ **Information technology** is the combination of machines, artifacts, procedures, and systems used to gather, store, analyze, and disseminate information for translating it into knowledge.

assembly line. Control is critical, and coordination is restricted to making the sequential linkages work in harmony.

■ WOODWARD'S VIEW OF TECHNOLOGY

Joan Woodward also divides technology into three categories: small-batch, mass production, and continuous-process manufacturing.[90] In units of *small-batch production*, a variety of custom products are tailor-made to fit customer specifications, such as tailor-made suits. The machinery and equipment used are generally not very elaborate, but considerable craftsmanship is often needed. In *mass production*, the organization produces one or a few products through an assembly-line system. The work of one group is highly dependent on that of another; the equipment is typically sophisticated; and the workers are given very detailed instructions. Automobiles and refrigerators are produced in this way. Organizations using *continuous-process technology* produce a few products using considerable automation. Classic examples are automated chemical plants and oil refineries.

From her studies, Woodward concluded that the combination of structure and technology was critical to the success of the organizations. When technology and organizational design were properly matched, a firm was more successful. Specifically, successful small-batch and continuous-process plants had flexible structures with small work groups at the bottom; more rigidly structured plants were less successful. In contrast, successful mass production operations were rigidly structured and had large work groups at the bottom. Since Woodward's studies, this technological imperative has been supported by various other investigations. Yet, today we recognize that technology is just one factor involved in the success of an organization.[91]

■ WHERE OPERATIONS TECHNOLOGY DOMINATES: THE ADHOCRACY

The influence of operations technological is most clearly seen in small organizations and in specific departments within large ones. In some instances, managers and employees simply do not know the appropriate way to service a client or to produce a particular product. This is the extreme of Thompson's intensive type of technology, and it may be found in some small-batch processes where a team of individuals must develop a unique product for a particular client.

Mintzberg suggests that at these technological extremes, the "adhocracy" may be an appropriate design.[92] An **adhocracy** is characterized by few rules, policies, and procedures; substantial decentralization; shared decision making among members; extreme horizontal specialization (as each member of the unit may be a distinct specialist); few levels of management; and virtually no formal controls.

The adhocracy is particularly useful when an aspect of the firm's operations technology presents two sticky problems: (1) the tasks facing the firm vary considerably and provide many exceptions, as in a hospital, or (2) problems are difficult to define and resolve.[93] The adhocracy places a premium on professionalism and coordination in problem solving.[94] Large firms may use temporary task forces, form special committees, and even contract consulting firms to provide the creative problem identification and problem solving that the adhocracy promotes. For instance, Microsoft creates new autonomous departments to encourage talented employees to develop new software programs. Allied Chemical and 3M also set up quasi-autonomous groups to work through new ideas.

■ **Adhocracy** is an organizational structure that emphasizes shared, decentralized decision making; extreme horizontal specialization; few levels of management; the virtual absence of formal controls; and few rules, policies, and procedures.

Information Technology and Organizational Design

Today, information technology (IT) and the computer are virtually inseparable.[95] Some even suggest that IT only refers to computer-based systems used in the management of the enterprise.[96] Certainly, the computer and extensions of the personal computer are a major force in most corporations. However, substantial collateral advances have also been made in telecommunication options. Furthermore, advances in the computer as a machine are much less profound than how information technology is transforming how firms manage.

It is important to understand just what IT does from an organizational standpoint—not from the view of the PC user.[97] From an organizational standpoint IT can be used, among other things, as (1) a partial substitute for some operations as well as some process controls and impersonal methods of coordination, (2) a capability for transforming information to knowledge for learning, and (3) a strategic capability.

■ INFORMATION TECHNOLOGY AS A SUBSTITUTE

Old bureaucracies prospered and dominated other forms, in part, because they provided more efficient production through specialization and their approach to dealing with information. Where the organization used mediating technology or long-linked technology, the machine bureaucracy ran rampant. In these firms rules, policies, and procedures, as well as many other process controls, could be rigidly enforced based on very scant information.[98] Such was the case for the post office: postal clerks even had rules telling them how to hold their hands when sorting mail.

In many organizations, the initial implementation of IT would displace the most routine, highly specified, and repetitious jobs.[99] The clerical tasks in bookkeeping, writing checks for payroll, and keeping track of sales were some of the first targets of computerization. Here IT was often initiated in the form of a large centralized mainframe computer. For instance, mainframe computers were still the major business for IBM well into the 1990s. Initial implementation did not alter the fundamental character or design of the organization. To continue the example of the post office, initial computerization focused mainly on replacing the hand tracking of mail. Then IT was infused into automated reading machines to help sort mail. This called for implementation of the ZIP code.

A second wave of substitution replaced process controls and informal coordination mechanisms. Rules, policies, and procedures could be replaced with a decision support system (DSS). In the case of a DSS, repetitive routine choices could be pro-

---

OB Across Functions

MARKETING

Will Salespeople and Distributors Be the New Clerical Casualties of the Web?

In just a few years the stock market value of amazon.com has surpassed that of industry leader Barnes and Noble, even though Amazon has no retail stores and sells fewer books. Firms in other industries are reexamining their channels of distribution and their reliance on internal sales units. Direct sales via the Web undercut the need for traditional dealers and provide direct access for consumers. At the same time, salespeople establish valuable relationships with customers. Yet, as amazon.com illustrates, many customers may want direct access. Now most corporate Web sites serve as window dressing for corporate images rather than marketing tools. But as Amazon exemplifies, that role is changing...and quickly.

grammed into a computer-based system. For instance, if you applied for a credit card, a computer program would check your credit history and other financial information. If your application passed several preset tests, you would be issued a credit card. If your application failed any of the tests, it would either be rejected or sent to an individual for further analysis.

The second wave of implementation brought some marginal changes in organizational design. Specifically, the firm often needed fewer levels of management and fewer internal staff. A small number of firms also recognized that they could outsource some internal staff operations. For instance, in many firms independent organizations actually do all of their employee payroll.

The emphasis on direct substitution was still the norm in many organizations well into the 1990s, and in smaller firms it continues today. This is much as one would expect with the implementation of a new-to-the-world technology. It takes decades to move from the lab to full implementation, and the first applications are often in the form of substitutes for existing solutions. For instance, autos were once just substitutes for the horse and buggy. Both computer technology and the auto took about 20 years to enter the mass market. However, IT, just as the auto, has transformed our society because it added new capability.

■ INFORMATION TECHNOLOGY AS A CAPABILITY FOR LEARNING

IT has also long been recognized for its potential to add capability.[100] For over 20 years, scholars have talked of using IT to improve the efficiency, speed of responsiveness, and effectiveness of operations. Married to machines, IT became advanced manufacturing technology when computer-aided design (CAD) was combined with computer-aided manufacturing (CAM) to yield the automated manufacturing cell. More complex decision support systems have provided middle and lower level managers programs to aid in analyzing complex problems rather than just ratify routine choices. Computer-generated reports now give even senior executives the opportunity to track the individual sales performance of the lowliest salesperson.

Now instead of substituting for existing operations, or process controls, IT provides individuals deep within the organization the information they need to plan, make choices, coordinate with others, and control their own operations.

Although simple substitution could proceed one application at a time, the real impact of adding IT capability could not come until it was broadly available to nearly everyone.[101] To use the auto analogy again, the real impact of the auto was felt only after Henry Ford sold hundreds of thousands of his Model T and new roads were constructed. For IT to have a similar impact on organizational design, the seamless use of computerized information across the organization was needed. The extremely powerful mainframe of the 1970s and 1980s was not up to the task simply because the information individuals required to do their jobs more quickly and better was often unique to them. They now needed a common technology with the capability for uniqueness. And nearly everyone would have to have it and use it in cooperation with others.

Enter WINTEL—that is, Microsoft Windows in combination with an Intel microprocessing chip. This combination provided a relatively cheap, easy-to-use personal computer with an almost standardized technology that could be individually tailored at a comparatively modest cost. WINTEL was the PC equivalent of the tin lizzie—Henry Ford's Model T designed for the masses.

With the adoption of WINTEL, three important changes occurred. First, IT applications for tasks found across many organizations were quickly developed and received board acceptance. Thus, the era of the spreadsheet and the word processing program began and displaced the old mainframes. Individuals could develop and transfer information to others with some assurance that the other party could read their output and duplicate their processes. Second, WINTEL expanded to incorporate existing telecommunications systems such as the Internet.[102] Thus, the era of connectivity also emerged. Married to parallel developments in telecommunications, a whole world of electronic commerce, teleconferencing—with combinations of data, pictures, and sound—and cell phones emerged. Third, IT was transformed from a substitute to a mechanism for learning.[103]

Collectively, the impact of IT organizational design was and remains profound. The changes can often occur from the bottom up. New IT systems empower individuals, expanding their jobs and making them both interesting and challenging. The emphasis on narrowly defined jobs replete with process controls imposed by middle management can be transformed to broadly envisioned, interesting jobs based on IT-embedded processes with output controls. A new series of coordination devices based on IT can displace the memo and the coordinating department as firms constitute temporary teams and task forces using "virtual meetings"—meetings via E-mail to solve cross-departmental problems.[104] The whole world of staff units has changed as bureaucratic professionals have adjusted to the new world of IT. And many middle managers replete with their staff assistants are no longer needed.

For the production segments of firms using long-linked technology such as in auto assembly plants and canneries, IT can be linked to total quality management (TQM) programs and be embedded in the machinery. Here data on operations can be transformed into knowledge of operations and used to systematically improve quality and efficiency. This also has meant that firms have had to rethink their view of employees as brainless robots. To make TQM work with IT all employees must plan, do, and control. Thus, we have taken special care to talk about job enrichment and job design, for combining IT and TQM with empowerment and participation is fundamental for success. For instance, in the mid-1990s two computer equipment manufacturers embarked on improvement programs combining IT and TQM. One manufacturer imposed the program on all employees. There was some initial success, but ultimately this program failed. The second combined the IT-TQM program with extensive empowerment and participation. Although implementation was slower, today the combination has produced a constantly improving learning environment.[105]

■ INFORMATION TECHNOLOGY AS A STRATEGIC CAPABILITY

A whole new series of firms has arisen in which IT is the business of the firm or the firm would not exist without sophisticated IT.[106] The whole computer and semiconductor business is the most obvious example. Where IT dominates, the firm is often designed as an adhocracy.

Perhaps IT's most profound effect can be seen in firms that rely on a mediating technology; banks, finance companies, dating services, and employment agencies are some examples. The job of the firm, as we know, is to facilitate exchange by matching types of individuals. In the case of banks, individuals who want to borrow are matched with those who want to lend by placing individual interests into categories. So those who have a savings account are put in a category of precisely that type of savings account and are pooled with others. IT can revolutionize the categorization process that underlies the matching by helping to create much more sophisticated categories and link these categories in new and novel ways. For example, IT lies behind the multibillion dollar secondary market for home mortgages. Until recent years, a bank or savings and loan (S&L) provided the funds for the mortgage from its depositors and would hold the mortgage until it was paid off. You would apply to a local bank or S&L for a mortgage. If they granted you a mortgage, you would pay the bank or the S&L that sold it to you. Much the same was the case for student loans. Now with IT, the bank or S&L can sell the mortgage to others, and normally does, so that it can recoup new funds to sell additional mortgages. It may even sell the right to "service" the loan so that you no longer send your money to the originating bank but to someone else. This change in information technology now allows all types of financial institutions to participate in lending money for mortgages. The job of the old banker or S&L manger has fundamentally changed. Now you can get a mortgage, a credit card, or use the ATM machine without ever contacting an individual.

Some financial firms could not exist without IT, which has become the basis for whole new industries. For instance, IT is the foundation for multitrillion dollar markets in international finance in which new exotic products are available which were nonexistent 15 years ago. A small handful of individuals in Connecticut working for a firm called Long Term Capital used sophisticated IT systems to bet several billion dollars on the interest spread between different kinds of bonds. Although they made several hundred million dollars in the mid 1990s, in 1998 their losses threatened the whole U.S. financial system to the point that the Federal Reserve (a quasigovernment agency) had to orchestrate a rescue. Long Term Capital had become too big to fail in an aspect of the global financial markets that barely existed in the 1980s. Few existing financial managers or regulatory agencies had the understanding of IT to develop effective controls for the global derivatives markets. Of course, IT has not developed in a vacuum, and its effective implementation often rests on others adopting common IT standards and operations. Just because IT presents a potential capability does not automatically mean the firm should adopt it or change its design to facilitate its use. The appropriate design also rests on external factors and the strategy of the firm. We turn to these issues now.

Environment and Organizational Design

An effective organizational design also reflects powerful external forces as well as size and technological factors. Organizations, as open systems, need to receive inputs from the environment and in turn to sell outputs to their environment. Therefore, understanding the environment has become important.[107]

The *general environment* is the set of cultural, economic, legal-political, and educational conditions found in the areas in which the organization operates. International concerns deal with the influences of the general environment, and throughout this volume we have shown examples of globalization. The owners, suppliers, distributors, government agencies, and competitors with which an organization must interact to grow and survive constitute its *specific environment*. A firm typically has much more choice in the composition of its specific environment than its general environment. It can develop policies and strategies that will alter the mix of owners, suppliers, distributors, and competitors with which it interacts. Although it is often convenient to separate the general and specific environmental influences on the firm, designers need to recognize the combined impact of both. Choosing some businesses, for instance, means entering global competition with advanced technologies.

■ ENVIRONMENTAL COMPLEXITY

A basic concern that must be addressed in analyzing the environment of the organization is its complexity. A more complex environment provides an organization with more opportunities and more problems. **Environmental complexity** refers to the magnitude of the problems and opportunities in the organization's environment, as evidenced by three main factors: the degree of richness, the degree of interdependence, and the degree of uncertainty stemming from both the general and the specific environment.

■ **Environmental complexity** is the magnitude of the problems and opportunities in the organization's environment as evidenced by the degree of richness, interdependence, and uncertainty.

Environmental Richness   Overall, the environment is richer when the economy is growing, when individuals are improving their education, and when those on whom the organization relies are prospering. For businesses, a richer environment means that economic conditions are improving, customers are spending more money, and suppliers (especially banks) are willing to invest in the organization's future. In a rich environment, more organizations survive, even if they have poorly functioning organizational designs. A richer environment is also filled with more opportunities and dynamism—the potential for change. The organizational design must allow the company to recognize these opportunities and capitalize on them.

The opposite of richness is decline. For business firms, a general recession is a good example of a leaner environment. Whereas corporate reactions vary, it is instructive to examine three typical responses to decline. In Japan, core manufacturing firms are reluctant to lay off core workers. Instead, they cut the hours of women employees, move some individuals to long-term suppliers, and initiate training for the remaining workers to prepare for a recovery. Since economic problems in Japan have lasted more than five years, however, these typical responses are starting to change. Japanese firms are looking more like their U.S. counterparts as they are giving employees early retirement options, cutting staff, and outsourcing more of their operations.

In the United States, firms have traditionally reacted to decline first by issuing layoffs to nonsupervisory workers and then by moving up the organizational ladder as the environment becomes leaner. As global competition has increased and new IT options have become more widely available, firms have also started to alter their organizational designs by cutting staff units and the number of organizational levels. This downsizing, though traumatic, can be minimized.

Many European firms find it very difficult to cut full-time employees legally when the economy deteriorates. In sustained periods of decline, many firms have therefore turned to national governments for help. Much like U.S.-based firms, European-based firms view changes in organizational design as a last but increasingly necessary resort as they must now compete with Asian and North American rivals.

Environmental Interdependence   The link between external interdependence and organizational design is often subtle and indirect. The organization may coopt powerful outsiders by including them. For instance, many large corporations have financial representatives from banks and insurance companies on their boards of directors. The organization may also adjust its overall design strategy to absorb or buffer the demands of a more powerful external element. Perhaps the most common adjustment is the development of a centralized staff department to handle an important external group. For instance, few large U.S. corporations do not have some type of governmental relations group at the top. Where service to a few large customers is considered critical, the organization's departmentation is likely to switch from a functional to a divisionalized form.[108]

Uncertainty and Volatility   Environmental uncertainty and volatility can be particularly damaging to large bureaucracies. In times of change, investments quickly become outmoded, and internal operations no longer work as expected. The obvious organizational design response to uncertainty and volatility is to opt for a more organic form. At the extremes, movement toward an adhocracy may be important. However, these pressures may run counter to those that come from large size and operations technology. In these cases, it may be too hard or too time consuming for some organizations to make the design adjustments. Thus, the organization may continue to struggle while adjusting its design just a little bit at a time.

■ USING ALLIANCES WHERE ENVIRONMENTAL FACTORS DOMINATE

In high-tech areas and businesses dominated by IT, such as robotics, semiconductors, advanced materials (ceramics and carbon fibers), and advanced information systems, a single company often does not have all the knowledge necessary to bring new products to the market. Often, the firms with the knowledge are not even in the same country. The organizational design must therefore go beyond the boundaries of the organization into **interfirm alliances**—announced cooperative agreements or joint ventures between two independent firms. Often, these agreements involve corporations that are headquartered in different nations.[109]

Alliances are quite common in such high-technology industries, because they seek not only to develop technology but to ensure that their solutions become standardized across regions of the world. In some cases, the fight for a dominant design pits one nation against another. For instance, Zenith joined forces with AT&T to develop one high-definition television (HDTV) system, and Toshiba, Sony, and some 30 other Japanese firms formed a strategic network to develop their own system. After a bitter contest the winner in the United States included the Zenith and AT&T group, who are likely get the lion's share of the estimated $20 billion HDTV market in North America.

Firms may also develop alliances to explore potentials for future collaboration. One of the largest and potentially most influential strategic alliances is the cooperation between West Germany's Daimler-Chrysler and Japan's Mitsubishi. The two companies agreed to share technology and to develop joint ventures,

■ **Interfirm alliances** are announced cooperative agreements or joint ventures between two independent firms.

market-based cooperations, or high-tech consortia, as the need arises. Yet some alliances to share technology date to the turn of the twentieth century.

In more developed industries, interfirm alliances are also quite popular, but they are often known by other names. In Europe, for example, they are called *informal combines* or *cartels*: Competitors work cooperatively to share the market in order to decrease uncertainty and improve favorability for all. Except in rare cases, these arrangements are often illegal in the United States.

In Japan, the network of relationships among well-established firms in many industries is called a *keiretsu*. There are two common forms. The first is a bank-centered keiretsu, in which firms are linked to one another directly through cross ownership and historical ties to one bank. The Mitsubishi group is a good example. In the second type, a vertical keiretsu, a key manufacturer is at the hub of a network of supplier firms or distributor firms. The manufacturer typically has both long-term supply contracts with members and cross-ownership ties. These arrangements help isolate Japanese firms from stockholders and provide a mechanism for sharing and developing technology. Toyota is an example of a firm at the center of a vertical keiretsu.

The network organization is beginning to evolve in the United States as well. Here, the central firm specializes in a core activity, such as design and assembly, and works with a comparatively small number of participating suppliers on a long-term basis for both component development and manufacturing efficiency. Nike is a leader in the development of these relationships.

More extreme variations of this network design are also emerging to meet apparently conflicting environmental, size, and technological demands simultaneously. Firms are spinning off staff functions to reduce their overall size and take advantage of new IT options. With these new environmental challenges and technological opportunities, firms must choose and not just react blindly.

Strategy and Organizational Design

For many firms, size, technology, and environment provide too many challenges and opportunities. Organizational design scholars recommend that the design follow the strategy of the firm and that the strategy take advantage of a combination of advantages offered by size, technology, and the environment.

Organizational strategy is the process of positioning the organization in its competitive environment and implementing actions to compete successfully.[110] The study of linking strategy, organizational design, and firm performance has a long tradition in organizational analysis. In the 1960s, Alfred Chandler studied the evolution of major U.S. firms and concluded that structure follows from the strategy established predominantly by senior management. More recent work suggests that the formula for success is much more complicated.[111] A winning strategy is more likely when the firm recognizes both the importance of a focus and the unique skills and abilities within the firm. Forming a strategy is an interactive process. Senior managers select those systems goals they believe should define corporate success, form these goals into a vision, select a target position within the general and specific environments, and develop a design to accomplish the vision.

■ **Organizational strategy** is the process of positioning the organization in the competitive environment and implementing actions to compete successfully.

■ COMPETENCY-BASED STRATEGIES

Once executives were told to develop a successful strategy by emphasizing one of a limited number economic advantages.[112] Today many strategists are emphasizing the skills and abilities the firms need to have to compete effectively; just saying you want your firm to be a technical leader and instituting an adhocracy does not get the job done.[113] Over time, the firm may develop specific administrative and technical competencies. As middle and lower level managers institute minor modifications and adjustments to solve specific problems and capitalize on specific opportunities, they and their firms may learn new skills. These skills may be recognized by senior management and give them the opportunity to adjust, modify, and build a so-called competency strategy.

The organization needs to build on and refine its unique experience and competencies. In this process, the firm may shift products and markets by relying on the creativity, innovation, and skills of all its employees. IBM was once known as a successful second-to-market imitator with the best service for its mainframe computers. It was not the technical leader, but it developed the standard for others, provided excellent service, and offered a wide array of mainframe products and services. Now IBM, or "Big Blue," is on the move. It has turned to flexible manufacturing for its personal computers to increase efficiency, accompanied by fewer levels of management and substantially greater participation. It is also reaching out to become the hub in a network of high-tech computer firms to service the expanding network computer market. IBM is fighting a long history of traditional management as it seeks to cut levels of management, reduce staff, stress innovation, and infuse itself with unique competencies.

Senior executives at such firms as Ford, AT&T, and Dow are now recognizing that an effective strategy builds on the competence of employees. Technical skills combined with astute management in an organizational design that reinforces employee contributions are fundamental to organizational success. This emphasis on individuals has also brought attention to the important topic of organizational learning. Executives now recognize that their firms must learn or die.

Footnotes

[1] See Michael Porter's three-volume series *The Competitive Advantage of Nations*, *Competitive Advantage*, and *Competitive Strategy* (New York: The Free Press, 1998).

[2] Kenichi Ohmae, *The Evolving Global Economy* (Cambridge, MA: Harvard Business School Press, 1995); Kenichi Ohmae, "Putting Global Logic First," *Harvard Business Review* (January–February 1995), pp. 119–125; and, Jeffrey E. Garten, "Can the World Survive the Triumph of Capitalism?" *Harvard Business Review* (January–February, 1997), pp. 67–79.

[3] William B. Johnston, "Global Workforce 2000: The New World Labor Market," *Harvard Business Review* (March–April 1991), pp. 115–127.

[4] See Porter, op. cit.; Kenichi Ohmae *The End of the Nation State: The Rise of Regional Economies* (New York: The Free Press, 1995); and William Greider, *One World, Ready or Not: The Manic Logic of Global Capitalism* (New York: The Free Press, 1998).

[5] For a discussion of FDI in the United States, see Paul R. Krugman, *Foreign Direct Investment in the United States*, 3rd ed. (Washington, DC, 1995). Statistics on FDI in the United States are available through the Bureau of Economic Analysis, International Accounts Data, [Online] *http://www.bea.doc.gov/bea/di1.htm*.

[6] "Just a Wee Bit of Life in Silicon Glen," *World Business* (March–April 1996), p. 13.

[7] Michael E. Porter, "Clusters and the New Economics of Competition," *Harvard Business Review* (November–December 1998).

[8] See "Alphabet Spaghetti," *The Economist* (October 3, 1998), pp. 19–22; 12 "The Atlantic Century," *Business Week* (February 8, 1999), pp. 64–67.

[9] "Europe Rising," *Business Week* (February 8, 1999), pp. 68–70.

[10] Sarita Kendall and Nancy Dunne, "Business Spurs All-America Free Trade Accord," *Financial Times* (March 22, 1996), p. 3.

[11] One view of the Asian economic crisis is reviewed in George Soros, "Toward a Global Open Society," *Atlantic Monthly* (January 1998).

[12] Michael M. Phillips, "Into Africa," *The Wall Street Journal* (September 18, 1997), pp. R6, R20.

[13] James A. Austin and John G. McLean, "Pathways to Business Success in Sub-Saharan Africa," *Journal of African Finance and Economic Development*, Vol. 2 (1996), pp. 57–76.

[14] Information from "International Business: Consider Africa," *Harvard Business Review*, Vol. 76 (January–February 1998), pp. 16–18.

[15] Robert T. Moran and John R. Riesenberger, *Making Globalization Work: So-*

lutions for Implementation (New York: McGraw-Hill, 1993); "Don't Be an Ugly-American Manager," *Fortune* (October 16, 1995), p. 225; and, "A Way to Measure Global Success," *Fortune* (March 15, 1999), pp. 196–197.

[16] "Working Overseas—Rule No. 1: Don't Miss the Locals," *Business Week* (May 15, 1995), p. 8.

[17] "Don't Be an Ugly-American Manager," op. cit., p. 225.

[18] Vanessa Houlder, "Foreign Culture Shocks," *Financial Times* (March 22, 1996), p. 12.

[19] Geert Hofstede, *Culture's Consequences: International Differences in Work-Related Values* (Beverly Hills, CA.: Sage Publications, 1980); and, Fons Trompenaars, *Riding the Waves of Culture: Understanding Cultural Diversity in Business* (London: Nicholas Brealey Publishing, 1993). For an excellent discussion of culture, see also Chapter 3, "Culture: The Neglected Concept," in Peter B. Smith and Michael Harris Bond, *Social Psychology Across Cultures*, 2nd ed. (Boston: Allyn & Bacon, 1998).

[20] Geert Hofstede, *Culture and Organizations: Software of the Mind* (London: McGraw-Hill, 1991).

[21] A good overview of the world's cultures is provided in Richard D. Lewis, *When Cultures Collide: Managing Successfully Across Cultures* (London: Nicholas Brealey Publishing, 1996).

[22] Benjamin L. Whorf, *Language, Thought and Reality* (Cambridge, MA: MIT Press, 1956).

[23] Edward T. Hall, *Beyond Culture* (New York: Doubleday, 1976).

[24] A classic work and the source of our examples is Edward T. Hall, *The Silent Language* (New York: Anchor Books, 1959).

[25] Allen C. Bluedorn, Carol Felker Kaufman, and Paul M. Lane, "How Many Things Do You Like to Do at Once?" *Academy of Management Executive*, Vol. 6 (November 1992), pp. 17–26.

[26] Edward T. Hall's book *The Hidden Dimension* (New York: Anchor Books, 1969; Magnolia, MI: Peter Smith, 1990) is a classic reference and the source of our examples. See also Edward T. Hall, *Hidden Differences* (New York: Doubleday, 1990).

[27] The classic work is Max Weber, *The Protestant Ethic and the Spirit of Capitalism* (New York: Scribner, 1930). For a description of religious influences in Asian cultures, see S. Gordon Redding, *The Spirit of Chinese Capitalism* (New York: Walter de Gruyter, 1990).

[28] Hofstede, op. cit. (1980). Geert Hofstede and Michael H. Bond, "The Confucius Connection: From Culture Roots to Economic Growth," *Organizational Dynamics*, Vol. 16 (1988), pp. 4–21.

[29] Hofstede, op. cit. (1980).

[30] Chinese Culture Connection, "Chinese Values and the Search for Culture-Free Dimensions of Culture," *Journal of Cross-Cultural Psychology*, Vol. 18 (1987), pp. 143–164.

[31] Hofstede and Bond, op. cit., 1988; and, Geert Hofstede, "Cultural Constraints in Management Theories," *Academy of Management Executive*, Vol. 7 (February 1993), pp. 81–94. For a further discussion of Asian and Confucian values, see also Jim Rohwer, *Asia Rising: Why America Will Prosper as Asia's Economies Boom* (New York: Simon & Schuster, 1995), and Chapter 3 on "China" in Lewis, op. cit. (1996).

[32] For an example, see John R. Schermerhorn, Jr., and Michael H. Bond, "Cross-Cultural Leadership Dynamics in Collectivism + High Power Distance Settings," *Leadership and Organization Development Journal*, Vol. 18 (1997), pp. 187–193.

[33] Nancy J. Adler, *International Dimensions of Organizational Behavior*, 2nd ed. (Boston: PWS-Kent, 1991).

[34] Trompenaars, op. cit. (1993).

[35] Alvin Toffler, *The Third Wave* (New York: William Morrow, 1980).

[36] Ibid.

[37] Information from "Sweatshop Wars," *The Economist* (February 27, 1999), pp. 62–63.

[38] Adler, op. cit. (1991).

[39] Information from Jennifer Scott, "Workers Being Sent Abroad Are Finding More Support," *The Columbus Dispatch* (March 8, 1999), pp. 10–11.

[40] Ibid.

[41] See J. Stewart Black and Hal B. Gregersen, "The Right Way to Manage Expats," *Harvard Business Review* (March–April 1999).

[42] See Rosalie Tung, "Expatriate Assignments: Enhancing Success and Minimizing Failure," *Academy of Management Executive* (May 1987), pp. 117–126; and Adler, op. cit. (1991).

[43] Nancy J. Adler, "Reentry: Managing Cross-Cultural Transitions," *Group and Organization Studies*, Vol. 6, No. 3 (1981), pp. 341–356; and Adler, op. cit. (1991).

[44] For a discussion of international business ethics, see Thomas Donaldson and Thomas W. Dunfee, *Ties That Bind* (Boston: Harvard Business School Press, 1999); Thomas Donaldson, "Values in Tension: Ethics Away from Home," *Harvard Business Review* (September–October 1996), pp. 48–62; and, Debora L. Spar, "The Spotlight and the Bottom Line," *Foreign Affairs* (March–April 1998).

[45] "Cracking Down on Overseas Bribes," *Business Week* (March 1, 1999), p. 41.

[46] "Business Ethics: Sweatshops," *The Economist* (February 27, 1999), pp. 62–63.

[47] Information from Council for Economic Priorities Accreditation Agency Web site: www.cepaa.org.

[48] Donaldson, op. cit. (1996).

[49] Ibid.; Thomas Donaldson and Thomas W. Dunfee, "Towards a Unified Conception of Business Ethics: Integrative Social Contracts Theory," *Academy of Management Review*, Vol. 19 (1994), pp. 252–285; and Donaldson and Dunfee, op. cit. (1999). For a related discussion see John R. Schermerhorn, Jr., "Alternative Terms of Business Engagement in Ethically Challenging Environment," *Business Ethics Quarterly* (1999), forthcoming.

[50] Geert Hofstede, "Motivation, Leadership and Organization: Do American Theories Apply Abroad?" *Organizational Dynamics*, Vol. 9 (1980), pp. 43+; Hofstede, op. cit. (1993).

[51] Two classic works are William Ouchi, *Theory Z: How American Businesses Can Meet the Japanese Challenge* (Reading, MA: Addison-Wesley, 1981); Richard Tanner and Anthony Athos, *The Art of Japanese Management* (New York: Simon & Schuster, 1981).

[52] See J. Bernard Keys, Luther Tray Denton, and Thomas R. Miller, "The Japanese Management Theory Jungle—Revisited," *Journal of Management*, Vol. 20 (1994), pp. 373–402; and "Japanese and Korean Management Systems," Ch. 13 in Min Chen, *Asian Management Systems* (New York: Routledge, 1995).

[53] An example is "Fall of a Keiretsu: How Giant Mitsubishi Group Lost Its Way," Special Report, *Business Week* (March 15, 1999), pp. 85–92.

[54] Wellford W. Wilms, Alan J. Hardcastle, and Deone M. Fall, "Cultural Transformation at NUMMI," *Sloan Management Review* (Fall 1994), pp. 99–113.

[55] See William A. Pasmore, *Designing Effective Organizations: A Sociotechnical Systems Perspective* (New York: Wiley, 1988).

[56] *The Economist* (October 17, 1998), p. 116.

[57] See Malcolm S. Salter and Wayne A. Edesis, "Wolfsburg at the Center," *Harvard Business Review* (July–August 1991).

[58] Peter Senker, *Towards the Automatic Factory: The Need for Training* (New York: Springer-Verlag, 1986).

[59] See Ramchandran Jaikumar, "Postindustrial Manufacturing," *Harvard Business Review*, Vol. 44 (1986), pp. 69–76.

[60] Michael Hammer, "Reengineering Work: Don't Automate, Obliterate," *Harvard Business Review* (July–August 1990), pp. 104–112.

[61] See Thomas M. Koulopoulos, *The Workflow Imperative: Building Real World Business Solutions* (New York: Van Nostrand Reinhold, 1995).

[62] For a good overview, see Michael Hammer and James Champy, *Reengineering the Corporation* (New York: Harper Business, 1993); and Michael Hammer, *Beyond Reengineering* (New York: Harper Business, 1997).

[63] Edwin A. Locke, Karyll N. Shaw, Lise M. Saari, and Gary P. Latham, "Goal Setting and Task Performance: 1969–1980," *Psychological Bulletin*, Vol. 90 (July–November 1981), pp. 125–152; Edwin A. Locke and Gary P. Latham, "Work Motivation and Satisfaction: Light at the End of the Tunnel," *Psychological Science*, Vol. 1, No. 4 (July 1990), pp. 240–246; and Edwin A. Locke and Gary P. Latham, *A Theory of Goal Setting and Task Performance* (Englewood Cliffs, NJ: Prentice-Hall, 1990).

[64] Gary P. Latham and Edwin A. Locke, "Goal Setting—A Motivational Technique That Works," *Organizational Dynamics*, Vol. 8 (Autumn 1979), pp. 68–80; Gary P. Latham and Timothy P. Steele, "The Motivational Effects of Participation versus Goal-Setting on Performance," *Academy of Management Journal*, Vol. 26 (1983), pp. 406–417; Miriam Erez and Frederick H. Kanfer, "The Role of Goal Acceptance in Goal Setting and Task Performance," *Academy of Management Review*, Vol. 8 (1983), pp. 454–463; and R. E. Wood and E. A. Locke, "Goal Setting and Strategy Effects on Complex Tasks," in B. Staw and L. L. Cummings (eds.), *Research in Organizational Behavior* (Greenwich, CT: JAI Press, 1990).

[65] See E. A. Locke and G. P. Latham, "Work Motivation and Satisfaction," *Psychological Science*, Vol. 1, No. 4 (July 1990), p. 241.

[66] Ibid.

[67] For a good review of MBO, see Anthony P. Raia, *Managing by Objectives* (Glenview, IL: Scott, Foresman, 1974);

[68] Ibid.; also, Steven Kerr summarizes the criticisms well in "Overcoming the Dysfunctions of MBO," *Management by Objectives*, Vol. 5, No. 1 (1976).

[69] For overviews, see Allan R. Cohen and Herman Gadon, *Alternative Work Schedules: Integrating Individual and Organizational Needs* (Reading, MA: Addison-Wesley, 1978); and Jon L. Pearce, John W. Newstrom, Randall B. Dunham, and Alison E. Barber, *Alternative Work Schedules* (Boston: Allyn & Bacon, 1989). See also Sharon Parker and Toby Wall, *Job and Work Design* (Thousand Oaks, CA: Sage, 1998).

[70] B. J. Wixom, Jr., "Recognizing People in a World of Change," *HR Magazine* (June 1995), pp. 7–8; and "The Value of Flexibility," *Inc.* (April 1996), p. 114.

[71] C. Latack and L. W. Foster, "Implementation of Compressed Work Schedules: Participation and Job Redesign as Critical Factors for Employee Acceptance," *Personnel Psychology*, Vol. 38 (1985), pp. 75–92.

[72] *Business Week* (December 7, 1998), p. 8.

[73] "Aetna Life & Casualty Company," *Wall Street Journal* (June 4, 1990), p. R35; (June 18, 1990), p. B1.

[74] Getsy M. Selirio, "Job Sharing Gains Favor as Corporations Embrace Alternative Work Schedule," *Lubbock Avalanche-Journal* (December 13, 1992), p. 2E.

[75] Ibid.

[76] "Making Stay-at-Homes Feel Welcome," *Business Week* (October 12, 1998), pp. 153–155.

[77] T. Davenport and K. Pearlson, "Two Cheers for the Virtual Office," *Sloan Management Review* (Summer 1998), pp. 51–64.

[78] "Making Stay-at-Homes Feel Welcome," op. cit.

[79] Carol Hymowitz, "Remote Managers Find Ways to Narrow the Distance Gap," *Wall Street Journal* (April 6, 1999), p. B1.

[80] Guynn, op. cit. (1998).

[81] Daniel C. Feldman and Helen I. Doerpinghaus, "Missing Persons No Longer: Managing Part-Time Workers in the '90s," *Organizational Dynamics* (Summer 1992), pp. 59–72.

[82] R. N. Osborn, J. G. Hunt, and L. Jauch, *Organization Theory: Integrated Text and Cases* (Melbourne, FL: Krieger, 1984), pp. 123–215.

[83] See Henry Mintzberg, *Structure in Fives: Designing Effective Organizations* (Englewood Cliffs, NJ: Prentice-Hall, 1983).

[84] For a comprehensive review, see W. Richard Scott, *Organizations: Rational, Natural, and Open Systems*, 2nd ed. (Englewood Cliffs, NJ: Prentice-Hall, 1987).

[85] See Peter M. Blau and Richard A. Schoenner, *The Structure of Organizations* (New York: Basic Books, 1971).

[86] Joan Woodward, *Industrial Organization: Theory and Practice* (London: Oxford University Press, 1965).

[87] Ibid.

[88] Gerardine DeSanctis, "Information Technology," in Nigel Nicholoson (ed.), *Blackwell Encyclopedic Dictionary of Organizational Behavior* (Cambridge, MA: Blackwell Publishers, Ltd., 1995), pp. 232–233.

[89] James D. Thompson, *Organization in Action* (New York: McGraw-Hill, 1967).

[90] Woodward (1965).

[91] For reviews, see Osborn, Hunt, and Jauch (1984); and Louis Fry, "Technology-Structure Research: Three Critical Issues," *Academy of Management Journal* 25 (1982): pp. 532–552.

[92] Mintzberg (1983).

[93] Charles Perrow, *Complex Organizations: A Critical Essay*, 3rd ed. (New York: Random House, 1986).

[94] Mintzberg (1983).

[95] Prashant C. Palvia, Shailendra C. Palvia and Edward M. Roche, *Global Information Technology and Systems Management: Key Issues and Trends* (Nashua, NH: Ivy League Publishing, 1996).

[96] DeSanctis (1995).

[97] P. Candace Deans, *Global Information Systems and Technology: Focus on the Organization and Its Functional Areas* (Harrisburg, PA: Ideal Group Publishing, 1994).

[98] Osborn, Hunt, and Jauch (1984).

[99] David A. Nadler and Michael L. Tushman, *Competing by Design: The Power of Organizational Architecture* (New York: Oxford University Press, 1997).

[100] David Lei, Michael Hitt, and Richard A. Bettis, "Dynamic Capabilities and Strategic Management," *Journal of Management* 22 (1996): pp. 547–567.

[101] Melissa A. Schilling, "Technological Lockout: An Integrative Model of the Economic and Strategic Factors Driving Technological Success and Failure," *Academy of Management Review* 23, No. 2 (1998): 267–284.

[102] Jack Veiga and Kathleen Dechant, "Wired World Woes:www.help," *Academy of Management Executive* 11, No. 3 (1997): 73–79.

[103] Jaana Woiceshyn, "The Role of Management in the Adoption of Technology: A Longitudinal Investigation," *Technology Studies* 4, No. 1 (1997): 62–99.

[104] Janice Beyer, Danta P. Ashmos, and R. N. Osborn, "Contrasts in Enacting TQM: Mechanistic vs Organic Ideology and Implementation," *Journal of Quality Management* 1 (1997): 13–29.

[105] Veiga and Dechant (1997).

[106] Michael A. Hitt, R. Duane Ireland, and Robert E. Hoskisson, *Strategic Management: Competitiveness and Globalization* (Cincinnati, OH: South-Western College Publishing, 1999).

[107] This section is based on R. N. Osborn and J. G. Hunt, "The Environment and Organization Effectiveness," *Administrative Science Quarterly* 19 (1974): 231–246; and Osborn, Hunt, and Jauch (1984).

[108] See R. N. Osborn and C. C. Baughn, "New Patterns in the Formation of U.S./Japanese Cooperative Ventures," *Columbia Journal of World Business* 22 (1988): 57–65.

[109] R. N. Osborn, *The Evolution of Strategic Alliances in High Technology*, working paper (Detroit: Department of Management, Wayne State University, 1997); and Shawn Tully, "The Modular Corporation," *Fortune* (February 8, 1993).

[110] L. R. Jauch and R. N. Osborn, "Toward an Integrated Theory of Strategy," *Academy of Management Review* 6 (1981): 491–498; Alfred D. Chandler, *The Visible Hand: The Managerial Revolution in America* (Cambridge, MA: Belknap, 1977); Karen Bantel and R. N. Osborn, "The Influence of Performance, Environment and Size on the Identifiability of Firm Strategy," *British Journal of Management* 6 (1995): 235–248.

[111] Hitt, Ireland, and Hoskisson (1999).

[112] M. E. Porter, *Competitive Strategy* (New York: Free Press, 1980).

[113] J. C. Spencer and R. M. Grant, "Knowledge and the Firm: Overview," *Strategic Management Journal* 17 (Winter special issue 1996): 5–10: Spencer and Grant (1996).

Source Notes

Information from "A Global Sightseeing Tour," *Business Week* (February 1, 1999), pp. ENT3.

Information from "Yahoo!," *Business Week* (September 7, 1998), pp. 66–76.

"Just a Wee Bit of Life in Silicon Glen," *World Business* (March/April 1996), p. 13.

Council on Economic Priorities Accreditation Agency Web site, www.cepaa.org.

Developed from Geert Hofstede, *Culture's Consequences* (Beverly Hills, CA: Sage Publications, 1980).

Developed from Fons Trompenaars, *Riding the Waves of Culture* (London: Nicholas Brealey Publishing, 1993).

Developed from Nancy J. Adler, *International Dimensions of Organizational Behavior*, 2nd ed. (Boston: Kent, 1991).

John R. Schermerhorn, Jr., *Management,* 6 ed. (New York: Wiley, 1999), p. 118. Used by permission.

"When Is a Temp Not a Temp?" *Business Week* (December 7, 1998), pp. 90–91.

Adapted from J. Richard Hackman and Greg R. Oldham, "Development of the Job Diagnostic Survey," *Journal of Applied Psychology*, Vol. 60 (1975), p. 161. Used by permission.

Based on Edwin A. Locke and Gary P. Latham: "Work Motivation and Satisfaction: Light at the End of the Tunnel," *Psychological Science*, Vol. 1, No. 4 (July 1990), p. 244.

Xerox (Canada): Information from Kerry Shapansky, "How Fact-Based Management Works for Xerox," *CMA Magazine*, Vol. 68 (December 1994/January 1995), pp. 20–22.

UPS: Information from Robert Frank, "Efficient UPS Tries to Increase Efficiency," *The Wall Street Journal* (May 24, 1995), pp. B1, B4.

Excite, Inc.: Information from Quentin Hardy, "Aloft in a Career Without Fetters," *The Wall Street Journal* (September 29, 1998), p. B1.

Gap, Inc.:Information from David Kirkpatrick, "The E-Ware War," *Fortune* (December 7, 1998), pp. 102-110.

George Anders, "Discomfort Zone: Some Companies Long to Embrace the Web But Settle for Flirtation," *Wall Street Journal* (November 4, 1998), pp. 1 and 14; and Jermiah Sullivan, "Functions of the Corporate Web," *Journal of World Business*, in press.

From the 1997 annual report of the Chase Manhattan Corporation and www.chasemanhattan.com.

Warner-Lambert Annual Report 1997, p. 24.

http://www.com/cgi-bin/cgi; Caree P&G Pursues Greatest Growth Ever (September 9, 1998); Douglas G. Shaw and Vincent C. Perro, "Beating the Odds: Five Reasons Why Companies Excel," *Management Review* (August 1992); P&G Annual Report, 1992, 1995, 1997.

www.solutions-4u.com/barter/49063a73.htm/.

THE OB Skills WORKBOOK

ARTICLE 1
The Company of the Future

by Robert B. Reich

It is a revolutionary notion: Talented people are joining up with fast companies to create "social glue"—the essence of both a winning business and a humane workplace.

Danielle Rios, 28, has it all—a BS degree in computer science from Stanford, a great track record as a software developer for IBM, and the energy and savvy to market herself. With all that going for her, Rios could be a free-agent winner in the new economy, adding value by juggling different projects with different firms. Or she could have her pick of well-established corporate launch pads for her career.

But for the last three years, Rios has worked with Trilogy Software Inc., a small, rapidly growing software firm based in Austin, Texas. Trilogy is on the cutting edge of sales-and-marketing software, and Rios is part of a team that shows potential customers how the software can work for them.

Joe Liemandt, 30, founded Trilogy in 1989, after dropping out of Stanford only a few months before graduation. To finance the startup, Liemandt charged up 22 credit cards. If Trilogy were to go public today, analysts say, it would be valued at more than $1 billion. Four years

ago, Trilogy had 100 employees; today it has almost 1,000—and plans to add another 1,000 before the summer of 1999. But to call Trilogy workers "employees" misses the point. They're all shareholders. They're all managers. They're all partners. That's how Liemandt, Trilogy's CEO, has chosen to run his company—and that's what makes it successful.

Liemandt knows that Trilogy depends on talented people. He also knows that people can go anywhere. Which means that his biggest competitive headache isn't companies like SAP AG, Baan Co., and PeopleSoft Inc.—businesses he has to face down in the marketplace. His biggest worry is holding onto people like Rios. "There's nothing more important than recruiting and growing people," he says. "That's my number-one job."

It's a seller's market for talent. People with the right combination of savvy and ambition can afford to shop for the right boss, the right colleagues, the right environment. In the old economy, it was a buyer's market: Companies had their pick of the crop, and the question they asked was "Why hire?" Now the question is "Why join up?"

As a result, the economy is fostering new kinds of organizations with new kinds of practices and operating rules for pulling people together. These companies offer many of the advantages of free agency: flexibility in how,

First appeared: Fast Company issue 19 page 124
Reprinted with permission from Fast Company Magazine.

when, and where you work; compensation linked to what you contribute; freedom to move from project to project. But they also offer the advantages of belonging to an organization in which mutual commitment builds continuity. They are the enterprises of the future.

What makes them so different? Consider again Danielle Rios and Joe Liemandt at Trilogy. In the old economy, Rios and Liemandt would have been on opposite sides of the table: employee and employer. They'd be there for years, locked in their conflicting roles. Liemandt would want steady, reliable work from Rios. Rios would want a fair wage from Liemandt and an opportunity to move up the company ladder. In the new economy, Rios and Liemandt sit on the same side of the table. And they've joined together—for a time—to create new value.

Ask leaders what their biggest challenge is, and you get the same answer: finding, attracting, and keeping talented people. Ask talented people what their biggest career challenge is, and you'll hear the same refrain: finding good people to work with—and to work for.

For Liemandt and Rios, and for everyone in the new enterprises of the free-agent economy, the crucial questions are: What leads them to work together in the first place, and what keeps them together? Here are the six "social glues" of the company of the future.

Money Makes It Mutual

The world is awash in money. Venture capitalists are pouring funds into startups at a ferocious rate. In 1997, for example, venture-capital firms raised $10 billion. That same year, 629 companies went public, with a total valuation of more than $39 billion. The stock market has softened in recent months, but it's still way up there—making possible a previously unthinkable market for acquisitions and IPOs.

All of this money has had an unavoidable impact on the job market, where money is a powerful motivator. Freshly minted MBAs from leading business schools are commanding a premium from blue-chip consulting firms: Signing bonuses and first-year salaries often run higher than $120,000. And the pay packages that large, successful companies are putting in front of their most talented executives are critical in the rapidly escalating war to keep talent—or to steal it away. Not long ago, in the kind of deal that one usually reads about only in the sports pages, one of Wall Street's premier stock analysts landed a one-year, $25 million contract—a $15 million increase over his 1997 pay package.

But for most people who are trying to decide which company to join, the name of the game today is stock options. Chalk it up as another legacy of Microsoft and that company's now-legendary cadre of millionaires: Across the landscape of the new economy, young, well-educated, talented businesspeople are joining up to get a piece of the action. They're willing to forgo larger salaries at bigger and better-established firms in favor of stock options in upstarts that may be worth a great deal down the road. The result: Even small, little-known enterprises can compete for top talent. In fact, startups promising high risk and huge gain are winning.

"Obviously, it's not just compensation that motivates people to come to work here," says David Stewart, 30, head of human resources at Tripod, a Web company (http://www.tripod.com) based in Williamstown, Massachusetts. "But stock options are a big motivator." Founded in 1992 by Bo Peabody, then a 19-year-old Williams College student, Tripod launched its site in April 1995. Today the company employs 60 people, produces one of the 10 most heavily trafficked sites on the Web, and boasts more than 2 million members. To keep ahead of the competition, Tripod depends on talent.

Stewart doesn't have a classic high-tech background. Before coming to western Massachusetts, he was a lawyer in Montreal. He had worked his way through law school in Toronto by doing stand-up comedy at night. In January 1996, his wife, Margaret Gould Stewart, was offered a job as creative director at Tripod. (Now 27, she has risen to become Tripod's vice president of media and community development.) Stewart recalls that he pulled out a map and tried to locate Williamstown on it. He couldn't.

His wife accepted Tripod's offer, and Stewart followed her to Massachusetts. He joined a small law firm in North Adams, about 10 minutes from Tripod. Almost inevitably, Tripod became one of his clients; Stewart saw huge possibilities in the startup, and he wanted in. "Because there was a lot of buzz around the company, people thought, 'Hey, this stock could be worth something someday,'" Stewart recalls. In August 1997, he decided to take a job in Tripod's human-resources department—a big career change. The salary at Tripod was a little lower than what he'd been making at the law firm. But the company included a "decent-sized grant package." If it weren't for the options, he might not have made the switch. Now, says Stewart, "when you combine salary and options, I make more than I did at the law firm."

Money played a similar role in bringing Kara Berklich to Tripod as the company's director of communications. Berklich, now 26, graduated from Williams College in 1994, worked as a consultant in Cleveland for six months, and then returned to Williamstown to join

Tripod. She knew Bo Peabody from her college days and would have joined up right after graduation—but at that point, Tripod not only couldn't offer options; it couldn't even offer a livable salary. When Tripod was able to put together a package that included options, says Berklich, the company suddenly became much more attractive. "You think that eventually those options will become publicly traded stocks, whether through an IPO or through a buyout by a public company," she says.

Stewart and Berklich bet right. Last February, Tripod was bought by Lycos, one of the contending search engines-cum-Web portals, for $58 million. After the acquisition, Lycos stock rose by some 25 points and reached a high of 107. About six months after the acquisition, Lycos's stock split. Stewart and Berklich have had their Tripod options converted into Lycos options—an arrangement that will nevertheless bind them to Tripod for some time. "I continue to receive options in the company that continue to vest," says Berklich. "Lycos remains a really terrific financial opportunity."

Of course, underlying the popularity of stock options are three simple propositions about the nature of competition today. First, the real competition is over talent. Second, if you want to attract and keep talent, you have to pay for it. And third, if you want talent to work for your organization with the enthusiasm that comes with ownership, then you have to trade equity for it. These days, money does more than just talk. It creates glue.

Mission Makes a Difference

Xerox Parc guru John Seely Brown said it best: "The job of leadership today is not just to make money. It's to make meaning." When it comes to attracting, keeping, and making teams out of talented people, money alone won't do it. Talented people want to be part of something that they can believe in, something that confers meaning on their work and on their lives—something that involves a mission. And they don't want that mission to turn into the kind of predictable "mission statement" that plasters many a corporate-boardroom wall. Rather, they want spiritual goals that energize an organization by resonating with the personal values of the people who work there—the kind of mission that offers people a chance to do work that makes a difference. Along with the traditional bottom line, great enterprises have a second bottom line: a return on human investment that advances a larger purpose. A powerful mission is both a magnet and a motivator.

Meet David Bellshaw, 37, who six years ago joined Isaacson, Miller, a Boston-based boutique head-hunting firm. Isaacson, Miller has undertaken various head-hunt-ing tasks—including, for example, placing Dave Olson as CEO for Patagonia Inc. But the firm has carved out a special niche for itself by advancing women and minorities into executive positions and by finding leaders for a wide range of civic organizations and not-for-profit enterprises.

Bellshaw launched his career at the California office of Heidrick and Struggles, one of the leading head-hunting firms in the United States. When his wife, Ava, got into the Tufts University School of Medicine in Boston, Bellshaw considered several jobs with big firms in that city. But tiny Isaacson, Miller—smaller then than its 50-person staff today—stood out. A major reason why he joined up was "the company's unique mission," he says. "We are vicariously saving the world through our clients. That's a very, very strong pull for me."

Isaacson, Miller isn't just a head-hunting firm—it also helps its clients understand their own unique missions. The firm applies a mixture of psychological counseling and missionary zeal, while being attentive to the practical realities of good management.

Bellshaw comes to this calling naturally: His father was a Baptist minister, and so was his grandfather. "I rebelled against my background, and I still do—very actively," Bellshaw says. "But in some funny way, given my genes and upbringing, my work is a secular way of doing what my family has done. Two generations of ministers, and I broke the mold. Yet there remains a mission-driven theme in my life."

In his six years with Isaacson, Miller, Bellshaw has matched some high-powered people with some great organizations. One assignment: to find a new dean for New York University's Wagner School of Public Service—a place that trains the very sorts of civic leaders whom Isaacson, Miller recruits. The assignment wasn't easy. The school needed someone who combined administrative skills, a deep knowledge of both the public and the not-for-profit worlds, and an ability to define the future challenges of civic leadership, especially in the New York City area, where most of the school's graduates work.

How did Bellshaw begin? By sending an 11-page "Invitation to Apply" to 100 potential candidates. Among those who are rumored to have responded were former Colorado representative Pat Schroeder and former Ohio governor Dick Celeste. After an intensive search, Bellshaw selected Jo Ivey Boufford, then a high-ranking official in the U.S. Department of Health and Human Services and the U.S. representative on the executive board of the World Health Organization. Why choose Boufford from a list of such prestigious candidates? According to Bellshaw, not only did she have a proven track record as a manager, but she also had both a demonstrable interest in public service and the "New York-style gutsiness" needed for the position.

Another assignment: to find a new head for the Lovelace Institutes, a biomedical-research institute based in Albuquerque, New Mexico. Founded more than 50 years ago, Lovelace had seen its mission lose focus, and it needed a leader with the vision to set a new course and the management skills to implement the necessary reorganization. Bellshaw's pick to lead the institute: Robert Rubin, who had been the vice president of research at the University of Miami, where he had a reputation for taking risks and for demanding results. Soon after joining Lovelace in the fall of 1996, Rubin devised a solution to its problems: Completely reorganize the institute, rename it the Lovelace Respiratory Research Institute, and turn it into a national respiratory-research center. He plans to make Lovelace the leading authority on every aspect of research into respiratory disease.

How deep is David Bellshaw's commitment to Isaacson, Miller? Last May, when his wife accepted a medical residency at the University of California at San Francisco, Bellshaw had to make another decision: Would he leave the firm for a larger, more traditional head-hunting outfit in California—one that could pay him a lot of money? Or would he strike out on his own? In the end, Bellshaw says, the power of Isaacson, Miller's mission won out. He came up with a third option: He opened a new, West Coast office of the firm.

"It was a chance to do something that was interesting on a moral dimension, as well as an opportunity to build an office," he says. "The result is a blend of mission and market. With this job, I have all the mission of the best not-for-profits, and I also have all the rigors of the corporate world."

Learning Makes You Grow

In a knowledge-based economy, the new coin of the realm is learning. Want to build a business that can outlive its first good idea? Create a culture that values learning. Want to build a career that allows you to grow into new responsibilities? Maintain your hunger to learn—and join an organization where you'll be given the chance to learn continuously.

It's a proposition that fast companies have already figured out: Talented people join up in order to learn. Of course, part of the lure of learning goes back to the first "glue"—money. Learn more now, earn more in the future. But again, money is only part of the story. Talented people also want intellectual challenge: They like being explorers on the frontiers of the knowledge economy. And as apprentices have known for centuries, it's easiest to learn on the job—by working directly with people who can teach you and who are committed to the same goals you are.

Consider John Jordan, 40, director of electronic-commerce research at Ernst & Young LLP's Center for Business Innovation in Cambridge, Massachusetts. The center, which houses 35 people on two floors in an office designed with the ultramodern look-and-feel of a learning laboratory, functions as an in-house research and brainstorming facility for the 82,000-person, $9.1 billion global accounting and consulting firm.

If learning is a core competency, then Jordan already possesses it. Consider his degrees: a BA from Duke in political science and history, an MA from Yale in ethics, an MA and a PhD from the University of Michigan in American studies. But all of that education left Jordan hungry for something else: an understanding of the real business world. He could have opted for independence—freelancing for several clients—or he could have chosen to pursue various consulting roles. At the center, Jordan found the perfect blend of intellectual stimulation and real-world application, and an environment that keeps him glued to interesting people.

Part of the learning comes from contact with supercharged experts. "Working here has given me a rich Rolodex," Jordan says. "I'm invited to participate in a lot of stimulating conversations that I wouldn't take part in otherwise." The center taps various fields to bring in visiting fellows: a neuroscientist, a science-fiction writer, a provocative business-school professor, a magazine editor. "It's a group that I could never assemble on my own," says Jordan.

Being part of a high-powered think tank hasn't deprived Jordan of his autonomy. He largely designs his own goals, and he works to achieve them at a comfortable pace. And he's enlarged the scope of his work. "The brand called John Jordan has limited viability," he admits. His new brand has a much wider appeal.

Another part of the learning comes from the quality of the problems that cross Jordan's desk every day. The center acts as a kind of filter—screening out trivial issues and letting through only the hardest conceptual challenges. "The institutional affiliation gives you the leverage to do things you couldn't do on your own," he says. "The learning curve is so steep—I'm learning too much here to make going out on my own an attractive option."

Jordan's boss is Chris Meyer, who is himself an accomplished learner: Meyer, 50, graduated from Brandeis University, studied economics for two years at the University of Pennsylvania in its PhD program, and earned an MBA from Harvard Business School. As the director of the Center for Business Innovation, Meyer recruits people who want to learn from one another—a process that makes Ernst & Young a desirable place to work. "People are attracted to the company because working here helps them become better than they could be otherwise," says Meyer.

Through its cutting-edge innovations, the center also offers its people a window onto the future. "By coming here, you're learning not just how to identify the issues of the future but also how to do the work of the future," Meyer says. "Working in the knowledge economy requires the ability to recognize patterns, to share ideas with people inside and outside your organization, to maintain relationships with people who have common interests, and to pull value out of those relationships." Learning how to master those skills may be the most important kind of learning there is.

Fun Makes It Fresh

When people work as long and as hard as they do in today's competitive companies, when the line between huge financial success and total economic failure looks as thin as it does today, there's only one thing that can keep the energy in a workplace flowing: fun. Very simply, if work isn't fun, it won't attract the best talent. The lesson is so obvious that it's easily forgotten: Friendship and camaraderie are basic adhesives of the human spirit.

When David Stewart made the decision to abandon his legal career, one of the things that attracted him to Tripod was its convivial atmosphere. "We're in this little town," Stewart says, referring to quaint Williamstown. "We have a really cool office space on the top floor of a big mill, with a lot of people who wear shorts and T-shirts all the time. It's very relaxed."

Look at other high-tech upstarts, and you're likely to see the same thing: hard work harnessed to shared enjoyment. And you don't need to be in high-tech for this glue to work. Nancy Deibler, 50, manages Sprint's small-business-sales division in Kansas City, Missouri. There, more than 150 people sell telecommunications services to smaller businesses. It can be tedious work: The salespeople work eight-hour shifts, making cold calls—the kind of job that can turn into a grind, resulting in high employee turnover and a lot of customer dissatisfaction.

But Deibler and her crew have found a way to counteract the tedium. They've created a strong rapport within the team by building fun into their work—and as a result, Deibler has been able to attract and keep top performers. "Many of us really look forward to going to work because of the other people on the team," Deibler says. "We relate to and get along with each other as friends."

Making fun a legitimate part of work isn't all that difficult, Deibler says. For example, Deibler's team might leave work at 3 P.M. to go bowling. "After doing something like that," she says, "the difference that it makes is measurable and it lasts for weeks." Add baseball games, cookouts, goofy hats, evenings of karaoke, mock casinos, zany sports, dressing up staffers in costumes to deliver morning coffee to salespeople—a host of ways to introduce positive energy and a spirit of playfulness into the all-too-often all-too-serious work world. Deibler knows that all of this may seem hokey to some people—and she doesn't care. "It lifts productivity," she says.

But if you want to see what fun looks like both as a way of working and as a business, visit Playfair Inc., a Berkeley, California-based international consulting firm that devises innovative team-building and stress-reduction programs. Its distinctive business model: Celebrate wackiness, incorporate zaniness into the work process—and in short, have fun. Playfair's clients include FedEx, Dupont, AT&T, Charles Schwab, and the Young Presidents' Organization—not exactly the kinds of places where you'd expect to find a lot of blue jeans-wearing, pizza-eating, fun-loving business types playing a game for laughs. Yet since its founding in 1975, Playfair has proven that there's real bottom-line value in putting fun into the workplace: Fun attracts talent, and it improves productivity.

Terry Sand is Playfair's "senior vice empress"—an intentionally irreverent title for an exceptionally talented woman. Sand, who is in her forties, has a master's degree in modern dance and theater from UCLA, and began her career performing in films and commercials. A founding member of several improv-comedy groups, she won San Francisco's All-Pro Comedy Award in 1984 and went on to become a popular local-TV personality.

Then, in 1986, Sand was diagnosed with systemic lupus, a painful arthritic condition. "TV is very stressful," Sand says. "I love it, and I still do it for fun sometimes, but having it be your career—basing your life on ratings—is extremly high-stress. I couldn't do that and also do the healing I needed to do." Still, Sand noticed that whenever she had the opportunity to conduct a comedy class or workshop, her condition would improve. "To stay alive, I had to figure out how to make a living and have fun," she says.

Playfair provided the answer. Sand joined the firm's small roster of keynote speakers and trainers in 1989, and now she uses comedy and performance to convey Playfair's insights about the power of fun to improve teamwork and productivity. Meanwhile, the opportunity to perform and practice her comedy has served as important therapy for Sand: Her disease is in remission, and she's had no significant relapse in seven years. "My relationship with Playfair lets me be more of who I can be," Sand says.

Playfulness is almost always purposeful, the people at Playfair argue. A great company will harness people's natural spirit of fun and focus that spirit where it can do the most good. "Like children, adults play to learn—and learn through play," says Sand. "There's a profound purpose to it."

Pride Makes It Special

Why choose to work for this company rather than that one? Why attend one college rather than another? Why root for this team rather than that other team? The answer is elemental: We all like to be affiliated with an organization that feeds our sense of pride.

It could be because the place is hip: Talk to the staff people at any House of Blues club, and you'll hear about the pride they take in their company's way of doing business. Or it could be because the place is proper and precise: Talk to the concierge at any Four Seasons hotel, and she'll tell you how proud she is to work for an organization that delivers world-class service. "The few, the proud, the Marines" could be rewritten as a recruiting slogan for any great enterprise that uses its prestige strategically to attract and keep great people—the kind of people who will build on that sense of pride and enhance that sense of prestige.

Pride was a key factor in bringing Kevin Perry, 28, to Red Storm Entertainment Inc. 15 months ago. Red Storm, a Morrisville, North Carolina-based software-development house that creates and markets multimedia entertainment products, including interactive computer games and board games, has already scored a number of accolades in the game industry. Last summer, Red Storm released Rainbow Six, an action-strategy game that was the genesis for the novelist Tom Clancy's recent book of the same name—the first time that a book has been derived from a game. (The book, published this year by Putnam, has topped both the *New York Times* and *USA Today* best-seller lists.) Red Storm will release three new games by the end of 1998, and eight more games are incubating for 1999.

Amid all of this creative energy, Perry enjoys a plum assignment: He leads a team charged with creating a new interactive computer game, ruthless.com, which should be out this season. The game, says Perry, replicates the big-money world of modern corporate raiding, blending high-stakes strategy with low-down ruthlessness: "It

combines the crushing grip of business expansion with rapier-like strikes of deceit, dirty tricks, and outright crime," he says.

But fast action isn't the only thing that makes Perry proud to be part of Red Storm. He had his choice of firms—including the choice not to commit to any one shop. What made Perry choose to join this company was the fact that Tom Clancy not only works with Red Storm—he also founded the company and chairs its board. "This is a cool place to work," Perry says. And Clancy's involvement "really helps us make a splash. People know that Red Storm is not some flash in the pan run by a 16-year-old out of his garage. Tom's association with the company really opens a lot of doors."

Red Storm Entertainment is quickly gaining a reputation not just for its bread-and-butter Tom Clancy military-strategy games but also as a top-notch developer of other kinds of computer games. The company is riding a virtuous circle: As Red Storm's reputation rises, it attracts more talent (like Perry)—and the more talent it taps, the more its reputation will continue to rise.

A different kind of pride attracts talented people to venerable institutions like Goldman Sachs, Yale University, General Electric, and Covington and Burling, a prestigious law firm in Washington, DC. What these institutions lack in hipness, they more than make up for in old-fashioned prestige. Membership in these enterprises confers status—and status is a form of capital.

But beware: The cycle can shift into reverse if an organization's prestige degenerates, leaving a once-proud brand in its place. Unless a firm continues to add real financial value—or is grounded in a strong ethical mission, in mutual learning, or in fun and excitement— what's "hot" or prestigious today can become unfashionable tomorrow. Status can turn stagnant, and no one wants to be affiliated with an organization that has lost its vital energy. When that happens, talented people can be as easy to lure away as they were to lure in—and the best people are usually the first to go.

Balance Makes It Sustainable

Talk to almost anyone in any company at any level, and you'll hear the same words: "I love what I'm doing, but I'm way too busy to get a life." Equal parts boast and complaint, that is the most pervasive refrain of the new economy. The problem is balance—or, more simply, sanity. And it's the last, but perhaps most important, adhesive that companies are using to lure and keep talented people. The best enterprises know this and are winning talented people by offering balanced work.

Easy to say it, easy to promise it. What distinguishes

the best companies, however, is not that they recognize how important balance is to attracting talent—it's how they create such balance in their organizations. Not long ago, any decent listing of "great places to work" would identify companies large and small that offered a preset "Chinese menu" of programs for balancing work and life: maternity and paternity leave, company-sponsored day care and elder care, regular retreats and periodic sabbaticals, flextime and even flexplace. In the new economy, the kind of balance that attracts people isn't a set of programs. Rather, it's a way of doing business. Balance is deeply embedded in the company's core—a compelling part of its corporate DNA.

Consider Great Plains Software, a leading vendor of financial-management software for midsize companies. Great Plains is headquartered in Fargo, North Dakota, in a two-story office building wedged between corn fields and a bingo parlor—not exactly a hip location. But Great Plains has attracted, developed, and retained some of the most talented people in its line of business. With 850 employees, the company has a turnover rate of 7% a year, which is almost unheard-of the famously volatile software industry. Great Plains also has a robust revenue stream—bringing in almost $86 million in fiscal 1998, up 50% over 1997—and a roster of loyal customers, including Adidas, the Detroit Lions, Cinnabon Bakeries, and the Girl Scouts of America.

What's the secret? Great Plains not only offers a balanced life—it lives one. Tami Reller, 34, has been with Great Plains since she graduated from Moorhead State University in Moorhead, Minnesota, in the spring of 1987. Her career with the company, where she began as an intern, is one long testament to the value of flexibility. "I was amazed at the company's level of commitment to helping interns succeed and stay with the company," Reller says. Her first assignment was in the company's finance operation at its headquarters in Fargo. Then she moved to San Francisco to train in sales. After seven years there, Reller felt ready for a move into the rank of corporate management—but she didn't want to leave California. No problem: Great Plains didn't want her to leave the company either, so it gave her a senior position in corporate marketing and allowed her to telecommute to Fargo—and, by the way, to finish an MBA while working part-time for three months.

That arrangement lasted until 1996, when, for family reasons, Reller moved to Minneapolis. Still no problem: Now she directs finance and investor relations from there. The next development: In a few months, Reller will give birth to her first child. Is she worried about balance? Not a bit—Great Plains lets its people take voluntary time off while keeping benefits.

"For me, balance means having the flexibility to choose what to accomplish and how I want to accomplish it—in my career, my job, my personal life," Reller says. "It's not simply an issue of not working 8-to-5. It's the ability to accomplish the big things in life—like finishing an MBA or having a child."

The Great Plains approach is to hire the best people it can find and then to give them maximum freedom to get their work done—however, whenever, and wherever they choose to work. "We have really smart people who know what they need to accomplish," Reller says. "You find a way to get the work done in the hours that you need. Sometimes that's 30 hours a week; sometimes it's 70 hours a week."

Doug Burgum, 42, Great Plains's chairman and CEO, explains how the system works. "We put people through a vigorous hiring process and through a lot of interviews. Once they're part of the team, we say, 'We trust you.' From day one, you get a key to the building. You get a laptop. You become an equal member of our community, and we trust that you're going to pull your weight."

None of that happens by accident. When Burgum began with the company in 1983, he understood that it needed something more than good software to become competitive. Great Plains's edge would be in the quality of its people—in their ability to provide first-class customer support and to develop strong relationships with suppliers and vendors. How do you attract the best people when your headquarters is in Fargo, North Dakota? By recruiting carefully, selectively, and rigorously—and then by giving those you hire the power to organize their work by themselves.

"Balance is not about taking off the day when your kid gets sick," Burgum says. Any company can give employees that sort of flexibility. "Balance is what's needed when your kids are playing in a softball tournament, and they really want you to be there. We want parents to be able to say yes to their kids. There's a huge amount of value in giving people the opportunity to say yes to things that are important to them but that may conflict with their regular working hours."

For Burgum, the idea of balance goes deeper than simply juggling tasks and appointments. "It's important to have flexibility over a life span or a career span," he says. "There has to be a deeper level of personal satisfaction, a sense that things are all right. If you can help people find that level, they tend to stick around." Burgum is proud of Great Plain's extraordinarily low turnover. "That's no small accomplishment in an industry where so much of a company's assets are linked to individual employees' knowledge," he says.

The 21st-Century Company

What do all of these new enterprises have in common? They are only as good as their most talented people. And they don't take the loyalty of those people for granted. They understand that talented people have never had more options. So these companies have developed strategies to recruit and keep people from whom they want total commitment.

What do the joiners have in common? They could have gone anywhere. They had their pick of the best. Many could have successful careers as free agents. They've chosen to join up—to commit themselves, at least for a time—because the mix of social glue in one organization was overwhelmingly strong.

The big change today, then, is not the absolute demise of loyalty in the workplace. Nor is it the evolution of free agency into the only way that people can work. The basic facts of work life are the same as they've always been: Everybody works for somebody or something—be it a board of directors, a pension fund, a venture capitalist, or a traditional boss. Sooner or later, you're going to have to decide whom you want to work for. And everybody works with someone else. The linkage may be tight, or it may be loose. But you've got to decide who to work with, as well as how strong the bonds of mutual commitment will be.

The big change is in the amount of choice and the variety of experiences available in today's workplace: Talented people are actively shopping for colleagues and bosses who meet their needs and match their values. The market for talent—the sellers of it, the buyers of it—is the most vital market in the modern economy. To attract and keep talented people, companies today are not just experimenting with how they approach the competitive marketplace of goods and services. They're also experimenting with how they approach the competitive marketplace of talent. Companies are testing the attractiveness of various combinations of social glue, and they are recognizing that unusual benefits attract unusual people—and that what works in one industry, or at one time, may not work in another industry, or at another time. Deployed carefully, these social glues become stronger through use: Each can attract talent in a way that makes an enterprise even more attractive to the same kind of talent in the future.

More fundamentally, companies are experimenting with a new operating system for the employer-employee relationship—one to replace the old set of practices that put employers and employees on opposite sides of the table. The model for the organization of the future aims to create tangible and intangible value that both sides can share and enjoy. It accepts as a core reality—rather than as a pleasant fantasy—the old saw that a company's people are its most important asset. And it builds on that reality to create a way of working that is profoundly human and fundamentally humane.

It is a revolutionary notion: Collaboration and mutual advantage are the essence of the organization. They can create flexibility, resiliency, speed, and creativity—the fundamental qualities of the company of the 21st century.

ARTICLE 2

Life In The Fast Lane

....

by Chuck Salter

To finish first, you have to work fast. Ray Evernham—NASCAR's top crew chief and the man behind racecar champ Jeff Gordon—offers lessons from the pit on teamwork, surprise, and the pursuit of perfection.

Business is more demanding than ever, more perilous than ever—and faster than ever. Every company is rushing to launch the next great product, to seal the next big deal. No company knows what's waiting around the next corner.

It Sounds a Lot Like Auto Racing

Ray Evernham knows a little something about business. He's a key player in an enterprise that generates millions of dollars in annual revenues, and he's lectured audi-

First appeared: Fast Company issue 18 page 175
Reprinted with permission from Fast Company Magazine

ences of business executives from DuPont, Digital, and Ingersoll-Rand. But Evernham knows even more about racing. He's widely considered to be the premier crew chief in NASCAR, the National Association for Stock Car Auto Racing. Over the past five years, he and his team have steered the DuPont-sponsored No. 24 car and its celebrated driver, Jeff Goron, from anonymity to unprecedented success in the Winston Cup Series—the big leagues of stock-car racing.

Evernham and Gordon burst onto the Winston Cup scene in 1993, when Gordon walked away with the Cup's Rookie of the Year honors. In 1994, Evernham was named Crew Chief of the Year. And in 1995, Gordon and Evernham hit the jackpot when Gordon won the Winston Cup Championship, the culmination of a grueling race for points that stretches from February to November. Gordon, then just 24, was the Winston Cup's youngest-ever champion. After garnering 10 wins in 1996 (good for second place that year), he and Evernham teamed up for another Winston Cup Championship in 1997. Their $4.2 million in prize money set a new record for total regular-season earnings in one year of racing. During their six years as a team, Evernham and Gordon have celebrated 37 victories, including wins in NASCAR's major races—the Daytona 500, the Coca-Cola 600 (three times), and the Brickyard 400 (twice).

Gordon's sudden dominance, combined with his youth, charisma, and leading-man looks, has made him the hottest commodity in the fastest-growing sport around. He's everywhere: on Leno and Letterman, on *People* magazine's 50 Most Beautiful People list. And on many Sundays, he's in victory lane. He gives much of the credit for his success to Evernham and to the pit crew know as the Rainbow Warriors. (Crew members wear rainbow-striped jumpsuits.)

Gordon is the star attraction, to be sure. But it's Evernham, 41, who pulls the whole act together. It's Evernham, an indefatigable perfectionist, who ensures that the No. 24 car—a 700-horsepower Chevrolet Monte Carlo—is the fastest on the track; who leads the daring pit stop that takes place with 20 laps to go; who pushes the Rainbow Warriors to be the best crew in the business, week after week.

Fast Company visited Evernham at the Hendrick Motorsports complex in Harrisburg, North Carolina, just north of Charlotte. In between signing autographs, speaking at a sponsor's lunch, and fine-tuning the No. 24 car, Evernham took time out to reflect on what it takes to finish first: painstaking preparation, egoless teamwork, and thoroughly original strategizing—principles that apply to any company that understands the need for speed.

New Teams Should Do Things in New Ways

One reason we got off to such a fast start when the Rainbow Warrior team was assembled five years ago was that, right from the beginning, we dared to be different. I didn't hire anybody for the team who had Winston Cup experience. Racing is racing; the right people can figure it out. I wanted people who had the desire and the intelligence needed to excel.

When you have a team with different kinds of people, you get a chance to do things differently. We came up with innovative ideas about the mechanics of the car—about things like suspension components and shock absorbers—partly because we didn't know any better. And we hired a separate crew to work solely in the pits. Traditionally, the same mechanics who worked on the car all week also suited up on Sunday to work as the pit crew. The car was the number-one priority: People relied on horsepower and driving talent to win the day. But I believe that the crew should be as important as the car.

We were also the first team to hire a coach specifically to train and rehearse the pit crew. People laughed at the way we trained: rope climbing, wind sprints, guys carrying each other on their backs. People said, "What in the world are you guys doing?" I'm sure that it all looked funny, but it worked. Typically, we pit in 17 seconds or less—about a second faster than other teams do. In one second, a car going 200 mph travels nearly 300 feet. So right there, we gain 300 feet on the competition.

You Win as a Team

When you coach and support a superstar like Jeff Gordon, you give him the best equipment possible, you give him the information he needs, and then you get out of the way. But racing is a team sport. Everyone who races pretty much has the same car and the same equipment. What sets us apart is our people. I like to talk about our "team IQ"—because none of us is as smart as all of us.

I think a lot about people, management, and psychology: Specifically, how can I motivate my guys and make them gel as a team? I surround them with ideas about teamwork. I read every leadership book I can get my hands on. One thing that I took from my reading is the idea of a "circle of strength." When the Rainbow Warriors meet, we always put our chairs in a circle. That's a way of saying that we're stronger as a team than we are on our own.

I also base rewards on team performance rather than individual performance. When our car wins, everybody shares in the prize money. And everybody gets a cut of what I make. I put a percentage of my bonus into the team account. When I sign a personal-service contract and I get paid to sign autographs or to give a talk, everybody shares in what I earn. I wouldn't be in a position to earn that income if it weren't for the team. Everyone should feel as if his signature is on the finished product.

Push for Perfection—but Accept Imperfection

This sport is so competitive that you must never stop trying to improve. Even when the car is running well, I make Jeff find something wrong with it. A lot of people who hear him talking to me on the radio think that he's complaining. He's not. I've got a series of questions that I ask him over and over. I'm pumping him for information. I'm trying to find out exactly how Jeff feels in that car. The only time when we stop working on our setup is when it's time to race.

We always try to make the car perfect. But the car doesn't have to be perfect to win; it just has to be less imperfect than everyone else's car. Last year, on the very first pit stop at the Coca-Cola 600, we dropped the car off the jack and banged up the front end, leaving the car aerodynamically flawed. It took us three or four pit stops to straighten the fender. But we still won. After all, we had hundreds of laps in which to recover from that mistake.

Take risks, but don't gamble. When we're going into a race, we always have a clear strategy. But we can't predict exactly what's going to happen. Change is part of racing. Sometimes during a race, it looks as if I'm making a daring call. Well, I may be taking a risk, but I'm not gambling. I've calculated everything beforehand. I'm constantly looking at four or five possible scenarios: At the next pit stop, are we going to put in all of the gas or only half of it? Are we going to add air to the tires or let some out? Are we going to raise or lower the track bar to adjust the "roll center"—which alters the steering? There are so many variables to consider, and the slightest adjustment can make a huge difference in the car's performance. A race may come down to whether we change two tires or four. I need to make the right call.

[*Editor's Note:* Two days after this interview, the Coca-Cola 600 came down to just such a decision about tires. With 21 laps to go and with Gordon trailing the leaders, a caution flag went up. While the other cars changed two tires, Evernham opted to take longer in the pit and to change all four. When the green flag came out, Gordon easily sped past the others—and on to victory.]

To Speed Up, Slow Down

I still have to prove this principle to Jeff sometimes, I'll say, "Go out and bust me a lap." He'll drive the car hard, really work it. He'll mash the pedal on a straightaway, drive down into a corner, jam the brakes, turn the corner, and mash the pedal again. Then I'll say, "Now take it easy, and drive a smooth lap." And by letting the car do the work, he actually improves his time.

The same principle applies to a pit stop. Watch Mike Trower, my best tire changer, at work, and you'll swear that the guy next to him will be done first. You'll be thinking, "I wish Mike would hurry up." But nobody can beat him. He just looks as if he's going slow. It's all the choreography. If you watch Mike change a tire, you'll see how efficient he is: He's so deliberate that he never has to hit a lug nut twice. It's "zzzt–zzzt–zzzt." Nice and smooth.

Don't Strut Your Stuff

There aren't many secrets in the Winston Cup, so you've got to protect as much information as you can. We want to have the fastest car on the track, but we don't want everybody else to know how fast we are. We don't show our hand until it's time to race or to qualify.

We also try to mix things up on race day. We don't want to fall into patterns or to tip off the competition about our next pit stop. Since everybody can hear us on the scanners, we might use a code word to signal whether we're changing two tires or four. Sometimes, when the car is running well, Jeff might get on the radio and complain to me that the steering's tight, even though he's about to pass another driver. And that driver's crew chief will fall for it: "Yeah, Gordon can't pass you right now, because he's tight." The driver will leave a little opening and—boom—we're past him.

To Win the Race, Drive by Different Rules

We attack certain race tracks differently from how everybody else does. If conventional wisdom says, "This corner is the best place to pass," we practice on the other end of the track, because nobody's expecting to get passed there. If you can hold your own where others plan to pass, and then sneak up and get by the others on another part of the track, you can gain an advantage.

We've done this at Darlington Raceway. Traditionally, at Darlington, you pass when you come off turn number two, because you can carry more speed into that turn than elsewhere. We worked hard at being good there, so we could avoid getting passed and so we could pass if we had to. But we also worked at being better around the rest of the track than most cars are. That extra work helped us win the Mountain Dew Southern 500 last year.

Face Down Your Toughest Competitor: Success

I have a saying posted in the shop: "Success is a ruthless competitor for it flatters and nourishes our weakness and lulls us into complacency." When you win, if you're not careful—if you don't pay attention to how your team is handling success—you'll stop doing the things that put you on top. You've got to be very critical of what you do. Remember, the other teams are looking at how you beat them last Sunday, and they're trying to figure out how to beat you next Sunday. You can't let up.

ARTICLE 3
Danger: Toxic Company

by Alan M. Webber

The problem isn't that loyalty is dead or that careers are history. The real problem, argues Stanford's Jeffrey Pfeffer, is that so many companies are toxic—and that they get exactly what they deserve.

According to Jeffrey Pfeffer, when it comes to the link between people and profits, companies get exactly what they deserve. Companies that treat their people right get enormous dividends: high rates of productivity, low rates of turnover. Companies that treat their people poorly experience the opposite—and end up complaining about the death of loyalty and the dearth of talent. These are "toxic workplaces," according to Pfeffer, 52, the Thomas D. Dee Professor of Organizational Behavior at the Stanford Graduate School of Business and the author of *The Human Equation: Building Profits by Putting People First* (Harvard Business School Press, 1998).

Pfeffer disputes much of the conventional wisdom in the current conversation about work and business. Loyalty isn't dead, he insists—but toxic companies are driving people away. There isn't a scarcity of talent—but there is a growing unwillingness to work for toxic organizations. Pfeffer also disputes the idea of the end of the career. "I don't believe that people are looking to go flitting from one job to the next," he says. "People are looking for the opportunity to have variety in their work and to tackle challenging assignments. The best companies are figuring out how their employees can have both opportunities—without leaving." When Fast Company interviewed the plain-talking, provocative Pfeffer in his Palo Alto office, he offered the following observations about the primacy of people in the new economy and about how you can detoxify your workplace.

The One Guaranteed Way to Get a 30% to 40% Productivity Gain

It mystifies me that so many companies think they can get a cheap competitive advantage by purchasing something on the open market! Anything that you can purchase on the open market is also available to your competitors. So the question is, How can you distinguish yourself in a world in which your competitors can copy everything you do?

The answer is, all that separates you from your competitors are the skills, knowledge, commitment, and abilities of the people who work for you. There is a very compelling business case for this idea: Companies that manage people right will outperform companies that don't by 30% to 40%. This principle even applies to the current IPO market: IPO firms that value their people have a much higher five-year survival rate than those that don't. Similar studies of the steel industry, the oil-refining industry, the apparel industry, and the semiconductor industry all demonstrate the enormous productivity benefits that come with implementing high-performance, high-involvement management practices.

Most people immediately understand this point. It's not as though I've discovered some mysterious black magic. There is conclusive evidence that holds for all industries, regardless of their type, size, or age. The results are the same. If you don't believe me, look at the numbers.

First appeared: Fast Company issue 19 page 152
Reprinted with permission from Fast Company Magazine

"Welcome to the Toxic Workplace! We Fire at Will!"

There is a lot of turnover in Silicon Valley, because there are so many toxic workplaces in Silicon Valley. These are companies that create the conditions that they deplore. Companies say to me, "Nobody who comes to work for us stays for any length of time. Loyalty is dead." Let's accept that premise for a moment—even though it's wrong. But if we do accept that premise, the question becomes, If loyalty is dead, who killed it?

Companies killed loyalty—by becoming toxic places to work! Start with the interviewing and recruiting process. What happens on a new employee's first day? The company asks the employee to sign an at-will employment contract that gives the company the right to fire the person at any time and for any reason. The document was prepared by a lawyer; the company tells the employee to have it reviewed by a lawyer before signing it.

Think about it: It's your first day on the job, and I've already told you that you don't have a permanent employment relationship with me, that your job is based on a contractual relationship—and then I wonder why, on your second day, you're not approaching me with a long-term perspective and a feeling of trust!

A Place Where People Come to Work to Get Rich Enough to Quit

Here's another example of a practice that creates the conditions that companies deplore: stock options. David Russo, the head of human resources for SAS Institute, gave a talk to my class. My students were dumbfounded to learn that this successful software-development company doesn't offer its people stock options. David said, "You must know lots of people who have gotten stock options. Why do they want them? Explain the logic."

Finally, one of my students raised his hand and said, "I can tell you the logic. For most people, stock options are like the lottery. People are hoping to strike it rich and then quit." David smiled and said, "What an interesting thing! We've built an organization in which your motivation for coming to work is to make a lot of money—so that you can get the hell out of the organization."

To me, that's an operational definition of a toxic workplace: It's a place where people come to work so they can make enough money so they can leave. Dennis Bakke, of Applied Energy Services Corp. (AES), likes to point to a photo of the top 20 people at his company. The photo was taken more than a decade ago, and today 17 of those 20 people are still there. They're all plenty wealthy—because AES has grown tremendously. They all could have quit. The fact that they didn't says a lot about that company.

Toxic Flextime: "Work any 18 Hours You Want."

Another sign that a company is toxic: It requires people to choose between having a life and having a career. A toxic company says to people, "We want to own you." There's an old joke that they used to tell about working at Microsoft: "We offer flexible time—you can work any 18 hours you want."

A toxic company says, "We're going to put you in a situation where you have to work in a style and on a pace that is not sustainable. We want you to come in here and burn yourself out—and then you can leave." That's one thing that SAS manages brilliantly: When you take a job there, you don't have to ask yourself, "Am I going to be a successful and effective SAS employee, or am I going to know the names of my children?"

What's the Difference Between a Factor of Production and a Human Being?

Another sign of a toxic workplace is that the company treats its people as if they were a factor of production. At a toxic workplace, the managers can reel off all of the various economic factors: "We've got capital that we invest, we've got raw material that we use, we've got the waste from the manufacturing process that we recycle—and, in the same category, we've got our people." It's a workplace that doesn't see people as people, but rather sees them as factors of production. And that's ironic, because what we celebrate as a competitive, capitalistic practice actually reflects a Marxist orientation: People are seen as a factor of production, from which a company has to extract an economic "surplus."

There is a huge difference between that perspective and the way AES, for example, looks at its people. Dennis Bakke even objects to the term "human resources." Dennis says that fuel is a resource—but that people aren't. Underlying this difference in language is a difference in philosophy that guides much of what a company does. If a company looks at you merely as a factor of production, then every day it must calculate whether your marginal revenue exceeds your marginal cost. That's how it decides whether or not to keep you.

If Your Company Is So Great, Why Doesn't Anyone Want to Work There?

You hear a lot about the shortage of talent. The thing to remember is that, for great workplaces, there is no shortage of talent. Companies that are short on talent probably deserve to be! Anyone who is smart enough to work in a high-tech company is too smart to work in a toxic workplace. And if they do work in one, as soon as they have a choice, they choose to leave.

For example, according to David Russo, SAS Institute had a 3% voluntary-turnover rate in 1997. SAS almost never loses one of its people to a competitor, he says. When it does lose people, it's usually because of a lifestyle change or because someone at the company has to move to a place where there is no SAS facility.

That kind of thing is happening across the economy. Hewlett-Packard has lower turnover than many of its competitors. The Men's Wearhouse has lower turnover than many other companies in the retail industry. Starbucks has comparatively lower turnover than other companies in the fast-food business. Of course, none of these companies is perfect. But a company that says, "We want to create a place that attracts people, that makes them want to stay," will have lower turnover than places that say, "We don't care about our people's well-being or about whether they stay." And then, when these toxic companies conduct themselves in this way, they wonder why people leave.

Which Is Better Business—Paying Signing Bonuses or Treating People Right?

High turnover costs big money. First of all, it costs money to go out and replace all of the people you've lost. If the companies in Silicon Valley that are losing people would stop paying $50,000 signing bonuses and instead do what's necessary to keep the people they've got, they would be much better off economically. Along with incurring replacement costs, when you lose people, you lose knowledge, you lose experience, and you lose customer relationships. Every time a customer interacts with your company, he or she sees a different person. I like to go to my branch bank because I know that I'll always make a new friend there: The turnover is so high, I'm always meeting new people!

There is nothing soft and sentimental about this part of the argument. This is simple economics. David Russo did a calculation in my class one day: A student asked him why SAS does so much family-friendly stuff. He said, "We have something like 5,000 employees. Our turnover rate last year was 3%. What's the industry average?" Somebody said 20%. Russo replied, "Actually, 20% is low, but I don't care. We'll use 20%. The difference between 20% and 3% is 17%. Multiply 17% by 5,000 people, and that's 850 people. What does turnover cost per person? Calculate it in terms of salary." The students estimated

that the cost is one year's salary and that the average salary is $60,000. Russo said, "Both of those figures are low, but that doesn't matter. I'll use them. Multiply $60,000 by 850 people, and that's more than $50 million in savings."

That's how Russo pays for the SAS gymnasium, for on-site medical care, for all of the company's other family-friendly items. "Plus," he said. "I've got tons of money left over." If you can save $50 million a year in reduced turnover, you're talking about real financial savings. This is not tree-huggery. This is money in the bank.

When You Look at Your People, What Do You See—Expenses or Assets?

You've got to ask a question that gets back to an old cliche: Do you walk the talk? It's easy for a company to say, "We invest in people. We believe in training. We believe in mutual commitments between the managers and the workforce. We believe in sharing information widely with our people."

Many organizations say those things—but in their heart of hearts, they don't believe them. Most managers, if they're being honest with themselves, will admit it: When they look at their people, they see costs, they see salaries, they see benefits, they see overhead. Very few companies look at their people and see assets.

In part, it's because of the financial-reporting systems that we've got. The fact is, your salary is an expense. If I buy a computer to replace you, I can capitalize the computer and then depreciate its useful life over many years. If I hire you, I take on an expense.

But there are other things that companies can measure. Whole Foods Market Inc. and AES, for instance, not only do employee surveys; they also take them seriously. I know of managers at Hewlett-Packard who were fired because they received such poor reviews from their employees.

Why Nothing Changes #1: Wishing Doesn't Make It So

Everybody knows what to do, but nobody does it. For example, a lot of companies confuse talk with action. They believe that, because they've said it, it's actually happened. One of my students did a research project on the internship program at a large Wall Street securities company. Under the program, the firm hired interns right out of college; then, after a few years, the interns would go back to business school. But the program was catastrophic. The firm treated the interns like dog doo, and that had two bad consequences. First, the interns didn't go back to work for the firm after business school, so the two or three years that the firm had invested in them were wasted. Second, and even worse, when the interns arrived at Harvard, Stanford, Chicago, or Northwestern, they would tell all of the other business-school students that the firm was horse manure—which made its recruiting difficult, to say the least. At some level, people at the firm understood these problems. So the senior leadership asked my student, who had interned there, to help the firm fix its program.

After she had done a bunch of interviews, she told them, "You have a model that says you're going to treat people with respect and dignity. Let me tell you the 30 things—and that's a low number—that you do to your interns that violate your model."

When the top people at the firm heard her report, they said, "This can't be. The core values of this firm are respect for the individual, treating the individual with dignity, and teamwork. We believe in these values." In effect, they were saying, "Because we believe it, it must be happening." These were not bad people. They just thought that their wishes had become reality.

Why Nothing Changes #2: Memory Is No Substitute for Thinking

There's another reason why companies don't do what they know they should: They fall prey to the power of precedents. They do something once, and then they get trapped by their own history: This is the way we do it because this is the way we've always done it. They substitute memory ("We did it this way before") for thinking ("Is this a sensible way to do it?").

Not long ago, I went to a large, fancy San Francisco law firm—where they treat their associates like dog doo and where the turnover is very high. I asked the managing partner about the turnover rate. He said, "A few years ago, it was 25%, and we're now up to 30%." I asked him how the firm had responded to that trend. He said, "We increased our recruiting." So I asked him, "What kind of doctor would you be if your patient was bleeding faster and faster, and your only response was to increase the speed of the transfusion?"

But what this law firm knew how to do was recruit. Over the preceding five years, it had created 162 partners—and it had lost 163 people in the same period. It preferred undertaking lavish recruitment efforts to dealing with the root causes of the turnover. People do what they know how to do. This law firm knows how to recruit—so it steps up recruiting. But what it hasn't thought about for five seconds is how to solve the underlying problem.

How to Make Something Change: Start with You

Where do you start? You start with a philosophy, and the rest follows from that. If you believe in training and developing people, you don't necessarily need a huge training budget. You begin by imparting knowledge in various ways—by holding meetings, by talking to people, by coaching them, by mentoring them. If you believe in reciprocal commitments, you start by building those commitments with the people you work with. If you believe in information sharing, you share information with the people you have the most contact with. In other words, you begin in your immediate sphere of influence. You start with your own behavior.

ARTICLE 4
Learning for a Change

by Alan M. Webber

Ten years ago, Peter Senge introduced the idea of the "learning organization." Now he says that for big companies to change, we need to stop thinking like mechanics and to start acting like gardeners.

It's been almost 10 years since Peter Senge, 51, pub-

First appeared: Fast Company issue 24 page 178

lished *The Fifth Discipline: The Art & Practice of the Learning Organization* (Doubleday/Currency, 1990). The book was more than a business best-seller; it was a breakthrough. It propelled Senge into the front ranks of management thinkers; it created a language of change that people in all kinds of companies could embrace; and it offered a vision of workplaces that were humane and of companies that were built around learning. Along the way, the book sold more than 650,000 copies, spawned a sequel—*The Discipline Fieldbook: Strategies and Tools for Building a Learning Organization* (Doubleday/Currency, 1994)—and gave birth to a worldwide movement.

But that movement hit a few speed bumps. People who adopted the themes and practices of *The Fifth Discipline* sometimes found themselves frustrated by the challenge of bringing about effective change—and sometimes found themselves out of work for trying. Now Senge and his colleagues have published *The Dance of Change: The Challenges to Sustaining Momentum in Learning Organizations* (Doubleday/Currency, March 1999). According to Senge, who is a senior lecturer at the Massachusetts Institute of Technology and a member of the Society for Organizational Learning (SoL)—a global consortium of companies and researchers who are examining learning and change—the new book presents "what we've learned about learning." The book begins with two key lessons: First, initiating and sustaining change is more daunting than the optimistic presentation that was offered in *The Fifth Discipline* had suggested. And second, the task of making change happen requires businesspeople to change the way they think about organizations: "We need to think less like managers and more like biologists," Senge argues.

To learn more about the evolving landscape of organizational learning, Fast Company interviewed Peter Senge in his office on the campus of MIT, in Cambridge, Massachusetts.

What's Your Assessment of the Performance of Large-Scale Change Efforts over the Past Decade?

Most leadership strategies are doomed to failure from the outset. As people have been noting for years, the majority of strategic initiatives that are driven from the top are marginally effective—at best. Corporate reorganizations are even more common than new strategies, but how many reorganizations actually produce companies that are dramatically more effective than they were before? Throw in mergers and acquisitions: Look at all of those that have failed. The traditional model of change—change that is led from the top—has a less-than-impressive track record.

And that's just the public track record. My own experience at MIT and at SoL has mostly been with big companies. How much change have they actually accomplished? If I stand back a considerable distance and ask, "What's the score?" I have to conclude that inertia is winning by a large margin. Of course, there have been enough exceptions to that conclusion to indicate that

change is possible. I can identify 20 to 30 examples of significant sustained change efforts in the SoL community. On the other side of the ledger, there are many organizations that haven't gotten to first base when it comes to real change, and many others that have given up trying.

When I look at efforts to create change in big companies over the past 10 years, I have to say that there's enough evidence of success to say that change is possible—and enough evidence of failure to say that it isn't likely. Both of those lessons are important.

Why Haven't There Been More Successful Change Efforts?

If it were simply a matter of more resources, people would have figured out how to get more resources. If it were a matter of more time, more money, more consultants, or just more effort, we probably would have been able to fill those needs by now. Or if the problem were intelligence—and you could simply assert that most bosses are pretty dumb or that most CEOs are just not very bright—then presumably the intelligent ones would succeed, their companies would rise to the top, and that would solve the problem. The marketplace would reward the bright ones who could change, and it would punish the dumb ones who couldn't.

But it doesn't seem as if any of those things are happening—which suggests that it's not a matter of resources or intelligence. In fact, I can tell you from firsthand experience that a lot of very competent executives fail at producing and sustaining momentum around change. That suggests to me that something more universal is at work here.

So What Is the Deeper Explanation for the Failure of Corporate Change Efforts?

At the deepest level, I think that we're witnessing the shift from one age to another. The most universal challenge that we face is the transition from seeing our human institutions as machines to seeing them as embodiments of nature. I've been thinking about this shift for 25 years or more: We need to realize that we're a part of nature, rather than separate from nature.

Think about any environmental problem that we face, from global climate and resource issues to population crises. Or look at the problems that seem to afflict people in organizations: Why are contemporary institutions so inhumane? And somewhere in the middle, between environmental issues and personal issues, there are institutional issues: Why do we view our organizations as rigid hierarchies rather than as communities of practice?

Whether you're talking at the macro, the personal, or the institutional level, the questions all point in the same direction: The real character of an age is evident in how it conditions us to think, and how it conditions us to think determines how it conditions us to act. The thinking and acting of the past 200 years—nurtured in Europe, accelerated in the United States, diffused throughout the world today—is a machine mind-set. That mind-set directly affects how we see organizations—and, therefore, how we think about creating change in those organizations.

What Implications Does a Machine Mind-Set Have for Companies that Seek to Undergo Change?

In the Machine Age, the company itself became a machine—a machine for making money. That's a key point in Arie de Geus's book, *The Living Company* (Harvard Business School Press, 1997). Ironically, the word "company" couldn't be more at odds with the idea of a machine. "Company" has roots that go back long before the Industrial Age. In fact, it has the same root as the word "companion": It means "the sharing of bread."

Somehow, during the course of the Industrial Revolution, this very humane sense of "company" changed, and the company became more and more machinelike. For the most part, seeing the company as a machine has worked. There are people who design this machine: They put it together and get it up and working. They are founders. There are people who operate or control the machine: We call them managers. The machine also has owners, and when it operates correctly, it produces income for those owners. It's all about control: A good machine is one that its operators can control—in the service of its owners' objectives.

The company-as-a-machine model fits how people think about and operate conventional companies. And, of course, it fits how people think about changing conventional companies: You have a broken company, and you need to change it, to fix it. You hire a mechanic, who trades out old parts that are broken and brings in new parts that are going to fix the machine. That's why we need "change agents" and leaders who can "drive change."

But go back and consider all of the evidence that says that most change efforts aren't very successful. Here is our first plausible explanation: Companies are actually living organisms, not machines. That might explain why it's so difficult for us to succeed in our efforts to produce change. Perhaps treating companies like machines keeps them from changing, or makes changing them much more difficult. We keep bringing in mechanics—when

what we need are gardeners. We keep trying to drive change—when what we need to do is cultivate change. Surprisingly, this mechanical mind-set can afflict those who seek "humane" changes through "learning organizations" just as much as it can afflict those who drive more traditional changes, such as mergers and reorganizations.

Where, Specifically, Does the Mechanical Approach Go Wrong in Effecting Change?

The easiest way to see this is to look at our interpersonal relationships. In our ordinary experiences with other people, we know that approaching each other in a machine-like way gets us into trouble. We know that the process of changing a relationship is a lot more complicated than the process of changing a flat tire on your car. It requires a willingness to change. It requires a sense of openness, a sense of reciprocity, even a kind of vulnerability. You must be willing to be influenced by another person. You don't have to be willing to be influenced by your damn car! A relationship with a machine is fundamentally a different kind of relationship: It is perfectly appropriate to feel that if it doesn't work, you should fix it. But we get into real trouble whenever we try to "fix" people.

We know how to create and nurture close friendships or family relationships. But when we enter the realm of the organization, we're not sure which domain to invoke. Should we evoke the domain of the machine? After all, much of our daily life is about interacting with computers, tape recorders, automobiles, and ATMs. Or should we evoke the domain of living systems—because a lot of our daily life is about interacting with family, friends, and colleagues?

There are those who come down firmly on the people side: They tend to be HR professionals and line managers—people who understand that relationships, teamwork, and trust are essential to effective operations. But high-level executives are frequently separated from the day-to-day stuff of the enterprise: They look at the organization from the perspective of numbers, financial statements, and prospective deals. Their number-one variable is the company stock price. That outlook distances them substantially from the living, human aspects of the enterprise. You end up with organizational schizophrenia. Some people operate the company as if it were a machine, and some treat it as part of the messy, living world.

What Happens When You See a Company as a Part of Nature?

It shifts profoundly how you think about leadership and change. If you use a machine lens, you get leaders who are trying to drive change through formal change programs. If you use a living-systems lens, you get leaders who approach change as if they were growing something, rather than just "changing" something. Even on a large scale, nature doesn't change things mechanically: You don't just pull out the old and replace it with the new. Something new grows, and it eventually supplants the old.

You see the same thing at the level of behaviors: If new behaviors are more effective than old behaviors, then the new behaviors win out. That insight gives us a doorway into a different way to think about how enterprises might change: What if we thought of organizational change as the interplay among the various forces that are involved in growing something new?

Looking at nature, we see that nothing that grows starts large; it always starts small. No one is "in charge," making the growth occur. Instead, growth occurs as a result of the interplay of diverse forces. And these forces fall into two broad categories: self-reinforcing processes, which generate growth, and limiting processes, which can impede growth or stop it altogether. The pattern of growth that occurs unfolds from the interplay of these two types of forces.

Looking at organizations, we find that one of the first things that changes is how we define the term "structure." *The Fifth Discipline* proposed a definition borrowed from system dynamics—which looks at structure in terms of feedback interactions within a system. Our new definition of that term is "a pattern of interdependency that we enact." Again, think about the relationships within a family rather than those within a company: People come to relate to each other in predictable ways, which form a pattern that then defines the structure of relationships—norms, expectations, taken-for-granted habits of communicating. Those patterns aren't fixed; they can change. And, more to the point, those patterns aren't given. Ultimately, the structures that come into play in our families are the result of the choices that we've made all along the way. We "enact" our families.

All of this applies directly to our ideas about leadership and, in particular, to the cult of the CEO-as-hero. In fact, that cult is one pattern that makes it easier for us to maintain change-averse institutions. When we enact the pattern of the CEO as hero, we infantalize the organization: That kind of behavior keeps everyone else in the company at a stage of development in which they can't accept their own possibilities for creating change. Moreover, it keeps executives from doing things that would genuinely contribute to creating significant change. The cult of the hero-leader only creates a need for more hero-leaders.

How Does Challenging the Idea of the Hero-Leader Promote Change?

Deep change comes only through real personal growth—through learning and unlearning. This is the kind of generative work that most executives are precluded from doing by the mechanical mind-set and by the cult of the hero-leader: The hero-leader is the one with "the answers." Most of the other people in the organization can't make deep changes, because they're operating out of compliance rather than out of commitment. Commitment comes about only when people determine that you are asking them to do something that they really care about. For that reason, if you create compliance-oriented change, you'll get change—but you'll preclude the deeper processes that lead to commitment, and you'll prevent the emergence of self-generated change.

Again, you end up creating a kind of addiction: People change as long as they're being commanded to change—or as long as they can be forced to change. But, as a result, they become still more dependent on change that's driven from the top.

If the Idea of the Hero-Leader Takes Us in the Wrong Direction, What's the Right Direction?

The first problem with all of the stuff that's out there about leadership is that we haven't got a clue about what we're talking about. We use the word "leader" to mean "executive": The leader is the person at the top. That definition says that leadership is synonymous with a position. And if leadership is synonymous with a position, then it doesn't matter what a leader does. All that matters is where the leader sits. If you define a "leader" as an "executive," then you absolutely deny everyone else in an organization the opportunity to be a leader.

But when we studied leaders inside the companies that are involved in the SoL consortium, that's not what we saw. We had several companies that were able to sustain significant momentum over many years, and there were no executives involved at all. In case after case, the most compelling lesson we learned was that if you want real, significant, sustainable change, you need talented, committed local line leaders. Find the people who are at the heart of the value-generating process—who design, produce, and sell products; who provide services; who talk to customers. Those value-generating activities are the province of the line manager, and if the line manager is not innovating, then innovation is not going to occur.

The next thing we noticed was that, in some organizations, the first round of change activities somehow led to second-order efforts. The original group would spawn a second group, and gradually new practices would spread throughout the organization. How did that happen? We identified people who were "seed carriers." They were internal networkers who knew how to get people talking to one another and how to build informal communities. In effect, they were creating communities of practice. These networkers represent a second type of leadership. Of course, we also found executives who were providing leadership by doing activities that were more mature and more profound than simply offering themselves as heroes. These were executives who focus on acting as a coach or as a mentor.

Out of these observations, we developed our own definition of "leadership." To me, the simplest definition of that word is "the ability to produce change": "We used to operate that way; now we operate this way." Then, using what we saw inside companies, we identified three leadership communities: local line leaders, internal networkers or community builders, and executive leaders. For significant change to take place, you need to create an interplay among those three communities. One community can't be substituted for another. Each community represents part of a necessary set.

What's the Best Way to Begin Creating Change?

I have never seen a successful organizational-learning program rolled out from the top. Not a single one. Conversely, every change process that I've seen that was sustained and that spread has started small. Usually these programs start with just one team. That team can be any team, including an executive team. At Shell, the critical generative work was done in a top team. Then, in a matter of a year or so, it spread to the top 150 managers, who percolated ideas among themselves—and they, in turn, formed new clusters of teams. At Ford, two teams started working almost in parallel. In case after case, the change effort begins small, and as it takes hold, networks form that carry change into wider groups.

Just as nothing in nature starts big, so the way to start creating change is with a pilot group—a growth seed. As you think about a pilot group, there are certain choices that you have to make in order to make the group work. The first choice goes back to the issue of compliance versus commitment: Will the change effort be driven by authority or by learning? To make that decision is to choose a central path. Then there are reinforcing elements: new guiding ideas; innovations in the infrastructure; theories, methods, and tools.

After a Pilot Group Forms, What Are the Next Steps?

Thinking about nature as the model again leads you to ask, "What are the self-reinforcing processes whereby the seed begins to realize its potential to grow? And what are the limiting processes that come into play as the seed interacts with the soil?"

There are a number of self-reinforcing factors that help a pilot program to take root. People develop a personal stake in it. People see that their colleagues take it seriously, and they want to be part of a network of committed people. There's also a pragmatic factor: It works. There are real business results—so it's worthwhile to become engaged. But the most fundamental reinforcer of a pilot program is hearing people say that they've found a better way of working. Most people would rather work with a group of people who trust one another. Most people would rather walk out of a meeting with the belief that they've just solved an important problem. Most people would rather have fun at work. It may be obvious, but what we've observed again and again is that personal enthusiasm is the initial energizer of any change process. And that enthusiasm feeds on itself. People don't necessarily want to "have a vision" at work or to "conduct dialogue." They want to be part of a team that's fun to work with and that produces results they are proud of.

But even if the pilot has potential to grow, there is no guarantee that growth will occur. All pilot groups encounter "challenges to initiating"—initial limiting processes that can keep growth from ever really starting. For example, it doesn't matter how promising a team is if its members don't have time to commit to the change effort, if they can't reorganize their schedules to accommodate weekly meetings, if they don't have time during which they can get together to reflect. Learning takes time. Invariably, you will get that time back—and then some—because most teams today waste lots of time, and therefore better learning capabilities will make them much more productive than they were before. But first you have to be able to make an investment of time.

Another example of an important potential limiting factor: A change effort has to have some relevance to people. It has to have some connection to them. It has to matter. Why should an engineer need to learn how to conduct a dialogue? Why should she care about that skill? The answer may be that the organization trips over certain technical issues that aren't really technical issues; rather, they're problems with internal conversations that lead to fights instead of creative resolutions. The point isn't to learn how to conduct a dialogue. The point is to invest some time and to get some help to change how people work together.

In Your New Book, You Identify the 10 Challenges of Change. Why Focus on Challenges?

The short answer: to produce effective leadership. In a natural system, the way to sustain growth is by paying attention to the interplay between reinforcing processes and limiting processes—and by paying special attention to the limiting processes. The limiting processes represent 90% to 98% of the real leverage in sustaining deep change. These 10 challenges are the limiting processes that we've seen again and again. They include processes that operate from the outset of a pilot—such as time and relevance—and they include processes that come into play once a pilot begins to succeed. After an initial success, things tend to get harder, not easier. So, if we want to have effective leadership, if we want to have humane communities that can sustain significant change, we need to learn how to focus on these types of challenges.

Are these the only 10 challenges? This is just the first cut; undoubtedly there are others. But if the discourse about change starts to focus on challenges and on strategies for dealing with those challenges, we may be able to build a body of knowledge that will allow for effective leadership and sustainable change.

Back to the First Question: A Decade after *The Fifth Discipline* Appeared, Do You Think that Big Companies Can Change?

Ultimately, organizational learning is about growing something new. Where does new growth take place? Often it happens in the midst of the old. Indeed, often the new grows out of the old. How will the old react? The only realistic expectation is that the traditional system of management, as [W. Edwards] Deming used to label it, will work harder and harder to maintain itself. But growing something new doesn't have to be a battle against the old. It doesn't need to be a fight between believers and nonbelievers. In any case, our Industrial Age management, our Industrial Age organization, and our Industrial Age way of living will not continue. The Industrial Age is not sustainable. It's not sustainable in ecological terms, and it's not sustainable in human terms.

It will change. The only question is how. Once we get out of our machine mind-set, we may discover new aptitudes for growth and change. Until then, change won't come easily.

Sidebar: The 10 Challenges of Change

In *The Dance of Change: The Challenges to Sustaining Momentum in Learning Organizations*, Peter Senge and his colleagues identify 10 challenges of change. Grouped into three categories—challenges of initiating change, challenges of sustaining momentum, and challenges of systemwide redesign and rethinking—these 10 items amount to what the authors call "the conditions of the environment that regulate growth."

Challenges of Initiating Change

"We don't have time for this stuff!" People who are involved in a pilot group to initiate a change effort need enough control over their schedules to give their work the time that it needs.

"We have no help!" Members of a pilot group need enough support, coaching, and resources to be able to learn and to do their work effectively.

"This stuff isn't relevant." There need to be people who can make the case for change—who can connect the development of new skills to the real work of the business.

"They're not walking the talk!" A critical test for any change effort: the correlation between espoused values and actual behavior.

Challenges of Sustaining Momentum

"This stuff is . . ." Personal fear and anxiety—concerns about vulnerability and inadequacy—lead members of a pilot group to question a change effort.

"This stuff isn't working!" Change efforts run into measurement problems: Early results don't meet expectations, or traditional metrics don't calibrate to a pilot group's efforts.

"They're acting like a cult!" A pilot group falls prey to arrogance, dividing the company into "believers" and "nonbelievers."

Challenges of Systemwide Redesign and Rethinking

"They . . . never let us do this stuff." The pilot group wants more autonomy; "the powers that be" don't want to lose control.

"We keep reinventing the wheel." Instead of building on previous successes, each group finds that it has to start from scratch.

"Where are we going?" The larger strategy and purpose of a change effort may be obscured by day-to-day activity. Big question: Can the organization achieve a new definition of success?

Sidebar:
Chronology of Learning Organization Concepts

1938 In his book *Experience and Education,* John Dewey publicizes the concept of experiential learning as an ongoing cycle of activity.

1940s The Macy Conferences—featuring Margaret Mead, Gregory Bateson, and Lawrence Kubie—bring "systems thinking" to the awareness of a cross-disciplinary group of intellectuals.

1940s Scottish psychologist Kenneth Craik coins the term "mental models," which later makes its way to MIT through Marvin Minsky and Seymour Papert.

1946 Kurt Lewin, founding theorist of National Training Laboratories, proposes the idea of a "creative tension" between personal vision and a sense of reality.

1956 Edgar Schein's research on brainwashing in Korea paves the way for an understanding of "process consultation."

1960 *The Human Side of Enterprise,* by Douglas McGregor, is published.

1961 Jay Forrester publishes *Industrial Dynamics.* This book, the first major application of system dynamics to corporations, describes the turbulence within a typical appliance value chain.

1970 Chris Argyris and Donald Schön begin work on "action science," the study of how espoused values clash with the values that underlie real actions.

1972 *The Limits to Growth: A Report for the Club of Rome's Project on the Predicament of Mankind,* by Donella Meadows and Dennis Meadows, is published. The book draws on Forrester's theories about system dynamics.

1971 to 1979 Erhard Seminars Training (EST) demonstrate the kind of powerful attitude shifts that can occur during a seminar that lasts several days.

1979 Consultant Charlie Kiefer, Forrester student Peter Senge, and researcher-artist Robert Fritz design the "Leadership and Mastery" seminar, which becomes the focal point of their new consulting firm, Innovation Associates.

1984 to 1985 Pierre Wack, scenario planner at Royal Dutch/Shell, spends a sabbatical at Harvard Business School and writes two articles about scenario planning as a learning activity.

1982 Senge, Arie de Geus, Hanover Insurance CEO Bill O'Brien, Analog Devices CEO Ray Stata, and other executive leaders form a learning-organization study group, which meets regularly at MIT.

1987 Peter Schwartz, Stewart Brand, Napier Collyns, Jay Ogilvy, and Lawrence Wilkinson form the Global Business Network, with a charter to foster organizational learning through scenario planning.

1989 Oxford University management scholar Bill Isaacs, an associate of quantum physicist David Bohm, introduces Senge to the concept of dialogue as a process for building team capability.

1989 *The Age of Unreason,* by Charles Handy, is published.

1989 The Center for Organizational Learning is formed at MIT, with Senge as director and with Ed Schein, Chris Argyris, Arie de Geus, Ray Stata, and Bill O'Brien as key advisers. The staff of the "learning center," as it's called, includes Bill Isaacs, Daniel Kim (whose research involves linking the learning organization work to the quality movement), and research director George Roth.

1990 *The Fifth Discipline* is published. The book draws on many influences: system dynamics, "personal mastery" (based on Fritz's work and the concept of creative tension), mental models (based on Wack's and Argyris's work), shared vision (based on work done at Innovation Associates), and team learning (based on David Bohm's concepts).

1990 Daniel Kim founds the "Systems Thinker," a newsletter devoted to "fifth discipline" issues. The following year, the newsletter's parent organization, Pegasus Communications, launches an annual conference series called Systems Thinking in Action.

1993 Harvard University professor David Garvin publishes an article on organizational learning in the *Harvard Business Review,* arguing that only learning that can be measured will be useful to managers.

1994 *The Fifth Discipline Fieldbook* is published. Authors of the book, which Senge edited, include Charlotte Roberts, Rick Ross, and Bryan Smith (president of Innovation Associates of Canada), and Art Kleiner (who serves as editorial director). The *Fieldbook* becomes a new management-book genre.

1994 The use of "learning histories" as a method of assessment begins at the Center for Organizational Learning.

1994 The first major Organizational Learning Center projects reach completion. Many of them have produced remarkable results. But a few have resulted in disappointing career prospects for some of the line leaders who were involved in them.

1995 Working with Dee Hock, the Organizational Learning Center begins a two-year process of building an ambitious international consortium called the Society for Organizational Learning, with Peter Senge as chairman.

1996 *The Age of Heretics,* by Art Kleiner, and *Synchronicity: The Inner Path of Leadership,* by Joseph Jaworski, are published.

1997 *The Living Company,* by Arie de Geus, is published.

1999 *The Dance of Change* is published.

CASES FOR CRITICAL THINKING

Drexler's Bar-B-Que

....

Developed by Forrest F. Aven, Jr., University of Houston—Downtown, and V. Jean Ramsey, Texas Southern University

Change seems to be a fact of life, yet in Texas some things remain the same—people's love for Texas-style barbecue. As you drive from Houston to Waco, for example, you will see many roadside stands asking you to stop by and sample different forms of bbq or bar b q (the tastes vary as much as the spellings, and both are often inspired). In the cities, there are many restaurants, several of them large chains, that compete with smaller, neighborhood businesses for the barbecue portion of individuals' dining out budgets.

Survival can sometimes depend on the restaurant's ability to identify and capitalize on "windows of opportunity." Small businesses are presumed to be more flexible, having the ability to react more quickly to changes when they occur—but the risk is also greater for them than for large organizations, which can more easily absorb losses. But although there may be differences in scale, an important question for *all* organizations is whether they have the willingness and the ability to take advantage of opportunities as they arise. On February 14, 1995, Drexler's Bar-B-Que, a small "neighborhood" restaurant in Houston, the fourth largest city in the United States, had an opportunity to test whether it had what it took.

Drexler's Bar-B-Que is located at 2020 Dowling Street in an area of Houston called the Third Ward—an economically disadvantaged neighborhood not far from downtown—and has been in the family "almost forever." The more recent history, however, begins in the late 1940s, when a great uncle of the present owners operated the establishment as Burney's BBQ. He died in the late 1950s, and an uncle of the present owners took the restaurant over and, because of a leasing arrangement with another popular barbeque restaurant in Southwest Houston, changed the name of the restaurant to Green's Barbecue. In the 1970s, James Drexler, 12 years old, began working with his uncle and learned the secrets of the old family recipes for the barbecue beef, chicken, and sausage. He learned the business "from the ground up." In 1982, when his uncle died, James and his mother took over the business, ended the leasing arrangement, and, in 1985, renamed it Drexler's Bar-B-Que. To this day, it continues to be a "family affair," but there has been increased specialization in tasks as business has grown. James Drexler continues to do all the meat preparation, his mother, Mrs. Eunice Scott, handles the other food preparation (the "standard fare" is potato salad, cole slaw, barbeque beans, and slices of white bread), and his sister, Virginia Scott, manages the "front operations"—customer orders and the cash register. There are only two or three other full-time employees, although sometimes during the summer a couple of nephews work part time.

Drexler's is a family business with strong underlying values. It is in the neighborhood and is *of* the neighborhood. Despite the success of the business and the increased patronage of individuals from other parts of the city (many of whom previously had few occasions to do more than drive through the Third Ward), the Drexlers have never considered moving from their original location. The culture of the organization, and the values underpinning it, are influenced by the current head of the family, Mrs. Scott. Her values of honesty, hard work, and treating people fairly and with respect—and her faith in God—permeate the atmosphere and operations of Drexler's. She moves through the restaurant inquiring about individual needs—equally for long-time customers and new ones—and always with a smile and warm greeting for all. She is there every day the restaurant is open and holds the same set of high standards for herself as she does for others who work in the restaurant.

Values also get played out in the way in which Drexler's Bar-B-Que "gives back to" the surrounding African-American community. Drexler's has, for many years, sponsored a softball team and a local Boy Scout troop. Youths from the neighborhood have opportunities to go camping and visit a local amusement park because the family believes that a business should not just involve itself in the community but has the

obligation to seek out aggressively opportunities to help others.

In some ways it would appear that Drexler's is not very flexible or adaptable. The restaurant is always closed at 6:00 P.M. and on Sundays and Mondays. The menu has remained the same for many years. Drexler's has always been well known in Houston's African-American community, especially that in the southwest portion of the city. Regular customers have frequented the restaurant for many years, and a successful side business of catering social functions has also developed. Business has improved every year. During the early 1990s, the business had grown to a point where the small, somewhat ramshackle, restaurant could no longer service the demand—there simply were not enough tables or space. So the decision was made in 1994 to close the business for six months, completely raze the building, and rebuild a new and modern restaurant (with additional space attached for future expansion into related, and unrelated, businesses by other family members). It was a good decision—upon reopening, business doubled. But the biggest test of the restaurant's ability to adapt to changes came on February 14, 1995.

Mrs. Scott has two sons, James and Clyde Drexler. James is the co-owner of the restaurant, and Clyde is an NBA basketball player. In 1994, Clyde Drexler appeared at the restaurant to generate publicity for the reopening. But on February 14, 1995, he was traded from the Portland Trailblazers to the local NBA franchise, the Houston Rockets. Clyde had played his collegiate ball at the local university and was popular in the city of Houston. He and Hakeem Olajuwon, the "star" of the Rockets team, had played together in college and were part of the team known as the Phi Slamma

Jamma. Clyde had been a very successful member of the Portland team; he had been selected to play on several all-star teams, had played for two NBA championships, and was a member of the original Dream Team that sent NBA players to the 1992 Summer Olympics.

The Houston Rockets, the defending NBA champions, were struggling during that winter of 1995. The acquisition of Clyde Drexler was seen as a "blockbuster" one and a key to helping the team repeat as NBA champions. The city was overjoyed with the idea that a local hero was returning home to assist the team in once more winning the championship.

The initial news of the trade brought many new customers to the restaurant. As the Rockets progressed through the playoffs during the spring of 1995, even more customers came. Some days, the restaurant had to close early because it ran out of food. During the semifinals with San Antonio and the finals with Orlando, there appeared to be as many newspaper articles and television reports originating from the restaurant as from the basketball arena. A radio station staged an event outside the restaurant for fans to earn tickets to the game. A major local newspaper gave the restaurant a favorable review in the food section. Many Rockets fans saw frequenting the restaurant as a way to "connect" to the ball team and came to hug Mrs. Scott or chat with her about her son, Clyde, or both. When the Rockets clinched their second NBA championship, everyone in the city knew about the Rockets, and many now knew of Drexler's Bar-B-Que.

The restaurant has since become the hub of several businesses located side by side. In addition to her two sons, Mrs. Scott has four daughters. Virginia Scott, who is heavily involved in the restaurant, is also co-owner of a beauty salon, with another sister, Charlotte Drexler. A bakery is owned and operated by a cousin, Barbara Wiltz. A bookstore with a sports emphasis is leased to a nonfamily member. In January 1996, a new addition was made to the building, and a significantly expanded catering business was begun. Meanwhile, the restaurant has increased its neighborhood involvement by offering free Thanksgiving and Christmas dinners to neighborhood residents in a neighborhood park.

Review Questions

1. Use the open systems model decribed in this chapter to show how Drexler's Bar-B-Que should operate as a learning organization.
2. How do the "values" of Drexler's Bar-B-Que relate to the ethics and social responsibility issues raised in this chapter?
3. What challenges of organization and managerial leadership face Drexler's in its current movement toward expansion? ■

C A S E   2
Sun Microsystems: "We're the dot in .com"

Developed by David S. Chappell, Ohio University

What does it take to foster a computer revolution? Bill Gates's Microsoft model, based on distributed personal computers with software (largely Microsoft's) loaded on each individual machine, may be slowly giving way to a networked system long championed by McNealy's Sun Microsystems. In fact, McNealy has been one of the few computer industry leaders to take on Microsoft directly with a zeal and tenacity that is legendary. Steven M. Milunovich, an analyst with Merrill Lynch and Company, argues that "If you want to know where the computer industry is going, ask Sun."[1]

Sun Microsystems

Sun Microsystems was founded by Andreas Bechtolsheim, Bill Joy, Vinod Khosla, and Scott McNealy in 1982. The first Sun system, the Sun-1, was a high performance computer based on readily available, inexpensive components and the Unix operating system largely developed by Joy while in graduate school at the University of California-Berkeley.

Note: The blue underscored words/ phrases in this case indicate Internet links provided in the online version. See the *Organizational Behavior, Seventh Edition* Web Site at http://www.wiley. com/college/schermerhorn.

From the very start, Sun resisted the so-called Microsoft Windows/ Intel (Wintel) model and concentrated on high-end workstations, suitable for engineering, designers, Wall Street traders, and CAD/CAM applications.

Scott McNealy took over as president of Sun in 1984 and since then has waged a constant war with Bill Gates and Microsoft. At first, Sun's market niche of high-end workstations kept it from competing directly with personal computers. However, over time PCs acquired more and more computing power, putting them in more direct competition with workstations. As a consequence, Sun has branched out into other computer areas, with an emphasis on the Internet.

Sun is the only major company that builds an entire line of computers based exclusively on its own designs, its own chips, dubbed Sparc, and its own software, a version of the Unix operating system known as Solaris. As such, Sun stands alone as the "pure" alternative to the Wintel world.[2] This strategy is not without its detractors, who point out that Sun handicaps itself by requiring huge R&D expenses compared to those firms relying on Windows and Intel. Sun spends 10.4% of its sales on R&D, compared to 4.5% at Compaq and 1.6% at Dell, who rely on Intel and Microsoft for much of their research.[3]

McNealy boasts that "there are three technology companies left in the computer world. Intel, Microsoft and Sun."[4] "They [Sun] are beginning to be viewed as much more credible as an end-to-end solution provider," says Joe Ferlazzo, an analyst at Technology Business Research. Sun offers an attractive alternative with the same operating system on everything from a $2500 workstation with a single Sparc chip to a $1 million server with 64 parallel chips delivering as much computing power as an IBM mainframe. "That's what's needed in the ISP environment and in corporate computing" he adds. In the opposite camp, Susan Whitney of IBM argues that "To believe that a single architecture will address all the business requirements is not a sound strategy."[5]

Undeterred, McNealy stays convinced of his mission, which is no less than to overthrow the personal computer. "The PC is just a blip. It's a big, bright blip," says McNealy. "Fifty years from now, people are going to look back and say: 'Did you really have a computer on your desk? How weird.'"[6] Analyst C. B. Lee of Sutro and Company and a former Sun manager argues that "McNealy shoots off his mouth too much. At some point, you've gotta be more mature."[7]

Offsetting McNealy's brashness is Ed Zander, chief operating officer for Sun, who exhibits a more conservative aura. "I think McNealy and Zander are kind of like yin and yang," says Milunovich from Merrill Lynch. "McNealy is the high priest of the religion. Ed is much more pragmatic. Having both is very good for Sun."[8]

One thing McNealy has been able to accomplish is the constant reinvention of Sun as times and external conditions change. Starting with workstations and their various components, he has now positioned the firm to offer top-of-the-line servers that power the Internet. With the development of Java and Jini, Sun is evolving into a powerful software machine that serves to drive the Internet and future "information appliances."

To do this, Sun recognizes the need for talented people. Many observers rate Sun's employees among the most talented in Silicon Valley. To keep them in a competitive marketplace, Sun emphasizes perks:

Family care: Adoptive parents receive financial assistance of up to $2000. Lactation rooms help new mothers return to work. In the San Francisco Bay Area, parents can take sick children to a special day-care center that cares for children with minor illnesses. Sun also offers a dependent-care spending account, a consultation and referral program, and an employee-assistance program providing short-term professional counseling.

Private workspace: When Sun designed its Menlo Park, California campus, the company asked employees for suggestions—and found that engineers prefer private offices over Dilbert-like cubicles. The engineers got the space they demanded for quiet development time.

Respecting employee time: Flexible hours and telecommuting help accommodate busy schedules and keep employees from wasting time on California freeways. Train travelers can catch a special shuttle to Sun facilities, and the company reimburses some commuting costs.[9]

Hard to Find Where the Sun Don't Shine

As early as 1987, Sun coined the phrase, "The network is the computer."[10] But it has only been recently, with the full advent of the Internet coupled with Sun's Java programming language, that all the pieces may actually be falling into place to make this vision a reality. "Microsoft's vision was to put a mainframe on everybody's desktop," claims McNealy. "We want to provide dial tone for the Internet. We couldn't have more different visions."[11]

In 1995, Java was introduced as the first universal software designed from the ground up for Internet and corporate intranet developers to write applications that run on any computer, regardless of the processor or operating system.[12] Most recently Sun has introduced Jini, a promising technology that lets computers and appliances connect to a network as simply as a telephone plugs into the wall.[13] Sun's objective is to make access to the Internet and computing as simple as picking up a phone and hearing a "Webtone".

Even Microsoft yielded to Java's appeal, licensing a version to develop its own line of software. Java's appeal is its ability to lower companies' IT costs because it runs unchanged on any device with a computer chip, enabling everything from wallet-sized cards to trucks to communicate over a network. However, Microsoft and Sun immediately got into a battle when Microsoft made a proprietary version of Java to run only on Windows programs. Sun sued and has won an initial ruling against Microsoft.

Sun claims that network computing will herald a shift away from personal computers to more friendly appliances such as phones, digital assistants, and televisions. It hopes Java will provide the link to its powerful network servers with these new network devices.[14] Microsoft prefers its Windows CE operating system to provide this link. In addition, it views Web appliances as "companions" rather than replacements to today's PCs.

The allure of a host of Internet devices is their ability to bring in more users. Their convenience and ease-of-use promotes a more ubiquitous presence for the Web and the information located there. Java goes after this "embedded" software market by powering the programs that run everything from phone switches to factory automation equipment.

Java-Powered Net "Appliances"

Network Computers
Stripped-down desktop computers run programs downloaded from the Internet.

TVs and Cable Set-Top Boxes
TCI will distribute 20 million Java-equipped set-top boxes to encourage communication over cable.

Screenphones
Simple devices for straightforward services such as grocery ordering.

Cellular phones and pagers
Cellular phone manufacturers plan to use Java to offer new services through their cellular devices.

Smart Cards
Java smart cards program routine processes, such as airline ticket purchases directly on the cards.

Cars
Navigation and diagnostic systems powered by Java programs.

Keys
Java-powered rings and pass cards.[15]

McNealy billed Java as the killer of Microsoft Windows. Sun claims Java is ideally suited for the "network computer" (NC) — a low-cost machine that has no hard drive, relying instead on a network that would supply it with small Java programs. Plummeting personal computer prices have stalled the takeoff of the NC, but McNealy and Sun remain committed to the idea. "Every day, 27,000 people (at Sun) get up and do one thing: network computing," claims Ed Zander. "That's a very, very powerful story."[16]

Sun-AOL-Netscape

In perhaps its greatest coup to date, on November 24, 1998, Sun signed an alliance agreement with America Online in association with its $4.2 billion purchase of Netscape Communications. Access to Netscape's e-commerce software allows Sun to hawk its servers and attract customers that want a more complete package.[17] In addition, Sun has access to one of the three largest portals on the Web. In exchange for providing $350 million

in licensing, marketing, and advertising fees for the deal, AOL agrees to buy $500 million in Sun servers over the next three years.

Open system advocates were originally concerned about AOL's involvement in the deal. They felt that AOL might hinder the free distribution of Netscape's browser. However, Stephen Case, AOL founder, assures doubters that the partnership will continue to allow free access to Netscape's browser technology. He intends to depend on Sun Microsystems to develop systems to provide Internet access over next-generation devices.

As a partner with AOL and Netscape, Sun is now in position to challenge IBM, Hewlett-Packard, and others in developing the systems that will let corporations rebuild their businesses in cyberspace. The challenge for Sun CEO Scott G. McNealy will be to behave like the top-tier industry leader that this deal may finally make him. And he'll need to make sure that Sun not only talks like a good partner but behaves like one, too.[18]

A major factor in Sun's favor is a world in which companies will choose to outsource anything that's not a demonstrably clear competitive advantage. Things such as human resources, financials, e-mail, and Web hosting all will clearly follow in the steps of payroll and facility security — that is, they'll be outsourced. Sun's been saying that the network is the computer for at least a decade. Oracle has been talking the talk for about three years. SAP was founded on the principle of centralized control in the early 1970s. But so far, no vendor has been able to convince any company that it should put its technological assets into someone else's hands. This is starting to change.[19]

The firm most strategically positioned to take advantage of this shift

is Sun or possibly IBM Global Services. Scott McNealy has stated several times that companies should never think about purchasing another server again. He means that companies should leave the costs of maintaining scalability and reliability of fundamental systems to someone that specializes in the technology.[20]

Even so, the Internet must continue to evolve in order for Sun to realize its vision. John McFarlane, head of Solaris software, puts it plainly. "We depend upon extreme reliability, availability and scalability as a market differentiator. . . . I know from my seventeen years as a Nortel employee how much it hurts when there's a service failure of any kind, and how great it feels when the network would take a licking and keep on ticking. The same ethic applies at Sun. We run our own company systems on Sun, and our average downtime is about 22 minutes per-employee-per-year. Another way to put it is we experience about 99.96% uptime for every company user. We won a contract with the New York Stock Exchange because of our ability to deliver their required 99.99% uptime — and so far we're at 100%. If the Internet is truly to succeed as the next great communication medium for mainstream users, and the WebTone is to truly represent the same level of connectivity as the dialtone, then that level of reliability must be our model for all users. We call it the utility model of computing."[21]

With all these changes going on, how does a company cope? McNealy sums up his strategy by arguing, "If everybody thought that what we were doing was the right thing, everybody would do what we are doing. If you are controversial and you are wrong, you've got a big problem. You have to be very controversial and very right to make lots of money."[22]

Review Questions

1. Discuss the authors' definition of high performance organizations. Is there anything you would add or delete?
2. Analyze Sun Microsystems based on the authors' five key characteristics of HPOs.
3. Does Sun represent a Greenfield or Redesign HPO?

References

1. Hof, Robert; Hamm, Steve; and Sager, Ira. "Is the Center of the Computing Universe Shifting?," *Business Week,* January 19, 1999, pp. 64–72.
2. Helft, Miguel. "Sun Succeeds with Market Savvy, Pragmatism," *San Jose Mercury News,* December 6, 1998.
3. Hof, Hamm, and Sager, op. cit.
4. Ibid.
5. Ibid.
6. Ibid.
7. Ibid.
8. Helft, op. cit.
9. Merrick, Amy. "Companies Go the Extra Mile to Retain Employees," *R&D,* September 1998, p. S3.
10. Hof, Hamm, and Sager, op. cit.
11. Ibid.
12. "Sun Microsystems Homepage—History," http://www.sun.com/corporate overview/who/html_history.html, April 20, 1999.
13. Hof, Hamm, and Sager, op. cit.
14. Helft, op. cit.
15. Hof, op. cit.
16. Helft, op. cit.
17. Hof, op. cit.
18. Sager, Ira; Yang, Catherine; Himelstein, Linda; and Gross, Neil. "Power-Play: AOL-Netscape-Sun," *Business Week,* December 7, 1998.
19. Taschek, John. "This Just In: The World Revolves Around Sun," *PC Week,* January 4, 1999, p. 48.
20. Ibid.
21. McFarlane, John. "Whose WebTone Is It, Anyway?," http://www.sun.com/corporate overview/news/webtone.html, May, 1998.
22. Helft, op. cit. ■

CASE 3
Crossing Borders
• •

Developed by Bernardo M. Ferdman, California School of Professional Psychology, San Diego, CA and Plácida I. Gallegos, Southwest Communication Resources, Inc. and The Kaleel Jamison Consulting Group, Inc.

This case study is based on the experiences of Angelica Garza, a woman of Mexican-American heritage who worked for 10 years in the Human Resource (HR) function of a multinational medical products company. This maquiladora plant was in Tijuana, Baja California, a large city directly across the U.S.-Mexican border from San Diego, California. Maquiladoras are manufacturing plants owned by foreign capital in the regions of Mexico bordering the United States, which have been set up to take advantage of favorable laws and cheap labor.

The Tijuana plant was one of a number of operations for USMed. Six other U.S. facilities were located in the Northeast, the Midwest, and Florida. In addition to her work in the manufacturing plant, where Angelica spent most of her time, she was also responsible for human resources for the small, primarily administrative facility in Chula Vista, on the U.S. side of the border. Eventually, there were 34 Americans—12 on the Mexican side and 22 on the United States side— and approximately 1100 Mexican nationals on the payroll.

There was little connection between Angelica and the HR managers at the other USMed plants, either in the United States or abroad. Angelica reported that USMed had no overall policy or strategy for dealing with human resources generally and diversity specifically.

The transition in Mexico was not a smooth one for Angelica. Nothing in her U.S. experience had prepared her for what she encountered in Mexico. Her Anglo colleagues had only vague knowledge about the operation in Tijuana and had little interest in understanding or relating to the Mexican workforce. Given her Hispanic upbringing in the United States, Angelica had some understanding of the culture and values of the Mexican employees. Her Spanish-speaking skills also enabled her to understand and relate to the workers. Although she had some understanding of the workers, however, the assumption on the part of U.S. management that her knowledge and connection to the Mexican workers was seamless was false. There were many aspects of cultural differences between herself and the Mexican employees that

Source: This is an abridged version of a case appearing in the Field Guide of E. E. Kossek and S. Cobel, *Managing Diversity: Human Resource Strategies for Transforming the Workplace* (Oxford, England: Blackwell, 1996).

the Anglo managers were unaware of:

In retrospect now, I can look back and [I'm] just amazed at what I was involved in at the time. I mean, I didn't have a clue. One of the things you find is that [people assume that Mexican Americans are most suited to work with Mexicans.] I guess just because I was of Mexican-American descent, it was like I would just know how to mingle with this total[ly] different culture.

As a result, Angelica experienced a great deal of frustration and misunderstanding. Her attempts to intercede between the management in Mexico and that in the United States often led to her disenfranchisement from her American colleagues, who did not value or appreciate her ideas or suggestions. Further complicating her experience in Mexico was the mixed reactions she engendered from the Mexican nationals. Because of her American status, Angelica was misunderstood and sometimes resented by Mexican employees and, at the same time, she lacked support from the U.S. organization.

I found that the Mexican women who were there [two women in accounting who were Mexican nationals, and had been there for about 5 years] were resentful. My saving grace was that I was an American because the Mexican women there looked at the Americans as being like a step above or whatever. And there was resentment of me coming in and taking away jobs. They perceived it as: They weren't doing a good job and we were coming in and taking responsibilities away from them. So me being a woman coming in, I was scrutinized by the two women who had been there. I couldn't get information from them. They gave me the least information or help they could and would be critical of anything I did once I took it from them.

You know, I look back and it was probably pretty frightening for them [the Mexican nationals] too, because we all came in and we knew what we had to do;

[USMed was] very straightforward about, you know, you fail to do this and you can lose your job and you've got to do that or you could lose your job, so getting them to follow these protocols and these operating procedures was very difficult. Change is difficult anyway but getting them to follow some of those rules [was] real challenging.

Angelica understood the employees' approach to the work as stemming from local conditions and from Mexican cultural styles. The great expansion of maquiladoras brought a number of changes, including new expectations and different cultural styles on the part of the managers. At first, potential employees were unfamiliar with these new expectations; the employers needed to train the workers if they were to meet these expectations. This was happening in the context of the meeting of two cultures. In her role, Angelica saw herself as more American than Mexican, yet also as different from her Anglo colleagues. She saw herself as bringing American training, expectations, and styles:

Well, see I'm American. I mean I was an American manager, and that's where I was coming from. But I was forced to come up with systems that would eliminate future misunderstandings or problems. Being a Mexican American I thought it would be easier working in Mexico because I had some exposure to the culture, but it was a real culture shock for me. It was a different group of people socioeconomically. A lot of those people came from ranchitos, [from] out in the sticks, where there were no restrooms or showers. There weren't infrastructures in Tijuana at all. It's pretty good now compared to what it was 10 years ago. We used to go to work through people's backyards and dirt roads. Dead dogs were marks for how to get there! And I think now, that if you go to Tijuana now—it's been 10 years of maquiladoras there—you can find more qualified Mexican managers or supervi-

sors or clerical people. [Finding] bilingual secretaries and engineers [was like] getting needles in a haystack back then.

I found myself being the only woman in an old-boy-network environment, and that was pretty tough. And it was also tough working in the Mexican environment. Because the Mexican men that I would deal with would look down on me because I was a woman. Again, my saving grace was because I was an American woman. If I had been a Mexican national woman, then I would have really had probably more problems. [For example] I had to work a lot, real close with the Mexican accounting manager, who was a male. And he would come to me and tell me how I had screwed up my numbers, or you didn't do this right, and stuff like that. I would go over the numbers and it was just a difference in terms of how things were calculated. Specifically, calculating an annual salary. He would do it by using 365 days, when I would do it by 52 weeks and you'd take your daily rate, it was different, it would always be off a little bit. But, I reported them the way the Americans would be expecting to see them.

Review Questions

1. What competencies are appropriate to ensure greater effectiveness of U.S. employees operating in a maquiladora or other non-U.S. organization?
2. What are some of the costs of not understanding diversity? What could the organization have gained by approaching the plant with greater cultural understanding?
3. From the HR perspective, what were the unique challenges that Angelica faced at various points in her work for USMed?
4. Angelica worked in a plant outside the United States. What do her experiences and perspectives tell us that applies to domestic operations? ∎

Never on a Sunday

Developed by Anne C. Cowden, California State University, Sacramento

McCoy's Building Supply Centers of San Marcos, Texas, have been in continuous successful operation for almost 70 years in an increasingly competitive retail business. McCoy's is one of the nation's largest family-owned and -managed building-supply companies, with sales topping $400 million. The company serves 10 million customers a year in a regional area currently covering New Mexico, Texas, Oklahoma, Arkansas, Mississippi, and Louisiana in 103 stores employing 1600 employees. McCoy's strategy has been to occupy a niche in the market of small and medium-sized cities. McCoy's was originally a roofing business started by Frank McCoy in 1923; roofing remained the company's primary business until the 1960s, when it began to expand under the management of son, Emmett McCoy.

McCoy's grounding principle is acquiring and selling the finest quality products that can be found and providing quality service to customers. As an operations-oriented company, McCoy's has always managed without many layers of management. Managers are asked to concentrate on service-related issues in their stores: get the merchandise on the floor, price it, sell it, and help the customer carry it out. The majority of administrative workload is handled through headquarters so that store employees can concentrate on customer service. The top management team (Emmett McCoy and his two sons, Brian and Mike, who serve as co-presidents) has established 11 teams of managers drawn from the different regions McCoy's stores cover. The teams meet regularly to discuss new products, better ways for product delivery, and a host of items integral to maintaining customer satisfaction. Team leadership is rotated among the managers.

McCoy's has a workforce of 70 percent full-time and 30 percent part-time employees. McCoy's philosophy values loyal, adaptable, skilled employees as the most essential element of its overall success. To operationalize this philosophy, the company offers extensive on-the-job training. The path to management involves starting at the store level and learning all facets of operations before advancing into a management program. All management trainees are required to relocate to a number of stores. Most promotions come from within. Managers are rarely recruited from the outside. This may begin to change as the business implements more technology requiring greater reliance on college-educated personnel.

Permeating all that McCoy's does is a strong religious belief, including a strong commitment to community. In 1961 Emmett McCoy decided, in the wake of a devastating hurricane, to offer McCoy's goods to customers at everyday prices rather than charging what the market would bear. This decision helped establish McCoy's long-standing reputation of fair dealing, a source of pride for all employees, and allowed the company to begin its current expansion perspective. In 1989 McCoy's became a drug-free company. McCoy's takes part in the annual National Red Ribbon Campaign, "Choose to Be Drug Free." McCoy's also supports Habitat for Humanity in the United States and has provided support for low-income housing in Mexico.

Many McCoy family members are Evangelical Christians who believe in their faith through letting their "feet do it"—that is, showing their commitment to God through action, not just talk. Although their beliefs and values permeate the company's culture in countless ways, one very concrete way is reflected in the title of this case: Never on a Sunday. Even though Sundays are busy business days for retailers, all 103 McCoy's stores are closed on Sunday.

Review Questions

1. How do the beliefs of the McCoy family form the culture of this company?
2. Can a retailer guided by such strong beliefs compete and survive in the era of gigantic retailers such as Home Depot? If so, how?
3. Is such a strong commitment to social responsibility and ethical standards a help or a hindrance in managing a company?
4. How does a family-owned and -managed company differ from companies managed by outside professionals? ■

CASE 5
MAGREC, Inc.

Developed by Mary McGarry, Empire State College
and Barry R. Armandi, SUNY-Old Westbury

Background

MagRec, Incorporated was started in the late 1960s by Mr. Leed, a brilliant engineer (he has several engineering patents), who was a group manager at Fairchild Republic. The company's product was magnetic recording heads, a crucial device used for reading, writing, and erasing data on tapes and disks. Need for the product and its future potential was great. The computer industry was in its embryonic stage, and MagRec had virtually no serious competition. In fact, almost all magnetic head manufacturers today use methods, techniques, processes, and so on, that were developed and pioneered by MagRec.

Like any other startup, MagRec had a humble beginning. It struggled during the early years, facing cash-flow and technical problems. After a slow start, it began growing rapidly. In the mid-1970s it had captured 35 percent of the tape head market, making it the second largest supplier of MegaComputer computer tape heads in North America. Financially, the company suffered heavily in the early 1980s because of price erosions caused by Far East competition. Unlike all its competitors, the company resisted and never moved its manufacturing operations offshore. By the mid-1980s, the company had accumulated losses to a point of bankruptcy. Finally, plagued by a no-win situation, the company entered a major international joint venture, in which foreign governments agreed to participate as minority owners (20% equity). The company received blanket sales orders from Japanese firms (GME, Victor Data, Fijitsu, etc.). Things looked good once again. But . . .

Pat's Dilemma

When Fred Marsh promoted me to Sales Manager, I was in seventh heaven. Now, six months later, I feel I am in hell. This is the first time in my life that I am really on my own. I have been working with other people all my life. I tried my best and what I could not solve, I took upstairs. Now it's different because I am the boss (or am I?). Fred has taught me a lot. He was my mentor and gave me this job when he became vice-president. I have always respected him and listened to his judgment. Now thinking back I wonder whether I should have listened to him at all on this problem.

It started one late Friday evening. I had planned to call my West Coast customer, Partco, to discuss certain contract clauses. I wanted to nail this one fast (Partco had just been acquired by Volks, Inc.). Partco was an old customer, in fact—through good and bad it had always stayed with us. It was also a major customer. I was about to call Partco when Dinah Coates walked in clutching a file. I had worked with Dinah for three years. She was good. I knew that my call to Partco would have to wait. Dinah had been cleaning out old files and came across a report about design and manufacturing defects in Partco heads. The report had been written

nine years ago. The cover memo read as follows:

To: Ken Smith, Director of Marketing
From: Rich Grillo, V.P. Operations
Sub: Partco Head Schedule

This is to inform you that due to pole-depth problems in design, the Partco heads (all 514 in test) have failed. They can't reliably meet the reading requirements.* The problem is basically a design error in calculations. It can be corrected. However, the fix will take at least six months. Meanwhile Ron Scott in production informs me that the entire 5,000 heads (the year's production) have aready been pole-slotted, thus they face the same problem.

Ken, I don't have to tell you how serious this is, but how can we o.k. and ship them to Partco knowing that they'll cause read error problems in the field? My engineering and manufacturing people realize this is the number one priority. By pushing the Systems Tech job back we will be back on track in less than six months. In the interim I can modify Global Widgets heads. This will enable us to at least continue shipping some product to Partco. As a possible alternate I would like to get six Partco drives. Michaels and his team feel that with quick and easy changes in the drives tape path they can get the head to work. If this is true we should be back on track within six to eight weeks.

A separate section of the report read as follows:

Confidential
(Notes from meeting with Dom Updyke and Rich Grillo)

Solution to Partco heads problem
All Partco heads can be reworked (.8 hrs. ea.—cost insignificant) to solve Partco's read problems by grinding an extra three thousandths of an inch off the top of the head. This will reduce the overall pole depth to a point where no read errors occur. The heads will fully

---

*Authors' Note: Error signifies erroneous reading, not an error message. For example, instead of "$200" the head reads "$3005.42."

meet specifications in all respects except one, namely life. Dom estimates that due to the reduced chrome layer (used for wear) the heads' useful life will be 2,500 hours instead of 6,000 hours of actual usage.

Our experience is that no customer keeps accurate records to tell actual usage and life. Moreover the cost is removed since Partco sells drives to MegaComputer who sells systems to end-users. The user at the site hardly knows or rarely complains about extra costs such as the replacement of a head 12 to 18 months down the line instead of the normal 2 years. Besides the service technicians always innovatively believe in and offer plausible explanations—such as the temperature must be higher than average—or they really must be using the computer a lot.

I have directed that the heads be reworked and shipped to Partco. I also instructed John to tell Partco that due to inclement weather this week's shipment will be combined with next week's shipment.

Dinah was flabbergasted. The company planned to sell products deliberately that it knew would not meet life requirements, she said, "risking our reputation as a quality supplier. Partco and others buy our heads thinking they are the best. Didn't we commit fraud through outright misrepresentation?"

Dinah insisted I had to do something. I told her I would look into the matter and get back to her by the end of next week.

Over the weekend I kept thinking about the Partco issue. We had no customer complaints. Partco had always been extremely pleased with our products and technical support. In fact, we were their sole suppliers. MegaComputer had us placed on the preferred, approved ship to stock, vendors list. It was a fact that other vendors were judged against our standards. MegaComputer's Quality Control never saw our product or checked it.

Monday morning I showed the report to Fred. He immediately recollected it and began to explain the situation to me.

MagRec had been under tremendous pressure and was growing rapidly at the time. "That year we had moved into a new 50,000 sq. ft. building and went from 50 or 60 employees to over 300. Our sales were increasing dramatically." Fred was heading Purchasing at the time and every week the requirements for raw materials would change. "We'd started using B.O.A.s (Broad Order Agreements, used as annual purchasing contracts) guaranteeing us the right to increase our numbers by 100% each quarter. The goal was to maintain the numbers. If we had lost Partco then, it could have had a domino effect and we could have ended up having no customers left to worry about."

Fred went on to explain that it had only been a short-term problem that was corrected within the year and no one ever knew it existed. He told me to forget it and to move the file into the back storage room. I conceded. I thought of all the possible hassles. The thing was ancient history anyway. Why should I be concerned about it? I wasn't even here when it happened.

The next Friday Dinah asked me what I had found out. I told her Fred's feelings on the matter and that I felt he had some pretty good arguments regarding the matter. Dinah became angry. She said I had changed since my promotion and that I was just as guilty as the crooks who'd cheated the customers by selling low-life heads as long-life heads. I told her to calm down. The decision was made years ago. No one got hurt and the heads weren't defective. They weren't causing any errors.

I felt bad but figured there wasn't much to do. The matter was

closed as far as I was concerned, so I returned to my afternoon chores. Little was I to know the matter was not really closed.

That night Fred called me at 10:00. He wanted me to come over to the office right away. I quickly changed, wondering what the emergency was. I walked into Fred's office. The coffee was going. Charlie (Personnel Manager) was there. Rich Grillo (V.P. Operations) was sitting on the far side of Fred's conference table. I instinctively headed there for that was the designated smoking corner.

Ken (Director of Marketing) arrived 15 minutes later. We settled in. Fred began the meeting by thanking everyone for coming. He then told them about the discovery of the Partco file and filled them in on the background. The problem now was that Dinah had called Partco and gotten through to their new vice president, Tim Rand. Rand had called Fred at 8 P.M. at home and said he was personally taking the Red Eye to find out what this was all about. He would be here in the morning.

We spent a grueling night followed by an extremely tense few weeks. Partco had a team of people going through our tests, quality control, and manufacturing records. Our production slipped, and overall morale was affected.

Mr. Leed personally spent a week in California assuring Partco that this would never happen again. Though we weathered the storm, we had certain losses. We were never to be Partco's sole source again. We still retained 60 percent of their business, but had to agree to lower prices. The price reduction had a severe impact. Although Partco never disclosed to anyone what the issues were (since both companies had blanket nondisclosure agreements), word got around that Partco was paying a lower price. We were unable to explain to our other customers why Partco was paying this amount. Actually I felt the price word got out through Joe Byrne (an engineer who came to Partco from Systems Tech and told his colleagues back at Systems Tech that Partco really knew how to negotiate prices down). He was unaware, however, of the real issues. Faced with customers who perceived they were being treated unequitably, we experienced problems. Lowering prices meant incurring losses; not lowering them meant losing customers. The next two financial quarters saw sales dollars decline by 40 percent. As the sales manager, I felt pretty rotten presenting my figures to Fred.

With regard to Dinah, I now faced a monumental problem. The internal feeling was she should be avoided at all costs. Because of price erosions, we faced cutbacks. Employees blamed her for production layoffs. The internal friction kept mounting. Dinah's ability to interface effectively with her colleagues and other departments plummeted to a point where normal functioning was impossible.

Fred called me into his office two months after the Partco episode and suggested that I fire Dinah. He told me that he was worried about results. Although he had nothing personally against her, he felt that she must go because she was seriously affecting my department's overall performance. I defended Dinah by stating that the Partco matter would blow over and given time I could smooth things out. I pointed out Dinah's accomplishments and stated I really wanted her to stay. Fred dropped the issue, but my problem persisted.

Things went from bad to worse. Finally, I decided to try to solve the problem myself. I had known Dinah well for many years and had a good

relationship with her before the incident. I took her to lunch to address the issue. Over lunch, I acknowledged the stress the Partco situation had put on her and suggested that she move away for a while to the West Coast where she could handle that area independently.

Dinah was hurt and asked why I didn't just fire her already. I recounted by accusing her of causing the problem in the first place by going to Partco.

Dinah came back at me, calling me a lackey for having taken her story to Fred and brought his management message back. She said I hadn't even attempted a solution and that I didn't have the guts to stand up for what was right. I was only interested in protecting my backside and keeping Fred happy. As her manager, I should have protected her and taken some of the heat off her back. Dinah refused to transfer or to quit. She told me to go ahead and fire her, and she walked out.

I sat in a daze as I watched Dinah leave the restaurant. What the

hell went wrong? Had Dinah done the morally right thing? Was I right in defending *MagRec's* position? Should I have taken a stand with Fred? Should I have gone over Fred's head to Mr. Leed? Am I doing the right thing? Should I listen to Fred and fire Dinah? If not, how do I get my department back on track? What am I saying? If Dinah is right, shouldn't I be defending her rather than *MagRec*?

Review Questions

1. Place yourself in the role of the manager. What should you do now? After considering what happened, would you change any of your behaviors?
2. Do you think Dinah was right? Why or why not? If you were she and you had to do it all over again, would you do anything differently? If so, what and why?
3. Using cognitive dissonance theory, explain the actions of Pat, Dinah, and Fred. ■

CASE 6
It Isn't Fair
. . . .
Developed by Barry R. Armandi, SUNY-Old Westbury

Mary Jones was in her senior year at Central University and interviewing for jobs. Mary was in the top 1 percent of her class, active in numerous extracurricular activities, and was highly respected by her professors. After the interviews, Mary was offered a number of positions with every company with which she interviewed. After much thought, she decided to take the offer from Universal Products, a multinational company. She felt that the salary was superb ($40,000), there were excellent benefits, and good potential for promotion.

Mary started work a few weeks after graduation and learned her job assignments and responsibilities thoroughly and quickly. Mary was asked on many occasions to work

late because report deadlines were moved forward often. Without hesitation she said "Of course!" even though as an exempt employee she would receive no overtime.

Frequently, she would take work home with her and use her personal computer to do further analyses. At other times, she would come into the office on weekends to monitor the progress of her projects or just to catch up on the ever-growing mountain of correspondence.

On one occasion her manager asked her to take on a difficult assignment. It seemed that the company's Costa Rican manufacturing facility was having production problems. The quality of one of the products was highly questionable, and the reports on the matter were confusing. Mary was asked to be part of a team to investigate the quality and reporting problems. The team stayed in poor accommodations for the entire three weeks they were there. This was because of the plant's location near its resources, which happened to be in the heart of the jungle. Within the three-week period the team had located the source of the quality problem, corrected it, and altered the reporting documents and processes. The head of the team, a quality engineer, wrote a note to Mary's manager stating the following: "Just wanted to inform you of the superb job Mary Jones did down in Costa Rica. Her suggestions and insights into the reporting system were invaluable. Without her help we would have been down there for another three-weeks, and I was getting tired of the mosquitos. Thanks for sending her."

Universal Products, like most companies, has a yearly performance review system. Since Mary had been with the company for a little over one year, it was time for her review. Mary entered her manager's office nervous, since this was her first review ever and she didn't know what to expect. After closing the door and exchanging the usual pleasantries, her manager, Tom, got right to the point.

Tom: Well, Mary, as I told you last week this meeting would be for your annual review. As you are aware, your performance and compensation are tied together. Since the philosophy of the company is to reward those who perform, we take these reviews very sincerely. I have spent a great deal of time thinking about your performance over the past year, but before I begin I would like to know your impressions of the company, your assignments, and me as a manager.

Mary: Honestly, Tom, I have no complaints. The company and my job is everything I was led to believe. I enjoy working here. The staff are all very helpful. I like the team atmosphere, and my job is very challenging. I really feel appreciated and that I'm making a contribution. You have been very helpful and patient with me. You got me involved right from the start and listened to my opinions. You taught me a lot and I'm very grateful. All in all I'm happy being here.

Tom: Great, Mary, I was hoping that's the way you felt because from my vantage point, most of the people you worked with feel the same. But before I give you the qualitative side of the review, allow me to go through the quantitative appraisal first. As you know, the rankings go from 1 (lowest) to 5 (highest). Let's go down each category and I'll explain my reasoning for each.

Tom starts with category one (Quantity of Work) and ends with category ten (Teamwork). In each of the categories, Tom has either given Mary a five or a four. Indeed, only two categories have a four and Tom explains these are normal areas for improvement for most employees.

Tom: As you can see, Mary, I was very happy with your performance. You have received the highest rating I have ever given any of my subordinates. Your attitude, desire, and help are truly appreciated. The other people on the Costa Rican team gave you glowing reports and speaking with the plant manager, she felt that you helped her understand the reporting system better than anyone else. Since your performance has been stellar, I'm delighted to give you a 10 percent increase effective immediately!

Mary: (mouth agape, and eyes wide) Tom, frankly I'm flabbergasted! I don't know what to say, but thank you very much. I hope I can continue to do as fine a job as I have this last year. Thanks once again.

After exchanging some departing remarks and some more thank yous, Mary left Tom's office with a smile from ear to ear. She was floating on air! Not only did she feel the performance review process was uplifting, but her review was outstanding and so was her raise. She knew from other employees that the company was only giving out a 5 percent average increase. She figured that if she got that, or perhaps 6 or 7, she would be happy. But to get 10 percent . . . wow!! Imagine . . .

Sue: Hi, Mary! Lost in thought? My, you look great. Looks like you got some great news. What's up?

Susan Stevens was a recent hire, working for Tom. She had graduated from Central University also, but a year after Mary. Sue had excelled while at Central, graduating in the top 1 percent of her class. She had laudatory letters of recommendations from her professors and was into many after school clubs and activities.

Mary: Oh, hi Sue! Sorry, but I was just thinking about Universal and the opportunities here.

Sue: Yes, it truly is . . .

Mary: Sue, I just came from my performance review and let me tell you, the process isn't that bad. As a matter of fact I found it quite rewarding, if you get my drift. I got a wonderful review, and can't wait till next year's. What a great company!

Sue: You can say that again! I couldn't believe them hiring me right out of college at such a good salary. Between you and me Mary they started me at $45,000. Imagine that? Wow, was I impressed. I just couldn't believe

that they would . . . Where are you going, Mary? Mary? What's that you say "It isn't fair"? What do you mean? Mary? Mary . . .

Review Questions

1. Indicate Mary's attitudes before and after meeting Sue. If there was a change, why?
2. What do you think Mary will do now? Later?
3. What motivation theory applies best to this scenario? Explain.

■

CASE 7
Amoco's Global Human Resource Systems

Developed by Ellen Ernst Kossek, Michigan State University

Headquartered in Chicago, Amoco, formerly Standard Oil of Indiana, began as a sleepy Midwestern U.S. refining company. Historically, Amoco has had a largely domestic focus in its human resources approach. "International human resources" primarily meant the personnel policies of U.S. expatriates—American citizens who work for Amoco abroad. Until several decades ago, most of Amoco's oil reserves were located in the United States; consequently, management had grown up with the view that most of the company's growth would come from within U.S. borders. Today, however, nearly 80 percent of new investment dollars are being targeted toward foreign operations.

Amoco mangement believes that developing a global approach necessitates transformation in attitudes, organizational processes, and human-resource systems. Drivers of global mandates for change in HR practices are as follows:

Global competition: Competitors are increasingly outside the United

States (British Petroleum, Royal Dutch Shell, ELF Acquitaine, BHP).

Major cash going overseas: Since most oil reserves and markets with most growth potential are now located overseas, operations will increasingly be done outside the United States.

Economic shift: The United States is no longer as dominant an economic base as it has been historically.

Global labor markets: A growing pool of talent will be hired beyond the U.S. labor market. There is also a need to manage cultural and politi-

cal constraints on travel, work permits, type of assignments, and labor market conditions.

Excessive cost of expatriations: Because of the rising cost of expatriates, Amoco must use the talent of local nationals to a greater extent. Yet, in some countries after the costs of social programs are entered into the analysis, staffing local nationals is not always necessarily cheaper.

Culture and value differences of global workforce: State-of-the-art U.S. practices may not favor applicants from non-U.S. cultures (e.g., targeted selection, individual reward and appraisal systems) or may have implementation problems. Expatriation of female employees is limited in some locations.

Increased pressures from foreign governments: Expectations have changed; foreign governments now demand that local nationals be employed.

Increasing need to have a global presence: In many cultures, a long relationship must be developed, and evidence of *staying power* must be shown in order to get business; lack of presence may affect future bids in a country.

Ethics: Amoco's values will not premit it to engage in bribing or violating U.S. laws when abroad, even if it is the custom.

The number one competitive pressure shaping human resource activities is the changing competition of the oil industry. Increasingly, Amoco's competitors are foreign companies, such as British Petroleum and Royal Dutch Shell. Since most investment for new business will be spent overseas, it is essential that Amoco's human resource systems adapt accordingly. Management must also no longer

Source: This is an abridged version of a case appearing in the Field Guide of E. E. Kossek and S. Lobel, *Managing Diversity: Human Resource Strategies for Transforming the Workplace* (Oxford, England, Blackwell, 1996).

view the United States as the premier economic base.

Because of the need for a global workforce, there will be significantly greater demand to integrate local nationals at all levels of an overseas subsidiary. Contributing to this view is the excessive cost of expatriations; that is, the high cost of moving U.S. employees abroad to run companies. Because of these financial pressures, Amoco must make greater use of the talent of local nationals. Yet, just hiring a great number of local nationals for managerial positions will not necessarily help a company globalize successfully; the ability to balance the parent company's view with local needs is a critical consideration. There is still a nagging (and some might say well-founded) fear in the minds of some Amoco executives that they must cautiously pick people who have allegiance to Amoco and not their local country's government. There is the tendency to be lean and mean in terms of placement of local nationals in key positions in developing countries. As a protective staffing strategy, even in developed countries, the vast majority of critical jobs are held by U.S. expatriates. In Norway, for example, some managers complain of a glass ceiling effect, a barrier that keeps nationals from moving into key positions. And the trend seems to be spiraling downhill, despite the fact that the country's operations are extremely successful, are stable, and mix relatively well with the United States. Even in Northern European countries, cultural differences remain that are barriers to developing a global workforce. Work and family values are different in European countries compared to the U.S. workaholic corporate norm. It is not uncommon to see Norwegian male employees leave at 3:30 in the afternoon to go pick up their children from school, a

practice that is still rare for male employees in the United States. Some U.S. managers have felt that if a lot of high-quality work needs to be done quickly in a short amount of time, U.S. managers are needed to get it done.

Developing worldwide human resource systems means analyzing cultural biases in "leading edge" practices developed with an American view. For example, targeted selection, whereby an interviewer asks questions that target the presence of key abilities found in successful U.S. managers, may not work well for individuals from countries that shun bragging excessively about one's strengths in an interview. Similarly, total quality management, which relies on self-empowerment, may require some modification before being applied abroad in cultures that value individualism less.

Over time, the amount of U.S. expatriation must decrease because of *de facto* cost pressures. Increasingly, a more cost-effective strategy might be to rely on the U.S. workforce more in the consultation role. Greater utilization of local nationals in running international operations might also better blend local laws and customs with Amoco's practices. Yet, typically, when planning new ventures, the human resource plan is usually the last one put in place.

There is also an increasing need to have a presence in a country, in order to get a concession or a government approval to begin energy exploration. In many cultures, a long relationship must be developed and evidence of staying power must be shown to in order to get business. The lack of presence may affect future bids in a country. As one employee commented, "We're very good at managing the technical aspects of the exploration busi-

ness—for instance we have led the industry in seismic techniques related to secondary tertiary recovery, but we're not very good at managing new cultures effectively to obtain entry." In Amoco's defense, some manager's argue that, realistically, Amoco may not know whether it will be in a new country 6 more months or 6 or more years. This uncertainty is dependent on whether a discovery is made, an endeavor that can fail 90 percent of the time. Some managers contend that it makes more sense to use talent from the United States until a discovery is found. Yet a key to developing marketing strength in new markets is to open an office in a country even before a discovery is made. Typically, however, Amoco will not open an office in a new country until after a discovery is made and concessions are given. Because of this policy, Royal Dutch Shell has a 10-month jump on Amoco in Romania, since it was there long before a concession was made. Given the fact that the entitlement and social programs in many countries are very much more costly than in the United States, a counter-argument can be made that it *does* make sense for a U.S. oil company to move slowly when hiring foreign employees. It would be extremely expensive to close a firm and pay off the former workers if no oil were found. Because of these conditions, contract employees are often used heavily in the early stages of development.

Still, many believe that it is not possible for a company the size of Amoco to open as many offices worldwide as larger competitors, such as Royal Dutch Shell or Exxon. Rather, Amoco should focus its efforts on opening offices early in selected countries. Instead of using its technical strengths *after* a discovery is made to gain business, Amoco should do a better job of making the world aware of its strength in applying technology well and leverage this capability to get new contracts.

Increasing pressures to hire locals are also being felt from foreign governments. Expectations today have changed. Foreign governments now demand greater employment of local nationals. This can be a problem in countries such as Trinidad, where lifetime employment is the norm. It is very difficult to be a low-cost operator when the biggest part of the costs come early; then, once the oil platforms are built and the growth is underway, the firm is left with a headcount that is not flexible.

An additional pressure stems from worldwide differences in ethics. Amoco values will not permit it to engage in bribing or violating U.S. laws when abroad, even if it is the custom and competitors are doing so. Ethics also affect the extent to which a multinational chooses to use techniques that minimize damage to the environment, even if there are no foreign environmental laws. Firms that are environmentally cautious may face much higher costs than their competitors. Yet some managers believe that Amoco's ethics could be turned into a competitive advantage to get new business, because many of Amoco's

environmental approaches are leading edge. In Pakistan, for example, the government would not allow the import of beride, a chemical used in the drilling of wells. Amoco spent an extra quarter million dollars on its wells in lining pits and putting up a dustproof room for the lead, which can be hazardous to the environment, if mixed. Similarly, in Burma, where operations were in a jungle, Amoco cut a very narrow path around the area for the oil well and then reforested. In the United States, where environmental regulations are considered to be the most strict in the world, Amoco strives not only to meet but to exceed environmental regulations. As one manager states, "If you spend more now, you'll save a lot later, because you'll be ahead of regulatory changes." Some believe that doing a better job marketing this record will increase global opportunities.

Review Questions

1. What is a global organization?
2. What are the key business pressures driving the globalization of human resource systems?
3. What are some HR practices that would help Amoco Production manage these tensions? ■

For one manager of software projects (based in Los Angeles) who oversees 11 people in a 50-person office based in Dallas, the answer is that telecommuting is very effective, although not without drawbacks. Our manager, a veteran of nine years of telecommuting, is in constant contact with her employees, software technical writers, and quality analysts–testers, through E-mail, with voice mailbox, phone, fax, and, at least once a month, face-to-face visits on site with each employee. One room in her home is fully outfitted as an office, one she can walk away from as a means of separating her personal and professional life. However, she is always connected to those whom she supervises. For example, on a weekend, if an employee has gone in to work, she can answer a question from home by merely walking into her home-based office.

To keep connected with her employees on a physical level, our manager meets individually with each employee on a monthly basis in Dallas. She spends an hour going over the priorities they have listed as activities for the month. Throughout the month, the manager and the employees are in constant contact. Through both physical and electronic communication our manager is able to get to know her employees well. As she has noted, meeting with them in person allows her to "see" them over the phone, judging their psychological "space" by voice intonation when there is no physical face to communicate with. Our manager also interacts with other managers and line personnel through telecommuting. For example, she negotiates over the phone what goes into a product, the time line, the product budget, and all other factors necessary to managing a product effectively.

While our manager likes telecommuting and is able to man-

CASE 8
I'm Not in Kansas Anymore

Developed by Anne C. Cowden, California State University, Sacramento

Telecommuting is defined as work done at home or in a remote location using technology as the link. Approximately 7.6 million people currently telecommute. The decision whether to allow employees to telecommute is controversial, owing to the number of managerial control questions raised by people working and/or managing off site.

age effectively, there are both good points and drawbacks. The advantages include the freedom from commuting every day in full office dress, the complexity and challenge to stay well connected with employees, and the time gained by staying at home. The drawbacks can be the isolation that some initially feel when not having daily physical contact with others. Another drawback may be "workaholism" if one is unable to separate life from one's job. Burnout can be a factor if one works all the time.

If you are thinking of telecommuting, our manager would advise the following: get a good headset for talking on the phone; be prepared for the initial feelings of isolation; and keep in daily, close contact with your employees.

Review Questions

1. Is telecommuting the wave of the future, or does top management lose too much control when people are off site?
2. How would you like being a telecommuter, as either a manager or one being managed?
3. Do you think telecommuting is effective for both the employee and the organization? Why or why not? ■

CASE 9
The Forgotten Group Member
....

Developed by Franklin Ramsoomair, Wilfred Laurier University

The Organizational Behavior course for the semester appeared to promise the opportunity to learn, enjoy, and practice some of the theories and principles in the textbook and class discussions. Christine Spencer was a devoted, hard-working student, who had been maintaining an A- average to date. Although the skills and knowledge she had acquired through her courses were important, she was also very concerned about her grades. She felt that grades were paramount in giving her a competitive edge when looking for a job and, as a third-year student, she realized that she'd soon be doing just that.

Sunday afternoon. Two o'clock. Christine was working on an accounting assignment but didn't seem to be able to concentrate. Her courses were working out very well this semester, all but the OB. Much of the mark in that course was to be applied to the quality of groupwork, and so she felt somewhat out of control. She recollected the events of the past five weeks. Professor Sandra Thiel had divided the class into groups of five people and had given them a major group assignment worth 30 percent of the final grade. The task was to analyze a seven-page case and to come up with a written analysis. In addition, Sandra had asked the groups to present the case in class, with the idea in mind that the rest of the class members would be "members of the Board of Directors of the company" who would be listening to how the manager and her team dealt with the problem at hand.

Christine was elected "Team Coordinator" at the first group meeting. The other members of the group were Diane, Janet, Steve, and Mike. Diane was quiet and never volunteered suggestions, but when directly asked, she would come up with high-quality ideas. Mike was the clown. Christine remembered that she had suggested that the group should get together before every class to discuss the day's case. Mike had balked, saying "No way!! This is an 8:30 class, and I barely make it on time anyway! Besides, I'll miss my 'Happy Harry' show on television!" The group couldn't help but laugh at his indignation. Steve was the businesslike individual, always wanting to ensure that group meetings were guided by an agenda and noting the tangible results achieved or not achieved at the end of every meeting. Janet was the reliable one who would always have more for the group than was expected of her. Christine saw herself as meticulous and organized and as a person who tried to give her best in whatever she did.

It was now week five into the semester, and Christine was deep in thought about the OB assignment. She had called everyone to arrange a meeting for a time that would suit them all but seemed to be running into a roadblock. Mike couldn't make it, saying that he was working that night as a member of the campus security force. In fact, he seemed to miss most meetings and would send in brief notes to Christine, which she was supposed to discuss for him at the group meetings. She wondered how to deal with this. She also remembered the incident last week. Just before class started, Diane, Janet, Steve, and herself were joking with one another before class. They were laughing and enjoying themselves before Sandra came in. No one noticed that Mike had slipped in very quietly and had unobtrusively taken his seat.

She recalled the cafeteria incident. Two weeks ago, she had gone to the cafeteria to grab something to eat. She had rushed to her accounting class and had skipped breakfast. When she got her club sandwich and headed to the tables, she saw her OB group and joined them. The discussion was light and enjoyable as it always was when they met informally. Mike had come in. He'd approached their table. "You guys didn't say you were having a group meeting," he blurted. Christine was taken aback.

"We just happened to run into each other. Why not join us?"

"Mike looked at them, with a noncommittal glance. Yah . . . right," he muttered, and walked away.

Sandra Thiel had frequently told them that if there were problems in the group, the members should make an effort to deal with them first. If the problems could not be resolved, she had said that they should come to her. Mike seemed so distant, despite the apparent camaraderie of the first meeting.

An hour had passed, bringing the time to 3 P.M., and Christine found herself biting the tip of her pencil. The written case analysis was due next week. All the others had done their designated sections, but Mike had just handed in some rough handwritten notes. He had called Christine the week before, telling her that in addition to his course and his job, he was having problems with his girlfriend. Christine empathized with him. Yet, this was a group project! Besides, the final mark would be peer evaluated. This meant that whatever mark Sandra gave them could be lowered or raised, depending on the group's opinion about the value of the contribution of each member. She was definitely worried. She knew that Mike had creative ideas that could help to raise the overall mark. She was also concerned for him. As she listened to the music in the background, she wondered what she should do.

Review Questions

1. How could an understanding of the stages of group development assist Christine in leadership situations such as this one?
2. What should Christine understand about individual membership in groups in order to build group processes that are supportive of her work group's performance?
3. Is Christine an effective group leader in this case? Why or why not. ■

CASE 10
NASCAR's Racing Teams
••
Developed by David S. Chappell, Ohio University

When asked to name the fastest growing American team sport, most people respond with basketball, baseball, football, or soccer. However, that distinction, based on total spectator audience, goes to stock car racing. The largest stock car racing group in the world is the National

Association for Stock Car Auto Racing (NASCAR). The NASCAR Winston Cup Series—its premier league with 34 events at 22 U.S. tracks—kicks off February 7 at Daytona International Speedway and runs through November 21 with the NAPA 500 at Atlanta Motor Speedway in Atlanta.[1]

NASCAR

The Daytona, Florida-based France family owns NASCAR, making it the only family-owned professional league in the United States. In 1998, NASCAR attracted 11 million fans to race tracks and another 252 million to watch races on television.[2] Attendance at NASCAR races has jumped 80 percent since 1990 and the league's television ratings placed second in 1998 behind the NFL in sports programming. Drivers are involved in seven cable network shows and three syndicated radio shows each week. NASCAR's official Web site, at www.nascar.com, is ranked among the five most popular sites on the Internet, receiving 35 million hits each week.[3]

Celebrating its 50th anniversary in 1998, NASCAR has become a marketing powerhouse, with races, merchandise, collectibles, apparel, and co-marketing tie-ins. The Coca-Cola Co. placed images of NASCAR racing teams and drivers on 30 million soda bottles in 1998. It was the biggest promotion the soft drink company had ever done and, the company said that it sold more bottles than its annual favorite starring Santa Claus. NASCAR-licensed products generated more than $900 million in sales in 1998, up from $80 million in 1990, for licensees in 150 categories, including apparel, gifts, accessories, toys and collectibles.[4]

The race cars themselves have been described by some as "200 mile-per-hour billboards." As an

---

*Note: The blue underscored words/phrases in this case indicate Internet links provided in the online version. See the *Organizational Behavior, Seventh Edition* Web Site at http://www.wiley.com/college/schermerhorn.

organized sport, NASCAR is unique in that its drivers are treated like independent contractors rather than employees. As such, they must behave in addition to seeking their own sponsors to finance their race teams.[5] Traditional NASCAR sponsors, including RJR Nabisco, Pennzoil-Quaker State, and General Motors have been joined by relative newcomers such as M&M/Mars, Lowe's, and Procter and Gamble. "If you look at where NASCAR was in 1993 and where it is today, you see it's a completely different sport," states Dave Elgena, senior executive vice president in charge of motorsports for MBNA. "Today you see lots of big corporations involved that wouldn't have been here six years ago."[6]

With a history of great drivers, including Richard Petty, Cale Yarborough, and Davey Pearson, a new crop of young drivers is exciting spectators. Compared to the "good-old-boys" who dominated the racing circuit for years, the new crop is younger and more sophisticated. One of the most successful young drivers in the league is Jeff Gordon, racing for Hendrick Motorsport's #24 Dupont Automotive Finishes.

Jeff Gordon—Racing Sensation

Jeff Gordon, on the Winston Cup racing scene since 1993, has been a sensation ever since he started racing go-carts and quarter-midget cars at the age of 5. In 1979 and 1981, he was the quarter-midget national champion, and in 1990 he won the 1990 USAC midget championship.[7] He has captured the imagination of race fans around the world, becoming the youngest driver ever to win three NASCAR Winston Cup overall championships and has over 40 individual race wins in a four-year span.

Gordon, 27, says his strong family upbringing in California and Indiana and his marriage to former Miss Winston beauty queen Brooke Sealy have made it easy. "There's no question Jeff has helped take our sport to the next level as far as image," said Ned Jarrett, a CBS analyst and two-time NASCAR champion during the 1960s. "He's helped raise the level of competition and also helped get the sport places it's never been before."[8] The question becomes, what does Gordon have that others have trouble imitating?

As the driver of a successful race car, Gordon represents the most visible part of an incredibly complex team of individuals—all with a contribution to make on raceday. "To build a winning team, you need three major ingredients—people, equipment and money," states Don Hawk, president of Dale Earnhardt Inc. "You can't do it with only one, not even with two, you need all three. Look at Gordon, his team has crew chief Ray Evernham and the Rainbow Warriors pit crew—their multicolored uniforms match Gordon's multicolored car, the best in the garage area, they have the fastest and most reliable Chevrolet on the track, and they have great finances from DuPont. You couldn't do what they've done with just a great driver, just a great car, or an open pocketbook. You must have all the elements meshing. I liken a winning racing team to a Rubik's Cube. All the pieces must fit, and be in the proper place."[9]

The High Performance TEAM

"Success is a ruthless competitor, for it flatters and nourishes our weakness and lulls us into complacency."

The quote above is found in the shop of Gordon's crew chief, Ray

Evernham, recognized by many in NASCAR as the premier crew chief in the business. While Gordon represents the star attraction, many believe that it's Evernham who pulls the whole act together. He is responsible for a group of over 120 technicians and mechanics and an annual budget estimated between $10 and $12 million. And he has strong opinions as to what it takes to consistently finish first: painstaking preparation, egoless teamwork, and thoroughly original strategizing—principles that apply to any high performance organization.[10]

You win as a team. Evernham believes that teams need to experiment with new methods and processes. When he assembled his Rainbow Warriors pit crew, none of them had Winston Cup experience and none worked on the car in any other capacity. With the use of a pit crew coach, the Rainbow Warriors provide Gordon with approximately one-second advantage with each pit stop, which at a speed of 200 miles-per-hour, equates into 300 feet of race track.

When you coach and support a superstar like Jeff Gordon, you give him the best equipment possible, you give him the information he needs, and then you get out of the way. But racing is a team sport. Everyone who races pretty much has the same car and the same equipment. What sets us apart is our people. I like to talk about our "team IQ"—because none of us is as smart as all of us.

I think a lot about people, management, and psychology: Specifically, how can I motivate my guys and make them gel as a team? I surround them with ideas about teamwork. I read every leadership book I can get my hands on. One thing that I took from my reading is the idea of a "circle of strength." When the Rainbow Warriors meet, we always put our chairs in a circle. That's a way of saying that we're stronger as a team than we are on our own.[11]

Evernham backs up this belief in

team by emphasizing team performance over individual performance. When the car wins a race, everyone shares in the prize money. In addition, when Evernham earns money through personal-service activities such as speaking tours and autograph signings, he shares what he earns with the team. "I wouldn't be in a position to earn that income if it weren't for the team. Everyone should feel as if his signature is on the finished product."[12]

The teamwork during a race can even include adversaries—as in other drivers. In an effort to make races competitive for fans, NASCAR uses several methods to make the cars approximately even in performance, thereby enhancing the competitive environment for the audience. To get ahead, racers depend on their friends in the form of cars that help aerodynamically "slingshot" them ahead of the pack. This may take the form of teammates (Wally Dallenbach and Terry Labonte for Hendrick Motorsports) or opponents.

Push for perfection but accept imperfection. High performance teams are constantly improving, even in small ways. Evernham makes use of every opportunity to learn something new. If the car is running well, Evernham asks Gordon to find something wrong with it. "We always try to make the car perfect. But the car doesn't have to be perfect to win; it just has to be less imperfect than everyone else's car."[13]

Don't strutt your stuff. In the past, most crews concentrated on the car and relied on horsepower and driving talent to win the race. Evernham takes a larger view that keeps the egos in check:

There aren't many secrets in the Winston Cup, so you've got to protect as much information as you can. We want to have the fastest car on the track, but we don't want everybody else to know how fast we are. We don't show our hand until it's time to race or to qualify.

We also try to mix things up on race day. We don't want to fall into patterns or to tip off the competition about our next pit stop. Since everybody can hear us on the scanners, we might use a code word to signal whether we're changing two tires or four. Sometimes, when the car is running well, Jeff might get on the radio and complain to me that the steering's tight, even though he's about to pass another driver. And that driver's crew chief will fall for it: "Yeah, Gordon can't pass you right now, because he's tight." The driver will leave a little opening and—boom—we're past him.[14]

To win the race, drive by different rules. Evernham attacks each race as different from the last. He is constantly looking for even the smallest advantage that can give his race car and driver the edge. The team practices passing cars in unsuspected areas of the track, when their competitors least expect it.[15]

High performance teams do not happen by chance; rather, they are the result of good recruiting and meticulous attention to learning every detail of the job. With 10 wins in 1997 and 13 wins in 1998, the Gordon recipe for success has resulted in three Winston Cup Series Championships. Jeff Gordon wins approximately one of every four races he starts, a pace unmatched in modern times. The question remains, can anyone catch him?

Review Questions

1. Evaluate Jeff Gordon's race team on dimensions discussed under the author's conversation on characteristics of high performance teams.
2. Discuss Jeff Gordon's race team on dimensions discussed under the author's conversation on methods to increase group cohesiveness.
3. Compare Gordon's race team on the methods of team building. Which one most applies to this situation?

References

1. Dodd, Annmarie. "The Fastest Sport on Earth—Fast-Moving and Fast-Growing, NASCAR Uses Its Loud, Folksy Appeal to Find New Racing Fans for the Future," *Daily News Record,* January 25, 1999.
2. Ibid.
3. Ibid.
4. Ibid.
5. Glick, Shav. "Dollar Signs: Sponsorships, Big Money Make NASCAR World Go 'Round," *The Los Angeles Times,* February 14, 1999, p. D1.
6. Yost, Mark. "Companies Use NASCAR Races as Means to Rub Elbows, Boost Their Business," *Wall Street Journal,* February 22, 1999, p. B17B.
7. Dodd, op. cit.
8. "NASCAR Online: Jeff Gordon," http://www.nascar.com/winstoncup/drivers/GordJ01/index.html, February 19, 1999.
9. Cain, Holly. "Gordon Becomes Driving Force," *The Seattle Times,* February 14, 1999, p. D1.
10. Glick, op. cit., p. D1.
11. Slater, Chuck. "Life in the Fast Lane," *Fast Company,* http://www.fastcompany.com/online/18/fastlane.html, October 1998.
12. Ibid.
13. Ibid.
14. Ibid.
15. Ibid.

CASE 11
First Community Financial

Developed by Mark Osborn, Arizona Chamber of Commerce

First Community Financial is a small business lender that specializes in asset-based lending and factoring for a primarily small-business clientele. First Community's business is generated by high-growth companies in diverse industries, whose capital needs will not be met by traditional banking institutions. First Community Financial will lend in amounts up to $1 million, so its focus is on small business. Since many of the loans that it administers are viewed by many banks as high-risk loans, it is important that the sales staff and loan processors have a solid working relationship. Since the loans and factoring deals that First Community finances are risky, the interest that it charges is at prime plus six percent or sometimes higher.

First Community is a credible player in the market because of its history and the human resource policies of the company. The company invests in its employees and works to assure that turnover is low. The goal of this strategy is to develop a consistent, professional team that has more expertise than its competitors.

Whereas Jim Adamany, president and CEO, has a strong history in the industry and is a recognized expert in asset-based lending and factoring, First Community has one of the youngest staff and management teams in the finance industry. In the banking industry, promotions are slow coming, because many banks employ conservative personnel programs. First Community, however, has recruited young, ambitious people who are specifically looking to grow with the company. As the company grows, so will the responsibility and rewards for these young executives. In his early thirties, for example, Matt Vincent is a vice president; at only 28, Brian Zcray, is director of marketing.

Since First Community has a diverse product line, it must compete in distinct markets. Its factoring products compete with small specialized factoring companies. Factoring is a way for businesses to improve their cash flow by selling their invoices at a discount. Factoring clients are traditionally the smallest clients finance companies must serve. Education about the nature of the product is crucial if the company is to be successful since this often is a new approach to financing for many companies. First Community's sales staff is well trained at understanding its product lines and acts as the client's representative as they work through the approval process.

To assure the loans or factoring deals fit within the risk profile of the company, First Community must ask many complex financial questions. Many small businesses are intimidated by credit officers, so First Community handles all of these inquiries through the business development officers. The business development officers, in turn, must understand the needs of their credit officers, who are attempting to minimize risk to the company while maintaining a friendly rapport with the client. By centralizing the client contract through educated sales representatives, First Community is able to ask the hard financial questions and still keep the clients interested in the process. A potential customer can easily be discouraged by a creditor administrator's strong questioning about financial background. Utilizing the business development officers as an intermediary reduces the fear of many applicants about the credit approval process. Thus, a sales focus is maintained throughout the recruitment and loan application process.

Internally at First Community Financial there is a continual pressure between the business development staff and the credit committee. The business development staff is focused on bringing in new clients. Their compensation in a large part is dependent on how many deals they can execute for the company. Like sales staff in any industry, they are aggressive and always look for new markets for business. The sales staff sells products from both the finance department and the factoring department, so they must interact with credit officers from each division. In each of these groups are credit administrators specifically responsible for ensuring that potential deals meet the lending criteria of the organization. While the business development officer's orientation is to bring in more and more deals, the credit administrator's primary goal is to limit bad loans.

The pressure develops when business development officers bring in potential loans that are rejected by the credit administrators. Since the business development officers have some experience understanding the credit risks of their clients, they often understand the policy reasoning for denying or approving a loan. The business development officers have additional concerns that their loans that have potential to be financed are approved because many of the referral sources of the sales staff will only refer deals to companies who are lending. If First Community fails to help many of a bank's referral clients, that source of business may dry up, as bankers refer deals to other lending institutions.

These structural differences are handled by focused attempts at improving communication. As noted before, the First Community staff experiences an extremely low turnover rate. This allows for the development of a cohesive team. With a cohesive staff, the opportunity to maintain frank and open communication helps bridge the different orientations of the sales staff and the administration divisions. A simple philosophy that the opinions of all staff are to be respected is continually implemented.

Since approving a loan is often a policy decision, the sales staff and the loan administrators can have an open forum to discuss whether a loan will be approved. CEO Jim Adamany approves all loans, but since he values the opinions of all of his staff he provides them all an opportunity to communicate. Issues such as the loan history for an applicant's industry, current bank loan policies, and other factors can be openly discussed from multiple perspectives.

Review Questions

1. What coordinative mechanisms does First Community use to manage the potential conflict between its sales and finance/auditing functions?
2. What qualities should First Community emphasize in hiring new staff to ensure that its functional organizational structure will not yield too many problems?
3. What are the key types of information transfer that First Community needs to emphasize, and how is this transmitted throughout the firm?
4. Why might a small finance company have such a simple structure while a larger firm might find this structure inappropriate?

■

CASE 12
Mission Management and Trust

Developed by Mark Osborn, Arizona Chamber of Commerce

With more than 500 business and political leaders in attendance from across the state of Arizona, CEO Carmen Bermudez of Mission Management and Trust accepted the prestigious ATHENA Award. The ATHENA, which is presented by the Arizona Chamber of Commerce, is annually awarded to companies that have a demonstrated track record in promoting women's issues within their company and the community. The 50-pound bronze statute that was presented to Mission Management and Trust was particularly special for the company's leadership because it was a tangible demonstration of their commitment to the community and to women's issues.

Mission Management and Trust is a small newly formed company of just eight employees that has already made great headway in an industry that is dominated by giant corporations. Mission Management and Trust opened its doors just two years ago, and it already manages over $45 million in assets. What makes Mission's development even more impressive is that Mission is the first minority- and women-owned trust company in the nation.

The trust management industry provides services to individuals, organizations, and companies who want their assets managed and protected by specialized outside firms. Mission management provides personal service to its customers at a level of sophistication that is unusual for a firm of its small size. Understanding that the trust management business is highly competitive, Mission developed a unique strategy that highlighted socially conscious policies combined with good business relations.

When the company was formed in 1994, it was created with more than the goal of just making a profit. Founder Carmen Bermudas started Mission with three principal goals in mind. "1. To run a top quality trust company; 2. To promote within the company and, by example, increase opportunities for women and minorities; and 3. To donate a portion of all revenue to charitable projects supported by clients and staff." As these statements demonstrate, Mission Management and Trust was created with a specific purpose in mind that was focused not just on the business of trust management but on the responsibility of being a good corporate citizen.

Even with these lofty goals, Mission faced the problem of finding clients who not only wanted quality services but were not hindered by some of the potential sacrifices a socially conscious investment company might make. Many investors want a high rate of return for their trusts, and social policy is of a much lesser concern. This was not the market Mission wanted to address, so it had to be selective in developing a client base.

Mission needed to find clients

that fit its social philosophy about investing and corporate responsibility. The ideal customers would be individuals and organizations that were committed to socially conscious policies and wanted an investment strategy that reflected this commitment. Mission found a perfect niche in the market with religious institutions. Churches and other civic organizations across the nation have trusts that they use to fund special projects and maintain operating expenses. They need effective service, but in many cases these organizations must be mindful of investing in companies and other projects that do not refelct their ideals. For example, a trust company that invests in companies in the highly profitable liquor and cigarette industries would not be consistent with the philosophy of many religious organizations. Mission services this niche by developing an organization that is structurally designed to make socially conscious decisions.

Mission has already begun to meet one of its principal goals, which is to donate a portion of its profits to charities. By the end of 1994, Mission had already donated $4500 to causes ranging from Catholic Community Services to the Jewish Community Center scholarship program. These donations not only fulfill a goal of the organization but assist in the socially conscious client recruitment. Mission's target client base will find Mission a much more attractive trust company because of its charity programs. A religious organization can be comforted with the reality that some of the dollars it spends on trust management will be recycled into the causes it promotes itself. The mission policy makes good social policy, but it also makes good marketing sense. Understanding your clients is crucial to developing a small business, and Mission has mastered this principle.

Mission makes the most of its commitment to charitable causes by keeping its clients informed about the trust's activities and, more importantly, its community activities. *The Mission Bell,* a regular publication of Mission Management and Trust, details news and issues about the trust industry, company activities, and, most importantly, how Mission's social responsibility philosophy is being implemented. The name *Mission Bell* is more consistent with a religious publication than a corporate investing sheet, but it is consistent with its clients' needs. The name of the publication and its content clarifies Mission's role and purpose. For example, the *Mission Bell Summer Issue* presented articles on new hires, breaking investment news, and an article about how Mission is working with other groups to support socially responsible corporate investing. Thus, the Mission philosophy is clearly defined in its marketing and communication strategies.

To be consistent with the goals of the organizations, Carmen Bremudez collected a small staff of highly experienced individuals whose backgrounds and principles fit Mission's ideals. She frequently comments that the best business decision she ever made was "giving preference to intelligent, talented, compatible people whose main attribute was extensive experience." Mission employees are not just experts in the field of finance but leaders in their communities. These dual qualifications fulfill three important requirements that are crucial for the company's success. With community involvement comes an appreciation of the investment sensitivities that are required by the organizations that Mission services. Second, individuals who are involved in the community have well-developed contacts that can be useful in

business recruitment. Finally, socially active employees are committed to the purpose of the organization and help unify the corporate culture within Mission.

Claire B. Moore, vice president of Mission Management and Trust, is a perfect example of how a corporate philosophy has been translated into practical personnel decisions. Claire was recruited because she had extensive banking experience, as demonstrated by her vice president position in Bank of America (Arizona). Her professional qualifications are augmented by her extensive involvement in the community, which includes the University of Arizona Foundation Planned Giving Council, Tucson Symphony, and the Junior League, to name a few.

The Mission case is a clear example of how matching a philosophy with a market can bear solid results. Mission's commitment to its ideals is evident and reflected in all of their business practices. When human resources, investing, marketing, and strategic planning decisions are made with unified goals in mind, the chances are good that a strong successful corporate culture will develop.

Review Questions

1. How do the mission elements of Mission Management differ from most firms?
2. Does donating to charity before the firm is fully established mean that Mission is not demonstrating financial prudence?
3. Could Mission's unique mission contribute to effective coordination as well as adjustment to the market?
4. Would Mission's unique mission still yield success with more traditional investors? ∎

CASE 13

Motorola: Is a High Performance Culture Enough?

Developed by David S. Chappell, Ohio University

Motorola Inc., world famous for its Six Sigma quality control program, was an early success story in the computer/electronics age. Motorola moved from being a decentralized but integrated, narrowly focused electronics firm at $3 billion in 1980 to being a decentralized and disintegrated broad portfolio firm at $27 billion in 1997.[1] Motorola is one of the world's leading providers of wireless communications, semiconductors, electronic systems, components, and services. Its cellular phone and pager products were identified among the very best in the early 1990s. However, increased competition, the Asian economic crisis, and its failure to fully embrace the digital revolution have severely tarnished its operating results and image. Can Motorola return to its high performance ways?

The Evolution of Motorola

Motorola Inc. was founded by Paul V. Galvin in 1928, as the Galvin Manufacturing Corporation. Motorola's long history of technological innovation began in the 1930s with the first car radio. Under the brand name "Motorola," suggesting "sound in motion" the company name was changed to Motorola, Inc. in 1947.[2] Being the sound of innovation, it was Motorola's goal to provide products that would give people the time and freedom to explore new worlds and handle daily tasks in the most efficient way.

Motorola represents a large number of firsts, including the first rectangular television picture tube, first practical car radio, pagers, and more. In 1988, Motorola won the first Malcolm Baldridge National Quality Award in recognition of quality in American business. This is the

same year that George Fisher (now president of Kodak) became president of the firm; he is credited by many with bringing Motorola into the cellular age.

Beginning in 1987, Motorola began the design of IRIDIUM. The system is a satellite-based, wireless communications network. It consists of 66 interconnected, low-orbiting satellites that deliver voice, data, fax and paging through a hand-held phone. The system will simplify communications for business professionals, travelers, residents and other users, permitting them to reach any destination on Earth. Along with Motorola, Sprint and Iridium Canada are contributing to the development of IRIDIUM system to the North American continent. The development of IRIDIUM will provide customers with high-quality service at a reasonable rate.

As Motorola continued to expand its worldwide presence in the global marketplace through products and services, the need for talented personnel to uphold these established standards has increased. In recognition of this essentiality, Motorola has demonstrated a high

Note: The blue underscored words/phrases in this case indicate Internet links provided in the on-line version. See the *Organizational Behavior, Seventh Edition* Web Site at http://www.wiley.com/college/schermerhorn.

commitment to seeking and developing a broad base of knowledgeable, highly trained employees, evident through their innovative training programs, through the establishment of Motorola University, and through the offering of expansive benefit plans to all associates.

The Importance of Organizational Culture to Motorola

In the early 1990s, Motorola was recognized as a true high performance organization with its innovations and socially responsible corporate attitude. Indeed, its organizational culture is identified as a source of competitive advantage for the firm. Working in quality teams, members strive to provide the highest level of customer satisfaction, measuring defects in incidents per billion. Motorola earmarks more than $100 million a year for training, with everyone in the organization, however humble, spending at least a week a year back in the classroom at Motorola University, courtesy of the company.[3]

Motorola lists its fundamental objective as total customer satisfaction: "To serve every customer better than our competitors do with products and services of excellent value and quality, and thereby earn continued enthusiastic trust and support."[4] It wishes to accomplish this objective with respect for the individual, a statement it makes clear in its shared beliefs.

People
To treat each employee with dignity, as an individual; to maintain an open atmosphere where direct communication with employees affords the opportunity to contribute to the maximum of their potential and fosters unity of purpose with Motorola; to provide personal opportunities for training and development to ensure the most capable and most effective work force; to respect senior service;

to compensate fairly by salary, benefits and, where possible, incentives; to promote on the basis of capability; and to practice the commonly accepted policies of equal opportunity and affirmative action.

Integrity and Ethics

To maintain the highest standards of honesty, integrity and ethics in all aspects of our business—with customers, suppliers, employees, governments and society at large—and to comply with the laws of each country and community in which we operate.[5]

From a proponent of <u>leadership training</u> to a leader in <u>quality control processes</u>, Motorola has created an internal climate that fosters high standards and a high performance culture. The firm depends on Total Customer Satisfaction Teams (<u>TCS</u>) to ensure the firm's commitment to quality. These teams are now made up of almost 30 percent of Motorola's 150,000 employees, and a goal of 10 times reduction of defects every two years puts pressure on them to constantly devise new ways to develop and deliver their products and services.

Motorola views itself as family and encourages employees to balance their work and family responsibilities. They support onsite <u>child care centers</u> and fund a <u>wellness program</u> for all employees.

Authors John Kotter and James Hesket's study on corporate culture shows that:

1. Corporate culture can have a significant impact on a firm's long-term economic performance.
2. Corporate culture will probably be an even more important factor in determining the success or failure of firms in the next decade.
3. Corporate cultures that inhibit strong long-term financial performance are not rare; they develop easily, even in firms that are full of reasonable and intelligent people.

4. Although tough to change, corporate cultures can be made more performance enhancing.[6]

Organizational culture can be a two-edged sword, however. Strong cultures may contribute to high performance for extended periods of time but may actually result in an inability to adjust when conditions change. It's important to foster a balance between stability and flexibility for change, an objective that is difficult to maintain. For many firms, success in the short term causes problems with inflexibility to changing situations in the long term.

So What Went Wrong?

In early June 1998, Motorola CEO <u>Chris Galvin</u> announced that the company would take a $1.95 billion charge and lay off 15,000 employees. Motorola's semiconductor business, which grew 23 percent in 1995, slowed to a 1 percent growth rate early in 1998. In recent years <u>Motorola's stock</u> has dropped 40 points, to a low of $50 in 1998, and its share of the U.S. cellular phone market has plummeted to 41 percent from 54 percent. "It's kind of depressing," moans one money manager. "It's not as though people weren't barking and screaming to management about what was going wrong."[7]

Maggie Wilderotter, a former top executive with <u>AT&T Wireless Services</u> and its predecessor, McCaw Cellular, lends insight into Motorola's troubles. In the early 1990s, 85 percent of the cell phones McCaw sold to subscribers were made by Motorola, whose flip phones, the most advanced at the time, were in hot demand. Around that time McCaw decided that the future of cellular was digital, and over the next few years Wilderotter met repeatedly with managers at Motorola's Schaumberg, Illinois,

headquarters and in her Seattle office, urging them to develop a digital phone. Motorola said it would work on it. So in the beginning of 1996, not long after AT&T Wireless had rolled out its digital network, Motorola unveiled its <u>StarTAC</u> phone: light, beautiful—and analog. AT&T had no choice but to turn to cellular phone manufacturers <u>Nokia</u> and <u>Ericsson</u> for digital handsets. By the end of 1997, fewer than 40 percent of AT&T Wireless' cell phones were Motorolas.

"It was bizarre," says Wilderotter, now CEO of Wink Communications, an interactive-TV company. "We were very forthright with what we wanted. I don't know if they didn't listen or they thought it wasn't going to happen. It is absolutely amazing to me that they lost their way."[8] In 1998, Nokia replaced Motorola as the leading supplier of mobile handsets, a position Motorola had held since the mobile phone industry began. Nokia sold 37.4 million units (an 81.5 percent increase from the previous year), representing a 22.9 percent market share compared to Motorola's 32.3 million units (only a 27.6 percent increase in volume), representing a 19.8 percent share.[9]

Much of Nokia's success is based on its digital technology, which accounted for 84.6 percent of the 163 million phones sold worldwide in 1998. Motorola remains the world leader in the declining analog handset sector, perhaps because of its presence in the U.S. market where digital has been slower to take off. Even with Motorola's introduction of a digital alternative to its popular StarTAC model, it retails for $500, compared to Nokia's 6100 at $200 and twice the battery life.[10]

Inspection of the company's IRIDIUM satellite system uncovers other weaknesses. The system eliminates "dead cells" by providing complete global coverage for cellular services. However, it comes with a price. The Motorola 9500 phone costs around $3000, and calls are priced anywhere from $1.75 to $7 a minute. The phone is bulky—about the size and weight of cell phones 10 years ago—with a thick, black antenna. In addition, the system needs an unobstructed view of the sky, with tall buildings and even dense foliage blocking transmissions.[11] With AT&T and others offering near unlimited long distance cellular service in the U.S. for under $90 per month, does the Motorola system make sense for anyone but the most remotely located employee?

Some of Motorola's problems are external, including a drop in semiconductor sales due to the Asian economic crisis, increased competition in cellular products, and a decline in pager sales. Motorola is attempting to restructure its operations in combination with cost-cutting measures. However, its situation illuminates the need for a culture that is both strong and responsive to external factors. In the quickly changing high-technology field, companies are forced to make difficult and costly choices among competing technologies.

Another concern for many is the presence of Chris Galvin, 48, as chief executive since January 1997. Unlike his predecessors, Chris has no engineering background; he studied marketing at Northwestern and rose through the sales side of the business. He intends to break down internal rivalries within the company and to create links between Motorola and other technology companies.[12] The question remains: Can Motorola regain its dominant market position without painful adjustments to its organizational culture? And can Chris Galvin lead them into a new era?

Review Questions

1. Discuss Motorola's relative success at the two functions/components of organizational culture discussed by the author.
2. Compare the various levels (observable, shared values, and common assumptions) of corporate culture at Motorola.
3. Discuss the various options managers might use in attempting to change the culture at Motorola.

References

1. Canavan, Patrick. "Motorola: Agility for the Whole Organization," *Human Resource Planning,* September 1998, p. 13(1).
2. "Motorola Homepage—Timeline," http://www.mot.com/General/Timeline/timeln24.html, March 4, 1999.
3. "Managing People: Nicely Does It," *The Economist,* March 19, 1994, p. 84. "Motorola Homepage—Culture," http://www.mot.com/Employment/stand.htm, March 19, 1999.
4. "Organizational Culture Alignment," http://www.msdev.com/culture.htm, March 7, 1999.
5. Ibid.
6. Roth, Daniel. "From Poster Boy to Whipping Boy: Burying Motorola," *Fortune,* July 6, 1998, p. 28(2).
7. Ibid.
8. Cane, Alan. "Nokia Seizes Top Spot in Mobile Phones," *Financial Times* (London), February 8, 1999, p. 22.
9. Ibid.
10. Peltz, Michael. "Hard Cell," *Worth,* March 1999, pp. 45–47.
11. Mossberg, Walter. "Cures for PC Boredom: A Truly Global Phone and a Better Palm Pilot," *Wall Street Journal,* March 11, 1999, p. B1.
12. Peltz, op. cit.

CASE 14
Perot Systems: Can a High Performance Company Have a Human Side?

Although computers have been around for decades, only in the 1990s has their full application potential been realized by companies around the world. Leading the way are internationally recognized Information Technology (IT) service firms, including IBM, Electronic Data Systems (EDS), consulting firms such as Andersen Consulting, Computer Sciences, and Cap Gemini. The U.S. Department of Commerce tabulated 1997 sales in the consulting, systems integration, and project management computer services industry at $90 billion.[1] A relatively recent but important entrant into this field is Perot Systems, which began in 1988 by Ross Perot. As the sixth largest IT firm in the world, can Perot Systems provide solutions for the elusive goal of fully integrated management systems in large, global organizations?

Note: The blue underscored words/phrases in this case indicate Internet links provided in the online version. See the *Organizational Behavior, Seventh Edition* Web Site at http://www.wiley.com/college/schermerhorn.

A Rich History

Ross Perot is one of the true masters of the American economic free enterprise system. Born in Texarkana, Texas on June 27, 1930, he has led a life filled with one significant achievement after another. Having lived his whole childhood in Texarkana, he entered the U.S. Naval Academy in 1949, where he served as class president and battalion commander, an experience that even to this day motivates him to hire many of his top company officers from ex-military personnel.

Upon his discharge from the navy, Ross married and began working for IBM's data processing division as a salesman. In 1962, with $1000, he started a one-man data processing company which he called Electronic Data Systems. Drawing on his experience in the military, in addition to recruiting a large number of ex-military personnel, Perot was able to build his firm into the premier data processing company in the U.S.

In 1984, EDS was sold to General Motors for $2.5 billion. GM wanted to greatly increase its use of technology in its manufacturing process and viewed its EDS purchase as an effective way of meeting this goal. As a result of the purchase, Ross Perot became one of the single largest holders of General Motors and a director in the company. However, Perot had great difficulty adjusting to GM's bureaucratic, autocratic management style, and he was eventually bought out of GM in 1986. After waiting the required two-year noncompete period, he started Perot Systems in 1988.[2] Interestingly, GM spun EDS off in 1996, as it became obvious that the two entities did not make a good fit.

Throughout his career, Ross Perot has always been a model of citizen volunteerism. In 1969, the U.S. government asked him to deter-mine what action could be taken to assist the prisoners-of-war in Southeast Asia. In recognition for his work, he received the Medal for Distinguished Public Service, the highest civilian award presented by the Department of Defense.[3] In 1992 and again in 1996, Ross Perot ran for president of the United States representing a new third party, the Reform Party, which he founded as an alternative to the Republican and Democratic parties.

Perot's campaign efforts forced him to step down from daily involvement in Perot Systems. That year, Mort Meyerson, who had helped him build EDS into a world-recognized leader in data processing, stepped in to assume the chief executive officer duties. Although he had worked closely with Perot at EDS, Meyerson did not share Perot's desire to recreate EDS's "young, male, military model" corporate climate at Perot Systems.[4] He was convinced that times had changed.

In purely financial terms, my seven years running EDS had been unbelievably successful. When I left, I was very proud of the people, the company, and our achievements. From the day I started as president in 1979 to the day I left in 1986, EDS never had a single quarter where we lost money. We never even had a quarter where we were flat—every quarter we grew like gangbusters. That kind of economic performance made a lot of our people very rich. I used to take enormous pride in the fact that I was instrumental in getting a lot of equity into the hands of the people at EDS.

What I realized after I left was that I had also made a lot of people very unhappy. Our people paid a high price for their economic success. Eighty-hour weeks were the norm. We shifted people from project to project and simply expected them to make the move, no questions asked. We called our assignments "death marches"—without a trace of irony. You were expected to do whatever it took to get the job done. In terms of priorities, work was in first place; family, community, other obligations all came after.[5]

Meyerson's concern was the emphasis on profit at the expense of people. He believed that technology, customers, the market, and what people in organizations wanted from their work had all changed from his previous time at EDS.[6] He asked himself two fundamental questions:

1. To get rich, do you have to be miserable?
2. To be successful, do you have to punish your customers?

Meyerson wanted to move Perot Systems toward a corporate model that recognized that the larger issues in life mattered as much as the demands for profit-and-loss. Listening to a senior manager talk about how they handled low performers on teams bothered him.

I heard talk of "drive-by shootings" to "take out" nonperformers; then they'd "drag the body around" to make an example out of them. They may have meant it only as a way of talking, but I saw it as more: abusive language that would influence behavior. Left unchallenged, these expressions would pollute the company's culture.[7]

Meyerson was fully aware that he had not only supported this environment at EDS, but encouraged it. As president for seven years, he had been largely responsible for the high performance atmosphere that demanded so much from EDS employees. He tells a story in which an employee named Max missed a day of work due to a snowstorm and how Meyerson himself called the employee at home to question his loyalty to EDS. The employee took the first opportunity he could and left EDS. He was Max Hopper, who later went on to design the highly successful SABRE reservation system for American Airlines.[8]

None of that happened by accident. I had helped design EDS to operate this way, using the compensation system to motivate people: I tied their pay to profit-and-loss performance. If you ran your project very profitably, you were richly rewarded. If you didn't, you weren't. I routinely spent an extraordinary amount of my time on compensation and rewards—roughly 15 percent. I did it because I knew that compensation mattered most.

The system worked; that is, we got exactly what we wanted. We asked people to put financial performance before everything else, and they did. They drove themselves to do whatever was necessary to create those results—even if it meant too much personal sacrifice or doing things that weren't really in the best interests of customers. Sometimes they did things that produced positive financial results in the short term but weren't in the company's long term interest. That's a charge you'd usually apply to a CEO—but I've never heard it said about individuals down to the lowest ranks of a company. Yet my pay-for-performance approach effectively encouraged that behavior from all of our people.[9]

Upon his arrival at Perot Systems, Meyerson inherited a company of 1500 employees and a revenue of $170 million. His initial effort went into meeting with the top 100 leaders in the company. Through these conversations, Meyerson concluded that he had heard "a laundry list of horrifying bad news."[10] He set about to change the company's culture, including a training seminar that over two-thirds of the firm's employees (including Meyerson) attended. Individuals who could not adjust were asked to leave. Meyerson's objective was clear:

We still tell people we'll give them everything we can in the way of financial rewards. In fact, more than 60 percent of our company is owned by the people who run the company. So if we go public someday, we'll still make a lot of our people very rich.

But we will have done it without having first made them miserable—by offering them another dimension they can't get in most other high performance companies: a human organization. If any of our people has an interest outside the company, we will encourage and support them; if they have needs outside the company, we will recognize them.[11]

Meyerson's other major concern was how EDS had treated customers. He described negotiations as intense, with EDS's desire to win every penny possible from the customer. Not just to win, but to dominate.[12] At Perot Systems, Meyerson promoted a much closer working relationship with customers and designed the reward system to reflect this newfound cooperation.

Here again, at Perot Systems, I turned to the compensation system to help us live the lesson. We use 360-degree evaluations for our people—asking boss, peers, and subordinates to participate—and always include input from our customers. We also ask our customers to give us report cards—and then we temper bonuses based on customer ratings of how well we support their needs.[13]

Similar to other information technology service firms, Perot Systems concentrates on particular industry groups in order to provide enhanced expertise. These include financial services, energy, travel and transportation, health care, communication, manufacturing, and construction.[14] Several of the contracts

---

Project: Avis Rent A Car

Avis Rent A Car System, Inc. selected Perot Systems Corporation to provide and maintain a state-of-the-art imaging and workflow solution for customer document processing in its Garden City, N.Y. World Headquarters and Virginia Beach, Va. Processing Center. The decision places Avis on the cutting edge of technological advancements, and the services agreement frees Avis to focus on what they do best, serving their customers.[15]

---

that Perot Systems obtained reflect this new corporate vision.

The change from data processing to systems integration has been motivated by globalization and the need for full supply-chain management. Companies depend on information systems to tie all the functional areas, including marketing, customer support, logistics, service, and operations together into a seamless whole. Rather than develop these competencies on their own, companies are increasingly depending on outside consultants such as Perot Systems to provide the expertise to run these complicated systems.

The New Face of Leadership?

Consistent with Mort Meyerson's new attitude toward business was a new emphasis on the shifting face of leadership. He concludes that the new leadership entails three jobs:

- **Make sure that the organization knows itself.** Meyerson suggests that the leader's primary purpose is to support and embody certain core principles that identify the organization. These values do not have so much to do with business strategy, tactics, or market share; rather, they have to do with human relationships and the obligation of the organization to its individual members and its customers.
- **Pick the right people and create an environment where those people can succeed.** In this sense, the leader is more coach than executive. This requires collaboration and teamwork among people at every level of the company. The leader is not viewed as the final authority in decision making; the team represents the source of knowledge.

- **Be accessible to the people in the organization.** Meyerson insists that he be in E-mail contact with all employees of the company. He personally answers thousands of E-mail messages every month. No longer is the leader an individual who shows up every six months to deliver a pep rally speech. And the leader must be accessible on issues and concerns that transcend the traditional boundaries of work and the company.[18]

Can a High Performance Company Have a Human Side?

While Mort Meyerson worked to develop his new view of leadership, Perot Systems struggled to earn a consistent profit. As one of the smaller players in the information technology field, Perot Systems' higher costs and lower net earnings troubled Mr. Perot. Operating margins at Perot Systems averaged 5.3

Project: California Electrical Grid

The ISO Alliance, a limited liability company owned jointly by ABB Power T&D Co. and Perot Systems Corp., has been awarded a contract to develop and implement one of the most critical new business systems the state of California will need to operate its electricity markets under deregulation. The new systems will help the state administer the bidding and manage the usage of its power grid to ensure reliable service—much the same way an air traffic control system coordinates take-off and landings at airports to maintain order and manage congestion. California is the largest power market in the United States, with approximately $27 billion in electricity commerce per year.[16]

---

percent versus 7.7 percent at rival EDS.[19] Since 1996, the company has gone through three management changes and in the strongest stock market in history—one led by technology issues—a public offering has been repeatedly delayed. Unhappy with these conditions, Mr. Perot chose to return to day-to-day operations in late 1997.

Initially announced as interim CEO, Perot has evolved into Perot Systems' full-time chief executive officer. "He has centralized reviews of spending and new contracts. He has directed every supervisor to attend a leadership training course that reinforces his precepts. He has cut expenses, stepped up recruiting from the military, reinstated mandatory drug testing, and assigned a reading list including his autobiography. He has promoted executives with military backgrounds who have been with him for decades, since his days as commander in chief of Electronic Data Systems. White shirts are in, and, under his current thinking, same-sex partners' health benefits will be out."[20]

Not everyone is convinced that Mr. Perot can provide the same type of spectacular returns as he did in his EDS heyday. "The wheel he's trying to reinvent is rusty," an executive at a rival company said.[21] When he stepped aside as Perot Systems' chief networked personal computers were just beginning to spread. E-mail addresses (Mr. Perot does not use E-mail; he relies on face-to-face communication) and Internet access were largely the domain of military overlords and university scientists, and Perot Systems was doing mostly standard corporate work on central computers.[22]

"At EDS, he built an organization that was based on command and control," said Allie Young, an analyst at Dataquest, the indus-

---

Swiss Air

March 4, 1997—Perot Systems Corporation today announced it has purchased a controlling stake from SwissAir Corp. in Icarus Consulting AG, a Zurich- and Frankfurt-based management consulting firm that serves the travel and transportation industries in Europe.

Founded in 1988, Icarus had been owned 55 percent by SAir Group, the holding company of SwissAir, and 45 percent by Icarus's management, respectively. After today's agreement, Perot Systems will have a 70 percent stake in Icarus, with a fixed option to purchase the remaining 30 percent from SAir Group over a three-year period.

As an example of its work, Icarus recently conceived and implemented a new air cargo system that combined the services of SwissAir and Sabena Airlines. Under this unique arrangement, Sabena has essentially sold its airline cargo space to SwissCargo, the SAir Group's cargo arm, giving up marketing and operational costs in exchange for a guaranteed revenue stream. SwissCargo gains added capacity and market share and can utilize its existing sales infrastructure much more efficiently.

"This is a good example of the consolidation of core competencies by major air carriers," said Ludwig Bertsch, the Zurich-based managing director of Icarus. "In the coming years we will see some airlines specializing in the design and management of hub systems and routes designs as network managers. Others will excel in flight operations. Still others will create strong niches in catering, cargo services, or maintenance."[17]

---

try research firm in San Jose, California. "It was 'my way or the highway.' At that time, that type of model worked. Companies wanted that. Today it's very different. Senior executives are involved in the decision making for contracts, very often the CEO. Information technology is a strategic decision. They don't want anything railroaded by them. They want a business partner."[23] The question is: Will Mr. Perot's command and control approach work in this new environment?

The IPO

On February 2, 1999, Morgan Stanley Dean Witter conducted Perot Systems' IPO at $16 per share, valuing it at $1.35 billion in the New York Stock Exchange flotation. By mid-afternoon, the price had risen $26 1/2 to a value of $42 1/2, thereby increasing Perot Systems' value to $3.6 billion. Analysts credited the movement to the current clamor for information technology shares and the glamour of Ross Perot's name. Perot's personal stake in the firm increased from $553 million to $1.4 billion on the move. (His personal wealth is estimated at $3.7 billion.)[24]

It remains to be seen whether Mr. Perot's leadership style can turn Perot Systems into a major force in the information technology field. With competitors over 12 times larger, competition remains intense. Can Ross Perot make the difference Perot Systems needs?

Review Questions

1. Compare Mr. Meyerson's leadership style versus Mr. Perot's based on the Michigan and Ohio State behavioral theories of leadership.
2. Utilizing Fiedler's Contingency Theory of Leadership, explain how either Meyerson's or Perot's style might be most appropriate based on specific characteristics of the situation at Perot Systems.
3. Evaluate the situation at Perot Systems from the point of view of the discussion on New Leadership.

References

1. John Mitchell. "Hoovers Industry Snapshot—Computer Software Industry," *Hoovers Online,* http://www.hoovers.com/features/industry/software1.html, February 5, 1999.
2. "Ross Perot Biography," *Perot Official World Wide Web Site,* http://www.perot.org/hrpbio.htm, December 17, 1998.
3. Ibid.
4. Allan Myerson, "Perot's Return to Business: The Vote's Not In," *New York Times,* February 22, 1998, p. 3:1.
5. Mort Meyerson, "Everything I Thought I Knew About Leadership Is Wrong," *Fast Company,* April/May 1996, pp. 5–11.
6. Ibid.
7. Ibid.
8. Ibid.
9. Ibid.
10. Ibid.
11. Ibid.
12. Ibid.
13. Ibid.
14. "Perot Systems Homepage," http://www.perotsystems.com, February 17, 1999.
15. "Avis Selects Perot Systems for Imaging and Workflow Solution," *Business Wire,* April 8, 1996, p. 4081260.
16. "Companies to manage California energy grid," *Electric Light & Power,* September 1997, p. 28.
17. "Perot Systems Takes Major Stake in SwissAir Unit; Consulting Organization, Icarus, Serves European Airlines," *Business Wire,* March 4, 1997, p. 03041322.
18. Meyerson, op.cit., pp. 10–11.
19. Wendy Zellner and Linda Himelstein, "Why Perot May Go with an IPO," *Business Week,* August 10, 1998, p. 65.
20. Meyerson, op. cit.
21. Ibid.
22. Ibid.
23. Ibid.
24. Andrew Cave, "Perot Systems' Shares Leap 165pc During Market Debut," *The Daily Telegraph,* February 3, 1999. ∎

CASE 15
Power or Empowerment at GM?

Developed by Aneil Mishra, Pennsylvania State University, Karen Mishra, Pennsylvania State University, and Kim Cameron, Brigham Young University

Introduction

Effective September 25, 1990, the management of the General Motors (GM) Parma, Ohio, stamping plant finalized another three-year local agreement with the United Auto Workers' Union (UAW), Local 1005. It was the second local agreement they had negotiated together *on time* and *without intervention* from Detroit, since Parma's self-described revolutionary agreement seven years previously. It was revolutionary because Parma's management and union had abandoned their old hostilities and incorporated a team-based approach to work, setting Parma in a new direction. The 1990 agreement formally documented their joint priorities of team-based work groups, extensive employee training, and a supportive working environment. The assistant personnel director for hourly employment, Bill Marsh, felt that, although this was another positive step in their ongoing relationship with Local 1005, the negotiating process seemed more "traditional" than the previous negotiation in 1987. Bob Lintz, the plant manager, agreed. Unexpectedly, the new Shop Committee chairman, who is Local 1005's prime negotiator, had introduced over 600 demands at the start of Parma's local contract negotiation. Even though management and the union were still able to finalize an agreement quickly, the tension created by the enormous list of demands still lingered. It could destroy the collaborative relationship that had been built over the past decade between management and the union leadership as well as the openness that Bob Lintz had managed to foster between himself and the hourly employees.

Background

In the early 1980s, Parma's corporate parent, GM, conducted a capacity rationalization study that concluded that almost 75 percent of Parma's operations should either be eliminated or tranferred to other GM facilities within three years. Despite a one-year lapse in formal relations, and with no contract in effect, Parma's management and Local 1005 responded to this threat to plant survival by conducting a joint effort to bring in new business. This joint effort led to a number of competitive assessments of Parma's operations that identified several noncompetitive work practices. To acknowledge

formally this new collaborative relationship, a new labor agreement was drafted and ratified in 1983 by Parma's rank and file that resulted in fewer work classifications and emphasized a team-based approach to managing work groups.[1]

To implement this agreement, Parma's top management and Local 1005 created the Team Concept Implementation Group, or TCIG, to introduce this new Team Concept and spent $40 million on extensive training of the entire workforce in problem solving, group dynamics, and effective communication skills. By 1990, the Team Concept had empowered hourly employees to assume more responsibility in their jobs and to focus on problem-solving and work-related matters and to move beyond status differences exemplified by position titles or neckties.

Roger Montgomery, who had chaired the Shop Committee from 1981 until 1990, felt that he had been able to put aside his past doubts of management's sincerity and work with Bob to create an environment based on teamwork and trust. He credits Bob's sincerity and openness with their ability to respect each other and work together for the good of the plant and its jobs. Roger believed that Bob had to overcome significant obstacles in creating this collaborative relationship at Parma, especially in convincing members of management and supervision. After years of open hostility between management and labor, Roger knew that Bob had supervisors and managers who didn't want to change. After years of fighting for employees by getting doors on bathroom stalls and eliminating hall passes, Roger felt that his union team had achieved greater consensus about the need for change. He felt lucky because even though some of his shop committee might not have agreed with

him about every detail, they did support his efforts out of loyalty to him and to his relationship with Bob. Bob Lintz also felt that his managers and Local 1005's leaders had worked hard to overcome decades-long hostilities and build a positive and collaborative relationship.[2]

Current Situation

Bob and his managers are concerned about the tension that has been created by the new Shop Committee chairman's large number of demands, especially because the union made only about 100 demands during the previous contract negotiations. Roger had publicly endorsed this new chairman of the Shop Committee, yet management was not certain that he would continue Roger's strategy of collaboration within the union and between management and the union. With several new individuals in the union leadership, Parma's management also had to consider the possibility that the entire union leadership was actually becoming more adversarial, especially as the two political factions within the union continued to compete for support among members of Local 1005. Relations between hourly and salaried employees on the production floor could also suffer.

The list of demands from the new chairman of the Shop Committee could have resulted from the uncertainty that existed with the recent announcements of plant closings by GM. Since the mid-1980s, six GM stamping plants had been closed, and Parma's employment level had fallen. These plant closings and pressure from GM were the result of GM losing 10 percentage points of market share in under 10 years and corresponding deterioration in GM's bottom line. By the fall of 1990, GM was losing more than $1100 for every vehicle it produced in North America, in part because of GM's high fixed costs. With over $700 million in sales, Parma is an important plant to GM, but there is no guarantee that it will not be closed if demand for GM's products does not improve. Wall Street is criticizing GM for not being more aggressive in closing plants to remove excess capacity. The corporation is pressuring all of its facilities to reduce expenditures significantly and to eliminate all overtime. Parma has made substantial progress in maintaining revenues amidst declining demand, but it still needs to make significant improvements in productivity. For example, it has still to better utilize the transfer presses that stamp automative doors and hoods. These presses were installed during the $600 million modernization in 1983, and in 1990 their uptime stood at 31 percent.

Parma also needs to improve its quality and customer satisfaction. In 1989, Parma began supplying the metal frame for the minivan produced at GM's Tarrytown, New York, facility. Arthur Norelli, general supervisor of Dimensional Control, remembers that in his first encounters with Parma, "I found them initially, very defensive, almost adversarial. They were always right until we proved them wrong. If we had a part that wouldn't go together properly, they would say 'Well, you're not putting it together right.' " Another customer, a transmission plant within GM's Powertrain Group, has concerns about Parma's ability to produce quality parts in a timely fashion. As recently as 1988, Parma was Powertrain's worst supplier for transmission components. Bill Hurles, a materials manager within the Powertrain Group, remembered Parma back then as "very dependable and very antagonistic."

In addition to pressures to improve costs, quality, and productivity, there are additional pressures on management from the union to bring stamping work in-house that has previously been outsourced. As Parma loses its prop shaft production to another GM facility, the union wants to bring back the production of sheet metal blankings, the first step in the stamping process. Blankings have been outsourced to a supplier, Medina Blanking, Inc., which produces an excellent quality product and has virtually become another department in Parma because of its highly responsive and capable delivery.

As GM closes plants and continues to downsize, Parma's salaried employees, too, are being affected significantly by efforts to reduce salaried employment and eliminate management layers throughout the organization. With fewer salaried employees, workloads are increasing even as promotional opportunities, compensation, and benefits stagnate. As is the case at most GM facilities, Parma's salaried employees are not unionized. As part of its efforts to cut costs, GM has eliminated the salaried year-end bonus, has sharply reduced merit raises, and is considering other benefit reductions. Profit sharing for both hourly and salaried employees has evaporated as losses in GM's North American operations have mounted to several billion dollars annually.

After 10 years of being a top manager at Parma and assuming responsibility for all of Parma's operations, Bob Lintz continues to fashion a top management team based on trust and openness. He also wants his managers to be committed to eliminating hostilities that linger between the stamping and components operations within the plant, as well as between hourly and salaried

employees. He is also looking for people who will support his informal and highly participative management style and who will work to increase the level of involvement among Parma's hourly employees. Although the TCIG has formally disbanded, its efforts are still ongoing. The weekly floor board meetings, where union officials and superintendents discuss plant floor issues, are still active and productive. The biweekly joint meeting of Bob and his staff, along with the Shop Committee chairman, the president of Local 1005, and the Shop Committee, are ongoing as well. These groups are representative of the Team Concept still at work at Parma.

Conclusion

Even though Bob's management team supports his desire to increase the level of involvement among Parma's hourly employees, Dean Baker commented, "Sometimes I get frustrated, though, because I wish he'd have a little bit more confidence in the management organization."

Parma's lead training coordinator, Pat Camarati, is concerned that many of Parma's managers and supervisors see the ongoing Team Concept training as more of a disruption than a necessity. Shop Committee member Ray Kopchak believes that, although they have made great strides, the biggest mistake the union and management can still make is to assume that their relationship can continue to improve without hard work. Seven years after beginning a new collaborative approach, he still feels that the easiest thing to do is "to go back to the old traditional way. But I don't want to do that, it's not necessary. We've proven that management and the union can work together."

Review Questions

1. How would you describe Parma's environment in terms of its level of uncertainty and complexity?
2. How would you characterize Bob Lintz's approach to communication, decision making, and the exercise of power to create change at Parma?
3. What are the most critical issues still facing Parma, and what should be done to address them?
4. How can resistance to change be overcome utilizing the existing workforce? ∎

References

1. *Harbour Report,* 1979–1989, p. 235.
2. *Harbour Report,* 1989–1992, p. 69.
3. It costs GM $795 more than Ford to produce a vehicle, [$396 of which is attributed to GM's stamping plants. GM's current contract with the International UAW, to which Parma and all GM's other facilities must adhere, provides union members 95 percent of their take-home pay for up to three years in the event they are laid off. This will cost the Corporation $4 billion over the three-year agreement. In addition, UAW members received wage increases of 17 percent, bringing unions wages and benefits to $36.60/hour.

CASE 16
The Poorly Informed Walrus

Developed by Barbara McCain, Oklahoma City University

"How's it going down there?" barked the big walrus from his perch on the highest rock near the shore. He waited for the good word.

Down below, the smaller walruses conferred hastily among themselves. Things weren't going well at all, but none of them wanted to break the news to the Old Man. He was the biggest and wisest walrus in the herd, and he knew his business, but he had such a terrible temper that every walrus in the herd was terrified of his ferocious bark.

"What will we tell him?" whispered Basil, the second-ranking walrus. He well remembers how the Old Man had raved and ranted at him the last time the herd had caught less than its quota of herring, and he had no desire to go through that experience again. Nevertheless, the walrus noticed for several weeks that the water level in the nearby Arctic bay had been falling constantly, and it had become necessary to travel much farther to catch the dwindling supply of herring.

Someone should tell the Old Man; he would probably know what to do. But who? and how?

Finally Basil spoke up: "Things are going pretty well, Chief," he said. The thought of the receding water line made his heart grow heavy, but he went on: "As a matter of fact, the beach seems to be getting larger."

The Old Man grunted. "Fine, fine," he said. "That will give us a bit more elbow room." He closed his eyes and continued basking in the sun.

The next day brought more trouble. A new herd of walruses moved in down the beach and, with the supply of herring dwindling, this invasion could be dangerous. No one wanted to tell the Old Man, though only he could take the steps necessary to meet this new competition.

Reluctantly, Basil approached the big walrus, who was still sunning himself on the large rock. After some small talk, he said, "Oh by the way Chief, a new herd of walruses seems to have moved into our territory." The Old Man's eyes snapped open, and he filled his great lungs in preparation for a mighty bellow. But Basil added quickly, "Of course, we don't anticipate any trouble. They don't look like herring eaters to me. More likely interested in minnows. And as you know, we don't bother with minnows ourselves."

The Old Man let out the air with a long sigh. "Good, good," he said. "No point in our getting excited over nothing then, is there?"

Things didn't get any better in the weeks that followed. One day, peering down from the large rock, the Old Man noticed that part of the herd seemed to be missing. Summoning Basil, he grunted peevishly. "What's going on, Basil? Where is everyone?" Poor Basil didn't have the courage to tell the Old Man that many of the younger walruses were leaving every day to join the new herd. Clearing his throat nervously, he said, "Well Chief, we've been tightening up things a bit. You know, getting rid of some of the dead wood. After all, a herd is only as good as walruses in it."

"Run a tight ship, I always say," the Old Man grunted. "Glad to hear that all is going so well."

Before long, everyone but Basil had left to join the new herd, and Basil realized that the time had come to tell the Old Man the facts. Terrified but determined, he flopped up to the large rock. "Chief," he said, "I have bad news. The rest of the herd has left you." The old walrus was so astonished that he couldn't even work up a good bellow. "Left me?" he cried. "All of them? But why? How could this happen?"

Basil didn't have the heart to tell him so he merely shrugged helplessly.

"I can't understand it," the old

walrus said. "And just when everything was going so well."

Review Questions

1. What barriers to communication are evident in this fable?
2. What communication "lessons" does this fable offer to those who are serious about careers in the new workplace? ■

CASE 17
Johnson and Johnson: Futuristic Decision Making

Developed by David S. Chappell, Ohio University

With brand names like Tylenol, Band-Aid brands, Neutrogena skin products, and Reach toothbrushes, Johnson and Johnson (J&J) represents the world's largest and most comprehensive manufacturer of health-care products serving the consumer, pharmaceutical, diagnostics, and professional markets.[1] Representative of its conglomerate business model, 15 company group chairpersons, along with their own management boards, oversee over 180 operating companies worldwide.[2] How does such a large company infuse its decision-making process with the energy of a small start-up company?

Johnson and Johnson

J&J was incorporated in 1887 through the combined effort of brothers Robert, James, and Edward Johnson. The brothers pioneered the surgical dressings industry based on work by Sir Joseph Lister, a noted English surgeon who identified airborne germs as a source of infection in the operating room. J&J developed a soft, absorbent cotton and gauze antiseptic dressing that could be mass produced and shipped in quantity to hospitals and every rural physician and druggist in the country.[3]

J&J has had an international focus to its business since its foray

into Canada in 1919. It launched a conscious product diversification program in the 1920s with the introduction of its Band-Aid brands and Johnson's baby cream. General Johnson, as the son of one of the original brothers was known, also created the famous J&J Credo around this time. The credo emphasizes the importance of ethical behavior and putting customers first and stockholders last. However, General Johnson was practical enough to infer that such an approach would benefit the owners of the firm in the long run.

J&J is perhaps best known for

its advancement of crisis management regarding the cyanide contamination of its flagship Tylenol painkiller. In September 1982, seven Chicago-area individuals died after taking cyanide-laced Extra Strength Tylenol capsules. Representing 7 percent of all of J&J sales and 17 percent of its profits, Tylenol represented a brand that the corporation could not afford to lose.[4]

J&J chose to take a very proactive approach to the crisis. It eventually recalled 31 million bottles worth over $100 million from retail stores, in addition to offering to exchange tablets for capsules for all customers at no charge. It pioneered the tamper-proof, triple-sealed packaging that is the industry standard today.

Immediately after the crisis, Tylenol's market share dropped from 35.3 percent of the pain reliever market to 7 percent; however, by May of 1983, its market share returned to 35 percent. The situation was repeated in 1986 when a Westchester, New York woman died of cyanide-laced Extra-Strength Tylenol capsules. Once again, the company recalled all capsules, vowing never again to offer any Tylenol except in the form of tablets or caplets.[5]

J&J does not view itself as just a pharmaceutical firm; it prefers to think of itself as a health-care organization. It represents an autonomous collection of independent entities whose decentralized structure fosters an entrepreneurial culture, insists CEO Ralph Larsen.[6] Not everyone agrees with J&J's conglomerate structure; Paine Webber analyst David Lothson, for example, complains that J&J should be three companies. Of particular concern is the ever-declining roles in sales and profits of the consumer-products line—falling from 44 percent in 1978 to only 28 percent of revenue in 1998. The stock, rather than trading at the attractive high multiples of

---

Note: The blue underscored words/phrases in this case indicate Internet links provided in the on-line version. See the *Organizational Behavior, Seventh Edition* Web Site at http://www.wiley.com/college/schermerhorn.

THE OB SKILLS WORKBOOK   **297**

Johnson and Johnson Conglomerate Structure

DIVISION	1998 SALES (in billions)	MAJOR PRODUCTS
Professional	$8.57	Coronary stents, minimally invasive surgery products, wound-closure products
Pharmaceutical	$8.56	Risperdal for schizophrenia, Levaquin for infections, Procrit for anemia
Consumer	$6.53	Tylenol painkillers, Band-Aids, baby products, Neutrogena skin products[8]

similar pharmaceutical firms, reflects a conservative valuation that is more similar to consumer-good behemoth Procter and Gamble.

Decision making requires the application of information, and perhaps more importantly, knowledge. "Data, information and knowledge are points along a continuum of increasing value and human contribution. Data—the signals about human events and activities that we are exposed to each day—has little value in itself, although to its credit it is easy to store and manipulate on computers.

"Information is what data becomes when we as humans interpret and contextualise it. It is also the vehicle we use to express and communicate knowledge in business and in our lives. Information has more value than data and, at the same time, greater ambiguity—as any manager will attest who has ever argued over how many interpretations the terms 'customer,' 'order' and 'shipment' can have inside the same company.

"Knowledge is information within people's minds; without a knowing, self-aware person there is no knowledge. Knowledge is highly valuable, because humans create new ideas, insights and interpretations and apply these directly to information use and decision making. For managers, knowledge is difficult to 'manage' in other people because (being mental) it is invisible and its extraction, sharing and use relies on human motivation."[7] Eventually, the companies that prosper with knowledge management will be those that realize that it is as much about managing people as information.

Larsen needs to convince people that his conglomerate business model as a source of knowledge is still practical. Most insiders agree that the strength of J&J is its diversity; the question becomes, how does the company make the most efficient and effective use of this diversity and its associated knowledge base as inputs into its decision making?

FrameworkS at J&J

Conceived in 1993 with the assistance of consulting firm McKinsey & Company, FrameworkS involves a series of focused dialogues between operating company executives, specialists, and most importantly, top management. "FrameworkS is an attempt to democratize how we make strategic choices, how we create our future," says Roger Fine, general counsel of J&J.[9] CEO Ralph Larsen states that never before has "a broad-based group of people been invited to be central, active participants in matters of very substantial corporate significance outside the direct responsibility of their operating companies."[10]

The first FrameworkS looked at the changing nature of the health care market in the U.S. J&J's nine executive committee members enlisted about 20 senior company executives to explore key topics. After splitting into teams to conduct research, they contacted customers, policy analysis, government officials, and academics regarding the marketplace and their competition. Reconvening after several months, they discussed major changes in how medical care is delivered in the United States, from fee-for-service to HMO institutional decision makers. Dennis Longstreet, head of J&J's Ethicon Endo-Surgery medical devices businesses, argued that the process "caused all levels of management to see things we had not seen before. We listened to our customers, and we looked to the core of our company, down to how we were organized."[11]

One of the critical findings of the investigation was that J&J's largest customers, such as hospital networks, government organizations, and managed care plans wanted a single J&J contract to coordinate purchases from J&J's diverse operating companies. As a result of this finding, in three months J&J created Health Care Systems, Inc. to support a single point-of-contact supplier to its customers. David Cassak, editor of a magazine that tracks the medical industry, states that "it's a truly unique and innovative structure, the perfect vehicle to address customer needs while retaining the culture of autonomous operating companies."[12]

In 1995, in an effort to increase its innovation, J&J launched a FrameworkS project focused on the qualities highly innovative companies exhibited. The team reviewed three J&J companies (Ethicon Endo-Surgery, Janssen Pharmaceutica and Vistakon) and three outside ones (Enron, Hewlett Packard and Nike).[13] They identified three types of innovative activities:

Type of Innovation	Example
Incremental	Glow in the Dark Band-Aid
Substantial (alters market demand with a new generation of product)	Reach Toothbrush
Transformational (alters industry structure)	Vistakon's disposable contact lens

The objective was to identify ways J&J could foster more substantial and transformational innovation in products, services, processes, and management.[14] "What's New" is the program that includes a "toolkit" of actions line managers can take to infuse innovation into their organizations. The intent is to "exercise core competencies and exorcise corporate rigidities."[15]

Does It Work?

While its hard to quantify the impact that FrameworkS has made on J&J's operations, most upper executives support the program. However, things don't always work out as planned. The year 1998 proved to be difficult, with six experimental drugs falling through late in development. J&J's coronary stent, responsible for $500 million of J&J's business, lost 90 percent of its market share to rivals; plans for a cholesterol-lowering margarine suffered a regulatory setback; and the company lost a battle over rights to a future version of a top-selling anemia drug.[16]

Calls to break up the company into separate operating units remain strong. Larsen resists these calls, claiming that "the future belongs to those companies that are broadly based."[17] Do the broad operating companies of J&J offer it a unique opportunity or an unwieldy anachronism? Does FrameworkS offer an institutional mechanism to capture its diversity into a useful and constructive process?

Review Questions

1. How is J&J able to incorporate its organizational diversity into its decision-making process?
2. How does the management of J&J hope that FrameworkS will help with creativity within the organization?
3. How does J&J attempt to infuse ethics into its decision making?

References

1. "Johnson and Johnson Homepage—1998 Fact Book," http://www.jnj.com/who_is_jnj /factbook/98fb_index.html, April 3, 1999.
2. Jones, Gladys Montgomery. "Framing the Future: How Johnson and Johnson Executives Keep in Touch with a Changing Marketplace—and One Another." *Continental Inflight Magazine,* March 1999, pp. 39–41.
3. "Johnson and Johnson Homepage—History," http://www.jnj.com/who_is_jnj /hist_index.html, April 3, 1999.
4. Hartley, Robert F. "Contrast—Johnson & Johnson's Tylenol: Great Crisis Management in Regaining Public Trust." *Management Mistakes and Successes.* New York: John Wiley and Sons, pp. 330–344.
5. Ibid.
6. Langreth, Robert and Winslow, Ron. "Johnson & Johnson Faces Question: Is It Merely an Unwieldy Anachronism?" *The Wall Street Journal,* March 5, 1999, pp. B1, B4.
7. "Is KM just good information management?" *Financial Times* (London), March 8, 1999, p. 2.
8. Langreth and Winslow, op. cit.
9. Jones, op. cit.
10. Ibid.
11. Ibid.
12. Ibid.
13. Ibid.
14. Ibid.
15. Ibid.
16. Langreth and Winslow, op. cit.
17. Ibid.

CASE 18
American Airlines: Trouble in the Air

Developed by David S. Chappell, Ohio University

As one of the major air carriers in the United States, American Airlines conducts thousands of flights daily. After years of operations under Chairman Robert Crandall, Donald Carty took over in May of 1998. One of his first strategic moves was to complete the acquisition of the small, Southwestern, low-fare regional carrier, Reno Air. As a result of this action, in

Note: The blue underscored words/phrases in this case indicate Internet links provided in the on-line version. See the *Organizational Behavior, Seventh Edition* Web Site at http://www.wiley.com/college/schermerhorn.

February 1999, the American Airlines pilots chose to conduct an unauthorized work slowdown, with over 1000 pilots calling in sick. This action served to effectively cripple American's ability to carry out operations at a loss to the carrier of over $150 million. How did the conflict between American and its pilots escalate to this level?

The Airline Industry

The modern era in the U.S. airline industry can be traced to 1978, with the deregulation of the United States' airline industry. Previous to 1978, major airlines had been regulated by the Federal Aviation Administration (FAA) and the Civil Aeronautics Board (CAB) essentially as a government-sponsored oligopoly. Competition was minimized, and entry into the airline industry was difficult, if not impossible. With deregulation, small, low-fare airlines sprang up in many markets, putting severe pressure on the operating profits of the older operators. The flying public benefited with improved service and lower fares, but the established airlines, with their higher operating costs, suffered.

Carrier Classifications

- **Majors**—The majors are airlines whose revenues exceed $1 billion annually. They generally operate international and domestic flights and service only major airports. The majors are characterized as long haul carriers.
- **Nationals**—National airlines are short-haul carriers. Their revenues generally are between $100 million and $1 billion. They fly shorter point-to-point flights that may include a few international flights.
- **Regionals**—Regionals generally make less than $100 million annu-

ally. They concentrate in certain areas of the U.S. and only service that area. They do not usually use large jets, so their capacity is smaller but it allows them to access smaller rural airports that aren't available to the larger carriers.[1]

The following is a listing of the top 10 passenger carriers:

1.	Delta	97,201
2.	United	81,863
3.	American	79,324
4.	US Airways	56,639
5.	Southwest	55,372
6.	Northwest	52,682
7.	Continental	35,743
8.	Trans World	23,281
9.	America West	18,130
10.	Alaska	11,758

Robert Crandall at American Airlines introduced the AAdvantage frequent flier program in 1980, now an industry standard. Intense pressure to slash prices (often to below cost), due to rising energy costs brought on by Gulf War sanctions, an economic recession, and corporate cost-saving measures that forced many business travelers out of first class and into coach led to unprecedented losses for the airlines.

Between 1990 and 1992, airline industry losses of over $5 billion exceeded the combined profits for the previous 67 years.[2] As a result of these losses, airline management pressured various unions representing pilots, flight attendants, and mechanics to agree to labor concessions. With the latter half of the 1990s providing very *attractive profits* for airlines, these unions are now becoming more and more aggressive to win back previous wages and benefits.

Employee salaries (consisting of cabin attendants, ground crews, and flight crews) represent 36 per-

cent of the operating costs for the airline industry. The next largest contributor is ticketing and promotional costs with 17 percent. Finally, fuel costs take 11.7 percent of the expense category. Net income is greatly affected by the fluctuations of these operating costs. Because operating expenses are controlled mainly by volatile forces, the net income of the industry is too dependent on factors outside of its control.[3]

As a result, airlines are looking for innovative ways to control costs, including ticketless travel, Internet sites, lowering or even eliminating travel agents commissions, application of new technology, extensive use of hub-and-spoke traffic systems, code sharing, and alliances. At the same time, labor disputes, including a pilot strike at Northwest in 1998, a narrowly averted flight attendant strike at America West in early 1999, and the American Airlines pilot "sick-out" all represent troubling times for airline passengers.

American Airlines

American Airlines, with its <u>rich history</u> of aviation firsts, is a division of AMR Corporation. With major hubs in Chicago, Dallas, and New York City, American Airlines serves about 160 destinations in the Americas and Europe (some through code-sharing alliances with foreign airlines); the airline also leads <u>Oneworld</u>, a global <u>alliance</u> with <u>British Airways</u> and other carriers. AMR operates American Eagle, a group of small regional airlines, owns low-fare carrier Reno Air, and holds 82 percent of the <u>SABRE</u> ("Semi-Automated Business Research Environment") Group, operator of the #1 travel reservation system.

Overall, American Airlines is the second largest domestic carrier behind only United in terms of total

RPMs (Revenue Passenger Miles) and total revenues from flight operations during 1997. Not only must American compete both domestically and abroad with its major brethren, it must also deal with regional and national upstarts, the scrappy entrant carriers to the market. These low-cost carriers usually go head-to-head with the major and regional airlines and try and gain market share by way of offering lower fare prices than the major airlines can. American estimates that as much as 47 percent of its bookings were impacted by competition from lower-cost carriers.

To capitalize on these growth opportunities, American entered into numerous alliances with both domestic and foreign carriers and is looking to expand into certain other markets by means of stock equity acquisitions. For instance, in 1996 British Airways (BA), the largest international passenger airline carrier in the world entered into a strategic alliance with American. Under the conditions of the agreement, both companies would use code sharing and combine some of their passenger and cargo operations, upon regulatory approval by the U.S. Department of Transportation (DOT) and the United Kingdom. Additionally, in 1997 the two companies agreed to implement a common frequent flier program. Finally, in September 1998, American entered into a strategic alliance called Oneworld, which is to rival United and Lufthansa's Star alliance. The members of the Oneworld Alliance include AA, British Airways, Canadian Air, Cathay Pacific, and Qantas.

In the deregulated era, airline competition has become, in part, a contest to build the most ubiquitous network. In that regard, one of American's most critical success factors is the implementation of a strong hub and spoke system. By linking markets on one side of a hub city to markets on another side, airlines are able to exponentially increase the number of origin-destination combinations they serve. The company's success can be linked to its operations at its hub cities which include Dallas/Fort Worth, Miami, Chicago and, to a lesser degree, San Juan, Puerto Rico.[4]

Since 1980, American has evolved from a domestic carrier into one of the world's foremost international carriers. In 1997, international flying generated more than 30 percent of American's passenger revenue. During that year they also did well in Latin America, attracting 7 percent more customers in that year than from the previous year.[5]

American's greatest shortcoming is its weak presence in the Asian market. Compared to many of their rivals, they fly very few routes in and out of Asia. Based on 1996 statistics, American possessed only a 4 percent share of U.S. airline traffic to and from the Asian region. Other weaknesses include their high-cost structure as measured in Cost/ASM (Available Seat-Miles) and Labor Cost/ASM. American's operating costs are among the highest in the industry, especially their labor costs.

The Pilot "Sickout"

Richard Aboulafia, aviation consultant at the Teal Group in Virginia, notes several items that encourage labor strife at the airlines, particularly at American. "Most of the labor-management disputes of the early 1990s were settled at a time of diminished profits for airlines and manufacturing, and now that things are looking up, labor is demanding its fair share."[6] He cites the militant elements of the Allied Pilots Association, especially in New York and Miami, a two-tier wage scale at American, and the difficulty the

Railway Labor Act creates in the way of hurdles to strikes. Left with few options, unions resort to various work slowdowns and stoppages. "It got quite adversarial, especially with American Airlines, and now American Airlines is paying the price for that adversarial atmosphere."[7]

American Airlines and its pilots had a close brush with a strike in February of 1997. Minutes after the strike deadline passed, President Clinton declared an emergency, appointed a Presidential Emergency Board, and ordered the parties to continue operating as usual while the board considered recommendations for a solution.[8] Pilots eventually ratified the agreement rather than have Congress impose a contract on them. In the summer of 1998, American pilots stopped volunteering for overtime, forcing American to cancel a small number of flights, when the union found out that American was placing more passengers on Canadian Airlines, one of its foreign partners, than was allowed in an agreement with the union. It was the purchase of small Reno Air that reignited the conflict between American and its pilots. American sought Reno to facilitate expansion into lucrative West Coast markets in addition to travel to the Far East.

The issue came down to how to integrate Reno's 300 pilots, who are paid less than American pilots, into the American system. American discussed the purchase with the Allied Pilots Association's union leaders but closed the deal on December 28, 1998 without first reaching agreement with the pilots union over how it would merge the two airlines.[9] American claims it needs 18 months to combine the two entities, due to crew training and a refit of Reno airplanes. The pilot's union argues that the company is dragging its feet in order to continue to pay Reno's pilots at lower rates, possibly setting a precedent for future acquisitions.[10]

The sickout began in earnest on February 6, 1999, and continued for 10 days, causing American to cancel over 6600 flights with a loss of over $150 million. As a major carrier, American's difficulties stranded huge numbers of passengers, many for days on end. American brought suit in court, and U.S. District Judge Joe Kendall of Dallas issued a temporary restraining order against the union. Kendall also found the union and two of its leaders in contempt of court for not encouraging the pilots to return to work immediately after his order. The judge ordered the union to post $10 million bond—and the leaders to post a total of $15,000—against potential contempt-of-court fines.[11] Eventually, the sickout was called off and pilots returned to their regular work schedule.

Where Do They Go from Here

One of American's primary competitors, UAL, is 60 percent owned by its employees. As a result, in the year 2000 a performance-based pay system for managers will partly be tied to worker satisfaction as measured by an outside survey firm. Coupled with customer satisfaction and on-time performance, the bonus system will account for more than half of what the top 635 UAL managers receive in compensation. Originally rejected by management, it was finally accepted after the union prepared a shareholder resolution,

which would have passed given the union's shareholder votes.[12]

In American Airlines' first employee satisfaction survey since 1993, a mere 23 percent said American does an excellent job of inspiring loyalty, while only 31 percent believe what senior management says. And only 30 percent think morale is good. So while 91 percent said they liked their jobs, the overall results were disappointing. Carty says he needs satisfied workers, because only they can provide the superior service that lures high-paying business travelers. Building a happy workforce "remains the last major frontier for us." Carty is already discussing survey details with employees, a first at American, and plans to bring managers and workers together to resolve problems. "Doing a survey like this probably hurts morale in a company unless it leads to some changes," he says. American clearly needs some changes and sooner, rather than later.[13]

Review Questions

1. Discuss the situation at American Airlines in regard to the stages of conflict the author presents.
2. Analyze possible conflict resolution methods using the direct conflict management techniques discussed in the chapter.
3. Suggest possible distributive or integrative negotiation approaches available to the two parties in the American dispute.

References

1. "Air Transport Association," http://www.air-transport.org/data/, March 22, 1999.
2. Johnson, Cynthia, "Hoovers—Airline," http://www.hoovers.com/features/industry/airline.html, March 22, 1999.
3. Ibid.
4. "AMR Corporate," http://www.amrcorp.com/annual/airline_group.htm, March 22, 1999.
5. Ibid.
6. Dine, Philip. "Airlines Face Labor's "Payback" Need: Workers Seek Rewards for Earlier Concessions," *St. Louis Post-Dispatch,* February 16, 1999, p. A1.
7. Ibid.
8. "AMR-Investor Information," http://www.amrcorp.com/annual/year_in_review.htm, March 22, 1999.
9. Zuckerman, Laurence. "Persistent Mistrust and Big Egos Lie at Heart of American Pilots Dispute," the *New York Times,* February 15, 1999, p. A14.
10. Ibid.
11. Pedersen, Daniel. "Stranded and Fuming," *Newsweek,* February 22, 1999, p. 39.
12. Leonhardt, David; Bernstein, Aaron; and Zellner, Wendy. "UAL: Labor Is My Co-Pilot," *Business Week,* March 1, 1999, p. 38.
13. Zellner, Wendy. "Blue Crew at American," *Business Week,* February 22, 1999, p. 8. ■

The New Vice President

[*Note:* Please read only those parts identified by your instructor. Do not read ahead.]

Part A

When the new president at Mid-West U took over, it was only a short time before the incumbent vice president announced his resignation. Unfortunately, there was no one waiting in the wings, and a hiring freeze prevented a national search from commencing.

Many faculty leaders and former administrators suggested that the President appoint Jennifer Treeholm, the Associate Vice President for Academic Affairs, as interim. She was an extremely popular person on campus and had 10 years of experience in the role of associate vice president. She knew everyone and everything about the campus. Jennifer, they assured him, was the natural choice. Besides, Jennifer *deserved* the job. Her devotion to the school was unparalleled, and her energy knew no bounds. The new President, acting on advice from many campus leaders, appointed Jennifer Interim vice president for a term of up to three years. He also agreed that she could be a candidate for the permanent position when the hiring freeze was lifted.

Jennifer and her friends were ecstatic. It was high time more women moved into important positions on campus. They went out for dinner to their every Friday night watering hole to celebrate and reflect on Jennifer's career.

Except for a brief stint outside of academe, Jennifer's entire career had been at Mid-West U. She started out teaching Introductory History, then, realizing she wanted to get on the tenure track, went back to school and earned her Ph.D. at Metropolitan U. while continuing to teach at Mid-West. Upon completion of her degree, she was appointed as an Assistant Professor and, eventually, earned the rank of Associate based on her popularity and excellent teaching.

Not only was Jennifer well liked, but she devoted her entire life, it seemed, to Mid-West, helping to form the first union, getting grants, writing skits for the faculty club's annual follies, and going out of her way to befriend everyone who needed support.

Eventually, Jennifer was elected President of the Faculty Senate. After serving for two years, she was offered the position of Associate vice president. During her 10 years as associate vice president, she handled most of the academic complaints, oversaw several committees, wrote almost all of the letters and reports for the vice president, and was even known to run personal errands for the president. People just knew they could count on Jennifer.

Review Questions

1. At this point, what are your predictions about Jennifer as the Interim Vice President?
2. What do you predict will be her management/leadership style?

3. What are her strengths? Her weaknesses? What is the basis for your assessment?

After you have discussed Part A, please read Part B.

Part B

Jennifer's appointment as interim vice president was met with great enthusiasm. Finally, the school was getting someone who was "one of their own," a person who understood the culture, knew the faculty, and could get things done.

It was not long before the campus realized that things were not moving and that Jennifer, despite her long-standing popularity, had difficulty making tough decisions. Her desire to please people and to try to take care of everyone made it difficult for her to choose opposing alternatives. (To make matters worse, she had trouble planning, organizing, and managing her time.)

What was really a problem was that she did not understand her role as the Number Two person at the top of the organization. The President expected her to support him and his decisions without question. Over time the President also expected her to implement some of his decisions—to do his dirty work. This became particularly problematic when it involved firing people or saying no to old faculty cronies. Jennifer also found herself uncomfortable with the other members of the president's senior staff. Although she was not the only woman (the general counsel, a very bright, analytical woman was part of the group), Jennifer found the behavior and decision-making style to be different from what she was used to.

Most of the men took their lead from the president and discussed very little in the meetings. Instead, they would try to influence decisions

Source: Adapted from Donald D. Bowen, et al., *Experiences in Management and Organizational Behavior,* 4th ed. (New York: John Wiley & Sons, Inc.), 1997.

privately. Often a decision arrived in a meeting as a "fait accompli." Jennifer felt excluded and wondered why, as vice president, she felt so powerless.

In time, she and the President spent less and less time together talking and discussing how to move the campus along. Although her relations with the men on the senior staff were cordial, she talked mostly to her female friends.

Jennifer's friends, especially her close-knit group of long-time female colleagues, all assured her that it was because she was "interim." "Just stay out of trouble," they told her. Of course this just added to her hesitancy when it came to making tough choices.

As the president's own image on campus shifted after his "honeymoon year," Jennifer decided to listen to her friends rather than follow the president's lead. After all, her reputation on campus was at stake.

Review Questions

1. What is the major problem facing Jennifer?
2. What would you do if you were in her position?
3. Would a man have the same experience as Jennifer?
4. Are any of your predictions about her management style holding up?

Part C

When the hiring freeze was lifted and Jennifer's position was able to be filled, the president insisted on a national search. Jennifer and her friends felt this was silly, given that she was going into her third year in the job. Nonetheless, she entered the search process.

After a year-long search, the Search Committee met with the president. The external candidates were not acceptable to the campus. Jennifer, they recommended, should only be appointed on a permanent basis if she agreed to change her management style.

The president mulled over his dilemma, then decided to give Jennifer the benefit of the doubt and the opportunity. He appointed her permanent Provost, while making the following, private agreement with her.

1. She will organize her office and staff and begin delegating more work to others.
2. She will "play" her Number Two position, backing the president and "echoing" his position on the University's vision statement.
3. She will provide greater direction for the Deans who report to her.

Jennifer agreed to take the position. She was now the University's first female vice president and presided over a council of 11 deans, three of whom were her best female friends. Once again, they sought out their every Friday night watering hole for an evening of dinner and celebration.

Review Questions

1. If you were Jennifer, would you have accepted the job?
2. What would you do as the new, permanent, vice president?
3. Will Jennifer change her management style? If so, in what ways?
4. What are your predictions for the future?

Part D

Although people had predicted that things would be better once Jennifer was permanently in the job, they in fact became more problematic.

People now expected Jennifer to be able to take decisive action. She did not feel she could.

Every time an issue came up, she would spend weeks, sometimes months, trying to get a sense of the campus. Nothing moved once it hit her office. After a while, people began referring to the vice president's office as "the black hole" where things just went in and disappeared.

Her immediate staff were concerned and frustrated. Not only did she not delegate effectively, but her desire to make things better led her to try to do more and more herself.

The vice president's job also carried social obligations and requests. Here again, she tried to please everyone and often ran from one evening obligation to another, trying to show her support and concern for every constituency on campus. She was exhausted, overwhelmed, and knowing the mandate under which she was appointed, anxious about the president's evaluation of her behavior.

The greatest deterioration occurred within her Dean's Council. Several of the male Deans, weary of waiting for direction from Jennifer regarding where she was taking some of the academic proposals of the president, had started making decisions without Jennifer's approval.

"Loose cannons," was how she described a couple of them. "They don't listen. They just march out there on their own."

One of the big problems with two of the deans was that they just didn't take no for an answer when it came from Jennifer. Privately, each conceded that her "no" sounded like a "maybe." She always left room open to renegotiate.

Whatever the problem, and there were several by now, Jennifer's ability to lead was being questioned. Although her popularity was as high as ever, more and more people on campus were expressing their frustrations with what sometimes appeared as mixed signals from her and the president and sometimes was seen as virtually no direction. People wanted priorities. Instead, crisis management reigned.

Questions

1. If you were president, what would you do?
2. If you were Jennifer, what would you do?

Conclusion

Jennifer had a few "retreats" with her senior staff. Each time, she committed herself to delegate more, prioritize, and work on time management issues, but within 10 days or so, everything was back to business as usual.

The president decided to hire a person with extensive corporate experience to fill the vacant position of vice president of Finance and Administration. The new man was an experienced team player who had survived mergers, been fired and bounced back, and had spent years in the number two position in several companies. Within a few months he had earned the respect of the campus as well as the president and was in fact emerging as the person who really ran the place. Meanwhile, the president concentrated on external affairs and fund raising.

Jennifer felt relieved. Her role felt clearer. She could devote herself to academic and faculty issues and she was out from under the pressure to play "hatchet man."

As she neared the magic age for early retirement, she began to talk more and more about what she wanted to do next. ∎

EXPERIENTIAL EXERCISES

My Best Manager

Procedure

1. Make a list of the attributes that describe the best manager you ever worked for. If you have trouble identifying an actual manager, make a list of attributes you would like the manager in your next job to have.
2. Form a group of four or five persons and share your lists.
3. Create one list that combines all the unique attributes of the "best" managers represented in your group. Make sure that you have all attributes listed, but list each only once. Place a check mark next to those that were reported by two or more members. Have one of your members prepared to present the list in general class discussion.
4. After all groups have finished Step 3, spokespersons should report to the whole class. The instructor will make a running list of the "best" manager attributes as viewed by the class.
5. Feel free to ask questions and discuss the results.

Graffiti Needs Assessment: Involving Students in the First Class Session

Contributed by Barbara K. Goza, Visiting Associate Professor, University of California Santa Cruz and Associate Professor California State Polytechnic University, Pomona. From *Journal of Management Education,* 1993.

Procedure

1. Complete the following sentences with as many endings as possible.
   1. When I first came to this class, I thought . . .
   2. My greatest concern this term is . . .
   3. In 3 years I will be . . .
   4. The greatest challenge facing the world today is . . .
   5. Organizational behavior specialists do . . .
   6. Human resources are . . .
   7. Organizational research is . . .
   8. The most useful question I've been asked is . . .
   9. The most important phenomenon in organizations is . . .
   10. I learn the most when . . .
2. Your instructor will guide you in a class discussion about your responses. Pay careful attention to similarities and differences among various students' answers.

My Best Job

Procedure

1. Make a list of the top five things you expect from your first (or next) full-time job.
2. Exchange lists with a nearby partner. Assign probabilities (or odds) to each goal on your partner's list to indicate how likely you feel it is that the goal can be accomplished. (*Note:* Your instructor may ask that everyone use the same probabilities format.)
3. Discuss your evaluations with your partner. Try to delete superficial goals or modify them to become more substantial. Try to restate any unrealistic goals to make them more realistic. Help your partner do the same.
4. Form a group of four to six persons. Within the group have everyone share what they now consider to be the most "realistic" goals on their lists. Elect a spokesperson to share a sample of these items with the entire class.
5. Discuss what group members have individually learned from the exercise. Await further class discussion led by your instructor.

What Do You Value in Work?

Procedure

1. The following nine items are from a survey conducted by Nicholas J. Beutell and O. C. Brenner ("Sex Differences in Work Values," *Journal of Vocational Behavior,* Vol.

28, pp. 29–41, 1986). Rank order the nine items in terms of how important (9 = most important) they would be to you in a job.

How important is it to you to have a job that:
____ Is respected by other people?
____ Encourages continued development of knowledge and skills?
____ Provides job security?
____ Provides a feeling of accomplishment?
____ Provides the opportunity to earn a high income?
____ Is intellectually stimulating?
____ Rewards good performance with recognition?
____ Provides comfortable working conditions?
____ Permits advancement to high administrative responsibility?

2. Form into groups as designated by your instructor. Within each group, the *men in the group* will meet to develop a consensus ranking of the items as they think the *women* in the Beutell and Brenner survey ranked them. The reasons for the rankings should be shared and discussed so they are clear to everyone. The *women in the group* should not participate in this ranking task. They should listen to the discussion and be prepared to comment later in class discussion. A spokesperson for the men in the group should share the group's rankings with the class.

3. (*Optional*) Form into groups as designated by your instructor, but with each group consisting entirely of men or women. Each group should meet and decide which of the work values members of the *opposite* sex ranked first in the Beutell and Brenner survey. Do this again for the work value ranked last. The reasons should be dis-cussed, along with reasons that each of the other values probably was not ranked first . . . or last. A spokesperson for each group should share group results with the rest of the class.

Source: Adapted from Roy J. Lewicki, Donald D. Bowen, Douglas T. Hall, and Francine S. Hall, *Experiences in Management and Organizational Behavior,* 3rd ed. (New York: John Wiley & Sons, Inc., 1988), pp. 23–26. Used by permission.

EXERCISE 5

My Asset Base

A business has an asset base or set of resources that it uses to produce a good or service of value to others. For a business, these are the assets or resources it uses to achieve results, including capital, land, patented products or processes, buildings and equipment, raw materials, and the human resources or employees, among others.

Each of us has an asset base that supports our ability to accomplish the things we set out to do. We refer to our personal assets as *talents, strengths,* or *abilities.* We probably inherit our talents from our parents, but we acquire many of our abilities and strengths through learning. One thing is certain: we feel very proud of the talents and abilities we have.

Procedure

1. Printed here is a T chart that you are to fill out. On the right-hand side of the T, list four or five of your accomplishments—*things you have done of which you are most proud.* Your accomplishments should only include those things for which you can take credit, those *things for which you are primarily responsible.* If you are proud of the sorority to which you belong, you may be justifiably proud, but don't list it unless you

can argue that the sorority's excellence is due primarily to your efforts. However, if you feel that having been invited to join the sorority is a major accomplishment for you, then you may include it.

When you have completed the right-hand side of the chart, fill in the left-hand side by listing *talents, strengths,* and *abilities* that you have that have enabled you to accomplish the outcomes listed on the right-hand side.

My Asset Base

ASSETS Talents, abilities, strengths	ACHIEVEMENTS AND ACCOMPLISHMENTS

2. Share your lists with other team members. As each member takes turn sharing his or her list, pay close attention to your own perceptions and feelings. Notice the effect this has on your attitudes toward the other team members.
3. Discuss these questions in your group:
   (a) How did your attitudes and feelings toward other members of the team change as you pursued the activity? What does this tell you about the process whereby we come to get to know and care about people?
   (b) How did you feel about the instructions the instructor provided? What did you expect to happen? Were your expectations accurate?

Source: Adapted from Donald D. Bowen et al., *Experiences in Management and Organizational Behavior,* 4th ed. (New York: John Wiley & Sons, Inc.), 1997.

EXERCISE 6

Expatriate Assignments

Contributed by Robert E. Ledman, Morehouse College

This exercise focuses on issues related to workers facing international assignments. It illustrates that those workers face a multitude of issues. It further demonstrates that managers who want employees to realize the maximum benefits of international assignments should be aware of, and prepared to deal with, those issues. Some of the topics that are easily addressed with this exercise include the need for culture and language training for the employees and their families and the impact that international assignments may have on an employee's family and how that may affect an employee's willingness to seek such assignments.

Procedure

1. Form into "families" of four or five. Since many students today have only one parent at home, it is helpful if some groups do not have students to fill both

Source: Robert E. Ledman, Gannon University. Presented in the Experiential Exercise Track of the 1996 ABSEL Conference and published in the *Proceedings* of that conference.

parental roles in the exercise. Each student is assigned to play a family member and given a description of that person. Descriptions of family members are given below.

2. Enter into a 20-minute discussion to explore how a proposed overseas assignment will affect the family members. Your goal is to try to reach a decision about whether the assignment should be taken. You must also decide whether the entire family or only the family member being offered the assignment will relocate. The assignment is for a minimum of 2 years, with possible annual extensions resulting in a total of 4 years, and your family, or the member offered the assignment will be provided, at company expense, one trip back to the states each year for a maximum period of 15 days. The member offered the assignment will not receive any additional housing or cost-of-living supplements described in the role assignment if he or she chooses to go overseas alone and can expect his or her living expenses to exceed substantially the living allowance being provided by the company. In your discussion, address the following questions:

   (a) What are the most important concerns your family has about relocating to a foreign country?
   (b) What information should you seek about the proposed host country to be able to make a more informed decision?
   (c) What can the member offered the assignment do to make the transition easier if he or she goes overseas alone? If the whole family relocates?
   (d) What should the member offered the assignment do to ensure that this proposed assignment will not create unnecessary stress for him or her and the rest of the family?
   (e) What lessons for managers of expatriate assignees are presented by the situation in this exercise?

Try to reach some "family" consensus. If a consensus is not possible, however, resolve any differences in the manner you think the family in the role descriptions would ultimately resolve any differences.

3. Share your answers with the rest of the class. Explain the rationale for your answers and answer questions from the remainder of the class.
4. (Optional) After each group has reported on a given question, the instructor may query the class about how their answers are consistent, or inconsistent, with common practice of managers as described in the available literature.

Descriptions of Family Members
Person Being Offered Overseas Assignment

This person is a middle- to upper-level executive who is on a fast track to senior management. He or she has been offered the opportunity to manage an overseas operation, with the assurance of a promotion to a vice presidency upon return to the States. The company will pay all relocation expenses, including selling costs for the family home and the costs associated with finding a new home upon return. The employer will also provide language training for the employee and cultural awareness training for the entire family. The employee will receive a living allowance equal to 20 percent of his or her salary. This should be adequate to provide the family a comparable standard of living to that which is possible on the employee's current salary.

Spouse of the Person Offered an Overseas Assignment (Optional)

This person is also a professional with highly transferrable skills and experience for the domestic market. It is unknown how easily he or she may be able to find employment in the foreign country. This person's income, though less than his or her spouse's, is necessary if the couple is to continue paying for their child's college tuition and to prepare for the next child to enter college in two years. This person has spent 15 years developing a career, including completing a degree at night.

Oldest Child

This child is a second semester junior in college and is on track to graduate in 16 months. Transferring at this time would probably mean adding at least one semester to complete the degree. He or she has been dating the same person for over a year; they have talked about getting married immediately after graduation, although they are not yet formally engaged.

Middle Child

This child is a junior in high school. He or she has already begun visiting college campuses in preparation for applying in the fall. This child is involved in a number of school activities; he or she is photographer for the yearbook and plays a varsity sport. This child has a learning disability for which services are being provided by the school system.

Youngest Child

This child is a middle school student, age 13. He or she is actively involved in Scouting and takes piano lessons. This child has a history of medical conditions that have required regular visits to the family physician and specialists. This child has several very close friends who have attended the same school for several years.

Cultural Cues

Contributed by Susan Rawson Zacur and W. Alan Randolph, University of Baltimore

Introduction

In the business context, culture involves shared beliefs and expectations that govern the behavior of people. In this exercise, *foreign culture* refers to a set of beliefs and expectations different from those of the participant's home culture (which has been invented by the participants).

Procedure

1. (10–15 minutes) Divide into two groups, each with color-coded badges. For example, the blue group could receive blue Post-it notes and the yellow group could receive yellow Post-it notes. Print your first name in bold letters on the badge and wear it throughout the exercise.

   Work with your group members to invent your own cultural cues. Think about the kinds of behaviors and words that will signify to all members that they belong together in one culture. For each category provided below, identify and record at least one important attribute for your culture.

Cultural Cues:	Your Culture:
Facial expression:	_____
Eye contact (note: you must have some eye contact in order to observe others):	_____
Handshake:	_____
Body language (note: must be evident while standing):	_____
Key words or phrases:	_____

Once you have identified desirable cultural aspects for your group, practice them. It is best to stand with your group and to engage one another in conversations involving two or three people at a time. Your aim in talking with one another is to learn as much as possible about each other—hobbies, interests, where you live, what your family is like, what courses you are taking; and so on, all the while practicing the behaviors and words identified above. It is not necessary for participants to answer questions of a personal nature truthfully. Invention is permissible because the conversation is only a means to the end of cultural observation. Your aim at this point is to become comfortable with the indicators of your particular culture. Practice until the indicators are second nature to you.

2. Now assume that you work for a business that has decided to explore the potential for doing business with companies in a different culture. You are to learn as much as possible about another culture. To do so, you will send from one to three representatives from your group on a "business trip" to the other culture. These representatives must, insofar as possible, behave in a manner that is consistent with your culture. At the same time, each representative must endeavor to learn as much as possible about the

Source: Adapted by Susan Rawson Zacur and W. Alan Randolph from *Journal of Management Education,* Vol. 17, No. 4 (November 1993) pp. 510–516.

people in the other culture, while keeping eyes and ears open to cultural attributes that will be useful in future negotiations with foreign businesses. (*Note:* At no time will it be considered ethical behavior for the representative to ask direct questions about the foreign culture's attributes. These must be gleaned from firsthand experience.)

While your representatives are away, you will receive one or more exchange visitors from the other culture, who will engage in conversation as they attempt to learn more about your organizational culture. You must strictly adhere to the cultural aspects of your own culture while you converse with the visitors.

3. (5–10 minutes) All travelers return to your home cultures. As a group, discuss and record what you have learned about the foreign culture based on the exchange of visitors. This information will serve as the basis for orienting the next representatives who will make a business trip.

4. (5–10 minutes) Select one to three different group members to make another trip to the other culture to check out the assumptions your group has made about the other culture. This "checking out" process will consist of actually practicing the other culture's cues to see whether they work.

5. (5–10 minutes) Once the traveler(s) have returned and reported on findings, as a group, prepare to report to the class what you have learned about the other culture.

Prejudice in Our Lives

Contributed by Susan Schor of Pace University and Annie McKee of The Wharton School, University of Pennsylvania with the assistance of Ariel Fishman of The Wharton School

Procedure

1. As a large class group, generate a list of groups that tend to be targets of prejudice and stereotypes in our culture—such groups can include gender, race, ethnicity, sexual orientation, region, religion, and so on. After generating a list, either as a class or in small groups, identify a few common positive and negative stereotypes associated with each group. Consider also relationships or patterns that exist between some of the lists. Discuss the implications for groups that have stereotypes that are valued in organizations versus groups whose stereotypes are viewed negatively in organizations.

2. As an individual, think about the lists you have now generated, and list those groups with which you identify. Write about an experience in which you were stereotyped as a member of a group. Ask yourself the following questions and write down your thoughts:

   (a) What group do I identify with?
   (b) What was the stereotype?
   (c) What happened? When and where did the incident occur? Who said what to whom?
   (d) What were my reactions? How did I feel? What did I think? What did I do?

   (e) What were the consequences? How did the incident affect myself and others?

3. Now, in small groups, discuss your experiences. Briefly describe the incident and focus on how the incident made you feel. Select one incident from the ones shared in your group to role play for the class. Then, as a class, discuss your reactions to each role play. Identify the prejudice or stereotype portrayed, the feelings the situation evoked, and the consequences that might result from such a situation.

4. Think about the prejudices and stereotypes you hold about other people. Ask yourself, "What groups do I feel prejudice toward? What stereotypes do I hold about members of each of these groups? How may such a prejudice have developed—did a family member or close friend or television influence you to stereotype a particular group in a certain way?

5. Now try to identify implications of prejudice in the workplace. How do prejudice and stereotypes affect workers, managers, relationships between people, and the organization as a whole? Consider how you might want to change erroneous beliefs as well as how you would encourage other people to change their own erroneous beliefs.

How We View Differences

Contributed by Barbara Walker

Introduction

Clearly, the workplace of the future will be much more diverse than it is today: more women, more people of color, more international representation, more diverse lifestyles and ability profiles, and the like. Managing a diverse workforce and working across a range of differences is quickly becoming a "core competency" for effective managers.

Furthermore, it is also becoming clear that diversity in a work team can significantly enhance the creativity and quality of the team's output. In today's turbulent business environment, utilizing employee diversity will give the manager and the organization a competitive edge in tapping all of the available human resources more effectively. This exercise is an initial step in the examination of how we work with people whom we see as different from us. It is fairly simple, straightforward, and safe, but its implications are profound.

Procedure

1. Read the following:

Imagine that you are traveling in a rental car in a city you have never visited before. You have a one hour drive on an uncrowded highway before you reach your destination. You decide that you would like to spend the time listening to some of your favorite kind of music on the car radio.

The rental car has four selection buttons available, each with a preset station that plays a different type of music. One plays *country music,* one plays *rock,* one plays *classical,* and one plays *jazz.* Which type of music would you choose to listen to for the next hour as you drive along? (Assume you want to relax and just stick with one station; you don't want to bother switching around between stations.)

_____
Source: Exercise developed by Barbara Walker, a pioneer on work on valuing differences. Adapted for this volume by Douglas T. Hall. Used by permission of Barbara Walker.

2. Form into groups based on the type of music that you have chosen. All who have chosen country will meet in an area designated by the instructor. Those who chose rock will meet in another area, etc. In your groups, answer the following question. Appoint one member to be the spokesperson to report your answers back to the total group.

Question

For each of the other groups, what words would you use to describe people who like to listen to that type of music?

3. Have each spokesperson report the responses of her or his group to the question in step 2. Follow with class discussion of these additional questions:

(a) What do you think is the purpose or value of this exercise?

(b) What did you notice about the words used to describe the other groups? Were there any *surprises* in this exercise for you?

(c) Upon what sorts of data do you think these images were based?

(d) What term do we normally use to describe these generalized perceptions of another group?

(e) What could some of the consequences be?

(f) How do the perceptual processes here relate to other kinds of intergroup differences, such as race, gender, culture, ability, ethnicity, health, age, nationality, etc.?

(g) What does this exercise suggest about the ease with which intergroup stereotypes form?

(h) What might be ways an organization might facilitate the valuing and utilizing of differences between people?

Alligator River Story

_____
Source: From Sidney B. Simon, Howard Kirschenbaum, and Leland Howe, *Values Clarification, The Handbook,* revised edition, copyright © 1991, Values Press, P.O. Box 450, Sunderland, MA. 01375. Send for a list of other strategy books from Value Press.

The Alligator River Story

There lived a woman named Abigail who was in love with a man named Gregory. Gregory lived on the shore of a river. Abigail lived on the opposite shore of the same river. The river that separated the two lovers was teeming with dangerous alligators. Abigail wanted to cross the river to be with Gregory. Unfortunately, the bridge had been washed out by a heavy flood the previous week. So she went to ask Sinbad, a riverboat captain, to take her across. He said he would be glad to if she would consent to go to bed with him prior to the voyage. She promptly refused and went to a friend named Ivan to explain her plight. Ivan did not want to get involved at all in the situation. Abigail felt her only alternative was to accept Sinbad's terms. Sinbad fulfilled his promise to Abigail and delivered her into the arms of Gregory.

When Abigail told Gregory about her amorous escapade in order to cross the river, Gregory cast her aside with disdain. Heartsick and rejected, Abigail turned to Slug with her tail of woe. Slug, feeling compassion for Abigail, sought out Gregory and beat him brutally. Abigail was overjoyed at the sight of Gregory getting his due. As the sun set on the horizon, people heard Abigail laughing at Gregory.

Procedure

1. Read "The Alligator River Story."

2. After reading the story, rank the five characters in the story beginning with the one whom you consider the most offensive and end with the one whom you consider the least objectionable. That is, the character who seems to be the most reprehensible to you should be entered first in the list following the story, then the second most reprehensible, and so on, with the least reprehensible or objectionable being entered fifth. Of course, you will have your own reasons as to why you rank them in the order that you do. Very briefly note these too.

3. Form groups as assigned by your instructor (at least four persons per group with gender mixed).

4. Each group should:
   a. Elect a spokesperson for the group
   b. Compare how the group members have ranked the characters
   c. Examine the reasons used by each of the members for their rankings
   d. Seek consensus on a final group ranking

5. Following your group discussions, you will be asked to share your outcomes and reasons for agreement or non-agreement. A general class discussion will then be held.

EXERCISE 11

Teamwork and Motivation

Contributed by Dr. Barbara McCain, Oklahoma City University

Procedure

1. Read this situation.
You are the *owner* of a small manufacturing corporation. Your company manufactures widgets—a commodity. Your widget is a clone of nationally known widgets. Your widget, "WooWoo," is less expensive and more readily available than the nationally known brand. Presently, the sales are high. However, there are many rejects, which increases your cost and delays the delivery. You have 50 employees in the following departments: sales, assembly, technology, and administration.

2. In groups, discuss methods to motivate all of the employees in the organization—rank order them in terms of preference.

3. Design an organization motivation plan that encourages high job satisfaction, low turnover, high productivity, and high-quality work.

4. Is there anything special you can do about the minimum wage service worker? How do you motivate this individual? On what motivation theory do you base your decision?

5. Report to the class your motivation plan. Record your ideas on the board and allow all groups to build on the first plan. Discuss additions and corrections as the discussion proceeds.

Worksheet

Individual Worker	Team Member
Talks	
Me oriented	
Department focused	
Competitive	
Logical	
Written messages	
Image	
Secrecy	
Short-term sighted	
Immediate results	
Critical	
Tenure	

Directions: Fill in the right-hand column with descriptive terms. These terms should suggest a change in behavior from individual work to teamwork.

EXERCISE 12

The Downside of Punishment

Contributed by Dr. Barbara McCain, Oklahoma City University

Procedure

There are numerous problems associated with using punishment or discipline to change behavior. Punishment creates negative effects in the workplace. To better understand this, work in your group to give an example of each of the following situations:

1. Punishment may not be applied to the person whose behavior you want to change.

2. Punishment applied over time may suppress the occurrence of socially desirable behaviors.

3. Punishment creates a dislike of the person who is implementing the punishment.

4. Punishment results in undesirable emotions such as anxiety and agressiveness.

5. Punishment increases the desire to avoid punishment.

6. Punishing one behavior does not guarantee that the desired behavior will occur.

7. Punishment follow-up requires allocation of additional resources.

8. Punishment may create a communication barrier and inhibit the flow of information.

Source: Adapted from class notes: Dr. Larry Michaelson, Oklahoma University.

Annual Pay Raises

Procedure

1. Read the job descriptions below and decide on a percentage pay increase for each of the eight employees.
2. Make salary increase recommendations for each of the eight managers that you supervise. There are no formal company restrictions on the size of raises you give, but the total for everyone should not exceed the $10,900 (a 4-percent increase in the salary pool) which has been budgeted for this purpose. You have a variety of information upon which to base the decisions, including a "productivity index" (PI), which Industrial Engineering computes as a quantitative measure of operating efficiency for each manager's work unit. This index ranges from a high of 10 to a low of 1. Indicate the percentage increase *you* would give each manager in the blank space next to each manager's name. Be prepared to explain why.

   ____ *A. Alvarez* Alvarez is new this year and has a tough work group whose task is dirty and difficult. This is a hard position to fill, but you don't feel Alvarez is particularly good. The word around is that the other managers agree with you. PI = 3. Salary = $33,000.

   ____ *B. J. Cook* Cook is single and a "swinger" who enjoys leisure time. Everyone laughs at the problems B.J. has getting the work out, and you feel it certainly is lacking. Cook has been in the job 2 years. PI = 3. Salary = $34,500.

   ____ *Z. Davis* In the position 3 years, Davis is one of your best people, even though some of the other managers don't agree. With a spouse who is independently wealthy, Davis doesn't need money but likes to work. PI = 7. Salary = $36,600.

   ____ *M. Frame* Frame has personal problems and is hurting financially. Others gossip about Frame's performance, but you are quite satisfied with this second-year employee. PI = 7. Salary = $34,700.

_____ *C.M. Liu* Liu is just finishing a fine first year in a tough job. Highly respected by the others, Liu has a job offer in another company at a 15-percent increase in salary. You are impressed, and the word is that the money is important. PI = 9. Salary = $34,000.

_____ *B. Ratin* Ratin is a first-year manager whom you and the others think is doing a good job. This is a bit surprising since Ratin turned out to be a "free spirit" who doesn't seem to care much about money or status. PI = 9. Salary = $33,800.

_____ *H. Smith* A first-year manager recently divorced and with two children to support as a single parent. The others like Smith a lot, but your evaluation is not very high. Smith could certainly use extra money. PI = 5. Salary = $33,000.

_____ *G. White* White is a big spender who always has the latest clothes and a new car. In the first year on what you would call an easy job, White doesn't seem to be doing very well. For some reason, though, the others talk about White as the "cream of the new crop." PI = 5. Salary = $33,000.

3. Convene in a group of four to seven persons and share your raise decision.
4. As a group, decide on a new set of raises and be prepared to report them to the rest of the class. Make sure that the group spokesperson can provide the rationale for each person's raise.
5. The instructor will call on each group to report its raise decisions. After discussion, an "expert's" decision will be given.

EXERCISE 14

Tinker Toys

Contributed by Bonnie McNeely, Murray State University

Materials Needed
Tinker toy sets.

Procedure
1. Form groups as assigned by the instructor. The mission of each group or temporary organization is to build the tallest possible tinker toy tower. Each group should determine worker roles: at least four students will be builders, some will be consultants who offer suggestions, and the remaining students will be observers who remain silent and complete the observation sheet provided below.

2. Rules for the exercise:
   a. Fifteen minutes allowed to plan the tower, but *only 60 seconds* to build.
   b. No more than two Tinker Toy pieces can be put together during the planning.
   c. All pieces must be put back in the box before the competition begins.
   d. Completed tower must stand alone.

Observation Sheet
1. What planning activities were observed?

   Did the group members adhere to the rules?

2. What organizing activities were observed?

Source: Adapted from Bonnie McNeely, "Using the Tinker Toy Exercise to Teach the Four Functions of Management, *Journal of Management Education,* Vol. 18, No. 4 (November 1994), 468–472.

Was the task divided into subtasks? Division of labor?

3. Was the group motivated to succeed? Why or why not?

4. Were any control techniques observed?

   Was a time keeper assigned?

   Were backup plans discussed?

5. Did a clear leader emerge from the group?

   What behaviors indicated that this person was the leader?

   How did the leader establish credibility with the group?

6. Did any conflicts within the group appear?

   Was there a power struggle for the leadership position?

EXERCISE 15

Job Design Preferences

Procedure

1. Use the left column to rank the following job characteristics in the order most important *to you* (1=highest to 10=lowest). Then use the right column to rank them in the
   order you think they are most important *to others*.

   ____ Variety of tasks   ____
   ____ Performance feedback   ____
   ____ Autonomy/freedom in work   ____
   ____ Working on a team   ____
   ____ Having responsibility   ____
   ____ Making friends on the job   ____
   ____ Doing all of a job, not part   ____
   ____ Importance of job to others   ____
   ____ Having resources to do well   ____
   ____ Flexible work schedule   ____

2. Form work groups as assigned by your instructor. Share your rankings with other
   group members. Discuss where you have different individual preferences and where
   your impressions differ from the preferences of others. Are there any major patterns
   in your group—for either the "personal" or the "other" rankings? Develop group consensus rankings for each column. Designate a spokesperson to share the group rankings and results of any discussion with the rest of the class.

My Fantasy Job

Contributed by Lady Hanson, California State Polytechnic University, Pomona

Instructions

1. Think about a possible job that represents what you consider to be your ideal or "fantasy" job. For discussion purposes, try to envision it as a job you would hold within a year of finishing your current studies. Write down a brief description of that job in the space below. Start the description with the following words—*My fantasy job would be* . . .

2. Review the description of the Hackman/Oldham model of Job Characteristics Theory offered in the textbook. Note in particular the descriptions of the core characteristics. Consider how each of them could be maximized in your fantasy job. Indicate in the spaces that follow how specific parts of your fantasy job will fit into or relate to each of the core characteristics.

   a) Skill variety: _____

   b) Task identity: _____

   c) Task significance: _____

   d) Autonomy: _____

   e) Job feedback: _____

3. Form into groups as assigned by your instructor. In the group have each person share his or her fantasy job and the descriptions of its core characteristics. Select one person from your group to tell the class as a whole about her/his fantasy job. Be prepared to participate in general discussion regarding the core characteristics and how they may or may not relate to job performance and job satisfaction. Consider also the likelihood that the fantasy jobs of class members are really attainable—in other words: Can "fantasy" become fact?

*Eggs*periential Exercise

Contributed by Dr. Barbara McCain, Oklahoma City University

Materials Needed

1 raw egg per group

6 plastic straws per group

1 yard of plastic tape

1 large plastic jar

Procedure

1. Form into equal groups of five to seven people.
2. The task is to drop an egg from the chair onto the plastic without breaking the egg. Groups can evaluate the materials and plan their task for 10 minutes. During this period the materials may not be handled.
3. Groups have 10 minutes for construction.
4. One group member will drop the egg while standing on top of a chair in front of the class. One by one a representative from each group will drop their eggs.
5. Optional: Each group will name the egg.
6. Each group discusses their individual/group behav-iors during this activity. Optional: This analysis may be summarized in written form. The following questions may be utilized in the analysis:
   (a) What kind of group is it? Explain.
   (b) Was the group cohesive? Explain.
   (c) How did the cohesiveness relate to performance? Explain.
   (d) Was there evidence of group think? Explain.
   (e) Were group norms established? Explain.
   (f) Was there evidence of conflict? Explain.
   (g) Was there any evidence of social loafing? Explain.

EXERCISE 18

Scavenger Hunt—Team Building

Contributed by Michael R. Manning and Paula J. Schmidt, New Mexico State University

Introduction

Think about what it means to be a part of a team—a successful team. What makes one team more successful than another? What does each team member need to do in order for their team to be successful? What are the characteristics of an effective team?

Procedure

1. Form teams as assigned by your instructor. Locate the items on the list below while following these important rules:
   a. Your team *must stay together at all times*—that is, you cannot go in separate directions.
   b. Your team must return to the classroom in the time allotted by the instructor.
   The team with the most items on the list will be declared the most successful team.
2. Next, reflect on your team's experience. What did each team member do? What was your team's strategy? What made your team effective? Make a list of the most important things your team did to be succesful. Nominate a spokesperson to summarize your team's discussion for the class. What items were similar between teams? That is, what helped each team to be effective?

Source: Adapted from Michael R. Manning and Paula J. Schmidt, *Journal of Management Education,* Building Effective Work Teams: A Quick Exercise Based on a Scavenger Hunt. (Thousand Oaks, CA: Sage Publications, 1995), pp. 392–398. Used by permission. Reference for list of items for scavenger hunt from C. E. Larson and F. M. Lafas, *Team Work: What Must Go Right/What Can Go Wrong* (Newbury Park, CA: Sage Publications, 1989).

Items for Scavenger Hunt

Each item is to be identified and brought back to the classroom.

1. A book with the word "team" in the title.
2. A joke about teams that you share with the class.
3. A blade of grass from the university football field.
4. A souvenir from the state.
5. A picture of a team or group.
6. A newspaper article about a team.
7. Compose a team song and perform it for the class.
8. A leaf from an oak tree.
9. Stationery from the Dean's office.
10. A cup of sand.
11. A pine cone.
12. A live reptile. (*Note:* Sometimes a team member has one for a pet or the students are ingenious enough to visit a local pet store.)
13. A definition of group "cohesion" that you share with the class.
14. A set of chopsticks.
15. Bring back three cans of vegetables.
16. A branch of an elm tree.
17. Find and share three unusual items with the class.
18. A ball of cotton
19. The ear from a prickly pear cactus.
20. A group name.

(*Note:* Items may be substituted as appropriate for your locale.)

Work Team Dynamics

Introduction

Think about your course work team, a work team you are involved in for another course, or any other team suggested by the instructor. Indicate how often each of the following statements accurately reflects your experience in the team. Use this scale:

1=Always   2=Frequently   3=Sometimes   4=Never

_____ 1. My ideas get a fair hearing.

_____ 2. I am encouraged for innovative ideas and risk taking.

_____ 3. Diverse opinions within the team are encouraged.

_____ 4. I have all the responsibility I want.

_____ 5. There is a lot of favoritism shown in the team.

_____ 6. Members trust one another to do their assigned work.

_____ 7. The team sets high standards of performance excellence.

_____ 8. People share and change jobs a lot in the team.

_____ 9. You can make mistakes and learn from them in this team.

_____ 10. This team has good operating rules.

Procedure

Form groups as assigned by your instructor. Ideally, this will be the team you have just rated. Have all team members share their ratings, and make one master rating for the team as a whole. Circle the items on which there are the biggest differences of opinion. Discuss those items and try to find out why they exist. In general, the better a team scores on this instrument, the higher its creative potential. If everyone has rated the same team, make a list of the five most important things members can do to improve its operations in the future. Nominate a spokesperson to summarize the team discussion for the class as a whole.

Source: Adapted from William Dyer, *Team Building,* ed. 2 (Reading, MA: Addison-Wesley, 1987), pp. 123–125.

Identifying Group Norms

Procedure

1. Choose an organization you know quite a bit about.

2. Complete the questionnaire below, indicating your responses using one of the following:

> (a) Strongly agree or encourage it.
> (b) Agree with it or encourage it.
> (c) Consider it unimportant.
> (d) Disagree with or discourage it.
> (e) Strongly disagree with or discourage it.

If an employee in this organization were to . . . *Most other employees would:*

1. Show genuine concern for the problems that face the organization and make suggestions about solving them . . . ____
2. Set very high personal standards of performance . . . ____
3. Try to make the work group operate more like a team when dealing with issues or problems . . . ____
4. Think of going to a supervisor with a problem . . .
5. Evaluate expenditures in terms of the benefits they will provide for the organization . . . ____
6. Express concern for the well-being of other members of the organization . . . ____
7. Keep a customer or client waiting while looking after matters of personal convenience . . . ____
8. Criticize a fellow employee who is trying to improve things in the work situation . . . ____
9. Actively look for ways to expand his/her knowledge to be able to do a better job . . . ____
10. Be perfectly honest in answering this questionnaire . . . ____

Scoring

A = +2, B = +1, C = 0, D = –1, E = –2

1. Organizational/Personal Pride
   Score ____
2. Performance/Excellence
   Score ____
3. Teamwork/Communication
   Score ____
4. Leadership/Supervision
   Score ____
5. Profitability/Cost Effectiveness
   Score ____

6. Colleague/Associate Relations
   Score ____
7. Customer/Client Relations
   Score ____
8. Innovativeness/Creativity
   Score ____
9. Training/Development
   Score ____
10. Candor/Openness
    Score ____

EXERCISE 21

Workgroup Culture

Contributed by Conrad N. Jackson, MPC, Inc.

Source: Adapted from Donald D. Bowen, et al., *Experiences in Management and Organizational Behavior,* 4th ed. (New York: John Wiley & Sons, Inc.), 1997.

Procedure

1. The bipolar scales on this instrument can be used to evaluate a group's process in a number of useful ways.

Use it to measure where you see the group to be at present. To do this, *circle* the number that best represents *how you see the culture of the group.* You can also indicate how you think the group *should* function by using a different symbol, such as a square (□), or a caret (^) to indicate how you saw the group at some time in the past.

2. (a) If you are assessing your own group, have everyone fill in the instrument, summarize the scores, then discuss their bases (what members say and do that has led to these interpretations) and implications. This is often an extremely productive intervention to improve group or team functioning.

   (b) If you are assessing another group, use the scores as the basis for your feeback. Be sure to provide specific feedback on behavior *you have* *observed* in addition to the subjective interpretations of your ratings on the scales in this instrument.

   (c) The instrument can also be used to compare a group's self-assessment with the assessment provided by another group.

1. Trusting	1 : 2 : 3 : 4 : 5	Suspicious
2. Helping	1 : 2 : 3 : 4 : 5	Ignoring, blocking
3. Expressing feelings	1 : 2 : 3 : 4 : 5	Suppressing feelings
4. Risk taking	1 : 2 : 3 : 4 : 5	Cautious
5. Authenticity	1 : 2 : 3 : 4 : 5	Game playing
6. Confronting	1 : 2 : 3 : 4 : 5	Avoiding
7. Open	1 : 2 : 3 : 4 : 5	Hidden, diplomatic

···· EXERCISE 22 ···

The Hot Seat

Contributed by Barry R. Armandi, SUNY-Old Westbury

Procedure

1. Form into groups as assigned by your instructor.
2. Read the following situation.

A number of years ago, Professor Stevens was asked to attend a departmental meeting at a university. He had been on leave from the department, but a junior faculty member discreetly requested that he attend to protect the rights of the junior faculty. The Chair, or head of the department, was a typical Machiavellian, whose only concerns were self-serving. Professor Stevens had a number of previous disagreements with the Chair. The heart of the disagreements centered around the Chair's abrupt and domineering style and his poor relations with the junior faculty, many of whom felt mistreated and scared.

The department was a conglomeration of different professorial types. Included in the mix were behavioralists, generalists, computer scientists, and quantitative analysts. The department was embedded in the school of business, which had three other departments. There was much confusion and concern among the faculty, since this was a new organizational design. Many of the faculty were at odds with each other over the direction the school was now taking.

At the meeting, a number of proposals were to be presented that would seriously affect the performance and future of certain junior faculty, particularly those who were behavioral scientists. The Chair, a computer scientist, disliked the behaviorists, who he felt were "always analyzing the motives of people." Professor Stevens, who was a tenured full professor and a behaviorist, had an objective to protect the interests of the junior faulty ad to counter the efforts of the Chair.

Including Professor Stevens, there were nine faculty present. The accompanying diagram on the next page shows the seating arrangement and the layout of the room. The ×s signify those faculty who were allies of the Chair. The +s are those opposed to the Chair and supportive of Professor Stevens, and the ?s were undecided and could be swayed either way. The circled numbers represent empty seats. Both ?s were behavioralists, and the + next to them was a quantitative analyst. Near the door, the first × was a generalist, the two +s were behavioralists, and the second × was a quantitative analyst. The diagram shows the seating of everyone but Professor Stevens, who was the last one to enter the room. Standing at the door, Professor Stevens surveyed the room and within 10 seconds knew which seat was the most effective to achieve his objective.

3. Answer the following questions in your group.
   (a) Which seat did Professor Stevens select and why?
   (b) What is the likely pattern of communication and interaction in this group?
   (c) What can be done to get this group to work harmoniously?

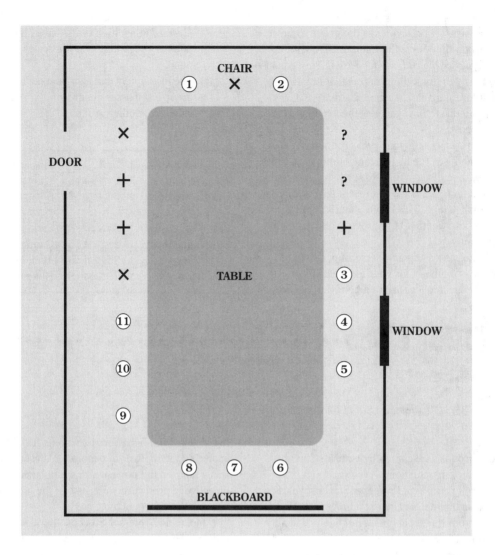

Organizations Alive!

Contributed by Bonnie L. McNeely, Murray State University

Procedure

1. Find a copy of the following items from actual organizations. These items can be obtained from the company where you now work, your parent's workplace, or from the university. Universities have mission statements, codes of conduct for students and faculty, organizational charts, job descriptions, performance appraisal forms, and control devices. Some student organizations also have these documents. All the items do not have to come from the same organization *Bring these items to class*.

Source: Adapted from Bonnie L. McNeely, "Make Your Principles of Management Class come Alive," *Journal of Management Education,* Vol. 18, No. 2, May 1994, 246–249.

(a) Mission Statement   (d) Job Description
(b) Code of Ethics   (e) Performance Appraisal Form
(c) Organizational Chart   (f) Control Device

2. Form groups in class as assigned by your instructor. Share your items with the group, as well as what you learned while collecting these items. For example, did you find that some firms have a mission, but it is not written down? Did you find that job descriptions existed, but they were not really used or had not been updated in years?

EXERCISE 24

Fast Food Technology

Contributed by D. T. Hall, Boston University, and F. S. Hall, University of New Hampshire

Introduction

A critical first step in improving or changing any organization is *diagnosing* or analyzing its present functioning. Many change and organization development efforts fall short of their objectives because this important step was not taken, or was conducted superficially. To illustrate this, imagine how you would feel if you went to your doctor complaining of stomach pains, and he recommended surgery without conducting any tests, without obtaining any further information, and without a careful physical examination. You would probably switch doctors! Yet, managers often attempt major changes with correspondingly little diagnostic work in advance. (It could be said that they undertake vast projects with half-vast ideas.)

In this exercise, you will be asked to conduct a group diagnosis of two different organizations in the fast food business. The exercise will provide an opportunity to integrate much of the knowledge you have gained in other exercises and in studying other topics. Your task will be to describe the organizations as carefully as you can in terms of several key organizational concepts. Although the organizations are probably very familiar to you, try to step back and look at them as though you were seeing them for the first time.

Procedure

1. In groups of four or six people, your assignment is described below.

One experience most people in this country have shared is that of dining in the hamburger establishment known as McDonald's. In fact, someone has claimed that 25th-century archeologists may dig into the ruins of our present civilization and conclude that 20-century religion was devoted to the worship of golden arches.

Your group, Fastalk Consultants, is known as the shrewdest, most insightful, and most overpaid management consulting firm in the country. You have been hired by the president of McDonald's to make recommendations for improving the motivation and performance of personnel in their franchise operations. Let us assume that the key job activities in franchise operations are food preparation, order-taking and dealing with customers, and routine clean-up operations.

Recently the president of McDonald's has come to suspect that his company's competitors such as Burger King, Wendy's, Jack-in-the-Box, Dunkin' Doughnuts, various pizza establishments, and others are making heavy inroads into McDonald's market. He has also hired a market research firm to investigate and compare the relative merits of the sandwiches, french fries, and drinks served in McDonald's and the competitor, and has asked the market research firm to assess the advertising campaigns of the two organizations. Hence, you will not need to be concerned with marketing issues, except as they may have an impact on employee behavior. The president wants *you* to look into the *organization* of the franchises to determine the strengths and weaknesses of each. Select a competitor who gives McDonald's a good "run for its money" in your area.

The president has established an unusual contract with you. *He wants you to make your recommendations based upon your observations as a customer.* He does not want you to do a complete diagnosis with interviews, surveys, or behind-the-scenes observations. He wants your report in two parts. Remember, the president wants concrete, specific, and practical recommendations. Avoid vague generalizations such as "improve communications" or "increase trust." Say very clearly *how* management can improve organizational performance. Substantiate your recommendations by reference to one or more theories of motivation, leadership, small groups, or job design.

Part I

Given his organization's goals of profitability, sales volume, fast and courteous service, and cleanliness, the president of McDonald's wants an analysis that will *compare and contrast McDonald's and the competitor* in terms of the following concepts:

Organizational goals
Organizational structure
Technology
Environment
Employee motivation
Communication
Leadership style
Policies/procedures/rules/standards
Job design
Organizational climate

Part II

Given the corporate goals listed under Part I, what specific actions might McDonald's management and franchise owners take in the following areas to achieve these goals (profitability, sales volume, fast and courteous service, and cleanliness)?

Job design and workflow
Organizational structure (at the individual restaurant level)
Employee incentives
Leadership
Employee selection

How do McDonald's and the competition differ in these aspects? Which company has the best approach?

2. Complete the assignment by going as a group to one McDonald's and one competitor's restaurant. If possible, have a meal in each place. To get a more valid comparison, visit a McDonald's and a competitor located in the same area. After observing each restaurant, meet with your group and prepare your 10-minute report to the executive committee.

3. In class, each group will present its report to the rest of the class, who will act as the executive committee. The group leader will appoint a timekeeper to be sure that each group sticks to its 10-minute time limit. Possible discussion questions include:
   (a) What similarities are there between the two organizations?
   (b) What differences are there between the organizations?
   (c) Do you have any "hunches" about the reasons for the particular organizational characteristics you found? For example, can you try to explain why one organization might have a particular type of structure? Incentive system? Climate?
   (d) Can you try to explain one set of characteristics in terms of some other characteristics you found? For example, do the goals account for structure? Does the environment explain the structure?

EXERCISE 25

Alien Invasion

Procedure

This is an exercise in organizational culture. You will be assigned to a team (if you are not already in one) and instructed to visit an organization by your instructor.

1. Visit the site assigned as a team working under conditions set forth in the "situation" below.
2. Take detailed notes on the cultural forms that you observe.
3. Prepare a presentation for the class that describes these forms and draw any inferences you can about the nature of the culture of the organization—its ideologies, values, and norms of behavior.
4. Be sure to explain the basis of your inferences in terms of the cultural forms observed

You will have 20 minutes to report your findings, so plan your presentation carefully. Use visual aids to help your audience understand what you have found.

Situation

You are Martians who have just arrived on Earth in the first spaceship from your planet. Your superiors have ordered you to learn as much about Earthlings and the way they behave as you can with-

Source: Adapted from Donald D. Bowen et al., *Experiences in Management and Organizational Behavior,* 4th ed. (New York: John Wiley & Sons, Inc.), 1997.

out doing anything to make them aware that you are Martians. It is vital for the future plans of your superiors that you do nothing to disturb the Earthlings. Unfortunately, Martians communicate by emitting electromagnetic waves and are incapable of speech, so you cannot talk to the natives. Even if you did, it is reported by the usually reliable Bureau of Interplanetary Intelligence that Earthlings may become cannibalistic if annoyed. However, the crash course in Earth languages taught by the Bureau has enabled you to read the language.

Remember, these instructions limit your data collection to observation and request that you *not* talk to the "natives." There are two reasons for this instruction. First, your objective is to learn what the organization does when it is simply going about its normal business and not responding to a group of students asking questions. Second, you are likely to be surprised at how much you can learn by simply observing if you put your mind to it. Many skilled managers employ this ability in sensing what is going on as they walk through their plant or office area.

Since you cannot talk to people, some of the cultural forms (legends, sagas, etc.) will be difficult to spot unless you are able to pick up copies of the organization's promotional literature (brochures, company reports, advertisements) during your visit. Do not be discouraged, because the visible forms such as artifacts, setting, symbols, and (sometimes) rituals can convey a great deal about the culture. Just keep your eyes, ears, and antennae open!

EXERCISE 26

Interview a Leader

Contributed by Bonnie McNeely, Murray State University

Procedure

1. Make an appointment to interview a leader. It can be a leader working in a business or nonprofit organization, such as a government agency, school, etc. Base the interview on the form provided here, but feel free to add your own questions.
2. Bring the results of your interview to class. Form into groups as assigned by your instructor. Share the responses from your interview with your group and compare answers. What issues were similar? Different? Were the stress levels of leaders working in nonprofit organizations as high as those working in for profit firms? Were you surprised at the number of hours per week worked by leaders?
3. Be prepared to summarize the interviews done by your group as a formal written report, if asked to do so by the instructor.

Interview Questionnaire

Student's Name _____ Date _____

1. Position in the organization (title):
2. Number of years in current position:
   Number of years of managerial experience:
3. Number of people directly supervised:
4. Average number of hours worked a week
5. How did you get into leadership?
6. What is the most rewarding part of being a leader?
7. What is the most difficult part of your job?
8. What would you say are the *keys to success* for leaders?

Source: Adapted from Bonnie McNeely, "Make Your Principles of Management Class come Alive," *Journal of Management Education,* Vol. 18, No. 2, May 1994, 246–249.

9. What advice do you have for an aspiring leader?
10. What type of ethical issues have you faced as a leader?
11. If you were to enroll in a leadership seminar, what topics or issues would you want to learn more about?
12. (Student's question)

Gender: M____ F____ Years of formal education____

Level of job stress: Very high____ High____ Average____ Low____

Profit organization____ Nonprofit organization____

Additional information/Comments:

Leadership Skills Inventories

Procedure

1. Look over the skills listed below and ask your instructor to clarify those you do not understand.
2. Complete each category by checking either the "Strong" or "Needs Development" category in relation to your own level with each skill.
3. After completing each category, briefly describe a situation in which each of the listed skills has been utilized.
4. Meet in your groups to share and discuss inventories. Prepare a report summarizing major development needs in your group.

Instrument

	Strong	Needs Development	Situation
Communication			
Conflict Management			
Delegation			
Ethical Behavior			
Listening			
Motivation			
Negotiation			
Performance Appraisal and Feedback			
Planning and Goal Setting			
Power and Influence			
Presentation and Persuasion			
Problem Solving and Decision Making			
Stress Management			
Team Building			
Time Management			

Leadership and Participation in Decision Making

Procedure

1. For the ten situations described below, decide which of the three styles you would use for that unique situation. Place the letter A, P, or L on the line before each situation's number.

   A—authority; make the decision alone without additional inputs.

   P—consultative; make the decision based on group inputs.

   L—group; allow the group to which you belong to make the decision.

Decision Situations

_____ 1. You have developed a new work procedure that will increase productivity. Your boss likes the idea and wants you to try it within a few weeks. You view your employees as fairly capable and believe that they will be receptive to the change.

_____ 2. The industry of your product has new competition. Your organization's revenues have been dropping. You have been told to lay off three of your ten employees in 2 weeks. You have been the supervisor for over 1 year. Normally, your employees are very capable.

_____ 3. Your department has been facing a problem for several months. Many solutions have been tried and failed. You finally thought of a solution, but you are not sure of the possible consequences of the change required or the acceptance of the highly capable employees.

_____ 4. Flex time has become popular in your organization. Some departments let each employee start and end work whenever they choose. However, because of the cooperative effort of your employees, they must all work the same 8 hours. You are not sure of the level of interest in changing the hours. Your employees are a very capable group and like to make decisions.

_____ 5. The technology in your industry is changing faster than the members of your organization can keep up. Top management hired a consultant who has given the recommended decision. You have 2 weeks to make your decision. Your employees are capable, and they enjoy participating in the decision-making process.

_____ 6. Your boss called you on the telephone to tell you that someone has requested an order for your department's product with a very short delivery date. She asked that you call her back with the decision about taking the order in 15 minutes. Looking over the work schedule, you realize that it will be very difficult to deliver the order on time. Your employees will have to push hard to make it. They are cooperative, capable, and enjoy being involved in decision making.

_____ 7. A change has been handed down from top management. How you implement it is your decision. The change takes effect in one month. It will personally affect everyone in your department. The acceptance of the department members is critical to the success of the change. Your employees are usually not too interested in being involved in making decisions.

_____ 8. You believe that productivity in your department could be increased. You have thought of some ways that may work, but you're not sure of them. Your employees are very experienced; almost all of them have been in the department longer than you have.

_____ 9. Top management has decided to make a change that will affect all of your employees. You know that they will be upset because it will cause them hardship. One or two may even quit. The change goes into effect in 30 days. Your employees are very capable.

___ 10. A customer has offered you a contract for your product with a quick delivery date. The offer is open for 2 days. Meeting the contract deadline would require employees to work nights and weekends for 6 weeks. You cannot require them to work overtime. Filling this profitable contract could help get you the raise you want and feel you deserve. However, if you take the contract and don't deliver on time it will hurt your chances of getting a big raise. Your employees are very capable.

2. Form groups as assigned by your instructor. Share and compare your choices for each decision situation. Reconcile any differences and be prepared to defend your decision preferences in general class discussion.

EXERCISE 29

My Best Manager: Revisited

Contributed by J. Marcus Maier, Chapman University

Procedure

1. Refer to the list of qualities—or profiles—the class generated earlier in the course for the "Best Manager."
2. Looking first at your Typical Managers profile, suppose you took this list to 100 average people on the street (or at the local mall) and asked them whether ___ (Trait X, quality Y) was "more typical of men or of women in our culture." What do you think *most* of them would say? That ___ (X, Y etc.) is more typical of *women*? or of *men*? Or of neither/both?[1] Do this for every trait on your list(s). (5 minutes)
3. Now do the same for the qualities we generated in our Best Manager profile. (5 min.)
4. A straw vote is taken, one quality at a time, to determine the class's overall gender identification of each trait, focusing on the Typical Managers profile (10–15 min.). Then this is repeated for the Best Manager profile (10–15 min.).[2]
5. Discussion. What do you see in the data this group has generated? How might you interpret these results? (15–20 min.)

Source: Based on Dr. Maier's 1993 article, "The Gender Prism." *Journal of Management Education,* 17(3), 285–314. 1994 Fritz Roethlisberger Award Recipient for Best Paper (Updated, 1996).

[1] This gets the participants to move outside of their *own* conceptions to their awareness of *societal* definitions of masculinity and femininity.

[2] This is done by a rapid show of hands, looking for a clear majority vote. An "f" (for "feminine") is placed next to those qualities that a clear majority indicate are more typical of women, an "m" (for "masculine") next to those qualities a clear majority indicate would be more typical of men. (This procedure parallels the median-split method used in determining Bem Sex Role Inventory classifications.) If no clear majority emerges (i.e., if the vote is close), the trait or quality is classified as "both" (f/m). The designations "masculine" or "feminine" are used (rather than "men" or "women") to underscore the *socially constructed* nature of each dimension.

Active Listening

Contributed by Robert Ledman, Morehouse College

Procedure

1. Review active listening skills and behaviors as described in the textbook and in class.
2. Form into groups of three. Each group will have a listener, a talker, and an observer (if the number of students is not evenly divisible by three, two observers are used for one or two groups).
3. The "talkers" should talk about any subject they wish, but only *if* they are being actively listened to. Talkers should stop speaking as soon as they sense active listening has stopped.

4. The "listeners" should use a list of active listening skills and behaviors as their guide, and practice as many of them as possible to be sure the talker is kept talking. Listeners should contribute nothing more than "active listening" to the communication.
5. The "observer" should note the behaviors and skills used by the listener and the effects they seemed to have on the communication process.
6. These roles are rotated until each student has played every role.
7. The instructor will lead a discussion of what the observers saw and what happened with the talkers and listeners. The discussion focuses on what behaviors from the posted list have been present, which have been absent, and how the communication has been affected by the listener's actions.

Source: Adapted from the presentation entitled "An Experiential Exercise to Teach Active Listening," presented at the Organizational Behavior Teaching Conference, Macomb, IL, 1995.

Upward Appraisal

Procedure

1. Form work groups as assigned by your instructor.
2. The instructor will leave the room.
3. Convene in your assigned work groups for a period of 10 minutes. Create a list of comments, problems, issues, and concerns you would like to have communicated to the instructor in regard to the course experience to date. *Remember,* your interest in the exercise is twofold: (a) to communicate your feelings to the instructor and (b) to learn more about the process of giving and receiving feedback.
4. Select one person from the group to act as spokesperson in communicating the group's feelings to the instructor.
5. The spokespersons should briefly convene to decide on what physical arrangement of chairs, tables, and so forth is most appropriate to conduct the feedback session. The classroom should then be rearranged to fit the desired specifications.
6. While the spokespersons convene, persons in the remaining groups should discuss how they expect the forthcoming communications event to develop. Will it be a good experience for all parties concerned? Be prepared to observe critically the actual communication process.
7. The instructor should be invited to return, and the feedback session will begin. Observers should make notes so that they may make constructive comments at the conclusion of the exercise.
8. Once the feedback session is complete, the instructor will call on the observers for comments, ask the spokespersons for reactions, and open the session to discussion.

"360" Feedback

Contributed by Timothy J. Serey, Northern Kentucky University

Introduction

The time of performance reviews is often a time of genuine anxiety for many organizational members. On one hand, it is an important organizational ritual and a key part of the Human Resource function. Organizations usually codify the process and provide a mechanism to appraise performance. On the other hand, it is rare for managers to feel comfortable with this process. Often, they feel discomfort over "playing God." One possible reason for this is that managers rarely receive formal training about how to provide feedback. From the manager's point of view, if done properly, giving feedback is at the very heart of his or her job as "coach" and "teacher." It is an investment in the professional development of another person, rather than the punitive element we so often associate with hearing from "the boss." From the subordinate's perspective, most people want to know where they stand, but this is usually tempered by a fear of "getting it in the neck." In many organizations, it is rare to receive straight, non-sugar-coated feedback about where you stand.

Procedure

1. Review the section of the book dealing with feedback before you come to class. It is also helpful if individuals make notes about their perceptions and feelings about the course *before* they come to class.
2. Groups of students should discuss their experiences, both positive and negative, in this class. Each group should determine the dimensions of evaluating the class itself *and* the instructor. For example, students might select criteria that include the practicality of the course, the way the material is structured and presented (e.g., lecture or exercises), and the instructor's style (e.g., enthusiasm, fairness).
3. Groups select a member to represent them in a subgroup that next provides feedback to the instructor before the entire class.
4. The student-audience then provides the subgroup with feedback about their effectiveness in this exercise. That is, the larger class provides feedback to the subgroup about the extent to which students actually put the principles of effective feedback into practice (e.g., descriptive not evaluative; specific not general).

Source: Adapted from Timothy J. Serey, *Journal of Management Education,* Vol. 17, No. 2, May 1993. © 1993 by Sage Publications, Inc. Reprinted by permission of Sage Publications.

Role Analysis Negotiation

Contributed by Paul Lyons, Frostburg State University

Introduction

A role is the set of various behaviors people expect from a person (or group) in a particular position. These role expectations occur in all types of organizations, such as one's

Source: Adapted from Paul Lyons, "Developing Expectations with the Role Analysis Technique," *Journal of Management Education.* Vol. 17, No. 3, August 1993, pp. 386–389. © Sage Publications.

place of work, school, family, clubs, and the like. Role ambiguity takes place when a person is confused about the expectations of the role. And sometimes, a role will have expectations that are contradictory. For example, being loyal to the company when the company is breaking the law.

The Role Analysis Technique, or RAT, is a method for improving the effectiveness of a team or group. RAT helps to clarify role expectations, and all organization members have responsibilities that translate to expectations. Determination of role requirements, by consensus—involving all concerned—will ultimately result in more effective and mutually satisfactory behavior. Participation and collaboration in the definition and analysis of roles by group members should result in clarification regarding who is to do what as well as increase the level of commitment to the decisions made.

Procedure

Working alone, carefully read the course syllabus that your instructor has given you. Make a note of any questions you have about anything for which you need clarification or understanding. Pay particular attention to the performance requirements of the course. Make a list of any questions you have regarding what, specifically, is expected of you in order for you to be successful in the course. You will be sharing his information with others, in small groups.

EXERCISE 34

Lost At Sea

Introduction

Consider this situation. You are adrift on a private yacht in the South Pacific when a fire of unknown origin destroys the yacht and most of its contents. You and a small group of survivors are now in a large raft with oars. Your location is unclear, but you estimate being about 1000 miles south-southwest of the nearest land. One person has just found in her pockets five $1 bills and a packet of matches. Everyone else's pockets are empty. The following items are available to you on the raft.

	A	B	C
Sextant	____	____	
Shaving mirror	____	____	
5 gallons water	____	____	
Mosquito netting	____	____	
1 survival meal	____	____	
Maps of Pacific Ocean	____	____	
Floatable seat cushion	____	____	
2 gallons oil-gas mix	____	____	
Small transistor radio	____	____	
Shark repellent	____	____	
20 square feet black plastic	____	____	
1 quart 20-proof rum	____	____	
15 feet nylon rope	____	____	
24 chocolate bars	____	____	
Fishing kit	____	____	

Source: Adapted from "Lost at Sea: A Consensus-Seeking Task," in *The 1975 Handbook for Group Facilitators.* Used with permission of University Associates, Inc.

Procedure

1. *Working alone,* rank in Column A the 15 items in order of their importance to your survival ("1" is most important and "15" is least important).
2. *Working in an assigned group,* arrive at a "team" ranking of the 15 items and record this ranking in Column B. Appoint one person as group spokesperson to report your group rankings to the class.
3. *Do not write in Column C* until further instructions are provided by your instructor.

Entering the Unknown

Contributed by Michael R. Manning, New Mexico State University; Conrad N. Jackson, MPC, Inc., Huntsville, Alabama; and Paula S. Weber, New Mexico Highlands University

Procedure

1. Form into groups of four or five members. In each group spend a few minutes reflecting on members' typical entry behaviors in new situations and their behaviors when they are in comfortable settings.
2. According to the instructor's directions, students count off to form new groups of four or five members each.
3. The new groups spend the next 15–20 minutes getting to know each other. There is no right or wrong way to proceed, but all members should become more aware of their entry behaviors. They should act in ways that can help them realize a goal of achieving comfortable behaviors with their group.
4. Students review what has occurred in the new groups, giving specific attention to the following questions:
   (a) What topics did your group discuss (content)? Did these topics involve the "here and now" or were they focused on "there and then"?
   (b) What approach did you and your group members take to the task (process)? Did you try to initiate or follow? How? Did you ask questions? Listen? Respond to others? Did you bring up topics?
   (c) Were you more concerned with how you came across or with how others came across to you? Did you play it safe? Were you open? Did you share things even though it seemed uncomfortable or risky? How was humor used in your group? Did it add or detract?
   (d) How do you feel about the approach you took or the behaviors you exhibited? Was this hard or easy? Did others respond the way you had anticipated? Is there some behavior you would like to do more of, do better, or do less of?
   (e) Were your behaviors the ones you had intended (goals)?
5. Responses to these questions are next discussed by the class as a whole. (*Note:* Responses will tend to be mixed within a group, but between groups there should be more similarity.) This discussion helps individuals become aware of and understand their entry behaviors.
6. Optional individuals have identified their entry behaviors; each group can then spend 5–10 minutes discussing members' perceptions of each other:
   (a) What behaviors did they like or find particularly useful? What did they dislike?

(b) What were your reactions to others? What ways did they intend to come across? Did you see others in the way they had intended to come across?
(Alternatively, if there is concern about the personal nature of this discussion, ask the groups to discuss what they liked/didn't like without referring to specific individuals.)

EXERCISE 36

Vacation Puzzle

Contributed by Barbara G. McCain and Mary Khalili, Oklahoma City University

Procedure

Can you solve this puzzle? Give it a try and then compare your answers with other classmates. Remember your communicative skills!

Puzzle

Khalili, McCain, Middleton, Porter, and Quintaro teach at Oklahoma City University. Each gets 2 weeks of vacation a year. Last year, each took his or her first week in the first 5 months of the year and his or her second week in the last 5 months. If each professor took each of his or her weeks in a different month from the other professors, in which months did each professor take his or her first and second week?

Here are the facts:

(a) McCain took her first week before Khalili, who took *hers* before Porter; for their second week, the order was reversed.
(b) The professor who vacationed in March also vacationed in September.
(c) Quintaro did not take her first week in March or April.
(d) Neither Quintaro nor the professor who took his or her first week in January took his or her second week in August or December.
(e) Middleton took her second week before McCain but after Quintaro.

Month	Professor
January	
February	
March	
April	
May	
June	
July	
August	
September	
October	
November	
December	

Source: Adapted to classroom activity by Dr. Mary Khalili.

The Ugli Orange

Introduction
In most work settings, people need other people to do their job, benefit the organization, and forward their career. Getting things done in organizations requires us to work together in cooperation, even though the ultimate objectives of those other people may be different from our own. Your task in the present exercise is learning how to achieve this cooperation more effectively.

Procedure
1. The class will be divided into pairs. One student in each pair will read and prepare the role of Dr. Roland, and one will play the role of Dr. Jones (role descriptions to be distributed by instructor). Students should read their respective role descriptions and prepare to meet with their counterpart (see steps 2 and 3).
2. At this point the group leader will read a statement. The instructor will indicate that he or she is playing

the role of Mr. Cardoza, who owns the commodity in question. The instructor will tell you
   (a) How long you have to meet with the other
   (b) What information the instructor will require at the end of your meeting
After the instructor has given you this information, you may meet with the other firm's representative and determine whether you have issues you can agree to.
3. Following the meetings (negotiations), the spokesperson for each pair will report any agreements reached to the entire class. The observer for any pair will report on negotiation dynamics and the process by which agreement was reached.
4. Questions to consider:
   (a) Did you reach a solution? If so, what was critical to reaching that agreement?
   (b) Did you and the other negotiator trust one another? Why or why not?
   (c) Was there full disclosure by both sides in each group? How much information was shared?
   (d) How creative and/or complex were the solutions? If solutions were very complex, why do you think this occurred?
   (e) What was the impact of having an "audience" on your behavior? Did it make the problem harder or easier to solve?

Source: Adapted from Hall et al., *Experiences in Management and Organizational Behavior,* 3rd ed. (New York: John Wiley and Sons, Inc.), 1988. Originally developed by Robert J. Hause. Adapted by D. T. Hall and R. J. Lewicki, with suggested modifications by H. Kolodny and T. Ruble.

Force-Field Analysis

Procedure
1. Choose a situation in which you have high personal stakes (for example: how to get a better grade in course X; how to get a promotion; how to obtain a position).
2. Using a version of the Sample Force-Field Analysis Form below, apply the technique to your situation.
   (a) Describe the situation as it now exists.
   (b) Describe the situation as you would like it to be.
   (c) Identify those "driving forces"—the factors that are presently helping to move things in the desired direction.
   (d) Identify those "restraining forces"—the factors that are presently holding things back from moving in the desired direction.

3. Try to be as specific as possible in terms of the above in relation to your situation. You should attempt to be exhaustive in your listing of these forces. List them all!
4. Now go back and classify the strength of each force as weak, medium, or strong. Do this for both the driving and the restraining forces.
5. At this point you should rank the forces regarding their ability to influence or control the situation.
6. In small groups share your analyses. Discuss the usefulness and drawbacks to using this method for personal situations and its application to organizations.
7. Be prepared to share the results of your group's discussion with the rest of the class.

Sample Force-Field Analysis Form

Current Situation:	Situation as You Would Like It To Be:

Driving Forces:	Restraining Forces:

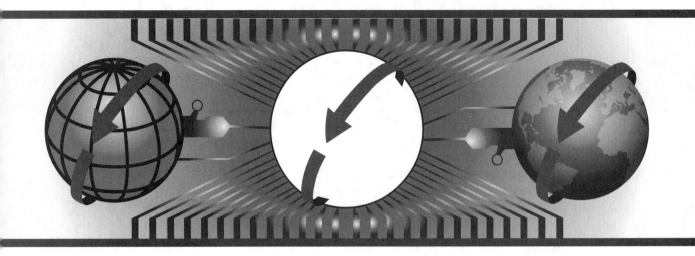

SELF-ASSESSMENT INVENTORIES

●●●●● **ASSESSMENT 1** ●

Managerial Assumptions

Instructions

Read the following statements. Use the space to the left to write "Yes" if you agree with the statement, or "No" if you disagree with it. Force yourself to take a "yes" or "no" position for every statement.

  1. Are good pay and a secure job enough to satisfy most workers?

2. Should a manager help and coach subordinates in their work?
3. Do most people like real responsibility in their jobs?
4. Are most people afraid to learn new things in their jobs?
5. Should managers let subordinates control the quality of their work?
6. Do most people dislike work?
7. Are most people creative?
8. Should a manager closely supervise and direct work of subordinates?

Source: Schermerhorn, John R. Jr., *Management*, 5th ed. (New York, John Wiley & Sons, Inc., 1996) p. 51. By permission.

9. Do most people tend to resist change?
10. Do most people work only as hard as they have to?
11. Should workers be allowed to set their own job goals?
12. Are most people happiest off the job?
13. Do most workers really care about the organization they work for?
14. Should a manager help subordinates advance and grow in their jobs?

Scoring

Count the number of "yes" responses to items 1, 4, 6, 8, 9, 10, 12; write that number here as [X = _____]. Count the number of "yes" responses to items 2, 3, 5, 7, 11, 13, 14; write that score here [Y = _____].

Interpretation

This assessment sheds insight into your orientation toward Douglas McGregor's Theory X (your "X" score) and Theory Y (your "Y" score) assumptions. You should review the discussion of McGregor's thinking in Chapter 1 and consider further the ways in which you are likely to behave toward other people at work. Think, in particular, about the types of "self-fulfilling prophecies" you are likely to create.

A 21st-Century Manager

Instructions

Rate yourself on the following personal characteristics. Use this scale.

> S = Strong, I am very confident with this one.
> G = Good, but I still have room to grow.
> W = Weak, I really need work on this one.
> ? = Unsure, I just don't know.

1. *Resistance to stress:* The ability to get work done even under stressful conditions.
2. *Tolerance for uncertainty:* The ability to get work done even under ambiguous and uncertain conditions.
3. *Social objectivity:* The ability to act free of racial, ethnic, gender, and other prejudices or biases.
4. *Inner work standards:* The ability to personally set and work to high-performance standards.
5. *Stamina:* The ability to sustain long work hours.
6. *Adaptability:* The ability to be flexible and adapt to changes.
7. *Self-confidence:* The ability to be consistently decisive and display one's personal presence.
8. *Self-objectivity:* The ability to evaluate personal strengths and weaknesses and to understand one's motives and skills relative to a job.
9. *Introspection:* The ability to learn from experience, awareness, and self-study.

Source: See *Outcome Management Project,* Phase I and Phase II Reports (St. Louis: American Assembly of Collegiate Schools of Business, 1986 & 1987).

10. *Entrepreneurism:* The ability to address problems and take advantage of opportunities for constructive change.

Scoring

Giving yourself 1 point for each S, and 1/2 point for each G. Do not give yourself points for W and ? responses. Total your points and enter the result here [PMF = _____].

Interpretation

This assessment offers a self-described *profile of your management foundations* (PMF). Are you a perfect 10, or is your PMF score something less than that? There shouldn't be too many 10s around. Ask someone who knows you to assess you on this instrument. You may be surprised at the differences between your PMF score as self-described and your PMF score as described by someone else. Most of us, realistically speaking, must work hard to grow and develop continually in these and related management foundations. This list is a good starting point as you consider where and how to further pursue the development of your managerial skills and competencies. The items on the list are recommended by the American Assembly of Collegiate Schools of Business (AACSB) as skills and personal characteristics that should be nurtured in college and university students of business administration. Their success—and yours—as 21st-century managers may well rest on (1) an initial awareness of the importance of these basic management foundations and (2) a willingness to strive continually to strengthen them throughout your work career.

Turbulence Tolerance Test

Instructions

The following statements were made by a 37-year-old manager in a large, successful corporation. How would you like to have a job with these characteristics? Using the following scale, write your response to the left of each statement.

> 4 = I would enjoy this very much; it's completely acceptable.
>
> 3 = This would be enjoyable and acceptable most of the time.
>
> 2 = I'd have no reaction to this feature one way or another, or it would be about equally enjoyable and unpleasant.
>
> 1 = This feature would be somewhat unpleasant for me.
>
> 0 = This feature would be very unpleasant for me.

_____ 1. I regularly spend 30 to 40 percent of my time in meetings.

_____ 2. Eighteen months ago my job did not exist, and I have been essentially inventing it as I go along.

_____ 3. The responsibilities I either assume or am assigned consistently exceed the authority I have for discharging them.

_____ 4. At any given moment in my job, I have on the average about a dozen phone calls to be returned.

_____ 5. There seems to be very little relation in my job between the quality of my performance and my actual pay and fringe benefits.

_____ 6. About 2 weeks a year of formal management training is needed in my job just to stay current.

_____ 7. Because we have very effective equal employment opportunity (EEO) in my company and because it is thoroughly multinational, my job consistently brings me into close working contact at a professional level with people of many races, ethnic groups and nationalities, and of both sexes.

_____ 8. There is no objective way to measure my effectiveness.

_____ 9. I report to three different bosses for different aspects of my job, and each has an equal say in my performance appraisal.

_____ 10. On average about a third of my time is spent dealing with unexpected emergencies that force all scheduled work to be postponed.

_____ 11. When I have to have a meeting of the people who report to me, it takes my secretary most of a day to find a time when we are all available, and even then, I have yet to have a meeting where everyone is present for the entire meeting.

_____ 12. The college degree I earned in preparation for this type of work is now obsolete, and I probably should go back for another degree.

_____ 13. My job requires that I absorb 100–200 pages of technical materials per week.

_____ 14. I am out of town overnight at least one night per week.

_____ 15. My department is so interdependent with several other departments in the company that all distinctions about which departments are responsible for which tasks are quite arbitrary.

Source: Peter B. Vail, _Managing as a Performance Art: New Ideas for a World of Chaotic Change_ (San Francisco: Jossey-Bass, 1989), pp. 8–9. Used by permission.

16. In about a year I will probably get a promotion to a job in another division that has most of these same characteristics.

17. During the period of my employment here, either the entire company or the division I worked in has been reorganized every year or so.

18. While there are several possible promotions I can see ahead of me, I have no real career path in an objective sense.

19. While there are several possible promotions I can see ahead of me, I think I have no realistic chance of getting to the top levels of the company.

20. While I have many ideas about how to make things work better, I have no direct influence on either the business policies or the personnel policies that govern my division.

21. My company has recently put in an "assessment center" where I and all other managers will be required to go through an extensive battery of psychological tests to assess our potential.

22. My company is a defendant in an antitrust suit, and if the case comes to trial, I will probably have to testify about some decisions that were made a few years ago.

23. Advanced computer and other electronic office technology is continually being introduced into my division, necessitating constant learning on my part.

24. The computer terminal and screen I have in my office can be monitored in my bosses' offices without my knowledge.

Scoring

Total your responses and divide the sum by 24; enter the score here [TTT = ____].

Interpretation

This instrument gives an impression of your tolerance for managing in turbulent times—something likely to characterize the world of work well into the next century. In general, the higher your TTT score, the more comfortable you seem to be with turbulence and change—a positive sign. For comparison purposes, the average scores for some 500 MBA students and young managers was 1.5–1.6. The test's author suggests the TTT scores may be interpreted much like a grade point average in which 4.0 is a perfect A. On this basis, a 1.5 is below a C! How did you do?

· · · · · · ASSESSMENT 4 ·

Global Readiness Index

Instructions

Rate yourself on each of the following items to establish a baseline measurement of your readiness to participate in the global work environment.

Rating Scale:

1 = Very Poor
2 = Poor
3 = Acceptable

4 = Good
5 = Very Good

____ 1. I understand my own culture in terms of its expectations, values, and influence on communication and relationships.

____ 2. When someone presents me with a different point of view, I try to understand it rather than attack it.

____ 3. I am comfortable dealing with situations where the available information is incomplete and the outcomes unpredictable.

____ 4. I am open to new situations and am always

Source: Developed from "Is Your Company Really Global," *Business Week* (December 1, 1997).

looking for new information and learning opportunities.

_____ 5. I have a good understanding of the attitudes and perceptions toward my culture as they are held by people from other cultures.

_____ 6. I am always gathering information about other countries and cultures and trying to learn from them.

_____ 7. I am well informed regarding the major differences in government, political, and economic systems around the world.

_____ 8. I work hard to increase my understanding of people from other cultures.

_____ 9. I am able to adjust my communication style to work effectively with people from different cultures.

_____ 10. I can recognize when cultural differences are influencing working relationships and adjust my attitudes and behavior accordingly.

Interpretation

To be successful in the 21st-century work environment, you must be comfortable with the global economy and the cultural diversity that it holds. This requires a *global mind-set* that is receptive to and respectful of cultural differences, *global knowledge* that includes the continuing quest to know and learn more about other nations and cultures, and *global work skills* that allow you to work effectively across cultures.

Scoring

The goal is to score as close to a perfect "5" as possible on each of the three dimensions of global readiness. Develop your scores as follows.

Items $(1 + 2 + 3 + 4)/4$

= _____ Global Mind-set Score

Items $(5 + 6 + 7)/3$

= _____ Global Knowledge Score

Items $(8 + 9 + 10)/3$

= _____ Global Work Skills Score

ASSESSMENT 5

Personal Values

Instructions

Below are 16 items. Rate how important each one is to you on a scale of 0 (not important) to 100 (very important). Write the numbers 0–100 on the line to the left of each item.

Not important				Somewhat important				Very important		
0	10	20	30	40	50	60	70	80	90	100

_____ 1. An enjoyable, satisfying job.

_____ 2. A high-paying job.

_____ 3. A good marriage.

_____ 4. Meeting new people; social events.

_____ 5. Involvement in community activities.

_____ 6. My religion.

_____ 7. Exercising, playing sports.

_____ 8. Intellectual development.

_____ 9. A career with challenging opportunities.

_____ 10. Nice cars, clothes, home, etc.

_____ 11. Spending time with family.

_____ 12. Having several close friends.

_____ 13. Volunteer work for not-for-profit organizations, such as the cancer society.

Source: Robert N. Lussier, *Human Relations in Organizations,* 2nd ed. (Homewood, IL: Richard D. Irwin, 1993). By permission.

_____ 14. Meditation, quiet time to think, pray, etc.
_____ 15. A healthy, balanced diet.
_____ 16. Educational reading, TV, self-improvement programs, etc.

Scoring

Transfer the numbers for each of the 16 items to the appropriate column below, then add the two numbers in each column.

	Professional	Financial	Family	Social
	1. _____	2. _____	3. _____	4. _____
	9. _____	10. _____	11. _____	12. _____
Totals	_____	_____	_____	_____
	Community	**Spiritual**	**Physical**	**Intellectual**
	5. _____	6. _____	7. _____	8. _____
	13. _____	14. _____	15. _____	16. _____
Totals	_____	_____	_____	_____

Interpretation

The higher the total in any area, the higher the value you place on that particular area. The closer the numbers are in all eight areas, the more well-rounded you are. Think about the time and effort you put forth in your top three values. Is it sufficient to allow you to achieve the level of success you want in each area? If not, what can you do to change? Is there any area in which you feel you should have a higher value total? If yes, which, and what can you do to change?

ASSESSMENT 6

Intolerance for Ambiguity

Instructions

To determine your level of tolerance (intolerance) for ambiguity, respond to the following items. PLEASE RATE EVERY ITEM; DO NOT LEAVE ANY ITEM BLANK. Rate each item on the following seven-point scale:

1	2	3	4	5	6	7
strongly disagree	moderately disagree	slightly disagree		slightly agree	moderately agree	strongly agree

Rating

_____ 1. An expert who doesn't come up with a definite answer probably doesn't know too much.

_____ 2. There is really no such thing as a problem that can't be solved.

_____ 3. I would like to live in a foreign country for a while.

_____ 4. People who fit their lives to a schedule probably miss the joy of living.

_____ 5. A good job is one where what is to be done and how it is to be done is always clear.

_____

Source: Based on Budner, S. (1962) Intolerance of ambiguity as a personality variable, _Journal of Personality,_ Vol. 30, No. 1, 29–50.

_____ 6. In the long run it is possible to get more done by tackling small, simple problems rather than large, complicated ones.

_____ 7. It is more fun to tackle a complicated problem than it is to solve a simple one.

_____ 8. Often the most interesting and stimulating people are those who don't mind being different and original.

_____ 9. What we are used to is always preferable to what is unfamiliar.

_____ 10. A person who leads an even, regular life in which few surprises or unexpected happenings arise really has a lot to be grateful for.

_____ 11. People who insist upon a yes or no answer just don't know how complicated things really are.

_____ 12. Many of our most important decisions are based on insufficient information.

_____ 13. I like parties where I know most of the people more than ones where most of the people are complete strangers.

_____ 14. The sooner we all acquire ideals, the better.

_____ 15. Teachers or supervisors who hand out vague assignments give a chance for one to show initiative and originality.

_____ 16. A good teacher is one who makes you wonder about your way of looking at things.

_____ Total

Scoring

The scale was developed by S. Budner. Budner reports test–retest correlations of .85 with a variety of samples (mostly students and health care workers). Data, however, are more than 30 years old, so mean shifts may have occurred. Maximum ranges are 16–112, and score ranges were from 25 to 79, with a grand mean of approximately 49.

The test was designed to measure several different components of possible reactions to perceived threat in situations which are new, complex, or insoluble. Half of the items have been reversed.

To obtain a score, first _reverse_ the scale score for the eight "reverse" items, 3, 4, 7, 8, 11, 12, 15, and 16 (i.e., a rating of 1 = 7, 2 = 6, 3 = 5, etc.), then add up the rating scores for all 16 items.

Interpretation

Empirically, low tolerance for ambiguity (high intolerance) has been positively correlated with:

- Conventionality of religious beliefs
- High attendance at religious services
- More intense religious beliefs
- More positive views of censorship
- Higher authoritarianism
- Lower Machiavellianism

The application of this concept to management in the 1990s is clear and relatively self-evident. The world of work, and many organizations, are full of ambiguity and change. Individuals with a _higher_ tolerance for ambiguity are far more likely to be able to function effectively in organizations and contexts in which there is a high turbulence, a high rate of change, and less certainty about expectations, performance standards, what needs to be done, etc. In contrast, individuals with a lower tolerance for ambiguity are far more likely to be unable to adapt or adjust quickly in turbulence, uncertainty, and change. These individuals are likely to become rigid, angry, stressed, and frustrated when there is a high level of uncertainty and ambiguity in the environment. High levels of tolerance for ambiguity, therefore, are associated with an ability to "roll with the punches" as organizations, environmental conditions, and demands change rapidly.

Two-Factor Profile

Instructions

On each of the following dimensions, distribute a total of "10" points between the two options. For example:

Summer weather   (7) ....(3) Winter weather

1. Very responsible job   (___) ....(___) Job security

2. Recognition for   (___) ....(___) Good relations
   work accomplishments   with coworkers

3. Advancement   (___) ....(___) A boss who knows
   opportunities at work   his/her job well

4. Opportunities to grow   (___) ....(___) Good working
   and learn on the job   conditions

5. A job that I can   (___) ....(___) Supportive rules,
   do well   policies of employer

6. A prestigious or   (___) ....(___) A high base wage
   high status job   or salary

Scoring

Summarize your total scores for all items in the *left-hand column* and write it here: MF = ____.
Summarize your total scores for all items in the *right-hand column* and write it here: HF = ____.

Interpretation

The "MF" score indicates the relative importance that you place on motivating or satisfier factors in Herzberg's two-factor theory. This shows how important job content is to you. The "HF" score indicates the relative importance that you place on hygiene or dissatisfier factors in Herzberg's two-factor theory. This shows how important job context is to you.

Are You Cosmopolitan?

Instructions

Answer the questions below using a scale of 1 to 5: 1 representing "strongly disagree"; 2, "somewhat disagree"; 3, "neutral"; 4, "somewhat agree"; and 5, "strongly agree."

____   1. You believe it is the right of the professional to make his or her own decisions about what is to be done on the job.

Source: Developed from Joseph A. Raelin, *The Clash of Cultures, Managers and Professionals* (Harvard Business School Press, 1986).

_____ 2. You believe a professional should stay in an individual staff role regardless of the income sacrifice.

_____ 3. You have no interest in moving up to a top administrative post.

_____ 4. You believe that professionals are better evaluated by professional colleagues than by management.

_____ 5. Your friends tend to be members of your profession.

_____ 6. You would rather be known or get credit for your work outside rather than inside the company.

_____ 7. You would feel better making a contribution to society than to your organization.

_____ 8. Managers have no right to place time and cost schedules on professional contributors.

Scoring and Interpretation

A "cosmopolitan" identifies with the career profession, and a "local" identifies with the employing organization. Total your scores. A score of 30–40 suggests a cosmopolitan work orientation, of 10–20 a "local" orientation, and 20–30 a mixed orientation.

·· ASSESSMENT 9 ·

Group Effectiveness

Instructions

For this assessment, select a specific group you work with or have worked with; it can be a college or work group. For each of the eight statements below, select how often each statement describes the group's behavior. Place the number 1, 2, 3, or 4 on the line next to each of the 8 numbers.

Usually	Frequently	Occasionally	Seldom
1	2	3	4

_____ 1. The members are loyal to one another and to the group leader.

_____ 2. The members and leader have a high degree of confidence and trust in each other.

_____ 3. Group values and goals express relevant values and needs of members.

_____ 4. Activities of the group occur in a supportive atmosphere.

_____ 5. The group is eager to help members develop to their full potential.

_____ 6. The group knows the value of constructive conformity and knows when to use it and for what purpose.

_____ 7. The members communicate all information relevant to the group's activity fully and frankly.

_____ 8. The members feel secure in making decisions that seem appropriate to them.

Scoring

_____ Total. Add up the eight numbers and place an X on the continuum below that represents the score.

Effective group   8 . . . 16 . . . 24 . . . 32   Ineffective group

Interpretation

The lower the score, the more effective the group. What can you do to help the group become more effective? What can the group do to become more effective?

Organizational Design Preference

Instructions

To the left of each item, write the number from the following scale that shows the extent to which the statement accurately describes your views.

> 5 = strongly agree
> 4 = agree somewhat
> 3 = undecided
> 2 = disagree somewhat
> 1 = strongly disagree

I prefer to work in an organization where:

1. Goals are defined by those in higher levels.
2. Work methods and procedures are specified.
3. Top management makes important decisions.
4. My loyalty counts as much as my ability to do the job.
5. Clear lines of authority and responsibility are established.
6. Top management is decisive and firm.
7. My career is pretty well planned out for me.
8. I can specialize.
9. My length of service is almost as important as my level of performance.

Source: John F. Veiga and John N. Yanouzas, *The Dynamics of Organization Theory: Gaining a Macro Perspective* (St. Paul, MN: West, 1979), pp. 158–160. Used by permission.

10. Management is able to provide the information I need to do my job well.
11. A chain of command is well established.
12. Rules and procedures are adhered to equally by everyone.
13. People accept authority of a leader's position.
14. People are loyal to their boss.
15. People do as they have been instructed.
16. People clear things with their boss before going over his or her head.

Scoring

Total your scores for all questions. Enter the score here [____].

Interpretation

This assessment measures your preference for working in an organization designed along "organic" or "mechanistic" lines. The higher your score (above 64), the more comfortable you are with a mechanistic design; the lower your score (below 48), the more comfortable you are with an organic design. Scores between 48 and 64 can go either way. This organizational design preference represents an important issue in the new workplace. Indications are that today's organizations are taking on more and more organic characteristics. Presumably, those of us who work in them will need to be comfortable with such designs.

Which Culture Fits You?

Instructions

Check one of the following organization "cultures" in which you feel most comfortable working.

1. A culture that values talent, entrepreneurial activity, and performance over commitment; one that offers large financial rewards and individual recognition.

Source: Developed from Carol Hymowitz, "Which Corporate Culture Fits You?" *The Wall Street Journal* (July 17, 1989), p. B1.

2. A culture that stresses loyalty, working for the good of the group, and getting to know the right people; one that believes in "generalists" and step-by-step career progress.
3. A culture that offers little job security; one that operates with a survival mentality, stresses that every individual can make a difference, and focuses attention on "turnaround" opportunities.
4. A culture that values long-term relationships; one that emphasizes systematic career development, regular training, and advancement based on gaining of functional expertise.

Scoring

These labels identify the four different cultures: 1 = "the baseball team," 2 = "the club," 3 = "the fortress," and 4 = "the academy."

Interpretation

To some extent, your future career success may depend on working for an organization in which there is a good fit between you and the prevailing corporate culture. This assessment can help you learn how to recognize various cultures, evaluate how well they can serve your needs, and recognize how they may change with time. A risk taker, for example, may be out of place in a "club" but fit right in with a "baseball team." Someone who wants to seek opportunities wherever they may occur may be out of place in an "academy" but fit right in with a "fortress."

Least Preferred Coworker Scale

Instructions

Think of all the different people with whom you have ever worked—in jobs, in social clubs, in student projects, or whatever. Next, think of the *one person* with whom you could work *least* well—that is, the person with whom you had the most difficulty getting a job done. This is the one person—a peer, boss, or subordinate—with whom you would least want to work. Describe this person by circling numbers at the appropriate points on each of the following pairs of bipolar adjectives. Work rapidly. There are no right or wrong answers.

Pleasant	8 7 6 5 4 3 2 1	Unpleasant
Friendly	8 7 6 5 4 3 2 1	Unfriendly
Rejecting	1 2 3 4 5 6 7 8	Accepting
Tense	1 2 3 4 5 6 7 8	Relaxed
Distant	1 2 3 4 5 6 7 8	Close
Cold	1 2 3 4 5 6 7 8	Warm
Supportive	8 7 6 5 4 3 2 1	Hostile
Boring	1 2 3 4 5 6 7 8	Interesting
Quarrelsome	1 2 3 4 5 6 7 8	Harmonious
Gloomy	1 2 3 4 5 6 7 8	Cheerful
Open	8 7 6 5 4 3 2 1	Guarded
Backbiting	1 2 3 4 5 6 7 8	Loyal
Untrustworthy	1 2 3 4 5 6 7 8	Trustworthy
Considerate	8 7 6 5 4 3 2 1	Inconsiderate
Nasty	1 2 3 4 5 6 7 8	Nice
Agreeable	8 7 6 5 4 3 2 1	Disagreeable
Insincere	1 2 3 4 5 6 7 8	Sincere
Kind	8 7 6 5 4 3 2 1	Unkind

Scoring

This is called the "least preferred coworker scale" (LPC). Compute your LPC score by totaling all the numbers you circled; enter that score here [LPC = ____].

Interpretation

The LPC scale is used by Fred Fiedler to identify a person's dominant leadership style. Fiedler believes that this style is a relatively fixed part of one's personality and is there-

Source: Fred E. Fiedler and Martin M. Chemers. *Improving Leadership Effectiveness: The Leader Match Concept,* 2nd ed. (New York: John Wiley & Sons, Inc., 1984). Used by permission.

fore difficult to change. This leads Fiedler to his contingency views, which suggest that the key to leadership success is finding (or creating) good "matches" between style and situation. If your score is 73 or above, Fiedler considers you a "relationship-motivated" leader; if your score is 64 and below, he considers you a "task-motivated" leader. If your score is between 65 and 72, Fiedler leaves it up to you to determine which leadership style is most like yours.

ASSESSMENT 13

Leadership Style

Instructions

The following statements describe leadership acts. Indicate the way you would most likely act if you were leader of a work group, by circling whether you would most likely behave in this way:

> always (A); frequently (F); occasionally (O); seldom (S); or never (N)

A F O S N   1. Act as group spokesperson.
A F O S N   2. Encourage overtime work.
A F O S N   3. Allow members complete freedom in their work.
A F O S N   4. Encourage the use of uniform procedures.
A F O S N   5. Permit members to solve their own problems.
A F O S N   6. Stress being ahead of competing groups.
A F O S N   7. Speak as a representative of the group.
A F O S N   8. Push members for greater effort.
A F O S N   9. Try out ideas in the group.
A F O S N 10. Let the members work the way they think best.
A F O S N 11. Work hard for a personal promotion.
A F O S N 12. Tolerate postponement and uncertainty.
A F O S N 13. Speak for the group when visitors are present.
A F O S N 14. Keep the work moving at a rapid pace.
A F O S N 15. Turn members loose on a job.
A F O S N 16. Settle conflicts in the group.
A F O S N 17. Focus on work details.
A F O S N 18. Represent the group at outside meetings.
A F O S N 19. Avoid giving the members too much freedom.
A F O S N 20. Decide what should be done and how it should be done.
A F O S N 21. Push for increased production
A F O S N 22. Give some members authority to act.
A F O S N 23. Expect things to turn out as predicted.
A F O S N 24. Allow the group to take initiative.
A F O S N 25. Assign group members to particular tasks.
A F O S N 26. Be willing to make changes.
A F O S N 27. Ask members to work harder.
A F O S N 28. Trust members to exercise good judgment.
A F O S N 29. Schedule the work to be done.
A F O S N 30. Refuse to explain my actions.
A F O S N 31. Persuade others that my ideas are best.
A F O S N 32. Permit the group to set its own pace.

A F O S N   33. Urge the group to beat its previous record.
A F O S N   34. Act without consulting the group.
A F O S N   35. Ask members to follow standard rules.
                    T _____   P _____

Scoring

1. Circle items 8, 12, 17, 18, 19, 30, 34 and 35.
2. Write the number 1 in front of a *circled item number* if you responded S (seldom) or N (never) to that item.
3. Write a number 1 in front of *item numbers not circled* if you responded A (always) or F (frequently).
4. Circle the number 1's which you have written in front of items 3, 5, 8, 10, 15, 18, 19, 22, 24, 26, 28, 30, 32, 34, and 35.
5. *Count the circled number 1's.* This is your score for leadership *concern for people.* Record the score in the blank following the letter P at the end of the questionnaire.
6. *Count the uncircled number 1's.* This is your score for leadership *concern for task.* Record this number in the blank following the letter T.

"TT" Leadership Style

Instructions

For each of the following 10 pairs of statements, divide 5 points between the two according to your beliefs, perceptions of yourself, or according to which of the two statements characterizes you better. The 5 points may be divided between the a and b statements in any one of the following ways: 5 for a, 0 for b; 4 for a, 1 for b; 3 for a, 2 for b; 1 for a, 4 for b; 0 for a, 5 for b, but not equally (2 ½) between the two. Weigh your choices between the two according to the one that characterizes you or your beliefs better.

1. (a) As leader I have a primary mission of maintaining stability.
   (b) As leader I have a primary mission of change.
2. (a) As leader I must cause events.
   (b) As leader I must facilitate events.
3. (a) I am concerned that my followers are rewarded equitably for their work.
   (b) I am concerned about what my followers want in life.
4. (a) My preference is to think long range: what might be.
   (b) My preference is to think short range: what is realistic.

5. (a) As a leader I spend considerable energy in managing separate but related goals.
   (b) As a leader I spend considerable energy in arousing hopes, expectations, and aspirations among my followers.
6. (a) Although not in a formal classroom sense, I believe that a significant part of my leadership is that of teacher.
   (b) I believe that a significant part of my leadership is that of facilitator.
7. (a) As leader I must engage with followers at an equal level of morality.
   (b) As leader I must represent a higher morality.
8. (a) I enjoy stimulating followers to want to do more.
   (b) I enjoy rewarding followers for a job well done.
9. (a) Leadership should be practical.
   (b) Leadership should be inspirational.
10. (a) What power I have to influence others comes primarily from my ability to get people to identify with me and my ideas.
    (b) What power I have to influence others comes primarily from my status and position.

Scoring

Circle your points for items 1b, 2a, 3b, 4a, 5b, 6a, 7b, 8a, 9b, 10a and add up the total points you allocated to these items; enter the score here [**T** = _____]. Next, add up the total points given to the uncircled items 1a, 2b, 3a, 4b, 5a, 6b, 7a, 8b, 9a, 10b; enter the score here [**T** = _____].

Source: Questionnaire by W. Warner Burke, Ph.D. Used by permission.

Interpretation

This instrument gives an impression of your tendencies toward "transformational" leadership (your **T** score) and "transactional" leadership (your T score). You may want to refer to the discussion of these concepts in Chapter 15.

Today, a lot of attention is being given to the transformational aspects of leadership—those personal qualities that inspire a sense of vision and desire for extraordinary accomplishment in followers. The most successful leaders of the future will most likely be strong in both "T"s.

ASSESSMENT 15

Empowering Others

Instructions

Think of times when you have been in charge of a group—this could be a full-time or part-time work situation, a student work group, or whatever. Complete the following questionnaire by recording how you feel about each statement according to this scale.

> 1 = Strongly disagree
> 2 = Disagree
> 3 = Neutral
> 4 = Agree
> 5 = Strongly agree

When in charge of a group I find:

____ 1. Most of the time other people are too inexperienced to do things, so I prefer to do them myself.

____ 2. It often takes more time to explain things to others than just to do them myself.

____ 3. Mistakes made by others are costly, so I don't assign much work to them.

Source: Questionnaire adapted from L. Steinmetz and R. Todd, *First Line Management,* Fourth Edition (Homewood, IL: BPI/Irwin, 1986), pp. 64–67. Used by permission.

____ 4. Some things simply should not be delegated to others.

____ 5. I often get quicker action by doing a job myself.

____ 6. Many people are good only at very specific tasks, and thus can't be assigned additional responsibilities.

____ 7. Many people are too busy to take on additional work.

____ 8. Most people just aren't ready to handle additional responsibilities.

____ 9. In my position, I should be entitled to make my own decisions.

Scoring

Total your responses; enter the score here [____].

Interpretation

This instrument gives an impression of your *willingness to delegate.* Possible scores range from 9 to 45. The higher your score, the more willing you appear to be to delegate to others. Willingness to delegate is an important managerial characteristic. It is essential if you—as a manager—are to "empower" others and give them opportunities to assume responsibility and exercise self-control in their work. With the growing importance of empowerment in the new workplace, your willingness to delegate is well worth thinking about seriously.

Machiavellianism

Instructions

For each of the following statements, circle the number that most closely resembles your attitude.

Statement	Disagree A Lot	A Little	Neutral	Agree A Little	A Lot
1. The best way to handle people is to tell them what they want to hear.	1	2	3	4	5
2. When you ask someone to do something for you, it is best to give the real reason for wanting it rather than reasons that might carry more weight.	1	2	3	4	5
3. Anyone who completely trusts someone else is asking for trouble.	1	2	3	4	5
4. It is hard to get ahead without cutting corners here and there.	1	2	3	4	5
5. It is safest to assume that all people have a vicious streak, and it will come out when they are given a chance.	1	2	3	4	5
6. One should take action only when it is morally right.	1	2	3	4	5
7. Most people are basically good and kind.	1	2	3	4	5
8. There is no excuse for lying to someone else.	1	2	3	4	5
9. Most people forget more easily the death of their father than the loss of their property.	1	2	3	4	5
10. Generally speaking, people won't work hard unless forced to do so.	1	2	3	4	5

Scoring and Interpretation

This assessment is designed to compute your Machiavellianism (Mach) score. Mach is a personality characteristic that taps people's power orientation. The high-Mach personality is pragmatic, maintains emotional distance from others, and believes that ends can justify means. To obtain your Mach score, add up the numbers you checked for questions 1, 3, 4, 5, 9, and 10. For the other four questions, reverse the numbers you have checked, so that 5 becomes 1; 4 is 2; and 1 is 5. Then total both sets of numbers to find your score. A random sample of adults found the national average to be 25. Students in business and management typically score higher.

The results of research using the Mach test have found: (1) men are generally more Machiavellian than women; (2) older adults tend to have lower Mach scores than younger adults; (3) there is no significant difference between high Machs and low Machs on measures of intelligence or ability; (4) Machiavellianism is not significantly related to demographic characteristics such as educational level or marital status; and (5) high Machs tend to be in professions that emphasize the control and manipulation of people—for example, managers, lawyers, psychiatrists, and behavioral scientists.

Source: From R. Christie and F. L. Geis, *Studies in Machiavellianism* (New York: Academic Press, 1970). By permission.

Personal Power Profile

Contributed by Marcus, Maier, Chapman University

Instructions

Below is a list of statements that may be used in describing behaviors that supervisors (leaders) in work organizations can direct toward their subordinates (followers). First, carefully read each descriptive statement, thinking in terms of *how you prefer to influence others*. Mark the number that most closely represents how you feel. Use the following numbers for your answers.

> 5 = Strongly agree
> 4 = Agree
> 3 = Neither agree nor disagree
> 2 = Disagree
> 1 = Strongly disagree

To influence others, I would prefer to:	Strongly Disagree	Disagree	Neither Agree nor Disagree	Agree	Strongly Agree
1. Increase their pay level	1	2	3	4	5
2. Make them feel valued	1	2	3	4	5
3. Give undesirable job assignments	1	2	3	4	5
4. Make them feel like I approve of them	1	2	3	4	5
5. Make them feel that they have commitments to meet	1	2	3	4	5
6. Make them feel personally accepted	1	2	3	4	5
7. Make them feel important	1	2	3	4	5
8. Give them good technical suggestions	1	2	3	4	5
9. Make the work difficult for them	1	2	3	4	5
10. Share my experience and/or training	1	2	3	4	5
11. Make things unpleasant here	1	2	3	4	5
12. Make being at work distasteful	1	2	3	4	5
13. Influence their getting a pay increase	1	2	3	4	5
14. Make them feel like they should satisfy their job requirements	1	2	3	4	5
15. Provide them with sound job-related advice	1	2	3	4	5
16. Provide them with special benefits	1	2	3	4	5
17. Influence their getting a promotion	1	2	3	4	5
18. Give them the feeling that they have responsibilities to fulfill	1	2	3	4	5
19. Provide them with needed technical knowledge	1	2	3	4	5
20. Make them recognize that they have tasks to accomplish	1	2	3	4	5

Source: Modified version of T. R. Hinken and C. A. Schriesheim, "Development and Application of New Scales to Measure the French and Raven (1959) Bases of Social Power." *Journal of Applied Psychology,* Vol. 74, 1989, 561–567.

Scoring

Using the grid below, insert your scores from the 20 questions and proceed as follows: *Reward power*—sum your response to items 1, 13, 16, and 17 and divide by 4. *Coercive power*—sum your response to items 3, 9, 11, and 12 and divide by 4. *Legitimate power*—sum your response to questions 5, 14, 18, and 20 and divide by 4. *Referent power*—sum your response to questions 2, 4, 6, and 7 and divide by 4. *Expert power*—sum your response to questions 8, 10, 15, and 19 and divide by 4.

Reward	Coercive	Legitimate	Referent	Expert
1 ___	3 ___	5 ___	2 ___	8 ___
13 ___	9 ___	14 ___	4 ___	10 ___
16 ___	11 ___	18 ___	6 ___	15 ___
17 ___	12 ___	20 ___	7 ___	19 ___
Total ___	___	___	___	___
Divide by 4 ___	___	___	___	___

Interpretation

A high score (4 and greater) on any of the five dimensions of power implies that you prefer to influence others by employing that particular form of power. A low score (2 or less) implies that you prefer not to employ this particular form of power to influence others. This represents your power profile. Your overall power position is not reflected by the simple sum of the power derived from each of the five sources. Instead, some combinations of power are synergistic in nature—they are greater than the simple sum of their parts. For example, referent power tends to magnify the impact of other power sources because these other influence attempts are coming from a "respected" person. Reward power often increases the impact of referent power, because people generally tend to like those who give them things that they desire. Some power combinations tend to produce the opposite of synergistic effects, such that the total is less than the sum of the parts. Power dilution frequently accompanies the use of (or threatened use of) coercive power.

ASSESSMENT 18

Your Intuitive Ability

Instructions

Complete this survey as quickly as you can. Be honest with yourself. For each question, select the response that most appeals to you.

1. When working on a project, do you prefer to:
   (a) Be told what the problem is but be left free to decide how to solve it?
   (b) Get very clear instructions about how to go about solving the problem before you start?

2. When working on a project, do you prefer to work with colleagues who are:
   (a) Realistic?

Source: AIM Survey (El Paso, TX: ENFP Enterprises, 1989). Copyright © 1989 by Weston H. Agor. Used by permission.

   (b) Imaginative?

3. Do you most admire people who are:
   (a) Creative?
   (b) Careful?

4. Do the friends you choose tend to be:
   (a) Serious and hard working?
   (b) Exciting and often emotional?

5. When you ask a colleague for advice on a problem you have, do you:
   (a) Seldom or never get upset if he or she questions your basic assumptions?
   (b) Often get upset if he or she questions your basic assumptions?

6. When you start your day, do you:
   (a) Seldom make or follow a specific plan?
   (b) Usually first make a plan to follow?

7. When working with numbers do you find that you:
   (a) Seldom or never make factual errors?
   (b) Often make factual errors?

8. Do you find that you:
   (a) Seldom daydream during the day and really don't enjoy doing so when you do it?
   (b) Frequently daydream during the day and enjoy doing so?

9. When working on a problem, do you:
   (a) Prefer to follow the instructions or rules when they are given to you?
   (b) Often enjoy circumventing the instructions or rules when they are given to you?

10. When you are trying to put something together, do you prefer to have:
    (a) Step-by-step written instructions on how to assemble the item?
    (b) A picture of how the item is supposed to look once assembled?

11. Do you find that the person who irritates you *the most* is the one who appears to be:
    (a) Disorganized?
    (b) Organized?

12. When an expected crisis comes up that you have to deal with, do you:
    (a) Feel anxious about the situation?

(b) Feel excited by the challenge of the situation?

Scoring

Total the number of "a" responses circled for questions 1, 3, 5, 6, 11; enter the score here [A = ____]. Total the number of "b" responses for questions 2, 4, 7, 8, 9, 10, 12; enter the score here [B = ____]. Add your "a" and "b" scores and enter the sum here [A + B = ____]. This is your *intuitive score*. The highest possible intuitive score is 12; the lowest is 0.

Interpretation

In his book *Intuition in Organizations* (Newbury Park, CA: Sage, 1989), pp. 10–11, Weston H. Agor states: "Traditional analytical techniques . . . are not as useful as they once were for guiding major decisions. . . . If you hope to be better prepared for tomorrow, then it only seems logical to pay some attention to the use and development of intuitive skills for decision making." Agor developed the prior survey to help people assess their tendencies to use intuition in decision making. Your score offers a general impression of your strength in this area. It may also suggest a need to further develop your skill and comfort with more intuitive decision approaches.

ASSESSMENT 19

Decision-Making Biases

Instructions

How good are you at avoiding potential decision-making biases? Test yourself by answering the following questions:

1. Which is riskier:
(a) driving a car on a 400-mile trip?
(b) flying on a 400-mile commercial airline flight?

2. Are there more words in the English language:
(a) that begin with "r"?
(b) that have "r" as the third letter?

3. Mark is finishing his MBA at a prestigious university. He is very interested in the arts and at one time consid-

ered a career as a musician. Is Mark more likely to take a job:
(a) in the management of the arts?
(b) with a management consulting firm?

4. You are about to hire a new central-region sales director for the fifth time this year. You predict that the next director should work out reasonably well since the last four were "lemons" and the odds favor hiring at least one good sales director in five tries. Is this thinking
(a) correct?
(b) incorrect?

5. A newly hired engineer for a computer firm in the Boston metropolitan area has 4 years' experience and good all-around qualifications. When asked to estimate the starting salary for this employee, a chemist with very little knowledge about the profession or industry guessed an annual salary of $35,000. What is your estimate?
$____ per year

Source: Incidents from Max H. Bazerman, *Judgment in Managerial Decision Making,* 3rd ed. (New York: John Wiley & Sons, Inc., 1994), pp. 13–14. Used by permission.

Scoring

Your instructor will provide answers and explanations for the assessment questions.

Interpretation

Each of the preceding questions examines your tendency to use a different judgmental heuristic. In his book *Judgment in Managerial Decision Making,* 3rd ed. (New York: John Wiley & Sons, 1994), pp. 6–7, Max Bazerman calls these heuristics "simplifying strategies, or rules of thumb" used in making decisions. He states, "In general, heuristics are helpful, but their use can sometimes lead to severe errors. . . . If we can make managers aware of the potential adverse impacts of using heuristics, they can then decide when and where to use them." This assessment offers an initial insight into your use of such heuristics. An informed decision maker understands the heuristics, is able to recognize when they appear, and eliminates any that may inappropriately bias decision making.

Test yourself further. Before hearing from your instructor, go back and write next to each item the name of the judgmental heuristic (see Chapter 3 text discussion) that you think applies.

Then write down a situation that you have experienced and in which some decision-making bias may have occurred. Be prepared to share and discuss this incident with the class.

Conflict Management Styles

Instructions

Think of how you behave in conflict situations in which your wishes differ from those of one or more persons. In the space to the left of each statement below, write the number from the following scale that indicates how likely you are to respond that way in a conflict situation.

1 = very unlikely	2 = unlikely	3 = likely	4 = very likely

____ **1.** I am usually firm in pursuing my goals.

____ **2.** I try to win my position.

____ **3.** I give up some points in exchange for others.

____ **4.** I feel that differences are not always worth worrying about.

____ **5.** I try to find a position that is intermediate between the other person's and mine.

____ **6.** In approaching negotiations, I try to be considerate of the other person's wishes.

____ **7.** I try to show the logic and benefits of my positions.

____ **8.** I always lean toward a direct discussion of the problem.

____ **9.** I try to find a fair combination of gains and losses for both of us.

____ **10.** I attempt to work through our differences immediately.

____ **11.** I try to avoid creating unpleasantness for myself.

____ **12.** I try to soothe the other person's feelings and preserve our relationships.

____ **13.** I attempt to get all concerns and issues immediately out in the open.

____ **14.** I sometimes avoid taking positions that would create controversy.

____ **15.** I try not to hurt others' feelings.

Scoring

Total your scores for items 1, 2, 7; enter that score here [*Competing* = ____]. Total your scores for items 8, 10, 13; enter that score here [*Collaborating* = ____]. Total your scores

Source: Adapted from Thomas-Kilmann, *Conflict Mode Instrument,* Copyright © 1974, Xicom, Inc., Tuxedo, NY 10987. Used by permission.

for items 3, 5, 9; enter that score here [*Compromising* = ____]. Total your scores for items 4, 11, 14; enter that score here. [*Avoiding* = ____]. Total your scores for items 6, 12, 15; enter that score here [*Accommodating* = ____].

Interpretation
Each of the scores above corresponds to one of the conflict management styles discussed in Chapter 15. Research indicates that each style has a role to play in management but that the best overall conflict management approach is collaboration; only it can lead to problem solving and true conflict resolution. You should consider any patterns that may be evident in your scores and think about how to best handle conflict situations in which you become involved.

ASSESSMENT 21
Your Personality Type

Instructions
How true is each statement for you?

	Not True At All		Not True or Untrue		Very True
1. I hate giving up before I'm absolutely sure that I'm licked.	1	2	3	4	5
2. Sometimes I feel that I should not be working so hard, but something drives me on.	1	2	3	4	5
3. I thrive on challenging situations. The more challenges I have, the better.	1	2	3	4	5
4. In comparison to most people I know, I'm very involved in my work.	1	2	3	4	5
5. It seems as if I need 30 hours a day to finish all the things I'm faced with.	1	2	3	4	5
6. In general, I approach my work more seriously than most people I know.	1	2	3	4	5
7. I guess there are some people who can be nonchalant about their work, but I'm not one of them.	1	2	3	4	5
8. My achievements are considered to be significantly higher than those of most people I know.	1	2	3	4	5
9. I've often been asked to be an officer of some group or groups.	1	2	3	4	5

Scoring
Add all your scores to create a total score = ____.

Interpretation
Type A personalities (hurried and competitive) tend to score 36 and above. Type B personalities (relaxed) tend to score 22 and below. Scores of 23–35 indicate a balance or mix of Type A and Type B.

Source: From *Job Demands and Worker Health* (HEW Publication No. [NIOSH] 75–160), (Washington, DC: US Department of Health, Education and Welfare, 1975), pp. 253–54.

Time Management Profile

Instructions

Complete the following questionnaire by indicating "Y" (yes) or "N" (no) for each item. Force yourself to respond yes or no. Be frank and allow your responses to create an accurate picture of how you tend to respond to these kinds of situations.

____ 1. When confronted with several items of similar urgency and importance, I tend to do the easiest one first.

____ 2. I do the most important things during that part of the day when I know I perform best.

____ 3. Most of the time I don't do things someone else can do; I delegate this type of work to others.

____ 4. Even though meetings without a clear and useful purpose upset me, I put up with them.

____ 5. I skim documents before reading them and don't complete any that offer a low return on my time investment.

____ 6. I don't worry much if I don't accomplish at least one significant task each day.

____ 7. I save the most trivial tasks for that time of day when my creative energy is lowest.

____ 8. My workspace is neat and organized.

____ 9. My office door is always "open"; I never work in complete privacy.

____ 10. I schedule my time completely from start to finish every workday.

____ 11. I don't like "to do" lists, preferring to respond to daily events as they occur.

____ 12. I "block" a certain amount of time each day or week that is dedicated to high-priority activities.

Scoring

Count the number of "Y" responses to items 2, 3, 5, 7, 8, 12. [Enter that score here ____.] Count the number of "N" responses to items 1, 4, 6, 9, 10, 11. [Enter that score here ____.] Add together the two scores.

Interpretation

The higher the total score, the closer your behavior matches recommended time management guidelines. Reread those items where your response did not match the desired one. Why don't they match? Do you have reasons why your behavior in this instance should be different from the recommended time management guideline? Think about what you can do (and how easily it can be done) to adjust your behavior to be more consistent with these guidelines. For further reading, see Alan Lakein, *How to Control Your Time and Your Life* (New York: David McKay), and William Oncken, *Managing Management Time* (Englewood Cliffs, NJ: Prentice Hall, 1984).

Source: Suggested by a discussion in Robert E. Quinn, Sue R. Faerman, Michael P. Thompson, and Michael R. McGrath, *Becoming a Master Manager: A Contemporary Framework* (New York: John Wiley & Sons, Inc., 1990), pp. 75–76.